Dedication

This novel is dedicated to my Grandmother
Mary Bennett 1904 - 1997

It is also dedicated to all those who devote their lives to the care of
our elderly, homeless, and dispossessed.

In memory of Peter Glancy
1936 - 2018
One of New York's bravest, and a son of Ireland.

Contents

Acknowledgements

The smallest project in life is always a product of, and indeed impossible without, the efforts, support, and sheer willingness of many people. As always, space allows me to mention only some of these, but my heartfelt gratitude goes to everyone who was part of realising my dream to bring this story from aspiration to realisation.

Many people, in both New York and Ireland are responsible for the completion of my book, through their assistance, kindness, hospitality and generosity, in every way.

Conor Power is my co-author, writing mentor and project expert. His professional wisdom, imagination, advice and enthusiasm always moved everything forward, up and over the hills and bumps. Without his ability to listen, his patience and attention to detail, this book would not exist. I thank him sincerely.

I owe a huge debt of gratitude and appreciation to my very good friends The Glancy Family, in Rockaway NY, headed up by the stalwart Peter and Rose. They are a shining example of all that is positive and good. Thank you all sincerely for everything you have done, with good hearts and spirit for so long.

I also thank Helen Rafferty for her editorial skills and her honesty. Her enthusiasm and willingness to jump on board, shaped and pointed things in the right direction.

The very dear friendship of Matthew and Liz Glynn has produced laughter, song, and the occasional tear along the way, during many pleasant, thought provoking evenings, with their friends and neighbors, in the warmth of their welcoming home in New York.

Margaret Mary (Muggsy) Glancy, one of our fellow travellers along the road, who's impeccable taste in wine sustained me on many a visit to the Big Apple. Long may her charm last.

I commend my dear friend Helen Smith. A lady of true character and boundless kindness. Her friendship and embrace has encouraged and supported me in a myriad of ways. She has defined various characters for me, as only she could.

Patricia Hunt was one of the first to read my early drafts. Her reviews and guidance were invaluable, and her interest was infectious. I shared moments with her over copious cups of tea, in Rossnowlagh, Co Donegal. Thank you Patricia for your continued support, practical observations and solid feedback.

PJ Curtis is a lifelong champion of the Arts in Ireland, over many decades, and many guises and genres. He is an old and true friend, and was the first to enlighten and guide me, many moons ago, through the hard path of criticism and rejection, and then recovery!

He has taught me to persevere and endure, and always carry on with my artistic endeavors, through thick and thin, ups and downs, in spite of all. Thank you PJ.

For their love, understanding, eternal friendship, and for the unique place we occupy together, I reserve a special thank you for Tommy and Marie, my loving and beloved parents. We continue to laugh, sing, and share stories along the journey from childhood to friendship.

I now know, thanks to one Kate Middleton, that New York's finest are the NYPD, and that New York's bravest are the NYFD. She enlightened me of these facts on her train journey from

Manhattan to Connecticut one evening after work, having noticed a little error on my behalf on an early manuscript, so I pass it on. Thank you.

Sincere thanks to Dr. Conor Reidy, whose extensive knowledge as a historical lecturer, and expertise as a literary editor, has proven an invaluable resource, both as editor and advisor during my final preparations prior to print.

Finally, the last words of acknowledgement are for my husband and life companion Colm. A funny, patient, and kind man, who has always smiled when I mention my next great project!

He continues to be my number one supporter, grammatical enforcer (endlessly trying to cure me of my use of non regulation capital letters!), and entertainer. For his love, I am always grateful, reassured and fulfilled.

MarieAnn Mc Loughlin Dwyer 2018

Prologue – "Awakening"

New York City, USA; Present Day.

"He's opening his eyes!"

"Where?"

"Ma'am, can you please sit down?" The female orderly's voice was clear and stern. "I'm going to have to ask you to sit down please. It's very important when someone is emerging from a coma not to alarm them. They may be frightened, they may be in pain...."

The words in Jack's head faded away into a soft white mist. There was a moment of clarity and now it was gone again. All these emotions coming and going. How many people were there? How many hours or days or weeks or years have I been here? Was there ever anything else before this? He felt sure that there was. Flashes of scenes went through his head. They were mostly of night-time scenes – Jack stirring a high-ball. Green light. Keeping control... don't drink too much... Harry Belafonte shaking his hand, saying something in drunken slurs... You're a great guy! Funny Irish accent. How come I didn't notice that before? Finding everything so hilarious. It's all right. You look after your clients and they'll always look after you. You gotta keep this going moving along. Where was he from? He didn't like being reminded of things like that. Belafonte laughing at my Irish accent. What Irish accent? I don't have one any more. I'll tell you where I'm from, Buddy! I'm from Main Street, from Upper East Side and Fifth Avenue. I'm from the Bronx, Queens, Midtown... I'm from Staten Fuckin' Island, if it's any of your goddamn business!

"Jack! Jack, can you hear me, Jack?" A familiar voice. The same as before only this time there was a pulse of recognition. He could see a face – the face associated with the voice. Alva. No... Analisa. "Jack!" It was one or the other. He couldn't tell which of the two. Two important ladies. Never the twain shall meet. Gotta keep them away, one from the other... You better believe it! His eyes began to open gingerly, slowly because of the pain. Too goddamn bright. Gradually, from the fog of the blurred white, forms began to emerge. The edge of a pillow and faces beyond, moving and trying to catch his attention. Dark hair, blond hair, questions and callings.

"Jack! *Il uomo destra mio*. You're awake."

"Analisa?"

"Yes, Jack. It's me. Oh Jack, I'm so happy you're awake!"

Something was wrong. Not quite wrong, just a little amiss. He looked around. Faces of orderlies, doctors or something. One or two. Then...

"Alva?"

"Yes." She immediately burst into tears. Jack stared at her. A sense of loyalty and something more. He could feel his heart filling with dark liquid. A sense of having messed up, maybe for good this time... More and more emotional and physical detail filled the empty spaces around her shaking form. Like a crowd of close friends suddenly entering a room, the memories and the incidents and the weight of everything became a three-dimensional reality and he understood why she was crying. He understood all the myriad of possible reasons why his wife was weeping here in this hospital room. His eyes looked from Alva to Analisa and back again. His head remained motionless on the large white pillow. A curved wisp stood above his head like a comical question mark on an otherwise neatly coiffed white head of hair. His blue eyes were sharp and alert, hooded by those constantly-frowning eyebrows. His nose hooked downwards just short of ugliness and lent him the distinction of one not to be trifled with. He smiled his sideways grin, displaying a set of neatly-arranged Americanised teeth, framed by a firm jutting jaw.

"Say," he said at last. "This is one helluva nice day."

Chapter 1 – "Fair City"

Dublin 1939

"Jack. Open your eyes. Wake up, darling. I brought you your favourite – toasted bread and beans, pet."

He remembered that he was meant to be feeling a little poorly and so ensured to prop himself slowly and carefully, as in the manner of a twelve year-old not quite feeling himself. He brushed back his wild shock of hair with his left hand and wiped his eyes as if only slowly coming around to his senses. His mother was standing at the foot of the bed, waiting and holding the plate with the beans and the toasted bread. Steam arose in a small comforting fog in the still cold air of the room.

"It's a bit cold in here, is it? I'll light the fire for you in a minute."

"No thanks, Ma. I'm really not cold." Jack smiled his cheeky smile and she smiled back with maternal satisfaction on her round face. She sat the plate carefully on the blanket covering his lap and fixed the bolster pillow so that he was sitting up straight. "Now," she said and kissed his forehead. She moved to exit the room, saying "I'll be back to check on you later, love."

There was such delicious delight in being here in bed with his mammy presenting him with warm beans on toast, knowing that all the other children would be sitting in class. They'd be going over their catechism with Fr Aquinas right now. He hated that class. He hated the way the priest held the book when he spoke, listing to one side like a stricken ferry boat, a lost look in his glazed eyes. He hated the way he moved and smelled when you got close to him – all hair oil and something private and fuggy. He could picture it now: 'Where's the Mills boy?' he would ask. 'Out sick, Father,' someone would answer. Then Fr Aquinas would nod his head and they would continue in their reading of Daniel in the Lion's Den for the umpteenth time and the questions of what was learned that were to follow. The tedium would finally be broken by the priest's customary burst of violence on whichever unfortunate boy who would forget some detail and so set himself up for a beating.

Delighted. Yes, delighted he was at not having to be there today. It was worth all the effort. He loved the sharp sweetness of the beans and the comforting sauce-flavoured goody they magically created from the ordinary bread they covered. Like a Midas touch of taste, he thought. Every time his mother made it, it always tasted exactly the same. A little later – when it was safe to do so – he'd get up and go and join his dad in the motor car. He loved getting a spin in the motor car. He loved the way it moved and smelled. It smelled of the future, of speed and power and rising above the mundane things that everyone seemed to think were so wonderful when they were just so dull. He loved the way it would pull along so strongly with a great noise, like there was some strong man tugging it with an unseen rope – like it was always going downhill, even when it was going uphill. He loved the way it trundled along so proudly. He liked staring out the window and catching the looks of people on the street. Some turned their heads to see what this thing was with such a great noise. Others completely ignored it like they'd seen a hundred motor cars in their life already and they'd had enough of it or like they just hated motor cars simply because they were motor cars. Then it would lurch forward again so thrillingly, snarling past a pony and trap on the wonderfully wide Baggot Street, passing out all the startled, panting people on their bicycles. It felt like it could go as fast as his father wished it to go. 'How fast are we going now, Da?' 'Oh, I'd say forty miles an hour, Jack.' Forty miles an hour! Wow!'

May Mills closed the door of Jack's room and returned to the kitchen. She smiled to herself. The poor boy seems to be fine now, she thought. He should probably be sent off to school but it was so nice to have him at home all to herself for the day, a day when she was off work as well. He would be more than able to catch up with his school work when he got back to school in the morning. A day away from school would hardly do him much harm. She sighed as she rinsed a wash cloth and proceeded to clean down the work surface next to the sink. It was a thick old butcher's block that her husband – Jack Senior – had salvaged from somewhere in his travels around the city. She liked it all the same. It was a fitting with character, she always thought – a working top that had seen hard work day-in and day-out over the years until it too began to sag a little with age. Not unlike herself, she thought, placing a hand on her hip and moving it around her waist. May was always dark and a little heavy-set but she had become a little more grey and little more heavy-set of late. She quietly lamented the onset of years and the withering of youth. It was never quite fair the way it struck women with more strength than it struck men.

The window over the deep Belfast sink looked onto the lane. It was a quiet lane that was only ever designed for discreet entrances to a series of stables and smaller houses. She hadn't particularly liked the look of the place when Jack first showed it to her. All she could think of were prostitutes and other undesirable types skulking around by night in search of victims. But it was a respectable part of town: like benign spies, they were right in the middle of some of the grandest addresses and residences and yet detached from it all in their own little house – a converted stable off the main thoroughfares. It was as peaceful – maybe even more peaceful – than Delvin, the little village in Westmeath where she grew up. 'My little Delvin Delight' is what Jack called her. She still liked to be called that and her mind drifted to her husband. She was thinking about what she would cook him for his tea and was wondering where he was right now. It was a funny thing, but she was possibly one of the few women with a husband who could never say for certain where her man was at any given time. It was one of the conditions of the job, she supposed. A taxi man is always a man about the town; someone who goes to wherever the fare takes him.

She remembered the first day they set eyes upon one another. It was during her first year at the Grand. If the kitchen was in any way quiet for a while, her gaze would be averted by people going past the large window to the tradesmen's entrance. She liked the look of him immediately. He wore a long tan-coloured coat like most delivery men. His hat was sitting to one side on his head and he had a twinkle in his eye when he looked at her that seemed to be just for her. She blushed and immediately turned away to concentrate on her kitchen duties once more.

There had been so many years in between. The Great War had come and gone. Then there was the terrifying upheaval of the Easter Rising. She would never forget that day. The bullets flew so close. Nobody seemed to know what was happening – not even Jack, who was usually the one to announce big news before it happened. One stray bullet had struck and killed the little grey-and-white tabby that used to come around looking for food. At first, they couldn't understand why such a healthy cat had seemingly dropped dead out of the sky, sporting just the neatest of cuts to his head. Then the postman said what had happened. He was certain it was a bullet, he said, before adding soberly that he had seen "many more of them, Missus... and in much worse circumstances too".

She turned away from the kitchen area and went over to the cupboard at the far end of the room – the "sitting-room" end, as Jack Senior had christened it. This was where he liked to sit and smoke his pipe on a Sunday morning after Mass, reading the paper. He was always giving out about something to do with politics. Generally, May would stay out of it. She wasn't interested in arguments that seemed to go around in circles, never doing anyone any good except setting people up for a fight of some sort. Hadn't this country seen enough fighting anyhow? She rarely offered an opinion on these matters. The last time she did, they ended up having the most ferocious argument. It was all about Dan Breen wanting to take away some rule about allegiance to the king. She liked the King of England. She said that he seemed like such a pleasant well-mannered gentleman and that the likes of Dan Breen with his big ugly face and gruff talk would do well to look up to him. That had set Jack off, all right. She tittered to herself as she remembered, covering her face and shaking her head. Boys and their politics... like big boys with wooden toys.

May went to the wardrobe in the corner where she kept her mending jobs. It was a great heavy coat made of pure wool. A British Army greatcoat, she guessed. Whether issued or captured, she couldn't tell. All she knew is that it would cost a guinea or two were it for sale in Brown Thomas in town. There was only the ripped sleeve to be mended and a button to re-sew. It wouldn't take long and she might even have time to finish the other dress afterwards. This was what she did with her spare time – earning a bit extra to ensure that Jack's school fees were paid and that he went out the door with food in his belly and books in his satchel.

She brought the coat over to the table and laid it out, then went over to the dresser, opened the lower section, removed her sewing box and brought it to the table to set to work, using the afternoon Spring light from the window.

The door opened suddenly and she gave a start. For the briefest of moments, she couldn't remember where she was or what she was doing. In her hands, was one of Jack Junior's large winter socks. The needle was stuck halfway through the toe of the sock that she had been darning.

"Hard at work, my little Delvin Delight?"

May's brain was still not fully engaged. Half of her struggled to comprehend while the other half tried to formulate a response. She lifted her hands slowly before her and stared at them like they belonged to someone else's body.

"Sure, don't worry, pet. I'm only joshin'. Don't I know well that you're workin' hard. As a matter of fact, it's too hard you're working, I'd say... by the looks of things." He was across to her where she sat in Jack's favourite spot and planted a kiss on her forehead.

"I only popped in for the cup of tea while I've two minutes to meself and I in the area." May rose to get out of her seat. "Don't get up, love. Aren't I well able to make it meself?" May stared at his back as he moved efficiently from sink to hob to cupboard and back, whistling a jaunty military score to himself.

"How are you doin', love? I see you're fixing a pair of socks there. Did you get through your pile of work today?"

She had to think where she was in her progress as her world and her precise position in it became clearer through the fog of slumber.

"I... No, I have a bit more to do. Jack is unwell so I kept him at home. What time is it, anyway?"

He whirled about to face her, pulling his watch from the breast pocket of his waistcoat. He always managed to look dapper. That was another thing that had always attracted her to him. He was a man who understood the importance of looking well turned-out, whatever the occasion and however one felt inside. Today he was wearing his mid-length grey coat sent over by his cousin in America, with the brown tartan hat and his grey trousers that he got in Brown Thomas for their style and hard wearing. He was still as fresh a charmer as he was the day he met her.

"Quarter to three on the button. What's wrong with the wee fella? Is he upstairs?"

"He had a sore throat and a bit of a cough and it's a cold enough sort of day. There's a lot of bad sicknesses about. Betty Harrington's boy was very bad the other night and they had to bring him to St Ultan's, they were terrified it was the flu. So I thought we shouldn't be taking any chances and leave him get better for the day."

"The sticky women's hospital, wha'? No, you did the right thing for sure, so you did. No takin' chances with the flu about, or anything that might look like it." He nodded his capped head solemnly and took a sip from his cup of tea. Like most men of his age, he deferred to what he perceived as the better judgement of his wife when it came to all matters concerning health and hygiene.

"Is he up above, so?" he asked, jabbing the forefinger of his left hand in the direction of the low ceiling.

"He is. Did you want to go up and see him?"

He ruminated for half a second, shifting the weight of his backside against the work surface. "Ah… D'you know wha? I won't." He finished his tea in one gulp, turned and spat out some tea leaves and rinsed out the cup before returning it upside-down on the draining board. "I'd better be off again. I've a couple of calls to make before the day is out."

He whisked across the floor to where she sat looking up at him, took both her shoulders, bent down to kiss her cheek, pulled back and smiled, running the back of his right hand across her cheek in a curious act of affection. Then, the door closed and he was gone. May sighed at something undefined that felt like benign spirit leaving the house.

Jack hated being late and he muttered curses to himself as he pushed on the throttle so that it eased past a coal-trap. The driver of the trap looked grimly ahead while the youngster helping him sat on the edge at the back, leaning against the bags of coal, staring blankly and open-mouthedly at Jack and his motorcar. Both were as blackened as young crows. He was heading east along Pembroke Road, trying to go as fast as he could without attracting too much attention. It seemed like a particularly quiet afternoon and it made him nervous for the fact that he would stand out all the more. He dreaded these moments before such an encounter – always afraid that someone that either he or May knew would clock him and talk about it afterwards. He knew that he could always say he was rushing to an appointment at such-and-such a place but he was never happy that it would fit. Besides, the guilt of it all gnawed at him. What would May think? Or little Jack? He shook his head to dispel the projected images of the aghast members of his family and concentrated on taking the turning to the right shortly before the big junction with Northumberland Road. He looked around. There was nothing approaching from either direction – just one or two people walking along the footpath. He daren't honk the horn and he pulled the wheel sharply so that the tyres made the slightest skid on the rough compacted surface. A middle-aged man on the pavement was startled as Jack's car took the turn no more than ten feet away from him. He gasped and looked directly at Jack. His surprise seemed to last even longer than the sudden start from a motor car travelling at such speed so close to him. Did he recognise him? Jack couldn't be sure. He slowed the car down slightly and continued. The entrance was along her somewhere. On the right, about 50 yards before him, he spotted the white post with the black post-box on top. He slowly manoeuvred the car onto the gravel drive. The city disappeared as if a curtain of trees had closed behind him and he pulled the Ford Model T to the side of the early nineteenth-century house, built to look like a grand farmhouse of the era. In the front left upstairs window, he saw the flash of a female figure. Dark hair. The curtain closed hurriedly. She had been waiting.

May gave a sudden start and sat up in bed. She wasn't sure what it was – a curious and subtle sort of wrenching, as if deep inside her soul; a hurting in her body that cut to the quick but without a specific physical place of injury. She sat in the darkness and listened for a moment. There was only the sound of her own heart pounding in her head. Gradually her rapid breathing subsided. Now she could hear Jack Junior snoring from the little room next door. Maybe that's what caused her to wake up so suddenly. She had often worried about how easily the sound travelled in this little place. She and Jack Senior didn't argue much, and they didn't seem to make love much anymore, but she still didn't want any of their private sounds to be heard by their son. Now that Jack would soon become aware of these things, it was even more important to be careful. She could picture her husband tutting his head at such talk. Sure didn't he often not only hear but see his own parents at it, he would say. And what harm did it do him? It was always a bit too much pressure for her. It wasn't in her nature to be so open about these things, even though these days, there were a lot of changes afoot in Ireland. Young men seemed a bit more worldly-wise and cheeky than in her day. Or maybe they were always like that in Dublin and not so much "down the country", as Jack would refer to anywhere outside Dublin. She gasped ever-so-slightly at the memory of those awful cards that Jack Senior got from his cousin who had been in the trenches: photos of brazen French harlots with everything open and on display for all the world to see. Had they no shame? What had got her thinking in circles like this? Thoughts going around in a loop that wouldn't let her mind settle. How late was it? She didn't dare go putting on any light lest she find it was even later than she thought. Once the light came on, she found it almost impossible to go back to sleep. Too many worries and she could never tell quite about what. They had enough money to keep things going, she knew they had, but she couldn't help worrying that she didn't know her own husband's mind. Maybe she knew him as well as any woman knew her husband, but it just didn't seem to be enough. Right now, for example, she was anxious that he wasn't there. She feared that he was somewhere that he shouldn't be. It wasn't even that she was afraid of him being attacked – she had seen him fend off an attacker once – it was something else. She clasped her hands together and hoped and prayed that there wasn't someone out there – some cheeky harlot – who would tempt him into her house. As soon as she thought it, she felt guilty for even dreaming it up. She shivered at the very thought of it, slumped back into her sleeping position, stared at the ceiling and wondered at what point worrying about the present took the place of dreaming of the future.

Jack Senior was in the room. He was moving about quickly and silently as was his wont – as stealthily and efficiently as a priest at Mass preparing for the final homily after the taking of the Eucharist; scurrying about with hurried reverence; cleaning, undoing, preparing amidst breathless whispers and clearing of throat. Then he was under the covers and in beside her. He assumed that she was still asleep, turned his back to her and sighed at length into a sleeping position.

"You were out late," she said from her side of the bed. Her words were not whispered but spoken softly.

"Oh, are you still awake, Pet?" He didn't move from his position. "I didn't wake you up, did I?"

"No. I couldn't sleep." She turned now towards him and moved her body closer. He smelled freshly washed – the result of a bedtime routine he had developed and which he always followed, of cleansing his face, neck and hands before coming to bed; especially when he had been out in the taxi of an evening.

"Ah, you poor pet. I hope you weren't worried, were you?"

"No… Not really… I'm glad you're home."

They said no more and fell into a satisfying sleep.

Jack Junior slumped into the chair and stared into the bowl of porridge. His feet touched the mature timber of the floor. It was a satisfying feeling, reminding him of the days when his feet wouldn't quite reach all the way down and he would swing them forward and back while eating his food. He stared at his food for a moment, considering his position like a chess player. He was hungry. Would he simply plunge his spoon into the bowl of stirabout and take the first mouthful? That was his instinct but he hesitated, wondering about whether or not he might go for a second day in the bed. He wasn't quite sure if he had the energy to do it, he wasn't sure if he'd manage it, get away with it. He wasn't even sure if he wanted to try. Nobody stays away from school for that long – not unless you've got polio like Daniel Masters, or even the croup, where you can't stop coughing and you die of coughing.

From her position standing in front of the sink, May stared over at her only child. A mild wave of panic went through her as she came to the realisation that he was becoming something else. What's that they called it? A changeling? No, that was for girls, wasn't it? It was all nonsense too. She recalled the famous case where a man killed his wife in Tipperary because he thought she was a fairy changeling. She shuddered at the thought and briefly wondered at the rapid run of her imagination. It was a strange thing – how slowly but surely change comes to us all. Jack Junior's magnificent head of curls was now no more. His sallow skin and curly head made him look so adorable. He still had that pout, that tightness of the lips but his curls were no more. He wouldn't tolerate them. She blamed his father more than the teasing of his classmates. It was the fashion now for hair to be kept short like that of a soldier. No more curls that bobbed with each hop, step and skip he made. He seemed to be spending an inordinate time staring at his porridge with the spoon in his hand. He lifted his head and caught her eyes. She looked away instantly as a knee-jerk reaction. It was all that talk of changelings and the supposed dangers of looking lovingly at your child for too long. They said that if you do that, then the fairies will take your child and replace it with one of theirs. Such nonsense, she thought, turning to look again at her beloved boy. She smiled. She had always promised herself that there would be no nonsensical *piseogs* in this house. In her lifetime, she had seen enough of the nastier side of traditional thought to know better. She would count her blessings every day and this boy was one of the greatest that you could ever be given and she would stare at him, admire him and tell him how beautiful and wonderful he was at every opportunity. That was something she had decided a long time ago. No harm can come from love – that was something she felt certain about. He would grow up to be the best of them and he was well on his way.

"Are you all right, pet? Will you be able for the schoolhouse today?"

He appeared to have been caught off guard for a moment. He had a mouthful of porridge and he nodded in a lively manner to confirm that he would be able to attend before dropping his head to one side, propping it up with his left hand and returning to the task of gathering another spoonful of the warm sweetened stirabout. It was at moments like this that she could clearly see the small boy in him once more and she silently thanked God for such a blessing.

Jack Junior stared at his feet as he trudged in his mannish manner along Mespil Road. Left, right, left, right. His clean new shoes clumped the hard footpath that ran alongside the canal wall. He noticed a blemish in the shoe on the left and stopped to take a closer look. It was just a droplet – probably fallen from a leaf overhead. He wiped it clear with his thumb, gathered his satchel of books once more, slung it over his shoulder and continued walking. He liked this part of the day. Unless it was a rainy windy morning, this was his favourite bit. He normally didn't meet anyone else going to his school along this road – he wasn't sure why but they all must have come from different parts of town that weren't where he lived.

He used to see some other children heading in the opposite direction to some other school. They would always walk on the other side of the street. They might look across at him but they never said anything to him and he didn't care to say anything to them. He liked the fact that there was only him amongst mostly grown-up people. They moved faster than he did. Some wore large heavy coats and clean hats like in the photos from his uncle in New York. He liked to imagine that he was like them – dressed in important clothes and hurrying to somewhere important. There were other people too – some were just walking slowly like they had nowhere to go. Occasionally, someone would go shuffling by with no shoes and dressed in rags. All the houses on the other side of the road had a garden in front and they looked like only rich people lived in them. Sometimes ladies would emerge in large dresses and old-fashioned wide-brimmed hats and get into a horse-drawn cab, with severe-looking men in moustaches accompanying them that stared you away. There were even motor cars sitting in the front gardens of some of them.

He preferred looking to see what was going on along the canal, however. There were always plenty of barges sailing by and people standing on the wide grass verge beside it, or children who didn't seem to need to go to school playing and shouting at the men in the barges. They carried just about everything – barrels of porter, coal, bricks, timber, iron... They chugged their way along slowly and he often tried to keep up with them on the footpath above them and maybe even go faster than them. If he caught the eye of a crew member or a tiller man at the back of the barge, he'd wave. They always waved back. They looked so happy and so sure of themselves, like they were really going somewhere exciting. He used to think that they were all heading out of Dublin and across the sea to America until his father laughed and told him that they weren't. They wouldn't be able to make it out of Dublin Harbour on those boats, he said. You needed to take an ocean liner or, better still, save up the money to get a spin on an aeroplane and you'd be there in less than a day. He had asked his father to take him to see an ocean liner and he promised he would, but he hadn't been to see one yet.

"Where are youse goin' with them books?" He had stopped to watch a long black-and-white barge laden with timber beams disappear into the dark arch of the Leeson Street Bridge. Just a little to his right, another barge was being loaded with heavy sacks from a cart next to the canal. A portly man was heaving the sacks onto the boat while a boy the same age as Jack was holding the reins of the horse. The horse was a heavy one with big white-fringed legs and big tattered blinkers covering his eyes. He remained completely still. It was the boy – only six feet from Jack – who had asked him the question.

"I'm going to school."

The boy spat on the grass in front of him. His spittle travelled a fair distance in one go. He could spit like a man. He wiped his mouth with the back of his hand. His face was grimy and he looked ten times tougher than Ger Stokes, the toughest scrapper in Jack's school.

"Youse are wasting your fuckin' time. You don't learn nothin' in school."

Jack wasn't too sure about that but he didn't want to get into an argument with this boy. He didn't want to be late for school either. He stared back at him for a moment.

"What are you lookin' at? Are youse some sort of poncy-boy or wha?" He made a sneer at Jack but he knew he wasn't going to chance letting go of the horse or he'd be in trouble with his father or his boss. He hadn't seen this boy before and reasoned that he wouldn't be able to give chase and that he probably wouldn't come across him ever again.

"I'm looking," he said, taking a deep breath, standing tall and looking down at the boy as much as he could, "at an ignorant fool."

"I'll fuckin' show yous-"

"What would you know about books, anyway? I bet you can't even read your own name!"

"Come here and say that youse poncy fuckin' bastard!"

Jack just pointed and laughed, backing away up the footpath. He whirled, turned right over the bridge, all the while maintaining eye contact with the boy, now fuming. Jack stopped halfway across the bridge. He cupped his hands and shouted: "Ignorant fool!" one more time and ran on up Leeson Street, laughing with giddy delight at doing such a thing.

At the school gate, the master Father Glynn was standing to attention. The children were arriving from different directions like tributaries of a minor river flowing begrudgingly from the South Circular Road. Each boy greeted him in turn with the words "Good morning, Father" like automatons. He nodded calmly in reply. In his long cassock, hands behind his back and the biretta on his head, he looked like a tall mysterious soldier, Jack thought – like the one who really commanded the other more "normal" soldiers who ran around in uniform and who carried guns. A lot of boys hated Glynn. He had piercing light blue eyes and he certainly moved like a soldier. He moved faster than you would imagine he could move. Jack never had any problems with him, though. He had never got on his bad side. He even thought that there was something almost heroic about him – like he had a whole series of amazing stories to tell, like the ones he mentioned only briefly about China. He had been there – the other side of the world where there was death and adventure and he had come back again and that really was something.

"Good morning, Father," Jack said cheerfully, his head high. "It's a very nice day today."

Father Glynn couldn't help the sliver of a smile escaping. This was a young lad who had cheek in him, he thought, but it was always directed in a positive way. He knew how to respect those in charge. He acted so much older than his years and he liked that in him. It was an unusual quality not to be encouraged so much ordinarily. Indeed, the other priests found him too full of himself and in need of being taken down a peg or two but there was something of a wisdom beyond his years that Father Glynn couldn't but admire in him. He suspected that it was something of a free spirit that didn't need to be suppressed; that would be better left to flourish and develop without hindrance.

"Good morning, Master Mills. Indeed, it is a fine morning. *Maidin breá atá ann*, for sure. I hope you haven't forgotten your catechism today?"

"No Father, I have not," Jack answered, deftly producing his penny catechism from his satchel, as if in anticipation of Father Glynn's request. He had forgotten it the previous week and was fortunate to escape a beating.

"Very good, young man." He winked and waved him through like a calm security guard at a village dance.

It was a long boring day in school. He hadn't wanted to be there and almost wished he was sick. He was leaning on his left hand, conscious of not attracting the attention of the boy who sat beside him all day and who always seemed to be coming down with something. Seán Davis had orange hair, freckles, permanently puffed red eyes and a constantly running nose. He didn't like looking at him most of the time and he didn't want to catch whatever he had now. They did have some fun together – Seán was a funny fellow and very good at imitating Father Aquinas. Another reason that made him such a tolerable classmate was the fact that his mother found it easy to blame him for passing on whatever germs were going around. She had even made representations to the schoolmaster Father Glynn to get the Davis boy moved away from Jack, but the priest would not give in to the strict school policy of not allowing any changes to such matters during the school year. No favouritism could be considered, she had to understand, and this, along with all general policies of the school, was one that had to remain constant and unchanged.

Jack sat up as Father Aquinas asked them to take out their English poetry books. Seán already had his out and was filling the small inkwell with what looked like a new bottle of blue ink.

"Could I have some?" Jack asked him. Seán shook his head.

"But I haven't any left. Why not?" Seán just sniffled and shrugged in reply.

"Come on! I'll get some tomorrow and give you back some." He glanced up at the teacher. He had better not talk too loud or Father Aquinas would leather him. "Seán!" he hissed under his breath. "Come on! I need it for the class!"

"No. You're always borrowing and not giving it back."

Jack had to think. He was probably right – the last time his mother gave him money to buy a bottle of ink, he'd kept it and spent half on sweets.

"All right. I'll give you a farthing if you give us some ink now."

"When?"

"Tomorrow."

Seán nodded, unscrewed the cap once more and put a small drop in his classmate's inkwell. Jack stared at it, the blue ink creeping ever-so-slightly up the minute cracks in its porcelain surface.

Seán looked at Jack as if about to say something, then like a dog realising that it had a grooming job needing attention first, he embarked on a long wipe of his nose using the sleeve of his jacked, from the elbow crease all the way to the end of the sleeve.

"*Ciunas!*" came the order for silence from Father Aquinas.

On the way back, Jack decided to take the longer route over Charlemont Bridge. It was partly because he fancied a slightly different walk home but mostly because he wanted to give a wide berth to the junction of the South Circular and Leeson Street just in case he came across that timber-merchant's boy again.

He trudged down Synge Street, heading south along the wide footpath. It was the mid-afternoon and ladies were out walking in pairs, chatting in whispers, carefully holding their backs straight, each with the similar dull straight coats and accompanying small handbags and hats. Every so often, Jack would try to look down into the level below the street. It always intrigued them – those kinds of houses, of which there were many in Dublin. They often had about five different families all living in the one house and all trying to ignore one another. These ones were all red-bricked and of the smaller variety; compared to the big houses on the South Circular Road in any case. They seemed to be houses just for one family, but it always looked something a bit more interesting would be going on in the lower levels. Maybe there were secret societies – Turkish spies and Russian anarchists plotting to bring the city to its knees; something that must be going on without everyone else knowing about it, like in that book his father had given him, The Riddle of the Sands. He grinned at the thought of it, jutting his jaw and catching himself talking to himself before a passing woman stared down at him. She looked severe in her grey check coat with tiny scintillations and her heavily rouged lips.

He re-fixed a frown, pulled up his satchel and said "Fine day, Ma'am." She suppressed a laugh with her gloved hand. He carried on, listening out for any clip-clop sounds and looking both ways in case of a motor car when he got to Lennox Street. He crossed the road and passed beside the smelly butcher's shop on the left as he entered the narrow alleyway of Lennox Terrace. He liked this street because it reminded him of his own street – a tucked-away and almost secret smaller version of the bigger streets. Like a spy, he thought, keeping an eye on the movements of the darker mysterious forces that meet in the basements of the unsuspecting well-to-do wealthy merchants.

For a moment, he wondered if he had been so lost in daydreaming that he hadn't noticed that he had walked all the way home. There, just a few steps ahead of him halfway down the street, was his father's motor car. He stopped in his tracks, squinted and stared at the markings on the back. There it was – YI0037. It was his father's Ford for sure. Jack looked behind again as if to double-check that he hadn't already arrived home.

This was excellent. He could find his father and get an unexpected spin in the motor car, all the way home. He would get him to drive back up Synge Street where the others would still be around, talking and playing marbles in the street. Daniel Burke didn't believe him when he told him that his father had a motor car. Now he'd see him and he'd believe him. They'd all have to believe him. He'd just wave at them nonchalantly like he was something special; something they never thought he was. He'd stun them. He'd shock them. Wait until he told his dad. He'd find it so funny. He hoped he would do it – just this once. Even if he just drove back up by the school and left him around the corner, he'd walk home from there. Jack started to hurry his steps towards the car. As he approached, his dad appeared on cue from the door of the house just beside it. There he was! He stopped and cupped his hands to call out to him before he disappeared into the motor car. Suddenly his father turned back to the door and there was a pair of arms around his father. A younger woman's arms. She reached up on her young tippy-toes. A green skirt and a white blouse. He saw the dark hair of the back of her head move over and back rhythmically as she kissed her father. A long kiss, no mistake. In shock, his eyes followed the line of his father's hands as they wrapped willingly around this woman's body.

He looked around again, wondering if this was a dream, a parallel world where everything was all wrong; back to front. Where had he come from? He looked behind him again. Was there no escape from this? He was aware of his breath becoming heavy and a sensation of his head parting from the rest of him and floating like a balloon in the sky. His mouth was dry. They were still there, whispering now with their heads together. Instinctively, he backed quietly and crouched behind a dustbin. He couldn't look anymore and slumped down, his back against the wall and the smell of rotting bin waste in his nostrils. He wanted to be sick. He put his head down and waited until he heard the sound of the motor car fade away as it turned the corner of a street somewhere.

Chapter 2 – "Pieces of Puzzle"

New York City, USA; Present Day

Dr Patel walked past the entrance to Ward No 7, where most of the stroke victims were housed. Most were over fifty-five but the occasional unlucky soul under that age ended up there too. He caught sight of the patient he'd seen the other evening – the talkative Irishman that everyone seemed to have an opinion on. He looked quiet enough at the moment. The doctor had his rounds down to a fine art and rarely wished to waste any time. He checked his watch: he was comfortably ahead of schedule and had a few minutes to spare before lunch break. He finished his apple, dropped it in the bin in the hallway and stepped inside.

"Mr Mills!"

There was no response. Doctor Patel stood at the end of the bed and stared at the craggy face of this most intriguing of patients and wondered whether he'd lost him again; whether he'd receded into the ether once more. That often happened with patients who suffered strokes. There was no way of telling precisely what damage had been done from the initial bleed, let alone any subsequent incidents that might have happened undetected. In some ways, that was what he had always loved about this career – there was no exact science when it came down to it; when it came to dealing with humanity in all its emotional and physiological mystery. Yesterday, this remarkable Irishman was wide awake and talking about the most extraordinary of lives. Today, he was staring into space and looking as if he might be lost there forever.

"I'm thinking! Jesus Christ, buddy... Didja never learn to give a guy ten fuckin' minutes on his own to think? Did they never teach you that in Gungha Din, or whatever corner of that roach-infested overbaked sub-continent they taught you how to be a doctor?"

Dr Patel smiled with relief, then laughed at the audacity of this man. With anybody else, he would take offence; he would stare back grimly with his excellent withering stare – a gift he got from his late father, another cranky old git – before turning down to his notes again and loudly pronouncing the prescription of the most unpleasant thing he could think of. But Jack broke all the rules. He cast them aside and made his own rules as he went along. It was great to see him in good form. Now he was smiling his crooked smile at him – jutting jaw, mad eyes. He knew damn well what he could get away with, even while he was getting away with it.

"Ahh!" Jack exclaimed with a dismissive wave of his good right hand. "You doctors are all the same! If you'd only leave people alone, maybe then they'd get better!"

"Well it looks to me like you're managing very well." Dr Patel approached, standing beside him now and scribbling the words 'no change' on the clipboard. "And all without my help, it seems." He busied himself studying Jack's chart and taking notes. He even put a thermometer up to Jack's ear just to make it look like he had some official business here and wasn't just there to shoot the breeze.

"Have your bowels moved this morning, Sir?"

"None of your fuckin' business," came the clear reply through gritted teeth. He continued to mutter under his breath. Dr Patel concentrated on his watch. The minute elapsed and he withdrew the thermometer, checked it and noted a normal reading in his notes. Jack had returned to staring into space.

"Say," Jack said suddenly, turning his head towards the doctor. "How long have I been in this goddamn dump?"

"What, do you mean New York in general or in this particular hospital?"

"Ha! Ha!" Jack's laugh staccatoed off the hospital ward walls like two shots from a small arms weapon. "That's a good one! You got a sense of humour – I'll give ya that! I'll give ya that..." His words tailed off as he wagged his finger and eyeballed him as nonchalantly as he could. His left side still refused to move as it should. It was paralysed since the stroke but when Jack moved like this, it was as if his entire body momentarily came to life; as if he was willing it back into obeisance by sheer dint of determination. At these moments, the doctor could clearly see Jack as a younger man, engaging in banter with one of the many illustrious members of New York society that used to frequent the club.

"Well I can tell you that you've been in this hospital for four weeks, three days and about two hours, Sir."

Jack furrowed his brow in an expression of disappointment, still staring ahead. "Four weeks..." he repeated, as if trying to allow the information sink in. "I gotta... I gotta get out of here and back to the club. You know? They need me there. I mean to say, if I'm not back there soon, the whole place will fall apart!" He opened his eyes wide and raised his right arm upwards. "How long more do they need to do all this stuff and make me better?"

"It's difficult to say, Sir. I think you'll be not much longer here, but I cannot say. You are getting better."

"Really? D'ya think so?" He looked up at Dr Patel with earnest bright blue eyes. "I gotta say... I feel like shit!"

They both burst into laughter. The laughing was infectious and a ripple of mirth spread about the ward, with all eyes on the Irishman and the Indian for a moment.

"I understand," Doctor Patel said, wiping his eyes once the laughing died down. "Listen, it will take some time. There's no point in worrying about your business. That will work itself out. The most important thing right now is you. You need to rest and get better. The sooner you get better, the sooner you can get back to work… But it will take time. Do you understand?"

"Yeah, yeah." He nodded and flashed a grateful glance the way of the doctor. He tried to shift to a more comfortable position using his right elbow, then gave up and sat back against the seat of pillows that the nurse had constructed for him earlier that morning. "I understand. Sure, sure. I'm gonna get back in the game, right?"

"Right." He smiled. "You know, one of the nurses was telling me that you're from Ireland. Is that true? I didn't know."

Jack looked around the room distractedly. He rubbed his hair as if checking that it was all in place. It hadn't been washed in a few days and had gone somewhat wild, sticking out in various places in white shocks.

"Yeah, yeah. It's true… but that was a long time ago. A long time ago."

Dr Patel nodded thoughtfully, his pen and clipboard down in front of his waist being held by both his hands. "I'm not sure about accents myself but you don't sound like an Irishman to me."

"Oh." Jack looked up again with mild surprise, before adding: "You don't think so, eh?" He smiled. "Like I say, it's been a while since I been back there… in the old country. You know?"

"Have you not been back to visit?"

"No, no. It's really not up to much. It's kinda poor and small… and besides, everything is here. I made my life here – my wife, my bar, the club… it's all here. It's all moving here, all the time. Over in the old place, nothing's moving. Everything's… kinda dead! Y'know?"

"I see." Dr Patel continued making notes on his patient's chart as he nodded his head, more as if he was biding his time rather than actually working. "And how is it that you say you knew so many famous people? I heard you talk about Frank Sinatra and John

Lennon... and the Kennedy's?"

"Oh! Ha ha! Who's been talkin' to you? Yeah, yeah. They all come to the club... you know; first one comes along. He likes it, he brings his friends or his lover or whoever. I don't care. I'm just there to look after them. Y'see? You gotta keep the customer happy. Isn't that what they say? Well, I was always about keeping the customer, treating him like a king, being there to make sure they're all nice and relaxed and having a good time, because let me tell ya, they ain't getting' treated like no king once they're back home."

"No?"

"No. Course not. That's why they come to me. That's what makes a place like mine the success that it is." He seemed to be growing with pride now, Dr Patel thought. His jerk of the head and twinkle of the eye had become that much quicker and sharper; a man so sure of himself that you will him to say something enlightening and profound every time he opens his mouth. What was the English word for that? Charisma. That's it – charisma.

"And did they all come to run away from the fame and photographers who chase them?"

"The paparazzi? Oh yeah, you better believe it! It's the price of fame, they say. But I always said to them: 'Not in my joint, it ain't! Here, you can act normal and be yourself. Leave your home life and your street life and every other life you got right outside the door cause we're not letting it in – only you! Sit down and tell me your troubles. Or don't... if you don't wanna. Ha ha! Yeaah..."

"It sounds wonderful. I think in many ways, you were like a doctor too – making the rich and famous of New York feel better, no?"

"Yeah. Yeah, I guess that you could say that. I certainly never thought of myself as a doctor before but now that you mention it... Yeah! Ha ha! They sure got plenty of medicine in my place!"

"Okay, Mr Mills. I think you're certainly making progress. The OT will be coming around later to go through your exercise regime –"

"The OT? Who the hell is that?"

"Your occupational therapist, Sir."

"Oh that fat girl with the freckles? Aww... Jeez!"

"She will help you get back the use of your left arm and leg. The exercises are very important."

"So you say. All she does is hurt me... and smell bad!"

"Quite. Anyway, I must go now and we'll talk again tomorrow. Okay?"

"Yeah, sure thing, buddy. Say... has any lady called looking for me?"

"Why, yes Sir. Your wife was here this morning."

"Really? Shit, I don't remember that."

"You were asleep so she went away again."

"Oh. Okay. Anyone else?"

"I'm not sure. I'll check with the orderly and let you know." Dr Patel strode across the floor to exit the ward in his long gangly stride. As he went through the door, the dark-haired handsome Italian lady who had been in the day before greeted him with a friendly smile.

Chapter 3 – "Alva's Ireland"

Dublin, April 1944

Jack looked both ways before crossing the wide junction. He had come from the direction of town, having decided to spend an hour or so rambling around St Stephen's Green as it was the first fine day this year that felt like summer. These days, the fuel rationing meant that it was quieter on the roads even than it was when he was a little boy, but those that did drive tended to drive fast and there seemed to be more bicycles than ever before. A rush of bicycles creaked and swished past like a small flock of low-flying birds. His eyes scanned the various people going about their daily business. He liked to clock them as quickly as possible, trying to imagine who they were and where exactly they were going. His attention was naturally caught by a pretty face and blond hair. She looked back at him as she went by, then suddenly her hand shot up to keep her hat from falling off and her front wheel wobbled slightly. A determined-looking middle-aged man in ragged shirt and hirsute face came by, laughing and shouted "Watch the birdie! Ha ha!"

Jack readjusted himself, smoothed back his hair and crossed the street when it was clear. He stepped onto the high pavement that curved around the junction of Camden Street and Charlotte Way. He looked up at the square clock hanging off the upstairs wall to check the time, pushed through the heavy black door of the Bleeding Horse Pub and walked in.

Éamonn was behind the bar cleaning glasses. Jack's youthful eyes adjusted quickly to the relative darkness within and the plump form of his boss materialised before the large mirrored wall. Jack caught sight of his own reflection and he adjusted a stray piece of forelock for neatness. He was taller than the average 16-year-old and could easily pass for 20, which he frequently did. His father said that he grew up faster and stronger than anyone he ever saw because "you didn't have to share your food with a gaggle of brothers and sisters like I did". He wondered briefly if he should have applied more oil.

"Jesus! If you keep lookin' at yourself in the mirror all day, it won't be any more use to the rest of us!" Éamonn was always bemused at this youngster. He was a decent enough worker – very tall and strong for his age – and he was ravenously hungry for work. He'd never seen the like of him for pure vanity and unwavering self-belief. He was a young man going places fast and had film-star looks. Éamonn had a slight envy of the way that Jack attracted the attention of the occasional women that came into the front bar, usually looking for a husband or a brother. They always did a double take, almost as if they were trying to guess what age he was. He could see that Jack loved the attention too. Some young fellas didn't know how to react to female attention, but this chap took it all as affirmation of how handsome he was. He was cocky, for sure, but maybe that wasn't such a bad thing.

"Sure I might as well look nice and clean for the customers."

"Christ I don't know. Half of them do be so drunk, they don't know if they're looking at the Mata Hari, Mussolini's mama or the Risen Christ."

"Well I'd rather look like the Risen Christ than Mrs Mussolini, anyway," Jack said, putting his comb back into his hip pocket and winking. He wasn't sure if his witticisms were on the mark but one thing he had learned from his father was that it was all about the delivery.

"Mind your lip, now, sonny. If you stick it out too far, it might just catch something nasty."

Jack just laughed. Éamonn was funny. He was officially his favourite "ould fella" in Dublin. He didn't mind the hard work and the long hours. He was delighted – meeting people and practising his barman-ship. This was a lot more exciting than the prospect of driving people around the city like his father. He couldn't imagine anything worse and he hoped to Christ that his da wouldn't mention it yet again. He cringed every time he could feel the question coming and no matter what the context – usually it was when they were sitting down comfortably to dinner – it always came out the same, word-for-bleedin-word, like a radio announcer before they gave you the news: "Would you not consider givin' the career of a *chauffeur* a go... like your ould man?" He would just say "No, da. Thanks." He really wanted to say something more definitive, like "No, da. I don't want to be driving around like a slave for people who are too rich and lazy to get themselves about and I don't want to be sneaking around the back streets like a coward, pretending to be someone that I'm not, thanks all the same." He was sick of it. The sooner he got out of this city, the better. He was already saving up.

"How much would a boat to America cost, Éamonn?"

Éamonn whistled low as he got out the big cloth for giving the counter the final decent polish, as he called it. "Boys, oh boys! I'd say you'd be talking about a hundred quid, maybe."

"A hundred pounds!?"

"Maybe, yeah. Let me think now... my sister went to America on a steam ship a couple of years after Independence and I'm fairly certain that she would have had to pay about forty or fifty pounds then, so I'd say it's after going up since then."

"Would it? Why?"

"Or, sure let me tell you... isn't it always the way. It's a bloody mystery so it is but things are always getting dearer. Even when you're getting less money like everybody is now, we're always having to pay more to keep somebody up there in the comfort."

"So who's the richest man in Ireland?"

"Christ I couldn't tell ya. I'd say it's probably Eamon de Valera. Or one of them bloody bishops."

"I'm going to America."

"Oh yeah? When?"

"As soon as I have the money saved."

Éamonn raised his eyes. He looked comical when he did that, with his dark bushy eyebrows and round bald head. "You'll be a while, Sonny. Anyway, there's no-one going anywhere much at the moment what with the war still on and the Brits have banned all people travelling from Ireland."

"Banned? Since when?"

"About a month ago. Did you not read the papers?"

"No." He was unsure if that even mattered or not. He didn't have the money to go to America or anywhere else much for that matter. Besides, couldn't you get a boat from Cork or some other port? Maybe the Germans were still firing torpedoes at everything that moved in the sea. He wasn't sure. The war was nearly over, they said, but from what he had seen on the newsreels at the Grafton the other night, there was still plenty of fighting going on.

"The Americans are goin' to have to batter the heads off them Russians next," said Éamonn, as if he was following Jack's thoughts. "Anyway, there's nothing much that we can do about all that. You can start ending the war by bringing up some more stout bottles from the cellar. I just finished a batch earlier this morning."

Jack snapped to attention, saluted dramatically and spun around on one heel, before marching away noisily to the door leading to the staircase. Éamonn laughed and shook his head.

Alva Blake struggled with the side door of the Bleeding Horse, leaning back as she pulled it towards her, then stepped quickly over the tiled surface and entered the pub before it closed behind her with a hush. It wasn't her first time inside the door of a public house but she always treated it with a certain degree of reverence and she stopped as if about to bless herself or effect some kind of acknowledgement before going any farther. She was dressed in a long print skirt with a green lambs-wool cardigan and light coat. Her medium-length brown hair fell in curved strands from her black beret, providing an oval frame for her strong features. She had what her mother described as "an artist's face" and a petite figure. Like most young women, she never particularly liked the look of herself but took some satisfaction in her dignified look that spoke more of a highborn beauty than the features of a sultry Mediterranean maiden. Alva looked around. The décor was of the classic Dublin Victoriana, with a touch of Bohemia about the place – the kind of interior she imagined in a Viennese café. She had never been but her father had described some place he had visited back in days of the Habsburg Empire. It was one of those stories from her father's travels that had somehow stuck out and captured her imagination and she longed to see what it was like for herself someday. It was a world of mysterious shifting nationalities, louche well-spoken foreigners and handsome counts. There seemed to be no-one about. She suddenly felt like an intruder and became self-conscious and her confident entrance now felt like an act of misplaced entitlement. The total silence unsettled her somewhat and she stood on the tips of her toes to look past the length of the dark timber bar to see if she could spot her brother.

Just then, Jack entered from a side door, whistling and moving swiftly over to the bar. He stopped when he saw Alva standing there.

"Hello," Jack said, decisively. He held his head up instinctively and leaned his elbow on the bar, maintaining a vaguely haughty professional distance that he felt was appropriate.

"Good morning," Alva gushed, joining her gloved hands together. She had expected to see someone older and fatter. She found it hard to look him in the eye and her eyes instinctively looked towards the floor. He couldn't be any older than me, she thought. "I was wondering," she started, looking up again. "I was looking for my brother. I thought that he might have come in here."

"There's hasn't been anyone in here yet, so there hasn't." He motioned with his extended hand to illustrate the emptiness of the pub. He smiled openly at her – a crooked and sardonic kind of smile but she found it immediately charming; confident yet inviting her to have a laugh at his expense if she so wished. He had a tall and noble bearing about him, she thought. One might almost say a young European count.

"Well... thank you and sorry for bothering you." She found herself resisting a curtsy and made to leave.

"Wait. Maybe if he comes, I'll keep an eye out for him for you, Miss...?"

"Miss Blake." She smiled. What a grown-up conversation they were having all of a sudden. She felt like she was acting like her mother. "Alva is my first name."

"Alva Blake." They stood and smiled at one another for a heartbeat. "Well my name is Jack. I'll write that down and so that way, if your brother comes in, then I'll know and... maybe if you come back again, I can tell you if he's been in here or not."

"Yes. That would be grand, thank you." The words emerging from her mouth sounded strange to her ears and she found herself at a loss as to whether or not she had said the appropriate thing.

"Very well... Alva – if I may call you that?" They both burst into smile. Jack liked the look of her – a fascinating face that blossomed into feminine beauty when she smiled or even talked. She looked clean and cultured and spoke like someone from Foxrock or Sandymount.

"You may."

Jack moved around inside the bar with, Alva thought, the measured swiftness of a ballroom dancer. "Well, I'll just get a pencil here and make a note of your name and… I hope you'll be back to us?"

"Maybe I will." She turned, pushed open the door and disappeared out into the street. Jack picked up the small block of pale surplus newspaper pulp that Éamonn had procured from his cousin in the Irish Press. With a pencil, he wrote the name Alva Blake on it. He tore it off and stared at it for a moment before folding it carefully and inserting it into his breast pocket.

"Alva! There's someone here to see you!" Alva's friend Jennifer gave a start as she stood on the thick speckled flagstone of the top step of the Blake household. Even though Alva's mother was very well-mannered and spoken, she had an indefinable edge to her that spoke of someone who would not suffer fools gladly. Jennifer's father had a bit of a thing for her. He always described her not as a beautiful woman but as a "handsome woman". She looked at Jennifer with her kind eyes and said "Oh, I do apologise… When I shout, I tend to shout a bit loud. It's not often I shout, but when I do… Alva hates it. She keeps telling me that I frighten away all the seagulls!"

"No, it's okay Mrs Blake." She looked around briefly at the Sandymount shoreline to see if she really had frightened the birds away.

"Anyway, never mind that. Come in, come in, please, dear!" Gwendoline Blake motioned her daughter's friend inside.

They stepped through the colourful porch with its soft window light and colourful floor tiles into the main hall. Jenny loved visiting this house. It was so much of what she aspired to. It was old, grand and so charming. It was pretty to look at from the outside with its red-bricked bay windows and fairy-tale chimney stacks but once you went inside, it was even more like the setting of a Noel Coward play or a house belonging to a character from an F Scott Fitzgerald novel. In reality, it was far less grand than all that but it was as close as she was to such a world. They even had a maid, who duly emerged from the kitchen, as if on cue. She was a middle-aged woman of blank expression named Angela.

"Angela," said Mrs Blake. "Would you bring us some tea, please? We'll be in the drawing room."

"Certainly, Mrs Blake."

Gwendoline motioned Jennifer into the drawing room. They sat down on the soft twin sofas facing one another over the coffee table.

"Are your parents well, Jennifer?" Gwendoline asked in a vaguely curious manner.

"Yes, thanks. Dad is still working away and Mam is mostly at home."

"She works too, I think. Alva mentioned that she was a secretary in a law firm?"

"Yes, but she does that on Tuesdays and Thursdays only. The way things are at the moment with the war and rations and all that, she says she may be down to one day a week soon. We don't know yet."

"I see." She glanced over to the door to see if her daughter might come through it. "And your father is still working for Arthur Guinness, yes?"

"Oh yes. He still works at Guinnesses."

"And all your family are well?"

"Oh yes, thanks."

Just then, the door opened and Alva came in.

"Ah! Here's the real lady of the house!" Gwendoline stood up to make way for her daughter, who sat down in her place.

"Yes, Mum. That's me!" She rolled her eyes only so that Jennifer could see it.

"I'll leave you two in peace," Gwendoline said. Even though Alva was the middle child, she had been the most precocious from birth and Gwendoline always gave her a little more leeway than the others. In moments like this one, she found herself as an observer in the room, wondering curiously as to why this mother didn't put her foot down more solidly with her middle daughter even though she had no trouble putting her foot down when it mattered with every other aspect of her life. It was just the way that their relationship had evolved over the years and they both seemed to hold a certain respect for one another that somehow knew where its limits lay.

"Thanks, Mum." Alva smiled up sweetly with genuine warmth at her mother, who returned the smile and exited the room.

"Your mum is so nice."

"Yes, I suppose... she can be a bit bossy sometimes."

"Well I think she's a splendid lady! You'd do well to follow her example, now." She said the last sentence in a high-pitched imitation of Sister Elizabeth – a cranky and wizened nun of small stature and thick glasses who croaked her way through science classes at Alexandra College in the city centre, where they were both boarding during the week. They both giggled. Alva put her hand to her mouth and tipped backwards.

"Oh Jenny! That's just like her!"

"So what's new with you in the last two days? Have you been thinking about what you're going to do with your future after the Leaving Cert, young lady?"

Alva giggled again at Jennifer's put-on generic teacher's voice. "Oh, I don't know. My mum wants me to do nursing and go to England but

I don't know."

"Maybe you'll marry a rich count from Poland."

"If there's any left now..."

There was a soft knock on the door that the two girls barely heard before Angela came in with the tea and scones. She silently put the tray down on the coffee table and left again.

Jennifer tasted the first one: "Mmmm... nice scones."

Alva poured the tea for both of them.

"Does your mother make these?"

Alva shook her head. "No, Angela makes them. Actually, I did meet someone sort of interesting over the last couple of days."

Jennifer's mouth was full of scone and she widened her big blue eyes and nodded quickly to encourage her friend to tell all.

"Well, I went looking for Daragh on Friday during the mid-morning break because I had to get money from him for the exam fees for school. Mum had given it to him to give to me because she thought that would be quicker than putting it in the post and my mother never puts any money in the post. Anyway, of course Daragh didn't show up with the money."

"How come?"

"Well, I thought that he must have spent it in the pub and then he was hoping to get some more money back on pay-day, which is Friday. I don't know – he's just a disaster really. So I thought I'd find him in the Bleeding Horse."

"Where's that?"

"It's only down the road from Earlsfort Terrace – it's on Camden Street, at a corner near the South Circular. Sure anyway, in I went to find him."

"And did you get the money?"

"No. Well yes I did later... that's another story... but when I went in, there was no-one else there and then this fella comes out!" She crouched down as if to make herself completely inaudible to the rest of the household. "Jennifer, he was fine!"

Jennifer crouched down conspiratorially, took a sip of tea and put her cup back on the saucer. "Who is he? What did he look like?"

"Well his name is Jack. I know that much. He's tall and dashing. He looks like he flies an aeroplane or something. He has this really lovely smile – like a film-star."

"Like James Stewart?"

"More like Cary Grant... or even Gene Kelly!"

"Oooh! So, what did you say? Did you talk with him?"

"Well, we didn't say much... It was more what we didn't say. I gave him my name."

"Alva!"

"That was all. I didn't tell him where I lived or anything."

"And then what happened?"

"He says 'I'll make a note of that, Madam, just in case he comes back again and I do hope I'll see you again'."

"He sounds awfully formal."

"Well he wasn't really. He was just... nicely mannered... strong and confident."

There was a silence while Alva stared intently into space and Jennifer stared at Alva, her teacup in hand, her mouth slightly open.

"I'm going to call on him again tomorrow!" They burst into suppressed giggles. Alva fell over in a hunch. Jennifer shook and held onto her teacup for fear of spilling anything on any surface of the drawing room.

"Who's… Alan Blake?" May Mills held her son's best work shirt in one hand and a small handwritten note in the other. She held it up to the light and away from her face, squinting to make out Jack Junior's tight writing. It brought back memories to her of when he was a six-year-old or thereabouts – trying to get him to loosen up his small tight writing so that it could be seen clearly by the teacher. Jack Senior had the stick approach. He used to smack his son's hand until he got it right. She wouldn't stand for that. She would prefer a thousand times that he keep his tiny squiggled writing rather than get a smack on the hand. He had certainly improved, she thought. His writing was still a bit tight but clear enough. It was with encouragement and not coercion, she reasoned. Now it was her eyes that had begun to betray her. She could hardly believe that she was at the age where she had to hold things back from her eyes like one of those old sisters in the convent where she was brought up.

"What? I don't know any… Oh wait a minute! Gimme that please, Mam!"

"Alva! It's Alva Blake!" She dropped her hand for a moment as she thought hard and ran through the different Blakes that she knew. Jack snatched the piece of paper from her. "Is that one of Jimmy Blake's girls?"

"Who? I don't know. I'm not sure. I don't think so." He hurriedly put the note into his bedside drawer and looked down at the floor and away to his left as he struggled to do up the top button on his second-best work shirt. Anything to avoid his mother's stare.

"Is she your sweetheart?"

"No!" He looked at her now. She stood unflinching at the door of his room, a bundle of his clothes gathered up in her arms for the Saturday morning wash. She was a plump but youthful-looking forty-four year-old. No grey hairs had yet invaded her dark head. To Jack Junior, she was simply old. "She's just a girl that I met in the pub. She came in looking for her brother."

May smiled. "I see, faith. I suppose you're not too young to be doing a line."

Jack scrunched up his face in disgust. "I'm not doing a line! Christ, that's a stupid thing to say!"

May was curious but felt that she was pushing things too much. They had had their talk about the facts of life many years ago and she didn't want to cause upset to her son.

"All right, pet. You know best what to do. All I can say is that it's lucky the woman who'll get you."

She disappeared downstairs and Jack shuddered with embarrassment. He stood up and walked over to his dresser with its slightly wonky drawers and creaking hinged mirror. He stooped his lanky frame forward slightly to angle it upwards so that he could get a better look at himself. He liked to keep things neat in his room. He wouldn't tolerate mess for any length of time and a stray sock on the floor wouldn't last two minutes. Even that old dresser – somewhat old and tatty though it was – had no clutter. On top of it were a black comb and a tub of hair oil. He opened the tin and took a little in his hand.

"A little dab will do," he whispered, mimicking the radio advertisement as he worked it in to his hair with his fingers and followed deftly through with a comb. "This is for you, Alva Blake. And don't forget to wear that nice skirt that swings from those hips like a big band sound! Yes Sir!" He winked at himself with an air of readiness and satisfaction, twirled 360 degrees and clicked his fingers in the air as if summoning a fantasy butler. He exited the room with his head held high.

Downstairs, May was scrubbing furiously on a pair of her husband's trousers. From behind, her form shuddered with the effort. Her sleeves were rolled up and the strings of her large apron jerked and waved like narrow snakes wriggling on a line.

"There's some stirabout on the hob and a boiled egg for you on the table," she shouted over her shoulder when she heard him come down the stairs.

He said nothing but went straight to the table and sat, eschewing the porridge for the boiled egg. He picked up the spoon beside it. He paused and was touched for a moment by a brief wave of love for his mother. It suddenly occurred to him that it didn't matter what would happen – what he would say or do or even think. She would always love him. He couldn't remember a day when he came to the breakfast table or the dinner table and there wasn't a boiled egg or a bowl of coddle or a bit of brown bread or something waiting for him. He picked up the spoon and wolfed into the large brown egg.

"Where's Da?" He asked once he had finished.

"He had to go on a run this morning," his mother answered nonchalantly. Inwardly, Jack pictured his father's car parked outside some other woman's house on some other narrow street in Dublin. His jaw set and he stared hard into the middle distance.

"My God, you've a stern face on you," his mother had come away from the sink for a moment. "She must have your heart set crossways!"

Jack took a deep intake of breath. "Mam! Jesus sake!"

"Careful now! I don't mind the swearing too much but you mustn't take the Lord's name in vain. No luck can come of that."

Jack threw his eyes up to heaven and got up to go. "I'd better go. Thanks for the breakfast, Mam."

"Are you not eating your stirabout?"

"No time. Éamonn'll have a sandwich for me at the pub." He planted a kiss on her cheek and disappeared out the door for his twenty-minute walk to work.

Jack turned up the small incline onto Leeson Street Bridge from Mespil Road. Saturday was a busy day in Dublin – busier than the weekdays in terms of the volume of activity on the street. Maybe it was only at the weekend that those with a motor car could afford to use it, such were the problems with the ration shortages. His father had a special dispensation, he had told him. He was very chuffed with that. He supposed that it was something to feel special about – having the income and the access to fuel that everyone else couldn't get. He hadn't noticed the car slowing down beside him on the bridge so that when it honked, he jumped with the fright.

"How's it going, young man? You're looking well, so you are."

Jack's father's face smiled at him through the open window of his car. A neat clean man with a pristine peaked cap on his head in the shiniest vehicle in Dublin.

"Howya, Da. Thanks. On me way to work."

"Sure, don't I know? Sorry I missed you this morning. I had to drop the boss man's wife out home to Killiney. I'm just heading back to the Shelbourne now."

"Yeah. Listen, I'd better keep walking. I can't be late for work."

"Good man. Listen, I might call in to the Horse later for a minute. Good luck, now."

He pulled off quickly leaving a small cloud of dust behind. Jack stared after the car, wondering why his father would want to call into a pub. Did he even drink? He wasn't sure.

"By Christ, you're eager!" Éamonn said, looking at the clock above the bar. "It's still only ten-too. There must be a fire after breaking out in the scratcher or something."

"Sure why wouldn't I be early? Isn't good honest work the granary bread of the working man?" he smiled cheekily, echoing one of

Éamonn's oft-repeated stock phrases. His boss raised his eyebrows comically in response.

"Now you're talking! Let's get some of that energetic wisdom into the working day. Here, let you be washing them glasses there while I go and shed a tear for Dear Old Ireland, as the fellah says."

Jack got to work while his boss visited the loo. He felt energised this morning for a reason that he couldn't quite identify. It was the tingle of possibility and of adventure, he sensed. He had been here before. It was always something to do with girls – a double-edged sword that might bring sweetness or misery. Maybe that was what was so exciting about such times – being on the verge of an event or a new direction that could be wonderful or horrible. There was something else too – something about having simply talked to Éamonn about going to America. Even though Éamonn was pouring cold water on the idea, the very fact of discussing it made it a realistic possibility in his head. People did it all the time, didn't they? He had relatives who went to America and there were supposed to be a hundred thousand American soldiers in the North right at this very minute while he was here in Dublin polishing glasses and putting them away. He was flying through them. He wasn't even sure if they were done as thoroughly as he normally did them. What did it matter? Éamonn liked him a lot and there would have to be several steps between such an indiscretion as not polishing a glass and getting the sack. Even the thought of deliberately doing things half-arsed for a whole day just to see how far he could go with it made him giddy. He felt that things were going to get better, maybe even brilliant, and it mightn't even have anything to do with Alva Blake. He looked directly in the mirror behind the bar and spoke her name out loud as he slowly dried the inside of a pint glass. It had a small crack in it, so he had to be careful in case he made it worse or broke it. Éamonn said that it was hard to get replacement glasses these days. Her name was brilliant, he thought. There was something sophisticated yet downright sexy about it. Alvaaa Blaaake...

"You do know that talking to yourself is the first sign of madness?" Éamonn had returned. Jack wasn't sure how long he had been on his own, thinking and talking to himself. He straightened up and looked away in faux nonchalance.

"Is that what you've heard?" he said. "I read that it was a sign of extreme intelligence, actually."

Éamonn just laughed and shook his head. "By Jaysus, you'll go far, sonny. How're you gettin' on with the glasses? Ah, good man!" He ran his eyes around the bar in a general ship-shape inspection. He seemed happy with the progress so far and took up a position of washing while Jack continued drying. Éamonn started whistling a love tune. He broke into singing.

"*Red sails in the sunset, Way out on da seeee...* Oh!" he said suddenly as if the memory had just entered his head. "There was a young lady looking for you this morning."

Jack's eyes darted over and back. "Really? Who was it?"

"I don't know. She didn't leave a name. A nice-looking girl with a soft southside accent, sweet as a nightingale. She had a friend with her."

"Oh yeah?" He asked the question in a casual manner as if it mattered little to him who this girl was or what she wanted, but inwardly, his heart leapt. He could feel his quickening pulse growing louder in his ears. His own reaction took him by surprise and he silently cursed the uncontrolled effect the news was having on him. Moments passed and he continued working away, drying methodically and stacking.

"Are youse not interested in the rest of it or have you that many lady friends in your life that it doesn't matter a shite to you who this young-one is?"

"No. I mean, Yes. What's the rest of the story?"

"She said that she'd be at the Pissery place beside the canal on South Richmond Street until twelve."

"The Pâtisserie?"

"That's the place. Me French isn't the best this morning, God help us. Tell you what… seeing as you arrived so early and you've been working so well, why don't you have a half-hour break and wander down there to have a look in the door?"

It was only a short walk up the street but Jack jumped on the back of a passing tram to save time. He jumped off right outside the black elegant façade of La Pâtisserie Continentale. He'd often passed by it but had never been inside. It had always seemed a bit too foreign, somehow – not so much because it had a slightly mysterious French name but for the people that seemed to frequent it. They were of a sort that would know what to say and do in such a place. He'd have one quick look inside to see if she was there, he reasoned as he jumped off the tram just outside the red-painted front of O'Connell's Pub. It was just about the only Dublin-looking institution in this little enclave of the city that his father always referred to as "Little Jerusalem" – part continental posh, part crumbling decay. He remembered one of his Jewish classmates Lenny who had come from near here telling him mysteriously one day that the Christian Brothers at the school weren't allowed to strike a Jew "because of what the Russians did".

As soon as he approached, he saw her sitting right beside the window. She looked different to the other day, he thought – more formal and plainer, perhaps. Her friend looked the more excitable sort and she gave a start as soon as she saw Jack. He grinned and strode inside.

There weren't many people in the dining room. A moustachioed waiter accosted him immediately.

"I'm just meeting some friends," Jack said, pointing to the table before the maître d'hôte could ask him anything. He moved over to the table the two girls were sitting at. They both stared at him with an expectant shadow of a smile, wondering he'd say next.

"May I take a seat," he said, already with his hand on the back of the chair.

Alva nodded with courteous approval. He sat down, pulled his chair towards the table and leaned forward, folding his elbows on the edge and looking from one to the other.

"This is my friend Jennifer... Jennifer Wilson."

Jack stuck out his hand smartly, straightened up and said: "Jennifer. It's a privilege and a pleasure to meet you, if you don't mind me saying."

Jennifer giggled. "Thank you very much, Mr Mills. Alva has told me so much about you."

Alva glared at Jennifer as subtly as she could.

"Is that right? All good, I hope." He winked conspiratorially at Jennifer. "Listen, I don't know about you two ladies, but I'd love a cup of tea." He turned around and clicked his fingers in the air. "Garsoon! Can I have a pot of tea here, please?"

Alva tried to settle her hands by her sides as nonchalantly as possible. Inside, she was already feeling an insidious sense of panic. She had hardly said a word yet and she couldn't think of what to say that wouldn't sound stupid or trite or ridiculous. He seemed so confident and carefree. And he seemed to be fundamentally different from the image she had retained in her head after the other day – a bit gruffer, perhaps. She wasn't sure. Maybe they were all a little bit nervous and had to just calm down a little.

"Well thanks for coming, anyway," she said suddenly. "Did you have to get off early? Does your boss know you're here?"

"Éamonn? Oh yeah, he's fine about it. He gave me an early break because I'd been in a bit early and we got all the bottles and glasses sorted faster than normal, you see. It's good to get that sort of stuff out of the way early. Then you're more in control, you know?"

"I never thought of that," said Jennifer. "I suppose you must spend hours cleaning up after all the customers. Is it hard work?"

"Ah no, it's grand."

"My father works in Guinness's, actually."

"Does he now?"

"Yes, they always give him a big huge crate of it at Christmas... every year."

"Yeah, they all have a dirty big bottle of it at the table on Christmas Day!" Alva interjected.

"Is that right?"

"No, don't mind me. I'm only joking."

Jack was glad he had come. He was afraid that Alva's friend would be some kind of mute chaperone, afraid to open her mouth and pouncing to snuff out any conversation that might be remotely flirtatious. But she was, as Éamonn might have put it, "a mad yoke" and was filling any awkwardness with a bit of chat.

"Your tea, Sir." The waiter had arrived and placed the teapot and cups on a tray in the centre of the table. It was a tall, brilliantly clean white enamelled pot with elegant fat curves, ornate floral design and gold-trimmed handle, top and spout. The waiter placed the cups and moved away.

"Begod, the tea should taste pretty nice out of this, what?" said Jack as he poured for the two girls – first Alva, who smiled sweetly at him, then Jennifer, then himself. "That's how you should have your tea – served from something of quality and beauty. What do youse think?" He ran his thumb along the gilt of the lid.

"Yes, it's lovely," said Alva.

"It's really beautiful. It's kindof like the one your mother has, isn't it? The one with the roses?"

"A bit, yeah. But this one's nicer... more French-style, I suppose."

"You can't beat a bit of French class all the same," said Jack. "Simple but elegant."

The girls nodded and sipped their tea.

"So, how long have you been working in the Bleeding Horse," Alva asked, looking straight at Jack. He liked her eyes. They were clear, pretty and honest. He decided immediately that it was the thing he liked about her the most. That was it. That was the thing he couldn't quite put his finger on, having met her again and wondering if it was the same person.

"Too bleedin' long!" His answer elicited a giggle from Alva and a suppressed guffaw from her friend. He liked the way she laughed, too. There was an honesty and unfettered attractiveness there too – something of an innocent little girl laughing at the antics of her favourite uncle.

"Well, it's a decent job. Éamonn is a great boss – you couldn't ask for better – and I'm looking to maybe move to the bar in the new airport soon."

"The airport out in Collinstown? Ooh... I'd love to go there. I've never been. Have you, Jenny?"

"No."

"Oh, it's great. It's deadly. There's a huge aeroplane that comes in from Liverpool twice a week. It's something else to see all those people getting out of the plane – people who were only maybe minutes before all in England."

The two girls' eyes were wide with delight. Jack sat back in his chair with a crooked smile.

"I might take youse both out there if I get the job I'm going for."

"Oh my God, that would be just ace, wouldn't it Jennifer? Imagine sneaking onto a plane going to America! Do they go to America?"

"I don't think so. Maybe after the war they will. Would you like to see America?"

"Oh, Jesus Mary and Joseph, I would! My uncle and cousins live there – in Chicago."

Jack's eyes settled calmly on hers. "It's my biggest dream," he said.

Chapter 4 – "Decay in the Apple Core"

New York City, USA; Present Day

Alva stood staring in the hallway of her apartment with her arms folded as the two ambulance men lowered her husband into the wheelchair. Her drawn face reflected a flat empty glass. Depressed. Humiliated. The words and associated images mind just paraded through her mind in an uninspiring fashion. Bereft. She was bereft of sympathy, of any empathy. Jack wasn't even looking at her. How long had it been since he'd gone beyond noticing, beyond caring, beyond offering the smallest piece of attention? He was manic. A maniac. He too was bereft, she thought; bereft of any warmth. With him, there were only lists of places to be and things to do. He was already compiling more of them. She could see that in his eyes that never stopped moving over and back in an attempt to put his world in order; to get everything that had become so disorganised back into its proper place. Was that all he craved? Where was the love and the tenderness that she was sure she once felt? There was a time when she felt like she was bathing in it, that there was some kind of world being created before her especially for her and that it was an endless sea of love. He may have even written her those words once. She wasn't sure.

She took a deep breath and tried not to think about any of it. There was no use. One thing that she had learned from all the time she spent with Jack was that there was no point in looking back. The past is past and the present is only a fleeting tingle. The future was all that counted and without an eye on the future, you're as good as dead. They were Jack's words again. It made her wonder if she'd lost the ability even to think for herself anymore.

"Ma'am?" The larger of the two men had just said something she'd missed. He was holding a clipboard with a yellow printed sheet attached to it. In the other hand, he held out a ballpoint pen. He looked like a kind man and his round dark face betrayed no emotion. His big brown eyes regarded her with a soothing professional calm. She guessed that he was probably a sixth or seventh generation New Yorker; that his relatives came up here from the South after the emancipation. Such horrors there were in the past, such misery and hatred and yet here they were all descended from their own various horrors and living in a calm and civilised present.

"I'm sorry, my dear. Am I to sign this?"

"Yes, ma'am. It's just to say that your husband is no longer in our care and that we have delivered him to you safe and sound."

"Well, I suppose he's not as perfect as I'd like him to be, but sure he'll do like that!" She made a half-hearted attempt to punctuate her joke with a laugh, uncertain if it would be understood or even if it was a joke at all.

The ambulance men smiled politely and disappeared through the doorway, closing it behind them.

Her stomach pulled downwards perceptibly at the suddenness of being left completely alone with Jack after the suspended existence of the last six months. For a moment, Alva considered a crazy thought of opening the door and simply pushing him out. She smiled at the notion. There was so much anger in her. She went behind her husband and released the brake. The chair moved smoothly over the polished parquet floor with the slightest of effort.

Alva brought her husband into the living room. She placed him just beyond the far end of the settee, faced him towards the television and applied the brake. She then went to sit at the opposite end of the settee. She drew up her legs and switched on the television.

Aside from a grunt of acknowledgement, Jack hadn't spoken a word since he returned to the apartment. Alva wasn't worried. She took it as a sign that he was very much aware of the depth of trouble he was in; of the gravity of the situation that they found themselves in. It was clear that he wasn't going back to work any time soon. The club was still closed and without Jack, there essentially was no club. George had been calling in and trying to keep the doors open as best he could since Jack's stroke, but he had his own commitments. Only the day before, he had called to say that he had the accountant wind up the operation and put everything in order. All the taxes were up to date and their money was safe in an account in Jack's name. Now she was a signatory too. She had to have access to the money in order to keep up with the mounting bills from the hospital. After the initial three months, the weekly payments had to increase ten-fold as their health plan ran short.

Alva wasn't going to say anything. She was surprised at her own steely determination not to utter a single word to him unless he spoke first. There was a time when she worried so much about what he was feeling, what was going on in his head. Was there a problem? Could she help? What was bothering him? He would always reply with some throwaway comment coupled with a sardonic smile, as much as to say that his problems were his own problems and it was nothing that she was equipped to cope with. Now she had some inkling. Now she understood that he had been living in his own life and in his own world that was quite apart from hers; from their life together.

She didn't even feel the burn of betrayal anymore. That was a smouldering presence that had been eating away at her for decades, without her being able to put a name on it or see it clearly. A slow death without formal identification. Now she had a face and a name in the form of that Italian woman who had come into the room and been acting like she was Jack's wife. Ms Serio was like a caricature, she thought. In Alva's eyes, she so closely resembled the embodiment of the 'other younger exotic woman' that her initial reaction was to suppress a laugh when she first saw her. It was with disbelief that it quickly dawned on her that this was no dream and that he really had been with her all this time. The humiliation she felt on that day that she had first laid eyes on her... she swore she wouldn't suffer it again.

On the television screen before her, an insane man was jumping up and down in some kind of gym, shouting instruction through a mawkish smile. Everyone was dressed in garish colours. She suddenly had a feeling of extreme nausea. This elfin hybrid of a creature with his false enthusiasm, false smile and false clothing seemed to represent everything she detested about America. False hopes, false dreams, false green fields on the other side of a long journey over the sea, false people, false husbands, false wives, false... fucking shit! She almost said the words aloud. She hated bad language. Here, people swore more disdainful abandon than they did in Ireland. She briefly considered the idea of going back but it only made her laugh. She never really had any intention of doing so and now she couldn't countenance the thought for a completely different set of reasons.

She needed to talk to her lawyer and take full control of the situation. She still hadn't even so much as looked in Jack's direction, even though she could feel his eyes on her every now and again; holding his face steady while his eyes peered across like someone lying in the undergrowth wearing camouflage – afraid to move lest he give his position away. Afraid and subjugated was how she wanted him to remain. She felt emboldened and empowered at the thought of what would surely lie ahead: a path of her choosing for once. She changed the channel. Two newsreaders were wearing enormous white-toothed smiles and laughing at something. All the newsreaders here are like performing seals, she thought. She sighed, wishing that she didn't feel so melancholic for something undefinable and out of reach.

"I don't suppose a fella could getta cup o' tea around here?" Jack spoke, looking at his wife hopefully but with his trademark smile that seemed to operate on an energy of its own. She reacted by turning up the sound on the television. Jack's gaze turned to the television as if mesmerised by the sight of the newsreaders talking about the birth of a baby elephant at Cincinnati Zoo, guffawing wildly but still maintaining a degree of professional control and polish. He thought of his own situation. He felt like a man on the edge of a cliff. The professional calm was important but he was struggling to keep it. He scolded himself inwards and pulled his jaw forward as if adjusting an unseen collar. Always look to the future. When would he be able to get back to the club? This was just temporary, he thought. I'll be out of here soon. His hand, he felt, had improved in the three months in hospital. Now that he was out of that goddamn place, he'd be able to exercise it normally without some dumbass orderly or nurse looking over his shoulder and moving it for him. Yeah. He'd get his hand going properly again, then his leg and he'd get the club open again. They'd all rush back to see him; to see how he's doing. There'd be a party in his honour. It would be a great occasion, with the New York Post and the Daily News taking pictures. My God, how have you been? What? Jesus Christ, we came as soon as we hear you were back, man! Great to see you. Really? You weren't able to move your left arm? Or your leg? That bad, huh? Who woulda thought it? All working now, eh? Sure, everything's in perfect order again... know what I mean? Ha ha, what a guy, that Irishman! Can't put you down that easy!

Yes, he would be back again. He straightened up in his chair as best he could. Why didn't he have one of those ones with the electric control so he could get around by himself?

"Jesus Christ, I need one of those wheelchairs that I can control myself." He said the words aloud, as if talking to himself but really directed at his wife. He tried pushing himself forward, jerking his upper body forward and trying to move the wheel with his right hand.

"The brake is on so it won't move," Alva said impassively. She sighed and got up to go to the kitchen, walking past in front of him as she did. His eyes followed her, like a dog seeking permission to go somewhere.

She would make his damned tea, Alva thought. It was only going to be one night here at any rate. Tomorrow, he'd be the problem of the people in the assisted living centre and he wasn't getting any sugar.

Chapter 5 – Dream Big

Dublin; January 1945

"Are you sure it's okay for me to stay here?" Alva's eyes were big and wild with excitement. They were seated opposite one another by the window with a view of the runway. Their left hands were joined midway across the table. Jack grinned. She liked the way the large window lit up one side of his face, she thought he looked like a film-star.

"Yeah. It's no problem – they're grand with that sort of thing."

Alva smiled and clasped Jack's hand with both her hands before squeezing and sitting up. It was her first time being at an airport. She was so excited to be here with Jack as her guide, chaperone and protector. She couldn't stop looking all around her. On the tarmac outside, a plane moved slowly across, busying itself like a giant bumble bee, going somewhere... It was all so mysterious. There was a constant humming of sounds and orders and words that you never saw anywhere else. It was a world so full of possibility. The bar was new and wonderful. It was an ordinary pub in so many ways and yet so completely different. For a start, it was called a "bar". Nobody used such a modern word to describe a pub in Dublin or possibly anywhere else in Ireland for that matter. This was surely for all the Americans that would be coming here once they got big enough planes and once the war was over. Even now, there was a collection of people here that looked impossibly international to Alva's eyes.

The seats were like something out of a hotel, only more modern, more... New York. They were soft, comfortable and new. The Bar was like any other only it too had a gleaming newness about it and it was like something ready to start dancing, with its shiny busy surface of deep orange and black patterns like tiles melting into one another. And the carpet – it was deep and soft, absorbing any noises and creating a luxurious hush.

"It's just that in some places, they don't like the staff fraternising with lady visitors." She emphasised the word 'fraternising' and frowned suggestively at the same time leaning forward into Jack's face.

Jack smiled at her coquettishness. She had a slightly mysterious and brazen attitude towards sexual matters – unlike any other girls he knew. She was reserved but with a controlled cheekiness beneath it and she seemed to know how to time such expressions so that they were all the sweeter for it. He held his head up in feigned haughtiness.

"Oh, now they've nothing against a bit of fraternisin' of a Friday night!" Alva giggled delightedly at Jack's attempt at mimicking his old boss Éamonn. "Provided you've your job done and sorted beforehand, mind." It didn't quite come out quite as witty and hilarious as he intended it would but Alva was laughing – that was the main thing.

Alva's thoughts flashed through the events of the previous weekend. She knew that no decent girl was supposed to 'fraternise' before marriage, but she didn't care. They had taken some precautions and they were going to be married soon anyway, so what did it matter? Besides, her father could hardly throw stones what with his carry-on. She wasn't supposed to know anything about that but she did. She had overheard her parents arguing on more than one occasion and it wasn't difficult to put together the pieces of the puzzle to get a clear picture of what was going on.

"What did you say your father did again?" Jack asked, as if reading her thoughts.

"He works for the Corporation."

"Does he now? Driving a lorry or something like that?" He couldn't imagine it. He had been in Alva's house and met her mother. Theirs was a fancy place. They even had a maid working for them.

"No, silly man! I already told you... he's high up in the housing department of the Corporation. He decides on giving people housing in Dublin. He knows absolutely everyone!"

"Oh yeah? He doesn't know me, though, does he?"

Alva laughed. "He probably does! No, he does know a lot of people. Any time we're out in town, like in a restaurant or going to Mass or something like that, he just has all these people coming up to him and talking to him. Even in the summer, if we go down to Bray to the seaside, he gets no peace from it, and neither do we."

Jack was smiling.

"What? What are you smiling at? Are you laughing that all these people keep coming up to us and talking to my father on the strand?"

"No. Well, yes, that is kindof funny all right, now that you mention it! No, I was just looking at the way your face goes when you're telling a story."

She squeezed his hand in mock punishment "What? What do you mean?"

He looked at her kindly, wearing a kind of genteel mature face – more suave and mature than your average 18-year-old Dubliner. "You look like that actress... Katherine Hepburn. Really nice."

"Katherine Hepburn? I do not! Would you go away out of that! Actually, my mother keeps telling me I look like Maureen O'Hara! Can you imagine?"

"Maureen O'Hara? Who's she?"

"She's an Irish film actress. She's not as beautiful as the American ones, mind you. My father actually knows her. Her real name isn't Maureen O'Hara at all, you know."

"Is it not?"

"No. It's a stage name."

"Funny stage name. Why didn't she pick something more… film-star, like?"

"I don't know. I can't actually remember what her real name is. Daddy knows it, though." She looked around thoughtfully. The bar seemed to have gone very quiet. There must have been about twentyother people besides them. They all looked like they were in their Sunday costumes and on their best behaviour. They were all talking quietly and respectfully as if they were at Mass or else not talking at all. There was one man over to her left who kept catching her eye. He wore a heavy expensive-looking patterned green top coat. His brown felt hat had a band around it that looked vaguely Germanic with a small white feather tucked inside it. He was about fifty or sixty, balding and with deeply sallow skin and he just stared into space, checking his wristwatch every five minutes and taking regular sips from what seemed to be a glass of whiskey.

"When will we tell them?" she asked.

"Your parents?"

"Yes. I want us to get married. I want to tell them."

"I suppose," he paused and cleared his throat, sitting up and uncoupling his hand from hers. "I suppose we should do it right and ask to see them together. What do you think?"

"Yes. That's what I thought we were doing. Daddy will be home this weekend. That's the best time – he's always busy during the week."

"Does he work long hours?"

She couldn't help tutting in a mild expression of disgust. "Yes, whatever he's at until the late hours. We never see him during the week." She lowered her head and they were silent for a moment, each averting their gaze towards the runway.

"I must tell you something," he spoke the words quietly but clearly and without moving his head. They looked at one another again. "It's just between us, mind, but... you might as well know. You should know, in fact..."

"Yes."

"I think... actually I know for a fact that my father... visits other women and my mother doesn't know about it. At least, I don't think she does."

Alva was shocked and her hand-made an involuntary movement towards her mouth. It wasn't that such a thing was unimaginable. It was because she didn't imagine that they would find themselves talking about such matters and it was quite amazing to find that the very same thing was happening in Jack's family as was happening in hers. Why was that? Was it just a coincidence? If so, it was an extraordinary one and it made her feel closer to him. Or maybe this always been the norm and she was just too blind or too young to notice it before?

Somehow, it didn't quite seem like any of their business and yet it was very much so and a very important thing to talk about. She also caught her breath in an effort to prevent herself from saying anything about her own father. Why she didn't want to talk about it, she wasn't quite sure. It was almost as if there was another presence beside her or within her – one that was placing a firm hand on her shoulder and telling her that this wasn't the time; that there would be other opportunities to talk about this during their life together. If she told him now what she knew to be going on – that her father also 'visited' other women – then it would all become a pointless place without a moral pillar. It would be too depressing; talking about plans and dreams and marriage when the very marriages that they came from were no more than castles made of sand. No. This talk would hold for another time.

"That's… a shame," she said finally, looking into his eyes pleadingly. "I'm glad you told me but it really doesn't matter."

He looked at her, unconvinced. His customary smile had turned downwards with twisted purpose in an almost comical inverted smile. He looked hurt and uncertain. She took his hands again in both of hers.

"You are not your father. Do you understand? I'm marrying you, Jack Mills Junior, and I'm really sorry for you and for your mother but you shouldn't have to be feeling ashamed of that. That's for your parents to think about and worry about."

Jack thought about the fact that he knew there was something going on, even as a child, but he never said anything to his mother – not once. He wanted to, but he didn't. Maybe Alva was right and it was basically his parents' business and not his. He pulled her hands up to his mouth and placed a kiss on them, looking up at her with one eyebrow raised.

"Would you like a drink from the bar, Madame?" he said, as suavely as he could manage. "A sherry, perhaps?"

"Sherry indeed! What would I do with a sherry?"

"I don't see why not. You're a very sophisticated young woman and I hear that you've plans of marriage."

Alva blushed and looked around in case anyone she knew had overheard. "Go on, so," she said, whispering conspiratorially. "I'll have a small one."

Jack arrived home later that evening to the sight of his mother asleep in the comfortable armchair with a ball of knitting in her lap. She woke with a start when he closed the door behind him. The door of the former stable building led directly into the street outside and it always left in a breeze that whisked across the whole ground floor at foot level.

"Sorry to disturb you, Ma. I'm only just back."

She moved her knitting aside from her swollen belly and wiped her eyes vigorously. "I must have fallen asleep. I get very tired with this one, whatever it is. I don't remember being half as tired with you. Did you have a nice time with Alva? She's a wonderful girl. So nicely mannered and lively."

He sat down in front of her before she could think about getting up.

"In fact, it's funny you should say how wonderful she is because," he stopped and grimaced at what he was saying, hardly recognising himself in his own speech. This wasn't as easy to just blurt out as he had planned. "Well, we were actually talking about getting married and... and we think that we want to."

May Mills was taken aback. Her first reaction was that it was all happening too soon. How long had they been doing a line? Barely a year if it was that. She couldn't quite remember but she knew that it was before she became pregnant. It was all so much to deal with and she couldn't find the words. Was she losing one child just as she was about to gain another? Nothing was coming out for what seemed like an eternity and the emotion welled up inside her.

It's... so soon. Well, I think it's fabulous." She stopped to collect herself and looked downwards to hide any tears that were determined to appear. She felt silly and selfish all at once. How could she not feel anything but ecstatically happy for her only son marrying a perfect girl?

"Ma. Come on, Ma... don't start crying. Please. We're just talking about it. Well, we want to get married soon but it might be for a while."

Jack sat forward in the chair. He didn't know whether to wait until she collected herself or touch her. Maybe that would set her off even worse. He lowered his head and decided to wait for a minute; wait for her to gather her thoughts and emotions. He knew that women found it hard to think clearly while they were pregnant. She just needed a moment to get over the shock. He had to think of his own future now. His mother would be here with the baby, whatever gender it turned out to be, and he would be gone to America with Alva. That was the plan. He longed to be rid of this place, with its tight walls that constricted around him day after day, and he longed to be rid of Dublin and Ireland too. Most of all, however, he longed to be away from this farcical situation; this pretend happy family with a father who had more interest in driving around fancy women than looking to his own nest. What was looking for? Why was he not happy enough with his son and his wife? One of these days, it would all come out and there would be more shame heaped upon this little place and this little family and he wasn't going to be here when that day came along. No Sir. He was America bound as soon as possible. Yes, he'd wait for his new sister or brother to arrive but then he was gone. He had never said so much to his mother directly or explicitly but she knew and that was why she was crying so much. The clock on the sideboard behind the settee his mother was sitting on ticked its flat beat through his mother's sniffles. He remembered that his father had acquired that sideboard somehow from a 'run' out to Lucan – some associate of his boss from the Shelbourne had it and wanted to get rid of it. It was the only piece of truly class furniture in the house, Jack thought. Art Deco. It always looked to him like something that was invited in momentarily and that it would never quite belong here.

"I'm sorry, pet. I don't know what's wrong with me. If your father saw me, he'd say it was me hormones acting up."

"Where is he, anyway? I thought he had the day off today?"

"He did but had a job to do on a run out to Bray."

Jack couldn't help snorting ever-so-slightly and smiling out of the corner of his mouth. He nodded, knowingly. "Yeah. Bray is a good run, all right."

"I'm very happy that ye're thinking about it. I really am. She's a lovely girl. I know I keep saying it but she really is and I think that you'll both be happy for many years together."

"Thanks, Ma."

"Have you made any plans? Have you talked to your father about it?"

"No, Ma. You're the first one I've told. I don't know. We're really serious about it and I've saved a lot of money from my time at the 'Horse' and even from the new job at the airport too so we thought that we would discuss it first, like, with our parents and see what happens then."

"Ah, you're very good. You were always a very good boy." The last word went up at the end involuntarily as she melted into tears once more. This time, Jack leaned forward and took her hands to comfort her. He wouldn't mention anything about going to America. Not this time – not yet.

"So, what do you think?" Alva asked Jennifer in the front room of the Blake family home in Sandymount. Alva was sitting forward in the armchair, her back to the front window. From Jennifer's viewpoint on the settee opposite, she could see the voile vision of the outside world, with the blurred outlines of seagulls flitting across the sky at regular intervals and she could just about make out the upper quarter of the famous Martello Tower – the one that her father told her had featured in an infamously banned book by that rogue of a writer James Joyce. She imagined that all kinds of illicit things went on there, that its thick walls and inexpressive squat exterior created an impenetrable seal from the normal Catholic-church-dominated workaday life of Ireland of the Emergency. It was one of those mysterious enclaves of an alternative world that was worrying and exciting in equal measure to her mind. Now, here was her best friend talking to her about launching herself into a real-life mystery of her own; about getting married and going away to America.

"Oh Alva! It's absolutely ace! I had a feeling... the very first day I saw you with him in that French place on Portobello. You really hit it off! Do you remember?"

Alva was nodding delightedly. They clasped hands, held them tight and released again.

"I haven't told my mother or my father yet," she whispered audibly and hurriedly.

"Oh. Why not?"

"I'm going to. Tonight. My father was working late and busy all week so... I'll talk to them tonight."

"Oh, Alva! What will it be like? Being married? Going to America?"

"Well, we hope we get to America."

"Oh, I don't know how I'd be. Maybe a bit scared...."

"Well, yes it is all a bit scary. I suppose. And do you know, the funny things is that when we decided it, he was all serious and wanting to talk about something. For a moment, I was half afraid that he might want to break us up."

"Really?"

"Well, he gets a lot of attention from other girls. Even when he was working in town, I used to see how other ladies would look at him – the older women as well as the younger ones. And since he was out at the airport, I just used to imagine all these English women sidling up to him with their expensive coats and make-up and their nylon stockings!"

"And did he go down on one knee?"

"No. He didn't really. Well, he did after we talked about it. It was a bit different – nothing like what I expected it would be like to have a man propose to you. We kind of talked about it. Like I said, he was all so serious and then he was talking about what we would do. I wasn't sure what he was saying for the first few minutes – I was only thinking 'so he's not breaking us up'. Then he was asking if his dreams were the same as my dreams; if I wanted to be part of the same dream."

"Oh Alva! That's awfully romantic, so it is! Part of the same dream!"

"I just said 'Yes' and then he got down on his knee and kissed my hand."

"Did he give you a ring?"

"Not yet. He said that he has one picked out for me. He's saved up money for the boat from here to England and then from England to America. We're going to tell our parents first... See how they react."

"They'll be happy. Sure, they love Jack, don't they?"

"Oh, yeah. My mother's mad about him and, as Daddy says, she's the boss."

Alva felt a strange kind of flatness in her elation. It all felt a little like it was no more than a dream. There wasn't quite enough substance to it – no reality to it. Maybe it would all change once they got their parents' blessings, but it felt as if they were just children playing make-believe. This could be a scene from when she was twelve years old, talking to Jennifer in her parents' front room about how she was going to be married to a young count and wear a white wedding dress and be whisked away in a horse-drawn carriage to a land far far away. The clock ticked its loud flat insistent beat on the mantelpiece and Jennifer's spoon tinkled around her tea cup. What was it about the whole scenario that seemed so surreal? She hadn't told Jack about thinking that he might be breaking up their relationship. Why would she? She was wrong about that anyway but he seemed to still enjoy getting smiles from other women and he chatted with them so easily, so casually... making them laugh and dream the kind of dreams that reflected in her eyes when she looked at him. Yet it was he who wanted to be married. He had asked her and she had said yes. He wasn't interested in any girl only in her. Otherwise, he wouldn't have decided; he wouldn't have talked to her about marrying and going to America. Yes, they did have the same dream and, in another year, or so, they would have enough money to make it real.

Jennifer sipped her tea and stared out of the window again, thoughtfully. "Yes, you're lucky that your parents like him. They're good, aren't they? I mean, my parents won't be happy until I'm hitched up with a doctor or a bloody barrister!"

Alva laughed. "Or a count!"

"Yeah! A count! Be like Countess Markievicz – with a gun and holster!"

"Ha ha! Ohhh... Jenny. Well if we do get to New York or wherever, I do hope you'll come and call on us. After you've trapped your barrister of course."

"Of course. I'd like to travel the world."

"Where would you go?"

"Everywhere that's spicy and exotic... Abyssinia! Indochina! Kuala Lumpur!"

"Well don't forget to work us into your schedule when you make your journey around the world, now."

Jennifer looked into Alva's eyes and wondered what would become of them. She could see everything happening at speed from now on. She didn't really want her to disappear and if she had to disappear, then she wasn't fully certain that she wanted her to disappear with Jack. To her, he looked too much like someone who would always be looking for something beyond the horizon. Yes, he was a kind and funny man and yes, he seemed to be devoted to Alva, but he wasn't happy to remain here in Dublin even though he had a steady job and plenty of money at a time when most people in the city seemed to be living on the bread line. His eyes were kind and warm too, but they were always looking about restlessly; looking beyond and over the shoulder of whomever he was talking to; looking past them, outside, through the streets, over the hills and over the sea. What would he be seeking when he got to America? Something more? She shuddered, lowered her head and shook it, feeling ashamed at herself for running away with her thoughts at a time when she should be thinking only celebratory thoughts for her friend.

"What is it? What's wrong?" Alva took Jennifer's hands.

"Oh, Alva. It's just that it's all so sudden and it's moving so fast. It only seems like a few weeks ago when you were talking about him and now you're talking about marrying and leaving for ever. I'll be broken-hearted to see you go, you're my best friend but I'm really happy for you. You're brave, so you are."

"Ah, here. Don't get all maudlin on me just yet. I'm not going anywhere for a while." Both of them had stopped talking and just looked into one another's moist eyes trying to ascertain one another's thoughts and feeling a growing sense of uncertainty and sadness.

There was a knock on the door and Angela walked in to clear the tray.

Jack stood with his back to the door to admire the view while he waited for someone to arrive and open it for him. He knew that he'd have a couple of seconds between the sound of approaching feet across the tiled floor of the inner porch and when the latch would be opened, giving him time to spin around to dramatic effect just like Cary Grant in His Girl Friday. He held the small bouquet of flowers with his right hand while with his left, he pinched the collars of his coat against the cold air that was moving in from the Irish Sea. On the horizon of the still grey water, he could make out the muddled masts of a mid-sized vessel – probably a trawler, he thought. It seemed to be heading eastwards, on the same route that he and Alva would soon be taking to England to get their passage to America. It was all that he could think of these days. He hoped that she was just as excited about it all as he was. She certainly seemed to be. There were other girls that he found more attractive. There seemed to be plenty of them these days and he tried to push those few that he had shared some passionate moments with right out of his head while he concentrated on Alva. She was still something special – someone who had a similar outlook on things. He wanted to go places, really go places and so did she. She didn't want to be stuck in this poverty-trapped oversized village any more than he did. He was beginning to see what his Uncle Tom in Meath meant by "hypocrites in soutanes and birettas". There were too many priests here and too many people falling over themselves to please them. America was a place where a man was in charge of his own destiny. He knew it. He could feel it in every twitching fibre of his body. He took a deep breath as if preparing for some sudden physical feat. He was about to spit in the direction of the sea but then realised where he was and thought that he had better not. A curlew wailed its evening song as the cold wind rose. A middle-aged man walked along the pavement and stopped at the gate. He had a large but well-trimmed moustache and looked straight at Jack as if he knew him. Jack was about to turn around when the man opened the gate and strode confidently up to him.

"You must be Jack!" he said with delight, removing his hat to reveal a thin sweep of receding dark hair tinged with grey on the sides.

"Yes," he said dumbly, switching the bouquet to his left hand as he answered the offer of a handshake.

"I'm Anthony Blake... Alva's father."

"Ah, hello Mr Blake. It's a pleasure to meet you."

"Likewise, likewise." He had a broad impish smile like a comical actor putting on a show for Jack. "And come here now – none of this Mr Blake nonsense. Call me Anthony. Please."

"Yes, Anthony." He forced it out of his mouth like a child being made to confess by a priest to a transgression he'd rather have not mentioned.

"I hope those aren't for me! Ha ha!" Alva's father pointed at the flowers and scrunched himself up into an energetic laugh. "Listen, come in, come in out of the cold!"

The head of the Blake household moved surprisingly quickly, and Jack was ushered past the stately hallway and into the warm front room before he knew it while Anthony went to hang up his coat.

Finding himself alone, Jack sat on the sofa and looked around again at the room, taking in its dimensions. It seemed even larger than the first time he had been here and he was noticing lots of things that didn't seem to have been there before. The piano in the corner was one. It was a brown upright type with the fallboard up ready to be played. He thought there had been some kind of table there the last day. Maybe it had been covered with a cloth. Maybe Anthony would be playing some raucous rugbyman songs on it later on – he seemed like the type. He was of that class of Dublin society that were at ease with life in Ireland. The things that bothered most people and hung around their necks like a bad spirit weighing them down through life just didn't bother people like Mr Blake, like Anthony. Jack wondered if he had been born into such an upbringing, would he still feel such a strong pull away from Dublin and towards America. Probably so, he concluded. Alva seemed to feel the same pull as he did. Maybe it just depended on your attitude. His own father certainly never showed any signs of wanting to move from Dublin. Maybe it didn't matter what you had, only what you wanted and what you wanted to be.

He scanned his costume quickly for any faults and fingered the knot on his tie to ensure that it hadn't slipped to one side or come undone. It was a brand new single-breasted navy suit that he had got from Lynch's on Aungier Street. Even the V-neck pullover underneath was new. The shirt was a work shirt, as was the tie. The door opened and Angela beckoned the young man to dinner.

Jack felt at home at the dinner table in the Blake household. The dark timber table was set out in beautiful white linen and heavy silver cutlery. It wasn't something that he hadn't seen before – just never in someone else's house. They even had had wine in solid crystal glasses. He hadn't cared much for it, however. It was his third or fourth time trying it and to his palate, it was sharp and acidic. James – his boss at the airport bar – maintained that most French wines brought into Ireland were "pure piss" by the time they made it here and that, anyway, "the Germans have been drinking all the good stuff since they took over the show."

Jack liked Mrs Blake's style. Her husband was full of giggles and winks and self-deprecating wit ("Sure, tis far from Chateau Lafite we were all reared, what?") but she had an unapologetic grace about it all. He could see some of the same characteristics in her daughter. Alva wasn't saying much throughout the meal – mostly smiling thoughtfully across the table. Maybe it was the dizziness caused by the wine, but he thought her particularly alluring tonight and he found himself trying not to gaze at her too much in the company of her parents.

"So tell me, Jack," Anthony began as the desserts were put in front of everyone, "what kind of clientele would you have at the airport bar? I'd imagine they'd be all well-to-do people with a few German spies thrown in? Ha-ha!"

"That sums it up pretty well, Mr Blake."

"Anthony, please!"

"Sorry, yes. Anthony, I'd say that there's about half of the people there waiting for a plane to go on it or to meet someone and the rest of them are just there to have a look at the place – you know, just tourists, if you like, having a look at what an airport looks like and feels like."

"Is that right, yeah." Jack smiled inwardly at the ultra-serious expression on Anthony's face. He caught a quick glance at Alva. She sipped her wine as if to suppress a chortle.

"Oh Daddy, it's very nice! You should see it. Everything brand new and right-up-to-the-minute fashion – the bar, the big comfy seats, the people there... everything."

"Begod I must have a jaunt out there soon, so. What do you think, Gwen? Will we take the motor car out to the airport the next fine Sunday afternoon?"

Gwendoline pushed out a polite smile to her husband before turning to Jack.

"Alva tells me that they've made you head barman there," she said.

Jack sat back in relaxed fashion, his right hand anchored on the table and holding the stem of his wine glass with his forefinger and thumb. "That's right, Mrs Blake. I was looking at my options before going there and I told them that I would take the job on the condition that I was made head barman."

Alva looked slightly puzzled. She hadn't heard that before.

"I see," said Gwendoline. "so the prospects are quite good, so?"

"Oh yes, Mrs Blake. Sure it's a busy place and do you know, it's only a matter of time before this terrible war comes to an end now that the Americans are really involved. After that, there'll be no stopping the place – flights to America, Rome, Paris... you name it."

"They've a bit of a way to go yet, those Americans," interjected

Anthony. "There'll be a bit of fighting but they'll get there all right."

There was a lull in the conversation and Anthony was the first to begin eating his ice-cream and blackberry pavlova. They all followed, eating in silence. Angela poured the tea.

Jack and Alva exchanged glances with one another and Jack took a short breath, cleared his throat and sat upright.

"Mr Blake –"

"Anthony!"

"- No, for now I think I'll just leave it at Mr Blake if you don't mind. Mr Blake, Mrs Blake. First of all, I'd like to thank you both for inviting me to your lovely home here tonight. As you might already suspect, I do have an ulterior motive for coming here and it has to do with your wonderful daughter."

Gwendoline's hand went instinctively to her chest and then up to her mouth to suppress any outpouring of emotion that she could already feel building up in her.

"I'm humbly asking you for your daughter's hand in marriage."

Gwendoline couldn't help the tears from coming. Anthony looked from her to Jack and back again as if he had genuinely not been expecting this to happen.

"Well I..." he began.

"Oh Jack! That's wonderful news!" Gwendoline stood up and opened her arms. Jack went over to receive the hug while Anthony applauded dumbly.

"Oh, I'd nearly marry him myself!" she said, as she released her son-in-law to be and moved to embrace Alva to her left. The two men looked on while the ladies cried tears of delight into one another's shoulders.

Chapter 6 – Breakaway

New York, Present Day

"And where is your husband at the moment?" Cheryl Rudder had a very distinctive way of asking questions. She was always completely deadpan, placing her arms in front of her on the desk in a non-threatening pose that left the interlocutor with the clear message that they had all the time in the world to answer carefully and correctly – whether it was the most innocuous question or one that had all kinds of powerful implications. When she spoke, it was always at speed and with her eyes closing momentarily to assist her concentration. She was always switched on and sharp – the best lawyer in the Upper East Side, according to Alva's friend Margaret. Margaret was a Mayo woman who had taken on much of the affectations and mannerisms of the New York intelligentsia and had even married a well-to-do banker. She was, Alva thought, a good soul behind it all. Even though her outward idiosyncrasies suggested someone shallow and false, she was pure gold as a friend and she trusted her advice on all matters of importance. Take this lawyer before her, for example. Had it not been for Margaret's recommendation, Alva would have not considered Ms Rudder for a second, with her frozen plasticsurgery lips and domineering schoolmistress style. She remained professionally passive before her, awaiting the answer to her question.

"Right now, he's in assisted living… in the West 86," Alva said finally.

"On the Upper West Side?"

"Yes."

"And how much did you say that was costing per month?"

"$5,300 a month."

Cheryl nodded thoughtfully and scribbled on her large yellow lined writing pad. Her head was lowered and her right hand moved furiously but the rest of her remained immobile. Over the last few months as she and Cheryl had been unravelling all of Jack's financial and legal affairs, they had exchanged some personal thoughts and information but she had never asked Cheryl's age. For some reason, it had never been relevant to any of their conversations, which were always overwhelmingly taken up with professional matters anyway. Cheryl was the kind of woman that simply did not exist in Ireland – or at least, not in the Ireland that Alva had grown up with. If she decided one fine day to up sticks and move her practice to Dublin, Alva felt quite sure that anyone she encountered there would take one look at her and decide that she was a madwoman. She was tall – with a masculine bird-like quality about her. Her small brown eyes peered at you through her soft-framed glasses. Her hair was naturally coloured, shoulder-length, swept back from her face and kept in place by the permanent fixture of a soft green headband. She could be forty-two... or even fifty-two...

"Mrs Mills, I don't believe that this situation is tenable... from a financial point of view, I mean."

"But there's enough money in the account now to cover his expenses for another few years, surely."

"Yes, I think that the next four or maybe five years will be fine. But you have to think about what's going to happen after that. Once that money is gone, there is no other income."

Alva knew this, of course. She had been thinking about nothing else since Jack had returned from the hospital a year and a half ago. She had needed to hear it confirmed to her by someone in a position of authority for it to warrant the next step, whatever that might be. She nodded thoughtfully.

"What does that imply? What does that mean for me?"

Cheryl straightened herself, crossed her legs and made a tent with her fingers, closing her eyes slightly.

"It means, Mrs Blake, that you need to take steps to ensure your own well-being: steps that will ensure the continuance of your home and of your lifestyle. You're not an elderly woman, Mrs Blake, and I'm sure you wish to continue living an independent lifestyle for as long as you can?"

"Yes. Of course."

"Then you will have to look at taking steps to ensure that that will remain possible. If not, I'm afraid that it can only end one way."

"Yes." She was like a member of a congregation in a Christian church in the Southern States, agreeing and almost giving praise to what she already knew to be the truth, to what she wanted to hear.

"This is going to involve some very difficult choices, Mrs Blake. There are options for you other than that of simply leaving your husband in the care of a private assisted living home. I understand that he's unable to walk?"

"That's right, yes. He's lost the use of his right leg and he has limited use of his right arm."

"I'm sorry to hear that. I presume that involved a lot of regular work from your point of view before he moved into assisted living?"

"A little, yes. But we did have a carer who used to come in and change his dressings, gave him a hand… took all kinds of verbal abuse." She tried to push out a laugh at the last sentence but it wouldn't come. There had been too many years of abusive language and so often she had been the brunt of his dismissive repartee. It wasn't jolly or funny or charming anymore. She only just seemed to realise that now; here in the clarity of this roomy office of expensive corporate furniture, shiny timber floor, Oriental rug and dark bookcases that ran either side of the picture window behind Cheryl

Rudder in cinematic fashion.

"So the option of him returning to your home without the carer would be difficult to contemplate too?" She let the words of the rhetorical question sink in for a few heartbeats. "You could, for example, have him made a ward of the State of New York. It would entitle him to regular care and housing in a designated centre and as someone in a state of pre-destitution and approaching retirement age, you'd have a clear argument in favour of such a move."

"What would that mean?"

"It would mean that the state would take charge of his accommodation and health and you would no longer be responsible for him –emotionally, professionally or financially."

Alva thought for a moment. What her lawyer was suggesting was abandonment. What would her family say if they ever got wind of that? Jack had certainly not been a good husband but was it right to abandon him now when he needed help?

"Don't think of it as an abandonment of any kind." It was as if Cheryl was reading her thoughts. "It happens much more often than you think. Mrs Mills... if one partner gets sick, then it can often lead to the other person becoming sick from the effort of trying to look after their spouse. You're both not getting any younger and looking after somebody who's infirm – even someone you know and love for many years – will take its toll."

On the short cab ride back home through town, Alva considered the words of her legal counsel. She took a deep breath and looked out at the afternoon crowds. It was always this river of energy that she loved most about New York. It was a human river that ebbed and flowed according to some unseen force through the straight concrete canyons of the city. It was like an enormous living organism and it never stopped going, never stopped giving off its endless ions of positive energy. Once you felt it and learned how to live with it, you could never do without it again, she thought, much like the presence of a real river by a house on a hill in the countryside. She took energy from it, even now at this later stage of her life. A home in the Irish countryside had been a fleeting dream of hers once – a very long time ago before she had even met Jack. But not anymore. She was a city girl for sure now. She and her friend Esther from Galway used sometimes talk about returning to Ireland. Esther always joked that it would destroy her in the same way in which the unfortunate Oisín was destroyed when he finally succumbed to leaving behind Tír na nÓg and came back home to Ireland. According to the well-known legend, the warrior had travelled from the Land of Eternal Youth only to be instantly transformed into a helpless old man as soon as his foot touched the soil of the land of his birth. She could never leave New York now. They had been here too many years and she had come to depend on its river of life that seemed to contain all the energy of the world concentrated into one place.

Alva paid the driver and alighted in front of their building. It was a six-storey block – not as tall as most of the buildings in the neighbourhood but this one had nice cut stone detail with an impressive curved façade that extended from the cream granite entrance steps right-up-to-the ornate cornice at the roof line. Even though she knew that Jack wasn't there, she couldn't help indulging in her years-old habit of looking up to the lounge window to see if Jack was at home and up and about. He used to lead such a vampire-like existence; only really coming to life in the afternoon before disappearing into his own private underworld at the club. It was a world that had become his sole domain more and more over the years. She sighed deeply and mounted the steps to the entrance. Harry the doorman was there with his usual smile to open the large tinted-glass door for Alva.

"Good afternoon, Mrs Blake. It looks like we won't be seeing any of that rain today."

"It looks like you were right, Harry. Keep those positive predictions coming."

"I'll certainly try, Mrs Blake. I'll certainly try."

As soon as Alva stepped inside the building, she felt a rush of anxiety. It was a cold kind of feeling like a chill wind that enveloped her and manifested itself as sure as an icy hand caressing the nape of her neck. She had a difficult decision to make. It was strange, but even as she searched her conscience and her heart for a feeling of remorse for the decision that she knew in her heart was already taken, she could find no regret and no compassion for a man whom she once adored. It was that very realisation that had shocked her so. That and an undeniable frisson of excitement that whatever was left of her life, she would now be in control.

Chapter 7 – "Flight to the Big Apple"

Dublin, October 1945

"Now, son… You have all the information before you. I can say no more except to say that it's a good offer and that you have a future here in Dublin. There's not many that can say that."

Jack Junior looked at his father straight in the eyes. For the first time in years, he felt something warm and positive towards his wayward dad. It wasn't from a sense of gratitude at the job offer his father was putting to him – he had been offered this a number of times before, maybe not in the same rather formal manner, but it was always an option for him that his father had made him aware of on several occasions. He knew that he would be able to take over the steady job of being the chauffeur of the owner of the Shelbourne Hotel. His father had got himself the position off the owner of Dublin's most exclusive hotel some time ago and it was no easy achievement. Jack knew that there would be a long line of people in Dublin who would give their right arm for an opportunity like this – an opportunity that would mean gainful employment in their own native city and country and not to have to go taking the boat out of here like so many others seemed cursed to have to do.

No. It wasn't a sense of gratitude because Jack didn't want to stay in Dublin, not under any circumstances that he could imagine at this point in his life. As he looked across the kitchen table and into the eyes of his father, he felt like he was looking at him man-to-man for the first time. It was as if their wordless spat that had lasted between them since childhood had come to an end now that they were both men. It was also the realisation that Jack Junior would soon be leaving Dublin and leaving his father behind and that maybe his father wasn't the worst person in the world after all. Maybe he just didn't get the chance to really know him. Maybe he just chose not to get to know him. In another world or universe – one where you can really start your next day completely afresh and free of everything you'd learned up to that point – he felt that he and his father would be close to one another. They might be like a father and son are supposed to be in the novels and pictures. Was that all complete folly or was it a realisable dream? He wished that he could say all of that and he wondered how to create such a place. Was it one that you must create yourself or was it one of those dreams that seem to be only just beyond the reach of the mortal man? Here they were with so much to say, yet it was all somehow reduced to a conversation involving his father once again offering him a job as a full-time chauffeur to Mr Joyce.

"Do you hear me, son? This is a full-time job this time, now. You'd be on a full wage that would beat any working-man's wage in Dublin and you'd be driving one of the most important gentlemen in town."

Jack Junior was sitting forward with his hands joined before him on the table. He stared straight down at the slight indentation in the edge of the wooden table. It had been there since he could remember. He sat back up straight, feeling like he really was looking at his father as one man looks at another for the first time in his life. It was empowering but soothing at the same time. He held his stare for a moment, his jaw set straight and his shoulders square.

"Dad, I don't think it's for me."

His father's head dropped slightly before he leaned forward. "What do you mean it's not FOR you? It's heaven-made for you! Look at you – you're a fine clean-cut handsome man with a friendly professional attitude on you. You're perfect for it as far as I can see."

Jack Junior had never had a conversation where his father had used so many positive superlatives all in one sentence. He could almost feel a tear welling up. He didn't want his father to see it. He glanced down briefly, cleared his throat, shook his head and looked at his father again.

"I know, Dad. Thanks. I know what you mean but... there are two things. For one, I just don't know if I'd stick it – I mean really stick it being a driver –"

"-chauffeur-"

"- a chauffeur for Mr Joyce. I'm used to dealing with different people, chatting to different people all day. That's something I like and I've got myself good work doing that. I know the money is better and it's a really handy number too with less effort involved and all, but I really like the bar work – meeting people and all that. I don't think that I'd be really happy with driving all day long, you know? I'd be goin' off me head!"

His father nodded his head resignedly.

"The other thing is this plan that Alva and me have for going to America. We're really doing it, so we are. It's not just some fancy dream that we have. We've been saving up and we might be going sooner, maybe before the year is out."

Jack's father just looked at him with kind eyes and extended his hand to his son across the table.

"Well son, then all I can say to you is 'good luck'. Good luck to the pair of youse. All right. I'd better be making me way to the scratcher. Your ma is a fierce woman for the snoring since she's been expecting so I'm hoping to get a few hours of kip anyway."

If this had been James Stewart saying goodnight to his father, there would probably be some kind of lively exchange involving one or the other saying something like "C'mere, you!" before a heartfelt hug. Instead, Jack Junior stood up awkwardly and said "Alright, Da" while his father mounted the stairs gingerly.

Jack was still thinking about his conversation with his father three days later, as he stood cleaning glasses during a quiet period of the mid-morning at Dublin Airport bar in Collinstown. He felt strange – as if something momentous had occurred even though it was such a simple and innocuous conversation that petered out into nothing. Deep within him, however, some kind of subtle rite-of-passage had happened and he now felt as if the whole plan to move to America needed to be accelerated. The sooner he and Alva got out of here, the better. There were too many distractions and heavy weights here. He felt surrounded by them all and he needed to go. Then there was the imminent birth of his brother or sister. He had been trying not to think about it, maybe hoping that it would disappear somehow. He thought about a funny joke that his colleague Trevor had told him about a young-one who was pregnant and had asked the doctor for something to "keep the swelling down". He laughed silently to himself, then thought about his mother's situation again. It was all very strange having a mother so old – almost fifty – and expecting a child. He could never imagine his parents doing it, least of all now when they barely seemed able for it in his eyes. There was going to be such an enormous gap between him and his new sibling. The whole thing was embarrassing and he could feel that everyone else around him was feeling it too. Alva's parents practically looked like they might get physically sick any time Jack's mother's pregnancy was referred to, while he and Alva barely talked about it and he hadn't mentioned it to anyone at work.

Just then, a flock of air hostesses came in and took one of the tables in the farthest corner. There were four of them with the captain. They were a class apart from the regular Irish men and women, he thought. So free in their expression – already half-American. One of them – Máiréad Tanner – clipped across the carpet to the bar.

"Hello, Jack,"

"Howya Máiréad. How's it going?"

She was a petite girl with fine pretty features, framed by shortish curly dark hair and brown eyes that always seemed to sparkle mischievously. He always thought that her body looked misplaced inside the slightly ill-fitting maroon uniform that the hostesses wore. The sleeves were so much broader than her arms surely were – like two melted drainpipes on either side of her and the big brass buttons looked so masculine. The only cute touches were the flight cap that sat still on her head as if by magic and the ever-so-slightly plunging neckline, whose V was filled with a very modern-cut white loose blouse.

"I'm very well, Jack," she smiled coquettishly, standing with her hands behind her back and swaying slightly like a small girl. He looked her up and down and recalled a conversation she had had with him a few weeks back when she brazenly informed him that a cousin of hers in America had sent over the bra she was wearing – the latest in American fashion. It certainly seemed to enhance her, he thought. He admired the way she held her chest proudly before her, unlike most Irish girls that tended to hunch and cover.

"Anything strange or startling in the world of aeroplane travel?" Jack leaned on the counter so that his eyes were level with hers.

"Not really, no." She sidled up to the bar stool and sat down softly on it. "We're off to Liverpool again. Captain O'Shea says we might be starting flights to London soon, though."

"Is that right?"

"Yes it actually is, Mr Jack the Barman." She had both elbows on the counter, her hands joining like a prayer flattened against the shiny counter, her grinning face turned up awaiting response.

"Well that's fairly exciting news all the same," he said slowly. "Is there anything you'd like me to get you?"

She laughed. "Yes, please. I'd like a hot port."

"Would you now? That should warm you up for the long journey across the cold Irish Sea, so it should. And your colleagues? A stiff treble whiskey for the captain, perhaps?"

She burst out laughing, giggling but trying to retain her composure, tickled at the thought of the pleasant but austere Captain Burke piloting the plane in a drunken state. It was hard to imagine him anything but sober and old before his twenty-seven years.

"Sure if he's too drunk to handle the old joystick, I could take over for youse." Máiréad emitted a screech of laughter. "I'm only here to please."

Jack was aware of the other air hostesses smiling and looking over towards him. A customer at the bar – a middle-aged man in a heavy overcoat – turned his head and smiled, took a sip of his cup of tea and said: "I think that lady has had enough to drink!" Jack smiled and winked at him conspiratorially.

"I'll have two more hot ports, please, a red lemonade and a cup of tea for the captain."

"Coming right up, Mademoiselle!"

"Oh, thank you!"

"Take a seat with your friends at the table there and I'll bring them down to you with a smile."

Jack went to get the drinks. These were the kind of moments he enjoyed as a barman, he thought, as if to confirm to himself that he was making the right decision and being true to himself. He looked over his shoulder as he warmed the spoon with the hot water. Máiréad was still looking at him, smiling. It was just a bit of harmless banter – a bit of fun and enjoyment of life. He took a spoon of honey and held it over the first toddy glass containing the heated port with cloves and poured some of the hot water over it so that it all ran into the glass. He gave it a quick stir and repeated it for the other two, put them on the tray quickly along with the lemonade, teapot, cup and saucer and sugar. He deftly laid his folded clean dish cloth over his left forearm, lifted the laden tray onto his right hand. With his head held high, he strode out from behind the bar over to where the Aer Lingus employees were sitting.

Trevor was standing with his hands on his hips when he returned contented-looking with the empty tray.

"What?" said Jack. "Something wrong?"

He stepped back behind the public area out of earshot of the customers and beckoned Jack to join him. "Your da telephoned. He says that you're to come home as soon as you can. He says the doctor says the baby is on the way."

Jack wasn't sure what to say. His initial reaction was to show only mild interest, as if the business had little to concern him. "Oh. Right, yeah."

"He sounded a bit bothered about it. Look, you can break off if you want. There's nothing much happening today. I'll cover you for the last couple of hours. Get yourself home, alright?"

"Yeah. Right enough." Jack didn't want to talk about it. He didn't want any questions about his mother's age, whether or not there were any other brothers or sisters, what his dad was like, what his mother was like, what his home was like. His head was spinning. He put aside the tray and the dish cloth and stared at them for a few seconds.

"A bit of a shock, I suppose? Listen, just take your leave. There's no problem here. Sure, there's fuck-all in today and it won't be gettin' any busier. You know?" He put his hand on Jack's shoulder and smiled. "So, be off with you. That's an order. See you on your next shift tomorrow evening all going well."

Jack was sitting waiting in the snug of Toner's on Baggot Street with a pint of porter before him. It was his third. He wanted to be anywhere but back at home, where everything had turned into a miniature birthing facility. All he knew from the moans and screams from upstairs was that his mother was in pain for hours. His father had gone out to Holles Street Hospital to get help with delivering the baby. As soon as the midwife arrived in a flurry of medical equipment and scents of sterility, he made straight for the door and ran through the wind and rain until he got to the pub. He had used the pub's public telephone box to get a message to Alva to meet him here. He couldn't quite tell Alva's mother what was happening. He couldn't really tell for sure what was going on anyway. It was all terrifying, disgusting and confusing and he just needed to get here and talk to Alva. Where was she? It must have been nearly an hour ago. He checked his watch but he wasn't sure if it had stopped after getting wet. He was still in his work outfit – white shirt and green tie. Staring ahead with his jaw set, he pulled his tie off roughly and cast it on the seat beside him. He didn't feel like leaving the quieter confines of the snug. He didn't feel like talking to anyone at the moment, least of all the smart-arse mouldy old literary types that frequented this place, he thought. He was suddenly aware of the fact that he was muttering to himself like an old man. He craned his neck to get a side view of the counter to see if by any chance Alva had come in and was standing waiting there. He had told her mother he'd be in the snug. Maybe she hadn't passed on the message or told her daughter not to be going out on such an awful night. That wouldn't do for her princess. He caught the attention of the barman, who raised his eyebrows quizzically.

"Another one, please." Jack raised his glass. The skinny barman in his grocer's navy apron raised his thumb in acknowledgement.

Suddenly Alva materialised through the open doorway of the snug to his left. She smiled uncertainly and folded her dripping umbrella.

"Alva! Jesus, you're a sight for sore eyes!" He got up and threw his arms around her before she had a chance to undo her wet coat, catching his foot on the leg of the table and tottering slightly as he did so like a drunken dancer.

Alva laughed at the impulsive gesture. "Oh Jack! Here, let me get my coat off." She took it off, left it on the seat opposite and sat down beside him, holding his hand. "Are you all right? What happened?"

"Oh, it's still going on... with the baby. I just had to get out. I... I had to see you. Jesus, your hands are frozen!"

"It's freezing outside. My mother told me to wait until tomorrow and not to be going out in the cold, but I just came out anyway. I got a cab. Did it arrive yet?"

"No. I don't know."

"Listen, I was thinking... maybe we should just go away. We could do it now, you know – just wave goodbye, get a boat to England and get our passage to America."

"Pint of porter!" The barman appeared at the counter and plopped the frothy glass of stout down. Jack handed him the eleven pence in change.

"How many have you had?" said Alva, looking at his eyes to see how merry he was.

"It's only my fourth."

"Only!" She giggled, squeezed his hand and leaned her head on his shoulder. "My hard-working hard-drinking man!"

"That's right, doll! You better believe it!" he said, doing his best James Cagney accent. He took a mouthful of beer. She planted a kiss on his cheek.

They talked and joked over the next hour and a half, making frivolous jokes, and giggling at the witty repartee from the other customers in the pub. They talked about what they would do next. Before they went back to their respective homes that evening, they had made a firm decision: that they would elope and make their way to America as soon as possible after the baby was born.

Jack arrived in the door, soaked and drunk just after midnight.

"Where were you?" Jack Senior was sitting in the armchair by the fire with a copy of the Irish Press in his hands. His reading glasses always made him look a bit comical, his son thought.

"Jesus, you look like William Churchill sitting there!"

"You mean Winston Churchill?"

"That's the man! Winston Churchill! C'mere... how's Mam?"

"Not too bad, thank God. She gave birth to a lovely little girl, Christina.."

Jack hadn't advanced more than two feet beyond the front door and he stared dumbly at his father, wavering on his feet like a tall tree in a storm. "A lovely little girl? Really?" He looked up towards the stairs and down again to his father with a blank, inebriated stare. "Well, that's that then, I suppose," he mumbled, almost to himself. "I'm off to bed." He climbed the stairs and plodded towards his bedroom. As he passed his parents' door, he heard the sound of a baby crying and his mother making soothing noises.

The next morning, Jack awoke. For a moment, he wondered if he'd dreamed everything from the night before. He remained prone with his hand on his head for what seemed like a long time. The ceiling, with its tattered central lampshade, seemed to keep sliding out of view. He cursed his physical state and the profound change in the house that awaited him as soon as he would get up. He knew he couldn't stay there all day, so he arose slowly, finding that he hadn't even worn a nightgown. He spent several moments staring at his tired naked self in the mirror of the wardrobe. Then he got dressed.

"Come in," his mother answered softly in response to his knock on the door. The curtain was still drawn and his mother looked small and insignificant amidst the jumble of pillows, blankets and towels. There was a wash hand basin on the night table beside her with a damp cloth resting on the lip. On the floor, there was a discreet pile of towels and other items to be washed. His mother's face was drawn and pale, like she had come close to death and was still returning slowly to life. The baby was so small, that he couldn't even see her at first. It was a slight darting movement of her hand that caught his eye. He moved closer and he could make out her prunish pink features. She was resting peacefully next to her mother's partially exposed breast. Jack felt suddenly awkward that his simple curiosity had led him to staring at a part of his mother's body that he wouldn't normally ever even glimpse.

"Are you... all right?"

"I'm a bit sore, pet. But I'm grand now. Isn't she beautiful?"

"Yeah. I suppose."

His mother laughed. "Ah, listen to you! you're a real man, now!"

"Well... I'd better make the tea. Would you like a cup?"

"Your father is making it, but thanks anyway."

He began backing towards the door. "All right. See you later Mam. I'd better be off."

He was very grateful that it was his day off as he made his way across South Lotts Road to catch the southbound tram on the other side of the street. All around him, life in Dublin was going on as normal as he waited at the stop, yet his whole world had shifted on its axis at the sight of his new sister, his first sibling. Family life as he had known it all his life was changed entirely.

On the opposite side of the street, the louche-looking unemployed men in grey hats and shabby overcoats stood outside the dark brown premises of T P Cullen, their bicycles lined up on the kerb, awaiting its opening. They looked like weary troops of some beaten army. Mothers in their head-scarfs pushing creaking prams and well-dressed professional gentlemen went by him at an unhurried pace. A young woman – not much older than Alva – was standing closest to him holding her baby, who was making protesting gurgles. There seemed to be babies everywhere today and he automatically scanned the faces of their mothers in vain to see if any of them were as old as his mother was. The field green-coloured Number Eight tram arrived and he hopped on, getting in ahead of the young mother and child.

Jack and Alva met in the front room of her parents' house to put a concrete structure to their plans of escape. They were sitting on the sofa, turned towards one another, both feeling the almost unbearable electric excitement and closeness that their semi-clandestine planning was giving them.

"I've asked all about it from Trevor at work," said Jack. He never felt so in love with her. They were as intimate as two people could ever be, he thought – more intimate than if they were naked together in bed. "Once we get to Holyhead, we get a train down to the south coast and get a steamer from Southampton."

Alva couldn't keep her eyes off him, hanging on every syllable like she was a small girl again, listening to her father telling those bedtime stories about the rabbits and the fox.

"Oh, Lord! I can't believe we're going – from England on a steamer! Maybe we can go and see Buckingham Palace?"

"Ha! I suppose we could if you'd really like to."

"Oh Jack! This is so exciting!"

Instinctively, they kissed deeply and longingly. Jack ached to be really alone with her again. There was a noise at the door and they stopped and turned, their faces bright red with a mixture of excitement and embarrassment. It was Alva's father.

"Oh, sorry to disturb you young lovers!How are your parents keeping, Jack?"

"They're fine, thanks Mr Blake."

"And I hear you've a new member of the family?"

"Yes. Yes, a little girl."

"A little girl! Sure that's wonderful news now. Listen, I'll stop blathering on now and leave you be and be sure to call again, Jack." He made a theatrical wink and pseudo-military salute and smiled as he left, closing the door behind him.

"When will we tell our parents, Jack?"

"I'll go down to the pier in Dún Laoghaire now and book our passage for exactly six weeks from today. Okay? That will give me time to hand in my notice at work and for us to get ready."

"Okay!" The tears welled up in her eyes. She felt sure, so sure now of everything; of him, of the adventure ahead and its dizzying possibilities. She felt certain that it would all work out and that her parents would be happy as long as she was happy. They embraced tightly and as close as if they were one wonderful being. "I love you, Jack," she whispered, her mouth in close to his ear.

"I love you too."

Jack practically ran out of the place before her mother – who was somewhere else in the house – had a chance to see him again. He skipped down the steps, ran to the garden gate and vaulted straight over. Breathlessly, he stopped with his hand still on the iron rail to see if Alva had seen him do it. She was standing at the bay window. She was laughing, shaking her head and with her hands to her mouth in the form of praying. She blew him a kiss and waved. He grinned and ran towards the bus stop.

At the harbour in Dún Laoghaire, Jack strode confidently over to the ticket office with his head held high like a man booking a first-class ticket of a round-the-world trip. In many ways, that was precisely his frame of mind because he could see no clouds on the horizon today and no reason why he wouldn't stop at New York. If one could make a decision to leave these shores and head across the Atlantic, then why stop there when you're already halfway around the world? The thought made him giddy with delight and he had visions of bliss and fun and sunny days and his unborn son by his side.

Even though his dad had told him that they had often visited here as a family when he was small, he had no memory of it at all and he looked around the portside area to see if he could find anything that might be vaguely familiar that would trigger a childhood memory. There was quite a bit of activity at the harbour, with dockyard workers transporting barrels of beer from train trucks towards the long pier where a large ship lay in dock. The markings "LE Irish Rowan" were clear in white lettering on the aft port side while, in larger lettering still was the word EIRE, emblazoned all along its flank, with an Irish tricolour at either side of the word. He knew that it was to ensure that it wouldn't be mistaken for a British vessel by German U-boat patrols. There was surely no further need for that now that the war was all but over. Farther along the quayside, a long austere-looking oil tanker was docked and a flexible pipe like a man-made umbilical cord connected it to a waiting lorry, behind which three more oil lorries were queued up awaiting their turn to be charged by the mother ship with the fuel that was vital for the country's needs.

The ticket office interior was a lot more sparse than he had imagined. It was a modest-sized room and the walls were decorated with framed photographs of ships, various official notices regarding the increasingly defunct travel bans and security warnings, as well as a framed notice with a candle burning in front of it, detailing a list of those who lost their lives in the sinking of the City of Limerick in 1940. Behind the clean timber counter, a deeply tanned man stared at him wordlessly with sky blue alcoholic eyes as he went through the transaction. Jack emerged into the patchy sunlight of the South Dublin afternoon, holding his large-format printed and signed tickets before him with both hands, scanning every detail and savouring their significance.

"It's a first step," he said aloud to himself before placing them carefully in the inside pocket of his coat and walking to the bus stop.

Jack and Alva's hands were joined on the kitchen table. Even though he had been in this house dozens of times by now, it was the first time that he'd set foot in the kitchen. He stared around at the brightly coloured décor – such a large room, he thought, immediately thinking to himself that he would have one equally as big when he had set up his own home with Alva. The dresser opposite him was a pristinely clean cream-painted behemoth with round brown knobs that seemed more useful for show than for practicalities. The willow-patterned plates lined up on the shelves had the appearance of having never been used to serve food. He imagined Angela spending an hour every day just cleaning them all individually before dusting the dresser from top to bottom. No escape from such duties for Angela. He wondered how long she had been working for Alva's parents. To his left, the large black range featured a drying rack above it, from which a couple of tea cloths hung, while the double Belfast sink off to his right was cleared of all the cooking pots and utensils that were hanging on a rack behind their heads. He felt Alva's hand squeeze his.

"Are you nervous?" Her voice was low, almost a whisper as she spoke the words. He turned his head and looked at her for a heartbeat before answering. He thought he could detect the slightest quiver in the light strands of her fair-brown hair.

"No," he said, assuredly. In truth, he wasn't quite sure how he felt. He didn't know if he was nervous or anxious or simply impatient. This was just another bridge to cross and another step to take and he wanted to have it done as quickly as possible. He felt glad that he was taking it with Alva.

"Not really, anyway... Are you?" He gave her a slightly haughty regard, the beginning of a smile emerging in the corner of his mouth.

"Yes!" They both laughed and squeezed their hands tighter.

"Listen. Don't be nervous. They'll understand and if they don't, well... they will. We're adults now and we can do what we want. Your parents are decent people."

"Yes. Yes you're right." She shot a look towards the door and nibbled at the nail on her free left hand.

"Listen. We talked about all of this already so we're ready for anything. I'm really glad we're doing this..."

"Me too."

"...and even if the worst comes to the worst and they disown you or disinherit you, we've enough money between us to get to America and to get a start. My Uncle Joe will help us get settled and it will all happen for us!"

She nodded her head. "Yes. Oh Jack!"

Gwendoline and Anthony appeared together at the door and came straight to the table. Jack and Alva straightened up. Jack stood up and shook their hands in formal fashion, looking each one straight in the eye as he always did.

"Well," Anthony began, glancing to his wife to see if she would prefer to have had the first word, "it seems you've something important to tell us."

Gwendoline remained silent. She had desperately tried, but failed to truly warm to Jack and was expecting the worst – an illegitimate pregnancy with her young daughter perhaps?

"Mr Blake, Mrs Blake," Jack found himself instantly relaxed once he began talking. He felt in control of the situation as soon as he saw the two anxious faces before him. It occurred to him that what he had just said to Alva really was true: it didn't matter a damn what the hell her parents said because they were about to leave on their own to New York and nobody on this earth could stop them. He felt himself straighten further and lift his chin as he spoke: "Your daughter Alva and I have made a decision. We're getting married at the registry office on Lombard Street on Tuesday morning and from there, we're taking the steam packet to Holyhead, getting a train down to London and Southampton and from there, we're sailing to New York."

Anthony frowned and looked at his wife. Her face was shocked but she looked straight at Jack.

"A registry office?" Her voice was loud but without emotion. She looked at her daughter. "Are you expecting?"

Alva's face turned crimson under the glare of a mother who could see inside her very thoughts and seemed to know that she had already been intimate with Jack. "What? No! No, Mother I'm not... expecting!"

"Then why are you running off? Leaving your family like this?" She turned to Jack. "Does your mother or your father know about this?"

"Yes, Mrs Blake, they do."

Anthony looked slightly lost and seemed to be sinking in his seat. "Look, Alva, there's no need for the hurry. What's the rush? Sure, couldn't we have a small proper wedding before ye go?" He looked appealingly to his wife. "There's no need to be going off to the registry office like... like I don't know what kind of people."

Gwendoline remained silent as the idea sank in. Perhaps, she thought, it wasn't such a bad idea after all. He was far from a suitable match for her but if Alva was determined to marry this ill-bred charmer, then maybe it was best that they got the formalities over with and moved away. She hadn't met Jack's parents and she had no desire to do so. A womanising cabman and a housebound orphan for a wife, having another child so late in life. It was for the best. It was so far away, though. Her heart stung at the thought of never seeing Alva for a long time – maybe never again. She looked down to compose herself. The gingham oil cloth stared back at her, seeming to mock her.

"Lots of people do it, Dad. What about Auntie Margaret?" Alva had found her voice.

"That was different," Anthony said. "She didn't want a big fuss and she was a few years older than you too. You're both so young..."

"We are quite young, Mr Blake, but we're old enough to be married and to make decisions for ourselves."

"So why have you decided to get married so suddenly?" Gwendoline asked the two of them.

"Well, Mrs Blake, we feel that now is the right time to go. The war is over and America is opening up again, looking for people to work there. We both want to go there and we're sure we can make a good go of it. We'll be staying with my uncle for a start and then we'll get a place of our own."

"Have you got a job over there?" Anthony asked.

"Yes, Mr Blake, I do."

"A barman's job?" Gwendoline's question was tinged with sarcasm.

"A barman's job pays well over in America, Mrs Blake. I've been told, in fact, that it's one of the best jobs going in New York." He hadn't been told any such thing but decided to say it anyway.

Gwendoline still only interacted with her daughter and soon-to-be son-in-law while her husband looked from her to his daughter, searching to find his true role in all of this. Gwendoline took a deep intake of breath.

"Well, you seem to have your minds made up and your bags packed too, no doubt, so I don't suppose there's any point in discussing the matter too much further." She turned to her husband finally and nodded: "We'll see to it that you're not short of help in getting started."

"Thanks, Mum."

"That's much appreciated, Mrs Blake, although we have enough put by between us two so we won't be stuck but thank you both all the same."

"Oh, you'll need help, young man. Let there be no doubt of that." Jack sneered back at her matronly tone. Let her give us the help, he thought. We'll soon be away from here, off to the greatest city in the world and making our own, starting our own family.

All the way home, Jack's mind spun like a whirligig. He had chosen the tram because it made a more circuitous route back home and he wanted to be alone with his thoughts for another while. His mind raced from his parents and new sister to Alva, to her parents, to taking the ship in just a few days' time, to America and back again. The meeting with Alva's parents that had seemed so terrifying and daunting turned out to be so... empowering. That was the word. He felt as though he were bursting with life. He felt like he suddenly realised that he was stronger, faster, cleverer, even more handsome than them. On the top deck of the tram at this hour of the evening, there was only one other person – an old lady up at the front. Nobody else was even slightly aware of the momentous transformation that was happening right here with him! Jack Mills! Off to America, making his mark and going places! Alva's father had looked so flustered and lost and frightened. Even his mother was not her usual assured self. It had been quite similar with his own family too. His mother looked so shell-shocked and his dad had searched for something positive to say about it all like a drunkard looking for change in his pocket to pay for a bottle of porter. Once he spoke the words and said it clearly that they were going, it was as if a magic wand had been tapped and the word was made real. Just like the way the priest taps the chalice and makes the words real at Mass, incanting mysterious Latin words. What is this magic he seemed to suddenly possess? The one that made people stop and listen and become lesser versions of themselves? He almost burst out laughing, he was so dizzy with the delight of it all. Was it even real or was it just his imagination? It certainly felt real.

His mother had used the word "selfish" when he had told her and his father in as brief a space of time as possible about his imminent departure for America. He couldn't remember exactly what she had said. It had been a flow of words that ultimately meant nothing as they weren't going to change anything but that word "selfish" had snagged on him and he resented it. There was nothing selfish about him. He was just looking to move on, to keep going. What was he expected to do? Stay at home and sit and stare at a tiny baby feeding and crying? That's what selfish would be – expecting him to give up all that he had going for him just to please his mammy; forcing him to cut down his momentum in flight like a leaping deer. He thought of Alva and about that one night of passion they had spent. He let his head rest against the cold window of the tram, the rain falling harmlessly on the other side of the glass and the rhythmic vibrations of the vehicle tingling through his head. He closed his eyes and he ached for her.

Southampton, England, Spring 1946

Jack and Alva stared up at the Queen Mary. The height of it was what they weren't prepared for. They more relieved than excited that they had finally made it to this point. Just as Alva's mother said she would, she sent them money. They really did need it too. Without it, they couldn't have got the embarkation tickets that Jack carefully held in his hands lest they get blown away by the stiff cool breeze. He opened the accompanying booklet that said Embarkation Arrangements on the front, with a colour painting of the ship on the top half depicting a New York skyline in the background and the words "Cunard White Star" on the bottom. He looked through it to see where

"You know, this is the same crowd that used to have the Titanic," Jack smiled teasingly."

"Oh now, please! Don't tell me you're going to try to frighten me all the way over to America!"

He threw his head back laughing, then kissed her and hugged her tightly.

"No. That's the complete end of it now. I promise!"

They were both wearing the same clothes that they had worn at the registry office in Dublin ten months beforehand – Alva in her purple dress suit with floral detail on the hat and Jack in his tan wool heavy coat and brown felt hat that he liked to wear tipped slightly up from his forehead like Roy Rogers. Alva looked her new husband up and down, feeling a slight tinge of jealousy at how he carried himself so confidently wearing a suit. She felt a little bit underdressed in these surroundings.

The last ten months had been up and down. But mostly up, she thought. Jack had had to take a job in Southampton. They had rushed into it all a bit too quickly and didn't have the price of the passage to America as well as start-up money, so they decided to gather together some more money while they were in England and while they waited for her mother to send them money too. There was much talk of babies. She wanted to have children straight away and she had visions of the first child being born in England but it didn't happen yet, even though they were doing it often enough. Everybody was so much more liberal here than in Ireland. They even had condoms. How can people buy such things without feeling completely awkward and embarrassed? It was different here – it seemed that you were free to be who you wanted to be. They had come across that woman who wouldn't put them up, though. Just because they were Irish. Maybe it was to do with the War of

Independence and the big war itself. She couldn't imagine and German people getting a nice reception here either. Most people were nice, though, and in any case, there would be plenty of time for children once they got settled in America. She had heard that it was often difficult to have children if you're not settled somewhere and your mind and body aren't ready for it. That was what her Aunt Maye from Foxrock had said and it's why they started so late, she and her ex-British-Navy husband Roger. He was her father Anthony's brother. He liked him well enough, even though he always referred to him as "a bit of a West Brit".

A porter had labelled and taken their bags for them so she had only her matching clutch bag. There seemed to be a lot of wealthy people here in England and particularly those getting onto the ship. There was an excited buzz about the dockside with the well-dressed crowds patiently making their way onto the gangplanks while up on the quayside, thousands had turned out to wish their friends or loved-ones goodbye. There were security wardens and police ensuring that everything went off without any trouble and journalists and photographers were appearing here and there through the crowd, stalking around like hunting dogs, taking photographs of the ship, the passengers and the crowd. There was a film camera set up at one end of the quayside, where a small group of official-looking gentlemen were gathered around the apparatus, seemingly ensuring that it was all being done correctly.

Some shouts came from away to their right and a new buzz rushed through the crowd. There seemed to be somebody famous boarding the ship. Alva craned her neck to see who it was but all she could see was a swish open-top car. Somebody got out, a hand waved to the crowd and they disappeared in a cloud of minders and chasing press men.

"Never mind, love," Jack said, moving close next to her ear, "We'll see plenty of famous people in New York." They faced each other and kissed.

"Aw' right, you two! You'll 'ave plenty of time for that sor' of fing once we're on board!"

A local wag like a caricature of a London spiv was the one encouraging them along. He had the pencil moustache, the slouched hat and the pin-striped suit. Jack and Alva just laughed and moved forward in the queue.

Chapter 8 – "Holding on with One Hand"

New York City, USA; Present Day

Jack sat on the edge of his bed and stared out the window of his third-floor apartment at the West 86 assisted living home. It was okay, he thought. In fact, it looks like it's gonna be one helluva day. This is just a temporary thing and it would soon change. Yeah, soon. Real soon. Yeah, the club will be back on its feet in no time. You betja. It wouldn't take too long, no siree. It takes a while to build it up like that. Nobody does it like me. Once they're your people, they don't go nowhere just like that. No way, buddy. They just fade away a little and then they're back right as soon as they hear you're open for business again. They're waitin' too… just waitin' to hear when old Jack is back at wheel. What's that, you say? Back already? Why that didn't take too long. Sure, you're lookin' as fresh as if you'd just gone down to the clinic for a check-up. Well whaddya know? Jack the Knife is back in town!

Yes, yes. There's progress. He sighed and stared down at his hands. In his right hand, he held an unopened tin of tuna. His left hand rested, limp and impotent on his left knee. The striped pyjamas that he had bought in Bloomingdales were wearing thin at the kneecap. They could do with a wash, he thought. Warm shafts of morning sunlight illuminated floating dust particles. Gotta get out of this place. I've had enough of it right now. Need help opening this goddamn can of tuna-fish. Where the hell is Analisa? Goddamn it. Haven't seen her in so long now. Did she say that she was not coming back? Yes. Yes, she did. She gives up too easily. That's the problem right there. No staying power, these Italians. Just like in the war. Ha ha! I just need some help with this fuckin' tin. My left arm is a bit tired today and I can't move it at all. It gets better around nine in the morning. Each day, there's a little bit more of it alive than there was the day before. Only I can feel it but it's there. What the hell time is it? He looked at the clock on the wall. 7am. In the old days, I'd be only going to bed by now. Maybe that's why I'm so hungry every morning – my whole metabolism and inner clock is outta whack.

On the floor before him, there were numerous open tins of tuna that were scattered as if left out for a colony of cats. The room was sparse. A large wine-coloured patterned rug covered a generous amount of the wooden floor. On the nightstand beside him sat a random collection of stale and half-eaten bagels. In the wardrobe hung a suit of clothes that he rarely put on. He wasn't able to do it on his own, anyway. The only other item of significance in the dusty room was a cardboard box containing a set of hard-covered books. Almost every day, he debated whether to get rid of them.

Jack reached towards the end of the bed and pulled his walker towards him. Time to get moving. He struggled to his feet. His dragged his left leg into a more dignified position like it was a drunken soldier on parade, grimacing as he did so from the sharp pain of the ulcer. He went to move towards the door and remembered his wallet. There's no good going nowhere in New York without some bucks in your wallet, buddy. He pulled open the drawer of the nightstand and took out the Aspinal black leather wallet. He had a flashback to the day he bought it – one of his most treasured possessions. Made in London at the world's finest leather-goods shop, the assistant had told him, pointing out the hand-made finishing work and the limited-edition "Visconti" markings. He lifted the wallet to his nose to get the reassuring smell of the leather. It was a scent that reminded him of well-off clients settling their tabs at the old airport bar back in the day. He thought he was such a high flyer back then! The girls would swoon and the gentlemen would say "That guy's all right", handing over their pressed pound bills or whatever. Jack ran his thumb through the notes to check that there were a few bills in case he needed them. He realised that there was nowhere today to get any more money. He had lost that particular battle but he wasn't going to waste his time thinking about that right now. He had been in trouble before, so he'd be back in business again. There was nothing surer, buddy. He had friends.

He put the wallet carefully into the pocket of his dressing-gown and struggled up to a standing position. He leaned and shuffled towards the door, opened it and went into the hall, shuffling past the door to the kitchen/dining room. He opened the heavy door and stepped out into the corridor. There was nobody for now. He took out his tuna tin again and sat down with his back against the wall. He tried in vain to get it open, using his right hand to place it into the palm of his left hand. He was sure that one of these days, that hand would close around it but not today.

He put the tin on the floor and, with his good hand he carefully approached the lip of the tin, latched the opener onto it and squeezed the handles of the opener so that the sharp point of it pierced the tin, making a barely audible puncture and hiss. He knew this was as far as he could go.

"Fuck!" He momentarily thought about throwing the whole thing against the wall but determination got the better of him. There was always someone passing along the corridor at this hour so he'd sit here and wait a few minutes. He always tried to change the times of his appeals for help or have it coincide with a social visit on one of the other rooms. He hated the idea of being a bum that always needed help with this or that so he never liked asking the same person twice.

The hall lights went out. He knew that if he just stood up, they'd come on again but he waited instead in the semi-gloom of the corridor, which was illuminated at the far end where there was a stair well and an outside window.

Any minute now, he thought. That dumbass cleaning lady or someone visiting someone else to take pity. Fuckin' can opener. Why don't they make these things so you can use them with one hand?

The lights came on suddenly. Someone was coming from the stairwell and he hadn't even heard her approach. Was his hearing going too? She was a middle-aged lady, below average height, who moved efficiently along the hallway and slowed down to have a look at Jack. She was dressed in a skirt, trainers and a light tan jacket. She had a small hold-all bag slung over her shoulder. Her hair had a freshly made-up look about it – neat and conservative like her overall appearance. She hunkered down, looked Jack in the eye and placed a hand on his limp left hand.

"Are you okay, Sir? Do you need some help?"

Jack twisted his body so that his hand pulled away from hers. "I'm fine! Who the hell sent you anyway?"

"Ehh, no-one…I'm a home help nurse. My name is Helen Bromley. I'm here visiting someone down the… Oh, I see! It's the can, isn't it? Here, allow me."

Before he had time to protest, it was in her hands and the opener was cutting through the thin metal top that had stood between Jack and some protein nourishment.

"So how long have you been here?" she asked, her hands busily opening his tuna. "You wanted to get a bit of air out here, huh? Those rooms can be stuffy – I know."

Jack looked at her with a jaundiced irritated eye. He was glad of getting the tin open but she asked a lot of questions and was, well, a bit forward. "Yeah, yeah. It's a bit fresher out here. I thought I might… yeah, get some air and, you know, it's nice to shoot the breeze with people too. I gotta keep that up in my profession – keep it all lubricated and fresh. You know?"

"What profession is that?"

"Jesus, you're a curious one! Well, it's a great club I... used to run. It's a midtown place over on fifty-first. Lotta famous faces go there all the time."

"Is that right?" She held the tin gingerly in one hand while with the other, her hand reached into her pocket and she took out a paper handkerchief to soak up the errant drips of oil. "Well I sure hope you get back there real soon. Is this your door here?"

"Yeah, that's mine. Here, gimme that!" He took the tin from her roughly and shoved himself up with one grim effort, using his good right leg and what little power remained in his left leg. He was quite tall when he stood up, she noticed. He looked almost comical, with his head raised as if he was reaching with his neck to become even taller, trying to offset his staggered stance.

"Do you need some help getting back into your apartment?"

"No. No, thanks. I'll be just fine." He gave her a fierce look, followed by a surprisingly seductive wink and crooked smile. She stared at him intently as he dragged himself to the door. He went to push down on the door handle with his good elbow. Without saying a word, she went ahead of him and opened it, putting an arm around his waist and guiding him through.

"Jeez, lady. Before we go any further, I've gotta say – I'm a married man!"

She couldn't help a short burst of laughter.

"And the walls are paper-thin... but I guess we can always say it was just a particularly rigorous physio-therapy session if the neighbours complain! Ha ha!"

She shook her head as she sat him down on the armchair just inside the door. He put the tin on the telephone desk beside him. She took a quick look around and peered ahead to see what the rest of the place was like. "Well, you certainly have no problem with your ability to talk!" He grinned and made a saluting gesture. "Okay, I've got to go now because I've a call to make and I'm late but I'll call to see you tomorrow. Okay?"

"Suits me, doll. I'll wear a pink carnation."

She disappeared through the door, smiling to herself as she shut it behind her.

Later that afternoon, Helen was back in Jack's apartment, sitting at his table over a cup of tea.

"I haven't heard from her since," said Jack, staring into the middle distance, "so I guess that's the end of our marriage. I don't know... women sometimes do that kind of thing. No offence, mind!"

"None taken." Helen Bromley – the daily-aid social worker who had come across Jack sitting in the corridor a few hours earlier had decided to call back to check on him again before she went home. Her client down the hallway needed far less help than this man clearly did and so she found herself sitting in his kitchen/dining room that was in dire need of a clean-up and some re-stocking of supplies.

"Of course, you're different, I can see... you're a real lady of class!"

"Well, thank you, Mr Mills. My mother taught me to never disregard a compliment. You know, there's an occupational therapist service here? For your arm and your leg? Have they told you about that?"

"Yeah, yeah... They sent some fuckin' gorilla-lady to hurt me but I didn't need her. They sent me another one too – mouthy girl, wouldn't stop yapping and hurting me. My leg pains a bit now and then but sure, my arm is comin' along fine. It's slow but it's getting there. I'll be back punching above my weight in no time!"

She nodded her head, unsure about his own physical assessment.

"Do I detect a hint of an Irish accent?"

"You sure do. Dublin born and bred, be the jaysus!" he saluted and winked again, a youthful sparkle in his eyes as he uttered the words in an exaggerated leprechaun-esque accent. "I haven't been back in a while, though. Used to run the bar at the airport."

"Really?"

"Yeah, yeah." He looked down at the frayed end of his dressing-gown cord, feeling the tattered material between his thumb and forefinger absentmindedly. "Maybe I should go back. It'd be like a whole different country now but maybe that's what I should do, now that my wife seems to have decided she don't want me anymore."

"I'm sorry that your marriage isn't going well."

"I'm not! I'm a free man now!" Helen put her hand to her mouth laughing. Jack cranked up the volume of his voice to shouting level. "Jesus Christ, if I'd have been jailed for murder, I'd ha' been out years ago! Ha ha ha!" His breathless wheezy smoker's laugh that spoke of a headlong enthusiasm for life was infectious. Helen couldn't but join in when she looked at his face contorted in a devilish grin, his whole body shaking, from his unruly shock of hair to his grubby slippers.

"Well," she said, wiping her eyes, "sometimes you have to be careful what you wish for."

"Ha ha! You sure got that right!"

She stood up to clear the table of the mugs and spoons. "You know, I'm going on a laundry run after this. Let me take your sheets and put them in with it. I'll have them back to you tomorrow. Do you have any spare sets?"

Jack was a bit taken aback. "Yeah. Yeah, sure I do." His mind ran through his bedroom to the other sheets that hadn't been cleaned in a while that were piled up in the corner of the bathroom. "That's a good idea. Here, let me give you something for your trouble." He pulled his wallet from the pocket of his dressing-gown as she quickly washed the ware and put it on the draining board.

"No, there's no need. Really." She held her hands up as she approached the table again.

"I insist." He gave her one of his piercing looks of pure defiance, like a man to whom such money was a thing of nothing; an impact that he would never feel. She couldn't but admire it and she took the $20 bill from his outstretched hand.

"Okay. I'll go gather the sheets. Where do you keep the clean ones?"

"They're… Tell you what — just take the ones in the bathroom first and maybe we'll wash the other ones the next day. I think that'd work out better. Yeah."

"Okay." She grabbed a bin liner and went through the bedroom and into the bathroom. It all needed so much cleaning and tidying. She bundled up the pile of sheets and, on her way back through the bedroom, she gathered up some of the random items of clothing scattered around the floor and put them all into the black plastic bag.

When she returned to the kitchen, Jack had gone to use the other toilet. His fine wallet was sitting on the table. She quickly picked it up and slipped the twenty dollars tidily back between its silk folds.

Two weeks later, Helen Bromley was passing through the reception area of the West 86. She had just delivered another pile of washing to her new unofficial "project" as her husband Fred called him. To her, however, Jack Mills was more than that. He was full of fight and vigour — he just needed the smallest leg-up and he'd get back on his feet. She couldn't stand to see people like that and there were so many of them in New York: people with potential and years of life left in them who were just abandoned like the fallen from a herd hurtling towards God-knows-where. Sometimes it was through no fault of their own and sometimes it was because of the cruelty and heartlessness of others but there was no excuse for it as far as she was concerned. Everyone deserved some basic dignity and a second chance. This man was his own worst enemy in many ways, she knew, but maybe all he needed was someone to take him by the hand and to get back to somewhere he can be safe and not just fade away into the distance to die a forgotten person. She loved his cantankerous complaining that never stopped and she loved his explosive sense of humour. He always skirted the fine line between being funny and being outrageous but a man of his age surely had the right to cross that line every now and again. In fact, part of his charm was that he knew that and took full advantage. She loved that he fancied himself as a ladies' man still.

She was thinking of all of this and still smiling to herself when she entered the community library that was attached to the building. It was there as a resource for the residents of the West 86 but it also served the wider community of people living in the neighbourhood. In fact, there was always a good crowd of people here because it was the only public library that served a densely populated part of the city.

She browsed through the travel section and immediately picked up a book on Ireland. It was a large coffee-table book with a lot of superb photographs of green fields, rugged wind-blown cliffs, sheep, ruddy-faced farmers and crumbling castles in the countryside. She wasn't aware of any Irish in her family – as far as she knew, she was a grand American melange of Italian tailors, English pilgrims and African slaves. Looking through the pictures in the book, she just couldn't see the sassy sophisticate from upstairs coming from this deeply green country.

"Oh, that's my home town!"

The voice came from over her shoulder. Helen turned around quickly to see a lady of short stature. She was late-middle-aged, she guessed but with a youthful porcelain complexion and bright blue eyes. Her white hair was short and neat, lending her a kind of proud energy that made it difficult to ascertain her age with certainty. She looked like she could have just stepped out of the book. She hadn't noticed her arrive.

"Sorry to startle you, my dear. I didn't mean to be prying – it's just when I saw the picture of Boyle Abbey, I got a shock myself!"

"Where?"

"Boyle Abbey. That's it there. That's my home town back in Ireland. It's called Boyle. Maureen O'Sullivan – you know Jane from the Tarzan movies – that's where she's from too."

"Sorry, I… Jane?"

"My apologies, dear. I'm talking awful rubbish, so I am. I didn't introduce myself. Violet Rooney is my name."

"Helen Bromley. Pleased to meet you."

She gave Helen a firm handshake with her right hand, while her left arm held her clutch bag. It was a classic -looking type, with a check pattern that matched the lady's green woollen coat.

"We're wearing green today because of the day's that's in it."

"Oh right. Saint Patty's Day?"

"Paddy's Day, yes. Are you Irish yourself?"

"Me, no. But I know an Irish man who's resident here in West 86. Are you living here too?"

"No, my dear. We live in a block over on West 93rd. We just call in now and again for the library service. I love books and so does my husband, and this is the nicest library on the Lower West Side, really. Well, PJ loves it in any case – it's his favourite."

A sprightly elderly man entered and went straight over to where the two ladies were standing talking – Helen holding the large coffee-table book on Ireland in her arms and Violet with her green check coat, dress and clutch bag.

"This is my husband PJ. Coming to fetch me out of the library in case I'd get lost! Ha ha!"

"Hello, how are you? Pleased to meet you." He was dressed in a smart dark suit with a dark green overcoat and a copious sprig of shamrock on the lapel.

"We'd better go, Helen," said Violet, slipping her arm into her husband's and heading towards the door. "I'm sure we'll bump into each other again."

Three days later, Helen, Violet and PJ were sitting at a table in the seating area of the library. The vase on the table contained an impressive but static collection of plastic flowers. From coming here regularly over the years, Helen knew that the only time the vase was refreshed was when the contents were replaced by plastic holly during Christmas.

"Well, he's just all alone. He's really smart but he's just down on his luck, you know? I don't know what to do with him because in another few months, he's going to be finished here and he'll have nowhere to go."

PJ tutted loudly and shook his head over and back. "Oh God, oh God, oh God! The poor guy.

"Yes. I do all his laundry for him. I wash his dishes, open his tins of tuna-fish... listen to his stories!"

"Does he have good stories?" Violet asked, her concern visible in her pursed lips and tilted head.

"Oh yes. He has really great stories about life at his bar in Manhattan, all the famous people who used to go there, that kind of thing. He's really funny – sometimes a little bit too funny! But he's great. He's just a guy who needs a little help and he doesn't really know where he's heading to. At least, he doesn't seem to be completely aware of his situation. Or else he ignores it... he just kind of carries on regardless, you know?"

"You should introduce us to him. We should get to know him," PJ sat forward. Like his wife of many years, he was also from Roscommon but from a small farm in the countryside, not from the busy shopping town of Boyle.

"Well, I could do... Only if he thought that I was setting him up in some way, he's the kind of guy who would just shut down. He's got a lot of pride and he wouldn't want to be treated charitably in any way, I think."

"I've got a better idea," said Violet, laying her hand on her husband's and winking at Helen. "You tell us where he lives and we'll just casually run into him one of these days."

"That's it, now," said PJ, his thick eyebrows rising emphatically as he spoke. They cut a dramatic presence against his kind facial features and neatly combed grey hair. "He'll probably love to be talkin' to someone from the Old Sod. Sure, all the Irish in New York are the same."

Helen nodded her head.

"And besides... Violet would talk the hind legs off of a donkey, so she would!" Helen put her hand to her mouth to suppress her laughing in a public library. "Sure, that's how she got a hold of me all those years ago! She started talking so much that I couldn't get a word in edgeways with a large shovel and sure the next thing I knew, I was standing before the altar saying 'yes' to the priest... and with stars in me eyes!"

Violet smiled and threw her eyes to heaven like she'd heard it all before a thousand times. Helen laughed quietly.

Jack exhaled noisily as he picked up the remote control of his television from the edge of his armchair in the lounge of his apartment. He stared at the slightly battered device with suspicion every time he pressed it lately because it had taken one fall too many on the floor or perhaps one kick too many under the coffee table. He frowned in an effort to remember. Whatever it was, the net result was that the side of the zapper had a shard of black plastic missing from it so that the red light was clearly visible each time he pressed a button to change channel and he wondered if it was some kind of dangerous laser that damaged your brain or caused blindness if you looked at it. He began to wonder at what point did lasers suddenly become benign. It seemed to him that it wasn't too long ago that the only reference to lasers was in the context of a futuristic gun or for a punishment being meted out to a suave hero in a spy movie. It used to be that it was all about shooting laser beams to destroy stuff. Now, it was lasers in medicine, lasers in your kitchen to cook your food and lasers that leaked out of the side of your TV zapper.

"Fuckin' stupid technology…" he mumbled to himself while he finally found the button that ran through each channel in succession each time you pressed it. His face was set in a cranky sneer as he looked for anything that would elicit any recognition or emotion in him.

"Jesus Christ, how come there's nothin' on here?" His words disappeared into the empty room, being absorbed by the furniture, the carpet and the high windows that looked out onto a small park and another apartment block that screened out the evening sun.

There was a ring at the door. For an instant, his heart leapt at the thought of someone coming and he felt that mild and undefined sense of agitation of the realisation that he was desperate for some company and even for some good news from another human being.

He moved onto his walker. That was a quick move, he thought to himself, pleased that there was some evidence that his mobility was improving.

"Yeah… getting better," he mumbled as he moved with regular practised pace out of the living room and into the small entrance hall. He peered through the spy hole and saw the back of what appeared to be an elderly lady walking farther down the corridor. He opened the door. She was suddenly lit up by the sensor lights and turned around to him.

"Oh, I'm sorry," she said. He recognised the Irish accent straight away. She even looked like she's just stepped off the steam ship, with her pale face and apologetic Irish way of holding herself. Just got her hair done and wearing her Sunday best. "I'm not sure I've even got the right floor. This is the third floor, right?"

"Yeah, yeah. This is the third floor."

"Oh, sure, janey mac. I'm completely wrong so. I was looking for the elevator. I'm after coming from the top floor down the stairs. I'm exhausted from it. I don't suppose I could trouble you for a glass of water?"

"Ehh… sure. Sure." Jack looked up and down the empty corridor. "Come inside and I'll get you a drink of water."

Violet stood at the kitchenette end of the living room while Jack steadily moved about on his wheeled walker, getting her a glass by the sink and filling it with water.

"Thank you very much," she said as he gave her the glass with a barman's smile. "It's nice to bump into someone from home too."

"Oh yeah. You picked up on that?" He grinned as he took a seat at the table opposite her, carefully easing himself down sideways from his standing position onto the chair.

"Oh sure, I always recognise another Irish person's accent," said Violet.

"You know, it's funny you say that because a lotta people have told me that I don't have any Irish accent anymore… including my wife! But, you know, maybe it's coming back to me now and again."

"That's often the way, so it is." Violet took a sip of the water. "Some people lose their accent the minute they set foot in America, others like me and my husband are the same all the time and then others lose it for a while and it comes back again. We're all different."

"Yep. We sure are. I have – well I used to have – a bar so I had to kinda adapt the way I spoke so that people could understand me better, you know?"

"Yes." She nodded, putting down her empty glass.

"Will I get you another?"

"Oh no. No thank you – you've been so good, so you have. It's lovely to meet another Irish person, I always think. You're never lost when you have someone else from home."

Jack looked at her thoughtfully. She seemed kind of scattered but he was glad to have someone call. It made him realise how much he missed talking to people and he felt a longing to talk to more people from Ireland too. He felt a soft wave push him slightly off centre. It had the taste of resignation and emotion and a clear sense of comfort, he thought.

"Say... How long have you been here? Do you know much about what's happening back home?"

"Oh Jesus Mary and Joseph, I don't, I'm afraid. I'm here with my husband a long time now. I don't know what's going on in Ireland anymore. Only the odd few bits and pieces from my niece in Dublin and then, sure it's only a few bits of gossip. I think it's all changed... more roads and more automobiles. More crime and scandals in the church!"

"Is that so? Well, maybe it's no harm to scandalise some of those guys. I was never a real fan of them, I'd have to say!"

"Oh! Well now, that's a conversation for another day." She quickly stood up and produced what looked like a ten-dollar bill after a brief rummage in her handbag. It was a plain but decent brand of bag,

Jack noted as she placed it under the empty glass. He couldn't help staring as the moment took him back to his days as a barman, watching customers slip tips under their glasses before they ordered another drink. It used to give him such a thrill, in those early days, to see such a uniquely American practice occur before him in real life. Sometimes, you forget where you were and how far you had come from home and then certain moments made it all crystal clear.

"What's that for?"

"That's just for the perfect little drink when I needed it and the appreciation of meeting someone decent from home!"

"There's no need... It's ridiculous."

"Just... think of it as a tip and you can buy me and my husband a drink the next time we see you."

She turned her back on the table and Jack and started to move to the hallway and the door out of the apartment. She lingered in the hall and he got up to follow her out.

"Well... I know better by now than to argue with an Irish woman!" He laughed out loud, following her into the hall. "Ha Ha! And now that you know where I am, don't be a stranger – you or your husband."

"I certainly won't." She shook hands formally and smiled kindly.

Violet and PJ were waiting in the lobby the very next day when Jack went on his daily journey to the ground floor to read whatever morning newspaper they had managed to get that nobody had already walked off with. He was beginning to do that more and more, he realised as he made his way out of the elevator. He automatically checked his look in the mirror as he did so. His hair could do with a cut but why was it that it seemed to grow faster as you got older? It should be the other way around. Maybe it was just that time moved faster as you got older. At least I've got a decent clean shirt, he thought. He still had a meagre-sized wardrobe but it was a quality one. That was something.

Helen had, of course, been ensuring that Jack had some clean item of clothing to wear most days. She had also ensured to let the Rooney's know of Jack's habits so it was no coincidence that they were sitting in the lobby when he came out of the lift, stopping to fix his hair and mumbling to himself.

"Well, hello there! Fancy bumping into you again!" Violet's broad Irish midlands accent echoed off the walls like a simple sweet familiar tune to Jack's ears.

"Ha! Jesus Christ! Twice in two days! What are the chances of that?" Jack moved across the dark tiled floor to where the Rooney's were seated, holding himself as straight as he possibly could. Violet and PJ stood up.

"This is my husband PJ... PJ, this is Jack – the man I was telling you about."

"Pleased to meet you, Jack. I see you're making your way around the building."

"Oh yeah. You gotta keep movin' around. You know? I just came down to see what they've got, stretch the legs, that sort of thing. Sometimes they got the morning paper, unless some bum has run off with it." He sat down on the sofa opposite them, a glass coffee table between them, on which were scattered various magazines and brochures on the assisted living complex. "So, are you from Boyle too PJ?"

"Oh no. I'm from out the country... near Tulsk, if you know it?"

"Tulsk. Yeah, sure I know it. One of the guys working at Dublin Airport was from there. Helluva nice guy he was too."

Violet excused herself and went to get coffee from the vending machine while the two men chatted. They were laughing by the time she returned to them.

"Hey, you're husband's a great man, Violet. I didn't know he was one of New York's bravest fire-fighting heroes! You must be proud. Let me guess… she saw you on a calendar and it was love at first sight! Ha ha! Mr July 1949! Ha ha!"

The noise of their laughter carried into the library next door, where a few people turned their heads in curiosity.

"Well it wasn't quite like that but there was a bit of a spark there all right," said Violet, taking her seat beside her husband and smiling as she sipped her hot coffee.

"Oh yes, there certainly was," said PJ, bumping affectionately off his spouse and taking his Styrofoam cup in both hands.

"Any kids?"

"Yes," said Violet. "Four daughters."

"Four colleens, eh? Beautiful." Jack nodded, picturing four identical red-haired young women.

"Yes," said Violet. "Four red-headed girls they are too."

"Really?"

"Rose is the eldest. She's a writer, living in California."

"Uh-huh." Jack's eyes were wide with interest. Ordinarily, he would have only a vague interest in other people's children, but he was too intrigued by the fact that they really were four red-headed Irish girls born and bred in America. It made him wonder for the first time in many years what a daughter or a son of his own might have turned out like.

"Then there's Agnes who's a teacher here in New York, at St Sophia's Catholic Girls School at Primrose Heights, if you know it."

"No."

"Then there's Catherine. She's an accountant. Works on Wall Street. And our youngest girl is Beth. She's a teacher too – she works in the same school as Agnes."

There was a silence for a few beats.

"Did you and your wife have children too?" PJ asked.

"No. No, we... never had any children." Jack's words tailed off and he looked around distractedly.

PJ and Violet looked at one another. "So, tell me all about that pub you used to have," PJ asked brightly.

"The bar? Yeah, it was one hell of a classy joint. You know... all the regulars used to come and bring their friends. Lots of famous guys — some of them whose names I couldn't even mention. Well, I could... but I'd have to kill ya! Ha Ha!"

The Rooney's listened while their new friend did most of the talking, transfixed by stories of Jack's Manhattan bar; of the fast-paced world of keeping the crowds coming and looking after regular customers; of managing the staff, watching out for the young men and young women of his employ; of stocking up and running out of water in the mid-fifties; of the whole bar watching the Moon Landing with two Russian spies amongst the crowd; of helping household movie stars to sober up or clean up before any member of the public or the press got a hold of them; of a life completely removed from the similarly hard-working but much more ordinary life that they had led since coming to New York. As they heard Jack tell the stories, his persona metamorphosed before their eyes. From the very first impression of an old man with faded garments and unruly hair struggling to get out of an elevator, there was virtually nothing left. His true first impression was his first burst of laughter, when his eyes glittered as they peered right into your soul and his true spirit was revealed. The rest was just a weary shell in which he was forced to live.

"Okay, Jack," said PJ as he got up to leave and held Jack's right hand in a firm, lingering handshake. "We'll see you again, no doubt." He glanced at his wife, who nodded and said goodbye to Jack in turn.

The regular visits that followed over the next few months were a source of reinvigoration for both the Rooney's and for Jack. They were great social occasions for different reasons. The Rooney's were thrilled and honoured to be making contact with this indefatigable fellow Irishman and helping him get on track again in their own small way. They always had a copy of the newspaper of the day with them when they visited, and they always had treat for him in the form of biscuits or cake or some left-over shepherd's pie or home-made salad from a family Sunday dinner. Violet would even bring pairs of socks and underwear for Jack, leaving them beside him at the end of their conversations in an unfussy manner. Helen visited him less often, but she continued to call on him regularly and together they looked out for him in the hope that he'd be soon back on his feet and possibly back home.

Jack loved the company. He loved an audience and he loved reconnecting with people from Ireland – something that he had studiously avoided since coming to New York. Was it that he saw himself above them or just that when he was in New York, he wanted nothing but to forge ahead and leave the old, tired country he knew behind him, along with everything that reminded him of it? He couldn't be sure. That was the thing, too, he thought one day after a conversation with his Roscommon friends – that was the thing that joined him and Alva. It was the thing that made them inseparable. It was that shared will to forge ahead together and to leave everything else behind that bonded them for so long. At least, it should have. At times, it was so hard to see what precisely happened. At the back of his mind lurked the truth like a stubborn drunken customer that won't go home – the truth that he had thrown it all away. He had pushed her out of his life. It wasn't a rejection and it wasn't a refusal. It was as if a cuckoo had got into the nest of his own head and of his own life. It pushed and pushed by degrees until he was out of the nest and it was now impossible to get back in.

The lift doors opened on the third floor. There was nobody there. He looked in the mirror to see himself staring back – just as gobsmacked and bewildered as he had been when he was a small child in school in Dublin being told about the ways of nature by his teacher and the phenomenon of what some creatures needed to do to survive. Were human beings really that simple? He gritted his teeth and stared back at himself defiantly. He would survive too, he thought. Alva had taught him a valuable lesson and it would soon be time to come home and to make amends. It wouldn't be pretty and it might not be very happy but he could feel a new chapter in his life beginning. Those people had been great to him and he was getting ready to leave here soon enough. It would all work out. He could feel it. He looked in the mirror again. He was smiling that old crooked smile. He felt himself practically glide out of the lift and down the corridor to his apartment.

Chapter 9 – Uptown Saturday Night

New York City, USA; April 1973.

Jack alighted from the taxi cab on West 42nd Street just outside one of the many seedy outlets advertising go-go girls inside. He liked to walk past them at this hour of the late afternoon, just before they began to get busy. There was still an aura of innocence about, even though it was starting to build up with the usual gathering of pimps and drug dealers hanging around, peering at anyone who hesitated to see if there was any business to be had. It was a warm Spring afternoon and he savoured the uncommon heat from the April sun. He felt an electrical thrill go through him. This, he thought, was where it was at. All life was represented in this short walk from the cab to his club. Along the broad sidewalk that skirted the eastern edge of Bryant Park, this walk contained for him the drama of all human joy and suffering in a journey of four blocks. He was as comfortable with the low-life as he was with the wealth that lived cheek-to-jowl in a manner completely unimaginable in Ireland. The constantly-moving kaleidoscope of colours, sounds, languages and music never failed to buzz through his whole body and remind him that he was alive and strolling down this great avenue in this great city. Here, he passed a theatre for the destitute, gaudily advertising 'live girls', where louche customers, addicts and amoral entrepreneurs would gather later in the evening as surely as the sun had risen that morning. In another block, he would pass theatres where a very different kind of clientele would gather at the same time, eager to see the latest play from Eugene O'Neill or Neil Simon.

He had got used to the heat of the city that his wife could never quite seem to cope with, despite having been here for the best part of three decades now and he looked every bit the suave New Yorker in his bespoke Alan David single-breasted suit and Italian shirt and tie. He caught a brief glimpse of himself in a window as he went by. He slowed down to adjust his hair. Slight greying around the sides but he was comfortable enough in it. He was a bit early for the club but he liked to get a head start on the day. He had felt a bit awkward around his young niece who was over staying with him for a few days with her mother; his younger sister. He hadn't met her since she was only a child herself. It felt all so strange to suddenly have her here in New York – such a real and immediate connection with the forgotten yesteryear, and with a child of her own too. It was an uncomfortable jolt from the past and his niece looked so much like the child he had always imagined that he and Alva would have had. So many years had zipped by already. It wasn't to be. He found himself mouthing the words and realised that he had stopped walking and was staring at his reflection in a huge Almart clothing store window, where a young female store assistant was adjusting a pair of hot pants on a mannequin. She smiled at him briefly before disappearing behind the curtain. He adjusted his collar and looked about him, momentarily lost, then looked up to see that the Empire State Building was still visible ahead of him on the left like a fantastic marker buoy in this sea of humanity. He continued towards the club.

Joe Zio was on security at the door. He was of a plump build with dark Mediterranean looks and a relaxed rounded countenance. He exuded calm but he was always alert. "Hi Joe. Howya doin'? Did you get any sleep last night? Ha ha!"

"No Sir! No rest for the wicked, right?"

"That's right! Now you're talking! Let's have a look at the state of this place. See you later, buddy."

"Sure thing, Mr Mills. Oh, and by the way, a Mr Shriver called this morning looking for you. I told him you'd be here in the afternoon and that you'd call him. Here's his number."

"Shriver, Shriver? Oh yeah! That's great, thanks."

He took the note, placed it in his inside jacket pocket and descended the stone steps to the basement club. The purple-coloured rope lighting along the walls has got to go, he thought to himself. It just looked a bit too cheap for a first impression. Nobody has this kind of lighting anymore. He made a mental note to remind Fran, his secretary, to investigate something with cleaner neon lines. Shriver, he remembered, was Arthur Miller's accountant who was getting him in on a condo deal in Queen's.

He instinctively reached for the doorway on the left at the bottom of the staircase, opened it and reached for the switch to light up the large bar area. He inhaled with satisfaction the smell of the smoke of thousands of cigarettes from the night before.

"Ahhh… that was a busy one for sure," he shook his head and laughed at the memory of one of the Broadway actors who had come in with a huge entourage of women after the show and proceeded to get incredibly drunk. He was a good drunk, though. Very funny guy, not one of those people who become unbearable or confrontational after a few drinks. He just got funnier and funnier. What the hell was his name? Someone famous… one of the Alda brothers. Towards the end of the night, he had stripped off his shirt, stood up on the table and recited a Shakespeare soliloquy from Hamlet.

Jack was shaking his head and laughing at the memory as he lit a Marlboro and walked through the door behind the bar and up a short metal staircase to his office. It was a haven of privacy and peace. There was a window out to the world – high up, barred and looking out onto an alleyway. The other window at the front had a view over most of the club from a lofty position. Very few people ever looked up to even notice it. When the lights were on, it was almost impossible to see it anyway. It was amazing the things that people got up in the corner sofas of the club when they didn't know that anyone was looking. New York seemed to have got a bit wilder in the last few years. It was as if people were behaving like they had nothing to lose. They were living in a bankrupt city with crime and general dirt about the place at what he hoped would be a peak. And yet, all of this seemed to create an irresistible creative buzz that was such an integral part of the soul of this great city. People were amazing. They always found a way of carrying on and of laughing at their own destiny, he thought as he stared around the floor and recalled various incidents of people canoodling in corners and sniffing cocaine or smoking marijuana. Some of the staff were arriving. He turned around to his desk, lit a cigarette and began going through his mail.

"Bills to pay," he muttered, opening each one and setting them aside neatly. He only used a secretary to type letters and always kept on top of most of the administration of the club. What was the point in owning a club if you couldn't look after a few bills? This had become a point of contention between himself and Alva, particularly over the last few years – the fact that he was working all hours and hardly ever spending time at home. I'm working for us, aren't I? Maybe in another few years it won't be so bad... If you're working for yourself, you have to work the hours you can. What was the problem, anyway? She had all her friends and boy, did they keep her busy! She was always going to somebody's house for some kind of party or get-together. All their friends were well-to-do, many of them were Irish. Jack didn't have too many close friends. The people he knew were more business associates and accomplices than friends, as such. He checked himself staring into the middle distance. He took a long drag on his cigarette and tapped the ash onto the silver ashtray – cleaned and sparkling for the new day. In any case, their intimacy had become spoiled by the growing certainty that they could not have children and he avoided it. That was the unspoken truth of the matter. Alva hadn't said that to him yet but he was only waiting for the moment when she would. She would throw it at him with arms out wide in the heat of an angry moment. He didn't want that moment to come. Maybe she also felt something similar. Was it time for them to live apart, therefore? Is this how it happens or does it all blow over after some time? The thought of talking it through tired him.

He knew that he had strayed but he always tried to rationalise about these affairs. To him, they were no more than associations on a business level. They were no more intimate, truly, than meeting someone for lunch and talking about condos in New Jersey or a new range of beer draught pipes. There was a meeting of minds, a connection was made and that was the end of it.

The phone rang. He picked it up and cradled it with his right shoulder and ear while his hands moved busily through the mail, catching up on his perceived daydreaming by hurriedly ripping open the remaining letters.

"Hello?"

"Hi. Is this Jack?" It was a woman's voice. He immediately pictured a seductive beauty.

"Well that depends on who's asking. With whom have I the pleasure of speaking?"

"Sorry?"

"Who's calling?"

"Jack. It's me – Analisa."

Jack frowned and rolled his eyes into the upper reaches of his memory, trying to keep the conversation from lulling into an uncomfortable silence as he did so. "Analisa! Hi! Howya doin'? Nice to hear from you."

"I'm fine, thank you! I just wanted to call to say hello and to say that I had a really good time the other night."

Pulses of familiarity washed over him. He stared at the letter before him. "Well, it's great you called… I had a fun time too, you know."

"I'm glad to hear it, Jack. I know you're probably busy now so I'll let you get back to your work. You're getting ready for the club tonight?"

"Yes, yes… I'm just, y'know, going through the mail – bills to pay and letters from the President. Just the usual stuff! Ha ha!" His eyes focused on the letterhead: Shearwater Fertility Clinic, Brooklyn, it read. His eyes scanned through the paragraphs… 'regret to inform you… Please don't hesitate… if you have any further questions… Doctor John Shearwater.'

"Ha, ha! Give President Nixon a kiss from me! Ciao!"

It came to him in a flash as soon as she put down the receiver. Analisa, the Italian from about a week ago at the club. How could he have forgotten her? A true intelligent beauty direct from the old country – not like the loud second-generation women of Little Italy who wore their heritage like a cheap perfume. Analisa… He recalled her having long dark hair and moving like a swan. Sweet intimate moments in some apartment in the western end of The Bronx. He replaced the phone and took the letter in his hands again, crumpled it up and threw it in the mesh waste paper basket beside him. He looked at it for a moment, then took it out again, tore it into pieces and put it back in the bin. He sighed deeply and picked up his handwritten 'to-do' list.

"That was another waste of three hundred dollars," he said aloud, almost cheerfully, switching his attention to the tasks at hand.

Later that evening, Jack came back into the club after a series of meetings across town. It was six pm and the bar was reasonably busy, mostly filled with regulars popping in for an after-work drink. The main bar was a long polished mahogany unit with a brass trim around the top and a brass foot rail running the full sixty-foot length of it. The high padded stools made in matching style were all occupied with people – overwhelmingly men in loosened ties fresh from their travails on Wall Street – while the cabaret-style small round tables that covered much of the surface of the main area were sparsely populated by a more mixed clientele. The tables along the edges of the main floor had padded partitions around them, offering a certain level of discretion to people. The Emerald Club's location and style meant that it naturally attracted a professional class of client, but Jack had always maintained a strict policy of keeping up a certain level of exclusivity and it had been very successful so far. No sloppily dressed people, no bums and nobody was allowed to get out of hand. A good club reputation took years to build up and weeks or possibly days to fall into ruin.

There was a dance floor area about three tables deep from the bar that was generally uncovered for those who liked to dance and it joined up with the small stage area in the corner. Jack had piped music all the time and live music on weekend nights. He kept it what he called a "classy" mix of jazz, swing and some select modern tunes. It proved to be good mixture and with more and more punk-style music around, the appetite for this kind of music with his clientele was becoming even stronger, it seemed. It had become more of a haven from the bad news, the fractured communities and the increasing dirt on the streets outside.

Off to the right of the main floor as one approached the bar, there was an archway leading to a smaller lounge area while a short corridor and doorway between there and the end of the bar gave access to the VIP lounge – the Green Room, where entry was on invitation only. It had its own separate bar – a smaller version of the main one – and featured luxurious seating in what people in Ireland would have referred to as "snugs"; enclosed rooms for those who could only find relaxation away from the madding crowds.

Jack gave a brief look around to see that all was as it should be: people relaxed, chatting and having a good time, a contented haze of smoke in the air while Frank Sinatra's 'One for my Baby and One for the Road' completed the comfortable ambience. He nodded contentedly and winked at Freddy Schaefer – the bar manager at the Emerald for over a decade now. Jack knew he was perfect for the job the first day he hired him. He was streetwise but calm and clearly spoken; a true New Yorker of German origin from the Bronx who had an easy way with all classes of people. He was tall and had that 'well-fed' American look and beamed back a broad smile as Jack approached.

"All ship-shape, buddy?"

"Yes Sir, Mr Mills. All good so far."

Jack flashed a crooked smile, leaned one elbow on the counter and surveyed the floor. "Yeah, yeah. Looks like a nice crowd. You got the Green Room all set up for later?"

"Sure have, Sir. We got about twenty-five people now. Sidney Poitier is bringing a few extra guests. Mr Poitier's agent called to see if that was okay? I said it was, right?"

"Oh yeah. Yeah, there's room enough for them. Gotta look after the big boys."

"Can I get you something, Mr M? A little Irish?"

"Jesus Christ, you take the words outta my mouth again! Set us both up there with a shot of Jameson!"

Freddy got two measures from the optics on the wall and turned around with the drinks. They clinked glasses.

"Good health, Freddy! And may all your dreams be really dirty! Ha ha!"

"Good health!" Freddy shook his head and laughed his characteristic deep chortle that made his whole body shake. He downed a mouthful.

"So, any big news with you these days?"

"Oh, not much, you know. The usual kinda stuff. We got my kid brother coming back from 'Nam next week... at least, that's what they tell us."

"Is that so? Are they still fightin' over there? I thought it was all over."

"It is mostly. My brother's in a PoW camp. They had an agreement in Paris a couple of months back to release all the prisoners but we gotta wait until now before they come home."

"Jesus. I didn't know that. Not easy doin' business with those gooks, I tell ya. Best of luck with it, yeah? I hope he comes home in good health. He's okay?"

Freddy nodded. "I think so." He raised his glass again. "To Harry."

"To Harry! May he come home to peace in one piece!"

"Amen to that, Mr Mills!"

Jack downed the rest of his drink. "Fix me up with another, will ya?"

Freddy got the drinks again and placed one in front of Jack.

"You know, when your brother gets back, he might need some work. Bring him in to see me, okay? We'll find something for him here for sure – until he gets on his feet at least. Then we'll see what he wants to do. Sounds like a plan?"

"Yes, Sir. I really appreciate that."

"No problem. I hear about a lotta guys who don't get any help from the Government when they get home and the way this city's goin'..."

"Oh, don't get me started, Mr M. Those guys at City Hall been runnin' this city into the ground for years. Years!" His nostrils flared and he took another sip.

"That's it, and all the while people like your brother are puttin' their necks on the line all the way over in fuckin' Gook-land. Cheers!" They both took another sip. "Tell me, what's goin' on with Poitier that he's bringing in such a crowd all of a sudden? Twenty-five people? He used always only have three or four in his party."

"Yeah, I think they're starting shooting a movie. Maybe they're already started. Mr Poitier's directing."

"By Christ! He's doin' well, so he is. All right, I'd better go and make some calls. See ya later, Freddy. And don't forget about what I said about your brother. Any brother of yours has a job here!" He knocked back the rest of his drink and moved to go to his office.

"I really appreciate it, Mr M."

Jack swivelled around with a theatrical look of deadpan seriousness. "Unless of course he's a complete fuck-up! Ha ha! Only kidding! See ya later, big fella." He waved, still laughing, as he mounted the stairs.

Alva sat at the kitchen table and turned the bottle of Bailey's over in her hand, examining every part of the label. It looked like some old Irish kind of drink but she was sure hadn't seen one before. She tried to think back to the days when Jack was working in bars in Dublin and in Dublin Airport. She thought it was all so sophisticated back then. Jack's younger sister had bought it at the airport but the way she was describing it made it sound like a completely different place to the one where Jack used to work back in the day. She felt like keeping it for herself. Jack was hardly there at all during her stay and it was Alva who ended up showing Jack's sister and niece around New York. She had come all the way from Ireland and her brother had barely spent two hours with her – dragging himself off to that bloody club at every possible opportunity. Even today, he barely said goodbye to his sister and niece before he was off again. "It only takes six fuckin' hours to get here nowadays," he had said dismissively when she challenged him about it. "She'll be back again when I'm not so busy." He was uneasy around his Irish visitors. There was an awkwardness and she knew that a lot had to do with her bringing one of her children. She obviously meant no malice in doing so but they had now probably both reached the end of their own potential child-rearing years and there she was accompanied by an example of what they could have had. So strange to see this little being that had come to visit; this soft-spoken, happy -go- lucky dream come true of what they had both longed for over so many years. She tried to think of the point in time when they both gave up on having children. She thought that she had done so before he did – maybe many years before. She was contented enough and accepted their fate much sooner than he had. He wanted to continue to fight for the dream, as was always his wish. They seemed to be fighting for diverging dreams now.

The other thing that had jolted both him and Alva was learning from his sister that their father wasn't living with their mother anymore. She had managed to kick him out, it seemed, and remained alone in the house. Christina and her husband Tom were keeping an eye on her but she seemed to be coping fine. She seemed to have enough money and she was even happy, according to Christina. All Jack had said was "well that was gonna happen someday" and nodded his head. But no matter how expected this development had been, his facial expression had betrayed something else entirely. It was a mask of shock and of dread.

The insistent rasp of the buzzer awoke her from her private thoughts. For a moment, she wondered who could be calling unexpectedly. Then she suddenly remembered. "Margaret," she said aloud. With all the excitement of the visitors from Ireland and of seeing them off earlier on, she had completely forgotten the day of the week and the fact that she had invited her best pal around for tea. She gave a quick look around to ensure that the place was presentable and got up to buzz her friend up.

By the time she had the kettle filled and placed on the stove, she heard the 'ding-dong' chime of the doorbell. She hurried out to the hallway, pausing to check her appearance in the full-length white beaded mirror on the way. The décor in their apartment was a melange of 1960s quality style and classic old Manhattan items such as the French-style antique mirror. "A bit like myself," she said aloud as she adjusted her hair and thought about getting it dyed to maintain its fading darkness. Lots of women were doing it nowadays. Margaret was even considering this new plastic surgery – something that seemed a step too far for Alva to think about seriously.

She turned the night-latch lock and the heavy door swung inwards smoothly.

"Hi, honey!" Margaret's big smile was always a tonic. They hugged and Margaret strode in energetically ahead of her friend, all big sunglasses, bangles and loose sleeves. She was always up to the minute with New York fashions and launched herself headlong into the next trend – whether it was the long-parted fringe and curled-back hair or the straight mid-length hair with a hairband. She had even taken to wearing the new tied shirt look with the tight jeans on occasion.

"So how were your visitations from Dear Old Ireland? You must tell me all, darling!" She took a seat at the kitchen table and put her sunglasses aside while Alva poured the tea. Margaret picked up the bottle of Bailey's. "Is this a gift offering from them?" She shook the bottle, her bangles jangling off the glass.

"Yes, they brought that. Do you know it?"

"Know it? Honey, I'm practically married to it at this stage! Rufus and I got some on our last trip to Europe. We went through Shannon Airport en route to Paris. I don't remember why. I think he had some business meeting to do with the bank. Anyway, you'll love this. When I tasted it, I thought 'finally, something wonderful and delicious from the Old Sod!'"

"Well now that's a great recommendation. I've also got some real Lyons tea for you here." She brought over the tray with steaming teapot, cups and milk.

"Jesus! You oughta have these people fly over more often!"

Alva poured and she sat down opposite her friend. "Yes, maybe we should but it's a big expense for them. Things still aren't so great back home."

"It's booming, honey!" She opened her clutch bag and produced a pack of Newport cigarettes and a gold lighter and lit up quickly. "Well, insofar as things can boom in Ireland. When was the last time you were over?"

"About ten years ago. It was when my mother wasn't well. Remember?"

"Oh yes! She had some problem with her nerves, wasn't it? Is she over that?"

"I think so. I'm really not sure but she seems to be well, going by her letters. I think she's come around to blaming my father for a lot of her problems. He wasn't the best husband, you know."

"Really? How do you mean?"

"Well... let's say he was a man who strayed from time to time."

Margaret's blue Galway eyes widened slightly. She exhaled out of the side of her mouth, took a sip of tea and replaced the cup gently on the saucer. "Alva, honey... you never told me about this before."

Alva was holding her cup with two hands and looking down into it. "Yes, I know. It was something I was ashamed of, I suppose. You know how it is in Ireland with that sort of thing – it doesn't get talked about."

"Jesus, Alva. You've no reason to be ashamed of anything like that. Look at how it is over here! People are breaking up and forming new relationships every day, so they are." Margaret's Galway origins came out much more when she spoke passionately about something, as she was now.

"Yes, I know, I know. It's ridiculous but I've always tried to ignore it. We all knew – me and my sisters – but we just hoped that it would go away and that Daddy would stop going with other women. I never even said it to Jack – even when he told me that his father used to do the same thing."

"When did he tell you that?"

"Oh, years ago. Not long before we were married."

"And how come you didn't say anything about your father after he telling you that?"

"I don't know... I just couldn't say it. I just thought 'well, it doesn't really matter. He's not the same as his father and I'm not the same as my father' and if we just put all of that behind us and keep looking forward, it will all be fine. It was... it was like... if I admitted there was something wrong with my household and my family too, that there'd be a curse on us; as if our marriage would be cursed."

Margaret inhaled deeply on her cigarette, the ash burning up its white length forming a long hot poker. She exhaled strongly, her eyes darting from side to side while Alva took a tentative sip of her tea.

"Alva, this is not like you." Margaret's cigarette hand jabbed a pointed finger at Alva. "This is not the Alva Mills I got to know and love. You're a stronger woman than this. You're not someone who believes in curses or superstitions. You're a strong woman and we're living in the era of women's lib, for Christ's sake! You ought to tell Jack about this, even if your parents are happy and content again."

"Well, I'm not sure they are."

"But you should talk to him about it. It's not your fault that if they don't get along and it's not your fault if your father is boinkin' some floozy from Phibsboro or wherever."

Alva couldn't help laughing. "Phibsboro! Where did you get that from? It's just funny imagining my dad heading over to the Northside for his... bits on the side." She spat the last words out bitterly and immediately took a mouthful of sugary tea as if to wash away what she said.

"Well, in my opinion you should talk to Jack. He'll appreciate it all the more, I think."

"His parents have split up."

"What? In Holy Catholic Ireland?" Margaret momentarily rested her cigarette on the edge of the ashtray and made an exaggerated outlandish effort at blessing herself, her eyes casting heavenwards in enraptured supplication.

"Margaret! You're a scream! It's true, though. Jack's sister was telling me all about it. She's kicked him out, apparently, and she's looking after herself without him."

"Good for her, I say! I think there should be more women in Ireland like her!"

"Really?"

"Course I do. Do you not?"

"I do, I do." She looked to her left, as if searching for a distant view that wasn't there as her back was to the window.

"Why should she have to put up with someone who's only ruining her life? Holding her back? There are too many women in Ireland like that – too many women like that over here too, mind. But that shouldn't be. In this day and age, there should be no room for that kind of thing. Life is short, girl! If Rufus ever did the dirty on me, I'd kick him out that bloody door as quick as I'd look at him!"

Alva looked into her friend's eyes to see if she really meant it.

"I would!" said Margaret, taking a drag on her cigarette and leaning forward to speak with wisps of smoke emerging with her words.

"And sure wouldn't I get half of his lovely big bag of bank money too, honey!"

The two women spontaneously fell backwards and burst out laughing, Margaret with her mad open-mouthed wheezy laugh and Alva with her shoulder-shaking high-pitched laugh. Later that evening, they would meet up with all the other friends from their local bridge club. Alva was in a wonderful mood and she felt so glad to have good friends. All through the evening, however, her mind was on Jack and on whether or not both of their short lives would be better if they were living apart.

At 5:15 am the following morning, Jack arrived back to the apartment. He got out of the cab and paid the driver. "Keep the change, buddy," he said, before wheeling about and striding off whistling the opening bars of 'Nel Blu dipinto di Blu'. As he entered the building, the night watchman saluted Jack just as he did most nights around this hour. Jack did a silent mime of a man opening fire on him with a submachine gun – something they both found hilarious in that context.

Jack opened the door of the apartment as silently as he could and closed it smoothly with a click. He took off his shoes, and went tip-toed to the ensuite bathroom, gave his teeth a quick scrub, took off all his clothes and snuggled in beside his sleeping wife. He was so tired that he'd decided not to bother with his customary wash of his face and neck before getting into bed.

In the half light, Jack could make out the still form of his wife's hair, half-exposed by the eiderdown that came up to her neck. He didn't approach too closely.

"You awake, honey?" he whispered.

"Sort of," she sighed. "Busy night?"

"Yeah. Busy, busy. Glad to be home, let me tell ya." He leaned over and planted a kiss on her neck. She gave a gentle moan of approval and he turned back the other way to settle down. He had the scent of a mixture of strong alcohol and Acqua di Parma lady's perfume. She sighed, shut her eyes tight and pulled the covers up over her ear.

Chapter 10 – The Dayroom

State Nursing Home, LongIsland, New York, USA; Present Day.

The sound of the pipe chimes shook Jack out of his daydream. The afternoon tea. Was it a sleeping dream? Had he been asleep? He wasn't sure. He fell back to sleep almost as immediately as he had awoken. He was back again at the Emerald. His body was fully functional and he was waltzing through the crowd on the dance floor. The people, the tables, the bar, the carpet, the wooden floor were a moving kaleidoscope of garish coloured lights, like giant confetti. Everybody was smiling. There was disco music playing because it was a new thing on Friday night that got everybody up dancing and because Robert Stigwood – a club regular and producer of Saturday Night Fever – had advised him to do so. Jack was waltzing through the crowds. He was dressed in his new tan-coloured tailored three-piece suit from Bresciani's, smoothly moving through the crowd, dancing an old step to a new beat, grabbing pretty girls to do a twirl, kiss their hand and move on. Everybody cheered as he waltzed his way through the crowd. Now he was on the tables, jumping onto the first one and pirouetting before leaping on to the next. The customers loved it, laughing and cheering at every antic from the impresario of impresarios. Look at him go! Glasses, ashtrays and bottles fell to the side and still everybody clapped and cheered. As he approached the bar, he saw Analisa sitting there. She was dressed like a 1950s high-school girl. He knew something was wrong but he moved towards her, inexorably like a moth to a flame. Her hair was tied back in a ponytail and she was chewing gum. "Giacomo," she cooed. "You are a dancer *straordinario*!" She uncrossed her legs, leaned back on the bar with her arms supporting her and began to slowly open her legs wide. "Ana! Jesus Christ, woman! What are you do…?" Suddenly Alva was there standing at the bar dressed in an apron, cleaning a glass. She looked old, hard… She glared at him and dropped the glass and towel. They fell to the floor and she made a grotesque face, making a gesture with her finger moving slowly across her throat. She then pointed the long finger at Jack.

"Mr Mills! Are you okay, Man? You sweatin'! It was just a bad dream."

For a brief moment, Jack felt suspended in mid-air, unsure if he was still dreaming or having a heart attack. He stared at the man before him, who was placing a tray on the table over his bed. It was Jerome. The name came to him reassuringly quickly. Jerome, the orderly from Jamaica.

"Jesus Christ, Jerome! You gave me a fright you crazy black bastard!"

"Now, now, Mr Mills. You know that it ain't right to be talkin' like that. I'll forgive you 'cause you just woke up from a bad dream but it ain't no use pickin' on me just because I is more beautiful than you."

"Ha ha! Well, you gotta say at this stage of the game, you're probably right!" He strained to pull himself up on the bed, using his good arm and being careful not to aggravate the open sore in his right leg. "What culinary fuckin' delights have you got for me?"

"Well now, Mr Mills, let me start by recommending these magnificent cheese-and-turkey sandwiches." Jerome waved his large hand slowly across the small array of food on the tray, smiling his large-toothed smile at Jack, who looked on with an intense look of disgust. "I believe that this purée of unidentifiable fruit is the perfect accompaniment and if you still have room for it, we have this wonderful jello to top off a really delightful dinin' experience! Yah-man!"

"Jesus Christ, Jerome! I'm kind getting' tired of this joke. What in the name of Jesus, Mary and Joseph is that?" He pointed to a clear plastic cup with an opaque milky-brown liquid.

"That, my good friend, is your tea."

"Tea? Jesus fuckin' wept! Looks like someone got sick in it." Jack stared up at Jerome pleadingly. His white hair was long and dishevelled and his body was a frail but determined leaning structure, even as he sat in the bed. In his brown eyes, his spirit remained untamed and ageless, with that crooked devilish sneer intact. "I think they're tryin' to kill me."

Jerome smiled. He was young-looking forty-something – tall and well-built with tied-up dreadlocked hair. His face was relaxed and open and his high cheekbones and long nose lent him an air of African nobility. "Ain't nobody tryin' to kill ya, man. They give the same stuff to everybody here."

"Maybe they're tryin' to kill us all. I mean, what kind of way is that to serve somebody a cup of tea? It wouldn't hurt just to use a china cup every now and again, would it?"

"Well, I'll put in a good word for ya, Mr Mills, but I tink they have a real small budget."

"Budget! Jesus, tell me about it! I gotta budget my way outta this dump. It's full of fuckin' retards and no-hopers. Not good for a man's soul, you know what I mean?"

"Well, we all got problems. What about your wife?"

"She's... I don't know where she is. Maybe she's dead. She won't have me anymore anyway. Locked the door and told me to fuck off... or as good as."

"Ain't you got no family here that can help you?"

Jack reached for one of the small triangular turkey-and-cheese sandwiches and stuffed it in his mouth unceremoniously. "They're all the other side of the world." He wiped the spittle from his mouth.

"In Ireland, right?"

"Yeah. Back in good old holy Ireland, where there's no money, only a bunch of priests in frocks and crooked politicians."

"Sounds a bit like Jamaica."

"Yeah? Except I'll bet the weather is a hell of a lot better there!"

"You don't get good weather in Ireland?"

"Naww… it's always fuckin' rainin'!" He was moving quickly now, ravenously scoffing the remaining sandwiches from the afternoon tea service. Jerome observed Jack. He had some serious physical problems but he was sharper than most of the other patients. He gave a quick look around to ensure that there was no-one else in need of assistance.

"Family is always important, you know? Maybe you could get word to someone in Ireland and they might come see you over here?"

"Yeah. Maybe. I dunno." He took a slurp from the milky tea and grimaced like he'd been stabbed. "Christ! It's cold too. You know, I used to know one of your guys at the club – a Jamaican, I mean. I like Jamaicans; always cool and respectful. And funny. Not like those wise-ass fuckers from Harlem – always full of attitude, always lookin' for something or to deal drugs in the club. I never had any of those bastards dealin' in my club – didn't matter to what colour their skin was."

"Who was your friend from Jamaica?"

"Harry Belafonte. You know him? Famous singer."

"Sure I do. You knew Harry Belafonte?"

"I still know him, for Christ's sake. Yeah, he was a regular at the club. Great friend. He was born here but his folks were Jamaican and he lived there for a while as a child. Great card player."

"Yeah?"

"Oh yeah. Fuckin' shark! And he's one hell of a practical joker – the funniest guy you'll ever meet. Do you know what he did to me one time?"

Jerome took a quick look around the ward and sat on the chair next to Jack's bed. There were three or four others, all eating quietly in their own worlds. "What?"

"He called me up at the office and put on this phoney Irish accent. I fell for it straight away, of course, like some kind of idiot. I don't know – it sounded kinda funny but I figured it was some kind of posh presidential type, you know? Anyway, he said he was the secretary of the President of Ireland and that the President was on a state visit and he wanted to come to the famous Emerald Club and that I was doin' a great job representing the people of Ireland and that he might be presenting me with a medal!"

"And what did you do?"

"He told me he was on his way. I didn't check any papers or nothin' to see if there was news about the Irish President coming. I couldn't even think who the hell the President of Ireland was. I just ran out of there, got a cab back home to change into something cleaner, something more presidential. So I get back to the club trying not to sweat so much and after pouring a bottle of cologne over me and I see this big limo outside with Irish flags on the hood. All the windows were blacked out so I couldn't see inside."

Jerome started shaking with laughter, making Jack laugh too. "As I came alongside, staring at the windows and trying to walk all dignified – Ha ha! – the fuckin' electric window comes down and I'm like 'Holy mother of Divine Christ! I'm late for the President of Ireland after coming all this way to see me!' Next thing, Belafonte sticks his head outta the window and starts singing *Take me home Kathleen*!"

"Ha ha ha! Harry Belafonte! Man, I don't believe it!"

"It's true, I tell you. He's one sharp cookie. Got me real good, so he did. Yeah, yeah… Yeah, I'll probably get things back in order if I can ever get out of this place. I don't know… do something about my leg so I get around a bit easier."

"You still thinkin' about the club?"

"Oh yeah. You gotta keep looking forward, right? No point in bitching about your misfortune."

"I suppose not."

"Course not!" He leaned closer to Jerome, lowering his voice conspiratorially. "Lots of cute little fishies in the sea, my Jamaican friend, and I ain't done fishin' yet! Ah-ha-ha-ha-ha!"

Jack's laugh exploded like a small arms fire in the confines of the ward and Jerome could only bend over double with laughter.

"All right, my friend," Jerome got up to leave. "You know that the first time I ever understand a whole story from you?"

"I can't imagine why… I've a very clear speaking voice, I'm told."

"Well, it's a bit of an Irish patois all da same! I'll leave you to have fun with your dessert. Don't be doin' too much tinkin' bout dem gyals. They only upset you. Remember… be nice and stay happy. One love. Irie." He clasped Jack's hand in his. The two grinned broadly at one another.

"Yeah, see ya later."

After his food, Jack had decided to go down to the dayroom, to have a look around and see if he found anything interesting to read in the newspaper or look at on TV. With the aid of his wheeled walker, he got himself to the elevator and down to the second floor. He avoided looking at his reflection in the mirror whenever possible. He never really recognised what he saw and looked away again quickly before he would let it get him down. There was nothing of the dapper club owner that once was. His clothes were those of a tired old man. He had no valuable possessions of any note and his appearance was dishevelled. He usually managed a rudimentary morning shave using his electric shaver, but his hair was long and unkempt. Sitting down was probably his best position. He could get his heavy atrophied left hand onto the table, sit up reasonable straight and appear to have all his limbs in perfect functioning order to anyone sitting across from him. The rest was the power of persuasion and he did a good job of continually persuading himself and everyone around him.

"Hi. How's it going?" He greeted the short Mexican nurse as he entered the Day Room. She was a cheerful woman of about fifty-five and Jack always made her giggle, even if it was just a brief greeting and a wink.

"Hi Mister Meels. Are you well today?"

"All the better now for seeing you, darling."

"Ha-ha-ha-ha-ha! I'm happy to see you too, Mr Meels. You're moving a leetle better today, I think."

"Oh, you better believe it! I got all the moves, honey!" He winked and she went off on her duties, giggling.

Jack looked around to see who was there and to find a free seat in the room. Just the usual crowd, he thought. It was such a collection of boring people. Not one of them had anything interesting to say. There was no sign of Mr Arnold – the only one he considered worth talking to. He always 'got' Jack in a way that other people didn't. Jack realised that just about everybody else considered him a crank and didn't want to talk to him. He laughed at the realisation of it. None of them had ever sat down to a real meal, he thought. Probably brought up on hamburgers, French fries and cold milky tea. No point in talking to them about culinary sophistication or fine clothing. Why is it only a small percentage of people in America are even worth bothering with? Maybe Irish people were just as bad. He wasn't sure – couldn't quite remember.

"Hi Jack!" It was that Benson lady – someone he didn't want draw upon himself without good reason to do so.

"Oh… hi there. I'm just lookin' for a paper."

"Here you go." She was sitting on the comfortable armchair in the corner. All the seating in the Day Room was a mixture of different types of chairs and seats seemingly cobbled together from ad-hoc purchases over a long period of time and/or donations from residents' relatives. She smiled and looked up at him through her large thick round glasses. Suddenly, he had a flash back to a girl he knew in primary school that used to plague him to get his attention. He didn't like her either.

"*Plus ça change…*"

"What was that, Jack?"

"Oh nothing. Just mumbling in French. Yeah, thanks for this. I'll go sit over there and read it."

He moved to the opposite side of the room where there was no-one. Altogether, there were only four people sitting around, reading or chatting quietly.

Jack opened the newspaper up on the table before him and started leafing through it, looking for something of interest in the Daily News to catch his eye. Just then, Dr Evelyn Coletto walked in. She was in her mid-length skirt, high heels and white medical coat and went over to another of the patients to tell him something whispered quietly. Jack's eyes perked up at the sight of the long-haired thirty-something beauty of Italian extraction. She glanced over at him and he caught her attention by raising his finger. She finished her chat and walked over to Jack. She smiled wryly at the mischievous eyes of the man before her, who otherwise had the outward appearance of a defeated old man.

"Hello, Mr Mills. Is everything all right?"

"Oh yeah. Everything's swell, thanks. You're looking particularly alluring today, if I may say so."

She looked into the chart she was cradling without answering but he could see the corners of her mouth move to suppress a smile.

"I was just reading here in the paper about how there's a famous Irish singer coming to town."

"I see."

"Yeah, and I thought it's the perfect opportunity for someone like you to experience such talent from the old continent. Do you have any Irish in you yourself?"

"Well... not that I know of..."

"I don't know if you're aware of it, but I'm from Ireland originally. I'd consider it an honour if you could join me at the Club 66 for dinner and a wonderful evening of entertainment. It's my all-time favourite piano bar, as a matter of fact. Just say the word and I promise you an evening you won't forget for the rest of your life."

"I scrub up real clean when I go out and I know every barman in Manhattan – they all used to work for me at some point."

Dr Coletto busied herself marking something on the chart which she cradled slightly awkwardly close to her chest. She looked up again and couldn't help smiling at Jack's confident raised eyebrow.

"Well, I'm very glad to see you in such high spirits, Mr Mills." She did an about-turn as nonchalantly as she could manage and strode purposefully towards the elevator.

"I love watching you walk away, honey!" Jack responded in a raised voice as she disappeared through the doorway. One of the other guests looked up from his newspaper and tutted.

"She has a gorgeous ass, don't you think?" Jack enquired of his disapproving fellow patient. He huffed in response, lifting his newspaper higher so that was banished from Jack's line of vision. Mrs Benson smiled a girlish smile to herself without looking up and continued reading her book.

It was early morning in the ward. Jack was sitting up staring into space and mumbling to himself, trying hard to piece together confused parts of a dream he had with memories of incidents that had happened years ago. Just how long he had been here, he couldn't recall. Sometimes it seemed like only yesterday when he was strolling down Fifth Avenue in his finest clothes. Analisa was on his arm and she was whispering something funny to him – something intimate about the night before. He loved the adoration. That was the thing. It wasn't the sex and it wasn't even that he was looking for a soul partner – he wasn't fully sure that he needed one. He thought Alva was his soul partner. They had so much in common but then... No, it was being adored by someone who was prepared to give him everything – body and soul – no matter what he did or said. Criticism of any kind was something he didn't have time for. Why, he wondered, did people spend so much time pointing out faults and trying to change people? He didn't do it. He just wanted to take the juice from life and taste it. Forget about the rest. It all turns to dust in the end, just like those priests used to remind him every Ash Wednesday when everyone who was Catholic had to go around with a piece of dust in the middle of their forehead. *Remember man you are but dust...* Where were they going that day? He remembered taking her through shops and buying her a necklace in Tiffany's. $500. Analisa loved the movie *Breakfast at Tiffany's* and they were living out the fantasy of it. She looked every bit as stunning as Audrey Hepburn and he felt like George Peppard. Only better. That was a great day – a day that made you feel glad to be alive; a day when you could taste the sweet juice of life in the greatest place in the world, as far as he was concerned. Was it that same day that he was having lunch with Analisa at the Tout va Bien on West Fifty-Third when Alva walked in? Very possibly. It was certainly one of those many *BreakfastatTiffany's* type of afternoons he spent with Analisa before going back to her place for a couple of hours. Alva had just marched straight to their table like she already knew they were going to be there. She glared at him – calmly, without hysteria. That was just like Alva – she would cry over the small things but when it came to the big stuff – the really big decisions – she was uncannily calm and focused on what needed to be done. She was even calm and accepting about their fate when they knew that they couldn't have children. He was the one who railed against facts and fought it all the way, but she looked at the large wave that was about to engulf them as a couple and stared at it with complete acceptance. He couldn't recall her crying over it. Neither could he remember her crying or causing a scene of any sort that day when she walked over to the table where he and Analisa were sitting, their adulterous fingers entwined on the white linen table cloth. Two glasses of Chateau d'Yquem before them. His immediate thought had been for the order of the restaurant and he looked straight at François the *maître d'hôte* to see that he was alert to a potential incident.

"That's enough," she had said. He had opened his mouth to say something but found no words. "I've had enough, Jack." He was so stunned by her reaction that he let Analisa's hand go and swore to himself as Alva turned and walked back out of the restaurant that things would change from that point on. They didn't, even though he swore it to Alva time and again during the months that followed. "Have things changed, Jack?" she would ask him calmly, her eyes seeming to look through him to a calm sea beyond him.

"Have they fuck!" he said aloud, causing one of the others still sleeping in the ward to groan loudly in complaint.

"Tryin' to sleep, here!"

"Blow it out your ass! It's morning! Fuckin' nothin' left now. All gone." He looked around him agitatedly. He lifted his leaden left arm with his right and felt along his bare wrist for a watch. He used to have a collection of expensive watches… Tag Heuer and Philippe Patek. "Where the fuck are they? Where are my watches? And my books? Who the hell took my books?! First they take everything you've got and then they try to kill ya!"

Someone reached for a button to call an orderly. Almost immediately, Jerome appeared and headed straight over to Jack's bed, smiling.

"Jesus Christ, that was quick! Look, it's already almost seven o'clock and I was looking for my stuff..."

"Jack, I dunno what you talkin' 'bout, man. I just came to let you know that you have a visitor."

Tara McCullough arrived at the Fair Street Nursing Home on Long Island, hoping against hope that she would find her uncle there. Having come over to New York from Ireland specifically to find her uncle, she had had a stressful week of it going from assisted living Home to Day Care Centre to nursing home and back again. It was thanks to one kindly employee at the West 86 Assisted Living Center who advised her to go to the Fair Street home that she found herself here.

"Yes, we have a patient by that name," the receptionist told Tara. "We do allow visitations but I'll need to see some ID to prove that you're related to Mr Mills."

Tara had been prepared and duly produced her Irish passport, along with a copy of her mother's birth certificate on which her maiden name of Mills was stated. "Mills... that's the name my mother had before she was married. She's Jack Mills' sister"

"Ok, so her birth name is Mills?"

"Her maiden name, yes."

The receptionist asked Tara to take a seat in the waiting area and twenty minutes later, the chief consultant Dr Sol arrived. He looked like a retired basketball player – beanpole tall with a shiny bald head and Slavic-like physical features. He looked like he'd outgrown his green scrubs and white coat slightly since he put them on and he wore a pair of round spectacles that perched on his long nose. He shook Tara's hand and sat on the seat next to her.

"Hi, Tara. I'm Dr Sol. I understand you're the niece of our patient Mr Jack Mills?"

"Yes."

"Well, we're delighted to have a member of his family come see him. He's quite a remarkable person."

"Yes, I know. Not always the most popular, though. Tell me doctor, how is he?"

"He does have a few ongoing problems but he's in good health and in good spirits. Oh, and by the way, there's something you must understand from the off: Mr Mills is now a ward of the State of New York."

"What does that mean?"

"It means that he is in the care of, and effectively belongs to, the State of New York. He arrived here in an agitated state wanting to go home. He was dehydrated and confused. We tried to take him home but I understand that he was refused entry to the place he said he lived…"

"Refused?"

"Yes, it was his wife, or his estranged wife, I believe."

"My God. I didn't realise it."

"Yes, well what it meant was that he was without any family, essentially. There was… nobody to claim him. So in those circumstances, the State of New York can pick up the baton, if you will. A New York state court appoints a court guardian and he gets placed in an institution like this one where we look after him as best we can."

"So he has a guardian? Who is that?"

"Uhh, yes he does. But it's just a formality really. In this case, it was a... Mr Theobold Solomon."

Tara searched her mind quickly but couldn't recall the name.

"Like I said, it's just a formality. Essentially, he's now in the care of the State of New York right here. We only allow visits from family members with ID. In fact, a lady has been calling to see him a few times. She's not allowed access to him but she has left some packages for him that we've passed on to Mr Mills – clothing and food mostly."

"Do you know the name of that lady – the one who drops off the packages?"

"I'm not sure… but I think one of the people in administration may be able to help you there. I think she's Helen something or other?"

Tara frowned, repeating the name a couple of times and shook her head again. "No, I don't know her. There hasn't been a woman from Italy called Analisa Serio in to see him?"

"I… I'm not sure. I don't think so. As far as I know, there's only been that other lady I mentioned and now you, but you need to double-check with the people in administration for that. Okay, I won't take up anymore of your time, Tara. I know you must be eager to meet your uncle again. Just bear in mind… he's in good spirits but he's lost a lot of mobility. "when was the last time you saw him?"

"Oh.. too many years to remember."

"Oh I see. Well… lotta changes so. The main two problems your uncle has are his left hand and his left leg. His left hand is more or less immobile after his initial stroke, and his left leg has limited mobility, being a diabetic he also has a very serious ulcer on his leg that we can't quite clear up. We manage it on a daily basis with cleaning and replacing dressing, antibiotics, diet and so on, we do our best to prevent further infection spreading but it's not something that's likely to get better any time soon. He won't let any of our female staff look after it – only male orderlies, he insists. He gets by pretty well. He's a real fighter. Like I said, he's quite the character here. He's certainly been teaching me a thing or two about fine wines and French dining etiquette!"

Jack made his way down to the Day Room, shuffling along with his walker and wincing at the pain that was acting up in his ulcer. He felt quite thrown by the news that he had a visitor – mostly excited but a little bit anxious as well. Someone coming to see him... Who was it? Maybe it was Alva. He couldn't imagine it anymore: whatever they said between them seemed to have been a definitive cutting off. Could it finally be Analisa? He was sure that he hadn't seen her in a long time – maybe since before he was in the assisted living place. She faded away at some point, almost unnoticed. Maybe it was because something had happened. Maybe she was sick too and maybe now she was coming back to see him – now that she could. He remembered the first time that he met her. It was on St Patrick's Day – March 17th. It was an unseasonably warm Spring that year. She had stood out amongst all the beautiful women that came and went at the Emerald Club. She had that strong mixture of grace and allure. *Something in the way*... That song by the Beatles was possibly even playing at the very moment he first saw her. Yes, he thought, there **was** something in the way she moved that caught his eye: Something that was confirmed when she smiled at him and that had him completely captured as soon as they began to speak to one another. She had had it rough, he was to learn later from so many long conversations – through her uprooted childhood from Apulia, her mother's death when she was only fourteen and then her unhappy marriage – but she had cast it off and turned her face towards the sun. He loved that about her; always seeking the silver lining, always interested in tasting the sweetness in life and disregarding all bitterness. Maybe she was his soulmate. Maybe it was Analisa that would turn up this morning to meet him once more and turn things back, reverse some of the damage of the years.

"No better woman to do it!" He said aloud in the confines of the elevator. He lifted his head and looked hard at himself in the mirror. He saw a grim determined crazy old man looking back at him. Shit! He thought. I haven't even shaved! He suddenly imagined the shock and the fright that Analisa would get when she saw him and it made him laugh. He couldn't stop the giggles and he bent over laughing like a madman alone in an elevator. He looked up at himself again and burst out laughing, barely controlling himself from farting, the thought of which made him giggle even more.

The elevator doors opened and he emerged with a grin, pains in his face and wiping tears from his eyes with a Kleenex from his pocket. As he shuffled through the doorway of the Day Room, a young dark-haired woman stood up to greet him. He smiled back.

"Analisa?"

"No. It's me Tara."

"Tara?"

"Your niece from Dublin. Remember? I came to see you years ago... with my Mam, your sister Christina; Christina McCullough."

The sudden recognition made his face light up with a broad smile. "Tara! Jesus Christ!"

They embraced and he spoke into her ear: "I'm so glad you came back. I can't believe you've come all this way."

She guided him over to the table in the corner, both with the same degree of astonishment, longing and mild awkwardness at the situation of family members connecting after a lifetime. They sat at right angles to one another – neither side-by-side nor facing each another but at the instinctive positions that this peculiar environment of familiarity and unfamiliarity dictated. With his right hand, he lifted his deadened forearm onto the table and joined his hands before him. After a short silence, Jack was the first to speak.

"So, did you come alone?"

"Yes. My husband Cormac is with me in New York but I came here alone."

"Well, bring him next time. Don't be hidin' him away in a hotel room. Ha ha." He looked around as if momentarily distracted, displaying the shock of hair at the back of his head that stood up like ridiculously as if someone had combed it that way as a prank. He turned to her again with a raised eyebrow. "You wouldn't know what he might be up to on his own! Ha!"

Tara laughed. "Well, it's good to see you haven't changed, Uncle Jack! Tell me first, how are you? How are they treating you in here?"

"Oh... I'm great. Yeah, yeah. I got this bad arm and my leg hurts like hell but they're pretty good at lookin' after me. If I get tired, Jerome, my right-hand man, excuse the pun! will push me around in a fairly fancy wheelchair. I had to put my foot down at the start, you know? That's the way you gotta do things sometimes – in business and in life too – but we've come to an understanding."

"I see."

"Yeah, they had this woman who used to just hurt me and acted like she was more used to dealing with elephants than human beings, you know? All rough and awkward. So I couldn't have that and I told them so and now it's okay. It's improving little by little... The food in here is terrible – it's just all slops that the pigs eat, really. They got me in these shitty clothes... I don't know. I don't think these people would know good food and a bottle of Chateau Lafitte if it jumped up and bit 'em in the ass!"

Tara put her hand to her mouth, not quite believing how loudly Jack was saying this.

Jack looked into Tara's eyes and smiled. "You know, you look a lot like your mother. The same eyes, same smile."

She nodded. "That's what everyone says. They say I look like Gran too."

"Yeah, yeah, God rest her soul." He instinctively struck his breast and bowed his head in a traditional Catholic manner that he hadn't used in years. "She was a good woman, so she was." Tara held his hand. "And what about Christina?"

"She's well. She's really great. She's back in Dublin at the moment."

"So they sent you over as a scout, eh? *Get over there to America and see what your man's got! See how much we can get off of him!* Eh? Ha ha!"

"Something like that!"

"Yeah, yeah. I don't think I'm the most popular in the family – a bit of a black sheep, eh? Ha ha! They probably sent you over to form a truce, with a white flag! Before any of the rest of them get on a plane."

"No, no, Uncle Jack. I decided to come on my own. We were a bit worried about you. It took a while to track you down, you know."

"Did it? Yeah, there've been a lotta changes in the last few years but I'm hangin' in there. Alva doesn't want me anymore so I can't go home. You know that?"

"Yes, I know."

"So I can't even remember how long I've been in here– must be a year or more."

"Have you got any private health plan? Maybe we could look at moving you to another place – somewhere better?"

"I don't know about that. They tell me I've no Medicare cover left – at least that's what that Dr Sol guy said. I don't really understand. I had lots of cover – used to cost me four hundred bucks a month or something like that. I guess Alva knows about that but..."

"And what about the club? It was really busy, wasn't it? Is there any income from it or from the sale of it?"

"I don't know. I know this guy George – he was a friend of mine – was running things for me for a while after I had the stroke, but I haven't seen him in a while. I'm sure it's been gone a while – closed up. Probably a Walmart's there now! Ha ha! Or some titty bar! Jesus, imagine that in the Holy Emerald Isle!"

Tara squeezed his hand. "Well… we'll see what we can do about it. Cormac and I will have a look into it."

"Sure. That's a good idea. Maybe we can get the place open again, eh? We've lots of clients who come all the time, again and again. Once they see me again, they'll all flock back like homing pigeons. Ha ha! Yeah, that's what they're like, in a way. We used to have all the big names call in. We're just in the right spot for it all, you know? All the guys from Broadway – Neil Simon, Arthur Miller, Alan Alda… I can't remember all their names right now. Then you had the movie stars too – mostly the likes of the new guys like Sidney Poitier – gentleman! – but we had 'em all, really. Even John Travolta turned up one night for our disco night."

"Disco night? I can't imagine that was your kind of music, Uncle Jack."

"Well it wasn't really. I didn't really like it but it was okay. Mostly it was jazz and crooners' stuff – that's what our clients liked, you know? Kept them away from the punk and the sugar-coated hard rock shit that was going on outside, excuse my French parlance. But we decided to have this disco night and we had it on late to give it the best chance, you know? When people are all tanked up, they think it's twice as exciting as it actually is! Then they tell all their friends about it and, believe you me, word travels really fast around this town. I mean really fast! Yeah, so Travolta comes in one night. All the girls' eyes were on him, of course, because it was at the height of the Saturday Night Fever craze but he was with this other guy the whole time. I put him in the Green Room for a while to chill out and not be disturbed by all the fans. Anyway, he comes out after a bit and, although he wasn't wearing his famous white suit, he just gets into the middle of the crowd when 'Stayin Alive' comes and starts doing all those moves in his white tee-shirt and blue jeans. The crowd went fuckin' **wild**! It was deadly."

Tara was smiling. "My God! That must have been amazing. Are you still in touch with any of the people from the club?"

"No! I don't know where they all are! Maybe it's like you say – nobody knows I'm here in this fuckin' Gulag. Who knows? Maybe they're all still there havin' a great time dancing with Rudolf Nureyev and Harry Belafonte and I'm in here oblivious to it all."

"Well, we'll have a look into it, Uncle Jack."

"Have you been to the club?"

"No, I only came here to see you and you took a while to find. I'd say you're hiding from the paparazzi!"

"Ha! Don't talk to me about those guys. It was a full-time job keepin' them out – them and their cameras. And you know, the trouble was that over the years, the cameras kept getting smaller and smaller. You can't let it happen, though. Once word gets out that you'll be photographed every time you go into the Emerald, you might as well shut the doors. I wish they'd shut the doors of this bloody place!"

A tall elegant man in his late sixties approached the table. Jack grinned up at him.

"Hey! Howya doin' Jack? I see you got a visitor."

"I certainly do. Tara… this is my good friend Mr Arnold: the only one in here with any sense – besides myself, of course!"

"Of course!" Tara laughed, stood up and shook hands with him.

"This is my niece Tara. Isn't she beautiful?"

"Very pleased to meet you, Tara." He had an instantly likeable soft-spoken manner and relaxed countenance. He indicated towards Jack with his head before adding: "I'm very sorry you have to put up with that guy."

"Hey! I heard that, you old Kike! Ha ha!"

"I don't know why he even calls me that. I'm not even Jewish. Okay, I just wanted to say hello. I'll leave you to it. Very nice to meet you again, Tara." He turned and walked out of the Day Room.

"He seemed like a nice person."

"'Yeah, he's a good old skin, as they say in Dublin. Very smart guy – good listener. He's had his fair share of struggles in life too, you know. You wouldn't believe it."

Tara and Jack spent another hour talking, getting up to speed with one another's worlds. She promised to come back with more visitors even though she wondered how many relatives were interested in even knowing much about Jack. He had been cut off from everyone else for so long and had little to do with anyone who had come to visit him, so wrapped up he was in his working life. Now she was the only real link between him and the rest of the extended family. She left some money at the nursing home to buy Jack some new clothes to replace the tired second-hand clothing that had come from charity donations and to pay a barber to come and cut his hair. She also asked to be contacted if Jack needed anything or if there was any change in his condition. From Alva, there was nothing at all and every indication made it clear that Jack's former wife would have nothing more to do with Jack.

Jack returned to his corner of the ward with a realignment in his perception of the world around him and a renewed sense of hope. He could almost taste it on his lips. He wondered at the realisation that there were people out there who still were concerned about him and who wished the best for him. Seeing his niece again evoked so many different emotions in him and so many memories of the past. They now seemed to take on a more defined three-dimensional form. He wanted to see his sister Christina again, feel the warmth of family members around him and maybe go back to Ireland again – just for a visit at least. In fact... no, he thought – no more than a visit. Going back to Ireland would be like visiting a foreign country as a defeated useless being and that was something he couldn't contemplate for a second. From the description that Tara had given him, it sounded like a totally different country now – more freedom, more money. Certainly, back in the forties and fifties, you couldn't imagine someone from Ireland just jumping on a plane, flying over to New York and then going back again. He was sitting on the side of his bed. Before him on the bed table was an opened package that had contained Oreo cookies, a bottle of wine and some fresh underwear – just like the package he'd got the month before. He was looking at the items laid out on the table, eyeing the label on the red wine bottle.

"Barton and Guestier," he said aloud in a low voice as if talking to an unseen dinner guest. "Mediocre and mass-produced. They haven't looked back since Roy Scheider and Richard Dreyfuss shared a bottle of it in 'Jaws'."

As he examined the small note that came with the package, he laughed at the recollection of Scheider telling him about it one night at the Emerald: how the director Spielberg had been so fascinated and excited to hear how many people had actually noticed what wine was in the scene and he had immediately started talking about using the idea to help finance his next film. You place the product and they will pay... Still, he thought, it's better than the warm water they serve you here. Just like the previous month, the note – crumpled up amongst the underwear – read simply: *Hope this finds you well. Regards, H.B.*

"Helen Bromley." The words came out so naturally and effortlessly that he wondered how it had been so hard to remember her name up to that point. He smiled with the warm assurance that someone he knew had been watching over him all the time, even though earlier that morning, he had considered himself long forgotten.

"Penny for your thoughts, buddy." Mr Arnold had walked into the ward in his usual quiet manner, his slippered footsteps making almost no sound on the LVT flooring.

"Jesus, you'd make a good assassin! I wouldn't have had the time to realise I was dead! Ha ha!"

"Well I didn't want to disturb you. You seemed lost in thought just there... talking to yourself. You know you're probably going crazy? I'd have that checked out if I were you."

"Ha ha! Not as crazy as you, you fuckin' Kike!"

Mr Arnold sat on the soft easy chair next to Jack's bed. "Is all this stuff from your niece?"

"This? No. It's actually from another lady. I only just figured out who she is. She's been sending me packages like this for months. She was good to me."

"That's nice. You need a friend every now and again. Especially one that sends you wine and cookies."

"Yeah, she even brought me from the other place to take me home that time... you know? I told you about all that. My wife wouldn't let me in – wouldn't even come down to talk to me. Helen just came back out to the taxi all ashen-faced and told me that I couldn't go home. Decades of marriage and suddenly she's the one who pulls the plug. Can you imagine?"

Mr Arnold shook his head.

"I dunno. I suppose I must have deserved it in her eyes. But Jesus, look at me! Wearing these rags and eating... fuckin' dog food and surrounded by a bunch of retards – present company excepted!"

His friend closed his eyes, smiled and nodded graciously.

"I didn't deserve this! Did I? I mean, kick me out of the apartment – sure – but what about my business and my work? I can't get it back. I don't know what's become of it; if it's all gone or not. It probably is. She probably sold the whole thing and took the cash. I didn't see any of that coming. Jesus Christ! Women!"

"Can't live with 'em, can't live without 'em."

"I think I'll try livin' without them for a while. Ha ha! See how that works out! What say we have a glass of BandG inferior paint stripper?"

"No thank you."

"Oh sorry, I keep forgetting. You don't mind if I have a glass myself do ya?"

"That's fine by me."

Holding the bottle between his legs, Jack unscrewed the cap and poured into the standard glass. "Here, you can have some of this fine, vintage, tepid water." He poured the water from the jug and they clinked glasses across the bed table.

"*Sláinte!*"

"*Gesundheit!*" Mr Arnold winked.

"See! I knew you were Jewish! You sneaky bastard!"

Mr Arnold laughed and shook his head. "No no. I'm just kidding. It's just an expression. There were a lot of Jews where I come from in Brooklyn."

Jack took a decent swallow of red wine. "Yeah, yeah. They don't mind their wine, that's for sure. What about your family? Have you had any visits lately?"

Mr Arnold shook his head stoically. "No, I haven't spoken to any of my family in many years." He looked earnestly at Jack. "I have a lot to prove to myself and to them before I can really be accepted back into their trust."

Jack soundlessly raised his glass and took another drink, draining the contents.

"I'm all right. I've got friends and I've got God."

"Well I've never met that guy. He's a hard one to find! Ha ha!"

"You just need to know where to look, my friend."

"Okay, okay. Stop talking like that or I'm gonna have to call security."

"No problem. Tell me, did you used to have a lot of problems when you were in the club with drunks out of control? I used to be a really lousy drinker."

Jack poured himself another drink. "Naw. Not really. We had a good manager in the bar – tough guy from your neck of the woods but a really intelligent fella who knew how to keep a lid on things. Know what I mean? He snuffed it out before it ever started. Yeah, occasionally we'd get some guy too tanked up tryin' to start a fight with everything around him but most of the time, we kept it all good natured. Things got a bit more aggressive in the mid-seventies with more people doin' cocaine but we had a low tolerance to that kind of thing. Kick the bums out and let the fun shine through! That was our modus operandi. Sláinte!"

"Mazel tov!"

"Ha ha! Funny guy!"

Jack drank deeply and stared downwards at an ill-defined space on the floor. "Yeah, I never had too many vices – I didn't drink too much, I didn't gamble... For me, it was just the women." He lifted his head and looked at Mr Arnold. "I couldn't help myself. I just like talking to girls, makin' them laugh, paying them some attention... Next thing you know, we're rolling around naked in some quiet corner somewhere. It might sound strange but it all seemed such harmless fun – making someone feel special and happy for a while... I dunno... I guess you're condemned to repeat the sins of your father, eh?"

"I can certainly relate to that." Mr Arnold held up his glass of water, then drank a sip.

"He ended up like me too, you know: cast adrift by my mother. I tell ya something – that's not an easy thing to do in Ireland where you're always expected to behave like a good Catholic and do whatever the priest tells you. She was a strong woman. She took what she needed and sent him to go figure it out for himself on his own, with or without his floozies. He had it coming a long time, but I never knew that my mother suspected a thing. I never told anyone else this but when I was twelve years old, I saw him. I saw him coming out of a house in this little back street in Dublin and kissing his girlfriend goodbye while my mother was at home. It turned me upside-down and inside out, I tell ya. I was a distraught, confused and disgusted – I was almost physically sick. I didn't know what to think, what to feel, whom to depend on... And poor mammy! And now here I am just like him. Everybody knows it; knows that I'm a cheat who just can't help himself. That's why nobody bothers to come and find me – except for my niece, that is – and she probably doesn't know the whole story. Sláinte!" He downed the remains of his glass, put it down on the table and went to pour another one, spilling a spoonful as he did so.

"You know," said Mr Arnold, "you can't blame yourself for just being a human being. What happened yesterday is yesterday's news and now you've got maybe another chance to make some connections with your past and with people who care for you. What about that woman with the packages? She believes in you, doesn't she? So you got her and your niece and maybe lots more people that you don't even realise you had fighting in your corner. That's what you gotta focus on. Hold onto that and everything else will fall into place."

"Yeah, maybe you're right." He threw back a double gulp of wine. "It better start falling into place pretty fast or I'm gonna die in here! Gesundheit!"

Chapter 11 – The Starfish

State Nursing Home, LongIsland, New York, USA; Present Day.

Analisa was there – far away at the end of the long corridor in the nursing home. He couldn't see her face and she was walking quickly away from him but he knew that it was her. Jack tried to shout her name but his voice wouldn't emit words. Instead, only bubbles came out. They floated into the air and he watched them pop, one by one, against the strip lighting on the ceiling. He leaned against his walking frame and pushed with all his might before she could turn left or right and disappear from view. He gritted his teeth and pushed hard but he barely moved. His right leg dragged and pulled him down. He tried again and again but it wouldn't move. He looked down at it and saw that there was a star-shaped hole in it as big as melon. Analisa was moving farther and farther away. Now he couldn't command his arms to move. They felt floppy, as if the bones in them had disintegrated. Then his good leg was stuck to the floor. It was covered with tiny suction cups and he suddenly realised that he was completely naked. He heaved but the more he heaved, the more stuck it became. All his limbs were now either completely useless or completely stuck to the surface of the floor or of the walking frame. He stopped struggling, closed his eyes and willed himself to move after Analisa. Suddenly, his eyes were open and he was zipping down the corridor after her. He was running; running faster than when he was a teenager running home from school along the wide footpath of the South Circular Road. He looked behind him and he could see the walking frame on the floor. Knocked over and sinking into the floor that had turned to liquid. And beside it was his old bad leg – a bloodied stump, bobbing on the surface of water. He had grown a new one – much better, stronger and faster. He ran on over this part of the corridor that was still solid. His left arm fell away and now he looked and a brand new one had grown back in its place. He laughed and laughed as he ran along the empty corridor. He wished that someone could see him. Where was everybody now when they had something wonderful to look at? When they had a different version of Jack Mills to see? This is the real me! He called out Analisa's name and this time his voice came out, strong and clear and she stopped and turned around. She was wearing the same dress that she had worn that day she had come to his hospital bedside when he had awoken from the coma. He was before her now, out of breath, smiling, panting.

"Look, Analisa! I'm renewed! I'm better! I knew you'd come back!" As he spoke, he didn't recognise his own voice. Analisa just stared back at him with the eyes of a stranger. He looked at his hands, his legs and his body. They were the body of a young man. He had willed himself into something else but she couldn't see through the façade.

"It's me, Analisa. It's Jack!" Jack reached out his hand to touch her. As soon as his hand touched the skin on her cheek, she popped like a burst balloon and her body dissolved into a puddle of salty water. He dropped to his knees and screamed and wretched on the floor of the hospital, staring at the wet pile of clothes where Analisa had stood. He continued to scream as the orderlies arrived from the doorways to return him to the ward.

"It's okay, Jack. You all right. No need to worry. We got you. That's right. Take it easy, mon. You safe now."

Jack opened his eyes to see Jerome sitting beside his bed with a hand placed gently on his shoulder.

"All right, Jack?" Jack blinked and looked up at the sparse expanse of ceiling with its familiar patterns of varying shades of grey waves from years of previous incidents of dampness and layered coats of paint. "Was you tryin' to escape from us?"

"I... I don't know."

"We found you lying down outside the door in the corridor but you're alright now. You went a long way without your walker. Pretty impressive, mon!"

"Am I alright?"

"You in perfect working order, man. You didn't hurt youself."

"Jesus! I had a dream! Weird fuckin' dream!"

"It must have been a strong one, man. The whole hospital heard ya!"

From another part of the ward came the sound of someone groaning, huffing and turning in their bed.

"Tell ya what, Jack. You relax now a while. I got to go now. You got your water beside ya here and breakfast comin' soon. All right, my friend?"

"Yeah, yeah." Jerome exited the ward and Jack took the cup of water and sipped it with his trembling hand. When he moved, he was suddenly aware of the fact that he was covered in sweat. He lifted the sheets and looked down at his right foot. A fresh bandage covered a large area of his foot and up along his leg to just below the knee. It was bigger than before. Not a good sign if the bandage is getting bigger. They get smaller as you heal. He lay awake for some moments and tried hard to remember his dream before reaching to his bedside locker. There was a battered copy of a biography of Napoleon and a small writing pad and pen. He took the pad and pen and wrote down the words "reaching out", "Analisa", "hope" and "starfish". He put the pen and paper aside and fell into a peaceful sleep.

Two weeks later, Jack was sitting in the Day Room, reading the New York Times at the table. His hair was neatly cut from the barber's visit that morning and he was wearing fresh new clothes – a clean blue shirt and navy check sports jacket and tan-coloured trousers. The room was busy with more patients than usual. He could see Mrs Benson out of the corner of his eye, sitting on the other side of the room, working her way methodically through her latest knitting project, keeping a steady eye on the evolving stiches through her thick horn-rimmed glasses. Her hair had turned a pink hue from a recent hairdresser's visit. Mr Arnold was playing chess with another new patient that Jack hadn't got to know yet. They were bent over the chess board that was laid out on a stool. It was mid-Spring and for the first time in months, the sun had climbed high enough to get above the back-yard wall. Its welcome rays came in warm shafts through the upper part of the high windows and reflected off the Magnolia-coloured ceiling and opposite wall.

Jack was absorbed in an article about the upcoming American presidential elections. The first primaries had started a couple of weeks beforehand and already people were talking about the new Republican candidate – a millionaire businessman with a strange wig – who was impressing voters wherever he went. "Jesus Christ!" Jack whispered as he stared at Trump's face, "that guy was one of the most annoying VIPs I ever had to deal with!"

"Howya, Jack! Happy St Patrick's Day!"

He looked up to see PJ and Violet Rooney standing before him. He stared at them for a moment and blinked to ensure he wasn't dreaming.

"Wow! Aren't you two a sight for sore eyes!" They went over to him and hugged him in turn before taking seats in front of him.

"Well, well, well. Look at you two!"

"Sure, we had to come and see you," said PJ, glancing at his wife. "We were getting on so famously in the other place."

Jack grinned at them both. "We sure were…"

"By God you weren't easy to find, Jack," said Violet. "We had to make a fair few enquiries. It was Helen Bromley who put us on the right track eventually. They're very strict in here, so they are. We had to say we were your Irish cousins! I don't think the woman at reception believed us but then this Dr Solomon or something came by and let us in to see you."

"We told him they couldn't keep the Irish from seeing each other on St Patrick's Day!" PJ added.

Jack was beaming with delight at the arrival of these two dear friends as if from nowhere: "Do you know what? I hadn't even realised what day it was. Fancy that! I was even readin' the paper and looking at the date on the top and everything. Never dawned on me. What an idiot! Ha ha!"

"So you're keeping well, Jack?" said PJ. "You're lookin' well, anyway so you are."

"Yeah, yeah. I'm not doin' too badly here. My niece got me some fresh clothes and stuff and I'm movin' on, you know? Still got lousy food and service in here but everyone's coming out of the woodwork to see me now and, y'know, it's all getting better. I was even thinking about the club again lately. Could be time for a change in direction again. But Jesus, it's great to see you two! I didn't think I'd see you again."

"Well we lost track of you after you left the other place," said Violet, nodding. "But tell us, is your family here or in Ireland looking after you a bit so?"

"Yeah, yeah. Like I said, my niece, she came to see me a few months back and she keeps writing to me and sending me stuff. Helen keeps in touch too. It's nice, you know... I can take care of myself fine but it's nice to get a little help now and again. It keeps them happy! Ha ha! And me too!"

PJ reached into a bag he had and produced a bottle of Paddy Whiskey and displayed it with two hands to Jack.

"Ahhh! I see you've brought along an old friend of mine! Now you're talking!"

"Well, seeing as it's Paddy's Day."

Violet went to get some glasses as Jack turned the bottle over in his hands. "Jesus, you know it really is a bit like meeting an old friend. I haven't seen one of these in... I don't know. A really long time, that's for sure. I probably haven't seen one since the club and even then, I don't think we used to stock Paddy. Did you bring it from Ireland?"

"Oh, indeed we did! Special delivery for Jack Mills the famous nightclub owner!"

"Ha ha! You old culchie! Here, crack it open there for me, would ya? I can't be doin' with waitin' too long."

PJ duly obliged and Jack inhaled briefly before taking a small swig. "Medicine! Ha ha!" Then, adding in a low voice with his head down and eyebrow raised: "Actually, I'm not entirely sure you're allowed drink alcohol in here."

"I'd better join you so." He winked and took a swig himself. "Are they treating you all right in here, Jack?"

"Not really, no. It's a real shithole but... what can you do? I'm hopin' that with Tara's help, I'll be outta here soon enough."

"That's your niece."

"Yeah, that's right. She's living in Dublin. She should be back over here in the next couple of weeks. You two outta meet her."

"Yes. Indeed we should. Maybe if you could give us her contact details, we could even write to her and we can all meet up or whatever the next time she comes."

"Yeah. I'll get her address and phone number for you. She won't mind. She's a good kid. Well, when I say 'kid', she's not exactly a kid anymore but she's got a great heart. You'll really love her."

Violet arrived back with two glasses in her hand.

"Mother of God, you didn't even need them, by the looks of things!" she said in mock admonishment.

Jack looked at her with a delighted mad stare in his eyes and his classic crooked smile: "It was him!" he said, lifting his hand to point the finger at PJ. "Your husband made me do it! Ha ha! I think he's got a drink problem there! You know? I can give you a few numbers that might be of help!"

Violet poured a generous measure into each glass and presented them to the men.

"You're not joining us then, Violet?" Jack enquired teasingly.

"Oh… I can't drink that stuff, that new Drumshanbo gin is far more my tipple! but sure I'll join ye in spirit."

"She'll join us in spirit," PJ added, "and we'll drink the spirits!"

The two men laughed and clinked glasses. PJ turned around and wished everyone in the room a Happy St Patrick's Day. They all responded with smiles and cheers of "Happy Saint Patty's!" and the three expatriated Irish in their little island at the far end of the Day Room spent the afternoon catching up, drinking whiskey and laughing.

Back in his bed later on that evening, Jack was in a regretful mood, with the after-effects of the first strong drinks he had had in a many months playing havoc with his mental well-being. For the first time in years, he was thinking about his trip back to Ireland. It had been during the time he was in assisted living and when he still had some money left. He had gone because his sister Christina had taken ill and he had departed on an expensive trip that he could ill afford, complete with his own agency nurse in tow. He had travelled in the vain hope of a change of direction and a reconnection with family and friends.

Jack arrived in an Ireland that he could barely recognise from the place that he had left sixty years before. On the flight over, he was mostly quiet and reflective; dealing with the concept of what was happening to him, with the enormity of it and yet the everyday nature of it for so many people. He flirted with the female cabin crew while they made a fuss over him and kept him comfortable during the flight.

He wasn't prepared for the size of Dublin Airport. The last time he had seen it, it was a relatively new building that was now morphed in size to the freshly-opened Terminal Two. He couldn't stop staring at the giant curves of its airy ultra-modern architecture and the enormous crowds from every corner of the world that were filing through it.

Neither was he prepared for the look of Dublin's streets; for the signs of prosperity and activity, for the multicultural mix in the people he saw in the city centre, for the motorway network with multiple lanes and spaghetti junctions of the kind that he hadn't quite realised even existed outside of the US.

From the airport, they cut through Dublin city centre to give Jack a look at his old stomping grounds. He asked the Nigerian taxi driver to make a diversion so that he could pass by the Bleeding Horse Pub – since renamed several times and returned to its old name once more – and past his old school on Synge Street. Of the small Coachhouse where he was born, a contemporary city loft apartment appeared. People had even stopped using the word "flat" and replaced it with "apartment" since he had last been home.

What did he achieve? He had hoped at that point to perhaps stay on in Ireland, but he quickly found that there was nothing left for him there. His behaviour over the years, his dismissal of his devoted mother, even after she poor woman had suffered an almighty stroke herself. He now discovered, had not only estranged his wife but had also estranged him from virtually every member of his extended family. Even Christina – the one with whom he had some sort of civil relationship – wasn't prepared or able to give him accommodation for any length of time. He and his nurse stayed at the Shelbourne Hotel – the most expensive in Dublin – and he had returned to the assisted living care in New York realising that all his bridges in Ireland had been definitively burned and fearing that he had also set fire to the most important bridge in his life in New York too.

Was that his last hurrah? He had survived up to now so there was no reason why he shouldn't keep going. Or was there? All these people connecting with him now – what did that mean? That there was another new chapter in his life about to come? The starfish. That was it. He was like a starfish that moves around at an almost imperceptibly slow speed on the ocean floor; that can grow a new limb if one falls off. The starfish defies everyone around them and survives one setback after another. They reinvent, regenerate, build up their strength and move on. They are difficult to trap because they sense when the danger is coming, they play dead and they plan for their next metamorphosis; their next stage in a life where they become something else. He tried to assess where he was now. If he was a starfish, what was his next move? He couldn't visualise one. He couldn't see where he was going to go. He had been trapped since the stroke. That was it: From that point on, he was heading downhill even though he didn't realise it. He felt suddenly gripped by a profound fear at the realisation of his predicament and of his dwindling list of options.

All his life, he had been ahead of the game. He had always looked forward like a sentinel perched high on the conning tower of a submarine. He always knew what lay ahead and when the optimum moment was to stay on the surface and when it was time to dive. He knew the waters and he knew which way the wind blew. He disregarded virtually all others, placing his unwavering trust in his own judgement and in his own ability.

Everything had worked out for such a long time since coming to

America. Everything had gone right, but up to what point? He couldn't get his mind away from the idea that he had been ensnared at some point. He tried to focus on any other signs of when the trap was first set. When was his fate sealed? Was it the stroke or was it before then only he hadn't noticed it?

Alva's voice – ever-present for so many years of his life – had been as silent as the tomb for maybe three or four years now. He looked down at his heavily bandaged limb that would never grow back like that of a starfish. Lately, he had noticed that it smelled of something rotten every time they changed the bandages and the stink lingered in a subtle form around him all day long like a determined grim reaper. He tried to think back to a point when Alva had been the one that he followed – his North Star. Those heady days in Dublin. Did he lead her, or did she lead him to America? Maybe they both decided together. It was so hard to tell and there seemed to have been so many conversations like this – all fallen into the dark fractures of his memory – where so many things he had taken for granted as fact weren't true at all. "You brought us here!" she had thrown at him on numerous occasions, as if all the negative things that had happened since they came to America had been his responsibility alone. Is that what she meant when she said that? Why are simple words so difficult to understand? He never placed much faith in words, only in actions. He tried to recall a quotation to that effect from Shakespeare's Julius Caesar. A "tide in the affairs of man"? He couldn't recall it for sure.

For all his success in New York, it was she who seemed to take to life in America better than he did. He stressed and worked so hard in the club that he became consumed by it. Life and work became one ill-defined obsessive headlong crazy adventure. There was no work without pleasure and there was no pleasure, it seemed, without some element of work being involved. Meanwhile, Alva had social gatherings and enjoyable occasions at Irish clubs, knitting clubs and

God knows what else with friends. They were real friends who spent time in one another's company, talking and expressing their innermost feelings. Was that a part of his work that he neglected? Aside from Mr Arnold and Jerome and the Rooneys, who did he have? He couldn't even say for sure that he'd never let any of them down or treated them any better than he did Alva. Nor could he say for sure that they were completely devoted to him.

For the first time in a very long time, he began to weep. At first he tried to suppress it and remain quiet. Little by little, however, the sobs took over. They shook his entire body, causing him to cry loudly, the tears coming down his face in unstoppable streams. The ward was in semi-darkness and from elsewhere in the room, he could hear somebody turning in their bed and whispering: "It's okay."

"Mr Mills. Can you hear me, Mr Mills? Are you awake?"

Jack awoke with a panic-stricken look in his eyes and a sharp intake of breath. He stared hard at the man hunched over him as if he had no idea who he was.

"Dr Sol?"

"That's right, Jack." He lay a hand on Jack's shoulder. "First of all...how are you? You look like you had an intense dream."

"Yeah, yeah. I'm fine, thanks. I was dreaming about my wife! A good dream mind you."

"Well... that's good! Not that I want you to tell me all the details, all the same! Haw haw!"

"It was freaky!"

"I understand. You are on strong painkiller medication for your leg so... it can sometimes be a side-effect to have some... unusual dream patterns."

"One minute she was kissing me and the next minute I was in this cage deep down under the ocean. I could see the stormy waves up on the surface." He looked up at Dr Sol with a mad mischievous stare, accentuated by his messy morning hair. "How do you interpret that?"

"I'm not sure, Jack. I'm not that kind of doctor – I don't specialise in dream analysis."

"She's got me rightly fucked, that's what it means!" His voice betrayed a strong Dublin accent this time. "Doc, I don't have a lot of options left, do I? Tell me – how bad is this leg?"

"Well, I was just going to talk to you about that, as a matter of fact. We have done our best for this leg of yours and given the state of your overall health, we've been trying to get you into somewhere you'll get more appropriate care. I've spoken with your niece in Ireland and we've managed to find you a place near here. It's on Long Island too – the Long Island Jewish Medical Center. It's what they call a tertiary care teaching hospital and they offer a really good level of care. I think they'll be able to give you the kind of service that we can't give you here."

"Yeah… Okay, that sounds good. They say the Jewish make the best doctors, don't they?"

"Haw haw! Is that what they say about us? Well I'll take any compliment I can get! It's not always easy to find a bed somewhere like that for a patient in your situation – without medical cover, I mean – but I fought and argued very hard on your behalf over the last few months and I'm happy to say that you'll be moving there in the next couple of days."

"Okay. That's great, Doc. I really appreciate it – everything you've done for me while I'm here and for getting me into this new Jewish place… you've been a true friend to me, you really have."

"Really, don't mention it. After all you've been through, it's the very least that you deserve, Jack. This isn't charity, Jack – it's the least you deserve. Between you and me, it makes me so mad sometimes, this country. I mean, we've got all the money in the world and we can't look after people properly – good honest hard-working people who dedicate their lives to fulfilling the great American dream, like you. Then three years later, they spit you out and put you somewhere like this to.... Look, don't mind me. I have a tendency to rant and rave sometimes. I just think that people deserve better, that's all."

Jack smiled weakly and nodded. "Well, better sounds wonderful to me right now." He extended his hand and they shook warmly.

Doctor Sol strode out of the ward again, leaving Jack alone with his thoughts. He wondered if this would be his final move. The dream of going back to Ireland was still alive. Maybe they'd patch him up well enough to send him across the Atlantic one more time. Maybe Tara would come with her husband and with Christina and he'd get back some energy once more. The accumulation of years coupled with his deteriorating leg were having their toll on him. He was spending more and more time just sleeping in his bed of late, without having the energy to get up and go down to the Day Room. He hadn't talked to Mr Arnold in days. Maybe he was gone. Maybe he'd managed to get out of this place and get back to picking the pieces of his life after all. He seemed to have been living a monastic life in here – saying very little about his past and just stoically getting on with doing his penance. What could he have done that was so bad? It was drink-related obviously, but much more than that, he had never revealed to Jack, for all the time that they spent together talking. Maybe it was because Jack talked too much and didn't listen enough. That's what Alva accused him of every time they argued. You don't listen... You never listen... If you'd only listen to me for once... She kept her accent all this time. Over fifty years living in New York and she still spoke with that cultured Southside Dublin voice that had so enticed him all those years ago. Time was such a treacherous thing, he thought. You can't feel the years passing. You make your plans and you lodge your dreams with your God or your imagination or whatever medium you choose. Then it all zips by and before you know it, your old friend Father Time has picked your pocket. Your dreams are gone and your body has been ravaged. He had been dreaming recently again about when he was a boy, running down the street in his short pants. There was a period when time didn't seem to matter, when it had no effect or dominion. Now it was his all-powerful enemy.

"Fuckin' Father Time!" he said aloud, smiling at how ridiculous it sounded – like some evil character in a comic book series. He wanted to remember some of the good times he had with Alva for a change. They did have so much fun in the early years of living in New York and along the way, there were many other good times. The first few weeks and months when they arrived had been difficult but they were young and their toils were all shared struggles; happy struggles for the most part.

They had been staying in a small apartment in Queen's with a spinster aunt of Alva's. Jack hated it there but it was all they could afford until he got a better-paying bar job. He was the one who was leading them, he remembered. He was the one who was the sole provider for this little team of two that were so united and so excited about the future. Their enthusiasm and belief drove them on, kept them together and motivated Jack to work all the hours that he could to save the money for a deposit so that they could rent an apartment of their own. He remembered waking up on a snowy Christmas morning in 1950 – their first Christmas together in their own apartment. It was a small two-room walk-up in Lower Manhattan; a ten-minute walk from Delancey Street subway station. It was still mostly bare but it was their very own love nest for just $33 a month. He recalled their intimacies that morning and afterwards, going out in the snow with a spring in his step to get bagels to go with their morning coffee and tea. He was already a convert to coffee while Alva remained a tea drinker all her life. They spent the remainder of the morning relaxing over a long breakfast in bed before he went to work in O'Casey's Bar in Midtown in the afternoon.

It was in O'Casey's that he had got his first education in working nights and looking after customers. O'Casey's had its fair share of troublesome drunks. Some of them were Irish and more of them were second-generation New York Irish – the real fighting Irish. Most of the Irish immigrants in that bar were hard-working and hard-drinking but rarely very troublesome. The trouble was always with the ones who had American accents who seemed to have a sense of in-built bitterness and entitlement about them. They were generally had what he always referred to as a more "well-fed" look about them, as opposed to the pinched overworked- looking Irish customers who loved being able to earn a decent living here but who always had one eye roving eastwards towards their native land across the Atlantic. They were cursed with the kind of nostalgic melancholy that Jack never adhered to.

Jack quickly built a reputation in O'Casey's as a charmer who could cajole the most boisterous and troublesome and who could defuse the most explosive situations. He also had an easy way with the female customers. Even though it was to be a long time after that before he first drifted into infidelity, his ability to get along with customers and keep them entertained and feeling special in a natural way was something that his boss Dermot noticed.

Jack recalled the time he came home to Alva to tell her the news about his promotion to senior bar manager at O'Casey's – "the youngest one we've had yet", Dermot had told him. Alva was so proud.

"Wah gwan, Jack! Something a bit nicer for breakfast today, mon! You daydreamin' again, my friend?" Jerome put the tray of food down on the bed table and swung it around slowly in front of Jack, who raised his upper body using the electric control pad. He looked at the breakfast ingredients to see what was different.

"Wow! Is that coffee?" He smiled up at Jerome and seemed to instantly become thirty years younger.

"It certainly is, my friend. See, none of us really tryin' to kill ya, after all. We all just want you to have a good breakfast. There's a French croissant there too, see?"

"Wow, wow, wow! That's fuckin' great! Crispy bacon! Jesus Christ, where did you get this stuff?"

Jerome grinned, lay a finger aside of his nose and tapped it.

"Ha ha! I see. Top secret, eh? Tell me, am I going to get this kind of treatment every day?"

"You never know, Jack! I thought I'd bring ya somethin' special. I hear you gonna be leavin' us soon."

"Word travels fast around this dump. Yep, that's what they tell me – the Jewish Medical Center or some such thing – Oh, sugar too!" He emptied the two sachets of sugar into the hot black liquid and stirred it. "It's not the Emerald Club but maybe the next step towards it." Jerome raised his eyebrows. Jack shrugged his shoulders. "Ah, who knows what's around the corner?"

Jerome sat down on the soft chair next to Jack's bed, stretched his legs out as if he'd decided to stop working for the day and folded his arms, looking around the room. It was empty of other patients, who had already taken their breakfast and dispersed to the Day Room or had been brought out by relatives. "Ya never know, Jack. Stranger things have happened at sea, mon."

"You much of a sailor, Jerome?"

"Not really, no. I used to go fishin' with my father in Trelawny Parish when I was younger. Hard work for very little money." He shook his head and sucked in through his teeth.

"Yeah, like I always said, the Jamaicans are like the Irish, only they got better weather than us."

"Oh there aren't too many differences! We just look a bit different to you with ya delicate pale skin!"

"Ha ha! You're all burnt down there! Too much sun, you have!"

"Ya can never have too much sun, mon."

"Isn't it true, actually, that they call Jamaica the Emerald Isle?"

"No, mon, that's Montserrat. They call the people there the 'Black Irish'."

"Oh yeah. That's it. I outta go visit there some time."

"Ya been back home to your own Emerald Isle, Jack?"

"Yeah. Just briefly a few years ago. I'm thinkin' maybe it's time for me to get back there now… pretty soon." They stared at one another for a heartbeat. "It's probably the right time for me to do that." Jack took a long sip of his hot drink. "Tell you what… this is the nicest fuckin' coffee I've had in New York ever! Ha ha!"

Days of sleep followed, punctuated by vivid dreams, clattering trays, perfunctory meals and visits from Dr Sol with news about his imminent move. Then, two new people arrived that he hadn't seen before, dressed in ambulance crew outfits with a hospital logo that included the Star of David.

"Is this the big day?" Jack asked.

"You might say that." It was the lady who answered. She was a bright and attractive woman in her late twenties or early thirties with an honest smile, Jack thought, deep brown eyes and short dark hair. He looked to her left hand and could see through the transparent rubber glove that she wasn't wearing a ring. He looked at her name tag and read her first name.

"I hope you're takin' me somewhere nice, Lorraine," he said with a wink, while they brought the stretcher alongside his bed and manoeuvred him expertly onto it. The man – a heavy-set man of roughly the same age with a tidy red beard and short cropped hair – grinned.

"Is this your boyfriend?"

They both laughed. "Well, it's nice to see you're looking forward to the move, Mr Mills," Lorraine said.

"Oh, there's always somethin' to look forward to in life." He looked at her co-worker. "Hey buddy, who did you have to kill to get to work with this beautiful creature?"

They both smiled professionally and continued the smooth transition of their charge from the ward out to the waiting ambulance.

A short ride later, they were bringing him out of the vehicle. Lorraine was holding the feet end of the stretcher. Jack was covered with a blanket and held in place with strapping across his body as she adjusted the wheels to get him onto the ground. It was a warm summer's day and Jack felt the welcome hot sun on his face as he emerged from the ambulance.

"What say I take you somewhere nice after I get outta this place? Have you been to the River Café?"

"I can't say that I have, Mr Mills." She had a suppressed smile, its crookedness almost mirroring that of Jack's. She kept her eyes on the task at hand and didn't look him in the eye.

"Well, you're in for a treat. They've got the best views in Manhattan. Right under the Brooklyn Bridge. It's the only place in town where you can get Stone Crabs from Florida and foie gras from France! The owner is an old friend of mine – Buzzy O'Keeffe. He's a Michelin Star genius and a hell of guy. He'll treat us like a king and queen. I'm already picturing you at the table in a beautiful red gown at sunset looking at that wonderful view across the East River!"

She shook her head and laughed. Jack smiled as they went through the automatic doors past the sturdy security guards and into the clean clinical smell of the bright interior.

"So whaddya say, lovely Lorraine?"

She was blushing now, trying to keep a lid on her giggling. "Well…" she answered, "That does sound really nice, Mr Mills. Tell you what, you look after yourself in here and once you're ready to go out, give me a call."

Jack looked at the male orderly and winked: "Sorry, buddy. You gotta move fast or you'll miss the opportunity. Hope you don't mind me cutting in."

"Not at all, Sir." He shook Jack's hand while his colleague dealt with the paperwork and officially handed him over to the care of the medical staff.

Jack took a good look around his new surroundings as he waited alone amongst the busying staff, ringing telephones, beeping machines, enquiring relatives, patients resting on chairs in the corridor and the regular gaggles of student doctors and nurses passing by being led like serious white-coated ducklings by senior doctors.

"Well, Jack," he whispered quietly, "Let's see what the next chapter brings."

Chapter 12 – Tara's Diary

Dublin; Present Day.

It was late June when I received word while I was abroad that Uncle Jack had been taken once again from the nursing home that he resided in to the Intensive Care unit of the Long Island Jewish Medical Center. Doctor Sol – the senior doctor in charge of his care at the nursing home – had fought hard to have him admitted. At this time Uncle J was under the guardianship of the State of New York and had absolutely no Medicare or any type of health Insurance cover. Everything had run out. For days, our good friends PJ and Violet Rooney had visited the hospital on my behalf and confirmed that he was going downhill. As non- family members, they knew that it was time for me to return stateside again, with the addition of my mother Christina. This visit had, as its main premise, to assist her brother Uncle Jack with his transition off the life support machine.

I flew back from Spain to Dublin, where I stayed a night with my parents before my mother and I boarded a flight to New York. We didn't know how much time we would need to reach his bedside, or indeed if we would make it on time at all.

We landed into JFK airport where PJ and his youngest daughter Beth met us at arrivals. My mother, now finding it difficult to walk herself without the assistance of a stick, had only heard news and updates of Uncle Jack from myself and the telephone messages received (with no onus upon them) from the Rooney family. She was already unprepared for seeing her brother and now she was going to see him as he lay dying. I had encouraged my mother to rest during the flight as I knew that we would have a long night ahead. I did my best to prepare her for his appearance in general.

On arrival at the hospital, as you can imagine, it all seemed sombre and unfamiliar. One of the strangest aspects of the experience in the hospital was the language they used. Although American words and expressions in general are very familiar to us from our visits over there and to the average Irish person from exposure to American television and films, their use of words in medical situations are particularly opaque in their meanings. For the average American, they're probably very appropriate and clear, but to us they sounded foreign and unclear and were of little comfort to us. This was particularly true for my now ageing mother. We heard the word "expire" repeatedly, for example – a word that is only ever used when you are using a debit or credit card in Ireland. "Don't be afraid to reach out," the doctor on duty would say. This meant that we could go to the nurses' station to ask a question if we needed to.

The Hispanic security men at the hospital reception would greet us each day on our daily pilgrimage. Every single morning, we would have to repeat the same information: What relative? What floor? What unit? Can I see your identity, please? Are you next of kin? All this, even though they met us every day and knew us from the previous day. They would never smile or show any kind of emotion. There was no small talk, and this was something we would find to be very difficult, as, I suppose, it's not only necessary but almost expected in the same situation back home in Ireland.

The first evening, having passed security, we waited for an elevator which brought us to the fifth floor. I remember noticing the colourful braids worn by a beautiful African lady, and a stethoscope draped across her neck. I would try to make out the various languages spoken as we exited the elevator making our approach to the ICU. Finally, we would be asked to follow an ICU Nurse to a room where we were instructed on how to "scrub and gown up", before being led to a dimly-lit room with just two patients. Here, amongst many beeping machines, my mother would see her brother for the first time in a long time.

Both my mother and I had partially trained as nurses earlier in our lives and I don't know if it was this fact or just an acceptance of life's twists and turns in general but seeing Uncle J lying with a machine assisting his breaths didn't stir either of us to tears. We were just happy, relieved and reunited. We had our own little circle of Dublin, in a very small space on Long Island.

We touched his hair. It was still thick and strong, unlike the rest of his poor body, or his leg that had well progressed into gangrene. The surgeon would later explain that amputation was futile and far too dangerous now anyway. Before our visit was concluded, we were told to prepare ourselves. Once the papers were verified, they said, his machine would be withdrawn. "Withdrawn": another strange, clinical and unfamiliar piece of American hospital jargon.

And so, we left. We now knew the time and the moment. None of it made sense. I couldn't help thinking how anyone could just decide on a time or a moment. Of course, if wasn't just anyone. The bureaucracy at the hospital – the legal people and the medical people – had made the decision. It was purely procedural for them. It was their job.

So it was six hours later that first day on a summer's day in July, that we re-entered the elevator again, going down. We stopped on the third floor – the maternity unit – to pick up a young mother in a wheelchair. There were bright blue balloons held in the hand of the man standing beside her and they smiled as they both looked down at their beautiful baby boy. We congratulated them, told them what a beautiful little baby they had. They asked us where we came from. "Ireland" we said. "Oh," they said, "where U2 are from?" "The very same place," I said!

PJ was waiting patiently outside the hospital, in a nearby loading bay ready to help my mother into his car. We headed back to the shelter of their home – our home from home – and the comfort of a family who cared for us for the duration of our stay.

So the day arrived. This was it. I had not trained to the heady heights of Intensive Care during my nursing days, so to be honest, I really wasn't sure what was about to transpire. Twelve noon, we were told. I did know however, that everyone was individual and would fight or pass in their own time, and that is exactly what happened.

Sitting patiently in the family annex, we waited while the tubes where extracted and Uncle Jack was made comfortable and presentable in his bed. The staff floated around the room silently, but very efficiently. There was a sense of confidence with each action. The process of dying was not obvious. Suited up in our white plastic gowns and gloves, we were once again given permission to approach him. As we approached, the nurse smiled and told us that our visit and conversations with him by his bedside the previous day had made a huge difference. Then his eyes opened and here he was back again! Back in the game!

"Hey, now listen carefully," he said, breathing slowly and heavily. "I'm gonna need your help to get outta this joint," he said. "I got plans." Well, my mother launched into stories of children, grandchildren, cousins, their parents, Ireland… I could see he was exhausted. This all finalised in a quietly sung version of "Two Little Boys"...*did* you think I would leave you dying, when there's room on my horse for two...before I gently suggested to my mother that it was time to let him rest. He was awake now. "Let's go and sleep ourselves for a few hours," I said. "We'll come back tomorrow."

That night I lay in bed thinking. I knew that we had some extra time, but that old saying "a change before death" was now very uppermost in my mind. I had to make some decisions about tomorrow. The doctors had told us that while it was a bonus that he was once again cognisant, it would only be fleeting. Perhaps he would pass in the night, they said. I looked over and Mam was asleep like a baby in the bed next to me. It was a balmy night. People were out late and firecrackers were going off as it was the fourth of July.

So the next day, freshly watered and fed, we set off once again on a clear, bright, beautiful day along a New York skyline, driving along water and over bridges, arriving at our destination. We had learned not to delay the security men with too much Irish small talk, and we were now almost getting into a routine.

To our delight, Uncle Jack was now propped up in the bed. The staff had made him so comfortable and presentable, gracefully shielding his leg from both his and our view. As we approached, I remembered that the night before as I lay in bed I had decided on a very definite plan. The plan was this: that if he chose to speak of death, if he chose to face it full on, then I too would face it with him; that we would hold hands and together speak of death. If on the other hand, he chose an alternative chapter to his life, then I would go with him there too.

Once again, gown and gloves went on and once again, Uncle J had rallied. Mam launched into stories of the very, very few neighbours they had left: stories of who lived where, who had emigrated, and finally she talked about her grandchildren, giving an individual account, one by one of each one's life. I could see him drifting, nodding... I could see him look down at his leg from time to time. The doctor approached and Mam shuffled off with him to tell him about her many grandchildren and great grandchildren, before finally letting the man discuss Uncle Jack.

I knew this was my chance. He looked at me sincerely. His sheets had moved and we could both see the open wounds of a disintegrating leg. It was bad. He knew it was bad and I knew it was bad.

"So," he said. "I gotta get this leg better before I can fly". "Yes," I said. "So, I'll rest up for a few days," he said. "I should be ready then." "Ready?" I asked. "Yes, ready to fly home to the old country. I have decided it's time to come home. Yeah, the time has come. Now can you make all the arrangements for me sweetheart?"

With that, I thought *Bless me father for what I am about to say*, and well, the plans just flowed.

We discussed coming home with "Irish Airlines" as he called it – first-class of course. Then it was straight to the Shelbourne Hotel on the Green – chauffeur driven, naturally. A small suite would be adequate and it was here he would base himself until I could secure a small centrally located apartment in Ballsbridge. I wouldn't of course book a grand steak dinner for his welcoming home party the first night because he would be jet lagged. We would put that in the diary for the second night. I took his measurements and he asked that I might dispatch myself to Louis Copland on arrival to pick up a couple of suits. He was quite specific about tie colours. Finally, he asked me to have a couple of full bodied bottles of red wine – preferably French – waiting on his arrival, leaving one uncorked for approximately 20 minutes if possible. "It shall be done," I said. He looked straight at me and said, "You're a beautiful lady...very classy." "Sure, didn't I learn it from the best?" I replied.

We left that day, all of us happy with life. I looked back through the window as we took our first few steps to leave. He signalled to me with his eyes as we walked away. Mam was chatting furiously about all the stories and people they had discussed.

A call came through from the hospital late during the night. The nurse said that he had only moments left. There was no time now except to say goodbye. As the night nurse put a phone up to his ear, my mother said goodbye. He was gone.

EPILOGUE

I wore the same black dress by his graveside on that late October morning some three months later. Jack had silently waited within a New York mortuary for his release papers. How ironic to release the released, I thought as I observed the slightly ruffled robes of Deacon O'Neill as he prayed for the souls of the faithful departed.

My eyes began to glaze as I slipped easily into a state of distraction as they slowly lowered Jack below ground. They nestled him gently within the safety of his Mother's final resting place.

Yes, my mind drifted to the very same dress that I had worn with pride on the first day we met at the nursing home. At least I knew for sure that my dress would meet with his approval. He did, after all, tell me that he liked it. I remembered the compliment and smiled. The wearing of the dress seemed like our unique and shared experience. It provided me with some remnant of tradition, which was of course none existent. So here we stood, the last bastion of organised humanity. Family. Jack's family. Small as we were in number, we now stood together to both welcome him home, and wish him farewell. And so on that late October morning amongst a vast sea of graves we prayed.

"Yes, though I walk through the valley of the shadow of death, I will fear no evil, for you are with me, thy rod and thy staff, they comfort me." Psalm 23:4

Jack was home. His circle was complete, without cause to ask permission. The net had been cast and our prodigal had returned.

Uncle, come now
Lie - in- peace
Rest a while, don't linger...

Our unknown hearts
Reborn, just new
The years did steal and hinder

Just found
Depart?
Away so soon?
The child inside I cry

To see you rest within this grave
My Uncle now has died

But I did love the thoughts of you
Imagined and aspired
An Uncle's image through a glass
Old pictures framed fireside

So go. Depart.
You held my heart
You gave your love to me

Not always clear, but now endeared,
My Uncle, my friend and me.

MarieAnn Mc Loughlin Dwyer

MarieAnn Mc Loughlin-Dwyer was born in Dublin Ireland in June 1966. One of seven children.

She is a songwriter, poet, and playwright.

She won "Best original song for a film" at the *American Tracks Music Awards* in Los Angeles, in May 2018. Her original compositions have featured twice on the BBC Radio Introducing series, in East Midlands UK.

This is her first novel. She lives in Rossnowlagh, Co Donegal Ireland.

To my greatest supporters:
Toni, Roy D., Vicki, Gretchen, Bill, Jim,
Marg, Graham, Gig, Eva, and Jim M.

CONTENTS

PREFACE

This book is primarily for secondary physical education teachers who want to develop the sport skills of their students in an efficient, sequential manner in the hopes that they will become lifelong participants in physical activity. While the book has been written from a physical education perspective, coaches will also find it useful in developing beginning skills in their athletes.

This is not a book on specific techniques of various sports, such as how to grip a football or how to position your feet in golf. There's already a plethora of excellent books available on technique. Particularly, I encourage readers to examine the *Steps to Success* series, published by Human Kinetics, for detailed descriptions of correct techniques for many sports, including some of the sports discussed in this book. As appropriate, I have referred readers to these sources for thorough explanations of techniques mentioned in this book.

This book outlines a sequence of progressions for teachers to follow as they work to develop skills in a sport. Each chapter begins with a background of the sport from the perspective of a physical education teacher. This is followed by a list of progressions covered in the chapter to give you a quick reference to the chapter's activities. Each sequential progression for teaching the sport includes the goal of each progression, the organization of the progression, a description of the activity, and ideas for ways to challenge your students further.

Having spent more than a quarter century in the physical education profession developing teachers of motor skill and observing teachers and coaches, I have seen that the most successful instructors teach sport skills in a sequential manner whenever possible, wasting little time in transitions and developing in their students strong foundational skills in each sport before adding more complex skills. The lead-up games and activities presented in this book are not the traditional ways of learning the sports. The activities put students directly into game-like situations in which they can develop the sport's basic skills. I find this works best toward promoting and maintaining student interest in the activities.

There has been limited attention given to progression development in the professional literature. As undergraduate programs move from developing skilled players of sport to instructors of sport skills, a clear need exists for efficient methods of presenting these skills. This book satisfies this need by presenting a step-by-step procedure for teachers to follow.

In presenting my material, I have tried to streamline the instruction of sport skills, based on the following assumptions:

- The teacher wants to develop sport skills.
- Students have a basic foundation in fundamental movement skills.

- Students are receptive to learning and developing sport skills.
- There is adequate equipment and space to ensure sport skill development. For example, there is a ball or racket for everyone. If students have to share rackets, teachers should reconsider teaching the unit unless it's taught along with another activity (such as half the class uses rackets while the other half works on fitness activities).
- There is adequate time to develop skills. A unit of 15 days in length (50-minute periods) is the minimum time students need to learn these skills. If maintaining interest is a major concern, then distributing units in small chunks over seven to eight days throughout the year is an alternative, though not an ideal one.

The book is organized in three parts. Part I outlines the concept of progressions, what skills to begin with, principles in delivering these skills, and how to maximize participation for greater efficiency and skill development. Part II covers teaching individual sports. Part III covers teaching team sports. Each chapter deals with a particular sport and includes detailed explanations on how to progress efficiently toward the desired goal of having students engage in the sport we are teaching.

I contend that physical educators are indeed educators, not just recreation directors. It is important to make kids feel good about participation in sports through not only teaching skills, which do build self-confidence, but also by making the class enjoyable; otherwise, students are less likely to play the sport after they leave the class. However, though we can try our best to make activities fun to do, sometimes the best way to develop a skill is through drills, which students often find tedious. I have found that a good mix of drills, exercises, simulated games, and real games (both cooperative and competitive) works to maintain my students' enthusiasm to participate, and I can only hope the same will be true for you.

All educators in a school, not just physical educators, work to develop self-esteem in their students. Students gain self-esteem from accomplishments, and our role as professionals is to assist students in developing motor skills and fitness, thereby increasing the possibility they will engage in lifelong physical activity with a sense of accomplishment.

This book sets out to fill a gap in the literature so that those in our charge improve their sport skills, which will improve their self-esteem, as we fulfill our educational mission. My hope is that teachers and prospective teachers find the material in this book helpful in bridging the learning gap for those students struggling in their classes.

ACKNOWLEDGMENTS

For many years my students have encouraged me to put my thoughts and ideas about progressions down in writing. Tired of procrastinating, I set out two years ago while on a sabbatical to get the job done. This book is the result. I owe thanks to many people who helped me along the way. At the top of the list is my close friend LeaAnn Martin, the greatest teaching partner any physical educator could have. Also, for their superior sports skills training during my undergraduate years, I thank the University of Wisconsin at LaCrosse. I am grateful to Martin Mulholland, Bonna Giller, Steve Card, and Julie Taylor for their sage advice on various chapters. I thank all my former students, especially the "Block" students who continue to challenge and inspire me. They are a phenomenal group and give me hope about the future of the profession. Finally, I am indebted to the faculty and staff of the department of physical education, health and recreation at Western Washington University under the driving force of Chair and close friend, Kathy Knutzen. I feel so fortunate to have been associated with such a professional group of people in what I believe is the best department of its kind in North America.

PART 1

The Progressions Framework

The Concept
of Progressions

For our purposes in this book, a *progression* is the sequential linking of one skill to another, leading to an acquisition of skills that permits a participant to perform in a game or game-like situation. As an analogy, think of an infant learning to walk. He or she doesn't just stand and suddenly begin walking. Rather, a clear and logical sequence of events and behaviors occurs (lifting the chin, lifting the chest, creeping, crawling, standing with assistance, and so on) that eventually culminates in unassisted walking. Another analogy is learning mathematics: you first learn addition and subtraction before progressing to multiplication and division. What holds true for teaching an infant to walk or helping a child learn mathematics also holds true for sport instruction. Ideally, one skill leads to another via an uninterrupted progression until the player can participate in the activity or sport or—as frequently happens because of limitations and constraints in the physical education context—in an activity that simulates the sport the student wants to play, such as a pick-up game of 3 v 3 basketball or volleyball or playing a round of indoor golf.

The concept of sequentially linking one skill to another, leading to an acquisition of skills that allows for successful performance in a game or game-like activity, might sound simple, but it isn't. How many times have you introduced a skill and witnessed students perform it correctly in a drill, only to watch in frustration as they neglect to perform the skill correctly while playing the game? It happens all the time. Upon examination, I have found that improper progression is often the culprit. The problem could be beginning the unit with the wrong skill, teaching skills out of proper order, or in some other way failing to equip students with skills they need to play the game correctly. Developing successful progressions is largely a trial and error process of seeing what works well and what doesn't; however, there are some basic principles to keep in mind. While these principles don't always apply for every sport (because each sport has its own idiosyncrasies), it's certainly worthwhile to review them.

Beginning With Essential Skills

One of the first questions to address when planning a unit is, "What skills do my students need to learn for success in this unit?" You then base the unit's length on your goals for the unit. Introducing too many skills for the time allotted gives students little chance to gain skill competency. Ask yourself what your students are realistically capable of accomplishing during the unit. Developing motor skills requires hundreds of sequential repetitions on a daily basis (or at least every other day). You can't just introduce a skill one day, practice it a few days, and expect it to be properly executed in a game.

A way to determine the essential skills of a sport is to scrutinize play in actual games. While we're all impressed by spectacular dunks in basketball or aggressive kills in volleyball, they are but small parts of the sometimes complex process leading up to them. What skills are *essential* to be taught? The next time you observe a sport, either live or on television, chart the skills used and compare them to what you're teaching. The skills that appear most often should signal to you the skills you should be teaching. Look for skills necessary to acquire in order to perform a part of the actual game so that students see the relevancy of developing these skills and will stay interested.

But which skill(s) should be taught first? One of the first rules for a teacher is to avoid beginning a unit with "dead-end" skills not essential for playing the basic form of the game. For example, in volleyball and tennis it's not uncommon for teachers to introduce the service first. While the serve is clearly an important skill to learn, it's not essential for playing some form of the game early in the unit (e.g., a tennis game could start by a drop serve and hitting a forehand ground stroke over the net; a volleyball game could start by tossing the ball over the net to begin a passing and setting game). I'd argue that in volleyball the pass followed by the set are most essential to play the game, while in tennis the forehand ground stroke is most essential. In basketball, shooting and dribbling are the most essential skills and should be taught first, though separately. Once students know how to shoot and dribble, the world of basketball opens for them, and you can then incorporate shooting and dribbling games into the unit.

Playing a form of the game might require learning only one essential skill or several essential skills. For example, in volleyball, students can play a 1 v 1 or 2 v 2 game after learning only the pass, but in softball, they need to learn to throw, catch, and hit before they can play a form of the game. In soccer, they must learn to pass, trap, and dribble before they can play a form of the game. In cases such as softball and soccer you need to practice skills separately before combining them in a game because it's very difficult for students to develop several skills at the same time. Plus, focusing on one or two skills at a time makes for more efficient practice, maximizing the number of trials each player receives. For example, in softball, it makes sense to combine throwing and fielding during practice, but hitting should be practiced separately because doing so reduces complexity and makes for more practice trials for each student (e.g., a fielder will get many more trials at fielding with a partner throwing back and forth than fielding a pitched ball from a batter).

Skills that are used in a game less often than essential skills, sometimes called secondary skills or "appendages," should be taught only after essential skills are performed successfully. Such skills as backsetting in volleyball, bunting in baseball, and heading in soccer fall into this category. They are part of the game but not essential to playing a form of the game. Often, these skills are best left to an intermediate or advanced class. Sticking initially to skills essential to playing the game helps maintain student interest. As physical educators, we're always concerned with keeping students excited, and nothing achieves this better than getting to some form of the game.

Chaining Skills Together

When possible, chaining or linking essential skills together makes for an easier progression that saves time and might speed up motor skill development, because more trials can be done in the allotted time. You can chain skills in two ways: within the skill itself (intrachaining) or between two or more skills (interchaining).

Intrachaining involves breaking down the elements of a skill and then linking them until the desired end is achieved. For example, a spike in volleyball is made up of several elements, including the approach, the take-off, and the hit. Intrachaining this skill entails teaching and practicing the approach first, then adding the take-off, and then adding the hit, until all the elements of the skill can be practiced together. Here are two scenarios in which intrachain progressions can be implemented in our volleyball example.

Scenario #1

- One-step approach, rocker step, arms back, gather and jump, imaginary hit at net.
- Two-step approach, rocker step, arms back, gather and jump, imaginary hit at net.
- Three-step approach, rocker step, arms back, gather and jump, imaginary hit at net.
- Individual practice of hitting ball down onto floor at wall.
- Three-step approach to net, hit ball off holder's hand (holder is standing on chair).

- Three-step approach to net, hit underhand tossed ball from center front over net.
- Center front tosses ball to self (self-tosses) and sets to hitter.
- Center back self-tosses and sets to center front setter, who sets to hitter.
- Short serve to center back, who passes to center front setter, who sets to hitter.

Scenario #2

- Individual practice of hitting ball down onto floor at wall.
- One-step approach, rocker step, arms back, gather and jump, imaginary hit at net.
- One-step approach, rocker step, arms back, gather and jump, hit ball off holder's hand (holder is standing on chair).
- Two-step approach, rocker step, arms back, gather and jump, hit ball off holder's hand (holder is standing on chair).
- Three-step approach, rocker step, arms back, gather and jump, hit ball off holder's hand (holder is standing on chair).
- Three-step approach to net, hit underhand tossed ball from center front over net.
- Center front self-tosses and sets to hitter.
- Center back self-tosses, sets to center front setter, who sets to hitter.
- Short serve to center back, who passes to center front setter, who sets to hitter.

While coaches might debate the merits of each of these progressions, the key point is that elements within the skill are chained together in a teaching sequence that includes short "baby steps" or "lead-ups" toward arriving at the desired end.

It's not always possible for intraskill activities to flow perfectly in line. For example, in the first scenario the flow of the lesson was interrupted when the hit had to be practiced separately before bringing it back into the flow of the lesson. The objective is for the teacher to find as many "baby steps" as possible to increase the chance of the learner acquiring the skill.

Depending on the activity, certain factors affect a skill's complexity and, by extension, the complexity of the intrachained progression toward learning the skill. For example, performance of a "closed skill," such as golf or archery, where the only external factors to consider are environmental elements (e.g., course design or weather), is less complex than performance of an "open skill," such as soccer or volleyball, where players must contend with defenders. This is not to say that golf is not difficult to develop—in fact, it's one of the toughest sports to develop—but think how much more difficult it would be if opponents were allowed to block your swing with their clubs. For activities or sports in which defenders try to disrupt a player's offensive endeavors, skill progression must eventually include overcoming the defenders if the game is to be played successfully.

Interchaining is the linking of two or more skills. Linking two skills, such as passing and setting in volleyball, results in less management time (because you don't have to organize two separate drills) and increases the number of repetitions for each student. This does not mean that both skills are initially taught together— rather, the two are linked *after* the student has developed each skill. For example, the pass might eventually be linked to the set, followed by adding another skill, such as the serve or the downball. In soccer, dribbling might be linked to passing and trapping while playing a 2 v 2 or 3 v 3 game requiring passing over an endline to score.

Some sports readily lend themselves to interchaining, especially closed-skilled sports such as golf. Since putting comprises the bulk of strokes performed on a golf course (up to 50 percent) and is a very safe activity to teach, a logical sequence would be to teach putting, then chipping, and then pitching before moving to driving. Linking these skills makes for an easy transition between skills as opposed to beginning with the drive, which is an extremely dangerous activity for the first day of a unit and is basically an end in itself. Although the sequence in the actual game is to drive, pitch, chip, and putt, reversing this sequence might work best in class, especially when considering your objectives of maintaining student interest and enforcing safety. By starting with putting (and perhaps holding a miniature golf tournament early in the unit), you maintain interest and safety. You then increase difficulty as the distance from the cup increases, until you cover the final skill: the full swing. For example, in one scenario, after (1) learning to putt and having played miniature golf, students would (2) learn to chip, (3) practice chipping, and then (4) link chipping and putting sequentially. They would then learn to pitch. After practicing pitching alone, they would link it to the previous two skills so that they can pitch, chip, and then putt in sequence. Likely, you'd teach driving separately because of lack of space on school grounds to link all the skills (driving, pitching, chipping, putting) in sequence. Of course, time and funds permitting, all skills are eventually linked on an actual golf course where students drive, pitch, chip, and putt as they play a round of golf.

Avoiding Gaps in Links

Overlooking skills that are essential to smooth progressions can stifle the progress your students have made. For example, a traditional middle-school physical education volleyball class might include the following progressions leading to a 2 v 2 pass and set halfcourt mini-game:

- Introduce passing and setting.
- Pass and set back and forth with partners, keeping the ball going.

- Play a 2 v 2 mini-game on a modified court using only passing and setting (play begins with a toss over).

This scenario is missing several key progressions necessary for student success. You must fill the gaps. To learn skills such as passing and setting, the ball needs to arrive consistently at the same place in the initial learning of the skill so that the receiver learns how to return the ball from that position before moving on to other receiving positions. Thus, it's essential that the tosser be trained in tossing the ball first so that a consistent toss can be expected. When the ball's flight is consistent, then the receiver can practice either the pass or the set but not in combination until each has been developed. Another factor sometimes overlooked is — foot movement, which is a skill in itself. Once receivers have success with balls being tossed to them, the next progression is to move to a ball and return it to the tosser using a toss. This skill requires proper footwork for court movement along with keeping shoulders in line of direction. Then add a ball and players return the ball to the tosser using both the set and pass. Players then progress to keeping a ball going in a designated space before eventually moving to a net, where partners cooperate 2 v 2 to keep a ball going using these two skills only. They then progress to an actual competitive game of 2 v 2. The sequence would look something like this:

- Partners practice underhand, tossing ball 10 feet high to each other.
- Partner underhand tosses to a stationary receiver, who returns ball with a 10-foot-high pass to tosser.
- Partner underhand tosses to a stationary receiver, who returns ball with a 10-foot-high set to tosser.
- Partner underhand tosses low or high to a stationary receiver, who chooses appropriate (pass or set) return to tosser.
- Players do a mass court movement drill with imaginary passing and setting with shoulders in line of direction.
- Partner underhand tosses to various areas around a receiver, who must move into position to return ball with a 10-foot-high pass to tosser.
- Partner underhand tosses to several areas around a receiver, who must move into position to return ball with a 10-foot-high set to tosser.
- Partner underhand tosses low or high to various areas around a partner, who chooses appropriate return (pass or set) back to tosser.
- Partners attempt to pass and set ball back and forth in a designated rectangular area.
- Partners are teammates and work with another set of partners to keep ball going over a net using only passing and setting.

- Partners compete in a game of 2 v 2 on halfcourt, using only passing and setting.

As you can see, there are many baby steps to take on the path toward game simulation. Many of these steps don't require extensive practice time, but if they are overlooked or ignored, it can mean the difference between student success and failure in developing the essential skills to play the game. It can take a bit of concentrated effort to break skills down into their subparts to determine what the baby steps are. Don't take anything for granted. For example, one skill consistently overlooked in teaching basketball is pivoting with the ball. Yet pivoting is essential right from the start so that players can protect the basketball from defenders. The same is true for shielding the basketball from a defender while dribbling. Other common teaching gaps might involve learning to get open to receive a pass in basketball or soccer, learning to receive and pass a served ball coming over the net in volleyball, and learning proper ready positions and court movement in racket sports, such as tennis and badminton.

Progressing
From Individual Skills to Partner Skills
to Small Group Skills to Team Skills

To reduce complexity in learning team sports such as basketball and soccer, it's important to begin learning skills in a closed setting, without defenders or other interference, and then progress to performing the skills in an open setting, with defenders. You can do this by progressing from (1) individual skill practice to (2) practicing with a partner, then (3) playing in a small group, and (4) playing with and against a team. To illustrate, in the initial stages of learning soccer, students need to get comfortable with possessing the ball, without outside interference, such as a defender trying to steal the ball. Adding a teammate or defender too early adds too much complexity too fast. The player's focus shifts from working on the skill to dealing with the defender, and what the player was learning is lost. Foot juggling, toe touching, dribbling, and just getting to know the ball should be the initial steps of learning. Follow this with skills done with a partner, such as passing and trapping, give-and-go skills, and the like.

Some sport skills, however, are best learned with a partner, because a partner can control speed and flight, while a wall cannot. For example, although it might seem efficient for a student learning a tennis forehand ground stroke to rally against a wall, most of the student's time is actually spent chasing down errant balls. He or she has not yet learned to control the ball. A partner tossing a ball consistently to one spot, with the student returning the ball to the tosser, is much more successful and efficient than using a wall. Walls are excellent for practice and warming up for players who already have good control of the ball.

For sports such as basketball and soccer, the ideal sequence of skills progresses from (1) practicing individual skills alone, then (2) adding a defender who only shadows (follows alongside the offensive player but does not interfere in any way with the ball or the offensive player) to (3) practicing skills against a live (competitive) defender to (4) 1 v 1 competitions. After this, players are introduced to partner skills (getting open to receive the ball, give and go, etc.) followed by 2 v 2 shadow and 2 v 2 competitive games. This then evolves to playing 3 v 3 or 4 v 4 competitions, practicing field concepts (balancing the field, maintaining a triangle, etc.), before culminating in playing the standard form of the game.

Implementing Game-Like Activities

As I've mentioned, making your drills game-like keeps your students involved, interested, and motivated. For example, playing a cooperative passing game where partners see how many successful passes they can complete in a row is more interesting than asking them to perform 25 passes.

You can create fun game-like drills yourself or find them in books, but be sure to look for books that focus on teaching within a physical education setting and not on coaching the sport. A coach is typically working with eager athletes who want to be there, and unfortunately this is not always your situation. Plus, coaches usually have fewer participants to manage than a teacher does. Most important, because coaches and their players are often fierce competitors, the drills they use, if applied in a physical education setting, can negate rather than induce learning. For example, a popular drill in physical education classes during basketball units is a full-court, fast-break drill in which a few players rebound the ball, then throw an outlet pass to players standing near the free-throw line, who then proceed down court to try to score. This is an effective drill in teaching rebounding, transition play, and outlet passing and works wonders in the coaching setting. But it fails in physical education. Why? Because the drill was created for a team of 12 to 14 well-skilled players who are in and out of play in short intervals. When applied in physical education, students spend most of their time on the sidelines waiting for their turn to participate.

As a physical education teacher, you need to discriminate in the choice of activities for your class. Often the best activities are those you create yourself or modify from books to fit the needs of your class. In one of my volleyball classes, I saw that students would not move more than one step if a ball came into their court space. After racking my brain for several days, I invented a game I called "Goalie Volleyball," in which a partner would underhand a ball about eight feet into the air so it landed in a designated court area that their partner was to protect. The receiving partner (the goalie) was to protect that area and not let the ball hit the floor; he or she could use only a pass or dig to get the ball back to the partner. Eventually these became contests to see who was best at protecting the space in five tries. As the students became more proficient, the tempo of the game increased, and soon the space was increased along with the speed of the ball (spiking was added from standing on a chair). The result was a marked improvement in court coverage during games. Creativity in designing game-like activities often results in significant skill improvement. Sometimes students don't even realize that what they are performing is a drill meant to improve their skills.

Summary

Your selection of the right skill progressions can mean the difference between success and failure for your beginning students. The principles of starting with essential skills, linking skills, avoiding gaps, progressing from individual to partner to small group to team skills, and making activities game-like will help your students enjoy success in their skill development on their way toward being able to play the game. Each sport is different, and what works for one sport might not work for another. There are always exceptions to the rule. As a teacher, it's up to you to apply these principles as you see fit and to modify and adjust them accordingly. Effective teachers are always looking for ways to reduce the complexity of skills and to invent new links in the chain so that students grasp the concept of each skill before proceeding to the next one.

Maximizing Potential for Successful Progressions

Y ou can ensure progression success through good teaching practice. In this chapter, I'll present some basics for you to consider and build on as you develop and implement your progression plan. No matter how successful you are already, if you're reading these pages, it's because you want to get better. There's always room for improvement on your way toward increasing your students' successes as you help them develop the skills necessary for playing the game.

Plan Throughout the Unit

Planning ahead pays great dividends. When developing motor skills, leave nothing to chance. Strong planning is the foundation for successful progressions; if you miss an essential progression, time is lost and student success is delayed. It takes time to create your plan and then to implement it throughout a unit, but the results can be rewarding. The teacher who plans well does not just throw out the ball, then sit back and let the class play with little feedback. The teacher who plans well expects progress from students and through specific steps helps them attain it.

One of the first matters to consider when planning a unit is how much class time to spend on games and how much on skill development. Here are some rules of thumb:

- First third of unit—spend 75 percent of class time on skill development and 25 percent playing mini-games.
- Second third of unit—spend 50 percent of class time on skill development and 50 percent playing mini-games.

- Last third of unit—spend 20 percent on combination drills or team practice and 80 percent playing the actual game.

Be sure that teaching is present and remains consistent throughout the unit, including during game-like play, game play, and, if appropriate, tournament play (when students apply in a competitive context all that you have taught them). One method of game-like play is the mini-game, in which students use the skills they have developed thus far in the unit, ideally imitating an aspect of the real game. For example, in basketball, after learning to dribble, students might play a game of dribble tag. After learning the skill of shooting the ball, they might play a game of Around the World (shooting from various spots on the floor). After you have worked on 1 v 1 offensive skills, students could play 1 v 1 games using only the skills they have developed thus far (e.g., using only the rocker step or driving strong or weak, with no outside shots).

By the last third of a unit, students should be using the basic skills necessary to perform in game-like settings. During these later stages, you should continue to teach, but focus less on skills and more on strategy and team concepts, patterns, and plays. Incorporate tournaments or league play as students become ready for them, but retain an educational component to the class, such as including a drill to start class that works on skills that still need development. You might follow this with a discussion of strategy or have teams practice set plays before game play begins. Once games begin, check all players to make sure they are using the skills and strategies you have taught them; modify the rules of the game if necessary to enhance learning.

Organize Practice Areas

Think ahead of time about how to use your practice space most efficiently. A technique I use is to divide my space into sections for practice areas. These areas might be the spaces between the five-yard line markers on a football field that run sideline to sideline, between the court lines on a gym floor, within the circles found on wrestling mats, or within the free-throw circles in gyms. You can also use cones, flags, or other markers to indicate practice areas or to designate areas in which students are assigned a safe place to practice and warn other students to stay out. Designated areas might also allow you to assign tasks to different groups if you wish to maintain a sense of order in the classroom.

Elementary teachers use the term "self-space." The concept of self-space allows for students to be dispersed for practice in an equitable fashion and eliminates the need for you to constantly ask groups to separate because one group is infringing on the space of another. By using designated practice areas, you can save an enormous amount of time in management, allowing more time to develop skills.

Organize and Disperse Appropriate Equipment

Having, organizing, and dispersing appropriate equipment increases the time available to your students for in-class practice and reduces stress caused by disorganization. The type of equipment available to your students can determine the success or failure of a unit. Are both senior and junior basketballs available? Are there trainer balls for volleyball players (trainer balls are a bit larger, lighter, and easier to handle than official volleyballs) and softball gloves for left-handers? Today, major suppliers of sports and physical education equipment carry modified equipment for all major sports offered in physical education classes, so there's no excuse for not having the proper equipment for each student.

Organizing and dispersing equipment can make a difference in the success of your class. Having equipment available for students to use when they enter class allows for more practice time. Similarly, a policy of controlling equipment in the students' hands when you're addressing them can make for a more efficient class. I like to have students put equipment on the ground so they're not distracted while I'm talking to them.

When dispersing equipment in class, designate groups or partners to retrieve the equipment needed to prevent long periods of wait time or fighting over equipment. Strategies such as "One partner go to the court and sit down while your partner gets the equipment, and when you both are sitting I'll know you're ready to start" or "Whoever is wearing something green can get their equipment first" work well for me. Use whatever strategy works for you, but planning ahead of time is essential. Otherwise, you lose precious time as students wait for equipment or while you search for equipment that should have been available at the start of class.

Having enough equipment on hand for each student to practice reduces wait time. While each student should generally have access to his or her own ball or piece of equipment, sometimes one ball per two or three players is best for a particular drill. When supplies do not allow sufficient equipment for each student, you'll need to modify, say by using playground balls to learn basketball dribbling.

Have Plenty of Successful Practice

If there's one sure thing that improves the skill level of students, it's plenty of successful trials. If students are to succeed at a skill, design activities for them to get hundreds of repetitions. In observing, tracking, and analyzing students in physical education classes, my physical education majors consistently find that students often receive fewer than 20 trials when attempting a particular skill—far short of what's needed for success. Think of a sport you now perform well and consider how many hours and trials it took before you were moderately successful. If necessary, reduce the number of skills you expect students to achieve to let them work more on developing the essential skills. Build the foundation first, and add appendage skills later.

You might want to do a little investigation to see if your students are getting enough repetitions. Try this—the next time you break students out after introducing a drill, step back, find an average student, and count the number of trials that student took during the time allotted. I think you might be surprised. What's more surprising is the number of trials that were successful. Was it 50 percent? Less? In general, if the success rate is lower than 70 percent, then that student is not ready to move on.

Better yet, look at the activity selected to develop a particular skill. Let's say it's a soccer pass and trap drill in which you have set up groups of four students, two to a side, one behind the other, 10 yards apart. The first person is to pass the ball to the first person in the other line, follow the pass, and line up in that line. Meanwhile, the student receiving the pass traps the ball and then passes to the remaining player in the starting line before following the pass and lining up in the opposite line. Sounds like a simple activity well suited to developing passing and trapping, right? Not necessarily. Note that there's a ratio of four people per ball, which translates into one person active while the other three are basically inactive. Students need to have enough opportunities to develop their skills, which won't happen if there's one ball per four or eight students. As a rule, the fewer students per ball, the greater the amount of trials. So, when designing activities for practice, design them with the fewest number of players needed and build from there.

Be critical of popular activities that don't really contribute to learning the skill. For instance, see if you can pick out the problem in this description of a badminton activity. The physical education class needs to work on the overhead clear, and the teacher finds an exciting drill that calls for teams of two across the court from each other. The shuttle is put into play with a deep serve, and the receiver returns the shuttle with an overhead clear and then gives her racket to her partner and steps out of the court. Meanwhile on the other side of the net, the student who served gives his racket to the next student receiving the shuttle and overhead clears the shuttle and repeats the same thing. The teacher watching this drill notes with satisfaction that the students are excited. Screams erupt and excitement fills the air as each court tries to keep the shuttle in the air. The question to be asked is, "Does this drill in any way enhance development of the overhead clear?" The answer is "not really." While there's interest, excitement, and enjoyment galore, little skill development is taking place. First, drills or activities should generally reflect the rules of the game for which they are intended. While the teacher can alter rules to enhance learning, this rule to require exchanging rackets contradicts basic badminton play—players never exchange rackets in a badminton game. Nor is this drill maximizing activity rates, because there are four people taking turns at hitting. A better solution would be for the teacher to begin with an activity in which just two people are involved—perhaps a deep serve followed by a competition to see who can keep the shuttle in play using only overhead clears that must travel into the back third of the opponent's court. This drill would fit the needs of the students and still maintain interest and excitement. As teachers, we need to ask ourselves what needs to be accomplished and how to best design an activity that reduces the number of players and increases the number of successful trials. Remember that practice alone does not improve skill. Plenty of successful practice trials is what leads to improvement.

Trim Wait Time

Related to plenty of perfect practice is the need to trim the length of time your students spend waiting for something to happen. As I've mentioned, having enough equipment for each student to practice with reduces wait time. Another way to trim wait time is to avoid using lines. While relays are popular with teachers, they can be havens of inactivity. Often, relays are run with the first student in line running to a designated place and back to his or her partner or team, and the activity is repeated until one team finishes. This form of relay has built-in wait time, as at least half the class waits for their teammates to return. A better way to run this relay would be to have the first person in line go in one direction only and after a certain distance the next one in line could go. Or you could switch relayers at the opposite end of the gym by forming a line for each team at each end of the gym. Better yet would be to eliminate relay lines entirely and have activities that don't require waiting, where everyone is practicing at the same time. For example, in practicing dribbling in basketball, instead of doing dribbling relays, play "dribble tag," in which all students are moving at once. In soccer, have each player dribble a ball, weaving in and out of cones that are set up in an oval so that the players dribble nonstop.

Waiting lines also provide a convenient hiding place for those "invisible" students you have in most classes. These are the students who refrain from indulging in any form of physical activity by hiding in the back of lines or passively going through the motions. Wait time does not refer only to waiting in lines but also to waiting within the activities themselves. Every class has its share of invisible students who do not want to get involved and who lose themselves in games, especially when there are large numbers of teammates, such as in an 11 v 11 soccer match. You can help prevent this occurrence by limiting the number of members on a team until students successfully perform the skills and their proficiency, efficiency, and confidence in the sport increases. Then additional players can be added.

Using roll call or warm-up to practice previous skills is another way to trim wait time. Efficient teachers set up routines for students to follow when they enter class that require them to practice skills that have not yet been successfully performed. After a certain number of repetitions, students can then move on to game-like activities before class begins. For example, students in the middle of a flag football unit might come to class, check the white board for the day's warm-up, get a partner and proceed to throw and catch from a stationary position a set number of times, and then run pass patterns a set number of times before adding a defender who covers the receiver.

Some units by their nature have wait time built in. Gymnastics and track and field events, which are not covered in this book, require an enormous amount of set-up and take-down time, which if done in class, reduces the amount of time available for practice. Similarly, these activities have equipment (e.g., uneven parallel bars) that limits the number of participants who can participate at one time. Plus, there's how-to and safety information to review for each piece of equipment and, in the case of track and field, time spent traveling between events. Using stations is probably the best way to teach these units. To reduce wait time, it's best to distribute the necessary information about each piece of equipment in short portions each day rather than give lengthy lectures. In addition to covering safety at each station, day one in a track and field unit might include lead-up activities (baby steps) for several events, such as

- distance running (jog one lap at a pace you can go all day and time yourself),
- shot (hold shot [softball] from a sideways standing position and put the shot),
- discus (roll discus on ground to a partner, making sure the discus comes off the index finger),
- high jump (one-step flop onto mat in "dead bug" position), or
- long jump (take one step onto take-off board and jump, landing on two feet in pit).

Trimming wait time is not difficult but requires a commitment from the teacher when planning and an ongoing vigilance to maintain high activity rates in each class.

Reduce Complexity

Learning a motor skill is not easy. The more you can reduce the complexity of the tasks, the less frustrated your students will be as they strive to grasp the skill. The addition of movement makes a skill much more complex than if it's done in a stationary position. Thus, a good strategy in teaching a skill is to progress from nonmovement to movement. For example, in learning the forehand ground stroke in tennis, students should begin moving to hit the ball only after successfully hitting the ground stroke from a stationary position. The rate of speed also adds complexity to learning and needs to be adjusted and controlled, along with the flight and path of the object. You should toss a tennis ball to one spot on the court at one speed until the student is successful—only then should you change the rate of speed and the path and flight of the ball. Adding equipment to a drill can be distracting, especially for middle-school students. Having students run through a drill empty-handed can allow them to focus on the directions of a complex drill or the patterns of a designed play. For example, asking students to run pass patterns in flag football without a ball in their hands results in crisp-run patterns; on the other hand, when students try to learn patterns while trying to catch a thrown ball on the run, they slow down once the ball is released to concentrate on catching the ball, and the pattern is quickly forgotten.

Similarly, the size of a piece of equipment might add complexity to learning motor skills. Equipment that does not fit a learner impedes development. Luckily, there are today many developmentally appropriate resources, including balls, baskets, rackets, and clubs, that meet the needs of all students. Reducing or enlarging the size of courts and fields is another way to add or reduce complexity. Progressing from a 3 v 3 volleyball game at halfcourt to full court is a sure way to add complexity to the game, while allowing servers to serve from the 10-foot line reduces complexity.

As noted earlier, adding a defender usually hampers learning a skill because the learner can get distracted, and there's the possibility that the defender stymies the performance of the skill; as a result, the learner's confidence in performing the skill diminishes. To help prevent this from happening, always teach offense first and defense last. As I'll discuss later in this chapter, adding competition too soon in a unit can add too much complexity to learning and do much more harm than good.

Teach to the Problem

Anticipating problems students might encounter in performing a new skill and focusing on those problems when introducing that skill gives students a greater chance of success. As an example, in tennis, two main problems students experience in learning the ground stroke have nothing to do with the stroke itself. The problems are getting into position to hit the ball and getting the racket back to begin the stroke. In learning the set shot in basketball, the potential problem to warn against is allowing the shooting elbow to be extended out to the side rather than in; in the drive in golf, the problem is in keeping the head down. If the teacher and students know ahead of time what problems they'll likely encounter when performing a skill, they can focus on just one or two points instead of trying to remember all the technicalities involved in the skill. As a teacher, becoming skilled in anticipating what the likely problems are requires a combination of educating yourself in the literature and learning on the job. There's no substitute for experience and training yourself to continually anticipate problems that students will have ahead of time and to teach to that problem.

Design Lessons for All to Succeed

If there's a range of skill abilities in your class, use a variety of teaching techniques to ensure success for all. One approach is to group by ability. Grouping by ability is not a dirty concept. Students need to be successful and at the same time challenged, and your job is to organize your class so that this happens for everyone. The best example I can give you is a soccer class with both beginning and advanced students. While it doesn't harm the advanced students to work on the fundamentals of the game, they eventually become bored with the pace of the class if you keep it at a beginner level. One approach is to have advanced students work with beginners on basic skills at the beginning of the unit. Once you feel comfortable leaving the beginners to work on their own, demonstrate the new skills you want the advanced students to work on and allow them to work on them in a separate part of the field.

Students can learn from many different methods of grouping. Sometimes it's perfectly fine to group beginners with advanced players, provided it's a learning experience for both. Other times it might be best to group by ability. Once beginners become more proficient in their skills and less intimidated by the advanced players, they'll have moderate success but make greater strides than if they had played at only their own level of skill (provided that restrictions are placed on the more talented students to include everyone on their team in the activity). It's more difficult, however, for more advanced players to improve if they constantly work with less-skilled players. A happy medium needs to be reached where more advanced players assist the learning of beginners but have the chance to improve also, whether it's through competing against like competition or working on advanced skills, such as using their nondominant hand or foot.

Grouping by ability is one of several ways to organize your students to reduce the risk of less experienced students being embarrassed. Avoid labeling groups such names as "majors" or "minors" and use a variety of grouping methods, such as randomly grouping students or allowing them to work in groups in which they feel comfortable.

Control Competition: Progress From Noncompetitive to Competitive

Competition can be healthy and good but only if it enhances rather than detracts from learning. Your task as a teacher is to ease the transition from learning a skill to being able to perform the skill in competition. The way to do this is to progress via steps from a noncompetitive environment to the desired competitive situation. First allow students to practice the skill on their own with added challenges ("See if you can . . .") from you.

Once students have developed a proficiency in a skill, they can progress to a cooperative activity with another student or students in which they cooperate together to achieve a goal (e.g., "See how many times you and your partner can keep the shuttle going using the underhand clear"). In this situation, time is not a factor, so students can relax and focus on keeping the shuttle in play. The teacher can then add a time limit to increase the tempo and the competitive aspect: "You have two minutes to see which team of partners can get the most underhand clears in a row." The students are now in a competitive situation but are cooperating by trying to give their partners a good return to increase the chance of defeating other teams in the class. From there, the next step is to have partners play a competitive game of 1 v 1 against each other using only the underhand clear. There's no magic to any of this—the process involves simply taking short steps before moving to the game itself.

Teach Offense Before Defense

The most common way to stymie progress in skill development is to teach defensive skills too early. Generally, defense is learned more quickly than offense, and since the excitement of the game comes from scoring, it's best to delay teaching defensive techniques until the offensive skills are performed well enough to give the offense a reasonable chance of success. Avoid combining the two, or the defense will dominate. For example, if you're teaching the spike in volleyball, don't teach the block at the same time because students will learn the block quite easily and stop all hits at the net. Offensive skills need time to develop; the more successful opportunities you provide, the better.

Of course, offensive skills eventually need to be practiced against a defender, but *eventually* is the key word here. Offensive skills need to be practiced on their own first, without the intrusion of a defender. Then they should be practiced against a shadow defender who merely follows the movements of the offensive player without interfering. Slowly the defender is allowed to be more aggressive, either by increasing speed from half or three-quarter speed to full speed or by reducing the restrictions placed on their technique or movement (e.g., hands kept behind back to full use of hands).

The key for you is to provide enough defense to allow the offense to continue developing but not so much defense that offensive skill development is impeded.

Continue Teaching in Games and Tournaments

Effective teachers carry teaching into the game itself and continue to improve the skills of their students, rather than merely managing at tournaments. I tell my students who want to become physical educators that such occasions are when the real teaching begins. When games begin, many students revert to their old playing habits and ignore skills they have been practicing. This doesn't have to happen. Before the competition, remind your students that you expect proper execution of the skills they have learned. Once the game begins, your job is to enforce and reinforce the skills and technique desired. As instructors, we have the power and duty to alter rules in order to meet our course objectives. To ensure that particular skills are practiced in a game, we can restrict players to using only those skills we want them to work on, as in the following examples:

- Tennis—allowing only the forehand ground stroke during a game.
- Volleyball—playing a game consisting only of passing.
- Flag football—allowing the curl, out, and post as the only pass patterns.
- Basketball—scoring off a pick and roll only.
- Soccer—disallowing heading to focus on trapping with the thigh or chest.

Restrictions might also require students to perform skills only in a certain pattern or sequence, as in these examples:

- Volleyball—to begin each play, the serve must be in the court, the receiving team must receive the serve with a pass, and then play begins.
- Badminton—each play begins with a short serve followed by an underhand clear followed by an overhead clear.
- Soccer—the ball must touch two of your teammates before you can shoot on goal.

Finally, restrictions might be used to build teamwork by requiring that every player must score in order for a team to win a game.

Another way to make game play more educational is to have each team or competitor select offensive plays to practice, thereby raising the quality of the game experience. You can extend the learning possibilities to include learning to scout another team, learning to referee and run the scorer's table, or taking turns as coach.

Teach Rules When Opportunity Knocks

Rather than spending a sizeable chunk of class time on teaching rules, teach rules as the unit progresses and the opportunity arises. For example, when introducing the short serve in badminton, teach where the serving area is and explain the lines on the court, but avoid teaching the intricacies of badminton scoring and who serves when. Instead, save this information for when it's most meaningful to students—when they're about to play a full game. We often overteach rules, which students quickly forget. If possible, teach the rule at the moment it appears in a game. For example, in soccer, the first time a shot on goal is missed and the ball crosses the endline is the perfect time to stop play for a 30-second explanation of what the rule is and where the ball is put into play.

Ensure Safety

Although there's no greater concern for physical education teachers than the safety of their students, teachers sometimes neglect this most important issue. For example, a teacher might instruct students on how to drive a golf ball but fail to have designated a "No Enter" safety zone around which the student is driving. Another teacher might allow a softball catcher to catch without a mask. The list of dangerous possibilities is seemingly endless, but adhering to basic guidelines significantly reduces the chance of injury.

- If an activity requires strength, match students according to ability and size so that one student doesn't overpower and possibly injure another.
- Before placing a student in a situation where danger might occur, always teach the student how to get out of the situation.
- Have an educational objective for everything you do. You can no longer pick an activity just because it's fun or the kids love it. There needs to be a designed educational motive for doing the activity.
- Keep an ongoing safety checklist for equipment, similar to the checklist fire departments use for checking fire extinguishers.
- Anticipate problems and take measures to avoid them. Be proactive.
- Actively supervise. Taking a phone call in your office during class is not active supervision. You must be there and be active. You can't supervise two gyms if there's a wall in between them. If you're expected to do so, raise your concerns in writing to your principal so that your complaint is on record.
- Always have a lesson plan ready in case your activities are ever called into question; document the safety information you cover with your students.
- Believe your students. If they tell you they're injured, reduce or eliminate their involvement and get them the first aid they need.
- Reinforce safety rules throughout your teaching. Don't expect students to understand and follow all safety rules that you tell them only once.
- Teach students that they are responsible for their own safety and the safety of their classmates.

Practice Equity

All students in physical education can develop skills, whether they're gifted athletes or students with special needs. Physical educators are educators of all students, not just some, and as educators we should base our every decision on one consideration: "What's best for all the students in my class?" To that end, no students should be excluded or placed in situations in which they feel detached from the group. On the other hand, tremendous differences exist among students, not only in skill levels but in physical and intellectual development as well, and students are well aware of these differences. Make sure these differences are not magnified and that students are not placed on display in your class.

All of this should not mean that students are never ability grouped or grouped by gender. Genders should be given equal opportunities for competition, as outlined in Title IX. You can implement a variety of groupings and pairings throughout a unit, but be sure to do it by design, not happenstance. By the end of the unit, everyone should have worked with everyone else, unless there are extenuating circumstances, such as safety concerns. Some days students are ability grouped; on other days, they get to pick their friends; on another day, you might split up kids with discipline problems and disperse them among students who model appropriate behavior; on other days, the girls might want to challenge the boys, and so on. The point is that students in your class should know that you're in charge of grouping students and that they are expected to work with all members of the class at some time. Most important, convey the message that each person in the class is to treat everyone else with respect. This message might be especially important in units such as dance, when students of the opposite sex are paired and feelings can be hurt when comments are made about a partner.

Much attention has been made of working with students with special needs. Students with special needs should be treated no different from other students and should be included within the framework of the class, not separated. All a student with special needs does to your class is extend one end of the ability spectrum. Students come into your class on each end of that spectrum. If a student enters your 10th-grade basketball class with Michael Jordan's ability, what would you do? You'd design your lesson so that student is challenged to improve his skills. The same needs to be done at the other end of the spectrum. Break down the skill you're working on into small parts and design inclusion activities that challenge everyone, remembering that not all students who have special needs or who are in special education are lower in ability (e.g., students who are speech or hearing impaired). Don't agonize over this issue; instead, look at it from the perspective of developing smaller steps in the skill progression framework, and treat that person as being lower skilled rather than as having a disability.

The concept of equity means that students have an equal opportunity to develop their skills. This means that one group shouldn't have an advantage over another in their practice trials or their game play. To ensure equity, make sure old-fashioned methods of instruction are removed from your methodology. One practice still too common is to eliminate students during activities. Doing this stems from our competitive sporting nature—we want to see winners and losers. This emphasis on competition with elimination *has no place in education.* This isn't to say that competition is evil, because it isn't. However, competition in which losers are labeled or eliminated from playing is not educationally sound. Do everything you can to ensure that all of your students receive an equal number of trials. This can't be done when winners remain on the court and losers sit out. Single-elimination tournaments do nothing to develop the skills of the losers. In fact, the winners get better because they have more opportunities and practice trials. What's needed are activities designed to keep students in play while still being exposed to competition. Round robin tournaments or, better still, leagues where everyone plays everyone in the class are good choices. Some activities—such as Knock Out in basketball (see p. 112), in which each player tries to control his or her ball by dribbling while also trying to bat another player's ball out of play—do require a player to be removed from the game. However, you can overcome this problem by recycling students back into play once they have been eliminated by having them do a skill related to the activity (dribble a ball with your nondominant hand 20 times before you re-enter a game of Knock Out) or a fitness activity such as jumping rope 30 times. This is much better than having students sit on the sidelines until a game ends. There are many recycling strategies to use to keep all of your students active.

Another tactic is to limit the number of times a player or team can remain on the field or court performing a skill. For example, if you have organized 3 v 3 games on each volleyball court with a team of three players waiting on the sideline to play the winner of the point (King of the Court), restrict the number of consecutive points one team can get to three, and then rotate teams to more equally distribute the number of trials each team receives.

Of course there will be times when better athletes get more opportunities simply because they are more efficient, aggressive, and have more control than their classmates. Just do as much as you can to ensure that all students are receiving maximum trials. Equity goes much farther than just equality in the treatment of individuals. Extending into the activity itself is the issue of whether each student is receiving an equal opportunity to develop his or her skills within the time allotted. Your job is to create an atmosphere that is truly free of bias and to provide opportunities for all students to develop motor skills to the best of their abilities. Any roadblock that prevents our students from pursuing this goal needs to be removed.

Summary

By organizing practice areas, allowing plenty of successful practice, trimming wait time, reducing complexity of tasks, controlling competition, teaching rules as opportunities arise, and ensuring safety and equity, you'll establish a solid foundation for successful lessons. All this, coupled with the use of strong sequential progressions, provides an excellent chance for beginning students to develop the essential motor skills of the sport they want to learn.

PART II

Progressions for Individual Sports

Badminton

Badminton is much more than a recreational activity played in the backyard. It's a sport that offers all the ingredients a person needs to lead an active, healthy lifestyle, including speed, dexterity, agility, power, endurance, decision making, competition, and skill. Many students like the game because they have played it with friends or family at home. Your challenge is to raise the level of their expectations for the game from a recreational activity to that of a highly skilled fitness activity. To achieve this, it helps to show them a video of elite competitive mixed doubles play at the national or international level. If showing a video is not convenient, then they need to watch players, preferably near their own age, competing at a high level. Once students have observed a higher level of play, use the progressions to develop the skills they need to play badminton competitively.

To play badminton adequately, your students need space to swing a racket safely. Teaching badminton in overcrowded conditions can result in injury and inefficient learning. For this badminton unit, there should be no more than one set of partners for each halfcourt (four players to each regulation badminton court with a net). You can often find unused space between courts that can serve as mini-courts— just line a string across to substitute for a net. Or you might use space outside the court areas for stations in which students can practice specific skills. If you don't have enough space to allow safe practice, I suggest dividing the class in half, with one half playing badminton and the other half doing other fitness activities; you can then rotate players between the two activities. To maximize use of space and to achieve high rates of trials while developing fundamental skills, players need designated practice areas. In this unit I have designated one-half a badminton court between partners as the minimum required space for partners to practice across from each other.

This brings up the question of practicing with a partner cross-court or directly opposite, especially in reference to serving. The purist would say that to practice serving to a partner directly opposite develops bad habits because all serving in badminton is done diagonally. While it's nice for each set of partners to have an entire court to themselves in order to serve diagonally and eventually to rally, this is not an option for most teachers. While early on in these progressions there's some diagonal serving practice tied to diagonal net play game, most serving is done directly across to a partner for rallies or game play in order to maximize use of court space and keep players active. Of course, if there's enough court space to allow one court for every two students, by all means introduce diagonal serving and play on the full singles' court as soon as possible. See *Badminton: Steps to Success* (Grice 1996, page 5) for a figure of a regular singles' and doubles' court noting the correct measurements and parts of the court.

After some introductory activities to develop familiarity with the shuttle, grips, and footwork, the progressions begin with the forehand short serve and the backhand short serve and net shots. Teaching badminton is one of the few times when you'll introduce the serve first. The reason for this is simple. Whereas in volleyball and tennis, the serve is difficult to return, in badminton, forehand and backhand short serves are easy to return with a net shot (forehand and backhand hairpin). Net shots also call for a player to move in order to hit the shuttle, and getting students to move in badminton is one of your main goals. By combining the short serve with net shots, students get practice trials in two essential skills of the game and can begin to play a form of the game early on. Another reason to initiate badminton instruction with a serve is that students have an easier time setting up situations for a partner by serving than if they attempt to throw the shuttle over the net (although at times a toss is more efficient in a drill).

For some players, contacting the shuttle during a forehand short serve is a nightmare: they repeatedly swing and miss the shuttle completely. When this happens, it's best to introduce the backhand short serve because it's easier to perform successfully. That a backhand short serve is mainly used in doubles play is irrelevant at this point.

From here it's up to you regarding the number of progressions your class can handle in each class. Ideally, on day one it's great to end with a short rally using the short serve and both net shots. Combining the forehand long serve with the forehand overhead clear also makes for an efficient lesson. However, if the skill level of your players warrants that each of these skills be taught separately, then do so before combining them. Because overhead clears, drops, and the smash all follow a similar set-up pattern, they are introduced sequentially for greater efficiency.

Badminton has everything a lifetime sport has to offer: athleticism, fitness, and great fun. The game is a teacher's dream from an organizational viewpoint in that you can stay with the same structure of partners on a halfcourt, bring players in to see the new skill, send them back out to have them practice that skill, then allow them to rally or play, using the new skill. Each skill is merely added to the previous skill, and soon students are playing the game.

In reviewing the progressions, keep in mind that they are for a group of beginning players; you might want to combine steps or jump ahead to suit the ability level of your players. As long as your students are successful, please go ahead. In addition, note that I've omitted several skills, including the backhand smash and clear, the around-the-head smash, and flick serves. While these skills are part of the badminton repertoire, I don't find them essential to perform beginning badminton. They are secondary skills, what I call "appendages" or "add-on skills" that accomplished players can learn once the fundamental skills of the game are successfully performed. You'll see that doubles play is introduced late in the progressions. This is because until students can successfully perform the basic skills of badminton, doubles play provides little, if any, activity for the student, and activities with lots of repetitions are generally at the top of my list. By playing halfcourt with a partner, students are given far more opportunities to develop their skills and are much more active and accustomed to performing on a smaller court area; they can later easily make the transition to doubles play. Finally, singles' play forces the hesitant or unassertive player to become involved because there's no partner to fall back on.

■ After following the progressions, beginning students should be able to play both singles and doubles using the following skills:
  - Forehand grip
  - Backhand grip
  - Racket-ready position
  - Grip change
  - Initial footwork
  - Forehand short serve
  - Backhand short serve
  - Net shots (forehand and backhand hairpin)
  - Net shot rally
  - King of the Hill
  - Aerobic net play
  - Forehand underhand clear
  - Backhand underhand clear
  - Forehand and backhand underhand clear rally
  - Halfcourt singles' game: short serve, forehand or backhand underhand clear, and net shots (hairpin drops)

- Forehand long serve
- Forehand overhead clear
- Long serve and overhead clear rally
- Short and long serves, forehand overhead clears, underhand clears, and net shot (hairpin drop) rally
- Forehand smash
- Short serve, clear, and smash
- Halfcourt singles' game: serves, clears, smashes, and net shots (hairpins)
- Overhead drop
- Overhead clear and overhead drop
- Short serve, underhand clear, overhead clear, overhead drop, and net shot
- Game: short or long serve, clears, drops, net shots (hairpin drops), and smash
- Forehand and backhand drive
- Four-corner drill
- Singles' game on full court: short or long serves, clears, drives, drop, net shots, and smash
- Defensive backhand
- Doubles' game: short or long serve, clears, drives, drop, net shots, and smash

3.1 Self-Volley: Forehand Grip

Goals

Develop the ability to grip the racket using the forehand grip and become familiar with the speed with which the shuttle rebounds off the racket; gain proficiency in controlling the shuttlecock; and lay the foundation for net shots, such as the hairpin drop.

Organization

Each player should have one shuttle and a racket, spread out in self-space (an area on the court where each player has room to swing the racket without hitting others). For this exercise, the space needed for each player is about the size of a basketball free-throw circle.

Description

Explain racket safety. Demonstrate the proper grip for a forehand stroke (same as Eastern forehand ground stroke or "pistol grip" in tennis; see *Badminton: Steps to Success* [Grice 1996, page 8] for a drawing of this grip). Tell the players to keep the shuttle in the center of the racket, gripping the racket loosely with the last three fingers, and pushing the shuttle up. Have players bounce a shuttle off the racket surface no more than three feet in the air 20 to 30 times while standing in one spot.

Challenge

Walk around the courts bouncing the shuttle off the racket surface while maintaining control of the shuttle.

3.2 Self-Volley: Backhand Grip

Goals

Develop the ability to grip the racket using the backhand grip and become familiar with the speed with which the shuttle rebounds off the racket. Gain proficiency in controlling the shuttle. Lay the foundation for net shots (hairpin drops).

Organization

Players spread out in self-space with one shuttle and a racket.

Description

Briefly explain and demonstrate the proper grip for a backhand stroke. Then have each player bounce a shuttle off the racket surface no more than three feet in the air 20 to 30 times, standing in one spot. Focus on moving the thumb to the top left bevel of the racket (right-handers), keeping the shuttle in the center of the racket, gripping the racket loosely with the last three fingers, while pushing the shuttle up.

Challenges

1. Have players walk around the courts, maintaining control of the shuttle.
2. Then tell players to walk around the courts alternating hits between forehand and backhand.

3.3   Short Serve and Net Shots (Hairpin Drops)

Goals

Develop the ability to perform the short serve (forehand and backhand) and net shots.

Organization

Players should be in partners on one-fourth of a court, one partner with his or her back to the net and the other at the baseline, each with a racket and with one shuttle for the two of them.

Description

Give an explanation and demonstration of the footwork and the stroke of the short serve (forehand and backhand) and net shot (forehand and backhand). Then have one partner short serve to the other partner, who returns the shuttle with the appropriate net shot. If possible, continue to rally using only net shots in the designated quarter of the court. If the shuttle goes out of the designated area, the nonserving partner serves. Tell players to keep the wrist locked; push the shuttle when serving. Always reach with the same foot as the racket on both net shots ("elbow and knee together").

Challenge

See how many shots each group can achieve in a row. Set an initial goal of 15. If they reach that, then time them to see how many consecutive hits they can get in one minute. Set a goal of 50. Have the player at the baseline gradually move back to extend the distance, one step at a time, no more than four steps.

3.4   Net Shot (Hairpin Drop) Rally

Goals

Develop the short serve and net shot (hairpin dropshot) in a rally over a net.

Organization

Players should be in partners across from each other on one half of a court. One player serves and the other gets in position to receive the serve. Each pair has two rackets and a shuttle.

Description

Explain the rules of serving and scoring and demonstrate player positions. Have players short serve and rally over the net using only forehand and backhand net shots. Tell the players to keep the shuttle no higher than four inches above and on either side of the net when it's returned. Use the predominant net shot, the backhand, for most hits. Remind players to step or lunge and that the lunge leg is always in tandem with the racket on that side (i.e., right-handed players lunge with the right foot). The shuttle can be put in play with either short serve. Emphasize that the shuttle should just barely make it over the net and that the shot is soft and shallow, not hard or deep (see figure 3.1).

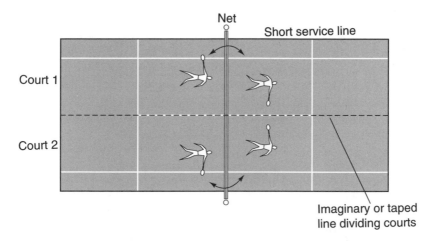

Figure 3.1   Setup for Net Shot (Hairpin Drop) Rally.

Challenge

Have players play a seven-point game using only net shots. The game begins with a short serve; only net shots at the net are allowed. Only the server can score. If the shuttle hits the net and travels over the net during the rally, play continues unless the shuttle hits the ground before being returned or it's out of play. If the shuttle hits the net on the service and goes into the receiving court, play continues. If the shuttle lands outside the service court, the shot is no good, and the receiving player serves. If a player can't return the shuttle, either the opponent scores a point or it's his or her turn to serve.

3.5 | King of the Hill

Goals

Develop diagonal serving and court movement.

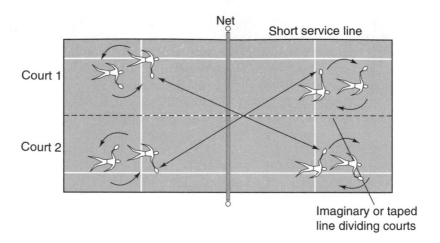

Figure 3.2   King of the Hill setup.

Organization

Two sets of partners (total of four), one pair, standing one behind the other, on halfcourt and the other pair, standing one behind the other, diagonally across the net from them on the other side on the other half of the court. Players line up behind the service line in I formation (see figure 3.2). (If this organization confuses your players, don't have them start diagonally. Instead have teams play directly opposite each other before moving to the diagonal.)

Description

The first player in line short-serves over the net diagonally to the first player in line for the other team and then goes behind his or her partner behind the service line. The first player in line (waiting behind the service line) of the receiving team returns the short serve with a lunge and net shot and does the same (moves behind partner behind the service line). Players move quickly into position to hit the shuttle, taking a lunge step and softly pushing the shuttle (no swinging the racket) in the direction they want it to travel. Only net shots are allowed. Players keep the rally going as long as they can. After several repetitions, have them switch courts so that they practice hitting the shuttle diagonally coming from another direction.

Challenge

Turn the game into a competition of team against team and play to seven points. Only the serving team can score. Switch sides of the court every five minutes.

3.6 Aerobic Net Play

Goal

Develop quickness using the lunge from the backcourt to the frontcourt to perform a net shot.

Organization

Players are in partners across from each other on one half of a court. One partner stands behind the baseline with a racket. The other partner stands at the net on the other side of the court with one shuttle.

Description

This is a fast-moving activity with no time for rest. Players move quickly, using lunge steps to get to the net to hit the tossed shuttle with a net shot, and then return quickly to the starting position. The player at the net tosses the shuttle over the net into the forecourt of his or her partner. The partner must wait until the shuttle is tossed before crossing over the baseline and coming to the net to hit the shuttle with a net shot back toward the partner who just tossed the shuttle. Once the shuttle is hit, the hitter quickly returns to starting position and awaits the next toss. Meanwhile, the tosser retrieves the shuttle (from wherever it goes, even crossing under the net if necessary) and then returns to the starting position to toss again. If the shuttle is not returned over the net, the hitter still returns to the baseline and awaits the tosser to retrieve the shuttle. Each player performs 10 successful hits, and then they exchange places.

Challenge

The first player to return five in a row successfully in the court using net shots wins.

3.7 Forehand and Backhand Underhand Clear

Goals

Develop the forehand and backhand underhand clear stroke from a short serve while in a stationary position.

Organization

Players pair off across from each other on one half of the court with a net between them. Each pair has two rackets and a shuttle.

Description

Explain and demonstrate the forehand and backhand underhand clear. Then have each partner take turns serving the shuttle over the net into the opponent's front service court using either the forehand or backhand short serve. The receiving partner returns the shuttle with either an underhand forehand clear or an underhand backhand clear high and deep into the backcourt. The receiver lets the shuttle land and then repeats the exercise back to the partner. Focus on getting the racket into position to hit the shuttle—using the shoulder and waist, not the wrist—and following through across the body and up, over the nonhitting shoulder, for the forehand.

Challenge

Mark off the back third of the court with court tape. Have players keep track of how many shots they can hit into this area using each stroke. Then challenge them to consistently return 7 of 10 into this area. If successful, have the server remain in place and extend his or her racket skyward. The underhand clears must go over the extended racket and into the back third of the court to count as a successful trial.

3.8   Forehand and Backhand Underhand Clear Rally

Goals

Move into proper position on the court to receive the shuttle; develop the forehand and backhand underhand clear stroke from various positions on the court.

Organization

Players pair off across from each other on one half of the court with a net. Each pair has two rackets and a shuttle.

Description

Players move to get into proper position on the court to return the shuttle and then, after the return, get back into racket-ready position at midcourt. Each partner takes a turn serving the shuttle over the net into the partner's front service court, using either a forehand or backhand short serve. The receiving partner returns the shuttle with either a forehand or backhand underhand clear, high and deep into the backcourt. If the shuttle remains in play, it's returned by the serving player, using an underhand forehand or backhand clear. If the shuttle falls short into the frontcourt, players may use a net shot to return the shuttle. Players rally until the shuttle goes out of play or can't be returned.

Challenge

Have partners keep the shuttle going for 10 consecutive hits. Increase the number of hits, as possible. Players should play a game up to seven points, using only underhand forehand and backhand clears and, when necessary, net shots.

3.9	**Halfcourt Singles' Game Using Short Serve, Forehand or Backhand Underhand Clear, and Net Shots (Hairpin Dropshots)**

Goals

Use the short serve and underhand clears and net shots in competition.

Organization

Players pair off across from each other on one half of a court with a net. Each pair has two rackets and a shuttle. The playing court consists of the center line, the baseline, and the singles' sideline (see figure 3.3). To determine who serves first, players can play Rock, Paper, Scissors. Only the serving player can score. Should a server score more than three points in a row, the opponent then serves. The game is played to seven points. You may choose to explain the rules of "setting" to avoid disputes should a tie occur. (If necessary, see *Badminton: Steps to Success* [Grice 1996] for an explanation of setting and lets.) Disputes are replayed with no questions asked.

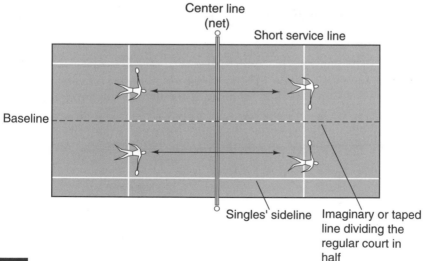

Figure 3.3 A modified playing court.

Description

One partner initiates play with a short serve. If during play the shuttle hits the net and travels over, play continues unless the shuttle hits the ground before being returned or goes out of bounds. If the shuttle hits the net on the service and goes into the receiving court, play continues. If on the serve the shuttle lands outside the service court area, the serve is no good, and the receiving player serves. Only short serves, underhand clears, and net shots are allowed. If a player uses another stroke, play stops as if the shuttle has been hit out of play. The focus is on knowing where on the court the opponent is located and using the appropriate stroke to hit the shuttle into the opponent's court (e.g., if the opponent is playing deep, place the shuttle in the forecourt; if he or she is playing close to the net, use an underhand clear to place the shuttle in the backcourt).

Challenge

Players perform the following sequence before play begins: short serve, net shot, and another net shot.

3.10 Forehand Long Serve

Goal

Develop the forehand long serve.

Organization

Players pair off across from each other on one half of a court with a net. Each player has a racket, and the partners share four shuttles.

Description

Explain and demonstrate the forehand long serve. (Show players how to start in the same racket position as the short serve in order to conceal the long serve.) Tell the players to drop, not toss, the shuttle away from the body and follow through over the opposite hitting shoulder. Each partner takes turns serving all the shuttles over the net, high and deep into the opponent's service court. The receiving partner allows all shuttles to land in the court and then returns them with forehand long serves of his or her own. Servers should try to consistently place the shuttle inside the back third of the opponent's service court.

Challenge

Mark off the back third of the service court with floor tape and ask players to keep track of how many shuttles land behind the tape. Set a goal of hitting 7 of 10 serves into the back third of the court. Have receivers extend their rackets straight up in the air to see if the serve can clear the racket and still have the shuttle land in the marked-off area.

3.11 Forehand Overhead Clear

Goals

Develop the forehand overhead clear; develop exerting enough power to drive the shuttle deep into the opponent's court.

Organization

Players pair off across from each other on one half of a court with a net. Each player has a racket and shares five shuttles.

Description

Explain and demonstrate the forehand overhead clear. One player long-serves high and deep to a partner. If the serve is in the singles' serving court and the receiver can get into position, the shuttle is returned with a forehand overhead clear, deep into the opponent's backcourt, as close to the baseline as possible. The server allows the shot to drop so that the hitter can see where it lands. If the serve is not playable with an overhead clear, it is replayed. After five successful overhead clears into the deep service court, partners exchange tasks. Have players focus on getting into position, bringing the racket back behind and in line with their racket shoulder, and transferring weight from the back foot onto the front foot at the same time they swing the racket forward in a straight line.

Challenges

Have partners compete with each other to see how many forehand overhead clears they can get to drop between the singles' and doubles' long service line in the opponent's backcourt. See if they can consistently return 7 of 10 shots into this area. If successful, have servers remain in place and extend their rackets skyward. The shuttle must go over the racket and land in the court to count.

3.12 Long Serve and Overhead Clear Rally

Goals

Use the forehand overhead clear in a rally. Get players to return quickly to center court after each return and get in racket-ready position to receive the shuttle.

Organization

Players pair off across from each other on one half of a court with a net. Each pair has two rackets and a shuttle. The playing court consists of the center line, the baseline, and the singles' sideline (see figure 3.3, p. 37).

Description

One partner initiates play with a long serve (high and deep). If the serve is in the singles' serving court and the receiver can get into position, the shuttle is returned with a forehand overhead clear high and deep into the opponent's court; the receiving player then returns with an overhead forehand clear, and a rally ensues. If the serve is not in the service court, the receiving player lets the shuttle drop and then serves back to the opponent. Players rally using *only* the forehand overhead clear until the shuttle lands outside the designated singles' court or until it's not returned with an overhead clear. Players alternate serving and use the single-court boundaries on their half of the court.

Challenges

Ask players to rally cooperatively for 10 consecutive forehand overhead clears. Then make the game competitive and have them rally using only forehand overhead clears, with a point scored for every clear that can't be returned or that's out of play. Alternate serving, with a point awarded each time a shuttle can't be returned or falls out of play (in this game, either player can score, not just the server).

3.13	**Short or Long Serves, Forehand Overhead Clears, Underhand Clears, and Net Shots (Hairpin Drops) Rally**

Goals

Use forehand overhead clears together with underhand clears and net shots (hairpin drops) in a competitive rally. Adjust as necessary to use the most appropriate stroke.

Organization

Players pair off across from each other on one half of a court with a net. Each pair has two rackets and a shuttle. The playing court consists of the center line, the baseline, and the singles' sideline (see figure 3.3, p. 37).

Description

One partner initiates play with a short or long serve. If the serve falls in the singles' serving court, play begins, and the receiving player returns the shuttle with the appropriate return shot. If the serve is not in the service court, the receiving player lets the shuttle drop and then serves back to the partner. Players rally using only underhand clears (forehand or backhand), overhead forehand clears, and hairpin drops (forehand and backhand) until the shuttle lands outside the designated singles court or can't be returned using one of these strokes. Players alternate serving and use the single-court boundaries on their half of the court. Count how many consecutive hits each group achieves. Set a goal for 10 and increase the number as appropriate.

Challenge

Change the rally to a competitive halfcourt game using only the strokes covered thus far. Play the game up to seven points, using regular badminton rules. To determine who serves first, have players play Rock, Paper, Scissors.

3.14 Forehand Smash

Goal

Develop the forehand smash.

Organization

Players pair off across from each other on one half of a court with a net. Each player has a racket and shares five shuttles.

Description

Explain and demonstrate a forehand smash, focusing on getting into position, bringing the racket back behind and in line with the racket shoulder, and transferring weight from the back foot to the front foot at the same time the racket swings forward in a straight line over the shuttle. One partner long-serves deep and high into the back third of the singles service court. The receiver returns the serve with a smash so that the shuttle travels in a fast, downward trajectory, just clearing the net. The server lets the shuttle land so the hitter can see where it falls. After five serves, partners trade tasks.

Challenge

Challenge players to successfully smash three out of five into their opponent's court.

3.15   Short Serve, Clear, and Smash

Goal

To get into proper position to hit a smash when the opportunity arises.

Organization

Players pair off across from each other on one half of a court with a net. Each player has a racket and shares five shuttles.

Description

One partner short-serves to the other on either the forehand or backhand side. The receiver returns the shuttle with the appropriate underhand clear. The server then gets into proper position, bringing the racket back behind and in line with their racket shoulder, transferring weight from the back foot to the front foot at the same time they swing their racket forward in a straight line over the shuttle, and smashes the shuttle back. The receiver lets the shuttle land so the hitter can see where it falls. After five serves, partners exchange tasks.

Challenge

If players are having success, have the partner receiving the smash attempt to return the smash by using a net shot to block the shuttle. If the net shot is successful, play continues with a rally using any of the skills learned so far.

3.16   Halfcourt Singles' Game: Serves, Clears, Smashes, and Net Shots (Hairpin Drops)

Goals

Use the short and long serve, the underhand forehand and backhand clears, the forehand overhead clear, and the smash in competition.

Organization

Players pair off across from each other on one half of a court with a net. Each pair has two rackets and a shuttle. The playing court consists of the center line, the baseline, and the singles' sideline (see figure 3.3, p. 37). To determine who serves, players play Rock, Paper, Scissors. Only the serving player can score. If a serving player scores more than three points in a row, the opponent then serves. Any disputes are replayed, no questions asked. Play games to seven points or for a set time, such as 10 minutes.

Description

Players start in racket-ready position. They move quickly into proper hitting position, and then return to the center of the court after returning the shuttle. One partner initiates play with a short or long serve. If the serve falls into the singles' serving court, the receiving player uses the appropriate shots learned so far (clears, net shots, and smash) to return the shuttle. If the serve does not fall into the service court, the opponent serves. Players continue to play until the shuttle lands outside the designated singles court or the shuttle can't be returned using the shots designated. Only the serving player can score.

Challenge

Award two points to any player, serving or not, if his or her opponent can't return a smash or if a net shot is successful after an opponent's smash.

3.17 Overhead Drop

Goal

Develop the overhead drop.

Organization

Players pair off across from each other on one half of a court with a net. Each pair has two rackets and five shuttles.

Description

Explain and demonstrate the overhead drop. One partner long-serves deep and high into the back third of the singles' service court. The receiver returns the serve with an overhead drop so that the shuttle travels downward and drops quickly over the net. The server allows the shuttle to land so the hitter can see where it hit (preferably just beyond the net; see figure 3.4). After five serves, partners exchange tasks. Focus on getting into proper position, setting up as if about to hit a smash, and slowing the stroke down at the last second.

Challenge

If players are successful, have hitter choose between using the smash or overhead drop, while the receiver tries to guess which stroke the hitter will use by moving into position to return the anticipated stroke. If hitters tip their hand as to which stroke they are about to use, the receiver tells the hitter what he or she is doing to give the shot away.

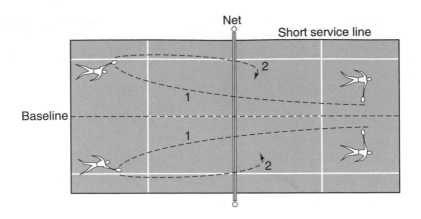

Figure 3.4 The overhead drop. (1) The shuttle's pattern; (2) where it drops.

3.18 | Overhead Clear and Overhead Drop

Goal

After serving long, players get into position to receive an overhead clear and then execute an overhead drop.

Organization

Partners stand across from each other on one half of a court with a net. Each pair has two rackets and five shuttles.

Description

One player long-serves to his or her partner. The receiver returns the shuttle deep with an overhead clear. The server then performs an overhead drop shot. The receiver lets the shuttle land so the hitter can see where it hits. After five serves, players exchange tasks. Players focus on getting into proper position, setting up as if to hit a smash but then slowing the stroke down at the last second.

Challenge

Once players are successful, allow the receiver to use either a drop, smash, or overhead clear, and if this shot is successful, players rally using the strokes covered so far.

3.19 Short Serve, Underhand Clear, Overhead Clear, Overhead Drop, and Net Shot

Goal

Combine several skills learned so far into a sequence that requires thought and performance.

Organization

Partners pair off across from each other on one half of a court with a net. Each pair has two rackets and five shuttles.

Description

One player short-serves to a partner on either the forehand or backhand side. The receiver returns the shuttle deep with an underhand clear. The server then performs an overhead clear back to the receiver, who returns the clear with an overhead drop shot. The drop shot is returned with a net shot. After five serves, players exchange tasks. Players should focus on returning to racket-ready position at center court after each stroke and avoid anticipating the next shot.

Challenge

If the net shot can be returned, players should return it and continue rallying, using only shots they have learned so far.

3.20 Game: Short or Long Serve, Clears, Drops, Net Shots (Hairpin Drops), and Smash

Goal

Use and further develop all shots learned so far, especially the drops (overhead and hairpin) in a game situation.

Organization

Partners pair off across from each other on one half of a court with a net. Each pair has two rackets and one shuttle. The playing court consists of the center line, baseline, and singles' sideline (see figure 3.3, p. 37).

Description

One partner initiates play with a short or long serve. If the serve is in the singles' serving court, play commences (using only shots covered so far) until the shuttle lands outside the designated singles' court or can't be returned. Players use the single-court boundaries on their half of the court. If the serve is not in the service court, the receiving player serves. Games are played to seven points or for a set time, such as 10 minutes. Players focus on returning to racket-ready position at center court after each stroke, getting into position to return the shuttle as quickly as possible, and avoiding the tendency to anticipate the next shot.

Challenge

Have players try to place the shuttle in an uncovered section of the court.

3.21 Forehand and Backhand Drive

Goals

Develop the forehand and backhand drive.

Organization

Partners pair off across from each other on one half of a court with a net. Each pair has two rackets and five shuttles.

Description

Explain and demonstrate the forehand and backhand drive, showing players how to use the arm, not the wrist, and keep the racket away from the body. One partner hits the shuttle in a flat trajectory over the net so that it arrives at the receiver somewhere between their shoulder and knee on either the forehand or backhand side. The receiver returns the shuttle with a drive so that the shuttle flies in a flat trajectory as it barely clears the net into the opponent's court. The shuttle is not returned. After five trials each to the forehand and backhand, partners exchange tasks.

Challenge

Rally using only the drive shot with a goal of achieving 10 in a row.

3.22 Four-Corner Drill

Goals

Develop the ability to react quickly to any shot hit to any area of the court, return the shuttle into the opponent's court using the appropriate stroke, and return to center court in racket-ready position with little hesitation.

Organization

Partners pair off on one halfcourt or one full regulation singles' court with net. Each player has a racket; one player has four shuttles.

Description

The receiving player stands in the middle of the court in racket-ready position. Player with the shuttles proceeds to hit each shuttle in rapid succession to various uncovered areas of the court. Receiving player reacts to each shot and moves quickly to return it before returning to center court in racket-ready position. Receiver then repeats the drill to his or her partner. Players focus on returning to center court in racket-ready position after each stroke, without trying to anticipate where the next shot will be hit. (Ask hitters to use the drive more than any other shot.)

Challenge

Avoid favoring or overplaying one area of the court. Increase the tempo of hits to receivers so they don't have time to think, only to move and react. Hit some shots right at the receiver's chest or hard flat drives to force them to use a drive shot.

3.23 Singles' Game on Full Court: Short or Long Serves, Clears, Drives, Drops, Net Shots, and Smash

Goal

Develop all the skills learned so far, especially drops (overhead and hairpin net shots) and diagonal serving, in a competitive singles' game using official badminton rules on a regulation size singles' court.

Organization

Partners play on a regulation singles' court with a net. Players each have a racket and share one shuttle. To determine who serves, have them play Rock, Paper, Scissors. Any disputes are replayed, no questions asked. Games are to seven points or every 10 minutes, at which time players rotate to play new partners. Players implement "setting" at the appropriate time in the game to avoid ties.

Description

Provide players with a discussion and demonstration on any rules, strategies, and situations not previously covered. Partners play a game of singles, using regulation rules. Players focus on returning to racket-ready position at center court after each return and using all the shots they have learned so far.

Challenge

Before each game, have all players write down a strategy they'll use against their opponents. Tell them to be ready with a backup plan should their first plan misfire. Afterward, have players write down their results: what worked and what didn't. If they had to play the same opponent again, how would they change their strategy, if at all?

3.24 Defensive Backhand

Goal

Develop the defensive backhand shot for use in doubles play.

Organization

Partners pair off with rackets, opposite each other on one halfcourt, one partner at net with five shuttles and the other at the baseline. Focus on reacting quickly to block the smash with the backhand.

Description

Explain and demonstrate the defensive backhand against a smash used in doubles' play. Have the partner at the net toss and smash the shuttle at the receiving partner, aiming for his or her racket. The receiver attempts to return the smash using the defensive backhand.

Challenge

Have receiver begin play with an underhand clear that travels into the opponent's front court. The opponent then smashes the shuttle back at the receiver, who attempts a defensive backhand shot.

3.25 Doubles' Game: Short or Long Serve, Clears, Drives, Drops, Net Shots, and Smash

Goals

Use the skills learned so far in a doubles' game and develop a sense of teamwork and strategy with a partner in a competitive doubles' game using official badminton rules on a regulation doubles' court.

Organization

Two sets of partners play against each other on one regulation doubles' court with a net. Each player has a racket with one shuttle per court. To determine who serves, players do Rock, Paper, Scissors. Any disputes are replayed, no questions asked. Games are to seven points or for a set time, such as 10 minutes. Players implement "setting" as necessary to avoid ties.

Description

Explain and demonstrate doubles' play rules, player positioning (up and back and side by side), rotation, and strategies. Have partners play a game of doubles, using regulation rules. Players are restricted to using only strokes covered in class. Players focus on using all the shots learned in class and communicating with their partner.

Challenge

Try to stay in the attacking, up-and-back position as much as possible, but if forced into the side-by-side defensive position, use the backhand as much as possible and hit to the opponent's weakness (i.e., if opponents are up and back, aim for the sidelines; if they're in a defensive side-by-side position, aim between the players). Use finesse rather than strength and work on placing the shuttle.

Reference

Grice, Tony. 1996. *Badminton: Steps to Success.* Champaign, IL: Human Kinetics.

CHAPTER 4

Golf

Always a challenge, seldom mastered, and played by millions of men and women into their twilight years, golf is truly *the* lifetime sport and a wonderful way for youngsters to maintain an active and healthy lifestyle. What better sport to teach young people than one that will challenge them all their lives, one they can play with friends, family, and future business associates? Golf's only drawbacks are bad weather and expense.

For the teacher, golf brings with it some concerns, primarily regarding safety. While one worry is flying golf balls, perhaps a more serious concern is swinging clubs. It's common for young people to want to swing the club around once they get it in their hands. It's also common for inexperienced golfers to forget to steer clear of swinging golf clubs. People have been killed from stepping into a club being swung. As a teacher, you need to be more careful and watchful than ever once you get your students out on the course. Repeat your safety rules often, and enforce them throughout the unit. Give special attention to students who miss class—don't let them touch a club until you have brought them up to date on what they missed, especially regarding safety. Also, once your students start chipping, pitching, and driving, you'll need to designate areas for them to practice so others don't wander into the space (see figure 4.1). Most golf injuries occur when people wander into a practice area behind an unaware golfer and are struck by a backswing or follow-through.

Golf is not a high-activity sport if you use a golf cart, but it's healthy if students walk the entire course (18 holes is no picnic) and even a bit strenuous if they carry their own clubs. If your class does use golf carts, and since (presumably) one of your goals in the class is to help your students develop aerobic fitness, you might

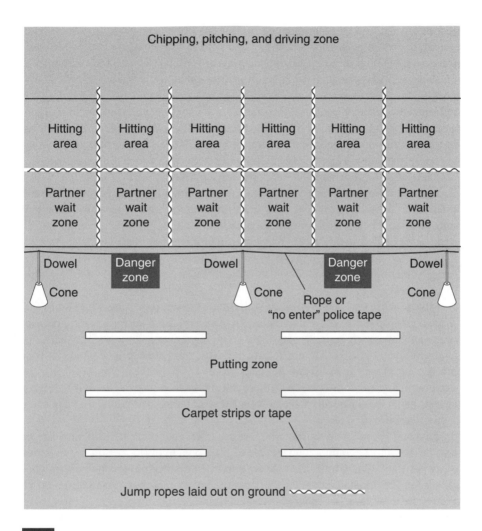

Figure 4.1 An example of roping off practice areas for safety.

want to set aside time before beginning each golf lesson for your students to do some aerobic activity.

While golf can be quite expensive, there are ways to reduce costs. Students might find used sets of clubs at garage sales for a good price. Also ask them to check their garages in case a parent's old clubs are gathering dust in a corner. You can chop old clubs into shorter lengths for your smaller students (this can also be done quite easily at any golf shop for a reasonable fee). Besides clubs, other equipment you'll need includes Wiffle® balls, regulation balls, tees, and mats or rugs for indoor hitting. You can find remnant rugs at carpet dealers (look for 4-inch-wide pieces 20 feet in length for practicing putting and 5-foot-square pieces for chipping, pitching, and driving). An outside playing field works well for chipping and pitching live balls provided the area is roped (or coned) off from outsiders. Ideally, you'll have several areas of a field set aside and groomed as practice greens for putting with different lies, but if this doesn't work for you, you can take the class to a public golf course instead. They often reduce rates for students. In many cases, the lawn in front of the school is well groomed, which works fine as a putting green. Ask a maintenance worker to mow the lawn extra short, if it's allowed. But do check with your principal before creating a putting green!

In the progressions for golf, I hope to keep students interested by involving them right away in one of the most satisfying parts of the game: putting the ball into the cup. I begin with putting, then proceed to chipping and pitching before addressing driving and tying them together in efficient progressions. This progression may go against the norm of learning golf, but by beginning with putting, many students are accommodated in a much safer environment while retaining their interest.

Most teacher texts on golf describe individual exercises golfers can do to improve their game and often also include nonhitting drills, such as practicing foot alignment, swinging an imaginary club, swinging a club at an imaginary ball, and so on. While these exercises are helpful and can improve technique, students generally want to see the results of their actions, so I've kept these types of drills to a minimum. Such exercises are best employed when students need to revisit skills or correct bad habits. Once they see how an exercise helps their game, they are more likely to do it with interest.

This unit begins indoors for two reasons: safety and control. Students learn to putt on day one, beginning with the use of lines on a gym floor or on 4-inch strips of carpet 10 to 20 feet long. This allows you to set up routines for the unit, emphasize safety, and keep students on task and in control as they practice the stroke they'll use more than any other (in a typical round of golf, 50 percent of the strokes are putts). After putting, students are introduced to chipping, either indoors or outdoors, before chipping and putting are linked. The same progression is followed for pitching, which is then linked to chipping and putting, preferably on a par three golf course.

The focus in the pitching progressions is on the full swing employing the two most used irons: the seven and nine. Once the class becomes familiar with these two irons and has some success, they move on to driving, followed by a round of golf on an actual course. Practice using lower irons is left up to you, once your students have experienced playing the game. On the course, students must select the appropriate club for each circumstance, demonstrate an ability to hit the ball using the proper stroke, keep score, and exhibit proper golf etiquette and safety.

■ After following the progressions, beginning students should be able to play nine holes of golf using the following skills:

- Putting
- Chipping
- Pitching
- Driving
- Scoring
- Obeying the rules
- Following proper etiquette
- Respecting safety issues

4.1 Imaginary Putting

Goals

Experiment with grips to see what's most comfortable; develop the basic principles of proper putting.

Organization

Give each player a putter and have them spread out in self-space in the gym.

Description

Explain and demonstrate safety rules, matching club length to the player, various putting grips (e.g., interlocking, overlap, baseball grip), stance, and the principles of proper putting. See *Golf: Steps to Success, 2nd edition* (Owens and Bunker 1995) for illustrations and more information on the various grips. Then spread players out in self-space and have them putt imaginary balls using the grips and styles you have demonstrated. Focus on setting up square to the target in a comfortable stance, body positioning over an imaginary ball, arms forming a triangle, and moving in a pendulum motion from the shoulders, not the hands.

Challenge

See if players can putt in a sweeping motion, keeping the sole (flat bottom of the club) the same distance in height from the floor (ground) throughout the stroke as opposed to starting high on the back swing, dipping low on contact, and ending high on the front swing.

4.2   Putt Following a Line or Carpet Strip

Goal

Consistently putt the ball in a straight line about 10 feet.

Organization

Players play with a partner, each with a putter and sharing three golf balls. Ask them to spread out in self-space in a gym. Self-space has either a court line about 10 feet long (floor must be even) or a 4-inch by 10-foot piece of carpet.

Description

Using the putting style they feel most comfortable with, players putt each ball, attempting to keep it on the line on the floor or within the 4-inch strip of carpet. Have partners at the receiving end return the balls in the same fashion. Focus on creating a triangle with the arms and a pendulum swing with the shoulders (not the hands).

Challenge

Have partners challenge each other to see who can most often keep the ball on the line or within the 4-inch strip of carpet.

4.3   Carpet Putt for Distance

Goal

Develop a sense of touch regarding how much force is needed to propel a ball a predetermined distance.

Organization

Spread out in a gym or a field, players pair off with partners, each with one putter and sharing three golf balls. If in a gym, use strips of carpet about 12 feet long. Make a starting line with floor tape (or anything else that doesn't interfere with the path of the ball) and from that line place three more lines every 3 feet.

Description

Explain and demonstrate putting for distance. Each player putts one ball at a time and tries to make it stop on or close to a marker. Have players start with the closest marker first and then try for the farther markers. Partners remove any balls that might get in the way. Focus on creating a triangle with the arms and a pendulum swing with the shoulders (not the hands).

Challenge

Play a game in which each partner calls out one of the three markers to be the target. Each partner putts, and the one who hits a ball closest to the target wins.

4.4   Putting to a Target

Goal

Consistently putt the ball in a straight line into a cup.

Organization

Players play with a partner in a gym, each with a putter and sharing six golf balls. In a 10-foot by 10-foot area, tape a tennis ball can or a paper cup to the ground (or use indoor practice golf cups if you have them), bottom against the wall and open end facing out. Players putt to the cup 10 feet away.

Description

Using their preferred putting style, players try to putt balls (three each) into the cup. Have them focus on lining up the ball with the cup and accelerating through the ball in a pendulum motion.

Challenge

Lengthen the distance (but no more than 25 feet).

4.5   Miniature Golf

Goal

Develop putting skills and incorporate the rules and etiquette of golf in a simulated game of mini-golf.

Organization

Players play in groups of two with one scorecard, two putters, and two balls. Set up the gym as a miniature golf course using tennis cans, paper cups, or indoor golf cups as holes. Have at least 9 holes and no more than 18 holes, with a par established for each hole. (To establish par, play a round yourself and come up with a reasonable yet challenging number.) The playing surface should be flat, but golfers should be forced to two-putt or three-putt the ball. Set up the course with obstructions to make it very difficult or even impossible to putt the ball directly into the hole. Have groups start at different holes so that no one is standing around.

Description

Explain and demonstrate scoring and golf etiquette (which ball is played first and so on). Then have partners play a round of golf, keeping score on scrap paper you have passed around. Ask players to concentrate on using the same setup routine for each putt and adjusting acceleration of each stroke to suit the distance of the putt.

Challenge

Have partners compete against other partners to see who can get the lowest score.

4.6   Putting Different Lies

Goal

Develop the ability to determine where to place and aim the ball when putting uphill or downhill on a green.

Organization

Each player plays with a partner, a putter, and a ball. Assign each pair of partners to make a mock uneven putting green using a 4-foot by 8-foot or longer neoprene gymnastics mat with no seams (a large wrestling mat can also be used) or equally large sections of carpet. The mat should be sloped slightly, using newspaper under the mat, with tennis cans or paper cups taped on each end to represent holes (see figure 4.2). The angle of slope should be no more than two to three degrees.

Description

Explain and demonstrate how to read a lie on a green and the tactics to employ when faced with an uphill or downhill lie. Show players the difference between target putting and playing a high line. Then players perform both uphill and downhill putts on their mats. Players should focus on accelerating through the ball if target putting ("never up, never in") and visualizing the pace of the ball if playing a high line.

Challenge

Change the slope of the mat to make it more challenging. Have twosomes play a round of mini-golf by moving from mat to mat.

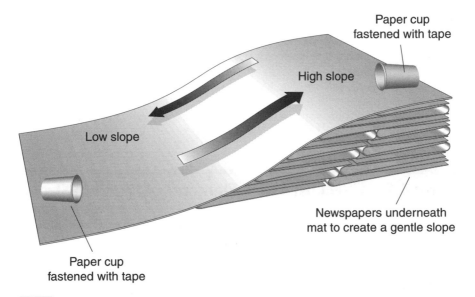

Figure 4.2 An example of the setup for Putting Different Lies.

4.7 Imaginary Chipping

Goals

Develop the proper swing for the chip shot and demonstrate proper safety procedures in the vicinity of a golfer using irons or clubs.

Organization

Players participate with partners or individually, each player with one chipping iron (nine-iron, sand wedge, or pitching wedge) in a roped-off (or coned-off) area either outside on the grass or inside on carpet squares. Roped-off areas should be about 5 yards by 10 yards using pylons and ropes on three sides to indicate the "no enter zone" (see figure 4.1, p. 51).

Description

Explain and demonstrate safety, in which the "no enter zone" is emphasized and players are reminded of the danger of walking behind a swinging golf club and of retrieving a ball before the release signal (e.g., "Go," "Begin") is given. Also provide a discussion and demonstration of the various grips and the purpose and mechanics of the chip stroke (see *Golf: Steps to Success, 2nd edition,* [Owens and Bunker 1995] for more information on the chip stroke). Players disperse into their "no enter zones" and practice the chip shot, hitting an imaginary ball. Have players focus on limiting their body movements.

Challenge

See if players can consistently use a short backstroke (no further than the 2 o'clock position) with minimal body action and keeping wrists locked at contact. Have partners watch each other and use the checklist (form 4.1) to give feedback.

Form 4.1   Checklist of Key Elements of the Chip Stroke

This checklist is to help you become a better golfer. It's not graded. Only you and your partner will share its contents so please be honest.

Place a √ only in the box that your partner does consistently. When your partner is finished, discuss the scoring and what you did and did not see consistently.

❑ Addressed the ball each time and had a set routine.

❑ Kept head still.

❑ Eyes were down.

❑ Everything worked as a unit (hands, wrists, arms).

❑ Feet were shoulder-width apart.

❑ Followed through.

❑ Kept wrists and elbows firm.

❑ Knees were flexed.

From *Sport Progressions* by Roy A. Clumpner, 2003, Champaign, IL: Human Kinetics.

4.8   Chipping a Wiffle Ball

Goal

Develop the proper swing and ball strike of the chip shot so the ball is lofted low and in a straight line.

Organization

Play can be inside or outside. Players pair off, each with a chipping iron (nine-iron, sand wedge, or pitching wedge) and four Wiffle golf balls within a 5-yard by 10-yard "no enter zone." If inside, form "no enter zones" with carpet squares.

Description

Review the chipping stroke, the importance of staying out of the "no enter zones" when a player is present, and the requirement that no one retrieves any ball until the release signal is given. Have players practice chipping a Wiffle ball, focusing on weight on the front foot, hands in front of the ball, and hitting down on the ball.

Challenge

See if players can chip five in a row in a straight line.

4.9   Chipping at a Target

Goal

Develop the proper swing and ball strike of the chip stroke to a target with a regulation golf ball.

Organization

Outside on grass, two partners (or individually if space allows), each with a chipping iron and six regulation golf balls, play within a "no enter zone." Five yards from the starting spot in the zone, spray (with biodegradable field paint, available from any major physical education supply company) a circle 20 feet in diameter. Inside that circle spray another circle 10 feet in diameter. Then inside the second circle spray a third circle 5 feet in diameter and inside that a fourth circle 3 feet in diameter. This last circle is the bull's eye (see figure 4.3).

Description

Remind players that the purpose of chipping is to get the ball rolling onto the green (target) so that it stops to be putted in with the next shot. Using the

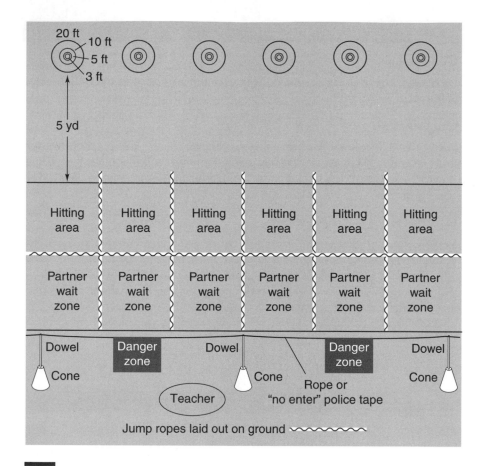

Figure 4.3 Setup for Chipping at a Target.

proper chipping stroke, have players try to loft the ball on a low trajectory so that it rolls into the circle (green) close to the bull's eye. Players can compete against each other. Points are scored for getting a ball into the circle (e.g., four points for the center circle, three points for the next circle, and so on). Players should focus on keeping their weight on the front foot and their hands in front of the ball, while hitting down on the ball.

Challenge

Move the starting line back (but no more than 10 yards from the outer circle).

4.10 Chipping Various Distances

Goal

Using the chip shot, adjust the swing and force of the club to the distance intended.

Organization

In roped-off practice areas, players practice alone or with a partner, each with a chipping iron and at least six balls apiece. On the field are four traffic cones, beginning 10 yards from the hitting line and every 5 yards thereafter (see figure 4.4).

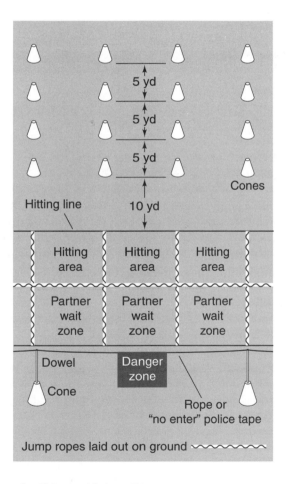

Figure 4.4 Setup for Chipping Various Distances.

Description

Using the proper chipping stroke, players attempt to loft the first ball low and have it stop between the first set of cones (10 to 15 yards). Players then hit a second ball and attempt to have it land and roll and stop between the next set of cones (15 to 20 yards) and so on. The third ball is then aimed to fall between the third set of cones (20 to 25 yards). Players should focus on shifting weight to the front foot, keeping hands in front of the ball, and hitting down on the ball.

Challenge

Only count the balls that hit the ground beyond the first cone. This mimics having to hit over an obstruction and make the ball "bite" (i.e., halt its rolling movement using backspin) so that it stays in the zone between the cones.

4.11   Target Chipping: Tic-Tac-Toe

Goal

Develop the ability to hit a chip shot that rolls and stops within a designated square.

Organization

Players play outside on grass with a partner and one chipping iron apiece. Use as many regulation golf balls as you have to spare (at least six apiece) and a Tic-Tac-Toe playing area. The playing area is laid out like a Tic-Tac-Toe game, consisting of nine squares; each area is 20 yards by 20 yards. You can also use grids on a football field with small traffic cones, hot spots, biodegradable field paint, or jump ropes to designate each boundary area. The distance from the hitting line to the beginning of the Tic-Tac-Toe grid is 10 yards (see figure 4.5). Give players a pencil and a copy of form 4.2: a diagram of a Tic-Tac-Toe grid.

Description

Partners play the game of Tic-Tac-Toe, using the chip shot. The spot where the ball *stops* determines the square, not where it initially lands. Players fill in their Os or Xs on form 4.2. The first player to get three squares in a row wins the game. Players focus on shifting weight to their front foot, keeping hands in front of the ball, and hitting down on the ball.

Challenges

Have players "call" the square they're aiming for before hitting the ball. Reduce the size of the square or place an obstacle, such as a track hurdle, for them to loft the ball over.

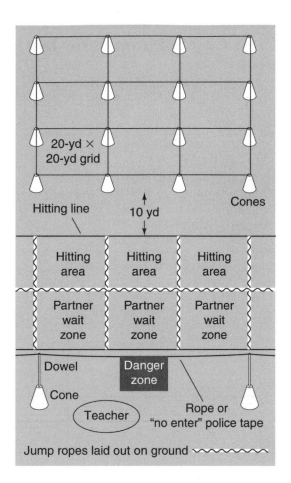

Figure 4.5   Tic-Tac-Toe grid.

4.12 Chip and Putt Game

Goal

Demonstrate proper chipping and putting skills in a simulated game.

Organization

Players play either outside on a field set up to simulate a chipping and putting green or at an actual golf course with a chipping and putting practice area. Each player has a scorecard, pencil, chipping iron, putter, and a ball. Players should begin no more than 15 yards from the green.

Form 4.2   Diagram of Tic-Tac-Toe

X = _____
Student name

O = _____
Student name

Tic-Tac-Toe directions: Partners decide who will be "X" and who will be "O." Place an X or O in the appropriate box after you chip the golf ball. The first person to line up all their Xs or Os vertically, horizontally, or diagonally in three consecutive boxes is the winner.

Description

Explain the etiquette of playing on the green. Players then proceed to chip and putt until they hole out. Players should keep score and practice golf etiquette. Focus on keeping quiet, who hits first, keeping bags off the green, pulling the pin, and marking ball placement.

Challenge

Have partners combine scores and compete against another set of partners for the lowest score; have players see if they can lower their score.

4.13 Imaginary Full Swing

Goal

Develop the proper mechanics of the full swing.

Organization

Players play outside with a partner (or individually if space permits), each with a seven-iron. Play is within a roped-off five-yard by five-yard "no enter zone."

Description

Review safety, emphasizing that players are not to enter the "no enter zone" area to retrieve a ball until the release signal is given. Then explain and demonstrate the mechanics of the full swing without a ball. Players then practice the mechanics of the full swing in their zones, pretending to hit imaginary balls. Emphasize the proper setup position (preparation) and execution phase, focusing on weight distributed evenly, hands in front of the ball, hitting down on the back of the ball, and letting the club do the work.

Challenge

Have partners watch each other for 10 swings and fill out form 4.3, a checklist of key elements for the full swing.

4.14 Pitch a Wiffle Ball

Goal

Develop the proper full swing of the pitch stroke so that the ball lofts high and in a straight line.

Form 4.3   Checklist of Key Elements of the Full Swing

This checklist is to help you become a better golfer. It is not graded. Only you and your partner will share its contents. Partner evaluating, please be honest. When you are finished, discuss the scoring with your partner.

Place a √ in the box that most accurately describes your partner's full swing.

	Consistent	Sometimes	Not observed
Addressed the ball each time and had a routine.	❏	❏	❏
Kept head down.	❏	❏	❏
Feet were shoulder-width apart.	❏	❏	❏
Had slow backswing.	❏	❏	❏
Accelerated through the swing.	❏	❏	❏
Hands and body led the club head.	❏	❏	❏
Followed through.	❏	❏	❏
Finished on balance.	❏	❏	❏

From *Sport Progressions* by Roy A. Clumpner, 2003, Champaign, IL: Human Kinetics.

Organization

Outside or inside. With a partner (or individually if space permits), each player has one pitching iron (seven-iron works best) and four Wiffle golf balls within a "no enter zone."

Description

Review the pitching stroke, focusing on the irons used for pitching, the importance of staying out of the "no enter zone" when a player is present, and the requirement that no one retrieves any ball until a release signal is given. Then have players practice using the full swing to pitch a Wiffle ball. Players focus on distributing weight evenly, keeping hands in front of the ball, hitting down on the back of the ball, and letting the club do the work.

Challenge

Have players try to pitch five in a row in a straight line.

4.15 Pitch at Targets

Goals

Develop the proper swing and ball strike of the pitch shot so that the ball lofts high, travels in a straight line, and bites when it lands (instead of rolling after landing). Be able to choose the best iron to achieve the distance desired using the full swing.

Organization

Players play with partners outside in a grass field at least 160 yards long. Each player has a seven-iron and a nine-iron and six regulation golf balls within a "no enter zone." Beginning 100 yards from the starting line and every 10 yards thereafter (up to 150 yards), set up markers (such as large traffic cones) at 10-yard intervals to form target zones.

Description

Using the proper full-swing motion, each player practices pitching to a target zone between a set of markers beginning with the target zone closest to the starting line. Players experiment with both the seven-iron and nine-iron to experience the difference in range each club provides. Ask players to focus on keeping their weight distributed evenly, keeping their hands in front of the ball, hitting down on the back of the ball, and letting their club do the work.

Challenge

Have partners compete against other teams of two to see which team can place a ball in all five target zones first.

4.16 Pitch, Chip, and Putt Game

Goals

Demonstrate proper pitching, chipping, and putting skills in a game-like situation, adhering to the rules and etiquette of golf.

Organization

Design a three-hole par three golf course with the distance between holes at least 100 yards. If there's not enough room at your school for this progression, skip to the next progression. Create a green at each hole (or, if this isn't possible, spray a circle the size of a hula hoop on the grass with biodegradable paint to represent the hole with a flag or cone in the center). Players group in foursomes with each player with a scorecard, pencil, pitching wedge, chipping iron, putter, and a ball. Assign each foursome a hole or station at which to begin. To reduce wait time, create practice stations between holes for each team to rotate to after they hole out. These stations could be putting greens, areas for chipping and pitching Wiffle balls, or even testing areas where you can check their stroke form.

Description

All players proceed to pitch, chip, and putt until they hole out, keeping score and practicing golf etiquette. Players maintain a routine for addressing the ball each time.

Challenge

Establish a par for each hole and challenge players, as teams and individuals, to see who can meet or score below par.

4.17 Imaginary Driving

Goal

Develop the proper mechanics of the full-swing drive.

Organization

Players can do this activity inside or at a driving range, with a partner or individually. Each player should have a driver within a roped-off "no enter zone" (five yards by five yards).

Description

Review safety—including the danger of walking into the "no enter zone" and of retrieving balls only after a release signal is given—and the mechanics of the full swing. Then, as you demonstrate a drive without a ball, ask the class to watch your body movements, particularly your head. Emphasize the setup position (preparation) and execution, focusing on keeping the head down and following through with the pendulum motion. Have players practice the mechanics of the full swing with a club in their zones, pretending to drive imaginary balls.

Challenge

Have partners watch each other using form 4.4, a checklist of key elements for the full-swing drive at an imaginary ball.

Form 4.4   Checklist of Key Elements
of the Full Swing for Driving

This checklist is to help you become a better golfer. It is not graded. Only you and your partner will share its contents. Partner evaluating, please be honest. When you are finished, discuss the scoring with your partner.

Place a √ in the box that most accurately describes your partner's full swing.

	Consistent	Sometimes	Not observed
Addressed the ball each time and had a routine.	❏	❏	❏
Head remained still and down.	❏	❏	❏
Feet kept shoulder-width apart.	❏	❏	❏
Knees were slightly bent.	❏	❏	❏
Had slow backswing.	❏	❏	❏
Arms, legs, and hands began as a unit at the start.	❏	❏	❏
Lead arm (left for right-handers) was straight throughout.	❏	❏	❏
Accelerated through the swing.	❏	❏	❏
Followed through.	❏	❏	❏
Finished on balance.	❏	❏	❏

From *Sport Progressions* by Roy A. Clumpner, 2003, Champaign, IL: Human Kinetics.

4.18   Driving a Wiffle Ball

Goal

Develop the proper full-swing drive so that the ball continues in a straight line down an imaginary fairway.

Organization

Players should do this indoors. If you're at a driving range, skip this progression. Players pair off with a partner, each with a driver and four Wiffle golf balls within a "no enter zone." Balls are to be hit off squares of carpet. Ask players to hit from the center of the gym toward a wall. Two lines of players can hit at once (with backs to each other), but designate zones separating the two and keep careful watch for players stepping backward into another player's zone.

Description

After once again reminding players that no one retrieves any ball until you give a release signal, have them practice driving a Wiffle ball using the full swing. Players focus on keeping the head down and using a full pendulum swing.

Challenge

Have players try to drive five in a row in a straight line.

4.19 Driving Balls Off a Mat

Goal

Drive a golf ball in a straight line using the full swing off a tee on a rubber mat.

Organization

Players practice at a driving range with partners. At each tee is a carpet with a rubber tee and an area directly ahead of the tee where players can drive off of tees on grass. Each tee is roped off for safety. Each player has a half-bucket of balls (25) and one driver. If a driving range is not accessible, you can use a field at least 250 yards long, but retrieving balls will waste much class time.

Description

After taking a few warm-up swings at the tee, players practice driving golf balls off the rubber tees on the mat using the full swing to try to drive the ball in a straight line. Partners switch after every five hits. The focus is on a smooth pendulum swing and keeping the head down.

Challenge

Have partners pick a target and challenge each other to see who can hit the straightest drive. Driving ranges usually have markers signifying distances—these work well as targets. Remind players that the contest is to see who drives the *straightest* ball. A ball that hits the target but which has been hooked or sliced is not straight. On a course, this shot would likely fall in the rough.

4.20 Driving Balls Off a Tee

Goal

Drive a golf ball in a straight line using the full swing off a tee.

Organization

Players practice at a driving range with partners. Each tee is roped off for safety. Each player has a half-bucket of balls (25), one driver, and tees. Usually there's an area directly in front of the driving mat where players can practice driving off a regulation tee. If not, ask the attendant where your players can practice driving on grass. If none is available, players can also do this activity at a grassy spot at school using Wiffle balls.

Description

Players practice driving golf balls off a tee they have set in the ground. They use a full swing in an attempt to drive the ball in a straight line. Partners switch after every five hits. Players focus on maintaining a pendulum swing and keeping their head down.

Challenge

Have partners compete against each other to see how many out of five drives they can drive straight without disturbing their tees.

4.21 Play Nine Holes of Golf

Goals

Demonstrate proper putting, chipping, pitching, and driving skills in a regulation game at a golf course while adhering to the rules and etiquette of golf.

Organization

After players have viewed the Professional Golf Association's video "The Spirit of the Game" (available from the U.S. Golf Association) on golf course etiquette and golf rules and have taken a quiz on rules, scoring, terms, etiquette, club selection, and key components of each stroke and error correction (form 4.5), assemble the class at a golf course. Group players into foursomes and stagger the tee times so they all don't begin together. Each player has his or her own set of clubs, tees, and balls.

Form 4.5   Golf Questions

Golf club selection

1. You are over 200 yards from the green. Which wood would you use?
   - (a) 1-wood
   - (b) 3-wood
   - (c) 5-wood
2. You are over 170 yards from the green and decide you would not like to use a wood. What iron would you use?
   - (a) 9-iron
   - (b) 1-iron
   - (c) 6-iron

Golf course etiquette (short answer)

1. After you hit your ball out of a bunker, what are you expected to do?

2. If you are a foursome and a twosome catches up to you, what is the acceptable thing to do?

3. When you are on the green and are taking care of the flag, where should you place it?

Terminology (short answer)

1. Eagle _____
2. Hook _____
   _____
3. Slice_____
   _____
4. Bogey _____
5. Birdie_____
6. Par _____

From *Sport Progressions* by Roy A. Clumpner, 2003, Champaign, IL: Human Kinetics.

Key components/error correction
1. Which of the following are important to success in putting?
   (a) Pendulum swing
   (b) Head over the ball
   (c) Stop the putter at contact with the ball
   (d) "Never up, never in"
2. While driving, you consistently miss the ball. What are you probably doing wrong?
   (a) Using the wrong wood
   (b) Swinging too softly
   (c) Holding your breath
   (d) Looking up as you swing instead of keeping your head down
3. Cross out the answers that don't apply.
   In a sand shot, it is important to:
   (a) swing fully
   (b) stop the club upon contacting the ball
   (c) follow through
   (d) look at the ball during entire swing
4. Which does not apply on an uphill lie if you are a right-handed putter?
   (a) Aim to the right because the ball will go left.
   (b) Play the ball off your back foot.
   (c) Increase the force of the club by two.
   (d) Play the ball off your front foot.

From *Sport Progressions* by Roy A. Clumpner, 2003, Champaign, IL: Human Kinetics.

Form 4.6   Golf Answers

Golf club selection

1. You are over 200 yards from the green. Which wood would you use?

   (a) 1-wood

   (b) 3-wood

   (c) 5-wood

2. You are over 170 yards from the green and decide you would not like to use a wood. What iron would you use?

   (a) 9-iron

   (b) 1-iron

   (c) 6-iron

Golf course etiquette (short answer)

1. After you hit your ball out of a bunker, what are you expected to do?

   Rake the area.

2. If you are a foursome and a twosome catches up to you, what is the acceptable thing to do?

   Allow them to play through.

3. When you are on the green and are taking care of the flag, where should you place it?

   Off the green out of the way.

Terminology (short answer)

1. Eagle two strokes less than par

2. Hook flight path of a ball that curves toward the midline of the golfer's body (i.e., right-handed golfer to the left, left-handed to the right).

3. Slice flight path of a ball that curves away from the midline of the golfer's body (i.e., right-handed golfer to the right, left-handed to the left).

4. Bogey one stroke over par

5. Birdie one stroke less than par

6. Par number of strokes assigned to each hole that represents what would be an expert's score on the hole

From *Sport Progressions* by Roy A. Clumpner, 2003, Champaign, IL: Human Kinetics.

Key components/error correction

1. Which of the following are important to success in putting?
   (a) Pendulum swing
   (b) Head over the ball
   (c) Stop the putter at contact with the ball
   (d) "Never up, never in"

2. While driving, you consistently miss the ball. What are you probably doing wrong?
   (a) Using the wrong wood
   (b) Swinging too softly
   (c) Holding your breath
   (d) Looking up as you swing instead of keeping your head down

3. Cross out the answers that don't apply.

   In a sand shot, it is important to:
   (a) swing fully
   (b) stop the club upon contacting the ball
   (c) follow through
   (d) look at the ball during entire swing

4. Which does not apply on an uphill lie if you are a right-handed putter?
   (a) Aim to the right because the ball will go left.
   (b) Play the ball off your back foot.
   (c) Increase the force of the club by two.
   (d) Play the ball off your front foot.

From *Sport Progressions* by Roy A. Clumpner, 2003, Champaign, IL: Human Kinetics.

Description

Players focus on maintaining their routine for addressing the ball each time and visualizing a perfect stroke and where the ball will go. When players arrive, have them practice putting on the practice green and, if possible, do some chipping. Ideally, they should also practice pitching and driving. Then have each foursome play nine holes of golf. Those who have to wait for their tee time continue to practice putting, perhaps creating games within their foursome. Those who finish first do the same while they wait for the others to complete their round.

Challenge

Have foursomes compete against each other by combining all their scores and comparing them to the combined scores of other teams.

Reference

Owens, DeDe, and Linda Bunker. 1995. *Golf: Steps to Success, 2d ed.* Champaign, IL: Human Kinetics.

CHAPTER 5

Tennis

Tennis is a sport that requires small successful steps to achieve and maintain student interest. When I first taught beginning tennis in a high school class, I sent the students out the first day to rally, expecting them to fall in love with the game, as I had. To my dismay, they quickly became discouraged after having little success. They spent most of their time chasing errant balls over the fence. Ideally, tennis should follow a unit on pickleball or racketball, where the shorter racket and smaller court surface reduce frustration and increase the chance for success. Once those units have been covered, try teaching tennis outdoors. When it rains, tennis can be played in a gym, but it's tough to keep students interested for more than a couple of days when all they're doing is practicing serving and rallying. Instead, I suggest playing pickleball on rainy days, as the game complements tennis perfectly. If you're unfamiliar with pickleball, refer to their Web site at www.usapa.org/pickleball.asp for an explanation of the game and the equipment required. Another alternative is to implement the United States Tennis Association's indoor tennis program, which uses short courts and foam balls. Check out their Web site at www.usta.com for information on the game and equipment.

I have included progressions in this chapter that delay the introduction of the serve and focus on the forehand and backhand groundstrokes. Once these are well developed, you can initiate the basic concepts of the game by putting the ball into play with a drop bounce serve using a forehand groundstroke. From there, other strokes including the regular serve can be added along with additional rules until the complete game is covered. As much as possible, the progressions avoid dead-end drills, such as serving a ball into a fence or wall, which most students find unappealing. Similarly, the progressions begin with an emphasis on controlling the ball, because no one likes chasing balls a long distance. To avoid lost balls, give out one ball to each player as students enter the class and hold them responsible for that ball when they exit the class. If a ball is hit over the fence, ask the student who hit the ball to retrieve it immediately, before he or she forgets where it landed.

When teaching, use all the space on the courts, not just the playing area. For example, many of the beginning progressions involve one player with his or her back to the net, tossing the ball to a partner (the hitter) stationed at the baseline. Using this setup, one court can accommodate eight players (see figure 5.1). Once players begin to hit over the net, only four players can be accommodated on a court, though additional players can be added if you use the space between courts. Some courts are laid out with fences set far back from the baseline. This is another area you can put to good use. Buildings adjacent to the courts can often provide adequate wall space for groundstroke development after students can control the ball and, in some cases, even parking lots can be blocked off for rally use.

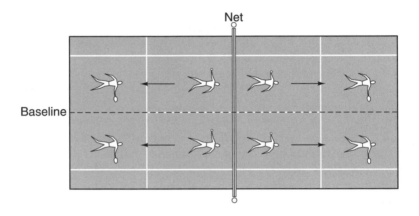

Figure 5.1   Court setup with tosser.

The progressions have partners initially playing a modified game of tennis over the net on a halfcourt serving and hitting groundstrokes directly across to a partner rather than diagonally (to make best use of court space). Ideally, you'd have one court per partner group, but this is unrealistic, so hitting diagonally is delayed until doubles play is initiated.

For more information about the techniques I introduce in these progressions, please refer to *Tennis: Steps to Success, 2nd edition* (Brown 1995).

■ After following the progressions described in this chapter, beginning students should be able to play both a game of singles and a game of doubles, using the following skills:

- Forehand and backhand groundstroke grips
- Ready position
- Shuffle step
- Crossover step
- Forehand return
- One- and two-hand backhand return
- Backscratch serve
- Overhead serve
- Forehand volley
- One- and two-hand backhand volley
- Rushing the net
- Forehand lob
- One- and two-hand backhand lob
- Smash
- Diagonal serve

5.1 Self-Volley With Forehand Groundstroke Grip

Goals

To experiment with the various forehand groundstroke grips and become familiar with the speed with which the ball rebounds off the racket and off the ground surface.

Organization

Players spread out in self-space, each with a ball and a racket.

Description

Briefly explain and demonstrate the various forehand groundstroke grips (Eastern, Western, and semi-Western grips), focusing on keeping the wrist rigid and locked. (For drawings of the various grips, please see *Tennis: Steps to Success, 2nd edition* [Brown 1995].) Then have each player bounce a ball off the racket surface no more than three feet into the air 20 to 30 times, then onto the ground in a controlled bounce 20 to 30 times while experimenting with each grip.

Challenge

Have players walk around the courts, using one of the forehand groundstroke grips, alternating between ground and air every couple of hits.

5.2 Self-Volley With Backhand Groundstroke Grip

Goal

To experiment with backhand grips to see which is most comfortable and which controls the ball best.

Organization

Players spread out in self-space, each with a ball and a racket.

Description

Briefly explain and demonstrate the proper one-hand (Eastern, Western, and semi-Western) and two-hand backhand groundstroke grips, focusing on keeping the wrist rigid and locked. Have each player experiment using these grips while bouncing a ball off the racket surface no more than three feet into the air 20 to 30 times, then onto the ground in a controlled bounce 20 to 30 times. (For examples of the various grips, please see *Tennis: Steps to Success, 2nd edition* [Brown 1995].)

Challenge

Players walk around the courts, using one of the backhand groundstroke grips, alternating between ground and air every couple of hits.

5.3 Mirror Ready Position, Crossover Step, Forehand and Backhand Groundstrokes (Stationary)

Goals

Develop the proper crossover step and forehand and backhand groundstroke form; make the appropriate grip change from forehand to backhand and backhand to forehand.

Organization

Players scatter around the court with their rackets in self-space in spots from which they can see you clearly at the front of the class. Be sure there's enough room for players to swing their rackets without hitting anyone. Have left-handers form one row in the back.

Description

Explain and demonstrate the ready position, crossover step, and the forehand and backhand groundstroke. Position yourself with your back to the class and, while giving cues to the class, proceed in slow motion from the ready position to perform a crossover step and forehand and then a crossover step and backhand on an imaginary ball. Make sure players can clearly see how you change your grip for the backhand. (Have players choose which backhand they prefer, the Eastern, Western, semi-Western, or two-hand backhand.) Have the class follow your motions and imitate each stroke you make. Keep your footwork to a minimum of one crossover step. As players grasp the mechanics of the stroke and the grip change, speed up the drill. Left-handed players in the back row follow along except they do a forehand when you demonstrate a backhand, and vice versa. Focus on returning to racket-ready position on the balls of the feet with knees bent ready to react quickly.

Challenge

Mix up the strokes so players don't relax.

5.4	**Mirror Ready Position, Shuffle and Crossover Step, Forehand and Backhand Groundstrokes (Moving)**

Goals

Develop the shuffle and crossover step with a forehand and backhand groundstroke.

Organization

Each player should have a racket in self-space in scattered positions and be able to see you at the front of the class. Be sure there's enough room for players to swing their rackets without hitting anyone. Left-handers form a row in the back.

Description

Explain and demonstrate the racket-ready position, shuffle, and the cross-step. Then position with your back to the class in racket-ready position and proceed at half-speed to perform a shuffle and then a cross-step with a forehand and then a backhand groundstroke on an imaginary ball. Move no more than three or four strides to the front, side, and back of the court, mimicking typical court movements in a game. Have the class follow your motions on the court and each stroke you make. As players grasp the footwork mechanics and the stroke, speed up and increase the distance you travel until it duplicates the normal movement patterns on a court in a game. Have left-handers in the back row go in the direction you move but use the opposite stroke (e.g., if you move right and do a forehand, the left-handers also move right but do a backhand). Remind them to always return to racket-ready position in the center of the court at the baseline. Focus on moving quickly and getting your racket back as you move.

Challenge

Speed up the activity and mix it up. Have a player lead the class and see if others can keep up. Remind them to always return to ready position.

5.5   Underhand Toss and Forehand Return (Stationary)

Goal

Develop the proper forehand groundstroke form and control before adding movement.

Organization

Players pair off in partners on a quarter of the court. Each partner has a racket, and each twosome has one ball. One partner (tosser) stands about two feet from the net with back to the net and holding a ball. The partner (hitter) stands on the same side of the net at the baseline in the middle of the halfcourt with racket in ready position (see figure 5.1, p. 78).

Description

The tosser underhand tosses the ball on one bounce to the forehand-side of the hitter so the hitter does not have to move. The hitter returns the ball under control directly back to the tosser, using the forehand groundstroke (either the Eastern, Western, or semi-Western grip). The hitter controls the ball so that the tosser doesn't have to move. Have players perform 10 trials, then rotate. If you find that balls are consistently being hit over the tosser's head, switch positions so that the tosser is at the baseline and the hitter at the net, thereby reducing time spent retrieving balls (because the fence or wall surrounding the courts stops the ball). Only do this if you need to, though, because the ideal setup is to hit toward the net, as this mirrors real tennis. Players focus on getting the racket back, locking the wrist, and swinging low to high.

Challenge

Speed up the tempo and increase the speed of the toss.

5.6   Underhand Toss With Backhand Return (Stationary)

Goal

Develop proper backhand groundstroke form and control before adding movement.

Organization

Partners pair off on a quarter of the court. Each partner has a racket, and each twosome has one ball (see figure 5.1, p. 78). One partner (tosser) stands with back to the net (about two feet from the net) with a ball. The other partner (hitter) stands on the same side of the net at the baseline in the middle of the halfcourt with racket in ready position.

Description

The tosser underhand tosses the ball on one bounce to the backhand-side of the hitter so the hitter does not have to move. The hitter hits the ball directly back to the tosser, under control, using a backhand groundstroke (Eastern, Western, semi-Western, or two-hand backhand). The hitter should control the ball so the tosser doesn't have to move. Players do 10 trials, then rotate. Players focus on quickly changing grips, getting the racket back, and keeping the lead elbow away from the body.

Challenge

Speed up the tempo and increase the speed of the toss.

5.7	Underhand Toss and Forehand and Backhand Return (Stationary)

Goals

Be able to change to the appropriate grip depending on the groundstroke and execute the proper form of the chosen groundstroke.

Organization

Partners pair off on a quarter of a court. Each partner has a racket, and each twosome has one ball (see figure 5.1, p. 78). One partner (tosser) stands with back to the net (about two feet from the net) with a ball. The other partner (hitter) stands on the same side of the net at the baseline in the middle of the halfcourt, racket in ready position.

Description

The tosser underhand tosses the ball on one bounce to the forehand or backhand side of the hitter without making the hitter move. The tosser mixes up the tosses so the hitter isn't sure which side the ball is coming to. The hitter hits the ball directly back to the tosser, under control, using the proper groundstroke. The hitter should control the ball so the tosser doesn't have to move. Players do 10 trials, then rotate. Players focus on returning to racket-ready position and changing to the correct grip while getting the racket into hitting position.

Challenge

Speed up the tempo and increase the speed by throwing the ball overhand over the net so that it bounces on the other side of the net.

5.8 Underhand Toss and Forehand and Backhand Return (Moving)

Goals

Be able to change to the right grip depending on the groundstroke and execute the proper form of the chosen groundstroke while moving.

Organization

Players pair off in partners on a quarter of a court. Each partner has a racket, and each twosome has one ball (see figure 5.1). One partner (tosser) stands with back to the net (about two feet from the net) with a ball. The partner (hitter) stands on the same side of the net at the baseline in the middle of the halfcourt in racket-ready position.

Description

The tosser underhand tosses the ball on one bounce to either the forehand or backhand side of the hitter so that the hitter has to move to get to it. The tosser mixes up tosses so the hitter can't tell which side the ball is coming to. The hitter, using the shuffle and cross-step, moves into position to return the ball and hits it back to the tosser, under control, using the proper groundstroke. The hitter then returns to the center of the halfcourt at the baseline in racket-ready position. The hitter should control the ball so the tosser doesn't have to move. Players do 10 trials, then rotate. Players focus on getting the racket back while quickly moving to get into position. They remain under control while hitting the ball and then return quickly to racket-ready position in the center of the halfcourt at the baseline.

Challenge

Speed up the tempo and increase the speed of the toss. Look one way and toss the ball overhand on the bounce to another area.

5.9 Overhand Toss Over Net and Forehand and Backhand Return (Moving)

Goals

Be able to change to the right grip for each groundstroke, move into proper position to return the ball, execute the proper form of the chosen groundstroke, and return to the baseline in ready position for the next toss.

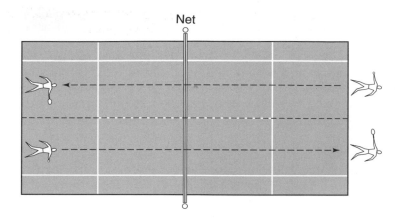

Figure 5.2   Setup for Overhand Toss Over Net and Forehand and Backhand Return (Moving).

Organization

Partners pair off on a halfcourt. One partner has a racket, and each twosome has one ball. One partner stands at one baseline (tosser), the other partner (hitter) stands across the net at the other baseline in the center of the halfcourt in racket-ready position (figure 5.2).

Description

The tosser overhand tosses the ball over the net, where it bounces on either the forehand or backhand side of the hitter. The tosser mixes tosses so the hitter can't tell which side the ball will come to. The hitter, using the shuffle and cross-step, moves into position to return the ball and hits it directly back to the tosser over the net on one bounce into the court, under control and using the proper groundstroke. The hitter then returns to the center of the halfcourt at the baseline and assumes ready position. The hitter should control the ball so that the tosser doesn't have to move. Players do 10 trials, then rotate. Players focus on getting the racket back while quickly moving to get into position, remaining under control when hitting the ball, and returning quickly to racket-ready position in the center of the halfcourt at the baseline.

Challenge

Speed up the tempo and increase the speed of the toss. Look one way and toss the ball overhand to another area. After tossing the first ball, have a second ball ready to toss as soon as the hitter is getting into ready position for the second hit.

5.10 Forehand and Backhand Rally Over Net

Goals

Be able to rally using forehands and backhands with proper form and footwork, change to the correct grip depending on the groundstroke, move into proper position to hit the ball, execute the proper form of the chosen groundstroke, and return to the baseline in racket-ready position for the next hit.

Organization

Partners pair off on a halfcourt. Each player has a racket, and each twosome has one ball (see figure 5.2, p. 85).

Description

Both players begin at their baselines. To begin, one player performs a drop bounce serve by dropping the ball to the ground on the forehand side and, on the rebound, hitting a forehand to the partner over the net, who then returns the ball after it bounces. Play continues as long as the ball bounces in play. Players should let the ball bounce and always use the correct groundstroke, keeping the ball in play as long as they can. This is a cooperative activity. Players focus on moving to the ball quickly and getting set up to hit the ball. On the backhand stroke, remind them to avoid getting too close to the ball.

Challenge

Have a contest to see which group of partners can rally the most times without an error.

5.11 Forehand and Backhand Game

Goals

Be able to rally using forehands and backhands with proper form and footwork, change to the right grip for each stroke, move into proper position to hit the ball, execute the proper form of the chosen stroke, and return to the baseline in racket-ready position. All of this is done under game-like conditions.

Organization

Partners pair off on a halfcourt (see figure 5.2, p. 85). Each partner has a racket, and each twosome has one ball.

Description

Explain tennis scoring and then have partners play a game of tennis as a competitive activity. The game begins with a drop bounce serve from the baseline. Play begins if the ball lands in the service court *directly opposite* the server. (Not diagonally—as I mentioned in the introduction, while serving diagonally is the official way to serve, more players can play on limited court space if serves are directly across. Players tend to make an easy transition from serving directly across to serving diagonally. Later, during games of singles, diagonal serving is introduced.) If the ball does not land in the service box, the player tries a second serve. If that one misses too, then the opponent serves. Once the ball is served into the service box, play begins. Players use either a forehand or backhand and should let the ball bounce. Any disputes are played over. Balls landing on the line are good.

Challenge

Rotate players on the outside courts one halfcourt clockwise every five minutes to expose players to different styles and speed of play.

5.12 Throw a Tennis Ball Into the Service Court

Goal

Develop the motion of the overhead service.

Organization

Players pair off across from each other behind the baseline with one tennis ball on one half of a court.

Description

Demonstrate an overhead baseball throw from behind the baseline into the partner's service court (directly across from partner, not diagonally). Then have partners throw the ball back and forth into each other's service court, allowing the ball to bounce before catching it, using the same arm that they intend to serve with. Players should focus on turning sideways to their partners, transferring weight onto the back foot as they bring the ball back into a 2 o'clock position, and transferring weight onto their front foot as they throw.

Challenge

Do the throw all in one smooth motion.

5.13 Serve Toss

Goal

Develop a toss for the serve that's consistently at the correct height and distance from the server.

Organization

Scattered positions on courts, each player with a ball and racket lined up behind the baseline.

Description

Briefly explain and demonstrate the stance, service toss, weight transfer, and racket position for a "backscratch" serve using the overhead throw as an analogy. Have players practice tossing the ball so it reaches the proper height for the serve (about 10 feet) and lands about a foot ahead of the front foot (left foot if right-handed). As the ball is tossed, weight transfers from the front to the back foot as the racket comes into the backscratch serving position. Players may mimic hitting the ball with the racket but should not come into contact with it. If they are incapable of doing both, just have them toss and do the weight transfer while getting the racket into position. Focus on keeping the tossing arm completely straight and not breaking the wrist.

Challenge

Place a hot spot (a circular piece of flat rubber) or draw a circle with chalk the size of a paper plate about a foot from the server's front foot. See if the server can consistently toss 8 out of 10 at the correct height using the serve toss, keeping the tossing arm straight, and having the ball land on the hot spot.

5.14   Toss and Backscratch Serve

Goals

Develop timing so that the racket contacts the ball at the proper height and angle. Learn not to hit balls that are not successfully tossed.

Organization

Partners pair off on a halfcourt, with one ball and rackets for each. The serving partner stands one large step in front of the baseline for a greater chance of success. The receiving player has heels on the baseline in the center of the court directly opposite the server in racket-ready position (see figure 5.3).

Description

Briefly explain the serving rules, including foot faults, and demonstrate the complete backscratch serve. Have players practice tossing a ball, transferring weight, and serving the ball from a backscratch position into the court directly across from each other. (If there's enough court space to allow just two players per court, go ahead and serve diagonally.) It's important for players not to try to serve a poorly tossed ball. Tell the players to catch the ball and re-toss it until it's tossed well. The receiving partner is in racket-ready position

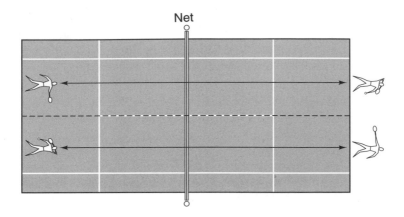

Figure 5.3 Setup for Toss and Backscratch Serve.

near the baseline. The receiver catches the served ball and serves it back to his or her partner. Focus on determining if the toss is a good one or not and stopping if the toss is not good.

Challenge

See if players can hit three out of five serves into the service court from behind the baseline without committing a foot fault (stepping on or over the line onto the court before contacting the ball).

5.15 Backscratch Serve and Rally

Goals

Serve the ball into the service court. The serve receiver develops the ability to decide if a serve is in the service court or out of it (and thus whether to return the serve) and whether to use a forehand or backhand in the return.

Organization

Partners pair off on a halfcourt, with one ball and rackets for each. For a greater chance of success, the server stands one large step in front of the baseline. Receiving player has heels on the baseline in the center of the court directly opposite the server (see figure 5.3).

Description

One partner serves using the backscratch serve. (Remind servers not to try to serve a poorly tossed ball.) If the backscratch serve falls into the service court, players rally the ball on the halfcourt, using forehands and backhands only.

The receiver is back in ready position near the baseline. If the ball isn't served into the service court, the receiver doesn't try to return the ball. Instead, the server continues to serve until the ball falls into the service court, at which time a rally ensues. After three successful serves followed by rallies, switch servers. When the server consistently gets three of four serves successfully into the service court, have them back up behind the baseline. Players focus on moving to return the ball and getting back into receiving position to return the next shot.

Challenge

Ask servers to try to serve the ball into the court near each sideline of the service court so that the receiver must use both forehands and backhands and not favor the forehand.

5.16 Halfcourt Backscratch Serve and Groundstroke Game

Goals

Learn basic tennis terminology and rules of singles' tennis and develop the backscratch serve and groundstrokes in a competitive situation.

Organization

Partners play on a halfcourt, with one ball and rackets for each. The server stands behind the baseline. The receiver has heels on the baseline in the center of the court directly opposite the server (see figure 5.3, p. 89). The server gets two chances to get the ball into the service court. If unsuccessful, the receiving partner gets one point. The server continues to serve from the same spot (since the game is being played on a halfcourt, there's no opportunity to move from one side of the court to the other). The basic tennis rules are followed in that once a player scores four points and wins by two points, the game is over, and the other player serves. Most of the rules of tennis can be applied. Please see *Tennis: Steps to Success, 2nd edition* (Brown 1995) for a more detailed description of scoring in tennis.

Description

Briefly explain the tennis rules for the halfcourt game. Players should move quickly to the ball, at the same time bringing their racket back. Once the ball is hit, the player returns to racket-ready position in the middle of the court at the baseline. Have players backscratch serve and play a modified game of tennis using only the strokes covered so far. Tell players the ball must bounce before they hit it. Have players focus on getting into racket-ready position as the opponent prepares to hit the ball.

Challenge

Have players try to hit the ball to a court space not covered by their opponent. If the class is picking up the concept of four points, introduce tennis terminology of love, deuce, and in and out, but only if they understand the concept of four points.

5.17 Full-Swing Serve Crosscourt

Goals

Develop the full-swing serve and get into proper position on the court to receive the serve.

Organization

Partners play on a halfcourt, diagonal to each other for the first time, with one ball for the twosome and rackets for each. The server stands behind the baseline on one side of the court as close to the center line as possible. Receiving player has heels on baseline or slightly behind, near the singles' sideline.

Description

Briefly explain and demonstrate the full-swing serve, the regulation service court, and the proper court position in which to receive a serve. Have players hit full-swing serves back and forth to each other, allowing the ball to bounce in the proper service court. Be sure to serve from each side of the court. Players focus on turning sideways to the direction they intend to serve to and contacting the ball at the 11 o'clock position.

Challenge

Have teams of two compete against each other to see who can get the most serves in. Each player counts the total number of serves he or she hits into the service court out of 10 serves (5 from each side). Combine the two scores out of 20 serves, and then let the other team serve.

5.18 Singles' Game on Full Court: Serve and Groundstrokes

Goals

Develop proper court positioning to receive the serve and forehand and backhand groundstrokes; execute the full-swing serve and forehand and backhand groundstrokes in competitive singles' play on a full court.

Organization

Two partners play at each full court with two balls and two rackets. (Players waiting to play can rally in the space between the courts, along the back of each court (safe space permitting), or hit against a wall. If the class is so large that there's extensive wait time, skip this section and go on to the next progression—or put those waiting to work as lines persons, umpires, and ball chasers.) To determine who serves first, have players play Rock, Scissors, Paper or flip a coin. If a served ball is outside the service box, the receiver shouts "out" to let the server know that the ball is not in play. A served ball on the line is considered a good serve.

Description

Review tennis rules, court etiquette, and scoring. Partners compete in singles' play, using "No Ad" scoring (i.e., the first player to win four points wins the game). The serve and forehand and backhand groundstrokes are the only skills players are allowed to use. The only other rule modification is that the serve must be hit into the service court to begin each point (a server can't lose a point for double-faulting). When two faults in a row are served, the server either moves in front of the baseline to serve or performs a backscratch serve (or both). Have players focus on hitting to open areas of the court rather than directly at their opponent. Have them hit to the backhand-side as much as they hit to the forehand-side of the court.

Challenge

Use regular scoring and serving rules. (See *Tennis: Steps to Success, 2nd edition* [Brown 1995].)

5.19 Forehand Volley

Goals

Develop proper form, racket position, footwork, and punching action of the forehand volley.

Organization

Two partners take opposite sides of the net, with no more than four players on each side of the net (eight players total on the court). The tosser stands no farther than 5 feet from the net. The player volleying stands 6 to 10 feet from the net on the other side (figure 5.4). Each partner group should have one ball and one racket.

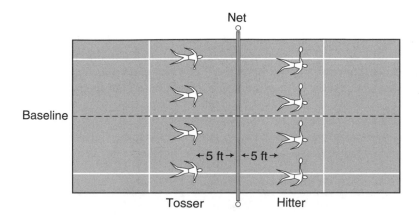

Net

Baseline

←5 ft→ ←5 ft→

Tosser   Hitter

Figure 5.4   Setup for four partner groups to a court.

Description

Explain and demonstrate the forehand volley; have the class shadow you as you show proper form. Then have one partner underhand toss the ball to the forehand side of their partner to a position where he or she can volley the ball back to the tosser. Focus on punching the ball instead of stroking the ball.

Challenges

Speed up the toss and vary the height. Toss directly at the chest of the hitter to force him or her to move into correct hitting position. If players are able, combine the forehand volley with the backhand volley (next progression) to save time.

5.20   Backhand Volley

Goals

Develop proper form, racket position, footwork, and punching action of the backhand volley.

Organization

Two partners take opposite sides of the net, with no more than four players on each side of the net (eight players total on the court). The tosser stands no farther than 5 feet from the net. The player volleying stands 6 to 10 feet from the net on the other side (see figure 5.4).

Description

Explain and demonstrate the backhand volley; have the class shadow you as you show proper form. Then have one partner toss the ball to the backhand side of their partner to a position where he or she can volley the ball back to the tosser. Focus on punching the ball instead of stroking the ball.

Challenge

Speed up the toss and vary the height. Toss directly at the chest of the hitter to force him or her to move into correct hitting position.

5.21 Forehand and Backhand Volley

Goal

Develop quick reactions to the side the toss is made, using the proper stroke to return the volley.

Organization

Two partners take opposite sides of the net, with no more than four players on each side of the net (eight players total on the court). The tosser stands no farther than 5 feet from the net. The player volleying stands 6 to 10 feet from the net on the other side (see figure 5.4, p. 93).

Description

Have one partner toss the ball either to the forehand or backhand side of the other partner to a position where he or she can volley the ball back to the tosser. Focus on punching the ball instead of stroking the ball.

Challenge

Speed up the toss and vary the height. Toss directly at the chest of the hitter to force him or her to move into correct hitting position.

5.22 Drop Bounce, Groundstroke, and Volley

Goal

Develop the ability to return a forehand groundstroke delivered from a long distance (baseline) by volleying at the net.

Organization

Partners on opposite sides of the net on a halfcourt. Players have two balls and two rackets.

Description

To begin, one partner standing at the baseline drop bounces a ball and hits it over the net (using a forehand) directly to the other partner, who is in a volleying position on the other side of the net, about 8 to 10 feet from the net. The receiving partner uses the appropriate volley (forehand or backhand), after which the ball is dead. The partner who begins the drill hits the ball directly to the receiver and doesn't try to avoid the receiver. After six volleys, partners switch positions. Players should get their rackets on the ball without swinging but rather punching the ball over the net.

Challenge

See if you can keep a rally going with one player at the net volleying and the other returning groundstrokes directly at the partner at the net.

5.23 Rush the Net and Volley

Goals

Develop the ability to rush the net after performing a groundstroke, get into proper position to volley, and execute a volley.

Organization

Two partners play on opposite sides of the net on a halfcourt. Each partner has a racket, and each twosome has one ball.

Description

Both partners begin at their baselines. One partner initiates play by a drop bounce and forehand drive deep into the other partner's court and then immediately rushes to the net to position for a volley. The receiving partner returns the ball with a forehand or backhand directly at the partner at the net, who then returns the shot with a volley. Play stops, and players repeat the drill. After six trials, partners switch positions. Get your racket on the ball and don't swing but rather punch the ball.

Challenge

Make the exercise a rally game, with a point won by the player whose opponent can't return the ball. No lobs are permitted. Alternate who initiates play with the drop bounce.

5.24 Rally With Groundstrokes and Volley

Goal

Use the volley in a game-like situation.

Organization

Two partners on one half of court, each with a racket and one ball for the twosome.

Description

This is a competitive activity. Both partners begin at their baselines. One partner initiates play with a drop bounce and forehand drive deep into the other partner's court. Players then rally, using forehands, backhands, and volleys. Players should hit no more than three groundstrokes in a row before they must rush the net for a volley. Players can hit the ball at or past the defender only chest high or lower (no lobs). Anything above chest high is declared out. Players focus on quickly getting to the net for a volley and getting their racket on the ball.

Challenge

When one partner goes to the net to volley, the other must do the same following the next hit.

5.25 Lob

Goals

Develop the touch needed to lob the ball with either the forehand or backhand, over the racket reach of an opponent at the net waiting to volley. Develop the ability when volleying at the net to turn and run to the backcourt to return a lob after it bounces.

Organization

Two partners with rackets and one ball play in a practice area on the court or on a halfcourt. The player who is lobbing stands at midcourt with a ball; the other player stands on the other side of the court near the net, as if ready to volley a return.

Description

Briefly explain and demonstrate the lob, focusing on lifting the ball on the racket. Then the player with the ball drop bounces it and lobs it (alternating forehand and backhand strokes) high over the racket reach of the partner waiting to volley at the net so that the ball lands in the back third of the partner's court. The partner at the net waits until the ball is hit, then runs back and attempts to return the lob with a forehand or backhand stroke.

Challenge

Lob the ball just high enough that it drops before the opponent poaching at the net can retreat and return it. Retreat back to return the lob with a groundstroke down the sideline of the court.

5.26 Rally Using Drop Bounce, Forehand, Rush the Net, and Lob

Goals

React to an opponent's rushing the net by implementing a lob stroke. When at the net, react to a lob by recovering and returning the lob after it bounces.

Organization

Two partners with rackets and a ball play on half a court. Each player begins from the baseline.

Description

This is a cooperative activity. From the baseline, one partner drop bounces and hits a forehand deep to their partner's court and then rushes the net. The receiving partner hits a lob (forehand or backhand) into the opponent's backcourt (ideally on backhand side) over the opponent's outstretched racket. If the opponent cannot hit the lob at the net, he or she recovers and runs to the back of the court and tries to return the lob with a forehand or backhand. Switch after five trials. Players should focus on getting into position to perform the lob and keeping the ball on the racket as long as possible.

Challenge

Every so often hit a groundstroke right at the person at the net instead of lobbing the ball; this keeps the player from inching back to return the expected lob.

5.27 Rally Using Groundstrokes, Rushing the Net, Volleys, and Lobs

Goals

React to an opponent rushing the net by hitting a lob. When at the net, react to a lob by recovering and returning the lob with a forehand or backhand. Play occurs in a game-like situation.

Organization

Two partners with rackets and a ball play on half a court. Each player begins from the baseline.

Description

This is a competitive activity. Play begins with a drop bounce and forehand from one of the players. Players then hit groundstrokes, volleys, and lobs, after each shot returning to the center of the court at the baseline in racket-ready position. Players try to keep their opponent off balance by hitting to areas not covered. Players use forehands, backhands, volleys, and lobs during play. Smashes are not allowed.

Challenge

Play a game keeping score, awarding two points for scoring with a lob.

5.28 Singles' Game Using Serve, Groundstrokes, Volleys, and Lobs

Goal

Use volleys and lobs in competitive singles' play on a full court.

Organization

Two players play at each fullcourt with two balls and two rackets. One player serves to the other. If the serve is out, the receiver shouts "out" to let the server know the ball is not in play. A serve on the line is considered a good serve. Regular serving rules apply (e.g., double-faults result in loss of point). Players waiting to play can rally in the spaces between the courts, along the back of each court (if it's safe) or against a wall. If the class is so large that there's extensive wait time, skip this section and go on to the next progression, or put those waiting to work as line judges, umpires, and ball chasers. (This singles' game is set up for two players on one court. If court space is limited, the game can be played on a halfcourt, with players serving to the service court directly opposite rather than diagonally—or play a doubles game, as described in the next progression).

Description

Players compete using No Ad scoring (the first player to win four points wins the game). The serve, forehand, backhand, volley, and lob are the only skills allowed—no smashes. Encourage players to rush the net and volley whenever possible. Players focus on getting back into receiving position at the baseline once a stroke is made and hitting to open areas on the opponent's court.

Challenge

Use regular scoring rather than No Ad scoring. Give a player an extra point if the volley results in an immediate score (a "winner").

5.29 Doubles' Game: Serve, Groundstrokes, Volleys, and Lobs

Goals

Exhibit an understanding of doubles play (rules and positioning) and execute the volley and lob as necessary. Experiment with up-and-back and side-to-side doubles' positioning and choose which works best with a partner.

Organization

Four players play on one court (one team on each side).

Description

Explain and demonstrate doubles' play, including player positioning (up and back and side by side), court lines, player and court rotation, and strategy. Have partners compete in doubles' play using No Ad scoring (first team to win four points wins the game). The serve, forehand, backhand, volley, and lob are the only skills allowed—no smashes. Partners should experiment with the up-and-back and side-to-side court positioning and choose whichever they feel most comfortable with (or alternate if players are ready for this). Encourage players to be aggressive and rush the net rather than stand in the backcourt. Encourage those players facing a net player to aim their returns down the sidelines to avoid giving the opponent an easy volley. Focus on taking advantage to rush the net when the ball forces an opponent deep.

Challenge

Alter the scoring, giving extra points for a volley that results in a winning shot or immediate score.

5.30 Smash

Goals

Move into proper position and demonstrate correct smash stroke form, timing, and placement.

Organization

Two partners with one racket and five balls play on half a court. The tosser stands at the service line on one side of the net. The player with the racket stands in the other court, halfway between the net and service line.

Description

Explain and demonstrate the smash and perform several shadow smashes. The tosser underhands the ball high to the smasher; the smasher smashes the tossed ball down over the net into the court with a high bounce. Players switch after five trials. Players focus on assuming the backscratch position and hitting the ball at the 11 o'clock position.

Challenge

Toss the ball so that the smasher has to cover more areas of the court. Have the smasher smash to various areas on the court.

5.31 Drop Bounce, Lob, and Smash

Goals

Move into proper position and return a lob with a smash, using proper technique, and place the ball in the opponent's court.

Organization

Two partners play with rackets and two balls on a halfcourt. The partner lobbing the ball is at one baseline, while the smasher stands on the other side of the net, about midcourt.

Description

From the baseline, one partner does a drop bounce and lobs to the player at midcourt, who smashes the ball back. Players do five hits and then rotate. Players focus on moving to get into position, getting the racket ready in the backscratch, and contacting the ball at the 11 o'clock position.

Challenge

Place the smash in an area where your partner is susceptible. Attempt to return the smash any way you can.

5.32   Drop Bounce, Forehand, Volley, Lob, and Smash

Goal

Use the smash in a game-like situation.

Organization

Two partners with rackets and two balls play on half a court. Both partners begin at their baselines.

Description

This is a cooperative activity. One partner drop bounces and hits a forehand deep to his or her partner and then rushes the net. The receiver returns the ball with a lob. The player at the net retreats to get into position and then performs a smash into the opponent's court. Players switch after three attempts. Players focus on moving into position, getting their racket into the backscratch, and contacting the ball at the 11 o'clock position.

Challenge

See if you can smash three of five in a row into your opponent's court.

5.33   Rally Using Groundstrokes, Volley, Lob, and Smash

Goal

React to a lob by recovering and returning the lob with a smash in a game situation.

Organization

Two partners with rackets and one ball play on half a court. Each player begins from the baseline.

Description

This is a competitive activity. Players rally back and forth, beginning with a drop bounce and forehand stroke. After each stroke, they return to midcourt at the baseline, racket ready. Players should hit forehands, backhands, volleys, lobs, and smashes at every opportunity. Encourage them to rush the net when the chance arises. Players focus on moving quickly to get into position to hit the ball while bringing the racket back.

Challenge

See if each player can use all the strokes in one rally.

5.34 Doubles' Game Using Serve, Groundstrokes, Volley, Lob, and Smash

Goals

Exhibit an understanding of doubles' play (rules and positioning) and execute the smash when appropriate.

Organization

Four players (two sets of partners) play on one court with two balls for the court and a racket for each partner.

Description

After an explanation and demonstration of doubles' play, including court positioning and strategy, partners compete in doubles' play using regular tennis scoring. Players should only use the skills they have learned, including the serve, forehand, backhand, rushing the net, volley, lob, and smash. Regular serving rules apply (double-faults result in loss of point). Encourage players to be aggressive and rush the net rather than play back the entire point.

Challenge

Alter scoring by giving extra points for a smash that results in a point.

Reference

Brown, Jim. 1995. *Tennis: Steps to Success. 2d ed.* Champaign, IL: Human Kinetics.

PART III

Progressions
for Team Sports

Basketball

$\mathbf{B}$asketball is one of the most difficult of all units to teach correctly and successfully because it involves so many complicated skills. For example, we often take a lay-up for granted, but if you break the skill down and analyze it, it turns out to be quite complicated. You have to be able to control a ball by dribbling it while moving with your head up. The lay-up also requires a great deal of timing and coordination of the eyes, feet, and hands. You must take off from the correct leg (inside leg) at the correct angle and distance from the basket while bringing the ball up and judging the exact moment you have achieved maximum height before releasing the shot. And this is just one skill! Add pivoting; passing and receiving; timing rebounds; and individual, dual, and team skills, and basketball becomes one of the most difficult sports to teach.

Two primary skills to teach right away are shooting and dribbling, as opposed to passing, rebounding, or defending. When a player receives the ball in a game, the first thing he or she does is look for an opportunity to shoot and score a basket, which is the object of the game. This is why you teach shooting at the beginning of a unit, along with dribbling, another essential skill. Dribbling allows a player to get past a defender for a higher percentage shot. Starting with shooting and dribbling also makes sense because players enjoy both of these skills and will naturally pick up a ball and shoot and dribble on their own without being asked. I don't remember ever seeing a player enter a gym, pick up a ball, and voluntarily practice rebounding or passing against a wall. Finally, by introducing shooting and dribbling at the start, you can correct bad habits and spend more time on developing these two most fundamental skills of the game.

Three other essential but commonly overlooked offensive skills you'll want to focus on are pivoting, freeing yourself to receive the ball through the use of V cuts, and screening/cutting (what to do when you don't have the ball). Beginning players generally don't know how to prevent a defender from stealing the ball from them once they have stopped dribbling (thus the need to pivot), how to free themselves from a defender to receive a pass (V cut), or what they should do when they don't have the ball (screen a defender or cut to an open area). If you practice these skills early on, you'll soon notice a marked increase in continuity of play along with an elevation in player confidence.

For the most part, basketball is made up of individual and dual offensive moves on a halfcourt, so our focus in this unit is on these skills. A light overview of rebounding and basic principles of man-to-man defense is appropriate, but the longer you can delay teaching defensive skills, the greater the chance your players will succeed in their offensive skills and not be thwarted by defenders. When you do introduce defense, I recommend starting with man-to-man. Leave zone defenses for more advanced classes. Skills such as fast-break play (boxing out, rebounding, and outlet passing), fullcourt presses, and halfcourt traps should also be left to the advanced class or the coach of a competitive team. Most schools don't have space to play fullcourt games without having players wait on the sidelines, which should be avoided whenever possible. Finally, I leave it up to you whether you want to include three-point shooting. I prefer to develop and emphasize the essence of offensive basketball: the ability to work together for a high-percentage shot using passing and screening. I'd save three-point shooting for an intermediate or advanced class. Besides, beginning players often don't have the strength to shoot a three-point shot using proper form. They tend to alter their form for the long shot, which leads to bad habits that are hard to break later on.

The progressions in this chapter move from individual skill development (1 v 1) to dual skills (2 v 2) and team skills (3 v 3) and end with 5 v 5 halfcourt play. Both regulation and junior basketballs should be available for all players, along with enough baskets so that no more than four players are shooting at each basket. You can increase the number of baskets by having them put up in each corner of the gym. If there's enough money, buy four portable goals and place them in the center circle of the basketball court.

I advise having beginning players develop their dominant shooting hand during class and leaving the nondominant hand for them to practice and develop outside of class on their own time. Experience has taught me that this skill is extremely difficult for beginning players to develop in class. Class time is better spent working on more functional offensive skills.

Many of the activities in the progressions require each player or a pair of players to have one basketball to work on the skill being introduced. I'll assume you know already to have enough basketballs on hand to meet the needs of your students. When an activity requires a player or pair of players to use more than one basketball, I'll mention this in the activity's Organization section.

■ After following the progressions, beginning students should be able to play in a game of halfcourt, 3 v 3 basketball, using all of these skills:
  • Set shot
  • Triple threat
  • Controlled dribble
  • Speed dribble
  • Directional dribble
  • Lay-up shot
  • Pivot
  • Rocker step
  • Drive strong and drive weak
  • Jab and crossover
  • Jab and shoot
  • Fake the shot and drive
  • Jump shot
  • Chest pass
  • One-hand push pass
  • Two-hand overhead flip pass
  • One- and two-hand bounce pass
  • V cut
  • Give-and-go
  • Backdoor
  • Pick and roll on the ball
  • Drive off screen (pick)
  • Pop out
  • Bounce pass off screen versus switch
  • Two-versus-two play
  • Pass and screen away
  • Pass high post, backdoor
  • Three-versus-three play
  • Moving without the ball
  • Five-versus-five play

6.1 On-the-Back One-Hand Set Shot

Goal

Have players develop proper elbow hinge action and wrist snap for backspin on the set shot.

Organization

Each player has a basketball; players scatter about the floor with space between them. Players are on their backs, with knees bent and feet flat on floor close to buttocks.

Description

Explain and demonstrate the one-hand set shot. Position the players' shooting hand on the ball properly with no guide hand. Finger pads are on one of the seams of the ball. Using the elbow as a hinge, players snap the wrist and propel the ball entirely with one hand up into the air three feet overhead. Look for proper backspin on the ball.

Once the proper hinge movement and snap of wrist adds backspin, add the guide hand, but make sure this hand is used only as a guide and does not interfere with the ball's flight (if there's no backspin, the guide hand probably interfered or the wrist did not snap). This is a perfect time for you to quickly make corrections in form. Focus on keeping the elbow in, finger pads across the seam, and a gap between ball and hand; snapping the wrist down; and putting backspin (not side spin) on the ball.

Challenge

See if players can set shoot 10 in the air 6 feet high and have the ball come back to them without their needing to move.

6.2 Triple Threat and Set Shot

Goal

Develop the habit of always beginning play in the triple-threat position and combining or coordinating use of the legs with the arm hinge action of the set shot.

Organization

Each player has a basketball 6 feet from and facing a wall with a line or spot on the wall at 11 feet.

Description

Explain and demonstrate the triple-threat position in which the player grasps the ball in set shooting position. The ball is held close to the body between the waist and chest. Feet are shoulder-width apart with the shooting-side foot slightly ahead of the nonshooting-side foot (toe to instep). This position allows the offensive player the triple option of passing, shooting, or dribbling (triple-threat position).

Have each player stand about 6 feet from a wall and shoot a set shot at a line or spot about 11 feet up on the wall. After each shot, the player retrieves the ball and shoots again. Or you might have players pair off about five yards apart throughout the gym and set shoot the ball back and forth to each other (have partner give feedback on elbow and wrist snap). The ball should be lofted about 11 feet in the air. After 20 to 25 successful trials, have players practice shooting the set shot from the triple-threat position at a basket no farther away than one giant step. Experiment shooting from directly straight on (no backboard) to the side at 45 degrees (use the box) to 90 degrees (no backboard). Explain the use of the box on the backboard when shooting bank shots. Focus on bending then extending the legs at the release, keeping the elbow in, and following through with the shooting hand in one smooth motion.

Challenge

In partners each player shoots 5 shots from the 5 angles and adds up the total number of baskets made for a team total out of 10. A basket does not count if there's no back spin on the ball. Each partner retrieves and gives helpful cues on form.

6.3 Shoot Around

Goal

Allow players to develop and practice their set shot in a noncompetitive atmosphere at a comfortable distance from the basket.

Organization

Tape 8 to 12 hot spots on the floor around each basket to indicate places from which to shoot. Distance from the basket depends on the ability of the players. Number the spots if you want players to follow a certain progression. If players are beginners, they should shoot from no farther than free-throw distance (15 feet).

Description

Using the triple-threat position, players practice set shots from various spots on the court in a noncompetitive activity. Players take no more than two shots at each spot before moving on. Have shooters follow a pattern, which helps develop a rhythm to the shot.

Challenges

Partners compete against other sets of partners. Have each partner shoot one set shot at each spot, and then his or her partner do the same. Combine the number of baskets for a total score. Then have partners compete directly against each other for a best score. Once players have achieved good form and are having some success, add a time element (but be ready to stop the if players start rushing shots in bad form).

6.4 Controlled or Stationary Protective Dribble

Goal

Become familiar with dribbling the ball with controlled protection, keeping eyes up and protecting the ball with the nondribbling arm from an imaginary defender attempting to steal the ball.

Organization

Each player has a basketball; players form a semicircle around the instructor.

Description

Explain and demonstrate proper body position of a controlled protected dribble. Lead players through a series of stationary controlled dribbling exercises, including an upright dribble with each hand before crossing over to protected dribbling. Focus on protecting the ball with the nondribbling arm, keeping the head up to look for defenders trying to steal the ball, and using only the pads of the fingers while pushing the ball to the floor in an arm-pumping action.

Challenge

Have players call out the number of fingers raised when you signal. A fist signifies a crossover dribble. Add a passive defender who walks around the dribbler, pretending to try to steal the ball. The dribbler must stay in one area but can move his or her body to stay between the ball and the defender.

6.5 Controlled Dribble While Moving and Cutting Using the Crossover

Goal

Become familiar with dribbling the ball with control while moving and cutting using the crossover dribble in all directions.

Organization

Each player has a basketball; players scatter around the floor with space between them.

Description

Explain and demonstrate controlled dribbling while moving and cutting (changing directions) with a crossover. Players walk, dribble, and cut in every direction throughout the gym, making sure to keep their heads up. As they approach another dribbler, they should avoid them, using a cut and crossover dribble to proceed in another direction. As players become more proficient, they can jog while dribbling.

Challenge

In partners, play follow the leader by shadowing the dribbling and cutting moves made by the leader around the gym.

6.6 Dribble Progression: Speed Dribble

Goal

Develop control of the basketball with each hand using a speed dribble while walking. Perform a 45-degree cut with a crossover dribble while running and speed dribbling.

Organization

Each player has a basketball. Players line up along a wall on one side of the court, facing the other wall. They spread out so that each player has a 10- to 15-foot area to dribble in. Designate these areas with tape, hot spots, or cones.

Description

Explain and demonstrate the speed dribble and then have players walk diagonally from one sideline of their area to the other, using a one-handed speed dribble. When each player reaches the sideline of their alley, they should perform a 45-degree cut while performing a crossover dribble to the other hand and then dribble diagonally to the other sideline in their alley. When they reach the wall opposite from where they started, they return to the start doing the same thing. Players can progress to a jog, then a run, as long as they remain in control.

Challenge

Speed dribble as fast as you can with no more than three dribbles in a row with one hand, then crossing over to the other.

6.7   Knock Out

Goal

Develop protective dribbling in a live competitive situation.

Organization

Each player has a basketball. Players scatter within a marked square or rectangle (size depends on number of players: for example, 20 players equals half a court).

Description

Review protective dribbling with your players. On a signal, have players continuously dribble around the inside of the rectangle using a protective dribble and shielding the ball from other dribblers with the body and nondribbling arm. If they are able, they can slap any other player's ball with their nondribbling hand provided they maintain control of their own ball. If their ball is knocked out of bounds, they must perform two sideline-to-sideline speed dribbles on the vacant halfcourt, using their nondominant hand before reentering the game. Focus on controlling the ball and continuously moving the body to stay between the defender and the ball while keeping eyes up to see approaching defenders.

Challenges

Make boundaries smaller or, for more aerobic work, expand boundaries and require players to jog or run. Reduce the number of balls so that two or three players play defense. If defenders manage to steal a ball, they switch positions with the player they stole it from.

6.8   Directional Dribbling

Goal

To identify which players look down at the ball while dribbling and encourage them to keep their eyes focused on the instructor for a signal to change dribbling hands.

Organization

Each player has a basketball. You'll need one chair and six traffic cones. The setup is similar to a baseball diamond. Place the chair at one corner of the basketball court where the base and sidelines meet, as if it is second base. Turn the back of the chair toward the wall, allowing room enough behind the chair for a player to dribble between it and the wall. Place a cone on each side of the chair about eight feet from the chair. Place another cone diagonally opposite the chair at the other end of the gym (this is home plate). Place a cone at the pitching rubber about 20 feet from home plate. Place the two remaining cones at first and third base but as close to the sideline wall as possible while still allowing enough room for a player to dribble between the wall and the cone. Line players up single file on the third-base sideline, with the first player positioned at home plate. Position yourself on the chair ready to signal dribbling directions (see figure 6.1).

Description

Provide a brief description and demonstration of the activity. Stand on the chair and give a start signal and point your finger either to the right or left side. The first player in line then begins to walk and dribble with the hand on the side to which you're pointing. If you switch to point in the other direction, the dribbler must cross-dribble over to that hand on the side to which you're now pointing. Once the first player reaches the first cone (pitcher's rubber), the second dribbler follows and does the same thing.

If players are able, they should jog or run but always under control. More adept players at dribbling may pass other players on the left but only if they can control the ball. Each player proceeds at a pace at which the ball remains controlled. Some players might have to walk. Players keep their eyes up and dribble in a straight line toward you. If they look down at the ball once a direction is given, switch again and they'll soon figure out that they need to slow down, control the ball, and keep their eyes on you. When dribblers approach the chair, they either go right or left, depending which direction you're pointing at that time. They then dribble between the cone and the chair you're standing on, continuing to dribble along the wall or sideline on the outside of the cones. The dribblers then get back in line until their next turn, dribbling continuously in line with their nondominant hand. Players

Figure 6.1 Directional Dribbling setup.
114

focus on going only as fast as they can while controlling the ball and not looking down at the ball.

Challenges

Increase the speed of directional pointing. Point more often toward the nondominant hand. Note that this is an excellent entry activity for practice. Additional skills can be added to the activity as players become more accomplished, and it soon can become an excellent comprehensive review or practice activity for most skills. For example, various shots can be assigned at every basket before returning to the starting line; passes can be performed against a wall in between baskets; players can knock out other players' balls as they cross in front of each other to shoot at baskets; and so on.

6.9 One Step and Shoot Lay-Up

Goal

Reduce the complexity of the lay-up by eliminating the dribble so that players concentrate on the angle, the proper take-off point, the take-off leg, and the shot itself.

Organization

Mark a spot on the floor with tape or a hot spot at a 45- to 60-degree angle about one giant stride from the backboard; this is where the shooter should take off. If your floor is marked with boxes, use the closest box to the basket on the free-throw lane (see figure 6.2). Players should be in single file, preferably on the side of their dominant shooting hand. The first player is one long stride from the floor spot, 45 to 60 degrees from the backboard.

Description

Explain and demonstrate shooting the lay-up with one step. Holding the ball in triple-threat position, have the first player take one step with the inside leg (the leg closest to the center of the court) onto the spot on the floor and leap off that leg into the air toward the basket maintaining the 45- to 60-degree angle. As the player ascends, he or she brings the ball up with the shooting hand behind the ball and the guide hand on the side (just as in the set shot). The ball is kept on the outside of the body, raised to a shooting position at the hairline, released with a set shot at the height of the leap, and banked off the top near corner of the box on the backboard. Continue until players are performing with confidence and developing a rhythm to the movement. Focus on taking only one step with the inside leg and going off that leg.

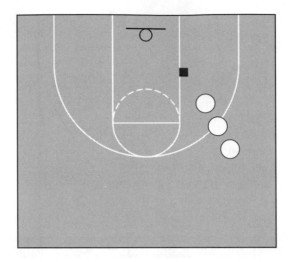

Figure 6.2   Setup for One Step and Shoot Lay-Up.

Challenge

Perform the same shot on the other side of the basket using the dominant hand. (Note that the take-off leg remains the same but is now on the outside.)

6.10   Two Steps and Shoot Lay-Up

Goal

Reduce the complexity of the lay-up by eliminating the dribble so that players focus on the angle, the proper take-off point, the take-off leg, and the shot itself with the addition of another step.

Organization

Mark a spot on the floor with tape or a hot spot, at a 45- to 60-degree angle about one giant stride from the backboard; this is where the shooter should take off from. If your floor is marked with boxes, use the closest box to the basket on the free-throw lane. Players line up in single file, preferably on the side of their dominant shooting hand (see figure 6.2). The first player is two long strides from the floor spot, 45 to 60 degrees from the backboard.

Description

Explain and demonstrate the skill. Holding the ball in triple-threat position, have the first player begin by taking one step with the outside leg followed by stepping with the inside leg onto the spot on the floor and leaping off that leg into the air toward the basket, maintaining the 45- to 60-degree angle. As the player ascends, he or she brings the ball up on the outside of the body with the shooting hand behind the ball and the guide hand on the side (as in the set shot) to a shooting position at the hairline. The ball is released with a set shot at the height of the leap and banked off the top near corner of the box on the backboard. Continue until players are performing with confidence and developing a rhythm to the movement. Focus on developing a smooth rhythm so that the sequence is smooth.

Challenge

Perform the same shot on the other side of the basket but with the dominant hand. (Note that the take-off leg remains the same but is now on the outside.)

6.11 One Dribble, Three Steps, and Shoot Lay-Up

Goal

Increase the complexity of the lay-up by adding one dribble without distracting players from the angle, proper take-off point, the take-off leg, and the shot.

Organization

Mark a spot on the floor with tape or a hot spot, at a 45- to 60-degree angle about one giant stride from the backboard; this is where the shooter should take off from. If your floor is marked with boxes, use the closest box to the basket on the free-throw lane. Players line up in single file, preferably on the side of their dominant shooting hand (see figure 6.2). The first player is three long strides from the floor spot, 45 to 60 degrees from the backboard.

Description

Explain and demonstrate the skill. Holding the ball in triple-threat position, the first player begins by taking one step with the inside leg while at the same time taking one dribble with the outside hand. At this point the player gathers the ball in both hands, with the shooting hand behind the ball and the guide hand along the side of the ball. The player takes a step with the outside leg and then the inside leg onto the spot on the floor and leaps from the inside leg into the air toward the basket, maintaining the 45- to 60-degree angle. As the player ascends, he or she brings the ball up on the outside to a shooting position at the hairline and releases with a set shot at the height of the leap. The shot should bank off the top near corner of the box on the backboard. Continue until players are performing with confidence and developing a rhythm to the movement. Players focus on developing a smooth, even rhythm that becomes almost second nature.

Challenge

Perform the same shot on the other side of the basket but with the dominant hand. (Note that the take-off leg remains the same but is now on the outside, and the ball is dribbled with the outside hand.)

6.12   Two Dribbles, Four Steps, and Shoot Lay-Up

Goal

Increase the complexity of the lay-up by adding two dribbles without distracting players from the angle, proper take-off point, the take-off leg, and the shot.

Organization

Mark a spot on the floor with tape or a hot spot, at a 45- to 60-degree angle about one giant stride from the backboard; this is where the shooter should take off from. If your floor is marked with boxes, use the closest box to the basket on the free-throw lane. Players line up in single file, preferably on the side of their dominant shooting hand (see figure 6.2, p. 116). The first player is four long strides from the floor spot, 45 to 60 degrees from the backboard.

Description

Explain and demonstrate the activity. Holding the ball in triple-threat position, the first player begins by taking one step with the outside leg and at the same time taking one dribble (with the outside hand), then another step with the inside leg while taking another dribble. At this point, the player gathers the ball in both hands, with the shooting hand behind the ball and the guide hand along the side of the basketball. He or she takes a step with the outside leg and then with the inside leg onto the spot on the floor and leaps from the inside leg into the air toward the basket, maintaining the 45- to 60-degree angle. As the player ascends, he or she brings the ball up on the outside of the body to a shooting position at the hairline and releases it with a set shot at the height of the leap. The ball banks off the top near corner of the box on the backboard. Continue until players are performing with confidence and developing a rhythm to the movement. Focus on developing a smooth, even rhythm that becomes almost second nature.

Challenge

Perform the same shot on the other side of the basket but with the dominant hand. (Note that the take-off leg remains the same but is now on the outside, and the ball is dribbled with the outside hand.)

6.13 Triple Threat, Dribble, and Lay-Up

Goal

Develop the complete lay-up from a triple-threat position, including the correct angle of approach, smooth steps, and take-off from the proper spot on the floor.

Organization

Each player has a basketball. On the floor at each basket mark a spot with tape or a hot spot at a 45- to 60-degree angle one giant stride from the backboard to indicate where the shooter should take off from. If your floor is marked with boxes, use the closest box to the basket on the free-throw lane. Players play at a basket of their choice or move around to various baskets.

Description

Explain and demonstrate the activity. Have players begin near the top of the key in triple-threat position and dribble the ball in for a lay-up at their own speed. Make sure that players are at the proper 45-degree angle and taking off from the spot marked on the floor. If players have difficulty with the steps, they should return to the point in the lay-up progression where they were successful and continue from there. Focus on making the initial dribble at a 45-degree angle rather than straight in at the basket in order to get the proper angle for the lay-up, thereby reducing the degree of difficulty of the shot.

Challenge

Perform the same shot on the other side of the basket but use the dominant hand.

6.14 Directional Dribbling and Lay-Up

Goal

To develop the ability to dribble with eyes up and perform lay-ups off the dribble.

Organization

Each player has a basketball. You'll need one chair and six traffic cones. The setup is similar to a baseball diamond. Place the chair at one corner of the basketball court where the base and sidelines meet, as if it is second base. Turn the back of the chair toward the wall, allowing room enough behind the chair for a player to dribble between it and the wall. Place a cone on each side of the chair about eight feet from the chair. Place another cone diagonally opposite the chair at the other end of the gym (this is home plate). Place a cone at the pitching rubber about 20 feet from home plate. Place the two remaining cones at first and third base but as close to the sideline wall as possible while still allowing enough room for a player to dribble between the wall and the cone. Line players up single file on the third-base sideline, with the first player positioned at home plate. Position yourself on the chair ready to signal dribbling directions (see figure 6.3).

Description

Briefly describe the activity to players. Players should maintain the correct angle as they approach the basket. Stand on the chair to give a start signal and point your finger either to the right or left side. The first player in line then begins to walk and dribble with the hand on the side to which you're pointing (left or right). If you switch to point in the other direction, the dribbler must cross-dribble over to that hand on the side to which you're pointing. Once the first player reaches the first cone (pitcher's rubber), the second dribbler follows and does the same thing. Players may jog or run but only if they can maintain control of the ball. Also, as long as they can continue to control the ball, more adept players at dribbling may pass other players on the left. Each player proceeds at a pace at which they can control the ball. Some might have to walk. Players need to keep their eyes up and dribble in a straight line toward you. If they look down at the ball once a signal is given, switch again and they'll soon understand that they need to slow down, control the ball, and keep their eyes on you. When each dribbler approaches the chair, they go either right or left (depending on the direction you're pointing), between the cone and the chair you're standing on and then along the wall or sideline on that side of the court. When they approach the cone at the corner (those who went left of the instructor) or midway down the court (those who went right of the instructor) they can then go to two of the designated baskets and shoot one lay-up each before returning to the start, where they get back in line until their next turn. They should dribble continuously in line with their nondominant hand. After the first player reaches the traffic cone 20 feet from the start, the next player starts. Players focus on maintaining and keeping the ball under control while directional dribbling and when approaching a basket.

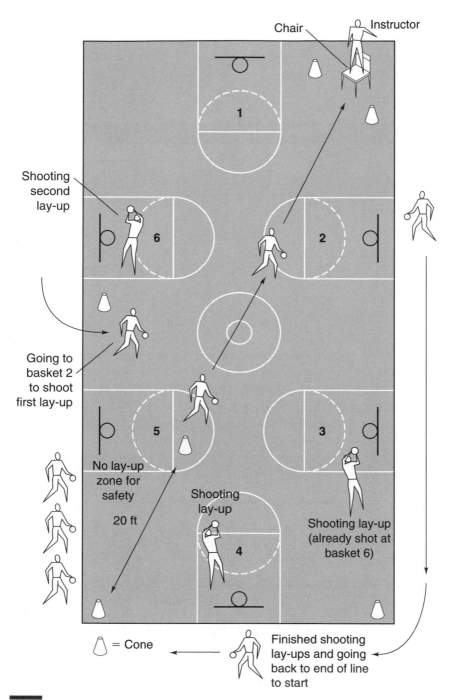

Figure 6.3 Setup for Directional Dribbling and Lay-Up.

121

Challenges

Increase the speed of directional pointing. Point more often toward the nondominant hand. Keep track of the number of baskets made in an allotted time.

6.15 1 v 0: Pivoting and Basic Rebounding

Goal

Develop pivoting and basic rebounding skills in a noncompetitive situation.

Organization

Each player has a basketball; players scatter around the floor with space between them.

Description

Explain and demonstrate the basic principles of pivoting and rebounding. Lead players through the following activities:

1. In triple-threat position, players establish one foot as their pivot foot and pivot up to 360 degrees in each direction, keeping elbows out to protect the ball from a defender. Repeat with the other foot as the pivot foot. Remind players to keep the foot nailed to the floor.

2. Players toss the ball to themselves high into the air, bend their knees, and jump up, swinging their arms upward. They grasp the ball (rebound) with both hands, hold onto it high (just above the hairline), and land on both feet simultaneously, with elbows out. They then establish a pivot foot and pivot. Repeat; this time after landing, players establish the other foot as the pivot foot.

3. Players toss the basketball to themselves high into the air, jump, rebound, and then land on one foot first, then the other. They then pivot on the proper foot (the foot that landed first) while protecting the ball. Repeat, this time landing on the other foot.

During the rebound, focus on timing the jump so that the ball is met at the height of the jump. After rebounding, players should protect the ball, keeping one foot nailed to the ground, with the ball near the hairline and elbows out.

Challenge

Toss the ball so that players have to run after the ball, jump, and land either on one foot or both feet and then pivot without traveling.

6.16 1 v 1: Pivot

Goal

Develop pivoting skills in a competitive situation.

Organization

Each set of partners has one basketball; partners scatter around the floor.

Description

Explain and demonstrate protecting the ball from a defender by pivoting. Have one partner on offense with a ball; the other partner defends. Inform offensive players that they have used up their dribble and must not allow their defender to get the ball. They cannot dribble, but they can pivot. Tell defenders to try to bat or grab the ball away, but they can't hit, slap, or hold the offensive player. Start and stop them after five seconds and switch positions. Continue alternating back and forth. Focus on keeping elbows out to protect the ball and keeping the body between the defender and the ball by pivoting quickly to get into position.

Challenge

The defender stands 10 feet away with the ball and underhand tosses the ball high into the air to the offensive player, who jumps into the air to retrieve the ball and comes down (on one foot or both feet). The defender then rushes to the offensive player and attempts to steal the ball. The offensive player uses pivoting skills to deny the defense the ball for five seconds.

6.17 1 v 1 Moves: Rocker Step and Drive Strong

Goal

Familiarize players with the rocker step so that it becomes automatic in a noncompetitive situation.

Organization

Players pair off in partners with a basketball. They should spread out around the basket no farther than free-throw line distance from the basket (see figure 6.4).

Description

Explain and demonstrate the rocker step and the drive to the strong side (the side opposite the pivot foot) against a passive defender. Have players individually perform a rocker step against their passive partner and then drive to the basket to shoot a lay-up. Switch from offense to defense after each trial.

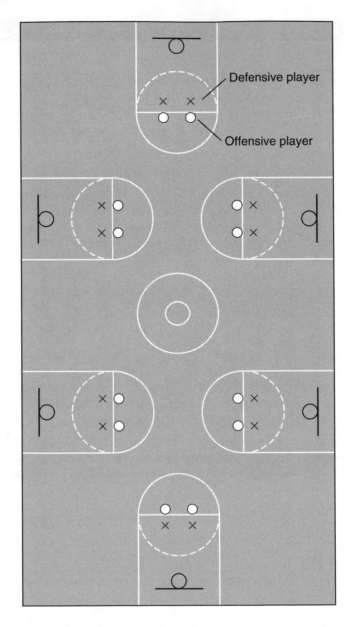

Figure 6.4 Setup for Rocker Step and Drive Strong.

Repeat, using the other foot as the pivot foot. Focus on keeping the ball in triple-threat position and driving as close to the defender's hip as possible, which allows the player to beat the defender.

Challenge

Have the passive defender toss the ball high into the air to the offensive player, who rebounds the ball, lands, establishes a pivot foot, and gets into triple-threat position. He or she then uses a rocker step against the passive defender and drives in for a lay-up.

6.18 1 v 1 Moves: Rocker Step, Crossover, Drive Weak

Goal

Familiarize players with the rocker step and crossover so that they become automatic in a noncompetitive situation against a passive defender.

Organization

Players pair off in partners, with a basketball. They should spread out around the basket no farther than free-throw line distance from the basket (see figure 6.4).

Description

Explain and demonstrate the rocker step, crossover, and drive to the weak side (the side of the pivot foot). Then have players individually perform a rocker step, then a crossover step, and drive to the basket to shoot a lay-up against a passive defender. Switch from offense to defense after each trial. Repeat, using the other foot as the pivot foot. Focus on keeping the ball in triple-threat position and driving as close to the defender's hip as possible, which allows the player to beat the defender.

Challenge

Have the passive defender toss the ball high into the air to the offensive player, who rebounds the ball, establishes a pivot foot, uses a rocker step against the passive defender, crosses over, and drives for a lay-up.

6.19 1 v 1 Moves: Rocker Step, Jab, and Set Shot

Goal

Familiarize players with the rocker step, jab, and set shot so that they become automatic in a noncompetitive situation.

Organization

Players pair off in partners, with a basketball. They should spread out around the basket no farther than free-throw line distance from the basket (see figure 6.4, p. 124).

Description

Explain and demonstrate the jab and set shot. Then have players individually perform a rocker step, jab, and set shot against a passive defender. Repeat, using the other foot as the pivot foot. Switch from offense to defense after each trial.

Challenge

Keep track of how many shots you and your partner can make out of 10.

6.20 1 v 1 Moves: Fake the Shot and Drive

Goal

Familiarize players with faking the shot and driving so these skills become automatic in a noncompetitive situation.

Organization

Players pair off in partners, with a basketball. They should spread out around the basket no farther than free-throw line distance from the basket (see figure 6.4, p. 124).

Description

Explain and demonstrate faking the shot and driving. Players individually practice faking the shot and driving against a passive defender. Repeat, using the other foot as the pivot foot. Switch from offense to defense after each trial. Focus on rocking back while looking up at the basket as if to shoot but without moving the ball from triple-threat position, then driving past the defender on the strong or weak side for a lay-up.

Challenge

Fake the shot, fake the drive with a jab, and come back and shoot.

6.21 1 v 1 Skills Practice

Goal

Develop 1 v 1 offensive skills against a passive defender so that the skills become a reflex action, depending on what the defender allows.

Organization

Players pair off in partners, with a basketball. They should spread out around the basket no farther than free-throw line distance from the basket (see figure 6.4, p. 124).

Description

Review and demonstrate when to use each 1 v 1 move learned, including the rocker step and drive strong; rocker step, crossover step, and drive weak; rocker step, jab, and set shot; and fake the shot and drive. Players practice 1 v 1 moves against a passive defender. The defender is to play loose or tight or to favor one side or another but in a passive mode, while the offensive player reacts accordingly. Play stops after each shot. After five trials, offensive players go to defense. Focus on letting the defender's actions determine the 1 v 1 move you'll attempt rather than making up your mind ahead of time what move you'll perform.

Challenge

Have defenders put their arms behind their backs and attempt to stop the offensive player from making the basket by just moving their feet to block the pathway the offensive player tries to take. Switch positions after each attempt.

6.22 1 v 1: Live Defender

Goal

Develop 1 v 1 offensive skills in a live situation so that they become automatic against a defender.

Organization

Players pair off in partners with a basketball. They should spread out around the basket no farther than free-throw line distance from the basket.

Description

Review and demonstrate when to use each 1 v 1 move learned thus far. Then have players practice 1 v 1 moves live against each other. The defender should play fairly tight and not favor one side or the other, and the offensive player reacts accordingly. Play stops after each shot. Do five trials and then switch from offense to defense. Focus on taking advantage of the opportunities that the defender gives you.

Challenge

Have the defender overplay the side that the offensive player is favoring.

6.23 1 v 1 Game

Goal

Develop 1 v 1 skills so that they are automatic from three areas on the court in an intense competitive situation.

Organization

Players pair off with partners with a basketball—three partner groups per basket. One partner group is at the free-throw line, and the other two groups are on each side at the wings.

Description

Explain and demonstrate how the 1 v 1 games are played, and tell players what's not allowed according to basketball rules (i.e., traveling, contact, etc.). Partners play games of 1 v 1. To begin play, the defense tosses the ball to the offensive player. The offensive player can do any of the individual 1 v 1 moves covered in class. Only one shot is allowed; after that, the ball is dead and the next partner group rotates in at one of the wings. The offense switches to defense after every play. After each partner group has played offense and defense once, teams rotate left to right (i.e., the left wing team goes to the middle, the middle goes to the right wing, and the right wing team goes to the left wing). If the defense steals the ball, the play is dead. Players call their own fouls. All fouls, violations, and disputes are replayed. Players keep track of their scores; the player with the most points at the end is the winner. Remind players to take advantage of what the defender gives them.

Challenge

Assign each player in a partner group either the number 1 or 2. At each basket there will be three players on team 1 and three players on team 2. Continue with the same activity as above, but add up the number of baskets made by the combined scores of each team (1 or 2) to determine a winner. Players waiting can coach and cheer on their teammates.

6.24 Jump Shot to a Partner

Goal

Concentrate on developing proper form in the jump shot.

Organization

Players pair off in partners, with a basketball. They should scatter about 10 feet apart.

Description

Explain and demonstrate the jump shot. Have players practice shooting a jump shot to each other beginning in triple-threat position without a dribble. Focus on using the legs to propel yourself vertically while bringing the ball up to a shooting position at your hairline.

Challenge

See if players can shoot the ball just as they reach the height of their jump (using exactly the same release of the ball as they do in the set shot) and land in the same spot from which they took off. This prevents players from drifting into defenders and fouling them during the shot.

6.25 Jump Shot at a Basket Close In

Goal

Maintain proper form in the jump shot while attempting to make a basket from various angles on the court.

Organization

Each player has a basketball at a basket.

Description

Explain and demonstrate shooting a jump shot from various areas and angles on the floor. Then, from a distance of no more than 10 feet from the basket, have players shoot jump shots from all angles. Be sure they bank the jump shot on shots of 45 degrees or less for maximum success. Focus on keeping the elbow in and shooting just before reaching the height of your jump.

Challenge

See how many baskets you can make out of five shots "around the horn" (straight on at the basket and on each side of the basket from 45 and 90 degrees).

6.26 Dribble, Jump Stop, and Jump Shot

Goal

Develop the ability to jump stop at the end of a dribble followed by a jump shot.

Organization

Each player is at a basket with a basketball.

Description

Explain and demonstrate the jump stop followed by a jump shot. From the top of the key (about 20 feet), have players, one at a time, slowly dribble in and perform a jump stop about 10 feet from the basket, followed by a jump shot. Progress the activity to a jog and then to a full run. Focus on being in control, landing on both feet at the same time, and coming to a complete stop before proceeding to shoot the ball.

Challenge

See if players can run, come to a jump stop, shoot the ball just as they reach the height of their jump (with exactly the same release of the ball as in their set shot), and then land in the same spot from which they took off. This prevents them from drifting into their defender and drawing a foul.

6.27 Directional Dribbling, Jump Stop, and Jump Shot

Goal

To develop the ability to dribble with eyes up and to perform a jump stop and jump shot.

Organization

Each player has a basketball; you'll also need one chair and six traffic cones. The setup is similar to a baseball diamond. Place the chair at one corner of the basketball court where the base and sidelines meet, as if it is second base. Turn the back of the chair toward the wall, allowing room enough behind the chair for a player to dribble between it and the wall. Place a cone on each side of the chair about eight feet from the chair. Place another cone diagonally opposite the chair at the other end of the gym (this is home plate). Place a cone at the pitching rubber about 20 feet from home plate. Place the two remaining cones at first and third base but as close to the sideline wall as possible while still allowing enough room for a player to dribble between the wall and the cone. Line players up single file on the third-base sideline, with the first player positioned at home plate. Position yourself on the chair, ready to signal dribbling directions (see figure 6.5).

Description

Briefly describe the activity to players. Stay under control when coming to a jump stop to prevent drifting into imaginary defenders.

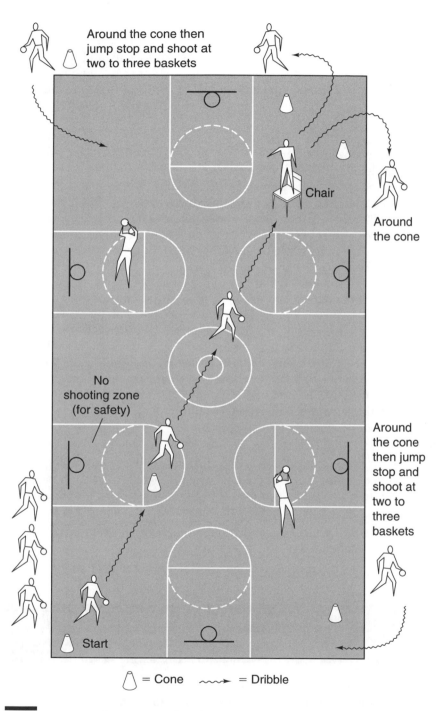

Figure 6.5 Setup for Directional Dribbling, Jump Stop, and Jump Shot.

Stand on the chair, give a start signal, and then point your finger either to the right or left side. The first player in line begins to walk and dribble with the hand on the side to which you're pointing (left or right). If you switch to point in the other direction, the dribbler must cross-dribble over to that hand on the side to which you're pointing. Once the first player reaches the first cone (pitcher's rubber), the second dribbler follows and does the same thing. Players may jog or run, as long as they can continue to control the basketball. Adept dribblers can pass other players on the left, but only if they can control the ball while doing so. Players proceed at a pace at which they can control the ball. Some may have to walk. They should keep their eyes up and dribble in a straight line toward you. If they look down at the ball once a signal is given, switch again, and they'll soon understand that they need to slow down, control the ball, and keep their eyes on you. When dribblers approach the chair, they go either right or left (depending which direction you're pointing), between the cone and the chair you are standing on, and continue dribbling along the wall or sideline on that side of the court. When they approach the cone at the corner (those who went left of the instructor) or midway down the court (those who went right of the instructor), they can then go to two of the designated baskets and perform a jump stop at the free-throw line followed by a jump shot. They then return to the start, where they get back in line until their next turn. While in line they should be dribbling continuously with their nondominant hand. After the first player reaches the traffic cone 20 feet from the start, the next player starts. Focus on maintaining and keeping the ball under control while directional dribbling.

Challenges

1. See if players can dribble and control the ball at full running speed without looking down at the ball when directed to switch hands and come to a complete stop on each jump stop before shooting. Keep track of the number of baskets players make in an allotted time.

2. Increase the speed of directional pointing. Point more often toward the nondominant hand.

3. Increase the distance from where they can shoot to the free-throw line.

6.28 | **2 v 0: Chest Pass, One-Hand Push Pass, Two-Hand Overhead Flip Pass, and One- and Two-Hand Bounce Pass**

Goal

Develop essential passing skills to play in halfcourt games.

Organization

Players pair off in partners with a basketball; players should form lines facing each other or be in scattered formation 15 to 20 feet apart.

Description

Explain and demonstrate each pass. Have players practice each pass, starting in triple-threat position. Players should focus on stepping forward with one leg to give more power to the pass and, with the exception of the two-hand overhead flip pass, keeping the ball in triple-threat position so defenders won't know if they're going to pass, dribble, or shoot.

Challenge

Increase the distance to no more than 20 to 25 feet.

6.29   2 v 1 Passing: Defender in the Middle

Goal

When being closely guarded, learn how to pass a ball past a defender to a teammate.

Organization

Three players (two offense, one defense) share one basketball. All three players straddle a line in single file. The two players on each end of the line are the offensive players, and the player in the middle is the defender. The two offensive players are no more than 15 feet apart.

Description

Explain and demonstrate the most susceptible areas for a defender to defend against a pass (one-hand push pass close to the defender's ears or a bounce pass). Then have the two offensive players attempt to pass the ball past the defender back and forth to each other without the defender touching the ball. Inform the defender what a proper defensive stance looks like but no more. The offensive players must straddle the line and may not be farther apart than 15 feet. If the defender touches the ball in any way, the player who passed the ball goes into the middle. If the offense completes 10 consecutive passes without the defense touching the ball, the defender rotates out to become an offensive player and is replaced by one of the offensive players. Begin with a passive defender until the passers get the idea, then play at regular speed. Passers always begin from triple-threat position and wait for the defender to be in a position to defend; the defender must guard the ball, not the receiver. The pass should be within the reach of the defender (i.e., the ball cannot be lofted high into the air well over the out-stretched hands of the defender).

Challenge

Play a game of horse. Each time a defender touches the ball, the passer gets a letter. The game ends when H-O-R-S-E is spelled.

6.30 Pass and Lay-Up

Goal

Develop the timing needed after receiving a pass on the run to gauge the number of dribbles it takes to be in the proper position to perform a lay-up.

Organization

One basketball per basket. Four players at a basket, two on each side at 45-degree angles to the basket.

Description

Explain and demonstrate the traditional lay-up drill. Have players line up, two per side, at the wings on each side of the free-throw line. One line begins (preferably on the dominant-shooting side) by dribbling the ball in for a lay-up. The first player in line on the other side rebounds the ball and passes to the next person in line, who waits for the pass at the wing. The rebounder then follows the pass around the outside of the court (rather than in front of the dribbler) to the back of the shooting line, and the shooter goes to the end of the rebounding line. Players use the chest pass. Once players are comfortable with the drill, move the shooting line back several steps. The shooter may now leave when the ball is rebounded but must receive the pass on the run at the free-throw line and then dribble the ball in for a lay-up. Focus on making crisp passes to the receiver and keeping the head up while dribbling the ball to the basket. The approach to the basket should be at the proper angle and the take-off from the correct distance from the basket, not underneath the basket.

Challenge

Bounce pass the ball to the receiver after the receiver has run past the free-throw line so that the receiver can't dribble the ball but must catch the ball, gauge the correct steps to take without traveling, and shoot a proper lay-up at the proper distance and angle from the basket.

6.31 2 v 0: V Cut and Give-and-Go

Goal

Develop the proper execution of the V cut and timing of each pass so that the receiver doesn't have to wait for the ball.

Organization

Players pair off in partners with a basketball on the right or left side of the key.

Description

Explain and demonstrate the V cut and the give-and-go. Then have players practice a V cut in open space on their own, followed by a V cut and give-and-go with a partner. To begin, one player with a ball stands just to the right or left of the top of the key, and his or her partner stands at the wing, about five feet from the free-throw line. The player at the top of the key with the ball is in triple-threat position. The player at the wing initiates play by doing a V cut toward the basket and comes back to receive the chest pass from the player at the top of the key. Immediately after the pass, the passer makes a cut directly toward the basket on the side of the pass, receives a return pass, and dribbles in for a lay-up (see figure 6.6). Begin with a walk, then progress to a jog and then to full speed. If there is more than one partner group per basket, alternate sides of the court after each trial. Focus on passing the ball to the V cutter while they're still moving out to receive the pass so that a defender has no chance of intercepting.

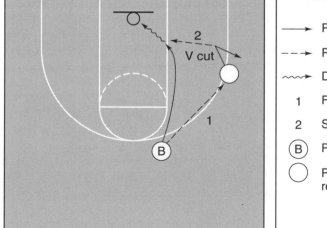
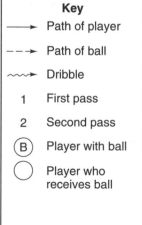

	Key	
→	Path of player	
- - →	Path of ball	
∿→	Dribble	
1	First pass	
2	Second pass	
Ⓑ	Player with ball	
○	Player who receives ball	

Figure 6.6   Setup for 2 v 0: V Cut and Give-and-Go.

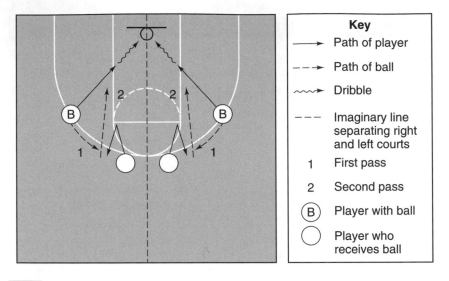

Figure 6.7   2 v 0: V Cut and Give-and-Go challenge.

Challenge

Have the player on the wing begin with the ball and pass to the player at the top of the key, who has performed a V cut. The passer on the wing then cuts to the basket, receives a pass, and dribbles in for a lay-up (see figure 6.7).

6.32   2 v 0: Backdoor

Goal

Develop the proper execution of the backdoor cut and timing of the pass so that the receiver doesn't have to wait for the ball.

Organization

Players pair off in partners with one ball on the right or left side of the key.

Description

Provide an explanation and demonstration of a backdoor after a V cut. Have players practice the move by themselves, starting without the ball in a slow jog. Once they're familiar with the move, they can practice the entire move on the court.

    To begin, one player with a ball stands just to the right or left of the top of the key, and his or her partner stands at the wing about five feet from the free-throw line. The player at the top of the key with the ball is in triple-threat position. The player at the wing initiates play by doing a V cut toward the basket, comes back as if to receive a pass, and then breaks to the basket in a backdoor move. The passer at the top of the key bounce passes the ball to the cutter, who dribbles in for a lay-up (see figure 6.8). Begin with a walk, then progress to a jog, then full speed. Focus on making the V cut as if you expect to receive the ball and then cutting explosively back to the basket to free yourself from a defender in order to receive the ball.

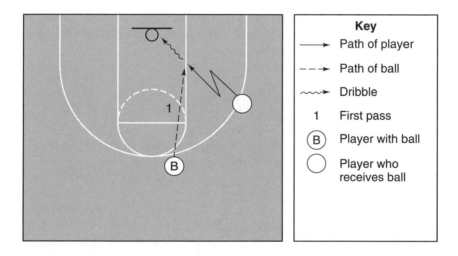

Figure 6.8   Directions for 2 v 0: Backdoor.

Challenge

The passer holds onto the ball as if the cutter is covered and waits for the cutter to continue past the basket and out to the wing on the other side of the court, where the pass is made to the cutter. The passer does a give-and-go, receiving a return pass and performing a lay-up. Since there is another partner group on the other wing, have each group alternate into the court to avoid collisions.

6.33 2 v 2: Give-and-Go, V Cut, and Backdoor With Passive Defense

Goal

Develop the ability of both the receiver (cutter) and the passer to react to defensive breakdowns and execute the V cut, give-and-go, and the backdoor while being guarded passively.

Organization

Four players play on halfcourt with one basketball—two on offense and two on defense. One offensive player is the point guard, and the other is a wing.

Description

Explain and demonstrate the 2 v 2 using the three offensive moves learned thus far. To begin, the wing does a V cut and receives the ball from the point guard, who then cuts to the basket (give-and-go) to receive a return pass from the wing for a lay-up (see figure 6.9a). If the point guard is not open, the point guard then abruptly stops and V cuts back out to the top of the key to receive the pass from the wing, who then performs a backdoor on his defender and receives a pass from the point guard for a lay-up (see figure 6.9b). If this is not feasible, the point guard can perform 1 v 1 moves on his defender or continue with give-and-go moves with his partner. Offensive players are restricted to using only the give-and-go, V cut, and backdoor moves. The defense merely shadows the offensive player and should intentionally create situations so that players get to practice all scenarios. This activity should be done at half-speed so players get the idea. Switch responsibilities every two trials so that everyone gets to practice each situation. This should be a cooperative, not a competitive, activity. If there are two groups of four players at each basket, have each group cycle in from halfcourt after each play. Focus on maintaining movement as opposed to standing and waiting for a pass. If no pass comes, then cut.

Challenge

See if players can make the activity flow so that it's nonstop until a basket is made.

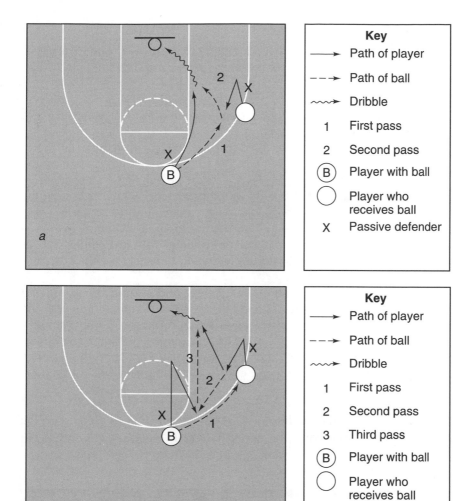

Figure 6.9 Options for 2 v 2: *(a)* V cut give-and-go and *(b)* backdoor with passive defense.

6.34 **2 v 2: Give-and-Go, V Cut, and Backdoor With Live Defense**

Goal

Develop the ability of both the receiver (cutter) and the passer to react to defensive breakdowns and execute the give-and-go, V cut, and backdoor while being guarded live.

Organization

Four players play on halfcourt with one basketball—two on offense and two on defense. One offensive player is the point guard, and the other is a wing.

Description

Explain and demonstrate playing 2 v 2 against live defenders using the V cut, give-and-go, and backdoor moves.

To begin, the wing does a V cut and receives the ball from the point guard, who then cuts to the basket (give-and-go) to receive a return pass from the wing for a lay-up. If the point guard is not open, the point guard then abruptly stops and V cuts back out to the top of the key to receive the pass from the wing, who then performs a backdoor on his defender and receives a pass from the point guard for a lay-up. If this is not feasible, the point guard can perform 1 v 1 moves on his defender or continue with give-and-go moves with his partner. Offensive players are restricted to using only the give-and-go, V cut, and backdoor moves.

The defense guards the offensive players and should try to prevent them from scoring. Once a shot is taken or the defense intercepts the ball, play stops, and the defensive team goes on offense. Otherwise, play is continuous. If there are two groups of four players at each basket, have each group cycle in from halfcourt after each play. First team to score five baskets wins. Focus on moving and not standing around waiting for a pass.

Challenge

Begin play in the corner with a forward passing the ball to a guard on the wing. The same basic principles apply (i.e., give-and-go, V cut, and back-door).

6.35   2 v 2: Live on Halfcourt

Goal

Execute 2 v 2 offensive moves in a competitive situation.

Organization

Four players play at halfcourt with one basketball—two on offense and two on defense.

Description

Explain and demonstrate the 2 v 2, using all the skills introduced thus far. Have one team begin at the top of the key, guarded by the defensive team. Play Rock, Paper, Scissors to determine who starts with the ball.

Play a game of 2 v 2 using only these skills: dribbling, lay-up, the set and jump shot, individual moves covered thus far (rocker step, drive strong and drive weak, crossover, jab and set shot, fake shot and drive), give-and-go, V cut, and backdoor. Play begins when the defense lightly underhands the ball to the offensive point guard, who can pass or dribble. No screening is allowed, and the three-second lane violation is enforced (no offensive player can remain in the lane for more than three seconds with or without the ball). Only lay-ups and close-in shots can be taken (from no farther than the free-throw line). Fouls or any possession disputes are replayed. No arguments are allowed! Only one shot is allowed. The defense switches to offense whenever a shot is taken (whether the shot is made or not), the defense steals the ball, or a turnover occurs. Teams keep track of their total number of baskets. If there are two groups of four players at each basket, have each group cycle in from halfcourt after each play. Focus on making crisp passes, keeping on the move, and beating the defender using any of the 1 v 1 moves.

Challenge

Allow play to continue if the shot is missed or the ball is stolen by the defense. If the defense gets the ball, they must dribble or pass the ball back past the three-point line, at which time they then can commence play on offense. Play continues until one team makes a basket; then switch sides or allow waiting teams to play.

6.36 Pick and Roll: On the Ball

Goals

Develop screening skills (setting and rolling) and the ability to drive off a screen.

Organization

Four players play with one basketball on a halfcourt—two passive defensive players and two offensive players. If no more than six players to a court can be accommodated, teams of two players cycle in and out.

Description

Explain and demonstrate a pick (setting a screen) on a defender, rolling off the defender, and driving off the pick. When screening, players should come to a complete stop at the defender's hip before rolling to the basket. Then have two offensive players stand about 15 feet from each other at the top of the key. The defensive players passively guard the offensive players in a man-to-man, no switching defense (i.e., they must guard the same player throughout). Refer to *Basketball: Skills and Drills, 2nd edition* (Krause et al. 1999) for an in-depth explanation of the pick and roll. Play begins with one of the offensive players with the ball in triple-threat position facing the basket. The offensive player's teammate lays a pick (screen) on the defender. Once the pick is made, the offensive player drives off the pick for a lay-up, while the screener rolls to the basket. Practice screening on each side of the court so that each player gets to practice coming off a screen in both directions. Focus on looking directly through the defender in triple-threat position without tipping off the defender that a screener is approaching.

Challenge

Have the screener begin from where the baseline and key meet and approach the defender at the top of the key from a blind side (almost a back screen). The offensive player with the ball must not give away the side the screener is approaching (i.e., he or she looks straight ahead in triple-threat position through the defender).

6.37 Pass, Pick, and Roll

Goals

Develop the ability to pass, set a screen on the receiver's defender, and roll. Develop the ability to drive off a screen.

Organization

Four players play with one basketball on halfcourt—two passive defensive players and two offensive players. If no more than six players to a court can be accommodated, teams of two players cycle in and out.

Description

Explain and demonstrate following a pass and screening, then rolling to the basket. Have two offensive players stand about 15 feet from each other at the top of the key. The defensive players passively guard the offensive players in a man-to-man, no switching defense.

Play begins with the offensive player with the ball passing the ball to a partner who has done a V cut to get clear of the defender. The passer follows the pass and sets a pick (screen) on the defender and then rolls to the basket. The receiver receives the ball and gets into triple-threat position, facing the basket and awaiting the pick. Once the pick is made, the offensive player drives off the pick for a lay-up, while the screener rolls to the basket. Please see *Basketball: Skills and Drills, 2nd edition* (Krause et al. 1999) for an in-depth description of the pass, pick, and roll. Practice screening on each side of the court so that each player gets to work on coming off a screen in both directions. Focus on laying the screen without a jump stop, as this takes more time.

Challenge

Have the receiver play a forward and receive the ball near the baseline in the corner. The passer then moves to the corner and screens the receiver's defender.

6.38   Pass, Pick, and Pop Out

Goals

One goal is to develop the passer's ability to pass, follow the pass, and recognize when a defense sags and get into position to receive the return pass from a receiver when the receiver is impeded from driving to the basket. A second goal is to develop the receiver's ability to recognize a defense sagging to prevent a drive to the basket off a screen and pass the ball back to a teammate who has popped out for a shot.

Organization

Four players play on halfcourt with one basketball—two passive defensive players and two offensive players. If no more than six players to a court can be accommodated, teams of two players cycle in and out.

Description

Explain and demonstrate the "pop out." Have two offensive players stand about 15 feet from each other at the top of the key. The defensive players passively guard the offensive players in a sagging man-to-man to prevent the drive or the pick and roll to the basket.

Play begins with the offensive player with the ball passing to a partner, who has done a V cut to get clear. The passer follows the pass and sets a pick (screen) on the defender (see figure 6.10a). The receiver begins to drive off the screen, but the path to the basket is blocked because both defenders have dropped back in a sag to prevent any driving. Seeing that the defender has sagged off to prevent penetration toward the basket, the passer, instead of rolling to the basket after the driver comes off the screen, steps back a few steps (pops out) away from the basket and awaits a return pass. He or she then gets set and shoots (see figure 6.10b). Practice on each side of the court so that each player gets to practice popping out in either direction. Rotate positions after each trial.

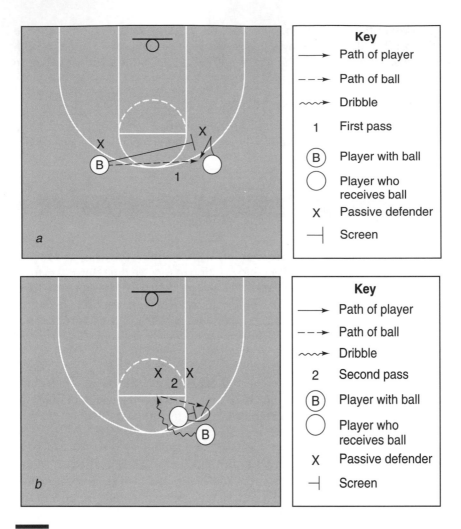

Figure 6.10 Movements of the players: *(a)* pass and pick, and *(b)* pop out.

Challenge

Have the receiver play forward and receive the ball near the baseline in the corner. The passer then moves to the corner and pops out in the corner when the defense sags to prevent the drive.

6.39 2 v 2: Pick and Roll Live Halfcourt

Goal

Develop all the offensive skills learned thus far in live 2 v 2 competition.

Organization

Four players play at halfcourt with one basketball—two on offense and two on defense. Four teams of two players can be accommodated per halfcourt. Teams rotate in and out after each trial, along with rotating positions.

Description

Review and demonstrate all the 1 v 1 and 2 v 2 moves the class has learned so far. Tell players that if they don't know what to do when their team has the ball to go lay a screen on the defender guarding the player with the ball. Have one team begin at the top of the key, guarded by the defensive team. Defense is man-to-man, with no switching. Sagging is permitted, but players should not overdo it. Play Rock, Paper, Scissors to determine who will have the basketball first.

Play a game of 2 v 2 using only these skills: dribbling, lay-up, the set and jump shot, individual moves covered thus far (rocker step, drive strong and drive weak, crossover, jab and set shot, fake shot and drive), give-and-go, V cut, backdoor, pick and roll (on the ball and pass and screen), and pop out (if the defense sags). Play begins when the defense lightly tosses the ball to the offensive player, who can pass or dribble. Screening is expected, and the three-second lane violation is enforced. Only lay-ups and close-in shots (from no farther than the free-throw line) can be taken. Fouls or any possession disputes are replayed. Defense switches to offense whenever a shot is taken (whether the shot is made or not), the defense steals the ball, or a turnover occurs. Teams keep track of their total number of baskets. Focus on moving and not standing around, waiting for a pass.

Challenge

Allow play to continue if the shot is missed or the ball is stolen by the defense. If the defense gets the ball, they must dribble or pass the ball back past the three-point line, at which time they can begin play on offense. Play continues until one team scores, at which time the other team gets the ball or, if teams are waiting, they come onto the court and resume play.

6.40 Pick and Roll Versus Switching Defense: Bounce Pass

Goal

Develop the ability when coming off a screen to read when a defender switches, see the opening created for a bounce pass, and bounce pass the ball to a teammate who has picked and is rolling to the basket.

Organization

Four players play with one basketball at halfcourt—two passive defensive players and two offensive players. If no more than six players to a court can be accommodated, teams of two players cycle in and out.

Description

Explain and demonstrate a switching man-to-man defense. Have two offensive players stand about 15 feet from each other at the top of the key. The defensive players passively guard the offensive players in a man-to-man, switching defense (defenders trade guarding offensive players whenever they're unable to continue guarding their player—such as when they're being screened by another player).

Play begins with a pass and screen by the passer on the player guarding the receiver or a screen on the player guarding the partner with the ball. Once the screen is made, the offensive player drives off the screen until stopped by the switching defender, at which point the offensive player leans back in the direction he or she came from and bounce passes the ball to a teammate who has rolled toward the basket for a lay-up. Practice screening on each side of the court so that each player gets to practice coming off a screen and passing in either direction. As the offense becomes more proficient, allow the switching defenders to play more aggressively. Each player gets two trials; then switch. Focus on the player rolling to the basket to keep the new defender at his or her back.

Challenge

Have defenders play a tight or switching man-to-man defense, but don't tell the offensive players.

6.41 2 v 2: Live at Halfcourt

Goal

Be able to select and perform the appropriate skill when the situation arises against a switching or tight man-to-man defense.

Organization

Four players play with one basketball at halfcourt —two on offense and two on defense. Four teams of two players can be accommodated per half-court.

Description

Explain and demonstrate playing 2 v 2 live, using all the skills the class has learned so far. Then have one team begin at the top of the key, guarded by the defensive team. Play Rock, Paper, Scissors to determine who has the basketball first.

Play a game of 2 v 2 using only these skills: dribbling, lay-up, the set and jump shot, individual moves covered so far (rocker step, drive strong and drive weak, crossover, jab and set shot, fake shot and drive), give-and-go, V cut, backdoor, and all pick and roll moves. Play begins when the defense lightly tosses the ball to the offensive player, who can pass or dribble. Screening is expected, and the three-second-lane violation is enforced. Only lay-ups and close-in shots (from no farther than the free-throw line) can be taken. Fouls or any disputes are replayed. Defense switches to offense when a basket is made by the offense, when a turnover occurs, or when the defense intercepts a pass or rebounds a missed shot. When a turnover occurs or the ball is rebounded by the defense, play continues, but the defense must bring the ball back outside the three-point line before attempting to score. The defense can play a tight or switching man-to-man and sag but should mix up the defenses. Teams keep track of their total number of baskets. When a team scores, the defending team becomes the offense (unless there's another group of players waiting, at which time they enter the game).

Challenge

Change the scoring to ensure that more lay-ups off screens occur by giving two points for a lay-up scored off a pick, while anything else (pop out, etc.) is awarded one point.

6.42 3 v 3: Pass and Screen Away

Goal

To balance out the floor by developing the ability to pass and screen away from the ball instead of always screening the ball.

Organization

Three players play on offense and three on defense with one ball on one full court. No more than nine players can be accommodated on this drill: six on the court and three waiting their turn.

Description

Explain and demonstrate how to screen away from the ball. Then have three offensive guards (two wings and a point guard) organize around the key with passive tight, man-to-man defenders.

The point guard initiates play, passing the ball to one of the wings, and then goes to screen the opposite wing's defender. The wing without the ball who's waiting to be screened keeps the defender occupied by making a few walking steps on the backdoor side of the defender and then, when the screen is laid on their defender, cuts directly off the screen heading straight down the free-throw lane toward the basket to receive a pass (chest or bounce) from a teammate on the other wing for a lay-up (see figure 6.11a). If the ball is not passed, the cutter continues through the lane along the baseline toward the teammate holding the ball. Once the first cutter has cleared the lane, the screener also rolls and follows the first cutter and receives a pass (this is the second option; figure 6.11b). If the screener can't receive the pass, he goes the opposite way of the first cutter. If neither pass can be made, the passer can either go one-on-one against the defender or give-and-go to the first cutter (see figure 6.11c). Begin the activity with a passive defender, and slowly have the defense tighten up. Players do two trials, then rotate positions or allow waiting teams to come in. Focus on keeping your defensive player occupied if you don't have the ball by using V cuts and moving to open areas on the court.

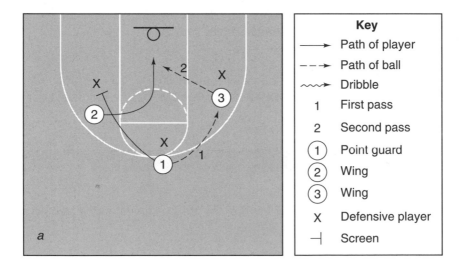

	Key
⟶	Path of player
- - ⟶	Path of ball
⟿	Dribble
1	First pass
2	Second pass
①	Point guard
②	Wing
③	Wing
X	Defensive player
⊣	Screen

Figure 6.11 Possible movements for 3 v 3: Pass and Screen Away.

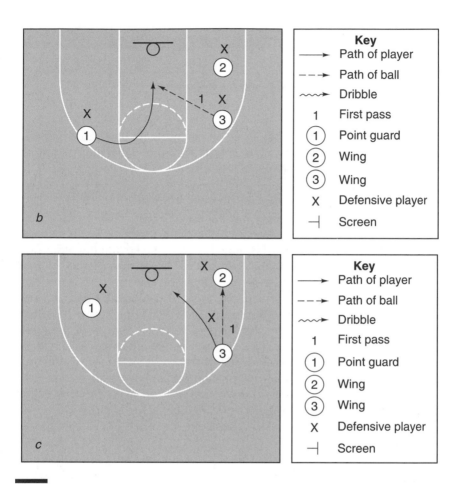

Figure 6.11 *(continued)*

Challenge

Have a point guard and a wing and forward on the same side; have the wing begin the play by passing to the point guard, then screening the forward.

6.43   3 v 3: High-Post Backdoor

Goal

Apply the backdoor and move to the high post.

Organization

Three players play on offense and three on defense with one basketball on a full court. No more than nine players can be accommodated on this drill: six players on the court and three waiting their turn.

Description

Explain and demonstrate the high-post backdoor move. Have two offensive guards on each wing and a forward. One guard brings the ball down on one side of the court. The other guard is directly across the key on the other side, with the forward positioned on that same side. The forward cuts to the free-throw line (but outside the three-second lane) and receives a pass from the guard. The off-ball guard waits until the forward catches the ball and performs a backdoor move toward the basket to receive a pass (two-hand flip, chest, or bounce pass) from the forward and perform a lay-up. It the cutter does not receive the pass, he or she continues through the lane and on to the same starting position on the other side of the court. If the forward cannot pass the ball, he or she then goes one-on-one with the defender or passes the ball to the remaining guard, who has switched positions with the other guard. Play two trials, then rotate positions or let waiting teams come in.

Challenge

Have the forward line up on one side and the guards bring the ball up the floor, passing back and forth. When the guards get into position and the ball is passed to the guard on the wing opposite the forward, the forward breaks to the high post to receive the ball and begin a backdoor.

6.44   3 v 3: Live at Halfcourt

Goal

Incorporate all skills in a 3 v 3 competitive game.

Organization

Six players play per halfcourt with one basketball—three on offense and three on defense. Twelve players can be accommodated on one court; six players wait while the other six play.

Description

Review and demonstrate all the moves that can be used in a game of 3 v 3. Have players play a game of 3 v 3 using only the following skills: dribbling, lay-up, the set and jump shot, individual moves covered thus far (rocker step, drive strong and drive weak, crossover, jab and set shot, fake shot and drive), give-and-go, V cut, backdoor, and all the pick and roll moves, including pass and screen away. Teams can have three guards or two guards and one forward.

Play begins when the defense lightly tosses the ball to the offensive player, who can pass or dribble. Screening is expected, and the three-second-lane violation is enforced. Only lay-ups and close-in shots (from no farther than the free-throw line can be taken). Fouls or any disputes are replayed. Defense switches to offense when a basket is made by the offense, when a turnover occurs, or when the defense intercepts a pass or rebounds a missed shot. If there's a turnover or the ball is rebounded by the defense, play continues, but the defense must bring the ball back outside the three-point line before attempting to score. The defense can play a tight or switching man-to-man. Teams keep track of their total number of baskets. If teams are waiting, they rotate in after each basket.

Challenge

Change the scoring to ensure that more lay-ups off screens occur by giving two points for a lay-up scored off a pick or a backdoor while anything else (pop out, etc.) is awarded one point.

6.45   5 v 5 at Halfcourt

Goals

Apply the individual and team skills covered thus far in class in a 5 v 5 setting; work and develop as a team.

Organization

Ten players play at halfcourt with one basketball—five offensive players and five defensive players.

Description

Review and demonstrate all possible situations that might arise in a 5 v 5 game. Provide each team with set plays on laminated cards, or allow them to design their own plays. After teams have practiced a basic set offense, teams get to work on their offense against another team, first with a passive defense, then a tighter defense, and finally a full defense. Each team gets five trials at scoring. Once teams are running their offense reasonably well, play competitive games of 5 v 5 on a halfcourt. Teams should use a three-guard and two-forward offense.

Play begins when the defense lightly tosses the ball to the offensive player, who can pass or dribble. Screening is expected, and the three-second-lane violation is enforced. Shots must be taken inside the three-point line. Fouls or any disputes are replayed. Defense switches to offense when a basket is made by the offense, when a turnover occurs, or when the defense intercepts a pass or rebounds an offensive missed shot. If there's a turnover or the ball is rebounded by the defense, play continues, but the defense must bring the ball back outside the three-point line before attempting to score. The defense can play a tight or switching man-to-man. Teams keep track of their total number of baskets. Each team is allowed one 60-second timeout to discuss strategy. Focus on keeping on the move and finding open areas on the court.

Challenge

To win a game, every player on the team must make a basket.

Reference

Krause, Jerry V., Don Meyer, and Jerry Meyer. 1999. *Basketball: Skills and Drills. 2d ed.* Champaign, IL: Human Kinetics.

Flag Football

American football is one of the few sports that must be completely modified to be appropriate for a physical education class. For one thing, a regulation game requires physically tackling an opponent—something not educationally sound or permitted in a classroom setting. In addition, regulation football requires helmets and other expensive equipment perhaps amounting to hundreds of dollars per individual. No physical education budget could handle that expense. Yet there's value in the sport from a physical education perspective. The game includes skills and tactics that can be used later in life in a city recreation league, at a family picnic, or even to increase the enjoyment of watching the Super Bowl. Using flags (strips of fabric that hang on each hip from a belt; "tacklers" pull the flag instead of tackling) makes the game as safe as any other field sport you might play in your class.

Flag football can be very active and exciting to teach if the game is modified to promote more activity and if the number of players on a team is properly minimized. Achieving this means emphasizing passing and receiving as the key skills to learn and delegating smaller roles to the skills of running, blocking, and kicking. When watching a typical 7 v 7 flag football game in a physical education class, you'll surely note one thing quickly: At the most, three players are active while the rest stand around and watch. Often it's the heavier and slower kids who end up blocking or centering while the swifter, more athletic types dominate the more active skill positions. The result? Well over half the class is unmotivated because they can see they're not part of the play and have little expectation that the football will come to them. While regulation football has 11 players on a team, most of these players don't participate in the most enjoyable part of the game, which involves getting to touch the football. Since our object is to educate by developing motor skills and fitness, we want to make sure that all of our students receive equal opportunities to develop their motor skills and fitness levels. This means we want all students enjoying the game enough to participate with enthusiasm. We can more likely achieve this goal by reducing the number of players per team, thereby increasing opportunities for enjoyment and learning.

The progressions involve all players by focusing on developing passing and receiving while playing mostly 3 v 3 games (one quarterback and two wide receivers) on 50-yard fields. Players begin with passing and receiving and proceed from nonmovement to movement, leading into various pass patterns. From there, a shadow defender is added to get the receiver accustomed to having a defender nearby before allowing the defender to guard live. Quickly, 3 v 3 games are introduced with set plays drawn up on cards to save time. At this point, the offense should dominate because defending the pass has intentionally not been covered to allow more scoring and to motivate interest. Once the offensive skills of passing and receiving have been developed, then man-to-man defensive coverage is practiced before returning to the 3 v 3 game format. Once passing, receiving, and man-to-man defending have been learned and players have some confidence, you can then add another player to the game. This opens up many prospects for instruction, including passing to a back out of the backfield (an offensive player who lines up behind the quarterback and primarily runs with the football, but in this instance they leave the backfield to go out for a pass), passing to a slot or flanker back (a back who instead of lining up in the backfield lines up five to eight yards on either side of the quarterback a yard behind the line of scrimmage), running with the football (using handoffs and pitches), centering the football, and blocking, among others. Since kicking involves at the most only two members of any team, this skill is saved for advanced classes. Usually there's no need to incorporate practicing the skill of stripping the football carrier of the flag, because players quickly learn what to do in the game itself. But if this skill is included, it should be delayed until the offense is having consistent success. The progressions end with games of 5 v 5 performing set plays drawn up on cards ahead of time; these plays should ensure that all players are potential pass receivers.

If the goal of the class is to teach the beginning basic skills of flag football with high rates of activity, then less is better, and focusing on passing and receiving is common sense.

Ideally, you would have enough space to play 3 v 3 games on 50-yard fields. For the initial teaching of receiving and catching, natural corridors are already present on a regular lined football field using the 5- and 10-yard markers. These lines keep students cognizant of keeping the football within those boundaries and reduces safety concerns. Similarly, to avoid controversy, I advise using official flags in which the entire belt comes off, but two-hand tag is also perfectly all right, especially if one of the goals of the class is for students to work out conflicts themselves (e.g., whether it was a two- or one-handed tag). Finally, understand the effect the size of the football can have on passing performance. Novices do much better with a junior football that's just a bit smaller than a regulation football, which allows them to grip the football with one hand and throw it with a tight spiral. A smaller junior football, while useful for teaching passing, is much harder to catch. Using sponge footballs (such as Nerf® balls) helps reduce a student's fear of catching. Be aware, though, that not all sponge footballs (or other modified footballs, such as "rag" balls) fly true, which can hamper skill development. Some are also more difficult to catch because they're slippery.

Many of the activities in the progressions require each player or a pair of players to have one football to work on the skill being introduced. I'll assume you know already to have enough footballs on hand to meet the needs of your students. When an activity requires a player or pair of players to use more than one football, I'll mention this in the activity's Organization section.

■ After following the progressions, beginning students should be able to play in a game of 3 v 3 and 5 v 5 flag football using the following skills:
- Passing with a three-step drop
- Passing while rolling out
- Receiving the football (facing, sideways, above and below the waist) while stationary and moving
- Running pass patterns, including
  - Streak
  - Out and in
  - Slant in and out
  - Post
  - Flag
  - Curl in and out
  - Banana in and out
- Defensive back stance and backpedal (man-to-man defense)
- Playing backfield
  - Handing off and receiving a football
  - Pitching and receiving a pitched football in the backfield
  - Running with the football and going in motion as a back from a position in the backfield or as a wide receiver
- Deep snap

7.1 Pass and Receive While Stationary

Goals

Develop the proper passing motion and football release while stationary so that the football flies in a tight spiral accurately to a partner; develop proper reception skills both overhead and above and below the waist.

Organization

Partners play in practice areas 10 yards long by 5 yards wide.

Description

Explain and demonstrate proper quarterback throwing mechanics and the techniques of receiving (overhead; above, at, and below the waist). Have partners practice throwing and receiving back and forth to each other from a distance no greater than 10 yards, without moving while facing each other. The receiver should give the passer a target with his or her hands (above the waist, at the waist, or below the waist). Focus on bringing the football up to the ear with both hands, pushing off the dominant foot, and stepping in the direction of the receiver with the nondominant foot as the football is thrown. When receiving, catch the football away from the body with the fingerpads and cushion or absorb the ball by drawing it back into your body as you catch it.

Challenges

Play a game of Target. If the receiver drops a catchable pass, a point is awarded the thrower. If the receiver has to move his or her hands (which have been positioned as a target to receive the football), the receiver gets a point. The football must be catchable (within easy reach) and not thrown hard. The first one to five points wins.

7.2 Pass and Receive While Moving

Goal

Develop the skill of leading a receiver with a pass and receiving a football in a sideways position while moving.

Organization

Partners play in practice areas 10 yards long by 5 yards wide.

Description

Briefly explain and demonstrate passing with a one-step drop, leading a moving receiver, and catching the football while turned sideways. Have players pass and receive back and forth, with the receiver walking between the two sidelines 10 yards apart. The passer is stationary and takes a one-step drop. The receiver gives the passer a target with both hands held shoulder height away from and ahead of the body.

Challenges

Have players pass the football with a tight spiral at about shoulder height a yard ahead of the body so that receivers don't have to break or alter their stride to catch the ball.

7.3   Three-Step Drop, Pass, and Receive While Jogging

Goal

Develop the skill of leading a receiver with a pass from a three-step drop and receiving the football in a sideways position while moving.

Organization

Partners play in practice areas 10 yards long by 10 yards wide.

Description

Explain and demonstrate the three-step drop and passing to a jogging receiver. Have the passer perform a three-step drop and pass to a receiver jogging from sideline to sideline (10 yards). Passer should be sure to lead the moving receiver so that he or she doesn't have to break stride. The receiver gives the passer a target with both hands held shoulder height away from and ahead of the body. Focus on quickly performing the three-step drop, planting the dominant foot, and transferring weight onto the front foot as you throw and lead the receiver.

Challenges

Have players pass the football (at about shoulder height a yard from the body) with a tight spiral so that the receiver doesn't have to break stride. See if they can succeed in three out of five trials. Challenge partners to see who can be the most accurate passer out of the five trials.

7.4   Running Pass Patterns Without the Football

Goal

Develop proper footwork for cutting and routes when performing the most commonly used pass patterns.

Organization

You can set this up in two ways. One way is for all the players to line up on a line three giant strides apart and have you lead the class through each pattern as a group. The other is to demonstrate each pattern, then have players practice in specified areas on the field. There's no need for a football. Players concentrate on making the appropriate cut and running the correct pattern rather than on catching the football.

Description

Explain and demonstrate the line of scrimmage, off-sides, how to run pass patterns, and the pass patterns themselves (including the streak, the out and in, the slant in and slant out, the post, the flag, the curl in and curl out, and the banana in and banana out [see figure 7.1, a–k]). Have players practice each pattern without a football so their focus is on making the proper cut with an upright stance. Focus on making crisp cuts and planting the correct foot when performing the out and in, slant in and slant out, post, and flag patterns and exploding off the plant to free yourself from a defender.

Challenge

Form groups of three, with one quarterback and two wide receivers (one on the left and one on the right of the quarterback about 10 yards from an imaginary center). The quarterback assigns a different pattern for each receiver, calls the signals ("Ready, set, go!"), and performs a three-step drop as the receivers run their routes. The quarterback throws an imaginary throw to one of the receivers. Any questions about routes can be ironed out at this time.

7.5 Running Pass Patterns With the Football

Goal

Develop timing between the quarterback and the receiver running pass patterns.

Organization

Players play in groups of three with two balls in a 30-yard by 30-yard area.

Description

Explain and demonstrate the three-step drop and throwing to a receiver running a designated pattern. Have the quarterback stand back from the line of scrimmage about 5 yards and call out the pattern to a receiver on the right side, who is lined up on the line of scrimmage about 8 yards from an imaginary center. The quarterback gives the signal ("Ready, set, go!"), and then

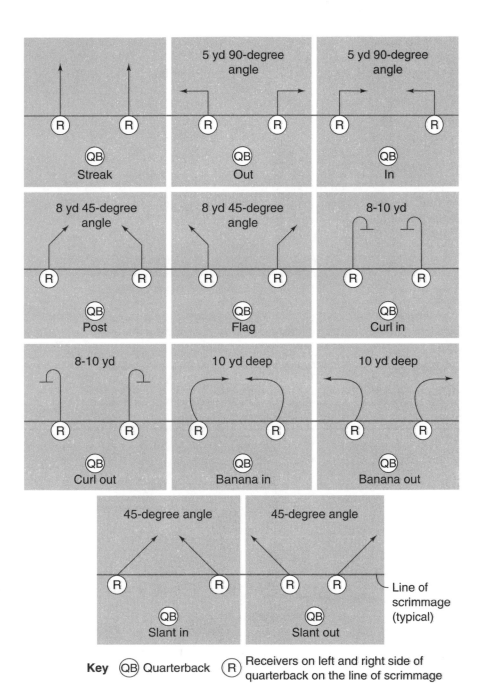

Figure 7.1 Pass patterns.

From *Sport Progressions* by Roy A. Clumpner, 2003, Champaign, IL: Human Kinetics.

performs a three-step drop and throws the football to the right receiver. The quarterback then calls a different pattern for the left receiver, using the second football, and the action is repeated. Players rotate positions after several attempts. Focus on leading the receiver so that the receiver does not have to break stride. For the receiver, focus on coming off the line of scrimmage at the same speed (fast) every play (so the defender is not tipped off) and making your cuts crisp.

Challenges

Keep track of the total number of receptions the team makes in a 10-minute period. See how many receptions a passer can make in a row to the two receivers. Receivers may not repeat a pattern.

7.6 3 v 0 Pass Patterns

Goal

Develop a routine of going to a huddle to determine the play to use, lining up on-side (staying behind the line of scrimmage until the football is put into play), remaining on-side as the quarterback calls the signals, taking off when the quarterback yells "go," and executing the play as it was drawn up.

Organization

Players play in groups of three (one quarterback and two receivers) with two balls in a 30-yard by 30-yard area. Passing plays are drawn up on 8.5- × 11-inch laminated paper (six to eight plays on each side) (see figure 7.2 for an example of one play).

Description

Explain and demonstrate a huddle, how to read drawn-up pass plays, and how to run a play. Have the teams of three huddle 10 yards from the line of scrimmage. The quarterback then points out the passing play to be run by the two receivers and breaks the huddle. Once the receivers are lined up (distance from imaginary center can vary from 5 to 10 yards) and the quarterback is in position 5 yards from the line of scrimmage, have the quarterback give the signal ("Ready, set, go!") and perform the three-step drop as the receivers run the pattern called for in the play. The quarterback throws to one of the receivers, who catches and runs with the football into the imaginary end zone (the endline of the 30-yard zone) and retreats back to huddle up with the same receivers to pick another play. A second group then approaches the line of scrimmage, having finished their huddle, and proceeds to run the play they picked. Players may not repeat a pattern until all patterns are tried,

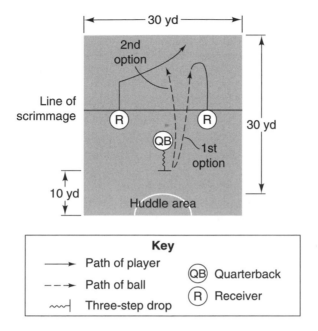

Figure 7.2 Pass play example.

can't receive more than two passes in a row, and must rotate positions after three attempts.

Challenges

1. Can the team in the huddle have their play picked by the time the other team has run their play?

2. Once the signal "go!" is given, can the quarterback throw the football within four seconds?

3. Add a second quarterback who throws to the other receiver after the first quarterback throws to increase the number of opportunities for quarterbacks and receivers.

7.7 3 v 0 Rollout

Goal

Develop the ability to throw the football on a rollout. A rollout is when the quarterback runs parallel to the line of scrimmage (but not over) to elude on-rushing defenders and gain time to stop and throw.

Organization

Players play in groups of three (one quarterback and two receivers) with two balls in a 30-yard by 30-yard area. Passing plays that require the quarterback to roll out are drawn up on 8.5- × 11-inch laminated paper (six to eight plays on each side).

Description

Explain and demonstrate a rollout and how to stop and throw the football to a receiver. Have teams of three huddle 10 yards from the line of scrimmage. The quarterback gives the play to the two receivers, then breaks the huddle. Once the receivers are lined up and the quarterback is in position five yards from the line of scrimmage, the quarterback gives the signal ("Ready, set, go!"), performs a rollout to the left or right, and throws the football to one of the receivers running the pattern called for in the play (see figure 7.3). The receiver catches the football and runs with it into the imaginary end zone (the endline of the 30-yard zone). After the throw, the quarterback returns to huddle up with the same receivers to pick another play. Meanwhile, a second group breaks from their huddle and approaches the line of scrimmage to run the play they picked. Players may not repeat a pattern until all patterns have been tried, can't receive more than two passes in a row, and must rotate positions after three attempts. For greater accuracy and power, focus on making sure to stop and plant before throwing the football.

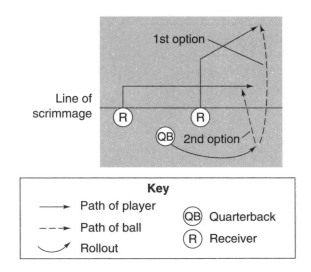

Figure 7.3 Pattern for a rollout.

Challenge

Can the quarterback roll out and be in a position to pass within four seconds?

7.8	3 v 3 With Passive Defense

Goal

Develop the ability to execute a drawn-up offensive pass pattern while being defended.

Organization

Players form one group of three players on defense and one group of three players on offense (one quarterback and two receivers) with two balls in a 30-yard by 40-yard wide area (see figure 7.4). Passing plays are drawn up on 8.5- × 11-inch laminated paper (six to eight plays per side). If needed, you can add a second group of offensive players.

Description

Explain and demonstrate playing 3 v 3 against a passive defense. Have teams huddle 10 yards from the line of scrimmage. The quarterback gives the play

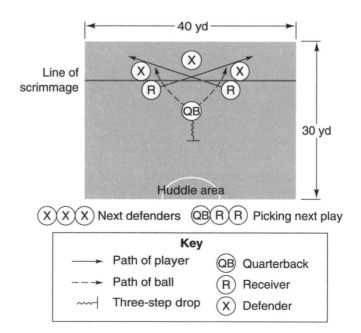

Figure 7.4   Setup for 3 v 3 With Passive Defense.

to the two receivers, then breaks the huddle. The three defenders shadow (passively follow) their assigned offensive player, meaning they can run with them but are not allowed to interfere with the play. One defender covers each receiver, and the remaining defender is the pass rusher who chases the quarterback. Once the receivers are lined up and the quarterback is in position five yards from the line of scrimmage, the quarterback gives the signal ("Ready, set, go!") and performs a three-step drop or a rollout as called for in the play. The receivers run their patterns. The two defenders covering the receivers line up wherever they want and shadow the receivers. The pass rusher guarding the quarterback must remain at the line of scrimmage counting to a set number but can begin rushing the quarterback once the set number is reached. The quarterback throws to one of the receivers, who catches and runs with the football into the imaginary end zone (the endline of the 30-yard zone), then retreats back to huddle up with the same receivers to pick another play. If there are two offensive groups, the second group now runs their play against the same defense. Players can't receive more than two passes in a row and must rotate positions when on offense after three attempts. The defense rotates onto offense after three plays. Receivers should focus on exploding off the line of scrimmage as fast as they can in order to close the gap (the cushion) between them and the defender. Then when they make their cut, the defender does not have enough time to recover and continue guarding them.

Challenges

Can the quarterback recognize when a receiver is not open and throw to the other receiver instead? If both receivers are covered, can the quarterback run? It's not necessary to give players a detailed explanation of running by the quarterback. Just inform them that if no receiver is open they should tuck the football under their arm and run rather than force a pass and have it intercepted.

7.9 3 v 3: Score in Three Plays

Goal

Develop the ability to execute an offensive pass pattern as drawn up while being covered by a live (not passive) defender.

Organization

Players form one group of three players on defense and one group of three players on offense (one quarterback and two receivers) with two balls in a 30-yard by 40-yard area (see figure 7.5). Passing plays are drawn up on 8.5- ×

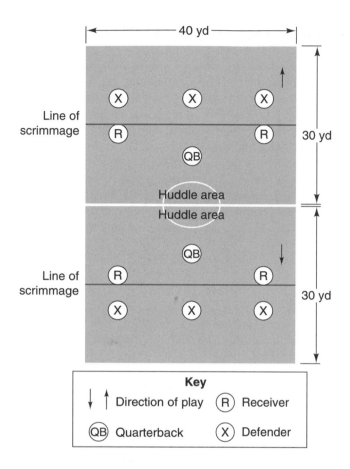

Figure 7.5 Setup for 3 v 3 Score in Three Plays.

11-inch laminated paper (six to eight plays on each side). If needed, you can add a second group of offensive players. All players wear flags for the first time.

Description

Explain using flags and demonstrate how to pull them; explain the rules of the game. Have teams huddle 10 yards from the line of scrimmage. Each team gets three chances to score. The quarterback names the play to be run to the two receivers, then breaks the huddle. Three defensive players guard their assigned receivers, running with them and doing anything that's legal to guard them, even intercepting the football. One defender guards each receiver, and the remaining defender is the rusher who chases the quarterback.

Once the receivers are lined up and the quarterback is in position five yards from the line of scrimmage, the quarterback gives the signal ("Ready, set, go!") and performs a three-step drop or a rollout as called for in the play, and the receivers run their patterns. The two defenders guarding the receivers line up wherever they wish and cover the receivers as best they can. The pass rusher guarding the quarterback must remain at the line of scrimmage counting to a set number but can then begin rushing the quarterback, trying to pull the flag. The quarterback attempts to throw to an open receiver. If the football is caught, the receiver continues to run until his or her flag is pulled by a defender or he or she reaches the end of the playing area for a touchdown. If the pass is incomplete, players form another huddle and make another play. An intercepted football is live, and the defender can return the football to his or her team's endline. Players can't receive more than two passes in a row and must rotate positions after three attempts. The defense rotates onto offense after three plays. The first team to score five touchdowns wins.

Challenges

Try setting the defense up for a particular play. For example: Run plays where a receiver runs the same pattern twice in a row. Then, on the third play, run almost an exact replica of that play, except this time the receiver plants and goes in the opposite direction.

7.10 3 v 3 With First Downs

Goal

Each team is able to move the football down the field and score without giving the football up in a turnover (interception) or a loss of downs.

Organization

Players form two teams of three players each (one quarterback, two receivers) on half a football field going sideline to sideline (about 40 yards wide by 50 yards long). Cones or field markers are placed on the sidelines at 10-yard intervals (see figure 7.6). Passing plays are on 8.5- × 11-inch laminated paper (six to eight plays on each side). All players wear flags.

Description

Explain and demonstrate the rules for playing 3 v 3. Tell the players to try to get everyone involved in the offense by throwing to everyone. Play begins at the offensive team's 10-yard line. The offensive team has four downs to reach the next 10-yard cone to receive a first down. If the offensive team does not reach the next cone for a first down, the defensive team takes over the foot-

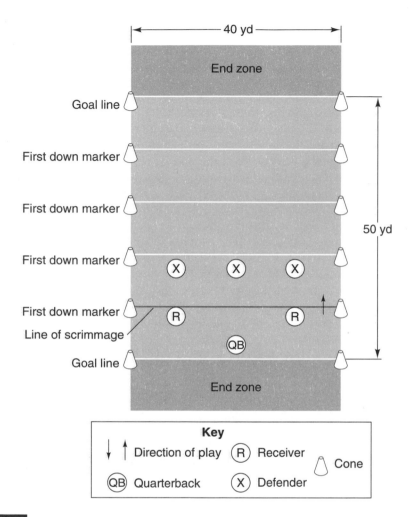

Figure 7.6 Setup for 3 v 3 With First Downs.

ball on their own 10-yard line. There is no kicking game. Players huddle 10 yards from the line of scrimmage, and the quarterback chooses the play. Three defensive players guard their assigned offensive player, running with them and doing anything that's legal to guard them, even intercepting the football. One defender covers each receiver, and the remaining defender is the pass rusher, who chases the quarterback. Once the receivers are lined up and the quarterback is in position five yards from the line of scrimmage, the quarterback gives the signal ("Ready, set, go!"). The defender guarding the quarterback then tosses the football to the quarterback, who performs a three-step drop or a rollout, as called for in the play, and the receivers run their patterns. The two defenders guarding the receivers line up wherever they wish and cover their receiver as best they can. After throwing the football to the quarterback to begin play, the pass rusher assigned to guard the quarterback remains at the line of scrimmage counting until a set number is reached, at which point he or she rushes the quarterback, trying to pull the flag before the ball is released. The quarterback attempts to throw to an open receiver. If the pass is completed, the receiver continues to run with the football until his or her flag is pulled by a defender or the end zone is reached (for a score of one point). After a score, the defensive team gets the football on their own 10-yard line. An incomplete pass comes back to the line of scrimmage. An intercepted football is live, and the defender can return the football to their end zone or until his or her flag is pulled. Players cannot receive more than two passes in a row. At least two players on each team must play quarterback at some time. A fumbled football is dead on the spot. Whichever team is ahead after a certain amount of time (say 20 minutes) wins unless the score is tied. If the score is tied, allow them to play the game out, with each team getting four chances to move the football the furthest up the field or score from the 10-yard line. There are no first downs. If the first team doesn't score, but the second team does, the game is over. But if the second team doesn't score either and does not match the first team's distance, the first team wins.

Challenge

Set a rule that if at the game's end everyone on a team caught at least one pass and scored, a bonus of two points is awarded.

7.11 Backpedal and Cut

Goal

Develop the proper backpedaling footwork and cutting required to guard a receiver.

Organization

Players line up on scrimmage line three giant strides apart.

Description

Explain and demonstrate the proper way for a defender to backpedal and cut when guarding a receiver. Have the entire group backpedal away from you about 10 yards; then point to the right or left, at which time players cut 45 degrees in the direction you're pointing (see figure 7.7). Players cut and run about five strides before stopping and returning to the starting line to begin

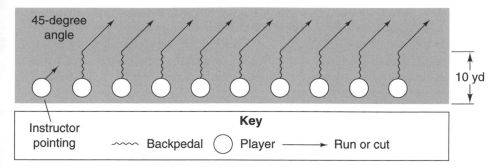

Figure 7.7   Setup for Backpedal and Cut pattern.

again. Focus on barely skimming the grass with your feet and pumping the arms.

Challenge

Once the defender has made the cut, point in the other direction, forcing the defender to cross over and go in a 45-degree angle in the new direction.

7.12   Guarding Receivers Without the Football

Goals

Develop proper backpedaling footwork; learn to maintain a cushion (the distance between the receiver and the defender guarding the receiver, in this case the defensive back) when guarding a receiver and turn and run at the appropriate time when the cushion breaks down. The rule of thumb is that whenever the distance between the receiver and the defender is five yards or less, the defender should turn and run rather than continue backpedaling.

Organization

Partners disperse throughout the field with enough room to practice pass patterns. There's no need for a football. Defensive players concentrate on proper backpedaling, maintaining a cushion of five yards from the receiver, and turning and running should the cushion break down.

Description

Explain and demonstrate the cushion and the need for the defender to maintain a five-yard distance from the receiver. Focus on keeping the five-yard cushion, but if it breaks down (the receiver gets closer than five yards), turn and run right away.

Have partners practice defending each other without a football. Receivers are to run any of the pass patterns learned thus far (streak, in and out, slant in and slant out, post, flag, curl in and curl out, banana in and banana out). They run each pattern without a football, focusing on technique; defenders focus on maintaining a cushion of five yards from the receiver. If the cushion breaks down, they turn and run.

Challenges

If the defender is having success, have him or her perform an Out and Up or Curl and Go on the defender to see if the defender can react. The Out and Up is an out pattern followed by the receiver turning upfield and running parallel to the sideline. In the Curl and Go, the receiver performs a curl that turns into a 360-degree turn and heads upfield looking for a long pass.

7.13 3 v 3 With Focus on Defense

Goal

In a competitive situation, develop the ability to cover a receiver, maintain a cushion, and turn and run should the cushion break down.

Organization

Players form two teams of three players each (one quarterback and two receivers). Play on half of a football field (about 40 yards wide by 50 yards long; see figure 7.6, p. 167). Place cones or field markers on the sidelines at 10-yard intervals. Passing plays are on 8.5- × 11-inch laminated paper (six to eight plays on each side). All players wear flags.

Description

Explain and demonstrate the activity and rules. Play begins at the offensive team's 10-yard line. The offensive team has four downs to reach the next 10-yard pylon and receive a first down. If the offensive team does not get a first down, the defensive team takes over the football on their own 10-yard line. There is no kicking game.

Players huddle 10 yards from the line of scrimmage. The quarterback gives the play to the two receivers and then breaks the huddle. Three defensive players guard their assigned offensive player, running with them and doing anything that's legal to guard them, even intercepting the football. Each receiver is covered by one defender, and the remaining defender is the pass rusher, who chases the quarterback. Once the receivers are lined up and the quarterback is in position 5 yards from the line of scrimmage, the pass rusher starts play by tossing the football to the quarterback and counting to a set number before he or she is allowed to rush. Meanwhile, the quarterback performs a three-step drop or a rollout, and the receivers run their patterns. The two defenders cover the receiver as well as they can. The quarterback attempts to throw to an open receiver. If the pass is completed, the receiver continues to run with the football until a flag is pulled by a defender or the end zone is reached for a score (of one point). After a score, the defensive team gets the football on their own 10-yard line. An incomplete pass comes back to the line of scrimmage. An intercepted pass is live until a flag is pulled or the defender can return the football to his or her team's endline. Players cannot receive more than two consecutive passes. At least two players on each team must play quarterback at some time. A fumbled football is automatically dead at that point. Any disputes are replayed. Focus on keeping a cushion of 5 yards from the receiver and turning and running if that cushion breaks down.

Challenge

Have defenders vary in how they guard their receivers from very tight at the line of scrimmage to loose coverage (upward of 10 yards off the receiver) to see if the quarterback sees the change and makes the correct adjustment (he or she should throw short when the defender plays off and throw long when the defender plays tight).

7.14 | Backfield Practice

Goal

Develop the backfield skills of giving and receiving a handoff, pitching and receiving a pitch, going in motion, and running with the football.

Organization

Players form teams of five players each in practice areas of 30 yards by 30 yards (see figure 7.8). Prepare running and passing plays on 8.5- × 11-inch laminated sheets.

Description

Explain and demonstrate handing off and receiving a football in the backfield, pitching and receiving a pitched football in the backfield, running with the football, and going in motion from a position in the backfield or as a wide receiver. Have teams practice plays that include these skills. All players rotate and practice each position. Focus on pitching the football with a two-hand underhand toss no higher than shoulders. Also focus on receiving a handoff with the near elbow up, delivering a handoff with both hands, running with the football, and going into motion.

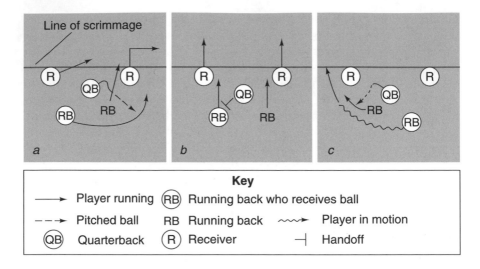

Figure 7.8 Setup for Backfield Practice. *(a)* Pitch to back, *(b)* handoff, and *(c)* running back in motion.

Challenge

Practice each play once with each player playing a different position—see if they can go through all positions without making a mistake.

7.15 5 v 5 Game

Goal

Use the offensive skills of running and passing the football in a competitive situation.

Organization

Players form two teams of five players each: one quarterback, two receivers, one back, and one flanker (a back who is split out to the sideline, one yard off the line of scrimmage and outside the end who is usually tight next to the tackle). The back can be a fullback or tailback, who lines up behind the quarterback in the backfield, or a halfback, who lines up in the backfield behind one of the guards. You also can use a slot back, but be sure to explain this position to your players (a back who lines up one yard off the line of scrimmage between the split end and the tackle on that side). Play is on one half of a football field (about 40 yards wide by 50 yards long). Place cones or markers on the sidelines at 10-yard intervals (see figure 7.9). Prepare passing

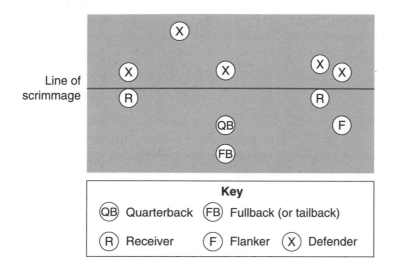

Figure 7.9   Setup for 5 v 5 Game.

and running plays on 8.5- × 11-inch laminated paper (six to eight plays on each side). All players wear flags.

Description

Review the offensive and defensive skills learned thus far and emphasize that you want to see them used in the game. Play begins at the offensive team's 10-yard line. The offense has four downs to reach the next 10-yard pylon and receive a first down. If the offense does not reach the next pylon in four downs, the defensive team takes over the football on their own 10-yard line. There is no kicking game.

Players huddle, and the quarterback chooses a play. Three players cover the wide receivers man-to-man; the remaining defensive players guard the quarterback and the back. The pass rusher tosses the football to the quarterback and remains at the line of scrimmage counting to a set number. When the number is reached, he or she can rush the quarterback and try to pull his or her flag. The other defensive player covers the back, who can run with the football, go in motion for a pass, or catch a swing pass. After a score, the offensive team receives one point and the defensive team gets the football on their own 10-yard line. An incomplete pass comes back to the line of scrimmage. An interception is live, and the defender can return the football to his or her endline for a score or until his or her flag is pulled. Players can't receive more than two passes in a row. At least two players on each team must play quarterback at some time. A fumbled football is dead on the spot it lands. There's no blocking. Any disputes are replayed. After 20 minutes or so, have teams play other teams. Focus on keeping the defense off balance by choosing plays they least suspect and probing their weaknesses.

Challenge

Give the offensive team only 30 seconds to huddle up and get the play off or else they receive a five-yard penalty.

7.16 Deep Snap

Goal

Develop a deep snap (passing the football between the legs back to a quarterback about five yards with a spiral).

Organization

Players play with partners, five yards apart.

Description

Explain and demonstrate the deep snap. Lead your players step by step through the deep-snap progressions:

1. Stand with your back to your partner about five yards apart; grip the football as if you are going to throw a forward pass.

2. Begin the motion of throwing the pass and at the same time bend over and throw the football between your legs back to your partner. Do not place the football on the ground or touch the ground with the football. The deep snap is nothing more than a forward pass between the legs.

3. Once you can consistently throw a spiral to your partner, bend over and place only the front stripe of the football on the ground. Proceed to propel the football as you just did with a forward pass between your legs.

Challenge

Add the nonthrowing hand on the football (on the side opposite the throwing hand) and lean forward, putting weight on the football. Propel the football back using the same motion with the throwing hand but adding the nonthrowing hand to give the football extra spin and velocity.

7.17 6 v 6 Game With Deep Snap

Goals

Incorporate the skill of the deep snap into a game and develop the offensive skills of running and passing the football in a competitive situation.

Organization

Players form two teams of six players each: one quarterback, two receivers, one back (either fullback, tailback, or halfback), one flanker or slot back, and a center (the player 5 yards in front of the quarterback on the line of scrimmage who initiates play with a deep snap). Play is on half of a football field (about 40 yards wide by 50 yards long). Place cones and field markers on the sidelines at 10-yard intervals. Prepare passing and running plays on 8.5- × 11-inch laminated paper (six to eight plays on each side). All players wear flags.

Description

Give players a quick overview of the rules for the game; emphasize being a good sport. Play begins at the offensive team's 10-yard line. The offense has four downs to reach the next 10-yard pylon to receive a first down. If the offense does not reach the next pylon in four downs, the defensive team takes over the football on their own 10-yard line. There's no kicking game.

Players huddle 10 yards from the line of scrimmage, and the quarterback chooses the play. Four players cover the wide receivers and center, man-to-man, with the remaining defensive players guarding the quarterback and the back. The pass rusher guarding the quarterback remains at the line of scrimmage counting to a set number. Once the number is reached, he or she runs toward the quarterback and attempts to pull his or her flag before the ball is released. Another defensive player covers the back, who can run with the football, go in motion for a pass, or catch a swing pass. The remaining defensive back covers the center. Play begins when the center deep snaps the football to the quarterback. A score is worth one point. After a score, the other team gets the football on its own 10-yard line. An incomplete pass comes back to the line of scrimmage. An interception is live, and the defender can return the football to his or her team's endline for a score or until his or her flag is pulled. Players can't receive more than two passes in a row. At least two players on each team must play quarterback at some time. A fumbled football is automatically dead on the spot it lands. There's no blocking. Any disputes are replayed. Play for 20 minutes or so before switching teams.

Challenge

Give the offensive team only 30 seconds to huddle up and get the play off or else they receive a five-yard penalty.

Slow-Pitch Softball

Softball is one of the most popular lifetime activities in North America. Students come to a softball unit having had exposure to the sport in some form or another every year since they entered grade school. However, the play they've been exposed to has not always been approached from an educational perspective. For one thing, the sport can be quite inactive when played by the standard rules of at least nine players on a team and lots of waiting between spurts of activity. Your job is further complicated by the notion held by some that softball is a leisurely sport played at family picnics and not an activity to be developed in a structured class. Your challenge then is to increase the activity rates and further develop skill. These progressions should do just that.

Softball poses a challenge when it comes to progression development. Like the skills of basketball, the skills of softball do not sequence well; consequently, some essential skills must be taught separately before they can be combined. The essence of slow-pitch softball is throwing, fielding, and hitting. While there are several approaches to take in teaching softball, I recommend practicing throwing and fielding separately from hitting before combining them.

As mentioned in chapters 1 and 2, the reduction in the size of fields or courts and the implementation of mini-games increases the opportunities and in turn the skill level of players. Slow-pitch softball, however, requires space to throw, hit, and field. Modifying or shortening field space can be done and is outlined in these progressions, but there are limitations. If the field is reduced too much, there remains little resemblance to the real game. Players need to take a full swing at a softball and see it travel out of the infield; fielders need to track and run under a deep fly softball.

Although it's not specified in the progressions, you should begin each day of your softball unit with fielding, throwing, and hitting practice—to the point that players are getting dozens of throws and catches and 30 to 40 swings at a softball with a bat each day.

Using stations to reduce wait time is highly encouraged. One of the inherent problems in teaching softball is getting enough batting practice. To have real batting practice for each student in class requires space and lots of time, which are luxuries for most of us. The progressions try to solve this problem by using batting tees, a piece of equipment even professional players use to refine their swing.

Some of the activities I've included do not exactly mirror the rules of softball. For example, one of the high-activity games is a 2 v 2 in which a batter can travel to either first or third base on a batted softball. While some might argue that the batter develops a bad habit by taking off in the wrong direction after contacting the softball, the benefits of hitting, running, and judging if one can make it home or not far outweigh the limitations.

You might also notice an emphasis on defense (fielding situations) over offense (hitting), which runs contrary to what I advocated in chapters 1 and 2. In this instance, the defensive skills of fielding and throwing must be introduced early on or there can be no progress. These skills are essential to the game. Fielding and batting should be taught concurrently and early on.

■ After following the progressions, beginning students should be able to play in a game of 9 v 9 or 10 v 10 slow-pitch softball using the following skills:

- Underhand pitching
- Catching
- Overhand throwing
- Fielding fly balls
- Fielding ground balls
- Forcing out the runner
- Hitting from a tee
- Hitting from a soft toss
- Hitting a pitched softball
- Running the bases
- Overhand throwing a softball from the outfield on one bounce to the catcher at the plate
- Backing up a throw from any position in the field
- Performing a rundown
- Performing cut-offs from the outfield as an infielder

8.1 Underhand Pitching and Catching While Stationary

Goal

Develop the proper motion for the underhand pitch and the proper execution of catching the softball above and below the waist.

Organization

With a softball, partners pair off 10 yards apart from other sets of partners in practice areas 5 yards by 10 yards.

Description

Explain and demonstrate proper pitching mechanics (including minimum and maximum height required on the arc, what constitutes a strike, and so on) and the techniques of catching. Have partners practice pitching and catching back and forth. The catcher should squat in a catcher's position and give the pitcher a target with his or her glove. After catching, the catcher becomes the pitcher. Focus on releasing the softball with an arc of at least 6 feet but no higher than 12 feet before it reaches the batter.

Challenge

The catcher gives the pitcher a target with the glove and shouldn't have to move the glove to catch the softball. Add a home plate and pitching rubber and play a game of balls and strikes in which one person pitches to an imaginary batter and the catcher calls balls and strikes. After one at-bat, the pitcher becomes the catcher, and the catcher becomes the pitcher. Each keeps track of the number of strikeouts they pitch (in this case a strikeout is when three called strikes are pitched before four called balls).

8.2 Overhand Throwing and Catching While Stationary and Moving

Goal

Develop proper overhand throwing and catching form.

Organization

With a softball, players pair off with a partner 10 yards from other partners in practice areas 5 yards by 15 yards.

Description

Explain and demonstrate proper overhand throwing and catching (direct and side-to-side technique). Partners throw and catch balls to each other from a distance of 10 to 15 yards without having the receiver move. Once they have gained proficiency, throwers make receivers move into proper position to receive the softball by throwing it to different areas in the practice area.

Challenge

Make your glove a target for your partner and see if he or she can hit the target in three out of five throws.

8.3 Overhand Throwing and Fielding Fly Balls While Stationary and Moving

Goal

Develop proper fielding of fly balls.

Organization

Partners pair off in practice areas of 5 yards by 15 to 50 yards.

Description

Explain and demonstrate the proper technique for moving into position and fielding fly balls. Partners throw and field fly balls back and forth beginning with light throws directly to the fielder, then right, left, up, and back. Focus on moving quickly into position to field the softball. Your hands should be positioned so that if you missed the ball, it would hit you at your hairline. Use two hands to catch the softball, not one.

Challenge

Play a game of Step Back. In practice areas 5 yards wide by 50 yards long (sideline to sideline of a football field), one player throws a high fly to his or her partner. If the receiver catches the fly inside the practice area, he or she takes two giant steps toward the thrower. If the receiver misses, the receiver recovers the ball and throws either from where it was recovered or from where it was dropped, whichever is farthest from the thrower. If the softball is thrown over the sideline, the receiver takes two giant steps forward from the point at which the ball crossed the sideline and throws the ball back. If the softball goes over the head of the receiver, the receiver must chase it down and stop it, at which point this becomes the throwing point, with no steps allowed. The ball *must* be a high fly. Award a point to the thrower if the softball reaches the end zone of the receiver.

8.4   Overhand Throwing and Fielding Ground Balls While Stationary and Moving

Goals

Develop the skills of moving in front of a ground ball to block the softball, judging a ground ball, and fielding various types of ground balls.

Organization

Partners practice in areas 5 yards by 10 yards with one softball.

Description

Explain and demonstrate proper technique for fielding ground balls and moving into position to field ground balls. Partners throw and field ground balls back and forth, beginning with one hop, then two, and then three, and so on to a stationary fielder. Once players are proficient, perform the same sequence but have the fielder move right, left, and forward. As the fielder becomes more competent, speed up the delivery of the ball.

Challenge

Play a game of HORSE in the practice area. Players throw grounders back and forth to each other. If a grounder gets past the fielder, he or she receives an H. All the fielder has to do is to stop the softball so that it stays in front of him or her, not necessarily catch it cleanly. The game is over when one player makes five errors and spells out HORSE. To make the game more competitive, expand the target area and throw from sideline to sideline (five yards wide).

8.5   Over the Line Grounders

Goal

Develop quick movement by fielders to get into position to field grounders, make the catch, and throw the softball to home plate.

Organization

You'll need four players, six cones, and a softball. Construct a miniature baseball field consisting of a home plate and a first base and third base 25 feet away from home. Instead of bases, place cones at first and third. Continue down the first and third baselines and place two more cones at 25-foot intervals (see figure 8.1).

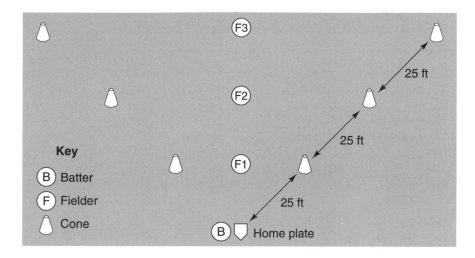

Figure 8.1   Setup for Over the Line Grounders.

Description

Explain and demonstrate the game. Have one person at bat and three fielders. Fielder 1 is behind the first set of cones (an imaginary line drawn through the first and third base cones), fielder 2 is behind the second set of cones, and fielder 3 is behind the third set. The object of the game is for the player at bat to throw grounders past the three imaginary lines created by the traffic cones. The fielders attempt to stop the grounders from crossing the lines using proper fielding technique. One point is awarded to the batter if the softball crosses the first line, two points if it passes the second line, and three points if it passes the third line. The fielders must hustle into position to get in front of the softball and completely stop it from going further (a deflected softball is not considered to be stopped). The softball must hit the ground before reaching the first line. Each player keeps track of his or her own score. Rotate positions after each throw. The batter becomes fielder 3, fielder 3 becomes fielder 2, fielder 2 becomes fielder 1, and fielder 1 becomes the batter. The first one to 15 points is the winner. The focus should be on quickly getting into position to stop the softball before it goes any farther.

Challenge

Award one extra point for the fielder if the softball is caught cleanly and not bobbled.

8.6 Around the Horn

Goal

Develop the ability to catch the softball while tagging a base, then turn and relay the softball to another base.

Organization

Five players (four infielders and a batter) play on a mini-infield with all bases and home plate. The distance between bases and home plate is reduced to 40 feet.

Description

Explain and demonstrate how to relay the softball and who covers the bag for each situation. Have the batter throw a grounder to one of the four infielders, who fields the softball and throws to first base. The first baseman tags the bag as the softball is caught and relays the softball to second base, where the action is repeated, then on to third, where it is again repeated, and then on to home, where the batter catches the throw. Rotate positions clockwise after each fielder gets two trials at each position. Focus on making sure to catch the softball and tag the base before turning to throw to the next base.

Challenge

Have the initial play made to third base and reverse the relay (e.g., third to second to first to home).

8.7 Force Out the Runner

Goals

Develop the skills of fielding grounders and throwing the softball to a base to complete an out. Help fielders sharpen their decision-making skills regarding where to throw the softball with a runner on base and if they should force out a runner.

Organization

Four players (two up to bat, two in the field) play on a mini-field with bases at first and third and a home plate (see figure 8.2).

Description

Explain the concept of a force-out and demonstrate stepping on a base or the plate to force an out after catching the softball. Have one team take the field while the other is up to bat. To begin play, the batter throws a grounder di-

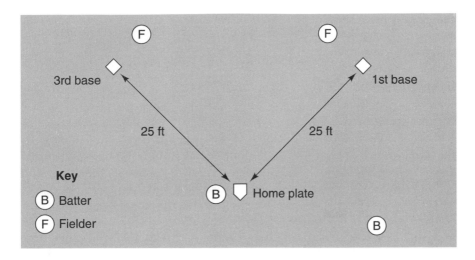

Figure 8.2 Setup for Force Out the Runner.

rectly at one of the two fielders, who are playing positions that approximate shortstop and second base. The batter (thrower) then runs either to first or third base, trying to reach the base before the fielders make a force-out. The fielder who fields the softball either runs to the base the runner has chosen to run to and causes a force-out (if he or she beats the runner there) or, if the runner is running to the other base, throws the softball to his or her partner, who is covering the other base for a force-out. Partners at bat each get four chances to bat before switching positions with the fielders. The first team reaching 10 force-outs wins. Focus on fielding and controlling the softball before deciding where to throw it.

Challenge

Instead of throwing the softball directly at the fielder, throw it so that the fielder has to move (but no more than two giant steps away).

8.8 2 v 2 Throwing and Fielding a Softball

Goal

Develop the skills of fielding ground balls, forcing out a runner, and making judgments about the speed of the base runner and your ability to throw the softball in time to force out a base runner trying to reach home plate.

Organization

Four players (two up to bat, two in the field) play on a mini-field set up with bases at first and third and a home plate (see figure 8.2).

Description

Explain and demonstrate the game. To begin play, the batter throws a ground ball anywhere between first and third base and runs either to first base or third base. If the runner reaches the base safely before being forced out, he or she remains on that base. The base runner cannot touch the base and immediately return home for a score. The base runner's teammate then comes to bat and similarly throws a grounder between first and third base; this player may run only to the vacant base. Meanwhile, the runner on base must return home to take his or her turn at bat. The fielder who is not fielding has a choice of going to the base toward which the runner is running (to receive the throw for a force-out) or going to home plate to cover the plate and prevent a score. The fielder must decide whether to force at home plate or at a base. With the exception of running to third base, most of the rules of softball are followed. After three outs, the side is retired. Focus on forcing at home plate whenever possible to prevent a score.

Challenge

Add infield fly balls (restricting the area in which they can be thrown), which requires learning how to tag up. ("Tagging up" is remaining on base until the softball is caught, and then taking off for the next base before the throw comes in.)

8.9   Hitting From a Tee

Goal

Develop proper hitting form and correct contact of the bat on the softball.

Organization

Designate a batting area with a batting tee for every two players (batter and retriever). You'll need six Wiffle balls or rag balls, one bat, and a fence or wall about five feet from the tee. The batting area should be about 10 yards wide and roped off with markers for safety to prevent others from entering (see figure 8.3).

Description

Explain the steps involved in hitting: the stance, swing, follow-through, and so on. Then have batters hit Wiffle balls off the tee into the fence or wall. The

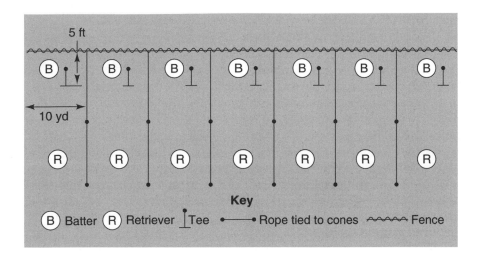

Figure 8.3 Setup for Hitting From a Tee.

batter should concentrate on hitting form. The retriever places a new Wiffle ball on the tee after each hit. Once all balls have been hit, the retriever rounds up all the balls and players trade positions.

Challenge

See if players can progress to hitting the Wiffle ball five times in a row without touching the tee.

8.10 Tee Softball

Goals

Develop hitting a softball off a tee in a semicompetitive situation; develop quick movement by fielders to get into position to field hits and throw to home plate.

Organization

Four players play with six cones, a bat, a batting tee, and a softball. Construct a mini-field consisting of the batting tee, which is home plate, and a first base and third base 25 feet away from home plate. Instead of bases, place cones at first and third. Continue down the first and third baselines and place two more cones at 25-foot intervals (see figure 8.1, p.181).

Description

Explain and demonstrate the game to your players. Have one player at bat while a partner feeds the tee. The two fielders position wherever they wish. An imaginary line is drawn between each set of cones. The object of the game is for the person at bat to hit the softball off the tee past the three imaginary lines created by the traffic cones. The fielders try to stop the ball from crossing the lines by fielding it and throwing it to the feeder at home plate to complete the play. One point is awarded to the batter if the softball crosses the first line, two points if it passes the second line, and three points if it passes the third line. Fielders must hustle into position to get in front of the ball and stop it from going further. Each team keeps track of their total score. Each batter gets four hits before exchanging positions with his or her partner, who is the feeder. After a total of eight hits, the batting team exchanges with the fielding team. Foul balls do not count as hits. Individual or team scores can be kept. The focus is on keeping your head down when hitting, and hitting down on the softball. Fielders should be in ready position to move as quickly as possible to prevent the softball from getting past them.

Challenge

Allow fielders to score points also. Award one point to the fielding team if the softball is caught cleanly, not bobbled.

8.11 Hitting From a Soft Toss

Goal

Develop the timing needed to swing the bat and hit a moving softball using proper hitting form.

Organization

You'll need six rag balls (or Wiffle balls), one home plate, one bat, and a fence or wall. One batter and a tosser pair off in a designated batting area with a home plate for every pair of partners. The batting area should be about 10 yards wide and marked off for safety to prevent others from entering.

Description

Explain and demonstrate the drill. Emphasize that the tosser needs to keep out of the range of the swinging bat. Have the batter assume a normal batting stance at the plate. The tosser kneels off to the side of the batter (at about a 25-degree angle) on the side the batter is holding the bat. To begin, the batter slow-motion swings the bat and stops the bat when it's pointing at where the tosser is kneeling; now the tosser knows the bat's extension. The tosser then backs up and kneels in a position where he or she is completely out of the range of the swinging bat. The tosser then softly underhands the rag ball up to the hitter, who judges the pitch, swings, and makes contact at the right moment. Once all the rag balls are hit, the tosser retrieves the balls, and players exchange positions. *Note:* While this is one of the best ways to develop hitting, this activity is dangerous if you have a group that does not follow instructions. If this is the case in your class, skip this activity or use a Wiffle ball, and have the pitcher toss underhand from five yards in front of or just to one side of the batter.

Challenge

Make good contact with the softball 50 percent of the time.

8.12 Over the Line Pitch and Hit

Goals

Develop the skill of hitting a pitched softball in a semi-competitive situation; develop quick movement by fielders to get into position to field a grounder and throw the softball to home plate.

Organization

You'll need a softball, a bat, and two teams of two players each. Construct a mini-field consisting of a home plate and a first base and third base situated 25 feet away from home plate. Instead of bases, place cones at first and third. Continue down the first and third baselines and place two more cones at 25-foot intervals. You can determine the width between the cones (see figure 8.1, p. 181). An imaginary line stretches between each set of cones. One team is in the outfield, and the other team has one player up to bat and one player pitching. The pitcher should be about 25 feet from home plate.

Description

Explain and demonstrate the game to your players. The object of the game is for the batter to hit the pitched softball past the three imaginary lines created by the traffic cones. The fielders try to stop the softball from crossing the lines by fielding it and throwing to the pitcher, who is covering home plate to complete the play. Award one point to the batter if the softball crosses the first line, two points if it passes the second line, and three points if it passes the third line. Fielders must hustle into position to get in front of the softball and stop it from going further. Each team keeps track of their total score. Each batter gets four hits before exchanging positions with his or her partner. After a total of eight hits, the batting team trades places with the fielding team. Focus on exploding on the pitched softball and keeping the head down.

Challenge

Also award one point to the fielding team if the softball is caught cleanly, not bobbled.

8.13 Pitch, Hit, and Field

Goals

Develop batting a pitched softball; develop pitching and fielding skills.

Organization

One mini-field set up in an area about half the size of a football field (see figure 8.4). This activity requires 5 players (a batter, a catcher, a pitcher, and two fielders), 10 softballs, a pitching rubber, and a home plate. The catcher must wear a mask.

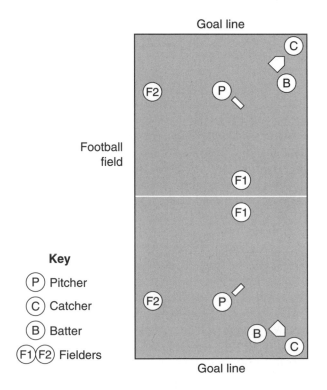

Figure 8.4 Setup for Pitch, Hit, and Field.

Description

Explain and demonstrate the activity. The pitcher pitches to the batter, who hits 10 softballs to the fielders, who field the softballs. If the softball is fielded in the infield, it's thrown directly to the catcher at home plate. If it's retrieved in the outfield, it's thrown on one hop to the catcher at home plate. Players rotate from catcher to batter, to left fielder, to right fielder, to pitcher to catcher. Foul balls do not count as hits. The focus is on maintaining a consistent swing, not trying to kill the softball but just making contact.

Challenge

Incorporate a first base: Have batters run on their 10th hit to try to get to first base before the pitcher receives the softball from the outfield.

8.14 | 2 v 2 Game

Goals

Develop the skills of hitting a pitched softball, tagging up on a fly ball, fielding grounders and fly balls, and forcing out a runner. Develop decision-making skills in the areas of (1) judging the speed of the base runner, (2) one's ability to throw the ball in time to force out a base runner trying to reach home plate, and (3) judging whether to try to score after tagging up.

Organization

Players form two teams of two players (two up to bat and two in the field). You'll need a softball and a mini-field (see figure 8.5) with bases at first and third, a pitching rubber, and a home plate. Place the pitching rubber at a comfortable distance from the plate (i.e., about 25 feet).

Description

Explain and demonstrate the game. Have one team take the field and the other be up to bat. To begin play, the pitcher (one of the fielders) pitches to the first batter, who hits the softball and runs either to first or third base. If the batter reaches a base safely before being forced out, he or she remains on that base. The base runner's teammate then comes to bat. This time, when the batter hits the softball, the batter can run only to the vacant base. Meanwhile, the runner on base must return home on a hit ball to take his or her turn at bat. The fielders have a choice of forcing out at home plate, thereby preventing a run, or forcing out at the base the batter is running to. As an example, say the first batter is Marcia. She hits the softball and arrives safely at third base. Her partner, Tashanna, then comes up to bat and hits a grounder to the fielder and must run to first base, while Marcia must try to get home and score. If the

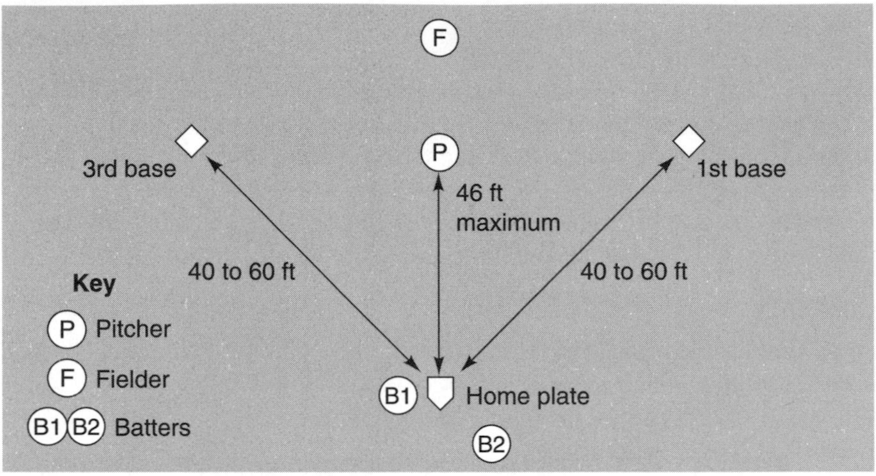

Figure 8.5 Setup for 2 v 2 Game.

fielder is close enough to first when she fields the ball, she can attempt a double play by tagging the bag for a force-out and then throwing home to the pitcher before Marcia arrives at the plate. If, however, Tashanna hits the softball to the pitcher, then the pitcher has to make the decision whether to throw to first, where her fielding partner has rushed to cover, or run home and force an out at home. With the exception of running to third base, most of the rules of slow-pitch softball are followed. After three outs, the batters take the field. There are no strikeouts. Foul balls are replayed. On a fly ball, the runner tags up, and the infield fly rule is in effect. Tell players to focus on stopping the batting team from scoring when they're out in the field and deciding ahead of time where they will go when the ball is hit and where they will throw if they are the one to make the play.

Challenge

Three strikes and the batter is out. All foul balls count as strikes, and a foul ball on a third strike is an out.

8.15 Back-Up

Goals

Develop the infielders' skills of backing each other up when ground balls are fielded; develop the proper technique for making a force-out at first base.

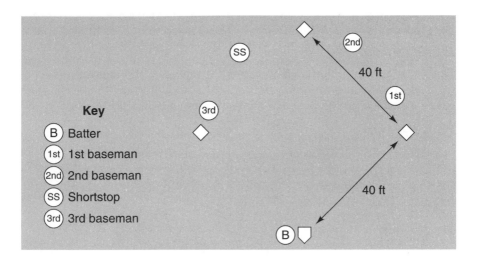

Figure 8.6 Setup for Back-Up.

Organization

Five players (four infielders and one batter) play on a mini-field with all bases and home plate. The distance between bases and home plate is reduced by a third to 40 feet (see figure 8.6).

Description

Explain and demonstrate infield positioning and backing up a fellow infielder fielding a softball. Have the batter throw a grounder to one of the four infielders, who fields the softball and throws to first base for the force-out. When the softball is thrown, the appropriate back-up fielder gets into proper backup position (third baseman is backed up by the shortstop, etc.). Since there's no pitcher, the first baseman fields the softball and tags the bag himself or herself. The batter (thrower) does not run to first base. Rotate positions clockwise after each fielder gets one fielding attempt. Tell players to focus on moving quickly into position and being ready to field the softball should the player they're backing up miss it.

Challenge

Have the batter run to first base to try to beat the throw.

8.16 Beat the Runner Around the Horn

Goals

Develop the ability of fielders to catch the softball while tagging a base as a runner approaches and turn and relay the softball to another base. Base runners develop proper baserunning technique in competitive play.

Organization

Five players (four infielders and a batter) play on a mini-infield with all bases and home plate. The distance between bases and home plate is reduced by a third to 40 feet (see figure 8.6). I recommend using rag softballs to prevent injury until fielders learn the skills.

Description

Review with players how to run the bases and then explain the activity. Have batters throw grounders to one of the four infielders and proceed to run around the bases as if their hit is a home run. The fielder fields the softball and throws to first base. The first baseman tags the bag as the softball is caught and relays the ball to second base, where the action is repeated, then on to third, where it is again repeated, and finally on to home, where the first baseman is covering the plate. The object for the fielding team is to relay the softball "around the horn" for a force-out at home plate before the runner arrives. The runner's goal is to demonstrate proper baserunning and arrive home before the fielding team can cause a force-out at the plate. Rotate positions clockwise after each trial. Tell players to focus on tagging the bag with their inside foot when baserunning. When fielders are relaying the throw, they should take care not to hit the runner with their throw.

Challenge

Keep score. Each player on the fielding team receives a point each time the team can relay the softball and force out the runner at home. The runner receives a point each time he or she reaches home before the throw.

8.17 Infield Situational Practice

Goal

Players develop their fielding skills by rehearsing (mentally and physically) each infield situation that might occur in a game. The goal is to eventually get to the point where fielders can automatically react correctly to each situation.

Organization

Seven players play on a regulation infield: one batter and a complete infield, including a pitcher and catcher.

Description

Explain and demonstrate the most common infield scenarios that can arise in a game, such as a runner on first and third, one out, and a grounder is hit to the second baseman, or an infield pop-up with no outs and a player on third. Have the player at bat call out a scenario (to make things run smoothly, you might want to give players laminated cards with common scenarios written on them) and then throw the softball accordingly. The fielders then execute what they believe is the correct response. If the response is not correct, the batter discusses the action that should have been taken, as noted on the laminated cards. Players rotate positions clockwise every four trials.

Challenge

Increase the numbers and put real runners on base. Have a runner for the thrower.

8.18   Rundown

Goals

Develop the ability of a fielder to tag a base runner caught in a rundown; develop a base runner's ability to proceed to the next base without being tagged.

Organization

Groups of three players play on a practice area about 5 yards wide by 20 yards long (see figure 8.7).

Description

Explain and demonstrate catching a runner in a rundown and putting the tag on him or her; have partners practice on each other before starting the activity. Designate bases as either first and second, second and third, or third and home. Put one fielder at each base with a base runner between them caught in a rundown situation. To begin, the base runner tosses the softball to one of the fielders and attempts to arrive safely at a base before being tagged. The runner is always trying to reach the next base, while the fielder is always trying to force the runner back to the original base. Rotate positions after each trial. Allow each runner about three to five trials. Tell partners the focus

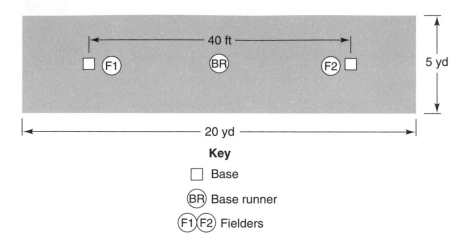

Figure 8.7 Setup for Rundown.

is always on forcing the base runners back to the base from which they came while keeping throwing to a minimum.

Challenge

Start runners between first and second. If they reach second safely, they get to try to reach third, and so on, with the object being to get home. Each base counts as a point. Whoever accumulates the most points wins.

8.19 3 v 3 v 3

Goals

Develop the fielding principles of players backing each other up, tagging runners, forcing runners back to base, relaying the softball to a base, and forcing a runner out in competitive play. Also develop the offensive skills of hitting a pitched softball, running the bases, and making good judgments in running the bases.

Organization

Nine players form three teams of three players to play on a mini-field. Team 1: catcher, pitcher, and first baseman; team 2: second baseman, shortstop, and third baseman; and team 3: batters. Place bases 40 feet from home plate (see figure 8.6, p. 191). Place pitching rubber about 25 feet from the plate.

Description

Explain and demonstrate the game. The batting team tries to hit the pitched softball past the infield on the ground and score runs as in regulation softball. A softball hit *over* the reach of the infielders is an automatic out for that batter. If a fielder catches a fly ball or pop-up, the batter is also out. If a fielder catches a grounder, his or her throw to the first baseman must beat the runner there or else the batter is safe at first. If there are any disputes, repeat the play. Balls and strikes are not called. Two full batting rotations equal half an inning. Teams then rotate clockwise (batters to second, shortstop, and third, and so on). Infield flies are ruled catchable, as are foul balls along the first and third baselines and behind the catcher. Each team keeps track of the total number of runs they accumulate. No sliding or bunting, but tagging the runner is encouraged.

Challenge

Inning ends immediately if a player gets caught in a rundown and is tagged.

8.20　Outfield Back-Up and Cut-Off

Goals

Outfielders develop reacting to a play by backing up an infielder if a grounder is hit; they also develop the skill of moving into position to catch a line drive or fly ball and throw it directly to a cut-off player. Infielders develop reacting to a softball hit to the outfield, transitioning to a cut-off player, and relaying the softball to home plate.

Organization

Groups of three players play in practice areas of 5 yards by 50 yards. The batter is at one end of the area near a designated home plate, a cut-off player (infielder) is in the middle, and an outfielder is at the far end of the practice area (see figure 8.8).

Description

Explain and demonstrate backing up the infield from the outfield and taking advantage of the cut-off player. The batter either throws a hard ground ball at the infielder or throws a line drive or high fly ball to the outfielder. If it's a grounder to the infielder, the outfielder must back up the infielder. If the softball is thrown to the outfielder, the infielder moves toward the fielder and calls "cut-off!" at which time the outfielder, upon making the catch, throws the softball directly to the cut-off player, who then relays the ball to the thrower at home plate. Rotate every four trials. Tell players the focus is on moving

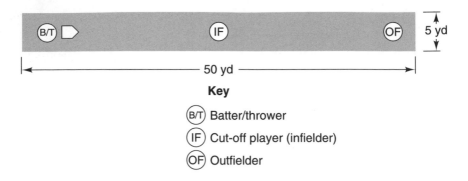

Figure 8.8 Setup for Outfield Back-Up and Cut-Off.

quickly to get into proper position as infielders and outfielders and making sure throws are accurate and catchable.

Challenge

Allow infielders to intentionally miss grounders to keep outfielders alert. Try to throw the softball past either of the two fielders but inside the sidelines and playable. Have each player keep track of the number of throws they manage to make the fielders miss.

8.21 Outfield Throwing: Cut-Offs at Home Plate

Goals

Outfielders react to the directions of the cut-off player and develop their one-hop throw to the plate. Cut-off players develop calling out instructions to the outfielders and their ability to relay the softball from the outfield to the plate.

Organization

Players play in groups of three players in practice areas of 5 yards by 50 yards. The batter is at one end of the field near a designated home plate, a cut-off player (infielder) is in the middle, and an outfielder is at the far end of the practice area (see figure 8.8). In this case, the batter should have a glove and not a bat.

Description

Review the one-hop throw to home plate; explain and demonstrate cutting off a throw from the outfield. Have groups of three players practice each situation as called out by the cut-off player (e.g., "Cut-off!" or "Home!"). Play begins with the batter throwing a fly, line drive, or ground ball deep to the outfielder. The cut-off player in the middle (infielder) moves out toward the outfielder and yells either "Cut-off!" or "Home!" If the call is "Cut-off," the fielder throws the softball directly to the cut-off player, who then relays the softball to the batter at the plate. If the cut-off player calls "Home," the outfielder hurls the softball to the plate on one hop so that the batter can easily handle the catch. Rotate every four trials. Focus on relaying the softball quickly by catching, whirling, and throwing on one hop to home plate all in one motion.

Challenge

Add ground balls to the infielder and intentionally try to throw the softball where the players aren't.

8.22 3 v 3 v 3 v 3 on a Regulation Field

Goals

Practice the fielding principles of backing each other up, tagging a runner out in a rundown or forcing the runner back to the original base, relaying the softball to a base, forcing out a runner, following the directions of the cut-off player, and throwing a one-hopper to home plate in competitive play. Develop the offensive skills of hitting a pitched softball, running the bases, and making good judgments on the basepaths in competitive play.

Organization

Twelve players play in four teams of three players on a regulation field. Team 1: catcher, pitcher, and first baseman; team 2: second baseman, shortstop, and third baseman; team 3: left fielder, center fielder, and right fielder; team 4: batters (see figure 8.9 where numbers indicate team members). The catcher should wear a mask.

Description

Explain and demonstrate the activity. Have the batting team try to score runs as in regulation softball. Balls and strikes are not called. Two full batting rotations equal one-half inning. Players rotate positions within their teams after each inning so that everyone gets to play each position. Each team keeps track of the total number of runs they accumulate. No sliding or bunting, but tagging the runner and force-outs are encouraged. Runners must tag up on a deep enough fly ball. The focus is on working together as a team and knowing ahead of time what you'll do in the field for each situation presented.

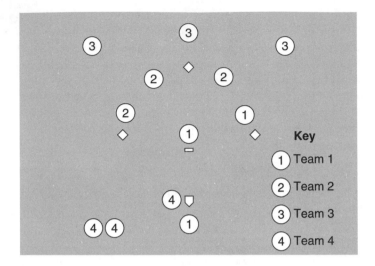

Figure 8.9   Setup of 3 v 3 v 3 v 3 on a Regulation Field.

Challenge

The inning ends immediately if a player gets tagged during a rundown or if an outfielder makes a one-hop throw to home in time for the catcher to tag the runner out.

8.23 | Practice the Scenarios

Goal

Players rehearse (mentally and physically) each scenario that might occur in a game to develop the ability to automatically react to most possible occurrences in a real game.

Organization

Ten players play on a regulation field. A batter throws softballs to a complete infield and complete outfield. In this case, the batter needs a glove and not a bat.

Description

Review and demonstrate backing each other up in the outfield; review some common scenarios presented thus far in the unit, especially if players have had any problems with the scenario (e.g., not knowing where to throw the softball with the bases loaded and no outs, etc.). The batter calls out a scenario (which might be written on a laminated card you've given him or her), such as "One person on first, no outs!" and then throws the softball to a spot of his or her choice. The batter does not run. The fielders then respond to the situation. If the players do not respond correctly, the batter tells them what should have happened on the play, based on the information on the laminated card. Players rotate clockwise every four trials. Tell players to focus on reacting quickly to the scenario and knowing ahead of time what to do in each situation.

Challenge

Create four teams of three (pitcher, catcher, and shortstop; three outfielders; first, second, and third basemen; and three batters). Call out scenarios written on laminated cards putting batters on base. The batter runs to first after throwing the softball into play. Rotate after each half inning. Continue playing until all teams have completed an equal number of at-bats.

8.24 9 v 9 Game

Goal

Use the skills thus far developed in a competitive game on a regulation diamond.

Organization

Eighteen players form two teams of nine players each to play on a regulation field. Catcher must wear a catcher's mask.

Description

Quickly review the game, asking players to answer questions about rules and strategy. Discuss areas that have proven tricky for the players or any common situations that might arise that haven't been reviewed. Have teams play a slow-pitch game with balls and strikes called by umpires you pick from the class.

Challenge

Have the batting team provide their own pitcher, and whenever an out is made the inning ends. The team coming in to bat does not have to wait for the fielding team to get set up but can bat as soon as their own pitcher is ready. This will result in players hustling in and out. Players must change their fielding positions every inning. An inning consists of everyone on the team batting. There are no balls and strikes called.

CHAPTER 9

Volleyball

Volleyball is a popular sport that appeals to a wide audience. Gone are the days of "jungle volleyball" when players hit with their fists, carried the volleyball by slapping with the hands, and generally took the game for a nice leisurely activity to fill time. Not anymore. Today's volleyball is one of the more physically demanding sports and is recognized throughout the world. As enjoyable as the game is, volleyball can be one of the most frustrating units for beginners. In many team sports, such as basketball or soccer, play usually continues after a misplay with little time for teammates to dwell on the mistake because they're too busy chasing the ball for a follow-up rebound or making the transition to defense. Not so in volleyball. When a player misplays a ball, play usually stops, and the player's error is evident to all. It's important, then, for beginning players to have success when learning the game of volleyball.

The progressions in this chapter are developed to reduce the possibility of failure. After a short footwork warm-up, the progressions begin with the most important skill: the pass. Before learning to actually pass, though, players need to learn how to toss (or set up) the volleyball for their teammates. When a player practices any of the basic skills, such as setting or passing, it's important that the volleyball is set to the same place each time so that the player can perform the skill consistently in the same way. One of the missing links in teaching volleyball is working on tossing the ball accurately so that a teammate can hit it at the same angle and from the same position over and over before complex skills are added. Don't take for granted that players learned this in elementary school and are able to do this. The best volleyball coaches and teachers I have observed always begin with teaching players to accurately two-hand toss underhand and don't allow their players to move on until they can consistently set up a partner. While it's true that a volleyball should never be caught, in the initial stages of developing the toss in these progressions, the receiver does catch the ball with two hands below the waist. However, this does not become a habit as the lesson moves quickly on from there to passing the volleyball back to the tosser.

Once students develop consistent setup skills, introduce the pass. A beginning player who acquires fundamental passing skills can join in any game and be reasonably successful. By introducing the pass before the set, beginning students learn right away to receive a volleyball coming over the net with a pass as opposed to a set, thereby reducing the potential for failure. The pass is much quicker and easier to develop than the set, and passing games over the net can be successfully implemented early in the unit. Closely follow the pass with the set (one of the most difficult skills to acquire) and then the serve. Failure at serving can be a humiliating experience, as can the receipt of an ace (failing to pass an oncoming serve). In the progressions the serve is delayed until the pass and set are developed; this helps students develop confidence and increase learning. The serve is added once students are fairly adept at 2 v 2 and 3 v 3 games. It is, however, okay to insert the underhand serve after the pass and combine these two skills in a serve-pass game. It's also all right in these progressions to skip the underhand serve progression and go directly to the overhand "pop" serve if students are physically capable because there's no link between the underhand and overhand serve.

It may surprise you to see that one of the last skills introduced in the progressions is the spike, or hit. Along with the pass, the spike is one of the most difficult skills for beginners to develop because few beginners have the size or the athletic, leaping, and timing abilities necessary to perform the skill well. Instead of the spike, the down ball is emphasized as an offensive weapon early on, introduced just after the serve, because all beginners are capable of performing it. One note: Even though it's within the rules, don't let your students "fist" the volleyball (hit it with a closed fist to get the ball over the net), as doing so invariably sends the ball at a high velocity in whatever direction it goes (which is hard to predict) and is a hard habit to break. Invoke your status as Commissioner of Volleyball in your class and rule fisting illegal. Case closed! Finally, in the last progressions, students learn to demonstrate team-play concepts such as the 4-2 and 6-0 offenses and team blocking.

Defense is not emphasized until late in the unit and then is lightly covered so that the offense has more success. Although I don't mention this in the progressions, all the skills can first be practiced without a volleyball so that you can check form, but do this at your own discretion. The use of trainer volleyballs, a somewhat larger and lighter volleyball, is highly encouraged so that players have early success and less tenderness in the forearms from repetitive passing. You might use beach balls and other types of balls also, but I think they hinder more than help because they do not fly true. If players complain of sore forearms, have them wear long-sleeved shirts or keep some old socks on hand with the toes cut off. Students can slip these over their forearms to cushion the impact. To ensure success, lower the net to a level where players have the most success. I would not set the net any higher than the women's regulation height of 7 feet, 4-1/8 inches. Most of the activities in the progressions require each player or a pair of players to have one volleyball to work on the skill being introduced. I'll assume you know already to have enough volleyballs on hand to meet the needs of your students. When an activity requires a player or pair of players to use more than one volleyball, I'll mention that in the activity's Organization section.

■ After following the progressions, beginning students should be able to play in a game of 6 v 6 volleyball using the following skills:
  • Ready positioning and court movement
  • Underhand tossing while moving and stationary
  • Passing
  • Setting
  • Underhand serving
  • Overhand serving
  • Down balls
  • Three-step approach and spike or down ball
  • Blocking
  • Tipping
  • Serve reception with a pass

9.1 Ready Position and Court Movement

Goal

Learn the importance of moving into position to receive the volleyball and develop proper body position and footwork.

Organization

Players scatter about the court facing the instructor. No equipment is needed.

Description

Explain and demonstrate the ready position for serve reception and court movement. Point to the areas of the court to which you want players to move using proper footwork. The focus is on staying low in an athletic position and returning to the starting point when the signal is given.

Challenge

Increase the tempo by pointing more quickly. At a signal, have players slap both hands on the floor and return to the starting position.

9.2 Underhand Toss and Catch to a Stationary and Moving Partner

Goals

Develop two-hand underhand tosses that are consistent in height and accuracy. The receiver gets positioned properly under the volleyball for a pass.

Organization

Partners play in practice areas 20 feet long by 10 feet wide.

Description

Explain and demonstrate the two-hand underhand toss and moving under and catching a tossed volleyball below the waist with two hands while stationary and while moving. Have a player two-hand underhand toss 10 feet high to a stationary receiver about 10 feet away. The receiver gets into the appropriate ready position to receive and catch the volleyball with two hands below the waist. Once both players are tossing consistently, have them toss the volleyball to the side, front, and back of the receiver, who moves with correct court movement and gets positioned to catch the ball with two hands below the waist as if to return the toss with a pass. Tell players to focus on being consistent with their toss by applying the same force to each arm, thereby making the pass more accurate.

Challenges

Speed up the tosses so that partners must move more quickly; mix up the tosses so that partners can't guess correctly where the toss is coming.

9.3 Underhand Toss and Return Pass While Stationary and Moving

Goals

Develop the ability to move into ready position to receive a pass and to accurately pass the volleyball back to the tosser using appropriate form so that the tosser doesn't have to move.

Organization

Partners play in practice areas 20 feet long by 10 feet wide.

Description

Explain and demonstrate how to pass a tossed volleyball, while stationary, back to the tosser so he or she doesn't have to move. Have one partner toss to a stationary partner in ready position, who passes the volleyball back to the tosser about 10 feet high, so that he or she is in a strong receiving position to pass. Once both players are making good passes consistently, have the tosser toss the volleyball to the side, front, and back of the receiver, who moves with correct court movement and positions himself or herself to pass the ball accurately back to the tosser. Players do 10 trials and then switch positions. Focus on getting into proper position with both shoulders facing the target and not swinging arms any higher than the waist.

Challenges

1. How many successful returns can a set of partners complete out of 10 trials each?
2. Have partners challenge another partner group.
3. Have partners challenge each other to a contest.
4. Increase the distance until the tosser is serving distance (about 20 feet) from the receiver.

9.4 Cooperative Pass Rally

Goal

Practice accurate passing in game-like conditions where the travel of the volleyball is unpredictable.

Organization

Partners play in practice areas 20 feet long by 15 feet wide.

Description

Explain and demonstrate passing the volleyball back and forth between two partners. Have play begin with one partner underhand tossing to the other partner, who passes back to the tosser. Partners continue to rally using only the pass within the confines of the corridor. Do 10 trials and then switch positions.

Challenges

See how many passes partners can do in a row.

1. Create a mini-court with a line down the middle to serve as a net separating the partners. One partner underhands the volleyball over the line, and the other receives the toss with a pass back to the tosser, and play begins. Only passes may be used. Introduce basic rules such as a ball on the line is in, no hitting the volleyball twice in a row, and so on.

2. Extend the dimensions of the court until it is a quarter the size of a regulation court.

3. Replace the line on the court with a low net and raise the net accordingly.

9.5   Underhand Toss, Catch, and Set While Stationary

Goal

Develop getting into ready position to receive a pass for a set, and accurately set the volleyball back to the tosser using appropriate form so that the tosser doesn't have to move.

Organization

Partners play in practice areas 20 feet long by 10 feet wide.

Description

Explain and demonstrate setting a tossed volleyball back to the tosser while stationary. Have a player softly underhand toss to their stationary partner in ready position who catches the volleyball in setting position. The setter then returns the ball in slow motion using proper setting technique. When the setter is consistent and using good form, have him or her speed up the return until they're no longer catching the volleyball but are legally setting it (without catching). Do 10 trials and then switch positions. The focus is on almost catching the volleyball with the pads of the fingers, bending the knees, and setting the ball back with a piston-like action.

Challenges

Increase the distance or the speed of the toss.

9.6 Underhand Toss and Set While Moving

Goals

Develop the ability to move into ready position to receive a pass on various areas of the court and to accurately set the volleyball back to the tosser using proper form so that the tosser doesn't have to move.

Organization

Partners play in practice areas 20 feet long by 15 feet wide.

Description

Explain and demonstrate setting the volleyball directly from an underhand toss while moving. Have one partner underhand toss the volleyball to an open area in the court; his or her partner moves under the ball to set it back to the tosser. The tosser should make the setter move up, back, and sideways. Players do 10 trials and then switch positions. Focus on moving quickly to get under the ball, set, and return to ready position in the middle of the court.

Challenges

1. Increase the distance (but no farther than halfcourt). How many successful returns can a set of partners complete out of 10 trials each?
2. Have partners challenge another partner group.
3. Have partners challenge each other to a contest to see who can return the most out of 10 trials back to the tosser without the tosser needing to move.

9.7 Cooperative Set Rally

Goal

Practice setting in game-like conditions where the travel of the volleyball is unpredictable.

Organization

Partners play in practice areas 20 feet long by 15 feet wide.

Description

Explain and demonstrate setting the volleyball back and forth between two partners. Play begins with one player underhand tossing to a partner who sets back to the tosser. Partners then rally using only the set.

Challenges

See how many sets partners can do in a row.

1. Create a mini-court with a line down the middle to serve as a net separating the partners. One partner underhand tosses the volleyball over the line, the other receives the toss with a set back to the tosser, and play begins. Only sets may be used. If you have not done so already, introduce basic rules such as a ball on the line is in, no hitting the volleyball twice in a row, and so on.

2. Extend the dimensions of the court until it's a quarter the size of a regulation court.

3. Replace the line on the court with a low net and raise the net accordingly.

9.8 Pass and Set Rally Alternating Hits

Goal

Pass and set in a game-like situation.

Organization

Partners play in practice areas 20 feet long by 15 feet wide.

Description

Explain and demonstrate cooperatively passing and setting the volleyball back and forth between partners. Have one player toss the volleyball to a partner, who passes the ball back to the tosser, who sets the ball back to the passer, and so on. This is a cooperative challenge to see how long partners can rally using passing and setting. Partners don't have to alternate setting and passing but should avoid favoring one over the other. They should count the number in a row they can achieve. Partners can play anywhere within the practice area and even exchange sides. If the volleyball should go out of the practice area, play stops for safety reasons (although in a game they'd be allowed to chase the ball and try to return it).

Challenges

1. Instead of cooperating with a partner, try to pass or set the volleyball to an area on the court that's open so that your partner can't reach it (the ball must always be hit at least 10 feet high).

2. Draw a line across the center of the court and have each player remain on his or her side of the court while volleying back and forth. Discuss basic rules such as double hits, ball landing on a line, and so on.

3. Increase the size of the court.

9.9 Pass and Set Rally Over the Net

Goal

Develop returning a volleyball coming over a net.

Organization

Each volleyball court with a net is divided into three 10-foot-wide courts. If need be, the space between courts can be used, too. The net is set at a height at which you think players can be successful but should be no higher than in women's regulation volleyball (about 7 feet, 4 inches; see figure 9.1). Players play in partners across from each other.

Description

Explain and demonstrate a pass and set rally over a net. Have one player toss the volleyball high over the net to the receiver, who passes back to the tosser, who sets or passes back to the passer. This is a cooperative challenge to see

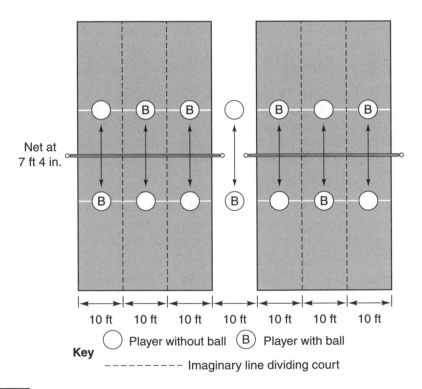

Figure 9.1 Setup for Pass and Set Rally Over the Net.

how many sets and passes can be made in a row. The initial toss over the net must be received with a pass, which reminds players not to get in the habit of receiving a serve with a set, which is a bad habit. Have players focus on moving into position quickly to receive the volleyball and sending it to a partner to maintain the rally. Tell them to control the ball when passing or setting and to aim it to their partner so that they can continue the rally rather than trying to make their partner miss.

Challenges

1. See if partners can perform five repetitions in a row.
2. Have partners challenge other partner groups to see who can reach five consecutive repetitions first.

9.10 1 v 1 Mini-Court Game

Goals

Implement passing and setting in a game situation. Develop receiving a serve (in this case a toss) with a pass rather than a set. Learn the basic rules of volleyball in a game situation. Begin to work on looking for areas uncovered by an opponent and trying to send the volleyball into that area of the court.

Organization

Each volleyball court with a net is divided into three 10-foot-wide courts. If need be, the space between courts can be used, too. The net is set at a height at which you think players can be successful but should be no higher than in women's regulation volleyball (about 7 feet, 4 inches). Players play in partners across from each other (see figure 9.1).

Description

Explain and demonstrate a 1 v 1 mini-court game. Play begins with a player serving (tossing) a volleyball underhand over the net or line at least 10 feet high to a partner who then must pass the ball back over the net into the server's court for play to begin. If the volleyball is not passed back, the serve is redone until the receiving side successfully passes the ball back over the net into the server's court. Once play begins, basic volleyball scoring continues. Only one hit is allowed per side. While this practice could lead to a bad habit (one hit and over), the need to get into some semblance of the game at this time outweighs the negative aspect of one-hitting. See *Volleyball: Steps to Success, 2nd edition* (Viera and Ferguson 1996) for a more detailed description of volleyball rules and regulations. Once the receiver passes the volleyball over the net, a pass or set can be used. Later, when 2 v 2 and 3 v 3 games are introduced, restrictions can be placed requiring two or more hits. Have players keep track of the score; rotate players after seven minutes or so. The focus is on moving into position quickly to receive the volleyball and then sending it to an area on the court that an opponent is not covering.

Challenges

1. Divide the class into two teams: A and B. In each partner group, assign one partner A and the other partner B. Have each player keep track of the total number of points he or she scores for his or her team during class. At the end of class, have each team (A and B) add up their total number of points to see who wins.

2. Create leagues and conduct 1 v 1 league play.

9.11 | Underhand Toss: Pass and Set

Goals

Begin developing team play skills with calling for the volleyball, passing to the center front, setting deep over the net, and rotating clockwise.

Organization

Players play in groups of three on one-half a volleyball court lengthwise with a net. One player (the server) is on one side of net, and the other two are side by side on the other side in the backcourt (see figure 9.2).

Description

Explain and demonstrate serve reception in the backcourt and passing the volleyball to the center frontcourt to a setter. Have the server two-hand underhand toss high and deep over the net to one of the two partners in the backcourt who are positioned to receive the tossed serve. The player receiving the serve passes to the center front near the net. The other receiving partner moves from the backcourt to the center frontcourt near the net to receive the pass and sets the volleyball over the net deep to the server, who repeats the serve. Rotate clockwise every five trials.

Challenges

1. The server lowers the trajectory of the toss to increase difficulty.

2. The server tosses to him- or herself then sets the volleyball over the net deep.

3. Add a third hit. The receiver passes to center front then goes either to the left or right front position. The center front (setter) then sets to the receiver coming to one of the front positions, who sets the volleyball over the net deep into the server's court.

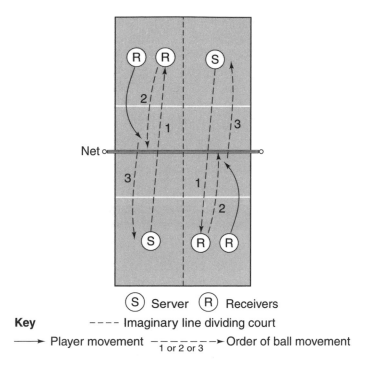

Server (S)   (R) Receivers

Key   - - - - Imaginary line dividing court

→ Player movement - - - - - - → Order of ball movement
                     1 or 2 or 3

Figure 9.2   Setup for Underhand Toss: Pass and Set.

9.12 2 v 2 Cooperative Rally

Goal

Implement passing and setting in a cooperative 2 v 2 situation similar to the real game but ensure that serves are always received with a pass and that partners are calling for balls.

Organization

Four players (teams of two on each side) play on half of a regular volleyball court with a net.

Description

Explain and demonstrate the activity. To begin the cooperative rally, have one team put the volleyball in play (serve) either with an underhand toss or toss to themselves and set the ball over the net at least 10 feet high deep into the other team's backcourt, where the other two players await. One of the backcourt players on the receiving team must pass the volleyball up to his or her partner, who has moved into the center front position at the net for play, who then sets the ball over the net to officially start play. If the serve is not passed then set, the serve is redone until the receiving side successfully sets the ball back over the net into the server's court. Once that occurs, the rally begins. During the rally, the receiving team must use at least two but no more than three hits per side. The object is to see how many consecutive hits over the net a team can accumulate. Tell players to focus on calling for volleyballs that they're taking so that their partner can move into position to receive their pass or set.

Challenge

Challenge other courts to see who can rally the most hits over the net.

9.13 2 v 2 Halfcourt Passing and Setting Game

Goal

Implement passing and setting in a competitive 2 v 2 situation similar to the real game but ensure that serves are always received with a pass and that partners are calling for balls.

Organization

Four players (teams of two on each side) play on half of a regular volleyball court with a net.

Description

Explain and demonstrate the activity. To begin the competitive game, have one team put the volleyball in play (serve) either with an underhand toss or a toss to themselves and set the ball over the net at least 10 feet high deep into the other team's backcourt, where the other two players await. One of the backcourt players on the receiving team must pass the volleyball up to his or her partner, who has moved into the center front position at the net, who then sets the ball over the net to officially start play. If this fails, the serve is redone until the receiving side successfully sets the ball back over the net into the server's court. Once the volleyball has been returned via a pass and set, the game begins. During the game, the receiving team must use at least two but no more than three hits per side. Regulation volleyball rules are in effect. Have players keep track of their score; rotate teams after seven minutes or so. The focus is on partners talking to each other and making sure that they're in position to cover the court equally while awaiting their opponent's return.

Challenges

1. Keep track of the total number of points each team accumulates for the entire class period; announce the winner at the end of class.
2. Create leagues for game play.

9.14 3 v 3 Halfcourt Pass and Set Rally

Goal

Develop backcourt serve reception play.

Organization

Six players (three on each side) play on half of a volleyball court with a net (see figure 9.3).

Description

Explain and demonstrate backcourt positioning (center back, left back, and right back) for serve reception and court movement once a backcourt player calls for the volleyball. Have teams rally on a halfcourt. To begin the rally, have one team put the volleyball in play (serve) by the right back player, either with an underhand toss or toss to themselves, and set the ball over the net at least 10 feet high deep into the other team's backcourt, where the other three players await in a W serve-reception formation. The center back player is the designated setter and immediately moves to the center front position once the service is made. The remaining two backcourt players are responsible for

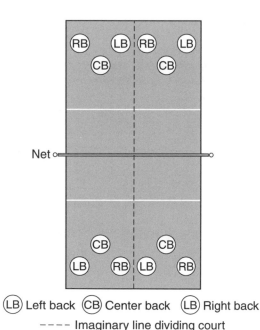

Key (LB) Left back (CB) Center back (LB) Right back
   – – – – Imaginary line dividing court

Figure 9.3   Setup for 3 v 3 Halfcourt Pass and Set Rally.

receiving the ball from the server. Whichever backcourt player receives the serve, his or her partner then goes to the net. The backcourt player who receives the serve passes the volleyball up to the setter, who then sets the ball to the remaining backcourt player, who then sets it over the net to officially start the rally. If this fails, the serve is redone until the receiving side successfully sets the volleyball back over the net into the server's court. Once the ball has been returned over the net via a pass and two sets, the rally begins. During the rally, the receiving team must use at least two but no more than three hits per side. Regulation volleyball rules are in effect. Players follow the standard serve rotation. Have players keep track of the number of consecutive successful hits they get over the net; rotate teams after seven minutes or so.

Challenge

Play "King of the Court" as an entry activity, with nine players per half court: three on one side, three on the other, and three on the sideline. Play begins when you toss the volleyball over the net into one team's court. The team passes, sets, and so on over to the other team, and play continues until one team makes a mistake (i.e., violates rules, commits a side-out, etc.). The team that has made the mistake is replaced by the team on the sideline. Designate one court the "winner's court" so that there's more movement. Winners get to remain no more than three times in a row. To make the game more competitive, have each team keep track of the total points they score.

9.15   Underhand Serve Over Net to Targets

Goal

Develop accuracy with the underhand serve with proper form.

Organization

Players play in partners across from each other on a third of a volleyball court. Three sets of partners can fit on one court, and another set can fit between courts. Begin with the net slightly lowered.

Description

Explain and demonstrate the proper underhand serve, emphasizing contacting the volleyball on the palm of the hand and foot opposition. Have players serve back and forth to each other starting from the 10-foot line. Each time they get three serves in a row into the court, they take two giant steps back until they reach the service line. Partners allow the volleyball to bounce in the court. The focus is on hitting the ball off your hand instead of tossing it up in the air and on keeping a consistent pendulum swing of the arm.

Challenges

1. Have your partner move to a different spot on the court each time. The server serves directly to the receiver, who runs into ready position and catches the volleyball with two hands below the waist, as if he or she is going to pass it. If the ball goes directly to the partner and the partner does not have to take more than one step to receive it, the server earns a point.

2. Section off the receiving court into four areas using markers, hot spots, or hula hoops. One partner calls out which spot to hit, and the server tries to hit the target. One point is awarded for each spot hit.

3. Play "Around the World." Section off the court into four squares. The first server to get "Around the World" by hitting each spot in a clockwise sequence wins.

4. Play tic-tac-toe with serves.

9.16 Serve, Pass, Set, Set

Goal

Develop serving and serve-reception team play.

Organization

Players play in groups of four on half of a volleyball court. One server is on one side of the net; three backcourt receivers are on the receiving side (see figure 9.4).

Description

Explain and demonstrate the activity. Review serve reception and rotation on the court. The server begins to serve from the 10-foot line and moves back two giant steps with success until he or she can serve the volleyball from the endline. The ball is served high and deep over the net to the backcourt. The center back player is the designated setter and, once the service is made, immediately moves to the net at the center-front position. The remaining two backcourt players are responsible for receiving the volleyball from the server. Whichever backcourt player receives the serve, his or her partner then goes to the net. The backcourt player who receives the serve passes the volleyball up to the setter, who then sets it to the remaining backcourt player, who then sets it over the net. The server retrieves the volleyball and serves again. Rotate clockwise every five trials. The focus is on players talking to one another about who's taking the serve (after the volleyball is served, not before) and who's going to the net to be the setter.

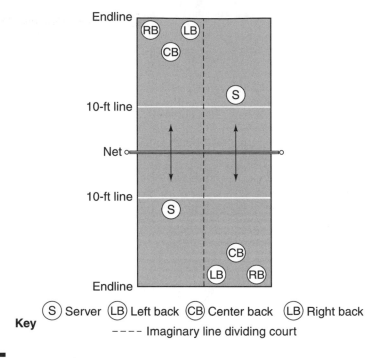

Figure 9.4 Setup for Serve, Pass, Set, Set.

Challenges

1. Count the server as part of the team and see how many times each team can serve, pass, set, and set again successfully. Begin with practice, then compete with other teams.

2. Don't have the server as part of the team but play a game keeping points. If the serve is not returned successfully with a pass, set, and another set, then the server gets one point. If the serve is not in the court, a point is awarded to each member of the receiving team. If the serve is returned with a pass, set, set, then each person on that team receives a point. Rotate after five trials.

9.17 3 v 3 Underhand Serve, Pass, Set Game

Goals

To help servers concentrate on getting their service into the opponent's court; to help the receiving team focus on receiving each service with a pass to the center front, which will set the stage for more complicated team tactics. Allowing the server to serve from where he or she is successful eliminates the automatic "side out" call for those not adept at serving. This forces the receiving team to return a serve with a successful pass before play can begin, eliminates the more effective servers from dominating play with aces (since the game will never begin if this happens), and promotes a cooperative atmosphere before moving on to a regular competitive game.

Organization

Two teams of three on a halfcourt (see figure 9.5).

Description

Explain and demonstrate the activity. Have players play a game of 3 v 3. To begin play each time, the serve must be in the court, and the receiving team must successfully pass the volleyball forward to their setter, who then sets the ball over the net. The receiving team must begin with a W serve-reception

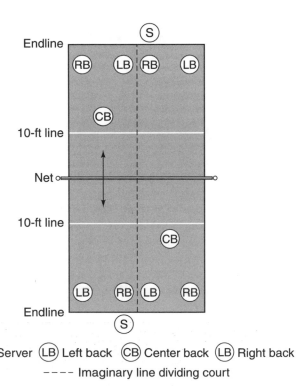

Figure 9.5 Setup for 3 v 3 Underhand Serve, Pass, Set Game.

formation. The center back player is the designated setter and, once the service is made, immediately stations him- or herself at the net from the center back position. The remaining two backcourt players are responsible for receiving the volleyball from the server. Whichever backcourt player receives the serve, his or her partner then goes to the net. The backcourt player who receives the serve passes the ball up to the setter, who then sets it to the remaining backcourt player, who sets it over the net to officially start the game. The server can serve from anywhere on the right side of the court. If the serve is not successful, the server takes a giant step closer to the net and repeats the serve. There must be at least two hits per side but no more than three. After the serve, only passing and setting are allowed (no spiking or blocking!). Teams follow standard serving rotation.

Challenge

Everyone on the receiving team must touch the volleyball before it goes over the net.

9.18   Overhand Pop Serve to a Partner

Goal

Develop the pop serve.

Organization

Players play in partners across the net from each other at the 10-foot attack line. No more than three partner groups on a court.

Description

Explain and demonstrate the overhand pop serve. In a pop serve, the server holds the volleyball in regular overhand serving position with the hitting hand behind the ball; as the ball is tossed (no more than a foot or two) the server draws the hitting hand back no farther than the ear and contacts the volleyball using correct form and follow-through. The pop serve is distinct from the complete overhand serve, in which the volleyball is tossed up high, and the hitting hand is drawn far behind the head in a "bow and arrow" style. Because the ball is not tossed very high, it is easier to control and have success. Partners lightly hit overhead pop serves over the net to each other. Each partner allows the volleyball to drop before returning it with the same proper form.

Challenge

Increase the hitting distance and height until the court resembles a regular volleyball court.

9.19 Overhand Serve Practice

Goal

Develop the overhand service.

Organization

Three sets of partners line up across the net from each other on a regular volleyball court (if you need more space, use the area between the courts, too). Players position on each of the 10-foot attack lines. Each practice area is about 10 feet wide (see figure 9.1, p. 208). You'll need two volleyballs per set of partners.

Description

Explain and demonstrate the overhead serve. Begin by having each player begin to perform the overhead serve but at the last minute miss the volleyball intentionally, allowing it to bounce on the floor. Once you see that players seem to have the correct action (the toss, weight transfer, timing, etc.), have them overhand serve back and forth to each other. Start them at the 10-foot line and move them two giant steps back whenever they get three serves in a row over the net and into the court. The receiver allows the volleyball to bounce in the court.

Challenges

1. Section off the receiving court into four areas using hot spots or tape. One partner calls out which spot to hit, and the server attempts to hit the target. Award one point for each spot hit.

2. Play Around the World. Section off the court into four squares. The first server to get "around the world" by hitting each spot in a specified sequential order wins.

9.20 Overhand Serve Reception Practice, Pass, Set, and Set

Goals

Practice overhand serving and serve reception team play by moving and calling for the volleyball, passing to the center front, setting deep over the net on the third hit, and rotating clockwise.

Organization

Groups of four—a server and three backcourt receivers—play on a halfcourt with a net (see figure 9.4, p. 216).

Description

Review service reception and rotation. Have the server begin serving from the 10-foot line and move back two giant steps with each successful serve until he or she can serve from the endline. The volleyball is served high and deep over the net. The center back player is the designated setter and, once the service is made, immediately moves to the net from the center back position. The remaining two backcourt players are responsible for receiving the volleyball from the server. Whichever backcourt player receives the serve, his or her partner then goes to the net. The backcourt player who receives the serve passes the volleyball up to the setter, who then sets the ball to the remaining backcourt player, who then sets the ball over the net. The server retrieves the volleyball and serves again. Since this activity is done on a halfcourt, the backcourt players will be much closer together than if they were on a full court. Rotate clockwise every five trials. Tell players the focus is on working as a team by talking to each other during play.

Challenges

1. Count the server as part of the team and see how many times each team can serve, pass, set, and set successfully. Begin with practice, then compete against other teams.

2. Don't have the server as part of the team but play a game keeping points. If the serve is not returned successfully with a pass, set, set, then the server gets one point. If the serve is not in the court, a point is awarded to each member of the receiving team. If the serve is returned with a pass, set, set, then each person on that team receives a point. Rotate after five trials.

9.21 3 v 3 Overhand Serve, Pass, Set Game

Goals

Develop accuracy in the serve; develop receiving each service with a pass, which sets the stage for more complicated team tactics.

Organization

Two teams of three play on a halfcourt (see figure 9.5, p. 217).

Description

Review court coverage and rules of play. Have players play a game of 3 v 3 on a halfcourt. To begin play each time, a player must overhand serve into the court, and the receiving team must successfully pass the volleyball to the setter at the center front position on the court. The server can serve from anywhere on the right side of the court. The volleyball is served high and deep over the net. The center back player is the designated setter and, once the service is made, immediately moves to the net from the center back position. The remaining two backcourt players receive the volleyball from the server. Whichever backcourt player receives the serve, his or her partner then goes to the net. The backcourt player who receives the serve passes the volleyball up to the setter, who then sets the ball to the remaining backcourt player, who then sets the ball over the net to officially start the game. Since this is on a halfcourt, the backcourt players are much closer together than they'd be on a full court. If the serve is not in the court, the server takes a giant step closer to the net and repeats the serve. There must be at least two hits per side but no more than three. Only passing and setting are allowed—no blocking or spiking.

Challenges

1. Everyone on the receiving team must touch the volleyball before it can be relayed over the net.
2. If the serving team scores three times in a row, a new server is rotated in.

9.22 Down Ball Practice at Net

Goal

Develop the top spin needed on a down ball at the net under a controlled setting.

Organization

Partners line up across the net from each other on a regular volleyball court about eight feet from the net. Each partner has a volleyball. No more than three sets of partners on a court.

Description

Explain and demonstrate the down ball. Have one person toss the volleyball above his or her head and perform a down ball over the net to his or her partner, who lets the volleyball bounce before doing the same back over the net. Focus on tracking the volleyball and setting up to hit it in a bow and arrow position, contacting it with an open hand and rotating the hand over the top of the volleyball to create top spin, which causes the ball to drop once over the net.

Challenges

1. Have partners toss the volleyball high into the air over the net and hit the ball back with a down ball.

2. Have partners move within an arm's length of the net and see if they can keep the volleyball going over the net continuously using passing and the down ball without letting the volleyball bounce and while staying within their practice area.

9.23 | Pop Serve, Pass, Set, and Down Ball

Goal

Gain realistic practice in performing a down ball after a pass-set series.

Organization

Groups of four players play on a halfcourt. The server is on one side of the net at the 10-foot attack line. Two receiving players are in the backcourt, with a setter at center front.

Description

Explain and demonstrate the activity. Have the server pop serve the volleyball to one of the backcourt players, who passes it to the setter at the net. The remaining backcourt player comes toward the net to receive the set from the setter and performs a down ball over the net and into the opponent's court, where the server lets it drop (ideally inside the 10-foot attack area). Rotate after three trials each. Have players focus on moving into proper position to receive the set in order to perform the down ball.

Challenge

After serving, the server goes to the net and puts his or her arms straight up in the air, forcing the player performing the down ball to make sure it's hit over the extended arms.

9.24 | 4 v 4 Halfcourt Game: Serve, Pass, Set, and Down Ball

Goals

Gain experience in a competitive volleyball setting; perform all the skills introduced thus far, particularly the down ball.

Organization

Teams of four play on a halfcourt in the positions of center front (the setter), left back, center back, and right back.

Description

Explain and demonstrate the activity. Have teams play a regular game of 4 v 4 on a halfcourt. To begin play each time, the serve must be in the court, and the receiving team must successfully pass the volleyball up to the setter; if the pass is successful to the setter, the game begins. The server can serve from anywhere on the right side of the court. If the serve is not successful, the server must take a giant step closer to the net and repeat the serve. There must be at least two hits per side but no more than three. Skills are restricted to the serve, pass, set, and the down ball (no spiking or blocking). An underhand serve is allowed, but encourage players to try their overhand serve.

Challenges

1. Anytime a team successfully performs a pass, set, and down ball from a serve, an extra point is awarded to their score when play stops.
2. If a down ball is successful on a second or third hit and is not returned, an extra point is awarded to that team whether they served or not.
3. If a down ball is hit successfully and lands in the court without anyone touching it on the other team, it's an extra point for that team, even if they didn't serve. If the serving team achieves this, they get two points instead of one.

9.25 4-2 Positioning and Play Practice

Goals

Develop a familiarity with regular volleyball court positioning for the 4-2 offense and implement a sequence of pass, set, and down ball in a regulation volleyball setting.

Organization

Players play in teams of six or seven. A team of six is organized in the W formation on one side of a court. If there's a seventh player, that player is on the other side of the net on the same court.

Description

Demonstrate the W formation and the 4-2 offensive formation. (Please see *Volleyball: Steps to Success, 2nd edition* [Viera and Ferguson 1996] for more information on the W or 4-2 formation and regulation volleyball rules.) Have teams set up the in the W formation and attempt a sequence of pass, set, and down ball from a toss. If six players are on the court, the center front player tosses to any of the three back players, who passes to the center front setter. The setter then has the option of setting to either of the front players, who must use a down ball. The tosser retrieves the volleyball. If there are seven players, the seventh player is on the other side of the net and tosses the volleyball over to begin the sequence and chases the final hit. Do four trials, then rotate clockwise following regulation volleyball rules.

Challenges

1. The center front (setter) changes from a toss to an overhead throw with a downward trajectory to begin play and slowly increases the velocity aiming for gaps in court coverage. This is effective for getting back position players to get low in ready position with their weight on the balls of their feet to move quickly.

2. The seventh player serves from the other side of the net, aiming for areas that aren't well covered. This can lead to a game where aces are scored for the server and points awarded to each member of the receiving team if the sequence (pass, set, and down ball) is successful.

3. Introduce the 6-0 offense and have teams practice having a setter come from the back row to the front. (Please see *Volleyball: Steps to Success, 2nd edition* [Viera and Ferguson 1996] for a more detailed explanation of the 6-0 offense.)

9.26 6 v 6 Game

Goals

Develop experience playing a regulation game on a regulation court, adjusting to the larger area; players have the opportunity to apply the pass, set, down ball sequence.

Organization

Teams of six play on a regulation court.

Description

Explain the activity. Teams of six compete in a volleyball game using a 4-2 formation. Skills are restricted to the serve, pass, set, and down ball (no spiking or blocking). Regular volleyball rotation and rules are in effect, but don't hesitate to make adjustments if there's trouble getting the serve into play or if players are just one-hitting. Play 10-minute games, keeping score; rotate teams after each game. The focus is on playing as a team, talking, and placing the volleyball into an uncovered area of the opponent's court.

Challenges

1. Any served volleyball that's in the court and hits the floor untouched earns an extra point for the serving team.
2. Any down ball that is in the court and hits the floor untouched earns an extra point for that team.

9.27 Spiking (Hitting) Volleyball Down Onto Floor

Goal

Develop appropriate contact for the spike along with correct wrist and arm action.

Organization

Each player is in a 10-foot-wide practice area 8 feet from a wall with a volleyball.

Description

Explain and demonstrate the final phase of the spike. Have each player complete the final phase of the spike by hitting the volleyball down onto the floor at a 45-degree angle so that it bounces off the floor into the wall and back to the vicinity of the player. Stop and repeat. The focus is on bringing the hitting arm up as you raise up on your toes and hitting the volleyball down, following through alongside your body (not across your body).

Challenges

1. Using only the spike, keep the volleyball going as it rebounds off the wall.
2. Time the volleyball's rise and jump into the air so that you hit the ball down at the height of your jump.

9.28 One-Step Approach, Rocker Step, and Jump

Goal

Practice and refine the final phase of the spike, especially the rocker step and gather.

Organization

Each player finds personal space in a practice area in the gym where they're not interfering with others; if there's room, have players line up facing the net, three giant strides apart and about two giant steps off the net.

Description

Explain and demonstrate the one-step approach, rocker step, and jump. Have players begin from a standing position. Each player then begins to take a one-step approach, then performs a rocker step, brings both arms back, gathers (bends down crouching to gather momentum), jumps, and spikes an imaginary volleyball at the height of the jump. Players practice this on their own until the movement is fluid, not mechanical.

Challenge

None.

9.29 One-Step Approach, Rocker Step, and Spike a Held Volleyball

Goal

Develop the difficult skill of combining the final act of contacting a held volleyball with the one step, rocker step, and jump.

Organization

Place four to six players on a halfcourt with a chair near the net. The net is lowered to a height that allows players to succeed. If you have more than one net, set each net at a different height, but no net should be higher than 7 feet, 4 inches. Let players decide for themselves which net they want to try. Have four volleyballs at each line. One player is on the chair, holding the volleyball to be spiked; a feeder is on the floor next to the holder, providing volleyballs; and the rest of the class is in line (see figure 9.6). The holder extends the volleyball out with one hand above the net, palm up, about a foot from the net.

Description

Explain and demonstrate spiking a held volleyball. From a standing position, have the first player in line take a one-step approach, then perform a rocker step, bring arms back, gather, jump, and, at the height of the jump, spike the volleyball down out of the hand of the holder over the net taking care not to hit the net or travel into it, land over the center line, or touch the chair. Volleyballs can be retrieved in two ways. If there's another group on the other side of the net practicing, the spiker retreats into the backcourt and retrieves

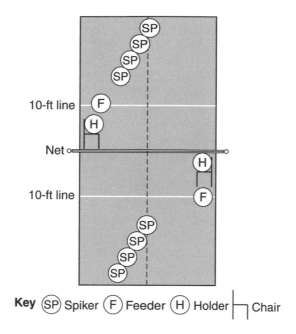

Key (SP) Spiker (F) Feeder (H) Holder ⌐ Chair

Figure 9.6 Setup for One-Step Approach, Rocker Step, and Spike Held Volleyball.

the volleyballs hit into the court by spikers on the other side of the net. If there's no group on the other side of the net, the spiker runs under the net and retrieves the volleyball and returns around the outside of the court before handing the volleyball to the feeder. For those unable to jump to a height at which they can spike the volleyball down, substitute a down ball for the spike. Feeders and holders for the spikers rotate after 10 hits.

Challenge

Have the holder toss the volleyball up slightly (no more than a foot) just before the hitter reaches the spiking phase.

9.30 One-Step Approach and Spike a Tossed or Set Volleyball

Goal

Develop the skill of combining the final act of contacting the volleyball with the one-step rocker step and jump, and timing this movement to a volleyball being tossed and set.

Organization

On each side of a net, players take positions so that there's one tosser/setter, one feeder, and a line of hitters. If there are three courts, you can have a total of six lines of hitters (two lines on each side of the net). Be sure the lines at each court are not directly opposite the line on the other side of that net. Lower the net to a height where players can succeed (although some may never be able to spike the volleyball and must substitute a down ball instead, which is fine). Have four volleyballs at each line. The tosser/setter is stationed at the center front position. The feeder is next to the tosser/setter, providing volleyballs.

Description

Explain and demonstrate spiking a tossed and set volleyball. Have the tosser two-hand underhand toss the volleyball up to a spiking position at the net. The spiker (first player in line) stands one stride from the net. As the volleyball leaves the tosser's hand, the spiker takes a one-step approach, performs a rocker step, brings arms back, gathers, jumps, and times the jump so that at the height of the jump the ball can be spiked down into the opponent's court. If players are having success with the toss, have setters set the ball by tossing to themselves and setting for the spiker. The spiker needs to be careful not to travel into or touch the net or land over the center line. If the volleyball is not in a perfect position to spike, perform a down ball instead.

Volleyballs are retrieved by the spiker, who retreats into the backcourt and retrieves the volleyballs hit into the court by spikers on the other side of the net. Feeders and holders for the spikers rotate after 10 hits.

Challenges

See if players can spike three out of five into the court, or have players compare to see who can spike the most balls into the court out of a specific number of tries.

9.31 Two-Step Approach and Spike a Set Volleyball

Goal

Develop the difficult skill of combining the final act of contacting the volleyball with the two-step approach from a set.

Organization

Place four to six players on a halfcourt with a setter near the net. The net is lowered to a height where players can succeed. Have four volleyballs at each line. A feeder is on the floor next to the setter, providing balls; the rest of the

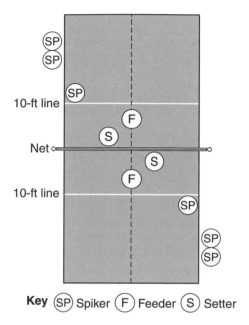

Key (SP) Spiker (F) Feeder (S) Setter

Figure 9.7 Setup for Two-Step Approach and Spike a Set Volleyball.

class is in line. The spiker (first player in line) stands two long strides from the net (see figure 9.7).

Description

Explain and demonstrate the two-step approach and spiking a set volleyball. Have the setter at the net self-toss and set the volleyball up to a spiking position at the net. As the volleyball leaves the setter's hands, the spiker takes a two-step approach, performs a rocker step, brings arms back, gathers, jumps, and times the jump so that at the height of the jump the ball can be spiked down into the opponent's court. The spiker needs to be careful not to travel into or touch the net or land over the center line. For those unable to jump to a height at which they can spike the volleyball down, substitute a down ball for the spike. Volleyballs are retrieved by the spiker, who retreats into the backcourt and retrieves the volleyballs hit into the court by spikers on the other side of the net. Feeders and holders for the spikers rotate after 10 hits. If the volleyball is not in a perfect position to spike, players hit a down ball instead. The focus is on taking off to do the two-step approach just after, not before, the setter sets the volleyball.

Challenge

The next spiker in line underhands the volleyball to the setter, who sets for the spiker.

9.32 Three-Step Approach to Spike a Set Volleyball

Goal

Develop the difficult skill of combining the three-step approach and spiking the ball after setting the ball to a setter.

Organization

Place four to six players in a halfcourt with a setter near the net. The net is lowered to a height where players can succeed. Have four volleyballs at each line. The spiker (first player in line) stands inside the sideline three long strides from the net (see figure 9.8).

Description

Explain and demonstrate the three-step approach and spiking a set volleyball. To begin, the spiker underhands the volleyball to the setter, who returns

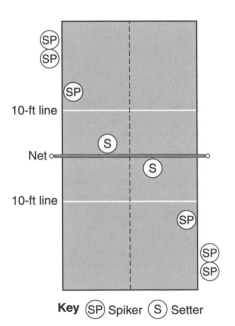

Key (SP) Spiker (S) Setter

Figure 9.8 Setup for Three-Step Approach to Spike a Set Volleyball.

it with a set to the spiker at the proper spiking position. As the volleyball leaves the setter's hand, the spiker takes a three-step approach, performs a rocker step, brings arms back, gathers, jumps, and times the jump so that at the height of the jump the ball can be spiked down into the opponent's court. The spiker needs to be careful not to travel into or touch the net or land over the center line. After spiking, the spiker retreats to the backcourt and retrieves volleyballs hit over the net by players on the other side of the net. For those unable to jump to a height at which they can spike the volleyball down, substitute a down ball for the spike. If the volleyball is not in a perfect position to spike, players hit a down ball instead. The focus is on timing the jump so that players spike the volleyball at the height of their jump.

Challenge

See if players can spike three out of five into the opponent's court.

9.33 | Pass, Set, and Spike

Goal

Experience and practice the timing of the spike when the volleyball is received in the backcourt.

Organization

Four players play on a halfcourt: one retriever on the other side of the court, one left or right front spiker, one center front setter, and one center back passer. The net is lowered to a height where players can succeed. Use four volleyballs (see figure 9.9).

Description

Explain and demonstrate the timing for spiking when the volleyball is received in the backcourt. Have the center front setter underhand toss the volleyball deep to the center back, who passes the ball back to the center front, who then sets to the spiker, who does a three-step approach and spikes the volleyball. Rotate on each spike. The spiker becomes the next retriever on the other side of the net, the retriever becomes the center front, the center front becomes the center back, and the center back becomes the spiker. If the volleyball is not in a perfect position to spike, players hit a down ball instead. Tell players to focus on staying back as a spiker until the last minute so that they don't catch themselves standing at the net waiting to jump up to spike.

Challenge

Overhand throw the volleyball to the center back with increased speed.

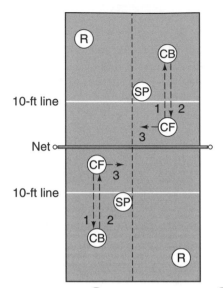

Key (CB) Center back/passer (CF) Center front/setter (SP) Spiker (R) Retriever
--- Imaginary line dividing court $\xrightarrow[\text{1 or 2 or 3}]{}$ Order of ball movement

Figure 9.9 Setup of Pass, Set, and Spike.

9.34 Serve, Pass, Set, and Spike

Goal

Experience and practice the timing of the spike when the volleyball is served over the net into the backcourt.

Organization

Four players play on a halfcourt. On one side of the net is the server/retriever. On the other side is one left or right front spiker, one center front setter, and one center back passer. Lower the net to where players can succeed (try 7 feet, 4 inches; see figure 9.10).

Description

Explain and demonstrate the activity. Have the server/retriever serve the volleyball deep to the center back, who passes the ball back to the center front, who then sets to the spiker, who does a three-step approach and spikes the volleyball. Rotate on each spike or after four turns. The spiker becomes the next server/retriever on the other side of the net, the server/retriever becomes

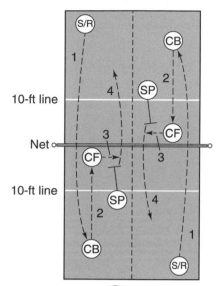

Key

(CB) Center back/passer (CF) Center front/setter (SP) Spiker
(S/R) Server/retriever ⊣ Player movement
--- Imaginary line dividing court ‾‾‾‾‾‾‾‾‾▶ Order of ball movement
1 or 2 or 3 or 4

Figure 9.10 Setup of Serve, Pass, Set, and Spike.

the center front, the center front becomes the center back, and the center back becomes the spiker. Have the server begin from the 10-foot line and move back as the receiving team has success. If the volleyball is not in a perfect position to spike, players hit a down ball instead.

Challenges

1. How many successful combinations of the serve, pass, set, and spike can your team do in five minutes?

2. Don't have the server as part of the team, but play a game keeping points. If the serve is not returned successfully with a pass, set, and spike, the server gets one point. If the serve is not in the designated halfcourt, a point is awarded to each member of the receiving team. If the serve is returned with a pass, set, and spike, each person on that team receives a point. Rotate after five trials. The first team to 10 points wins.

9.35 Offensive Practice: Serve, Pass, Set, and Spike

Goal

Organize and implement a 6-0 formation for your team in a rally situation.

Organization

Teams of six players on each side of the net play on one volleyball court with one volleyball (see figure 9.11).

Description

Explain and demonstrate the 6-0 offense, including player positioning and strategy. (See *Volleyball: Steps to Success, 2nd edition* [Viera and Ferguson 1996] for a detailed description of the 6-0 offense.) Then have each team practice this offensive set. Each player on one team gets to serve the volleyball to the other team, and a rally ensues. Once everyone on one team serves, the other team serves.

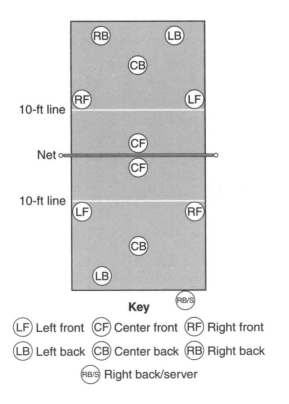

Key

(LF) Left front (CF) Center front (RF) Right front

(LB) Left back (CB) Center back (RB) Right back

(RB/S) Right back/server

Figure 9.11 Setup of Offensive Practice: Serve, Pass, Set, and Spike.

Challenges

1. See if players can get through one rotation (all six players serving once) of performing a successful serve, pass, set, and spike series.

2. Play a game keeping points. If the serve is not returned successfully with a pass, set, and spike, then the server gets one point. If the serve is not in the court, a point is awarded to each member of the receiving team. If the serve is returned with a pass, set, and spike, each player on that team receives a point. Rotate after each serve to keep the group active. First player to win 11 points is the winner.

9.36 6 v 6 Game: Serve, Pass, Set, and Spike

Goal

Players experience a regulation game as a member of a team that has practiced together and make adjustments as they attempt to execute the pass, set, and spike sequence.

Organization

Players play in two teams of six on a full court.

Description

Review volleyball rules and regulations. Have teams of 6 compete in a game using either the 6-0 or the 4-2 offensive set. Skills are restricted to the serve, pass, set, down ball, and spike. Regular volleyball rotation and rules are in effect. However, don't hesitate to make adjustments if players have trouble getting the serve into play or are only hitting the volleyball once and over.

Challenges

1. Any served volleyball that's in the court and hits the floor untouched wins an extra point for the serving team.

2. Any spike that's in the court and hits the floor untouched wins an extra point for that team.

9.37 Hit and Block

Goal

Blocker experiences the final blocking action and develops proper technique at the net before adding the jump.

Organization

Partners (one blocker and one hitter) scatter throughout the gym (see figure 9.12).

Description

Demonstrate the use of the arms in the final blocking technique. Have the blocker stand and raise his or her arms above his or her head into the final blocking position. The hitter stands directly in front of the blocker (no more than arm's-length away) and hits the volleyball using the overhand serve hard into the blocker's hands. The blocker performs the correct blocking technique as the volleyball is prevented from getting past the arms. Players do five blocks and then rotate. Begin softly and increase in velocity with success.

Challenge

None.

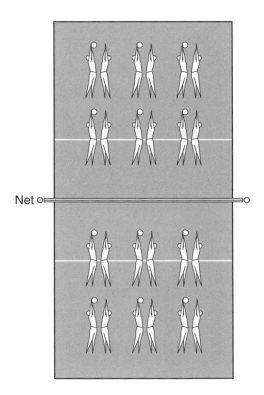

Figure 9.12   Setup for Hit and Block.

9.38 | Partner Net Block

Goal

Players combine the entire blocking technique and time their leap with a partner.

Organization

Players play in partners across from each other at the net, which is set at a height so that players can jump up and reach both hands over the net (see figure 9.13).

Description

Demonstrate the timing for blocking. Have partners count to three and jump up together on each side of the net and clap hands together using proper blocking technique, land, and repeat.

Challenge

Have players slide-step in one direction around the ends of the net, continuing to jump and block with the oncoming person on the other side of the net.

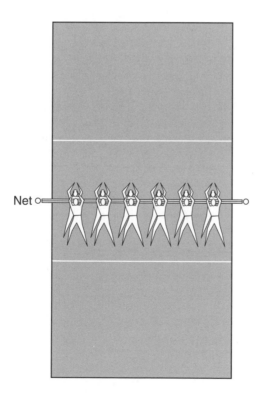

Figure 9.13   Setup for Partner Net Block.

9.39 | Pass, Set, Spike, and Block

Goal

Experience and practice the timing of the block when an opponent is attempting a spike.

Organization

Four players play on a half court: one blocker/retriever, one left or right front spiker, one center front setter, and one center back passer (see figure 9.14). Use five volleyballs.

Description

Explain and demonstrate the activity. Have the center front setter underhand toss the volleyball deep to the center back, who passes the ball back to the center front, who then sets to the spiker, who does a three-step approach and spikes the volleyball. The blocker on the other side of the net begins in the center front position, moves laterally to time the jump with the spike, and blocks the volleyball. After five trials, the blocker retrieves the volleyballs

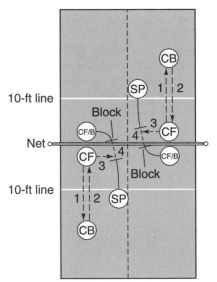

CB Center back/passer   CF Center front/setter   SP Spiker

Key   CF/B Center front/blocker   ⊣ Player movement

– – – Imaginary line dividing court $\frac{\text{- - - - - - - ➤}}{1 \text{ or } 2 \text{ or } 3 \text{ or } 4}$ Order of ball movement

Figure 9.14 Setup for Pass, Set, Spike, and Block.

and then rotates to become the center front, the center front becomes the center back, and the center back becomes the spiker. The spiker becomes the next blocker on the other side of the net. Tell players to focus on keeping their hands held up in the "stick 'em up" position ready to block rather than down where they might interfere with the net as they raise them up to block.

Challenge

Eliminate the center back and have two spikers, a left front and a right front. One of the spikers tosses or sets high to the center front setter, who can then set to either spiker. Setter must turn shoulders in line of direction and may not set backward. The blocker now has to slide much more quickly to where the set is made in order to make the block.

9.40 6 v 6 Double Block Positioning

Goal

As a team, develop the skill of double blocking at the net.

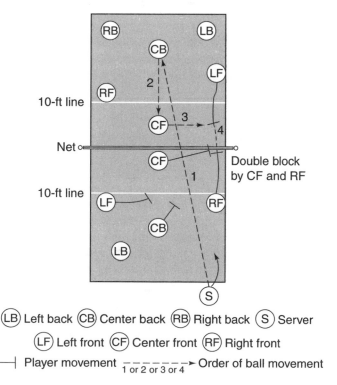

Figure 9.15 Setup for 6 v 6 Double Block Positioning.

Organization

Two teams of six on one full court (see figure 9.15).

Description

Give players an overview of player positioning on the double block. Have one team serve and then position themselves in the appropriate double-block position when the receiving team attempts to spike the volleyball. Only spikes are allowed—no tips. Alternate serving between teams every five trials. The focus is on moving quickly to double up with a teammate at the net when you see the direction the other team is spiking.

Challenge

Play a game in which a spike that gets through the block (not a tip) counts as one point and a block counts as two points.

9.41 6 v 6 Game: Serve, Pass, Set, Spike/Down Ball, and Block

Goals

Players compete in a regulation game as a member of a team that has practiced together; the team makes adjustments as they attempt to execute the pass, set, and spike/down ball sequence along with team blocking in a competitive situation.

Organization

Two teams of six play on one full court.

Description

Review 6 v 6 play and what you want to see players doing during the games. Have teams of six compete in a volleyball game using either the 6-0 or 4-2 offensive formation. Restrict skills to the serve, pass, set, spike, down ball, and block. Regular volleyball rotation and rules are in effect. However, don't hesitate to make adjustments if players have trouble getting the serve into play or if teams are doing too much one-hitting.

Challenges

1. Any served volleyball that's in the court and hits the floor untouched wins an extra point for the serving team.
2. Any spike that's in the court and hits the floor untouched wins an extra point for that team.

9.42 Partner Tip

Goal

Develop the mechanics involved in the tip.

Organization

Partners are directly across the net from each other in six-foot practice areas with one volleyball. One player is a blocker and the other a tipper.

Description

Explain and demonstrate tipping the volleyball. Have partners practice tipping the volleyball to each other by self-tossing the ball and tipping it first with no blocker and then, when they have success, adding their partner as a blocker. The blocker begins flat-footed and, if the tipper is successful, is allowed to jump and block. As tippers develop the tip, they then can toss the volleyball to themselves higher so that they can add a jump. The tipper gathers, jumps, and tips the volleyball at the height of the jump, up and over the fingertips of the blocker so that the ball lands in the proper area of the court. Alternate trials.

Challenge

Give the hitter the option of tipping or spiking the volleyball.

9.43 Pass, Set, and Tip Over Block

Goal

Experience and practice the timing of the tip when a blocker prevents a spike.

Organization

Four players play on a halfcourt: one blocker, one left or right front spiker, one center front setter, and one center back passer (see figure 9.16). Use five volleyballs. Lower the net to a level at which players have success.

Description

Explain and demonstrate the activity. Tell players to focus on making it look as if they are going to spike the volleyball before pulling up and tipping. Have the center front setter underhand toss the volleyball deep to the center back, who passes the ball back to the center front, who then sets to the spiker, who does a three-step approach and tips the volleyball over the attempted blocker. The blocker on the other side of the net begins in the center front position and moves laterally to time the jump with the spike and, if possible,

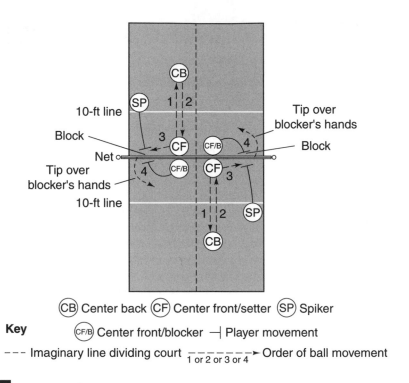

Figure 9.16 Setup for Pass, Set, and Tip Over Block.

blocks the volleyball. After five trials, the blocker retrieves the volleyballs and then rotates to become the center front, the center front becomes the center back, and the center back becomes the spiker. The spiker becomes the next blocker on the other side of the net.

Challenge

Let players decide whether to spike or tip the volleyball.

9.44 6 v 6 Game: Serve, Pass, Set, Spike/Down Ball or Tip, and Block

Goals

Players compete in a regulation game as a member of a team that has practiced together; the team makes adjustments as they attempt to execute the pass, set, spike/down ball, or tip sequence.

Organization

Two teams of seven play on one full court (this number takes into consideration that there's usually a player missing on most teams).

Description

Review what you want to see players doing in the games and go over any rules you want to reiterate. Have teams of six compete in a volleyball game using either the 6-0 or 4-2 offensive formation. In playing a regular volleyball game of 6 v 6, it's inevitable that some teams will have more than six players. One way to handle this is to put more people on a court, such as 7 v 7 or 8 v 8. This does not help in learning the game, as bad habits develop and laziness can set in. Another way is to rotate players out. For example, if a team has seven players, the seventh player rotates out of the game from the right front position and rotates back in on the next rotation into the right back position. Or the seventh player could be the designated server who stays off the court after serving but rotates back into the game the same way. Restrict skills to the serve, pass, set, block, spike, down ball, and tip. Regular volleyball rotation and rules are in effect, but make adjustments as necessary.

Challenges

1. Any served volleyball that's in the court and hits the floor untouched wins an extra point for the serving team.
2. Any spike that's in the court and hits the floor untouched wins an extra point for that team.

Reference

Viera, Barbara, and Bonnie Jill Ferguson. 1996. *Volleyball: Steps to Success. 2d ed.* Champaign, IL: Human Kinetics.

CHAPTER 10

Soccer

Soccer is a fantastic unit for physical education because it requires high levels of physical activity while being relatively inexpensive, requiring only field space, soccer balls, and goals (for which you can easily use traffic cones if you don't have nets). To maintain high rates of activity, the progressions here lead to games with no more than five players, plus a goalie, per side. If the class is made up of highly skilled soccer players, then it's fine to proceed to 8 v 8 and 11 v 11 play because players are more efficient and skillful and tend to become more involved in the game. But playing 11 v 11 with students who are not well skilled leads only to great chunks of inactivity for those who need it the most. They're left standing around watching the skilled players control the game.

The premise behind the progressions is to develop the basic skills of soccer and, in particular, have students maintain proper balance and spacing on the field when on offense. The essential offensive skills covered are dribbling, passing, trapping, shooting, shielding, volleying (full and half), chipping, the throw-in, forming a triangle, and moving without the soccer ball. Heading, which is recognizably an important skill when elite levels play, is taught but appears only late in the progressions. Although I've included heading, you might prefer to omit it if you have concerns about safety (for instance, there is some evidence that too much heading can harm the brain). Defensive techniques and tactics such as channeling and support are covered late in the progressions after the offense has developed some confidence. Goalie skills are also delayed until the end of the progressions. Only a few students per class will be goalkeepers in a game, so spending a lot of time on goalie skills is inefficient. Plus, it's important for students to have offensive success when shooting on goal, so it makes sense to put off defensive skills and give the offense time to build some confidence. Similarly, slide tackling (a defensive skill in which a player attempts to disrupt the offensive player with the soccer ball by sliding feet first into the ball, often contacting the offensive player) is not permitted because it can cause injury and impede the development of offensive skills. Teachers who want to delve into the intricacies of heading, volleying, slide tackling, goal keeping, and defensive skills and tactics are encouraged to develop these skills in an advanced class once players have achieved fundamental skills.

In soccer, it's important to remember that more space equals more success. When learning offensive soccer skills, the bigger the space for players to practice, the easier it is to develop skills. This applies not only to field space during practice but also to the width of the goals. Begin with the goals quite wide to promote success and reduce them accordingly as proficiency increases. Creating separate work areas on a field is made easy with the use of World of Soccer "donuts" (half-cones; www.gophersport.com). These markers work better than cones because one person can carry 40 or 50 of them, and they don't present tripping hazards.

Most of the activities in the progressions require each player or a pair of players to have one soccer ball to work on the skill being introduced. I'll assume you already know to have enough soccer balls on hand to meet the needs of your students. If possible, shin pads should be provided for each player. When an activity requires a player or pair of players to use more than one soccer ball, I'll mention that in the activity's Organization section.

■ After following the progressions, beginning students should be able to play in a game of 6 v 6 (five players and a goalie) soccer using the following skills:
- Dribbling
- Passing (inside and outside)
- Trapping (inside, outside, sole, body, chest, and thigh)
- Shielding
- Triangle passing (give-and-go)
- Throwing in
- Two touching (deflect and touch)
- Shooting on goal (instep and top of foot)
- Volley and half-volley return
- Chipping
- Heading
- Catching, punting, decreasing angle, and hurling (goalkeeper skills)

10.1 Toe Touches

Goal

Warm up and focus on the need for quick feet in soccer.

Organization

Players are in self-space inside the 18-yard penalty box in front of the goal or a practice area about 18 by 24 feet with lines, donuts, or cones for boundaries (see figure 10.1). Each player has a soccer ball, and there are six players in each box.

Description

Explain and demonstrate toe touches. Have players alternate touching the soccer ball with the sole of their foot as quickly as possible. Focus on touching the soccer ball lightly with the sole of the foot.

Challenge

Have players see how many touches they can get in 20 seconds.

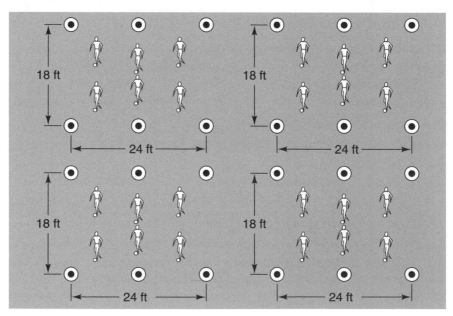

Key ⊙ Donut marker

Figure 10.1 Setup for Toe Touches.

10.2   Slalom Touches

Goal

Experience the kind of control you can get with the inside of the foot.

Organization

Players are in self-space inside the 18-yard penalty box in front of the goal or in a practice area about 18 by 24 feet with lines, donuts, or cones for boundaries (see figure 10.1). Each player has a soccer ball.

Description

Explain and demonstrate slalom touches. Players should attempt to tap the soccer ball back and forth using inside foot taps (like a flipper on a pinball machine). Focus on maintaining control and getting into a rhythm.

Challenges

See how many touches they can do before they have to stop.

10.3   Drag and Pull Back the Soccer Ball

Goal

Familiarize the foot with the soccer ball and develop a technique for changing direction.

Organization

Players are in self-space inside the 18-yard penalty box in front of the goal or in a practice area about 18 by 24 feet with lines, donuts, or cones for boundaries (see figure 10.1). Each player has a soccer ball.

Description

Explain and demonstrate dragging and pulling back the soccer ball. With the inside of the foot, drag the foot over the soccer ball until the ball is on the outside, and then return. Then with the sole of the foot, pull the soccer ball back. Alternate feet. Focus on dragging the sole of the foot over the top of the soccer ball.

Challenge

Have players go over and back five times as fast as they can go without losing control.

10.4 Dribbling With the Inside Foot

Goal

Get introduced to controlling the soccer ball (dribbling) using the inside of the foot while moving.

Organization

Players are in self-space inside the 18-yard penalty box in front of the goal or in a practice area about 18 by 24 feet with lines, donuts, or cones for boundaries (see figure 10.1, p. 246). Each player has a soccer ball.

Description

Explain and demonstrate dribbling with the inside of the foot. Walk around dribbling using the inside of each foot while keeping the ball under control with eyes up to avoid running into others. Focus on touching the soccer ball to direct it to the other instep rather than dragging the ball with the instep.

Challenge

See if players can slowly begin to jog, always keeping the soccer ball under control.

10.5 Dribbling With the Inside and Outside of Foot

Goal

Become familiar with controlling the soccer ball while moving (dribbling), using both the inside and outside of the foot.

Organization

Players are in self-space inside the 18-yard penalty box in front of the goal or in a practice area about 18 by 24 feet with lines, donuts, or cones for boundaries (see figure 10.1, p. 246). Each player has a soccer ball.

Description

Explain and demonstrate dribbling with the inside and outside of the foot. Focus on finding a walking speed that allows for controlling the soccer ball. Don't walk so fast that you lose control. Walk around dribbling, alternating using the inside and outside of each foot while keeping the soccer ball under control with eyes up to avoid running into others.

Challenge

Slowly begin to jog while maintaining control.

10.6 Continuous Inside and Outside Weave Dribble

Goal

Become familiar with controlling the soccer ball while moving (dribbling), using both the inside and outside of the foot through a designated pathway.

Organization

Set up markers (cones or donuts) in an oval formation five feet apart with two markers per player in the class. Each player has a soccer ball and stands at every other marker (see figure 10.2).

Description

Explain and demonstrate weaving and dribbling the soccer ball in a continuous path. If the ball is consistently uncontrolled, slow down. Players dribble the soccer ball in and out of the cones in a continuous weave using the inside and outside of the foot as required while keeping the ball under control. Change direction after a few minutes. Focus on maintaining control of the soccer ball.

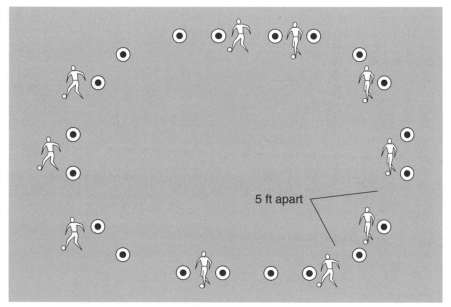

Key ⦿ Donut marker

Figure 10.2 Setup for Continuous Inside and Outside Weave Dribble.

Challenge

See if they can pass the person ahead without disrupting.

10.7 Speed Dribble

Goal

Recognize that by touching the soccer ball every three to four steps, you can cover greater distances more quickly.

Organization

Players spread out on the sidelines of a football or soccer field, each with a soccer ball.

Description

Explain and demonstrate the speed dribble. Players speed dribble (one touch of the soccer ball to propel it ahead and a touch thereafter every three to four steps) in a straight line, alternating feet as much as possible, until they reach the other sideline, where they stop the soccer ball using the inside of foot or sole trap and return to the start. Repeat for one minute. Focus on touching the soccer ball so that it goes no further than three to four steps so that you can quickly get to and control it should a defender close in on you.

Challenges

1. Have players keep track of how many trips from sideline to sideline they can do in one minute.
2. Have players stop when you blow the whistle, change direction, and go back.

10.8 Outside-Foot Sidestep and Fake-and-Speed Approach

Goal

Get past an invisible defender by getting him or her to commit in one direction, allowing the dribbler to cut diagonally in an opposite direction past the defender.

Organization

Players spread out on half a football or soccer field, each with a soccer ball.

Description

Explain and demonstrate the outside-foot sidestep and fake-and-speed approach. Player slightly nudges the soccer ball with the outside of the foot, steps over the ball with the same foot, and performs an instep dribble to cut diagonally opposite with a speed dribble. Focus on going slow in the beginning until the skill is perfected before exploding at the cut.

Challenge

Perform with each foot from sideline to sideline until the dribble becomes smooth with a sudden burst of speed at the cut.

10.9 Dribbling Changing Directions

Goal

Develop change-of-direction dribbling techniques.

Organization

Players spread out on half a football or soccer field, each with a soccer ball.

Description

Explain and demonstrate dribbling techniques used to change direction. Use dribbling techniques learned thus far to change direction (e.g., pull back, drag, speed dribble, outside-foot sidestep, fake-and-speed approach) to elude an invisible defender. Players should practice all these skills and change direction on their own continuously in the area indicated and not just dribble around aimlessly. Focus on keeping the head up to see other players and changing directions continuously using all the skills but especially the ones proving difficult.

Challenge

Distribute cones throughout the field for players to dribble toward (not between), changing directions at the last minute whenever they reach a cone.

10.10 Dribble Past a Stationary Defender

Goal

Work at changing directions using both dribbling techniques to avoid a defender while maintaining control of the soccer ball.

Organization

Partners pair off in 10-yard practice areas 10 to 15 yards long. One partner is in the middle of the practice area as a stationary defender, and the other has the soccer ball.

Description

Explain and demonstrate dribbling past a stationary defender. Using the dribbling skills learned thus far, players try to get by the stationary defender situated in the middle of the practice area without losing the soccer ball or stopping. The defender can only attempt to kick the ball away from the offensive player while maintaining a stationary position. Focus on maintaining a steady pace to get past the defender rather than slowing down and stopping to protect the soccer ball.

Challenge

Allow the defender to move, first at half-speed and then full speed.

10.11 Shielding the Soccer Ball From a Defender

Goal

Develop correct shielding technique (e.g., leaning into defender) against a live defender.

Organization

Partners pair off with one soccer ball in self-space inside the 18-yard penalty box in front of the goal or in a practice area about 18 by 24 feet with lines, donuts, or cones for boundaries (see figure 10.1, p. 246).

Description

Explain and demonstrate shielding. After practicing shielding with a soccer ball without a defender, add a defender. The offensive player must shield the defensive player from the soccer ball for a set length of time (about 15 to 30 seconds). The defender begins by just shadowing the offensive player, then runs at half-speed before going full speed. You might want to introduce rules regarding physical contact at this time. Focus on leaning into defenders to keep them away from the ball.

Challenges

1. Have the defender go full speed.
2. Play Knock Out, in which dribblers control their own soccer ball while attempting to knock someone else's ball out of a practice area (the size

of which allows players enough room to maneuver while still forcing dribblers to protect their ball from other dribblers). If a player's soccer ball is knocked out, he or she must perform a skill of your choice (e.g., 25 speed dribbles on the adjacent field) a set number of times before reentering the activity.

10.12 1 v 1 Mini-Game

Goal
Use the skills of dribbling and shielding in a competitive situation.

Organization
Partners spread out on mini-fields (about 18 by 24 feet set up with cones, donuts, or boundary lines; see figure 10.1, p. 246).

Description
Explain and demonstrate the activity. Have players play a 1 v 1 mini-game of modified soccer, the object of which is to dribble the soccer ball under control across the opponent's endline for a score. The defender tries to take the soccer ball away and score at the other endline. The dribbler uses the shielding techniques covered. After a player scores or the soccer ball goes over the sideline, the other player dribbles the soccer ball back into play. The defender gives the offensive player a five-yard buffer to resume play, but once the dribbler begins to dribble, the defender can resume guarding close. Focus on keeping the head up to see what the defender is doing and trying all the techniques introduced thus far, not just the ones already performed well.

Challenge
Place two stationary defenders on the field who can take or kick the soccer ball away as long as they don't move.

10.13 Inside-Foot Pass and Inside-Foot Trap While Stationary

Goal
Develop stationary passing and trapping using the inside of the foot.

Organization
Partners pair off in practice areas 10 yards by 8 to 10 yards with one soccer ball.

Description

Explain and demonstrate the inside-foot pass and the inside-foot trap. Stationary partners pass and trap the soccer ball using the inside of the foot. Alternate feet each time. Focus on absorbing the soccer ball for control rather than blocking it.

Challenge

Extend the distance to 12 to 15 yards.

10.14 Outside-Foot Pass and Outside-Foot Trap While Stationary

Goal

Develop stationary trapping and passing using the outside foot.

Organization

Partners are side by side in practice areas 10 yards by 8 to 10 yards with one soccer ball.

Description

Explain and demonstrate the outside-foot pass and the outside-foot trap. Stationary partners pass and trap the soccer ball using the outside of the foot. Alternate feet each time. Focus on developing a rhythm of trapping and then passing without much hesitation between.

Challenge

Extend the distance to 12 to 15 yards.

10.15 2 v 0: Two Touch (Deflect and Touch) and Pass While Stationary

Goal

Develop the skills of deflecting a pass, touching the soccer ball, and then passing the ball.

Organization

Partners spread out on half a football or soccer field, each with a soccer ball about 10 to 12 yards apart.

Description

Explain and demonstrate deflecting the soccer ball (controlling an incoming ball, then directing it to a place where it's in a better position for the player to operate) and touching the ball before passing. Then have partners pass and trap, but make the rule that they must touch the soccer ball twice (first with a deflection, then a touch) before passing.

Challenge

Time players for one minute and have them count how many soccer balls they can deflect and pass during that time.

10.16 2 v 0: Two Touch (Deflect and Touch) and Pass While Moving

Goal

Develop skills of two touch (deflecting then touching) and then passing on the run using inside- and outside-foot traps and passes while remaining onside.

Organization

Partners are on one sideline of a football or soccer field in 10-yard practice areas with one soccer ball (see figure 10.3).

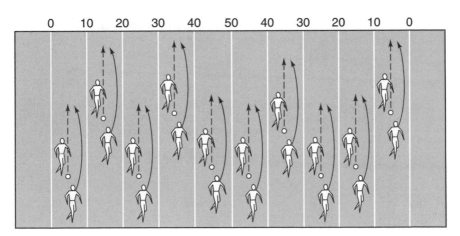

Key - - - ► Ball movement   ——► Player movement

Figure 10.3 Setup for 2 v 0: Two Touch (Deflect and Touch) and Pass While Moving.

Description

Explain and demonstrate the offsides rule: In a regulation game, a player is *offsides* when he or she does not have two defensive players between himself or herself and the goal when receiving the soccer ball from a teammate (Mood et al. 2003). For the purpose of this drill, the player receiving the soccer ball from a pass must remain behind the passer until the ball is passed. Have partners pass and two touch (deflect and touch) on the run from sideline to sideline using both inside- and outside-foot traps and passes. If a player is offsides, play stops for the player to get onside and then resume play. Have players focus on staying behind the passer until contact is made on the soccer ball.

Challenge

Consistently maintain a 10-yard distance between partners while maintaining momentum with no one offsides.

10.17 Triangle Passing: The Box Drill

Goal

Develop the habit on offense of always forming a triangle from the soccer ball to allow for passing lanes and balancing the field. Develop the principle of give-and-go to an open area of the field.

Organization

Arrange 15-yard by 15-yard or 20-yard by 20-yard areas (boxes) over the field. At each corner is a traffic cone or donut for a marker (see figure 10.4). Three players play with one soccer ball.

Description

Explain and demonstrate triangle passing. Have each player pick a corner at which to stand to begin play, with one corner left vacant. The player with the soccer ball must pass diagonally to the right or to the left corner but not directly ahead to the corner opposite. Once a pass is made to one of the corners, the remaining nonreceiving corner must leave that corner and go to the vacant corner. The receiver then has the option of passing to the newly occupied corner or back to the player who just put the soccer ball into play. Each time a player receives the soccer ball, there should be a player diagonally on each side so that a triangle is formed.

Challenge

See how many successful passes a team can do in two minutes.

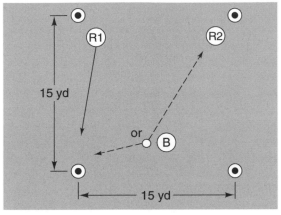

Key (B) Player with ball (R1)(R2) Receivers

– – → Pass option ● Donut marker ○ Ball

Figure 10.4   Setup for Triangle Passing: The Box Drill.

10.18 Box Drill v Defender(s)

Goals

Develop the habit on offense of always forming a triangle from the soccer ball; when being pressured by a defender, perform the give-and-go, passing the soccer ball to the open corner.

Organization

Arrange 15-yard by 15-yard areas (boxes) over the field. At each corner place a traffic cone or donut for a marker (see figure 10.5). Four players play with one soccer ball.

Description

Explain and demonstrate triangle passing against a defender. The box drill is modified by adding a defender in the middle of the field who can roam to any area of the field to intercept a pass. After five successful passes, or if the defender intercepts a pass, players rotate. Focus on trapping, seeing where the defender is, and passing to the open corner.

Challenge

Add a second defender with the rule that one defender must always challenge the soccer ball (both defenders can't just guard the corners).

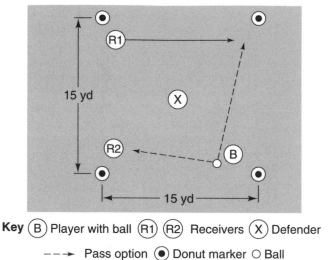

Key (B) Player with ball (R1) (R2) Receivers (X) Defender

- - -→ Pass option ⦿ Donut marker ○ Ball

Figure 10.5 Setup for Box Drill v Defender(s).

10.19 3 v 1 Attack

Goal

Use the principles of maintaining a triangle against one defender on a larger field and avoiding offsides in a game-like setting.

Organization

Groups of four players (three offense and one defense) play on a field 30 yards wide by 50 yards long (sideline to sideline on a football field; see figure 10.6).

Description

Explain and demonstrate the 3 v 1 attack. Have three offensive players begin on one sideline and try to move the soccer ball up the field and dribble over the other sideline against one defender. The offensive player with the soccer ball is to dribble until the defender commits, at which point a pass is made and the passer runs into open space while maintaining the triangle. If the defender intercepts the soccer ball, stop play, and the offense resumes from that point. Rotate positions at each end. Because there's no goalie, offensive players receiving a pass must have the defender between them and the goal when receiving the soccer ball or it's offsides. Focus on knowing where the defender is and using the triangle-passing concept while maintaining a balanced field.

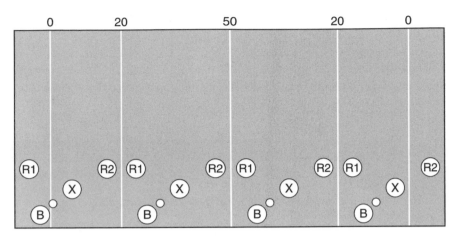

Key (R1)(R2) Receivers (B) Player with ball (X) Defender ○ Ball

Figure 10.6 Setup of 3 v 1 Attack.

Challenge

See if a team of three can go down the field without the defender touching the soccer ball.

10.20 3 v 2 Attack

Goal

Use the principles of maintaining a triangle against two defenders on a larger field and avoiding offsides in a game-like setting.

Organization

Groups of five players (three on offense and two on defense) play on a field 30 yards wide by 50 yards long (sideline to sideline on a football field; see figure 10.6).

Description

Explain and demonstrate the activity. Have three offensive players begin on one sideline and try to move the soccer ball upfield against two defenders by dribbling over the other sideline. The offensive player with the soccer ball is to dribble until the defender commits, at which point a pass is made to the open partner. The passer then runs into open space while maintaining the triangle. If defenders intercept the soccer ball, stop the action, and have the offense resume play from that point. Rotate positions at each end. Focus on maintaining the triangle and balancing the field.

Challenge

See if players can maintain possession of the soccer ball from one sideline to the other.

10.21 Throw-In, Two Touch (Deflect and Touch), and Pass

Goals

Develop proper technique of the throw-in; receive a soccer ball on the bounce with a two touch followed by a pass.

Organization

Partners play in 10-yard by 15-yard practice areas.

Description

Explain and demonstrate a proper throw-in and a two touch then pass return. Have one player perform a throw-in to a receiver five to seven yards away. The thrower then runs diagonally to the right or left of the receiver to receive a return pass. The receiver returns the soccer ball off the bounce with a two touch followed by a pass to the open area to which the thrower is running. Exchange positions after five trials. Focus on having the thrower toss the soccer ball lightly in the beginning so that the receiver has success in two touching and then passing.

Challenge

Vary the distance and speed of the throw-in so the receiver must adjust.

10.22 Throw-In: 2 v 1

Goals

Put into practice the skills of the throw-in and two touch; develop an understanding when to pass and when to dribble in a game-like competition.

Organization

Three players play on a 15-yard by 15-yard practice area: two partners and a defender.

Description

Explain and demonstrate performing a throw-in versus a defender. Have one partner stand behind a designated sideline and use proper technique for the throw-in to a moving partner guarded by a defender. The receiver performs a two touch followed by a return pass to the partner who, after the throw-in, moves to an open area to receive the pass. If the partner who performed the throw-in is covered, the receiver continues upfield dribbling the soccer ball until he or she decides to attack the ball, at which point the ball is passed. The object is for the offense to move the soccer ball up the field 10 yards under control against the defender for one point. If the defender intercepts the soccer ball, play stops. Play resumes again at the sideline. Rotate players after two trials. Focus on having the player who receives the throw-in make sharp cuts to clear himself or herself to receive the throw-in; after the throw-in, players move to an open area to receive a pass.

Challenge

Lengthen the field to 20 yards and see if the offense can move the soccer ball without being stopped.

10.23 3 v 3 Shadow (Passive)

Goal

Teams of three employ all skills learned thus far, particularly the throw-in, and overlap against a shadow defense.

Organization

Two teams of three players play on fields 25 yards wide by 50 yards long (sideline to sideline of a football field). If there's not enough field space, have extra teams line up on the sideline and wait their turn. The activity is designed so that there's little wait time for those on the sideline.

Description

Explain overlapping (offensive player from the middle of the field runs forward past the partner with the soccer ball and waits for a pass) to your players. Have one team at a time proceed to move the soccer ball down the field against a team of shadow defenders, using the skills introduced thus far with the goal of dribbling past the endline for a score. Play begins with a throw-in. Once past midfield, the next team can move down the field against another team of shadow defenders. Once all teams reach the far end, teams switch roles, and the drill is repeated back to the start. Players rotate positions. This is a good time to emphasize and call offsides. The defense is not allowed to interfere with the soccer ball but only to shadow their opponent using a person-to-person defense.

Challenge

Each player on the team must receive and pass the soccer ball twice before a score.

10.24 3 v 3 Over the Endline

Goal

Employ the skills of dribbling, passing, trapping, shielding, two touching, the throw-in, the give-and-go, overlapping, and triangle passing in a competitive game-like situation.

Organization

Mini-fields with goals on each end are dispersed over the playing area. Each field is about 30 yards wide by 40 yards long. Two groups of three players play on each field.

Description

Explain and demonstrate 3 v 3 games. Play 3 v 3 using skills learned thus far: dribbling, passing, trapping, two touching, the throw-in, shielding, the give-and-go, overlapping, and triangle passing. To score, a team must dribble the soccer ball over the opponent's endline. Whenever one team gains possession of the soccer ball, the defense must back off for five seconds to avoid everyone converging on the ball. This gives the offense time to transition and set up. Do not allow slide tackling or heading the soccer ball. If a handball (a ball touched intentionally with the hand) occurs, an indirect kick (a free kick from which a goal cannot be scored unless touched by another player) is awarded. Play man-to-man defense. If there are any disputes, do the play over or have one team get the call the first time and the other team the next time. Begin at half-speed or use a shadow defense at first and then progress to half-speed and full speed. Perform Rock, Paper, Scissors to begin. Focus on keeping a balanced field and staying in a triangle formation on offense.

Challenge

Reduce the size of the field to make the game more difficult.

10.25 Shoot and Trap While Stationary

Goal

Develop proper shooting form and shoot the soccer ball from various distances and angles toward a target (goal).

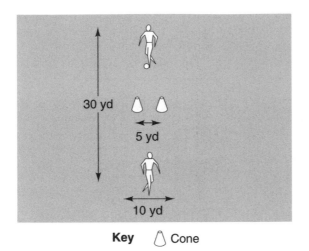

Key △ Cone

Figure 10.7 Setup for Shoot and Trap While Stationary.

Organization

Partners play in 10-yard by 30-yard practice areas. Place two cones at midfield 5 yards apart (see figure 10.7).

Description

Explain and demonstrate shooting on goal using the top-of-the-foot technique. Have partners practice shooting (driving) a stationary soccer ball at a target (between the cones) back and forth to each other. The receiver runs and traps the oncoming ball using the appropriate trap and shoots from that point. Alternate shooting feet.

Challenge

Have players two touch the soccer ball as it comes to them. Deflect it, touch it, and shoot.

10.26 Two Touch, Dribble, and Shoot

Goal

Develop shooting on goal off a dribble from various distances and angles toward a target (goal).

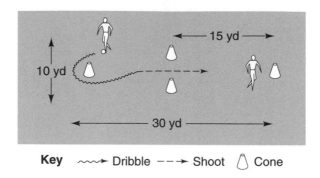

Key ∿→ Dribble --→ Shoot △ Cone

Figure 10.8 Setup for Two Touch, Dribble, and Shoot.

Organization

Partners play in 10 yard by 30 yard practice areas. Place two cones at midfield five yards apart. Place two additional cones opposite each other 15 yards from midfield equidistant from the sidelines in the middle of the field (see figure 10.8).

Description

Explain and demonstrate the two-touch, dribble-and-shoot activity. Have partners dribble, then shoot at a target (between the cones) back and forth to each other. The receiver two touches the oncoming soccer ball, then dribbles around the cone 15 yards back from midfield, and shoots at the goal. Alternate shooting feet.

Challenge

If time allows, the receiving partner can charge up between the goals and become a goalie.

10.27 Two Touch, Pass, and Shoot a Moving Ball

Goal

Develop shooting a moving soccer ball from a pass from various distances and angles toward a target (goal).

Organization

Four players (in two-partner teams) play in practice areas 20 yards wide by 30 yards long. Place two cones at midfield 5 yards apart (see figure 10.9).

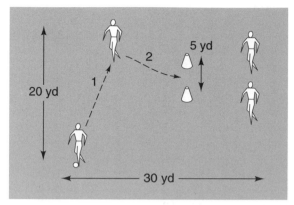

Key – – –► Pass/shoot 1 First pass 2 Shot on goal △Cone

Figure 10.9   Setup for Two Touch, Pass, and Shoot a Moving Ball.

Description

Explain and demonstrate the activity. Have teams of two practice shooting on goal from a pass, back and forth to each other. The receiver approaches the soccer ball and performs a two touch, then passes to his or her teammate, who proceeds to shoot the ball on the run between the cones to the other team, who repeats the action. Alternate shooting feet. Focus on adjusting for the speed of the pass and keeping the head down when shooting.

Challenge

If time allows, a partner can charge up between the goals and become a goalie.

10.28   3 v 3 With Goals

Goal

Employ the skills of dribbling, passing, trapping, shooting, shielding, throwing in, the give-and-go, overlapping, crossing, and triangle passing in a competitive situation.

Organization

Set up mini-fields with goals on each end throughout a playing area. Each field should be about 40 yards long by 30 yards wide. Place four cones at each field to serve as goals (set them about five yards apart—or wider if there's

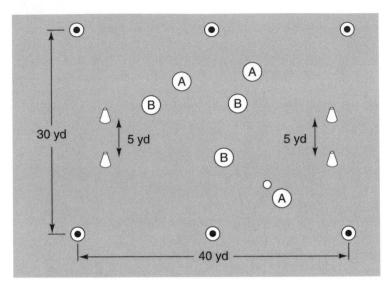

Key (A) Team A (B) Team B (●) Donut marker ○ Ball ⋀Cone

Figure 10.10   Setup for 3 v 3 With Goals.

little success; see figure 10.10). Two groups of three players play on each field.

Description

Explain and demonstrate crossing (for this class, crossing means kicking the soccer ball from the wings to a teammate cross-field). Players play 3 v 3 using only the skills learned thus far. Do not allow slide tackling or heading the ball. Whenever one team gains possession of the soccer ball, the defense must back off for five seconds to avoid everyone converging on the ball at once. This gives the offense time to transition and set up. If a handball occurs, an indirect kick is awarded. Play man-to-man defense. If there are any disputes, do a play over or have one team get the call the first time and the other team the next time. Begin at half-speed or, if they're not ready, begin with shadow defense and progress to half-speed then full speed. Focus on looking for a teammate open on the wing rather than downfield.

Challenges

Reduce the size of the field or the distance between goals to make the game more difficult. Allow whichever defender is closest to the goal to be a goalkeeper (but he or she can't remain as a regular goalie).

10.29 Individual Juggling

Goal

Develop juggling, which is the foundation for the volley and half-volley.

Organization

Players are in self-space on half a football or soccer field. Give one slightly deflated soccer ball to each player.

Description

Explain and demonstrate foot and thigh juggling. Have players attempt to keep a soccer ball in the air by juggling, predominately with their feet. Players are to use each foot and not favor one over the other.

Challenge

See if players can juggle five times in a row using each foot and using the thigh no more than once.

10.30 Toss: Volley, Half-Volley, and Heading While Stationary

Goal

Develop proper timing and contact with the soccer ball using the volley, half-volley, and heading while stationary.

Organization

Partners play in practice area 10 yards by 25 yards.

Description

If you decide not to include heading, have players do only volleys and half-volleys. Explain and demonstrate the volley (meeting the soccer ball in the air with a part of the body, usually the instep, and deflecting it to a teammate or at the goal), half-volley (same as the volley except off a bounce), and heading the ball (hitting the soccer ball with the top of the head or forehead to a teammate or at the goal). Have one partner toss the ball in the air to a stationary partner five yards away, who returns the ball with a volley or header or, if the ball bounces, a half-volley. Do four trials with each before switching. Focus on quickly getting into position to receive the soccer ball.

Challenge

Increase the distance of the toss.

10.31 Toss: Volley, Half-Volley, and Heading While Moving

Goal

Develop proper timing and contact with the soccer ball using the volley, half-volley, and header while moving.

Organization

Partners play in a practice area 10 yards by 25 yards.

Description

Explain and demonstrate the activity. From about 10 yards apart, have one partner toss the soccer ball in the air so that his or her partner must move to get into proper position to return the ball with a volley or header or, if the ball bounces, a half-volley. Do four trials each before switching. Focus on moving into proper position to enable the soccer ball to be returned.

Challenge

Play a game of volley tennis using all three skills. On a volleyball or tennis court (you need a hard surface) or indoors on a gym floor, play 3 v 3. Tennis rules apply. To begin, the server stands behind the baseline, tosses the soccer ball in the air so that it bounces behind the baseline, then kicks the ball into the regular service court. The game proceeds from there using the same rules as tennis except that the soccer skills of volleying and kicking are employed. The soccer ball can't bounce more than once. Passing to partners is legal. Begin with trainer volleyballs or old volleyballs.

10.32 Chip to a Partner While Stationary

Goal

Develop the chip using proper form and contact with the ball.

Organization

Partners play in practice areas 10 to 15 yards by 25 yards.

Description

Explain and demonstrate chipping (lobbing the ball over the head of an opponent with the foot). Have partners, about 20 yards apart, chip a soccer ball back and forth to each other, alternating each foot. The receiver uses the appropriate trap to stop the oncoming soccer ball before returning it. Focus on keeping the head down at contact.

Challenges

1. On both ends of a regular football field, partners chip the soccer ball between the goalposts back and forth to each other.

2. Play Keep the Ball Out of the River. Designate a 10-yard-wide area in the middle of the field (the river); partners chip back and forth to each other across the river.

10.33   **Clean Up Your Own Backyard: Trap, Dribble, and Chip to a Target**

Goal

Develop the chip off of a dribble.

Organization

On a football field, space 20 cones on each 45-yard-line marker equidistant from each other from sideline to sideline. Divide the class in half with each team lined up on their 40-yard line, 5 yards behind their own set of cones (see figure 10.11). Provide one soccer ball for every two players.

Description

Explain and demonstrate the game. Have players line up on their 40-yard line behind their cones. Emphasize that players must remain behind this line at all times. Distribute soccer balls equally between the two teams. When the signal is given, players have two minutes to chip soccer balls from their 40-yard lines toward their opponent's cones. The receiving player must wait for the oncoming ball to pass over his or her 40-yard line before using the appropriate trap to stop the oncoming soccer ball and then dribble and chip the ball back from behind the 40-yard line. Players must remain behind their 40-yard line and aren't allowed to interfere with any oncoming soccer ball that could hit one of their cones. Any cones knocked down inadvertently by a player's own team remain down and count against the team. The team that knocks down the most cones wins. A cone must be hit directly by a chip for it to count. If a soccer ball is chipped that might hit an opposing player, the kicker yells "Fore!" to make players aware of an oncoming soccer ball.

Challenge

Add a rule change: After trapping the soccer ball, players pass or deflect the ball to a teammate, who then traps and chips.

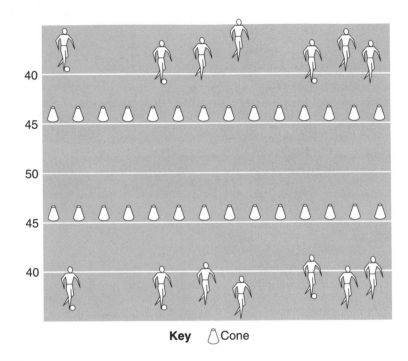

Key ⌂ Cone

Figure 10.11 Setup for Clean Up Your Own Backyard.

10.34 Dribble and Chip to a Moving Partner

Goal

Develop chipping in a large and realistic setting with large areas of the field to cover.

Organization

Partners distribute themselves throughout the field no more than 15 to 25 yards apart.

Description

Explain and demonstrate the activity. Have partners chip a soccer ball back and forth while running throughout the field. The receiver traps the soccer ball using the appropriate trap and chips off the dribble or stops the ball before chipping. Partners must be alert to other players on the field and avoid interfering with them. Alternate feet as much as possible and maintain spacing while avoiding offsides. Focus on stopping the soccer ball before attempting a chip.

Challenge

Set cone goals at each end of the field; have partners chip and trap up and down the field and attempt a shot on goal.

10.35 Throw-In: Chest, Foot, and Thigh Trap While Stationary

Goals

Choose the appropriate trap to use on an incoming soccer ball in flight; control the ball so that it can be passed or dribbled.

Organization

Partners play in practice areas 5 yards long by 10 yards wide.

Description

Explain and demonstrate the throw-in and the activity. Have one partner use the throw-in technique to a partner's chest, thigh, or foot area, forcing the partner to choose the best trap to use (chest, thigh, or foot) before the soccer ball hits the ground. Focus on keeping both feet on the ground when throwing and making the throw a continuous motion with both arms.

Challenge

Increase the distance and speed of the soccer ball so that the receiver must make decisions quicker.

10.36 Throw-In: Top of the Foot, Inside of the Foot, Chest, and Thigh Trap While Moving

Goals

Develop accuracy in performing a throw-in to a moving target. Move quickly to get into position and choose the best trap to use on an incoming soccer ball in flight; control the ball so that it can be passed or dribbled.

Organization

Partners play in practice areas 5 yards long by 10 yards wide.

Description

Explain and demonstrate the activity. Have one partner perform a throw-in to their moving partner, who chooses the appropriate trap to use. Partners are

10 yards apart. Alternate thigh and foot. Focus on leading the receiver with the pass and making the pass easy to handle.

Challenge

Increase the distance and speed of the soccer ball so that the receiver must make decisions quicker.

10.37 3 v 3 Full Speed

Goal

Develop and employ the skills of dribbling, passing, trapping, shooting, shielding, two touching, throwing in, the give-and-go, overlapping, crossing, chipping, volleying (full and half), and triangle passing in a full-speed competition.

Organization

Arrange mini-fields with goals on each end throughout a playing area. Each field should be about 40 yards long by 30 yards wide. Place four cones at each field to serve as goals; space them about 5 yards apart—or wider, if there's little success. Two groups of three players play on each field (see figure 10.10, p. 266).

Description

Explain and demonstrate the activity. Play 3 v 3 using only the skills learned thus far. Whenever one team gains possession of the soccer ball, the defense must back off for five seconds to avoid everyone converging on the ball at once. This gives the offense time to transition and set up. Do not allow slide tackling. If a handball occurs, an indirect kick is awarded. Play man-to-man defense. If there are any disputes, do the play over or have one team get the call the first time and the other team the next time. Play 10-minute games at full speed, then rotate teams. At the end of each game, the losing team sings a song to the winning team (the winning team gets to choose the song). Focus on moving, not standing around, and keeping the triangle when on offense.

Challenge

Reduce the size of the field or the distance between goals to make the game more difficult. Allow whichever defender is closest to the goal to be a goalkeeper (but he or she must move out and play the role of attacker after a save).

10.38 Goalkeeping: Catching, Hurling, and Punting

Goal

Familiarize and develop the skills of goalkeeping.

Organization

Three players play on practice areas 10 yards wide by 40 yards long. Place two cones 5 yards apart at one end for a goal.

Description

Explain and demonstrate the basic techniques of goalkeeping (catching, hurling, and punting). Have players take turns practicing these three skills of goalkeeping. Players are positioned as follows: one player is the goalie, another player stands about 10 yards from the goal, and the third player is about 30 yards from the goal. Play begins with the player 10 yards from the goal rolling the soccer ball, then lightly tossing it toward various areas in the goal. The goalie practices catching and hurling the soccer ball out from the goal to the remaining player situated 30 yards from the goal. Finally, the goalie catches and then punts the soccer ball down the field to the farthest player. Rotate after 10 to 15 trials. Focus on being in ready position and moving quickly to stop the soccer ball.

Challenge

Increase the speed of the throws.

10.39 Dribble and Shoot on Goalie

Goals

Develop goalie and attacking skills in a live situation.

Organization

Set up mini-fields 20 yards by 30 yards with modified goals with crossbars. Goals should be 5 yards wide and no higher than 7 feet and should have a wall or net behind it to stop soccer balls. You can use large cones for the goals with a 6-inch dowel inside each cone with a rope attached at the top connecting the two dowels. If indoors, tape an outline of a goal on the wall. Four players (one goalie, three shooters) play with three soccer balls.

Description

Explain and demonstrate how a goalie can reduce the odds of an attacker scoring by reducing the angle of attack. Distribute players about 20 yards from the goal in a semicircle and proceed, one at a time, to shoot on goal in a specified order, such as left to right. The goalie tries to stop the attempts and, if successful, hurls (or, if space allows, punts) the soccer ball back to the attackers. No player can shoot until the goalie points directly at the attacker, acknowledging it's that player's turn. After all players are comfortable with shooting from various positions on the field, have them back up 10 yards and dribble in and shoot from the same distance (20 yards). Shooters retrieve their own soccer balls. Goalie rotates after five trials. Focus on cutting down the angle of the shooter.

Challenge

Have players create targets in each of the four corners of the goal and try to hit each of them. Players earn two points for hitting a target, one point if they kick the soccer ball past the goalie, and a bonus five points if they hit each of the four targets. The goalie gets one point for each shot blocked. Whoever gets 10 points first is the winner.

10.40 2 v Goalie

Goals

Develop a rhythm and flow between two players as they combine dribbling, passing, trapping, and shooting on a defended goal. Develop goalie skills of catching and blocking shots and cutting down the angle of the shooter.

Organization

Set up mini-fields 20 yards by 30 yards with modified goals with crossbars no higher than 7 feet and 5 yards wide; there should be a wall or net behind the goal to stop the soccer balls. If indoors, you might tape an outline of a goal on the wall. Teams of three players play: two attackers and one goalie.

Description

Explain and demonstrate the activity. Starting 30 yards from the goal, partners dribble, pass, trap, and shoot on a defended goal. The shooter retrieves the soccer ball and returns to the start with a partner to make another attempt. If the goalie stops the soccer ball, the goalie returns it to the start with a hurl after the players have returned to their starting positions. If the soccer ball is shot and blocked by the goalie but still in play, play is stopped. Rotate positions after five to eight attempts on goal. Focus on getting the goalie to attack the dribbler before making the pass.

Challenge

Reduce the width of the goal and back attackers up another 10 yards.

10.41 2 v 1 Plus Goalie

Goal

Develop a rhythm and flow between two players as they combine dribbling, passing, trapping, and shooting on a goal defended by a back and a goalie.

Organization

Set up mini-fields 20 yards by 30 yards with modified goals with crossbars no higher than 7 feet and 5 yards wide; there should be a wall or net behind the goal to stop the soccer balls. Teams of two players each play: two attackers, one defender, and one goalie.

Description

Explain and demonstrate the activity. Start 30 yards from the goal; partners dribble, pass, trap, and shoot on a goal defended by one back (the defender located farthest back near the goalie) and a goalie. The shooter retrieves the soccer ball and returns to the start with his or her partner to make another attempt. If the goalie stops the soccer ball, he or she returns it to the start with a hurl after the players have returned to their starting positions. If the soccer ball is shot and blocked by the goalie but still in play, play is stopped. Rotate positions after five to eight attempts on goal.

Challenge

Reduce the width of the goal and extend the size of the field.

10.42 3 v 3 Controlled Attack and Defend

Goal

Develop defensive skills of channeling, chasing, and pressuring attackers and pushing the soccer ball away and to the sidelines upfield.

Organization

On one-third of a soccer field (30 by 50 yards), set up a goal (two cones 5 yards apart) with a penalty box (about 10 yards wide by 5 yards long). Two teams of three players each play: three attackers on offense and two defenders and a goalie on defense (see figure 10.12).

Description

Explain and demonstrate the defensive tactics of channeling, chasing, and pressuring attackers; demonstrate the defender's job of pushing the soccer ball away and to the sidelines upfield. Starting from midfield or farther,

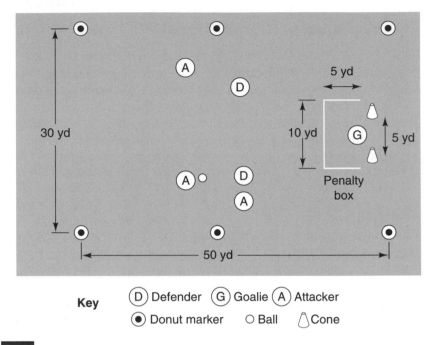

Key (D) Defender (G) Goalie (A) Attacker
(●) Donut marker ○ Ball △ Cone

Figure 10.12 Setup for 3 v 3 Controlled Attack and Defend.

attackers get five attempts to score. The defenders try to stop them and at-tempt to kick the soccer ball out to the sidelines in order to proceed upfield. Rotate attackers and defenders after five trials. Award one point for each score the offense makes. Focus on channeling and pushing the soccer ball to the sidelines.

Challenge

Allow the defense to take the soccer ball upfield and try to score on another goal set up at the end of the field.

10.43 4 v 4 Game

Goals

Employ the skills of dribbling, passing, trapping, volley and half-volley, shield-ing, two touching, throwing in, the give-and-go, chipping, triangle passing and shooting on a defended goal, goalkeeping, and the defensive skills of channeling, chasing, and pressuring attackers in a competitive game-like situation.

Organization

Set up mini-fields with goals and a penalty box 10 yards wide by 5 yards long. Each field is about 30 yards wide by 50 yards long. Two teams of four players play on each field. Each team has a goalie.

Description

Explain the game, the rules, and the type of play you want to see from your players. Have teams of four (three players plus a goalie on each team) compete using the many skills they've learned thus far. Play man-to-man defense. If there are any disputes, repeat the play or have one team get the call the first time and the other team the next time. If the soccer ball is shot and blocked by the goalie but still in play, play continues. A ball stopped by the goalie is then cleared using a hurl or a punt, with the goalie allowed only four steps. Soccer balls that go over the touch line (sideline) are put back in play with a throw-in. Soccer balls that go over the goal line last touched by the offender are put into play by an indirect kick by the defense from the goal line rather than the corner of the penalty box because of space restrictions. Soccer balls that go over the goal line and are last touched by the defender are put into play by the offense at the nearest corner flag with a penalty kick using a chip. No slide tackling is allowed. If a handball occurs, play stops and an indirect kick is awarded.

Challenge

Decrease the size of the goal or increase the size of the field to make the game more difficult.

10.44 5 v 1 Team Offensive Practice

Goal

Players practice playing each position, performing the appropriate skill as necessary and demonstrating a triangle setup and overlapping as their team moves the soccer ball upfield to score.

Organization

Teams of six players are on fields 40 yards by 50 yards with one soccer ball and regular (or reduced size) goals at each end with nets and a penalty box.

Description

Explain and demonstrate offensive field positioning for teams of five, emphasizing the importance of the triangle and overlapping. Have teams begin at one goal line and move the soccer ball upfield to shoot on goal. They then do the same thing back to the start. Players are designated as forwards/strikers, who are the attackers (no more than two); midfielders/halfbacks, who play in the middle two-thirds of the field; and defenders/backs (usually one); teams can determine the number of each. Players rotate positions when they return to the start. Goalie is at one end of the field.

Challenge

Each player must touch the soccer ball before a score can be attempted.

10.45 6 v 6 Offensive and Defensive Practice

Goal

Players demonstrate the ability to play each position on both offense and defense using appropriate skills and strategies covered.

Organization

Two teams of six players each (five attackers, five defenders, and two goalies) play on fields 40 yards by 50 yards with goals (with nets) at each end and a penalty box.

Description

Review defensive principles such as chase, pressure, and channeling as they apply to five defenders plus a goalie. An offensive team attempts to move the soccer ball upfield and score against five defenders and a goalie. The defensive team implements the team defensive principles of chasing, pressuring, and channeling. If the offense scores, the defense becomes the offense and attempts to score at the other goal. If the defensive team gets the soccer ball, it becomes the offense and attacks the other goal with no defense. Players are designated as forwards/strikers, midfielders/halfbacks, and defenders/fullbacks, the number of each to be determined by the team. Players rotate positions when they return to the start.

Challenge

When the defense stops the soccer ball and proceeds downfield, allow one player on the former offensive team to drop back and become a goalie.

10.46 6 v 6

Goal

Employ the skills of dribbling, passing, trapping, volley and half-volley, shielding, two touching, throwing in, the give-and-go, chipping, triangle passing, heading, shooting on a defended goal, goalkeeping, and the defensive skills of channeling, chasing, and pressuring attackers in a competition.

Organization

Two teams of six players each (five attackers, five defenders, and two goalies) on fields 40 yards by 50 yards with one soccer ball and goals at each end with nets and a penalty box.

Description

Explain the activity and tell players what you want them to focus on. Have teams of six (five players plus a goalie on each team) compete using all the skills learned thus far. No slide tackling. Play man-to-man defense. If the soccer ball is shot and blocked by the goalie but still in play, play continues, but the goalie gets only four steps. A soccer ball stopped by the goalie is cleared using a hurl or a punt. Soccer balls that go over the sideline are put back in play with a throw-in. Soccer balls that go over the goal line and are last touched by the offender are put into play by an indirect kick by the defense from the goal line rather than the corner of the penalty box because of space restrictions. Soccer balls that go over the goal line and are last touched by the defender are put into play by the offense at the nearest corner flag with a penalty kick using a chip. If a handball occurs, play stops and an indirect kick is awarded. Play for two 20-minute halves or more. Goalies can play that position for only 10 total minutes so that they get extensive running activity.

Challenge

Allow teams one 10-minute timeout per game, at which time they must make adjustments to player positioning to improve their team's performance.

Reference

Mood, Dale P., Frank F. Musker, and Judith E. Rink. 2003. *Sports and Recreational Activities, 13th ed.* Boston: WCB McGraw-Hill.

Roy **A. Clumpner,** PhD, is a recognized expert on skill development through progressions. He is a professor of physical education, health and recreation at Western Washington University. Since 1977, Dr. Clumpner has taught methods to physical education teachers and presented numerous workshops and lectures on developing progressions. He also has taught physical education and coached sports at the junior high, high school, and college levels.

CORNEL WEST

BLACK PROPHETIC FIRE

In Dialogue with and Edited by
CHRISTA BUSCHENDORF

BEACON PRESS
BOSTON

BEACON PRESS
Boston, Massachusetts
www.beacon.org

Beacon Press books
are published under the auspices of
the Unitarian Universalist Association of Congregations.

23 22 21 20   8 7 6 5 4

This book is printed on acid-free paper that meets the uncoated paper
ANSI/NISO specifications for permanence as revised in 1992.

Text design and composition by Kim Arney

Chapter 2, "The Black Flame—W. E. B. Du Bois," was published in an earlier form
as "'A Figure of Our Times': An Interview with Cornel West on W. E. B. Du Bois"
in the *Du Bois Review* 10, no. 1 (2013): 261–78. Chapter 3, "Moral Fire—Martin
Luther King Jr.," was published in an earlier form as "We Need Martin More Than
Ever" in *Amerikastudien/American Studies* 56, no. 3 (2011): 449–67; a shortened
version was published in the German political journal *Die Gazette* (Summer 2013).

Photography credits: *Frederick Douglass*, c. 1850–1860; *W. E. B. Du Bois*, 1918, by
Cornelius Marion (C. M.) Battey (1873–1927); *Martin Luther King Jr.*, 1964; *Ella
Baker*, 1964, by Danny Lyon (Magnum), reprinted here with permission; *Malcolm X*,
1964, by Marion S. Trikosko; *Ida B. Wells*, 1893, by Mary Garrity. Photographs are
from Wikimedia Commons/Library of Congress, unless otherwise noted.

Library of Congress Cataloging-in-Publication Data
West, Cornel.
    Cornel West on Black prophetic fire / in dialogue with and edited by Christa
Buschendorf.
        pages   cm
    Includes bibliographical references and index.
    ISBN 978-0-8070-1810-1 (paperback : acid-free paper)
    ISBN 978-0-8070-0353-4 (ebook)
    1. Douglass, Frederick, 1818-1895—Political and social views. 2. Du Bois,
W. E. B. (William Edward Burghardt), 1868–1963—Political and social views.
3. King, Martin Luther, Jr., 1929-1968—Political and social views. 4. Baker, Ella,
1903–1986—Political and social views. 5. X, Malcolm, 1925–1965—Political and
social views. 6. Wells-Barnett, Ida B., 1862–1931—Political and social views.
7. African Americans—Biography. 8. Prophets—United States—Biography.
9. Revolutionaries—United States—Biography. 10. West, Cornel—Interviews.
I. Buschendorf, Christa. II. Title. III. Title: Black prophetic fire.
    E185.96.W47 2014
    920.009296073—dc23
    [B]
                                                                2014010359

To the memory of two spiritual giants
always full of Black prophetic fire:

David Walker and Harriet Tubman

That man has a truly noble nature
Who, without flinching, still can face
Our common plight, tell the truth
With an honest tongue,
Admit the evil lot we've been given
And the abject, impotent condition we're in;
Who shows himself great and full of grace
Under pressure. . . .

—GIACOMO LEOPARDI

winds of change are blowing
i know because of the revolutionaries and most of all the
people—
    the wretched of this earth
       will be free

—ERICKA HUGGINS

CONTENTS

Why We Need to Talk About Black Prophetic Fire

Are we witnessing the death of Black prophetic fire in our time? Are we experiencing the demise of the Black prophetic tradition in present-day America? Do the great prophetic figures and social movements no longer resonate in the depth of our souls? Have we forgotten how beautiful it is to be on fire for justice? These are some of the questions I wrestle with in this book.

Since the assassination of Martin Luther King Jr., it is clear that something has died in Black America. The last great efforts for Black collective triumph were inspired by the massive rebellions in response to Dr. King's murder. Yet these gallant actions were met with increasing repression and clever strategies of co-optation by the powers that be. The fundamental shift from a we-consciousness to an I-consciousness reflected not only a growing sense of Black collective defeat but also a Black embrace of the seductive myth of individualism in American culture. Black people once put a premium on serving the community, lifting others, and finding joy in empowering others. Today, most Black people have succumbed to individualistic projects in pursuit of wealth, health, and status. Black people once had a strong prophetic tradition of lifting every voice. Today, most Black people engage in the petty practice of chasing dollars. American society is ruled by big money, and American culture is a way of life obsessed with money. This is true for capitalist societies and cultures around the world. The Black prophetic tradition—along with the prophetic traditions of other groups—is a strong counter-force to these tendencies of our times. Integrity cannot be reduced to cupidity, decency cannot be reduced to chicanery, and justice cannot be reduced to market price. The fundamental motivation for this book is to resurrect Black prophetic fire in our day—especially among the younger generation. I want to reinvigorate the Black prophetic tradition and to keep alive the memory of Black prophetic figures and movements. I consider the Black prophetic tradition one of the greatest treasures in the modern world. It has been the leaven in the American democratic loaf. Without the Black prophetic tradition, much of the best of America would be lost and some of the best of the modern world would be forgotten.

All the great figures in this book courageously raised their voices in order to bear witness to people's suffering. These Black prophetic figures are connected to collective efforts to overcome injustice and make the world a better place for everyone. Even as distinct individuals, they are driven by a we-consciousness that is concerned with the needs of others. More importantly, they are willing to renounce petty pleasures and accept awesome burdens. Tremendous sacrifice and painful loneliness sit at the center of who they are and what they do. Yet we are deeply indebted to who they were and what they did.

Unfortunately, their mainstream reception is shaped according to the cultural icon of the self-made man or the individual charismatic leader. This is especially true for the male figures. This is not to say that they did not fulfill the function of leaders and speakers of their organizations. But I want to point out that any conception of the charismatic leader severed from social movements is false. I consider leaders and movements to be inseparable. There is no Frederick Douglass without the Abolitionist movement. There is no W. E. B. Du Bois without the Pan-Africanist, international workers', and Black freedom movements. There is no Martin Luther King Jr. without the anti-imperialist, workers', and civil rights movements. There is no Ella Baker without the anti-US-apartheid and Puerto Rican independence movements. There is no Malcolm X without the Black Nationalist and human rights movements. And there is no Ida B. Wells without the anti-US-terrorist and Black women's movements.

There is a gender difference in regard to men's and women's roles assigned in social movements. This shapes their reception in history books and in popular culture. Male figures are prominent on the basis of their highly visible positions. They often are chosen to represent the movement, usually due to their charismatic qualities. Yet despite the charisma of many women leaders, it is difficult for them to be chosen to represent the movement. They are often confined to untiring efforts in organizing the movement. As a consequence, even when women give speeches, even when they contribute to the political thinking of movements, their words are not taken as seriously as they ought to be. One of the aims of our dialogues about the Black prophetic tradition is to bear witness to the fiery prophetic spirit of Ida B. Wells by presenting examples of her fearless speech and action, and to bear witness to the deep democratic sensibilities of Ella Baker, who understood better than any of the others the fundamental role of movements in bringing about fundamental social change.

This book becomes even more important in the age of Obama, precisely because the presence of a Black president in the White House complicates our understanding of the Black prophetic tradition. If high status in American society and white points of reference are the measure of the Black freedom movement, then this moment in Black history is the ultimate success. But if the suffering of Black people—especially Black poor and working people—is the ultimate measure of the Black freedom movement, then this moment in Black history is catastrophic—sadly continuous with the past. With the Black middle class losing nearly 60 percent of its wealth, the Black working class devastated with stagnating wages and increasing prices, and the Black poor ravaged by massive unemployment, decrepit schools, indecent housing, and hyperincarceration in the new Jim Crow, the age of Obama looks bleak through the lens of the Black prophetic tradition. This prophetic viewpoint is not a personal attack on a Black president; rather it is a wholesale indictment of the system led by a complicitous Black president.

∎ ∎ ∎

The Black prophetic tradition highlights the crucial role of social movements in the United States and abroad. The Occupy Wall Street movement was a global response to the thirty-year class war from above, which pushed the middle class into the ranks of the working class and poor, and even further exacerbated the sufferings of working-class and poor people. The 2008 financial crisis, primarily caused by the systemic greed of unregulated Wall Street oligarchs and their bailout by the Wall Street–dominated US government, revealed the degree to which American society is ruled by big money. And the fact that not one Wall Street bank executive—despite massive criminality on Wall Street—has gone to jail, while any poor and, especially, Black person caught with crack goes straight to prison, shows just how unjust our justice system is. The realities of the power of big banks and corporations are hidden and concealed by a corporate media that specializes in generating weapons of mass distraction. This systemic concealment also holds for the military-industrial complex, be it the Pentagon or the CIA. Rarely are the death-dealing activities of both institutions made public to the American citizenry. And courageous whistle-blowers—such as Chelsea Manning, Julian Assange, John Kiriakou, and Edward Snowden—who reveal to the public the corrupt activities of the US government are severely punished. Even the recent discussions about drones dropping bombs on innocent civilians remain confined to American citizens. The thousands of non-American civilian victims—including hundreds of children—receive little or no attention in the corporate media. The Black prophetic tradition claims that the life of a precious baby in Pakistan, Yemen, Somalia, Haiti, Gaza, Tel Aviv, Lagos, Bogotá, or anywhere else has the same value as a precious baby in the USA.

The Black prophetic tradition accents the fightback of poor and working people, be it in the United States against big money, be it in the Middle East against Arab autocratic rule or Israeli occupation, be it against African authoritarian governments abetted by US forces or Chinese money, be it in Latin America against oligarchic regimes in collaboration with big banks and corporations, or be it in Europe against austerity measures that benefit big creditors and punish everyday people. In short, the Black prophetic tradition is local in content and international in character.

The deep hope shot through this dialogue is that Black prophetic fire never dies, that the Black prophetic tradition forever flourishes, and that a new wave of young brothers and sisters of all colors see and feel that it is a beautiful thing to be on fire for justice and that there is no greater joy than inspiring and empowering others—especially the least of these, the precious and priceless wretched of the earth!

—CW

■ ■ ■

It was November 1999. On the occasion of the publication of *The Cornel West Reader*, Harvard's African American studies department honored the author for his outstanding academic achievements, and it was announced that Cornel West would give a talk in Emerson Hall, the home of Harvard's philosophy department, in Harvard Yard. I was on sabbatical doing research in the Harvard libraries, revising a book-length manuscript on the US reception of the German philosopher Arthur Schopenhauer. I decided to seize the opportunity to hear one of the stars of the widely praised "dream team" that Professor Henry Louis Gates Jr. had brought together. I had heard much about West, but I had read very little—and I was in for a great surprise.

In his talk, West directed the audience's attention to the life-size portraits of Harvard's Golden Age of Philosophy, which adorn the walls of the lecture hall. They include, among others, William James and Josiah Royce, who figure prominently in West's book about American pragmatism, *The Evasion of American Philosophy*. Then, to my amazement, West started to talk about Royce's lifelong struggle with Schopenhauer's profound pessimism. Royce, he explained, was convinced that one had to come to terms with this philosopher's dark yet realistic view of the omnipresent suffering and sorrow in human life. But, West claimed, as much as Royce wrestled with Schopenhauer, he would not give in to Schopenhauer's hopelessness but, rather, would resort to the only option to Schopenhauerian pessimism: a leap of faith. I couldn't believe my ears!

After the lecture I introduced myself to Cornel West and said that my work-in-progress was related to Schopenhauer (and to Royce, for that matter). He answered, "Well, I heard there is a woman in Germany who works on the reception of Schopenhauer in America." "Yes," I said, "that's me." "We have to talk," he said. And since then we have been in conversation.

By now I am, of course, aware of the fact that given Schopenhauer's focus on human suffering and his great compassion with all living beings, Cornel West's interest in his work does not come as a surprise. Nor does his attention to Royce because notwithstanding West's unflinching acknowledgment of the deep sense of the tragic in human lives, he has remained what he calls a "prisoner of hope." In fact, West's strong affinity to these philosophers derives from the fact that the questions they raised have been fundamental to his own thinking and, moreover, to his understanding of American democracy. After all, as West confesses in the lecture "Pragmatism and the Tragic," he believes, like Melville, that "a deep sense of evil in the tragic must inform the meaning and value of democracy."[1] If, as West expounds in the same text, "a sense of the tragic is an attempt to keep alive some sense of possibility. Some sense of hope. Some sense of agency. Some sense of resistance in a moment of defeat and disillusionment and a moment of discouragement,"[2] then who is better qualified to understand this than Black people? After all, as West reminds us, Malcolm X's definition of a "nigger" is "a victim of American democracy."[3]

But in contrast to Schopenhauer, Royce, and Melville, Cornel West is an activist not just of the word but also of the deed. This is why the twentieth-century Marxist thinker Antonio Gramsci and his concept of the organic intellectual is a key figure in these dialogues on the Black prophetic tradition. As West has professed repeatedly, his own thinking and activism have been inspired by the Gramscian notion that intellectuals should be rooted in or closely tied to cultural groups or social organizations. Again, this is not surprising, for the practical counterpart to Gramsci's theoretical concept is the long history of the Black struggle for freedom, in which the firm entrenchment of leaders in their group's organizations has been a vital practice.

My own contributions to our transatlantic dialogue have been very much shaped by the theory of the French sociologist Pierre Bourdieu. Black prophetic leaders are clear-sighted observers of the various kinds of violence Black people experience as a group and as individuals. Consequently, they tend to look at the evils of their day through a lens resembling a sociological view, which allows them to lay bare the power imbalances deeply ingrained in society. Yet they do so without ever losing sight of the concrete suffering of Black people. To understand their "logic of practice" (a term coined by Bourdieu that refers to the need to overcome the binary opposition of theory and practice) and, more generally, to reach a better understanding of the situation of Black people in America, I have found Bourdieu's concepts immensely helpful. Bourdieu assumes that there is a correlation between the structures of the social world and the mental structures of agents, so that divisions in society—divisions that, for example, establish and reproduce power relations between the dominant and the dominated—correspond to the principles of vision and division individuals apply to them. In addition to an insight into the thoroughly relational character of the social world, which implies a refutation of the myth of individualism, Bourdieu also offers precise analyses of mechanisms of power. One of the core concepts of Bourdieu's theory is the notion of symbolic violence. Being soft and inconspicuous, this type of symbolic force is an apt means to naturalize the social order and thus sustain its inherent inequalities. There is a striking passage in one of Bourdieu's major books, *Pascalian Meditations*, in which he draws on a passage from James Baldwin's essay "Down at the Cross" in *The Fire Next Time* in order to illustrate the subtle psychosocial mechanisms of symbolic violence and their function and consequences in the socialization of a Black child. According to Bourdieu, Baldwin's description shows how Black parents unconsciously pass on the dominant vision and division of the social world, as well as their intense fear of that dominant power and the

no-less-terrifying anxiety that their child will be harmed by trans-
gressing the invisible boundaries. Baldwin writes:

> Long before the Negro child perceives this difference, and even
> longer before he understands it, he has begun to react to it, he
> has begun to be controlled by it. Every effort made by the child's
> elders to prepare him for a fate from which they cannot pro-
> tect him causes him secretly, in terror, to begin to await, without
> knowing that he is doing so, his mysterious and inexorable pun-
> ishment. He must be "good" not only in order to please his par-
> ents and not only to avoid being punished by them; behind their
> authority stands another, nameless and impersonal, infinitely
> harder to please, and bottomlessly cruel. And this filters into the
> child's consciousness through his parents' tone of voice as he is
> being exhorted, punished, or loved; in the sudden, uncontrolla-
> ble note of fear heard in his mother's or his father's voice when
> he has strayed beyond some particular boundary. He does not
> know what the boundary is, and he can get no explanation of it,
> which is frightening enough, but the fear he hears in the voices
> of his elders is more frightening still.[4]

Baldwin, himself a powerful prophetic voice in the Black literary tradition, addresses both the structural power imbalances and injustices
of the social order, and the terror the dominant evoke in the dominated, who suffer from the violence exerted upon them be it physical
or symbolic.

And so do each of the great six prophetic figures we discuss in
our dialogues. Obviously, they are all prophets of the past who bat-
tled against very specific ills of their day. But though these particular
evils may have vanished—owing in part to the very battles the prophets fought and the sacrifices they made—the power differential and
resulting inequalities are still deeply ingrained in the social order,
although they exist under a different name. To give but one example,
the symbolic violence of signs reading "whites only," which once divided social space into privileged and unprivileged sites and erected
boundaries that served the functions of excluding, denigrating, and
controlling the dominated, today is exerted in the practice of racial

profiling called "stop and frisk." Thus, though we have to contextualize the historic figures we talk about so that we may appreciate their merits, as well as understand their shortcomings, we should also be aware of their exemplary natures, which enabled them to transcend the horizon of their times and become relevant to us today.

Given that we touch upon current political events in these talks, we decided to print the conversations in the order they were recorded rather than in the chronological order of the historical figures we discuss.

As outstanding intellectuals, all the Black prophetic figures in this book offer astute analyses of the mechanisms of power that help us discern these very mechanisms in the different shapes they take today. As organic intellectuals and activists, they reflect on problems of organizing and mobilizing that may provide useful insights for today's freedom fights. And as prophets who compassionately and fearlessly face both the evils of our world and the powers that be, they inspire us to do the same.

This is why we need to talk about Black prophetic fire!

—CʜB

Frederick Douglass, c. 1850–1860

CHAPTER ONE

It's a Beautiful Thing to Be on Fire

FREDERICK DOUGLASS

Our conversations on the Black prophetic tradition started in 2008 during Barack Obama's presidential campaign, when, on many occasions, the senator from Illinois would identify himself with Abraham Lincoln. And in his inauguration speech, in January 2009, President Obama strengthened the association with the sixteenth president by using the phrase "a new birth of freedom" from Lincoln's Gettysburg Address as a theme. Which Lincoln did Obama have in mind? Did Obama acknowledge the role Frederick Douglass and the Abolitionist movement played in making Lincoln the great president we remember? And how could Douglass's prophetic witness be carried into Obama's presidency?

The ascendancy of Barack Obama could easily dampen Black prophetic fire and thereby render critiques of the American system to be perceived as acts of Black disloyalty. Ironically, the incredible excitement of the Obama campaign could produce a new sleepwalking in Black America in the name of the Obama success.

We recorded our dialogue on Frederick Douglass in the summer of 2009.

CHRISTA BUSCHENDORF: Undoubtedly, Frederick Douglass is a towering figure of nineteenth-century American history in general and African American history in particular. His extraordinary ascent from a slave to the much-admired orator and prominent activist in the Abolitionist movement and the women's suffrage movement, best-selling author and successful editor of an influential newspaper, United States Marshal, Recorder of Deeds in Washington, and Minister to Haiti, has inspired innumerous African Americans. On the cover jacket of W. E. B. Du Bois's autobiographical essay *Dusk of Dawn* there is a photograph showing Du Bois standing before a huge framed portrait of Douglass, which seems to be a strong statement regarding the impact of Douglass on Du Bois. What is your general assessment of Douglass's influence on both African American and American culture at large?

CORNEL WEST: Frederick Douglass is a very complicated, complex man. I think that Douglass is, on the one hand, *the* towering Black freedom fighter of the nineteenth century; on the other hand, he is very much a child of his age, which is not to say that he does not have things to teach those of us in the twenty-first century, but he both transcends context and yet he is very much a part of his context at the same time. I think that's part of the complexity in our initial perception of his influence on America, on Black America, on Du Bois and subsequent freedom fighters.

CHB: What are the factors we should consider, when you call him a child of his age, and would you say that these factors contribute to reducing his status in a sense?

CW: I think that his freedom fighting is very much tied to the ugly and vicious institution of white supremacist slavery. Those of us in the post-slavery era experienced Jim Crow and other forms of barbarism, but that's still different from white supremacist slavery, and we learn from Douglass's courage, his vision, his willingness to stand up, the unbelievable genius of his oratory and his language. And yet there is a sense in which with the ending of slavery, there was a certain ending of his high moment. He undoubtedly remained for thirty years a very important and towering figure, but for someone like myself, he peaks. It's almost like Stevie Wonder, who peaks, you know, with *Songs in the Key of Life*, *The Secret Life of Plants*, despite his later great moments. There are moments when people peak, and that peak is just sublime; it's an unbelievable peak. I don't think any freedom fighter in America peaks in the way Douglass peaks. And that's true even for Martin Luther King in a certain sense. And yet Douglass lives on another thirty years; that's a long time. Martin peaked and was shot and killed. Malcolm peaked and was shot and killed. But what if Martin had died in 1998 saying, "Well, what am I? Well, I'm a professor at Union Theological Seminary teaching Christian ethics." There are different stages and phases of their lives. So it's not a matter to reduce Douglass, but to contextualize him, to historicize him. And any time you historicize and contextualize, you pluralize; you see a variety of different moments, a variety of different voices. His voice in the 1880s is very different than his voice on July 4, 1852, July 5, 1852.

CHB: Yes, when he gave his famous speech "What to the Slave Is the Fourth of July?"[1] But while you love the militant Douglass—as did Angela Davis, for example, when she referred to him in the late 1960s[2]—others seem to appreciate him for his later development, for his integrationist policies. And often Douglass the "race man" is juxtaposed to Douglass the "Republican party man." Did he become too pragmatic a politician? Was he in his later years out of touch with the ongoing suffering of African Americans? Had he adopted a bourgeois mentality? Did his second marriage to Helen Pitts play a role in his development, as some critics claim?

CW: I think that the old distinction between the freedom fighter against slavery early on and then the Republican Party man later on might be a bit crude, but it makes some sense, because Douglass in his second stage, the later stages of his life, certainly is significant and never entirely loses sight of trying to fight for the rights of Black people and, by extension, the rights of women and rights of others. But the relevance for us is that he is less international, he is less global in those later years. You see, when he spends time with the Chartist Movement in Britain in the late 1840s—when he is pushed out of the country twice, after publication of the first autobiography, and then following John Brown's raid on Harper's Ferry—he makes his connections in Europe, makes the connection between the planetizing, globalizing of the struggle for freedom; whereas in the later phase of his life, Douglass became such a nationalist and a patriot and so US centered. He is so tied in to the machinations of the Republican Party and willing to make vulgar compromises, and he is relatively silent against Jim Crow, and his refusal to speak out boldly, openly, publicly, courageously against barbarism in the South is troubling.

CHB: But what about his speech against lynching?[3]

CW: Yes, but it was a somewhat isolated thing. For example, at the great Freedman's Memorial ceremony in 1876, when they unveiled Lincoln's grand statue,[4] Douglass hardly makes any reference to what was happening in the South at that time. He says Lincoln is the white man's president, you are his children, Black people are his step-children, seemingly beginning with a critique. But the twenty thousand Black folk who were there waited for him to say something about the present: nothing, nothing. And then, you see, to allow himself to be used and manipulated by Rutherford B. Hayes,[5] so that at the final withdrawal of American troops he is right away appointed to the honorable position of US Marshal of the District of Columbia, as if that were a kind of symbolic exchange, you see.

You say: "Oh Frederick, Frederick, oh my God! How could you allow that to take place, given who you are, given the tremendous respect that is so well earned that people have for you, especially Black people but all freedom-loving people, and the degree to which once you get caught in the machinations of any political party in the United States as a freedom fighter you are going to be asked to make tremendous concessions, compromises." The shift from prudence to opportunism looms large. And I think you can see this also in terms of his role in the American imperial apparatus: as he became the minister to Haiti and so on. It's just hard to be that kind of bold, free-thinking, free-speaking, freedom fighter we witness in the early Douglass when you are caught within the political system.

CHB: I agree. Yet one might still consider that the conditions for fighting for the cause had changed so dramatically that he may have decided to try whatever he could to assist Black people rising within the power system. You said in a recent interview with Jeff Sharlet, one will not find *you* in the White House.[6] But that's a decision, and once you make a different decision, you will have to compromise. Moreover, we have to historicize again, because there had not been any African American in such eminent political posts before. That in itself was highly significant and symbolic, just as today it is symbolic that Barack Obama is president.

CW: That's true. But you can also see the ways in which the political system could seize on *the* towering Black freedom fighter of the nineteenth century, absorb him, incorporate him, diffuse his fire, and make him a part of the establishment, so that the next generation that comes along would have memories of the fiery freedom fighter of the 1830s, 1840s, 1850s, and 1860s. But during those last thirty years he is an incorporated elite within a Republican Party, which itself is shot through with forms of white supremacy, not to mention male supremacy, and imperial sensibility. For example, what would a Frederick Douglass in the later part of his life have looked like and what legacy would he have left if he had sided with the populist movement, if he had sided with the working-class movement, multiracial, the way he sided with the multiracial women's rights movement in Seneca Falls in 1848? It would have sent a whole different set of signs and signals, so that the mainstream would have had difficulties incorporating him. I remember reading Michael Lind's book on the new American nationalism a few years ago, and *the* hero is Frederick Douglass.[7] He is a hero because he is a representative American;

he has got a white father, a Black mother who dies when he is seven; he's got Native American blood in his mother; he becomes the multicultural icon of America so that he can be incorporated in the latter part of the twentieth century as this patriot, nationalist, multicultural liberal. I mean, he is just tamed; he is defanged in terms of his real power and his buoyancy as a militant freedom fighter. And Michael Lind has grounds for that; Douglass provides grounds for that. Then, of course, when he marries sister Helen Pitts—he marries a white sister—all kinds of controversy break out as well. And part of it has to do with the way he manages that: he just tells the truth about his personal life—out of respect for the people who respected him. He wants some kind of rest and calm and serenity, too, a peaceful place in a luxurious mansion in Anacostia that last decade of his life. But I just wonder what kind of a multiple legacy he would have left if he hadn't taken the Republican route. Even though, you know, people are who they are and not somebody else.

CHB: And yet he is very much this heroic icon because people remember his first years.

CW: There is nobody like him. I mean, I don't know of any figure in American history whose language and oratory is so full of fire and electricity focusing on a particular form of injustice. I think Douglass stands alone in that regard. He really does. And he was somebody with no formal schooling at all, probably the most eloquent ex-slave in the history of the modern world.

CHB: Owing to these extraordinary accomplishments, he has often been considered a self-made man. In fact, in 1859, he begins delivering his successful lecture "Self-Made Men" on a tour through the Midwest.

CW: Now, his attempt to view himself as being a self-made man—a reference made famous by Henry Clay—I am also very critical of that, though. I don't like this notion of being self-made. I love the degree to which he attempts to make himself in a context where he is dependent on others, but this notion of some isolated monad or some isolated autonomous entity feeds into the worst of American ideology. I prefer Melville's notion of "mortal inter-indebtedness."[8]

CHB: Yes, American individualism is such a central facet of the American mind. But what I admire in Douglass is that, on the other hand, in his autobiographies, he seems to be quite interested in the factors that both hindered him and furthered him, societal factors that shaped him. He talks a lot about the conditions under which he grew up and which made it harder or easier for him to become what he became, and in that respect he is almost like a sociologist, I think, because he analyzes the system. He is very perceptive when it comes to revealing the master-slave relationship and power structures and so on, and in that sense, I think he is still relevant for us, because those power structures are not yet overcome, after all, even if they were cruder then than they are now. But they still exist.

CW: That's true. Yet there are two sets of issues here for me. One is what you rightly note, which is Douglass's sensitivity to the institutions and structures that serve as obstacles for his flowering as a person and, therefore, by extension the flowering of other persons. But the other side of this is, when you stress those institutions and structures but still view yourself as self-made, it can feed into the worst kind of individualism, even given the sociological analysis that is subtle. For example, you can hear Clarence Thomas talk about what he has overcome. So if he gave an analysis of Jim Crow, if he gave an analysis of institutional racism and discrimination, he would point out the fact that he overcame all of that, he is still a self-made man. There is a sensitivity to the sociological factors, but it is still him in and of himself who triumphs like Horatio Alger. For example, you notice Douglass never mentions his first wife, Anna, in terms of the crucial role she plays in his escape. She is the one who gave him money; she is the one who bought the hat and the clothes; she is the one who gave money to the chap who bore a resemblance to Douglass, who served as the person who bought the pass.

Now, how are you going to omit that in your narrative if you are going to be true to the social character of who you are and consequently sensitive to the social structures and the institutions of society?

There is a sense in which the Horatio Alger ideology can be sociologically astute and still ideologically backwards because of the self-made agent at its center. Douglass tends to feed into that ideology that we associate with Abe Lincoln and going back to Henry Clay all the way up to Clarence Thomas, and it's a very blinding, obscuring, and obfuscating ideology that, for me, is quite dangerous. There is a sense in which, for me, piety is central. Piety is but a way of talking about the reverent attachment that we have to those in family, in social movements, in civic institutions, in various social networks who help make us who we are. So Douglass should be the first who would have to say he was made, in part, by the Abolitionist movement. There is no great Frederick Douglass without William Lloyd Garrison. But on the other hand, he helped make the movement. There is no great Abolitionist movement without Frederick Douglass, you see. There is no great Frederick Douglass without Wendell Phillips—Phillips and Garrison, of course, the two who wrote the dedicating narratives for the first autobiography.[9] But once you take this kind of socially infused notion of piety that I accent—and I spent a lot of time on this in my memoir[10]—then you recognize what goes into that self as a supposedly self-made person, and then you are also sensitive to the structures and institutions as well; then you get, it seems to me, a much fuller and truer treatment of who we are as persons, as individuals, socially mediated persons and individuals. So that, again, I don't want to appear too obsessed with his limitations, but I'm very sensitive to his limitations given his iconic status.

ChB: In contrast to you, though, historians have emphasized the self-made man concept. I have hardly come across any comments that stressed the interrelation between the individual Douglass and society, or that underlined Douglass's own acknowledgments of what he owed to others. It is true, indeed, and it has been criticized often, that he hardly ever mentions the women who loved and supported him. Besides his first wife, Anna, and his second wife, Helen, there is, for example—

CW: Julia Griffin and the German sister, Ottilie Assing.

CHB: Right. But, nevertheless, he gives us many facts about his life recognizing circumstances where it is not due to him but to others that he can go forward.

CW: Take his name itself, "Douglass," from Sir Walter Scott's "The Lady of the Lake," from the chap in New Bedford whose name was Johnson. Remember, he says, "Too many Johnsons in town; it's too many Johnsons in town." He gives him a new name, "Douglas," and Douglass adds an "s" because he remembers a street in Baltimore. That's part of the inter-dependency; that's part of the piety in terms of acknowledging that one is indebted to and dependent on others in shaping you, and it becomes a source of good in your life, and it becomes the very launching pad for you in terms of your future, the wind at your back in the present. So, you're right that he notes those. But I don't think he accents those. I think that's one of the reasons why historians so easily assimilate him into this very narrow individualistic ideology, you see. And it could be that Douglass deliberately crafted himself in such a way that he would be acceptable to an American culture that tends to accent self-made men and later on maybe women, and that to me warrants criticism, you know, because it's just not the truth of who we became over time.

CHB: Yes, you are right. But as someone with a special interest in relational sociology, I am trying to pay attention to the analysis of the societal structures he provides, as well as to the contingent elements in his life. For example, when he is on the plantation of Master Lloyd, he happens to have frequent contact with the youngest son of Master Lloyd, Daniel, and in the first autobiography, he remarks only in passing that it was due to that contact that he learned standard English. Whereas in the first autobiography, he emphasizes that Master Daniel would protect him and divide his cakes with him,[11] and in *My Bondage and My Freedom*, he writes that Master Daniel "could not give his black playmates his company, without giving them his intelligence, as well,[12] it is only in *Life and Times*, the third autobiography, that he explains at length what to many Northerners was a mystery, namely, how he "happened to have so little of the slave accent in my speech."[13] He acknowledged then that, owing to his companionship with Daniel, he had learned the dominant language and thus was able to turn into a successful orator immediately after he had fled the South, which I doubt he could have, if he had acquired only the Black vernacular. That's just one example.[14]

CW: I like that. I think you are onto not just something, but you are onto a lot. There is probably a lot more buried in the text that has been overlooked because of the narrow lens of the ideology of self-made men that Douglass has so much contributed to.

CHB: Douglass was highly critical of "the *slaveholding religion* of this land,"[15] repeatedly castigating the hypocrisy of Christian slaveholders. But one also wonders when reading his three autobiographies, how important religion was to his own worldview. It seems to me that he is very much a man of the Enlightenment.

CW: You know, I just preached at the Mother Zion in Harlem on 138th Street. Its pastor, Gregory Robeson Smith, was a student of mine; he is the grandnephew of the great Paul Robeson. This is the church that Paul Robeson's brother pastored for thirty years. Talking about the AME Zion Church tradition that produced Harriet Tubman, Paul Robeson, Frederick Douglass, and John Coltrane, I said, "My God, even as a Baptist, we don't have anybody who was comparable to all four of them." But it raises the question of the role of religion in the shaping of Frederick Douglass and whether, in fact, he was much more secular than one would think. I was on a committee for a dissertation at Union Theological Seminary thirty years ago. It was on Douglass and Feuerbach. Douglass fell in love with Ludwig Feuerbach. That was the first set of texts that you saw in his library, both in Rochester as well as in Anacostia in Washington, DC. It's quite interesting. The first thing he wanted to do when he got to Britain was to meet Marian Evans, who was, of course, the great George Eliot, who translated *The Essence of Christianity*[16] and was also the great author of *Middlemarch* and other novels. She was obsessed with Feuerbach, too. She and Lewes, George Henry Lewes—a grand journalist—they were living together and really made a difference in the intellectual life of England and Europe. But the thesis was that even though Douglass did speak and preach in AME Zion Church, was deeply shaped by it and would say so quite publicly, that privately he was an agnostic, and that after reading Feuerbach he began to use Christian themes and motifs, narratives and stories, but did not have a cognitive commitment to the claims, and he could never really put this out in public, but he had a lot of private discussions, and so in that sense, one of the points you make, he seems much more a figure of the Enlightenment than he would be if he had remained tied to religious authority.[17] I didn't introduce all of this in my Mother Zion sermon. AME Zion Church, they still have a right to claim him, you know. But of course, Coltrane was not a Christian either; he was ecumenical and spiritual and so forth, but he was shaped by the AME Zion Church. His grandfather was an AME Zion pastor, and Coltrane grew up in the parsonage there in Hamlet, as well as in High Point in North Carolina at the AME Zion Church. This issue of how secular was Frederick Douglass deserves further investigation.

CHB: He seems to shift his position, but what to me is rather prominent are his references to humanism; as if he wanted to say, you don't really need religion; it's enough if you believe in human dignity, the right to freedom, and other values established by the Enlightenment. But as you said, he could not admit as much. He indicates it quite often, but he could not tell the public, "I'm a non-believer."

CW: Exactly. When he went to Great Britain, you know, one of the places he wanted to go was the birthplace of Robert Burns, because Burns meant so much to him,[18] and then from Burns, he goes on to say, "But my favorite of all favorites is the great Lord Byron."

CHB: Oh yes, and he quotes him on freedom.[19]

CW: Absolutely. And when you actually look closely at Byron, he really almost worships the imagination as he affirms the eclipse-of-God talk. Which is to say that there is a certain kind of secularization in such a Romantic poetic position, and I do think that Douglass was deeply influenced by Byron in that regard, freedom fighter first and foremost, and it's about the imagination, it's about transgression, it's about transformation, and not God, and yet he couldn't be explicit in the secular mode. I don't think that this dissertation on Douglass and Feuerbach was ever published. I know the professor, his name is John Grayson, he teaches at Mount Holyoke.[20] But your question about Douglass being a child of the Enlightenment or even a child of secular Romantic thinking is a very important one. Because then the question becomes, well, in the Black intellectual tradition, what legacy does he leave regarding secular thinking? I think *the* most secular thinker the Black tradition has ever produced is Richard Wright, and it would be interesting to look at Richard Wright's writings on Douglass.

CHB: In his famous speech we mentioned before, "What to the Slave Is the Fourth of July?," Douglass draws a distinct line between his white "fellow-citizens" and himself as someone "identified with the American bondman," a disparity that culminates in his words: "This Fourth of July is *yours*, not *mine*."[21] This statement is connected to the vital question of the possibility of African Americans to identify with the American nation. Even after Emancipation, the sense of belonging to the nation-state has been both a crucial and a controversial issue for African Americans. One answer is the idea of the brotherhood of men, humanity, as a community everybody belongs to and on the basis of which Black people admonish America, the nation, to come up to its promises.[22] You find this thought in many Black writers besides Douglass, for example, in Ida B. Wells's or W. E. B. Du Bois's autobiographies. What is your position on African American national identity?

CW: If you have a notion of the potential nation, of a nation that has the potential and possibility of being free, equal, and just; treating other nations with respect; and multilateral in its foreign policies, then I find the idea of African American national identity in part desirable, that's true.

CHB: "In part" means what?

CW: In part. It means that you are still a bit too tied to the most powerful ideology of modernity, which is nationalism. And I am so suspicious of nationalisms, be they potential or actual. If internationalism tied to the "wretched of the earth"[23] had become much more powerful in the latter part of the nineteenth and the early twentieth centuries, the twentieth century would have been less barbaric, less fascistic, less chauvinistic, you see. And even these days, when globalism and internationalism are much more popular, more buzzwords, they tend to still be easily colonized by capitalism and a lot of other more mainstream ways of looking at the world.

CHB: But isn't the notion of humankind, humanity, the counternotion to what you are criticizing? Or what would you say? What is your solution if you want to avoid the nationalisms?

CW: Well, for me, the three major counter-voices against the nationalisms, be they potential or actual, would be Marxism, radical democratic movements and views, or a prophetic religious view. So, in the Marxist tradition, you have at the center an internationalism and a globalism that are always tied to working-class movements and so on. That is one of the reasons why I resonate so deeply with that tradition. And the second, the radical democratic one, you're still concerned with everyday people, no matter where they are, no matter what the national context, no matter what boundaries they find themselves in terms of land and space. And in terms of prophetic religion—but for me, especially, prophetic Christianity—you've got the symbol of a Cross, which is the catastrophic, the mutilated body of this particular Jew in the face of the Roman Empire, that is tied to a love, connected to a concern for the least of these, and every flag is subordinate to that Cross; every nationalism, every ideology, even, is subordinate to that Cross; and that Cross is nothing but the scandalous, the calamitous, the horrendous, the catastrophic in the human condition, which is suffering. And how do you transfigure that suffering into some voice, some vocation, some vision to empower the least of these (as in the twenty-fifth chapter of Matthew)?[24] So, for me, all three are intertwined; so the Marxism is indispensable, and the radical democracy is indispensable.

CHB: But I wonder why you do not include the Enlightenment ideas of human brotherhood, of universalism. Is it because they are too optimistic in that the belief in progress comes with that particular historic movement of Enlightenment and the rationality that is also part of it, and that you would consider too one-sided?

CW: Well, it depends on which particular figures. When you're thinking of Voltaire's *Candide*, you don't get a deeper critique of optimism, Pangloss and so forth. It would also be true of *Rameau's Nephew*, of Diderot. I think that the greatness of the European Enlightenment was precisely the shattering of the tribalism and clannishness, the nationalism, to turn instead to grand visions of justice, and I see that in Voltaire; I see it in Diderot; I see it in Kant, in his own very complicated conceptions of autonomy and rationality; I see it in Lessing.[25]

CHB: But what is your apprehension, why don't you include it in your list—except if you claim that it is in Marx anyway?

CW: Yeah, I think, Marx, for me, would be one of the grand fruits of the Enlightenment but also of a certain Romanticism. I don't want to downplay Romantic thinkers; I think the Byrons and Shelleys are magnificent. Shelley died for Greek independence, but it was an independence of Greeks that was tied to the call for the independence of all peoples who are under forms of the yoke of oppression. So I don't really want in any way to disparage the best of the Enlightenment or the best of Romanticism. Of course, I don't know enough about the East, Islam. I'm sure they have great humanist traditions too. So, I'm with you on that.

CHB: In an essay on Douglass, John Stauffer comments on Douglass as an intellectual as follows:

> Throughout the book, Douglass quotes or paraphrases famous white writers: Coleridge, Sir Walter Scott, Shakespeare, Lord Byron, Aristotle, Milton, Martin Luther, William Cowper, Longfellow, and Whittier; and there are at least thirty-five separate biblical references. These references reveal not only Douglass's growing intellectual powers, they highlight his efforts to break down the color line. He anticipates W. E. B. Du Bois, who declared in *The Souls of Black Folk* (1903): "I sit with Shakespeare and he winces not." Like Du Bois, the Douglass of *My Bondage* seeks to become a "co-worker in the kingdom of culture," dwell above the veil of race, and merge his double self—a black man and an American—into a better and truer self.[26]

But there are others who would think of Douglass more as an activist than an intellectual. You have written on the predicaments of Black intellectuals. What kind of an intellectual was Douglass? You have propagated the Gramscian concept of the "organic intellectual."[27] Would you call him one?

CW: He is definitely an intellectual. He is not an academic, but he is certainly an intellectual. Douglass, I think, represents the height of modern eloquence, what Cicero and Quintilian call "wisdom speaking," or a memorable and moving utterance that touches not just mind but also heart and soul, both to think and act, and I can't think of someone who is able to do that and not be an intellectual in a certain sort. Absolutely. I think he is also an organic intellectual. He is an intellectual who was shaped by a movement, the Abolitionist movement, one of the greatest social movements in the history of America, maybe even of modern times, the nineteenth century certainly. To have someone who was molded, shaped, and formed in that movement—you can just see it over time, the intellectual exposure, the readings of a variety of different thinkers as he is trying to promote the cause of the movement, the cause of freedom and justice. I mean, it's very rare that you have a kind of Gramscian-like organic intellectual who does not go to school, who learns how to read and write and think in a serious way in the context of a movement. That's a rare thing, you know. It's not even true for Marx himself. When he is writing his dissertation on "The Difference Between the Democritean and Epicurean Philosophy of Nature," he's not part of a movement at all, not as of yet.

As to Douglass, one wonders whether he is reading William Cobbett, one of the great cultural social critics who was tied to working-class, populist concerns.[28] I don't know if he's reading Hazlitt.[29] I don't know if he's reading Ruskin.[30] Did he read William Morris?[31] One wonders. We know he loved Carlyle. This is very interesting. Carlyle's book *On Heroes and Hero Worship* meant a lot to Douglass, and the Carlyle between *Sartor Resartus* up unto maybe *The French Revolution* does have some very important things to say in terms of his critique of society. He later became much more conservative, and by the time we get to the pamphlet on niggers, Carlyle is really degenerated.[32] I'm telling you, sometimes it is best just to die early.

CHB: Well, there is a link to Emerson, I would think, because Emerson liked Carlyle, too.

CW: Absolutely, absolutely. Do we have evidence, though, of Douglass reading Emerson?

CHB: Yes, yes.

CW: Widely, though?

CHB: Oh, I can't tell you. For example, there is the idea of representative men, which James McCune Smith takes up in his introduction to the second autobiography. He explicitly alludes to Emerson's *Representative Men* by claiming that Douglass himself is "a Representative American man—a type of his country men."[33] I remember Douglass read *English Traits*, but that was later in his life, in 1886.[34]

CW: I wonder how widely, how deeply. But I know that they were on platforms together for the celebration of British emancipation of slaves in the West Indies; I remember they are mentioned in the Gay Allen biography.[35] Historians make much of that, as my dear friend at Harvard, Lawrence Buell, who wrote that wonderful biography of Emerson, did.[36] You can see the overlap there with Douglass, but it's not tight; it's not close. Emerson wasn't close to anybody, including his wife. But it would be interesting, if they had spent more time together. But, you know, this recent work[37] that you note between Douglass and Melville . . .

CHB: Yes, it is quite fascinating to see how many scholars have considered comparing the two.

CW: Well, I haven't read the new collection; I know Sterling Stuckey and others had talked about the Black elements in, as well as Black influences on, Melville in *Moby-Dick* and other texts, but Douglass and Melville, wow, I'd be quite interested.[38] There is nobody like Melville in American literature, I'm telling you. There is this new book by William Spanos on Melville. That is powerful. On Melville's critique of American imperialism. He's got a Heideggerian reading, too, and a critique of the metaphysical tradition and the openness to concrete, lived experience not being subsumable under any kind of philosophical system. But William Spanos, my dear brother, he was a teacher of Edward Said at Mount Hermon, when Said was a prep school student,[39] and, you know, Spanos founded *Boundary 2*, the first postmodern journal. I was blessed to be on the board together with Paul Bové, Jonathan Arac, Donald Pease, and the others. But Spanos has got two huge volumes out on Melville, one just on *Moby-Dick*, and the recent one is on the later fiction. It is called *Herman Melville and the American Calling*,[40] and it is about Melville's resistance to the American call for nationalist, chauvinist, exceptionalist discourse. It's a fascinating read. But Melville is just so profound, and to juxtapose him with Douglass, who has his own kinds of profundities but is very, very different, is a complicated matter.

CHB: One possible aspect of comparison would be their concepts of power, how they describe power relations, and I think in that respect they would be equal.

CW: That's interesting.

CHB: Of course, the other reference would be their ways of being prophets.

CW: Oh yes, that's true. That's very true.

CHB: As you defined it, to be a prophet is not about predicting an outcome but rather to identify concrete evils, and both did.[41]

CW: Absolutely, in that sense both would be deeply prophetic. And yet, Douglass was such an activist, and Melville was hardly an activist at all, or not a political activist. You could say he was an activist in language, and, my God, identifying those concrete evils was a form of activism. I'm quite intrigued by how these folk are connecting Melville and Douglass.

CHB: But to come back to the question of nationalism, there is another interesting recent study on Douglass, a chapter in a book by one of the editors of the collection of essays on Douglass and Melville, Robert Levine: *Dislocating Race and Nation*.[42] Levine investigates the critique of Douglass that you share as to his commitment to the nation in the later years, to American patriotism and so on. One of the issues usually mentioned in this context is the annexation of Santo Domingo, later known as the Dominican Republic. Douglass was involved in exploring the possibilities of an annexation, that is, he was a member of a government committee that went there and interviewed the people, and he is always criticized in that he seemed to encourage the annexation in dialogue with President Grant. Levine takes a close look at the contemporary debate and shows that those people, for example, Charles Sumner or Carl Schurz, who were against the annexation, were against it partly for the wrong reasons from Douglass's point of view.[43] Their arguments based on climate theory were racist in fearing that annexation would add "tropical" Blacks, who allegedly were unfit for civilization to the US nation. According to them, certain regions of the earth were preserved for specific races and one should not mix them.

So, their anti-imperialist arguments seem to be progressive, but they were racist as well. In contrast, Douglass argued for the annexation, granted that the Blacks of Santo Domingo would consent to it, and he believed they would. As you know, it never came about, but it was a very concrete plan at the time, and Levine tells a much more complex story than most historians who complain about Douglass, asking, "How could he ever be in favor of the annexation?"

CW: Well, I think that even if Douglass had his own good reasons, if he's acting as an agent of the US government, there is a good chance that the US government does not have the same reasons that he does. And in the end their reasons will prevail in terms of the effects and consequences of the policy.

CHB: That's right. But Levine goes into the papers of the president, and there is a "Memorandum" in his personal files, a list that he made for himself of "Reasons why San Domingo should be annexed to the United States."[44] Well, what are his reasons? What are good reasons for the annexation? You're right, they are economic reasons.

CW: Absolutely. Resources.

CHB: Exactly. But the interesting thing is that, in this list, there is also the issue of race and, for example, the reflection that it would be favorable in terms of fighting slavery that still existed in Brazil if the US were less dependent on Brazilian goods.

CW: That's interesting. No, that's true. It's very true, because we have to keep in mind that Douglass had encountered some very ugly racism within the Abolitionist movement himself, you know, reducing him from person to symbol and spectacle and "stay away from philosophy, you just give the facts," as John Collins used to tell him all the time.[45] Now, it's true, people like William White saved his life, so that there's a white brother and a Harvard grad who really sacrificed himself to save Douglass's life, and Douglass almost got killed in Pendleton, Indiana.[46] So he had some white comrades who he knew cared for him. But the racism within the Abolitionist movement was something he was quite sensitive to. And, therefore, you can understand how he would also be sensitive to some of the anti-imperialist arguments that were also racist. It's true that those kinds of complications always need to be acknowledged, even though in the end, I would want to come down on the anti-imperialist side with good reasons rather than on the US government side with good reasons. See, Douglass situated himself historically on the wrong side. It reminds you of James Weldon Johnson in Nicaragua, who wrote *The Autobiography of an Ex-Colored Man*.[47] Remember, when he is in Central America—that's where he writes that novel—he's an agent of US imperialism. He's pushing, supporting the companies down there, and then still reflecting on various forms of oppression in the metropole, in the US itself. So it's interesting how you get those kinds of contradictions. But, I guess, we're all shot through with contradictions.

CHB: Let us talk about the significance of Douglass in this particular historical moment. In a recent interview with Tavis Smiley on Public Radio International, you talked about Douglass's attempts to influence President Lincoln, trying to push him toward more forceful action with regard to Emancipation. Discussing the prospects of the Obama presidency, you suggested that we need a Douglass today as well, a Douglass who would put pressure on President Obama as to the recognition of today's problems of African Americans—and, by extension, Americans of all colors who suffer from the effects of neoliberal politics. Obama refers to Lincoln and to Douglass.

CW: Yeah, I think my dear brother Barack Obama has got the wrong Lincoln in mind. And Douglass could help him here. And I think by keeping track of Douglass, when Douglass called Lincoln a representative of American racism or when Wendell Phillips famously called Lincoln the "slave hound from Illinois," you wonder what is going on here. You see what I mean. That's not the Lincoln that people want to take seriously, but it is the Lincoln who is part of the historical record. So that when I say Obama has got the wrong Lincoln, you know, he thinks that is the Lincoln who is concerned with reaching out to rivals, especially on his Right. So you bring in people from the opposite political party or the opposing political group or constituency, and you don't recognize that Lincoln was not only a child of his age but that one of his heroes was a slaveholder, Henry Clay, from Kentucky; his best friend is a slave-trader, Joshua Speed, with whom he sleeps in the same bed for four years, visits him over and over again. Lincoln has his own slave that Joshua Speed gives him when he goes and spends time with him in Kentucky.

That is not to say that Lincoln didn't hate slavery, but it is to say that he was quite complacent and willing to defer. He doesn't oppose the Black Codes in the State of Illinois, where Black people had to pay money in order to enter the state. We know his history of voting for the slave trade in Washington, DC, in the House; we know of his strong support of the Fugitive Slave Act of 1850. That was really, one could say, the straw that broke the camel's back for the Abolitionists. We know that in the first inaugural address he talked about supporting the first proposed Thirteenth Amendment, which was to make slavery permanent in the South as a concession to the South, the unamendable amendment. He said, "Yes, I will accept that." And Douglass, of course, was ready to go to Haiti because of that. That's one of the moments when he calls Lincoln the pro-slavery president.

Most historians don't deal with that Lincoln. They don't want to deal with that Lincoln. Well, Obama needs to recognize that that is an integral part of the Lincoln that he is crazy about, and that the Lincoln Douglass calls pro-slavery goes on from that: he is the Lincoln of colonization; he supports not just either going to Liberia or Cow Island—where he provides the money and over three hundred Black folk die—or to Columbia, which is now Panama, the isthmus there; Lincoln supports colonization. The Lincoln that most of us really cherish is the Lincoln of just the last two and a half years of his life, and that's because of the Abolitionist movement; it's because of Harriet Beecher Stowe; it's because of Wendell Phillips; it's because of Charles Sumner, and Frederick Douglass at the top. So that you say to President Obama, "Now, wait a minute, you not only support the Republican ambassador to China, you got him in your Cabinet. You feel like you got your team of rivals in this little truncated, domesticated, tamed version of Lincoln." You say, "No, there is no great Lincoln without the social movement," and Barack Obama is very, very suspicious of social movement people. He is mesmerized by the establishment. He wants to reassure especially the financial establishment; he is mesmerized by Wall Street; he is seduced by these neoliberal economists, by the economists who have been rationalizing elite interests for the last fifteen or twenty years. And, you see, the great Lincoln was not mesmerized by these kinds of people; he really wasn't. The great Lincoln would say: "Frederick, you got a point. Harriet, you are the one who got us into this mess. Sooner or later I've got to take you all seriously, you know. I'm not an Abolitionist, but I do hate slavery. I didn't believe that we could overcome white supremacy and create a multiracial body politic until the last few days of my life, but I am influenced by the social movement." And you say, "OK, but which social movements influence Barack Obama?" The green movement, that's the one movement. I think, he is very good on green issues; he really is.[48] But when it comes to the Black freedom movement, he is trying to neutralize if not tame it, you see. He's got a very, very ambivalent relation to it, he really does.

CHB: And you think it is more than just strategy, because you might realize as an American politician, and especially as a president, that your means are limited, that if you go too far, especially too far to the left, that that's the end of you. So how do you steer in-between?

CW: I think, in the end, it's fundamentally a question of style, and here, as Frantz Fanon used to say, style does help to define who you are and help to define your being. Barack Obama is someone who likes to be liked by everyone, and he likes to be able to create some kind of middle-ground synthesis that brings people together without really coming to terms with the deep conflicts. Here he could learn a lot from Douglass. He might quote Douglass all day and all night about power conceding and so forth, but Douglass understood the depth of it, that you don't find truth in the middle of the road; you find truth beneath the superficial, mediocre, mainstream dialogue, and the truth is buried, is hidden beneath that, and when you connect with that truth, you have to take a stand. When you take a stand, you're not going to be liked by everybody; people will try to crush you, people will try to lie on you, people will try to kill you. Now, Obama still gets assaults in the media all the time, but I think he really doesn't want to be someone who just takes a principled stand and risk and is able to withstand all those bows and arrows. That's not his personality. I would argue that the Black freedom movement has produced a lot of different styles and strategies, but the great figures in the Black freedom movement, like Douglass, know they can't be liked by everybody. When you think of figures like Martin Luther King, Fannie Lou Hamer, Ella Baker, Malcolm X, that's not the strand that Barack Obama is comfortable with at all.

CHB: There is this great statement by Douglass you just alluded to from which Obama takes these famous lines: "Power concedes nothing without a demand. It never did and it never will."[49] But in the same speech Douglass also says: "Those who profess to favor freedom and yet deprecate agitation are men who want crops without plowing of the ground; they want rain without thunder and lightning."

CW: That's powerful. So Douglass understood.

CHB: And he goes on to say, "Find out just what any people will quietly submit to and you have found out the exact measure of injustice and wrong which will be imposed upon them, and these will continue till they are resisted with either words or blows, or with both. The limits of tyrants are prescribed by the endurance of those whom they oppress." If that's not powerful . . . But Obama doesn't quote it.

CW: He didn't go that far. No. Well, you see, some of those particular words are not part of the soul of Barack Obama. And, you know, everybody is who they are and not somebody else.

CHB: But you could say that he wouldn't be where he is if they hadn't been who they were.

CW: That's right. Absolutely. He wouldn't be head of the American empire as a Black man if he followed the fiery Douglass. That's absolutely right. And that's both the strength as well as the severe limitation of Barack Obama.

CHB: And the system wouldn't allow it either.

CW: That's exactly right. In fact, that's probably the most important thing: the system that wouldn't allow and concede his ascendency, which is still historic, and that's the reason why I supported him. But we ought to be honest, the truth that led many of us to support him is the same truth that lead many of us to criticize him and the system, and I think that's something that the early Douglass would understand, though, later, Douglass could be appropriated by Obama and would be very consistent. In a certain sense, he's heading the very system that was appointing Douglass.

CHB: Maybe one more thing. In his autobiography Douglass emphasizes the moment when he fights against the slave breaker Edward Covey, and he says one of the preconditions was that he was ready to give up his life. He refers back to Revolutionary times and that famous phrase "Give me liberty or death."[50] So to be ready to give up your life for freedom is also a thought that Douglass cherishes, and it is like a red thread in his work, at least its first part.

CW: A deep commitment.

CHB: Yes, and I thought it was interesting because you refer to something like that yourself.

CW: Absolutely. But this sense of giving up one's life was the ultimate cause, but there's also a penultimate cause in the life you live before you die, and that to me is just as important a question, you know. How do you use your time and your energy? And the time and energy that you have available to you before death puts an end to the whole thing, and there again you got this creative tension between truth and power and a commitment to telling the truth, bearing witness to the truth and yet easily being marginalized versus trying to gain access to political power, economic power, cultural power, and oftentimes easily being absorbed and incorporated, and how do you deal with that to and fro, moving back and forth. It is like the early Ralph Bunche, you know—Marxist, leftist, powerful critic of US capitalism—and the later Ralph Bunche, who is one of the Black bourgeoisie to the core, Nobel Peace Prize winner hanging out in the upper-middle-class circles in Black and white DC, caught up in the establishment. We see a similar shift in Douglass: Shakespeare Society on the fifteen-acre Cedar Hill that looks like the White House in Anacostia, all of the different teas there, having the very genteel dialogues about a variety of delicate subjects while Jim Crow is raining terror on Black folk.

Did you see this new book called *Slavery by Another Name*?[51] It's a hell of a text. The author is actually the Atlanta bureau chief of the *Wall Street Journal*, and he is a white Southern brother and his name is Blackmon. Fascinating ironies of life. But he is a kind of centrist guy who follows the white and Black members of the family of Green Cottenham in a book of about five hundred pages that won all these awards. I couldn't put it down because this guy really concludes that Jim Crow was a form of slavery, a view confirmed by many Black and progressive scholars years ago, for instance, Leon Litwack's book *Trouble in Mind*, which is still the best thing ever written on Jim Crow.[52] People were saying nothing has been written since Litwack—that's not true—but this guy says something like, "This is slavery by another name, this is the most vicious form of terrorism I could conceive alongside slavery," and he's telling a story beginning in the latter part of the nineteenth century of the white and Black members of the Cottenham family, how their lives are intertwined. The Black members of the family get caught in this Jim Crow system, and it is quite ugly. The book focuses on the human dimension to it. It is not an analysis solely, but Blackmon is telling the archetypal story of what happened generation after generation. And you say to yourself, Douglass is dead in 1895, but by the 1870s, it is beginning to take shape, crystallizing in the 1880s, legalized in the 1890s, and was in place until the 1960s, and you say, well, where is the voice of that early Douglass in the nation as Jim Crow is developing in the 1870s and '80s?

CHB: But even so, someone like Ida B. Wells speaks out for Douglass and acknowledges him in this respect. I don't know whether she idealized him, but she takes him seriously as a fighter for the cause, even in the later years.

CW: Yes, that's true. And you couldn't get a grander crusader for justice than Ida in the face of American terrorism as manifested in Jim Crow.

CHB: And she was the person who convinced him that the reasons given for lynching were not the true ones. As you know, she studied the statistics and specific cases, and she told him, and that made him aware that he should not stick to the propaganda, and he changed his mind, and then he gave this speech, which you mentioned earlier.

CW: I mean the last speech that he gave, "Lessons of the Hour," 1894, that's a great speech. A powerful speech, there's no doubt about that. I remember when I first read it. He is looking back; it is almost a self-critique too. He is looking back saying, "Don't be duped by this kind of false bread of freedom given to emancipated slaves. We got new challenges. America, you either have to come to terms with this or you are going under." But what I think Ida B. Wells has in mind and what Du Bois has in mind—and you pointed out that on the cover of Du Bois's *Dusk of Dawn*,[53] he is standing before a portrait of Douglass—is that it is inconceivable to be a freedom fighter in the United States and not have Frederick Douglass's spirit as integral to what you are doing. That is part of the grand achievement of those twenty-three years. And that is just there. He could have gone off and played golf after Emancipation like William Lloyd Garrison and a lot of the others. For them it was over.

CHB: And that is what, for a moment, he had thought about. Why not go to a farm and lead a quieter life?[54] Haven't I done enough—

CW: —Enough in one lifetime. You can understand that. Absolutely right. Even though you can't ever conceive of Martin
or Malcolm doing that in their later lives. You just get the
impression that they were so on fire that they would have just
burned till the end, no matter what, till sixty-five, seventy, and
Du Bois was like that too. At ninety-five he is still on fire, you
know. There's no doubt about it. Very much so. It's a beautiful
thing to be on fire, though. It really is.

W. E. B. Du Bois, 1918

CHAPTER TWO

The Black Flame

W. E. B. DU BOIS

With a Black president in the White House, the question arose as to what this meant for the Black prophetic tradition. Was it possible that Black people would mistake this symbolic achievement for a wholesale victory? Could it be that, overjoyed by the iconic recognition of Blackness, they would ignore—notwithstanding the undeniable effects of the financial crisis—the continuing or rather growing inequality between whites and Blacks, rich and poor in terms of decent income, housing, education, health care, jobs? In this situation, the incorruptible voices of the Black prophetic tradition needed to be heard. We decided to continue our dialogue, and W. E. B. Du Bois, as undeniably the most important Black intellectual of the twentieth century, was the obvious choice. We agreed to explore the more radical facets of his thinking and expose his uncompromising critique of the United States, which has often been considered too painful to become part of the American (or even African American) collective memory. The title of this chapter, "The Black Flame," refers to Du Bois's little-known trilogy of historical novels, which he wrote in the last decade of his life.[1]

CHRISTA BUSCHENDORF: Given W. E. B. Du Bois's long and eminent career, his versatility and productivity, any assessment of his life work is a challenging, if not daunting, undertaking. It seems to be appropriate to start out by evoking some of the points you have made in your own writings on Du Bois. You have written extensively on Du Bois. In your study on American pragmatism, you characterized Du Bois as "the Jamesian organic intellectual,"[2] and in your essay "Black Strivings in a Twilight Civilization," you called him "the towering black scholar of the twentieth century"[3] and "the brook of fire through which we all must pass in order to gain access to the intellectual and political weaponry needed to sustain the radical democratic tradition in our time."[4] In addition, you put forth an extended critique of some of Du Bois's basic tenets.

CORNEL WEST: Absolutely. Let me start off by saying that W. E. B. Du Bois, alongside John Dewey, is *the* towering public intellectual in the first half of the twentieth century in the American empire. And when looked at through the international lens, he is even more important than Dewey, because Du Bois understood the centrality of empire, and he understood the centrality of white supremacy and the shaping of the US empire in a way that John Dewey did not. And when we look fifty, a hundred, a hundred and fifty years from now, when the American Gibbon puts pen to paper to the "Decline and Fall of the American Empire,"[5] it will be Du Bois's work that will be seen as most insightful, as opposed to Dewey or even William James or some of the other great figures that we know. And so in that sense we may not even be yet in a position to fully appreciate the breadth and the scope and the depth of W. E. B. Du Bois as a scholar, as a public intellectual, as well as an activist, as someone who offered an astute critique of capitalism and class hierarchy and understood the latter's intimate relation to white supremacy and racial hierarchy. And so I think we are still very much in the early stages of the kind of appreciation of Du Bois's contribution to our understanding, especially, of a post-American world or a world in which the American empire is no longer at the center. And in that regard, I think, we have to proceed very tentatively, provisionally, and yet also firmly to try to understand the variety of different dimensions and aspects of this towering genius.

CHB: It's interesting that it took him a while to get to the internationalization of the problem, as he mentions in his autobiography, *Dusk of Dawn*.[6]

CW: That's true. I think it is the 1915 book *The Negro* where he really begins to understand the centrality of empire and again race in the US empire.[7] You can just see him beginning to become awakened, and any time he becomes awakened there are two fundamental consequences. One is the radical character of what he has now to say, and the second is the problem of how to come to terms with the marginal status of such a radical perspective. After all, most of America, and especially the American academy, is just not ready. They can't assimilate, they can't incorporate, they can't render intelligible the radical message that Du Bois is putting forward. I think this is going to be true for a whole subsequent slew of figures, including myself.

CHB: It certainly was true during Du Bois's lifetime, when he was not recognized adequately in the academy, though he was one of the foremost sociologists of the time, a man who came up with a new method: interdisciplinary empirical studies.[8] If he had been a white man, this breakthrough would have been celebrated, and he complains that he was not even published, and that when his book on the Negro in Philadelphia came out, there were no reviews.[9]

CW: Yes, the 1899 classic *Philadelphia Negro*, it's true. But I think that even if Du Bois had been white, his radical view would still have been very difficult for mainstream America and most difficult for the American academy to come to terms with. Being Black made it even more difficult. There is no doubt about that. So the response has been to domesticate Du Bois, sanitize and sterilize him, and to make him part of a kind of a domesticated view about Black Nationalism on the one hand and integrationism on the other hand. And of course, there was the issue of his dispute with Booker T. Washington, especially Washington's reluctance to promote civil rights, voting rights, and liberal education for Blacks. And those are part and parcel of who he is, but they are just small slices of what his project was, and I think in the twenty-first century, it's up to us to begin to see what he was actually about. How is it possible for this emerging cultural freedom—that comes out of an enslaved and Jim-Crowed people—to present a challenge to an imperial power with very deep roots in white supremacy, one driven by a capitalist project or driven by capitalist forces and tendencies? For Du Bois, this becomes the central problematic, and it very much is our problematic today. I think there is a sense in which W. E. B. Du Bois is the most relevant figure from the twentieth century for us in the twenty-first century, and we ignore him at our own peril. Very much so. And in that sense, you know, we all stand on his shoulders. When I had written fifteen years ago that he is the towering Black scholar of the twentieth century, there was no doubt about that, and I'm more convinced of that fifteen years later than I was then.

CHB: You have just remarked that it is from the position of an outsider, or, as he himself calls it, a "group imprisonment within a group,"[10] that he could analyze the empire, and actually, I think he is of the conviction that it is *only* from the margin that one can criticize society because of the distance one necessarily has from it.[11] One does not fully identify with it. So that though, in general, there is a great disadvantage in being at the margin, in this one respect there is an advantage in marginality, and I would think that you have that view on your own condition as well.

CW: Yes, I think that's true. Of course, you can be marginal and an outsider and still get it wrong. But in terms of those who are willing to tell some of the most painful truths about the emergence and sustenance of the American empire alongside the precious American democratic experiment within the American empire and the tension between those two, certainly being on the margins or an outsider is almost a precondition. I think he is right about that. The problem is when it comes to solidarity and its preconditions, which is to say the conditions under which collective insurgency can emerge, the conditions under which agency among the oppressed can emerge, oftentimes it becomes a rather depressing matter because, you see, it seems as if there is a relative impotence or relative powerlessness. The emergent agency is so often pacified, and folks suffer generation after generation with unjust treatment, unattended to, and then layers of suffering begin to mount, just like in the ninth thesis of Walter Benjamin's "Theses on the Philosophy of History," that history of catastrophe, the piling of wreckage, generation after generation, all of those precious lives lost, wasted potential, witnessed generation after generation.[12]

One wonders how Du Bois, who lived ninety-five years, was able to witness that wreckage, see the US empire shipwrecked at the very moment when it viewed itself as victorious and sailing uncontested in the sunshine. You can imagine what a tearing of the soul that must have been for him. Of course, he began as a much more naïve Enlightenment figure, naïve Victorian figure, who was initially tied to empire and tied to the West in its contemporary incarnation. He never gives up on the West; he never gives up on the Enlightenment; he never gives up on the Greeks; so the legacy of Athens, the legacy of Jerusalem, the legacy of the Enlightenment mean much to him. But once he really discovers the Marxist critique of capitalism, once he discovers the variety of critiques of empire and weds it to his profound resistance and critique of white supremacy, he's in a different space. I think he began to realize that after the lynching of Sam Hose.

CHB: He acknowledges himself that he was naïve and that he had to go through stages.[13] In the beginning, he thought you just have to teach people; you just have to tell them the truth, and they will accept it and they will change. But then he acknowledged that there was irrationality, that there was habit you have to cope with.[14]

CW: Absolutely, the cake of custom and the gravitas of habit. I think in a certain sense the early Du Bois had a naïve conception of evil—evil as ignorance, evil as not knowing the facts—as opposed to the later Du Bois, who saw evil being tied to interest, evil being tied to power and privilege within various social structures that have to be contested politically, organizationally, collectively. And, you know, *that* Du Bois is the Du Bois that remains *our* Du Bois; he is a figure of our times. I mean, it's amazing that it has taken American history fifty, seventy-five years to begin to catch up with Du Bois in terms of this problematic of the US empire that will decline as political system, will be broken as culture, will decay, if it does not come to terms with the kind of very deep democratic reforms and structural transformations required for that empire to revive and become something that's worthy of affirmation.

CHB: One of his ideas of how to try to accomplish that was that he believed in a special role for African Americans. He believed, maybe idealistically, naïvely—I wonder what you think about that?—that due to their tradition, due to roots in Africa and the communal spirit that he thought derived from that African culture and was in a way transposed to the New World, that African Americans could and actually should be a counterforce to American capitalism by forming communal and economic projects by deliberate separatism—a controversial word, of course. His ideas remind me of Malcolm X's notions of how African Americans should create their own businesses and keep them separate so that whites would not be able to further exploit and profit from their labor, suggesting that anti-capitalist forces might be based on the African American community, something not often taken up, I think.

CW: Yes, I've never been convinced of that aspect of Du Bois or Malcolm in that regard. It seems to me that these Black businessmen and -women tended to be just as deferential to capitalist forces and just as ready to embrace the market forces on the capitalist conditions as anybody else.

CHB: But maybe there is a difference between Malcolm X and Du Bois in that the latter really means no compliance with the

capitalist system but introducing a communist—Du Bois
didn't call it that—but a communist way of doing business,
without profit; you know, oriented toward the community
and its needs without giving in to capitalism.[15]

CW: Yes, at the normative level I can see Du Bois putting that
forward. It reminds me in some ways of the Honorable Elijah Muhammad, whose economic cooperatives were going to
be different than the competitive capitalist models. And yet,
when you actually look at the practice of Black businessmen
and -women, some of whom may have partly even been influenced by Du Bois—very few probably, but those few who
are—they still find themselves caught within the ravages of
the capitalist market. And therefore, at the aspirational utopian level it may make sense, but it's just hard to see how
that's translated on the ground. I do think that one of the
most important texts Du Bois ever wrote is *The Gift of Black
Folk* [1924]. It's a classic that tends to be overlooked and underappreciated like so much of Du Bois's magisterial corpus,
and there, I think, he is on to something. He talks about the
gift of Black folk to America and the world as being a reconstruction of the notion of democracy looked at from the
vantage point of enslaved or Jim Crowed people, or a reconstruction of the notion of freedom from that vantage, and
then a cultural gift as well, in song and story and tradition
and art. Each one of those contributions is quite powerful,
and they certainly constitute counter-hegemonic forces in
making American capitalist democracy a more fully inclusive
capitalist democracy; there is no doubt about that. The question is how these gifts did become counter-hegemonic in a
more radical way, you see.

Now one of the things that has always fascinated me
about Du Bois—and I have been quite insistent in my critique of Du Bois—is that when it comes to popular culture,
he was in love with the "sorrow songs," to use his wonderful
phrase in the last chapter of *The Souls of Black Folk*. He was in
love with the spirituals. But I've never been convinced that

he had an appreciation, let alone a deep comprehension, of the blues and jazz. We know he was very, very suspicious of blues and jazz; he distanced himself from them. And yet, for me, they constitute crucial, indispensable counter-hegemonic forces in terms of keeping alive ideals of humanity, ideals of equality, ideals of humility, ideals of resistance and endurance in the face of the catastrophe that the US empire has always been for the masses of Black people, be it slavery, Jim Crow, or be it the new hyper-ghetto that our dear brother Loïc Wacquant has written about better than anybody else,[16] or the hyper-incarceration that has targeted poor people, specifically Black men. When you look at the forms of agency of those particular brothers and sisters, the music has been central, and it's not spirituals for the most part, because they are unchurched, most of them; most of them are un-mosqued and un-synagogued; they don't have any ties to religious institutions at all. So it's fascinating to me that there is still a certain relic of cultural elitism in the radical democratic, anti-capitalist, anti-imperialist project of Du Bois, and this creates a tension for me.

CHB : The reason I see for why he was so distanced from that part of the African American tradition is that he was so much afraid of hedonism, of entertainment as something that is just distraction, part of capitalist consumer culture, distracting people from what they should try to become, and he probably didn't see the serious contribution to cultural work that jazz and blues ultimately makes.

CW : I think that's a very good point. There is an irony here, because you know the great August Wilson used to say that Black people authorize reality by performance, that performance in a communal context, where call and response is central, creates a form of agency, creates a form of self-confidence and self-respect that are preconditions for the creation of new realities. You see that in churches in the past under slavery. We've seen it in communal artistic practices under Jim Crow, and we see it today in hip-hop. They are not revolutionary forces, but they do constitute spaces, spaces that are very rare, because most of the spaces in the US empire are already colonized. But to have certain spaces by means of performance can provide a view of a different sense of who you are: You're human as opposed to subhuman. You're human as opposed to being a commodity. You're human as opposed to being an object. You're human as opposed to being an entity to be manipulated. And that's, again, the profound role of Black music, especially within those communal contexts. I'm not sure Du Bois understood that because of his fear of hedonism and cheap entertainment and the stereotype of Black people as, you know, born singing, born dancing, born moving, and so forth and so on.

CHB: And another point might be his own upbringing. He was from New England, and it's really funny to read his account when he first came to the South and was overwhelmed by how his people—and he calls them "his people"—behaved. But he is completely alien to their traditions, for example, in church.[17] It was difficult for him. This reticent gentleman, he had problems; he embraced the culture, but it never became part of his own habitus.[18]

CW: Absolutely. One of the great ironies of W. E. B. Du Bois is that he is the greatest—and will probably always be the greatest—Black intellectual ever to emerge out of the US empire, and the problematic that he ended up wrestling with about the US empire—the centrality of race and class and gender, but especially the capitalist core—needs to be hit head-on. But he was not the spiritual extension or the spiritual property of the very people that he was willing to give his all for, the very people he was willing to live and die for. Billie Holiday would have scared him to death; James Brown would have sent him into conniptions; and he just would not have been able to fully embrace brothers George Clinton and Bootsy Collins. And the Funkadelics would have generated a heart attack. If he had shown up at a Parliament-Funkadelic concert, with Garry in diapers and brother George and all his colors,

Du Bois would have gone crazy. Or if he had listened to a Reverend C. L. Franklin sermon when the whooping began, he would have been ashamed, you see. You would want to say, "Du Bois, this is the spiritual genius and part of the very people you're talking about." And yet at the same time we know that there could be no Franklin, there could be no Clinton, there could be no Funkadelics without the genius of W. E. B. Du Bois, because he has given his all, his intellectual wherewithal, his political activism, his time, his energy to affirm the humanity of the Clintons and the James Browns and the C. L. Franklins and the Jasper Williams and Manuel Scotts and all of the great cultural geniuses, the Cecil Taylors, and so forth. So that's a fascinating irony.

One of the things that I have been able to really both revel in and benefit from—and you see it probably more in *Democracy Matters* than in anything else[19]—is trying to unite this radical intellectual legacy of Du Bois that hits the issue of empire and white supremacy with the popular cultural expressions of genius and talent—be it in music, be it in dance, be it among the younger generation or older generation—so that you actually have a kind of an interplay between, on the one hand, Du Bois's radicality and militancy when it comes to politics and economics, empire and race, and, on the other hand, the antiphonal forms of call and response, the syncopation, the rhythm, the rhyme, the tempo, the tone that you get in the best of Black cultural forms that are requisite for sustaining Black dignity and sanity, sustaining Black people as a whole.

CHB: He was so afraid of "uncivilized" behavior, he would probably have taken much of what you are talking about to be just that. And his concern with education—and maybe we could talk about his idea of the Talented Tenth—was quite different from any attempts at grassroots political socialization or education in general.

CW: Absolutely. Of course, Du Bois should consider Louis Armstrong, Ma Rainey, or Bessie Smith part of the Talented Tenth, you see. Bootsy Collins, George Clinton, Aretha Franklin, they are certainly part of the Talented Tenth. Stevie Wonder is part of the Talented Tenth, but given Du Bois's elitist conception of education, they would be considered mere entertainers. So I do resonate with his need for a conception of education that has to do with awakening from sleepwalking, with wrestling with reality to transform it so that that illuminates and liberates. I do resonate with that. But because of his conception of who would be candidates for that, it seems to be still too narrow for me. The irony is that for Du Bois, the nonliterate or illiterate slaves who created the spirituals would probably be candidates for the Talented Tenth, because when we look closely at his readings of their products, their songs, their expressions, he sees their genius. He really does!

CHB: In the expression of suffering.

CW: Yes, yes.

CHB: It is here that his empathy shows. There is a piece, a conversation Du Bois has with a white person, I think, who does not understand what Jim Crow is like, even in 1920.[20] And he explains it in terms of his own daily experience and how humiliating it can be. This is his way of expressing the suffering of the people under oppression.

CW: Very much so. You could be alluding to what I consider to be one of the most powerful essays that he wrote—and he wrote so many powerful essays and texts—but "The Souls of White Folk" is probably the most militant, radical, illuminating, and counter-hegemonic text that we have.[21] I know it was a favorite of the great John Henrik Clarke, who was a great Pan-Africanist and who viewed Du Bois as one of his precursors, but again fascinating that John Henrik Clarke viewed Du Bois as a precursor in the same way that William Julius Wilson, concerned about class but more about integration, would view Du Bois as a precursor. In the same way, an NAACP liberal integrationist would view Du Bois as a precursor, so that Du Bois is rich enough and his work polyvalent enough, subject to multiple interpretations enough, that he ends up with all of these different progeny. But that essay, "Souls of White Folk," is a devastating thing. I remember the first time I read this, I said, "Oh my God, this is a Du Bois we don't really get a chance to look at too closely." He writes:

> It is curious to see America, the United States, looking on herself, first, as a sort of natural peacemaker, then as a moral protagonist in this terrible time. No nation is less fitted for this rôle. For two or more centuries America has marched proudly in the van of human hatred,—making bonfires of human flesh and laughing at them hideously, and making the insulting of millions more than a matter of dislike,—rather a great religion, a world-war cry: Up white, down black; to your tents, O white folk, and world war with black and parti-colored mongrel beasts![22]

That's just one moment.

CHB: There is yet another one, where there is the perspective of the daily life of Blacks and their suffering from discrimination, etc. He exposes that in a dialogue that is really powerful. Which brings me to another point, namely, that within the limits of his concept of culture, he, in principle, would have agreed with you that it is not enough to explain something scientifically but that one should also try to express it by other means, in different styles. This is what he did in his work, be it in his novels or in his very early essays in *The Souls of Black Folk*, where he combined scientific essayistic writing with the poetic. And the reason for this was really that he wanted to reach out. He knew he could not reach people otherwise, though one would doubt that he could reach them today with his at times lyrical *Suada* [German for "harangue"].

CW: No, but there would be other artists who would appropriate his work and make it more popular, because they could see the genius at the center of it. One of the things that makes me smile is Du Bois putting on these pageants, these plays, you know, thousands of Black people, trying to get them to see the greatness of African civilization, hundreds of actors and so forth. I mean, that's popular culture at its core, and it's, again, his attempt to reach out. I love his passion to communicate by any means relative to what he thinks are going to be the most effective means.[23]

CHB: True, and also, as to media, in his time he was avant-garde as an editor of the *Crisis*. This is what he could do as an activist.

CW: Absolutely. That was popular. Any of us who try to expand the public spheres into film and music and books and magazines and some of television and, of course, radio—I think we're building on Du Bois, even if we have slightly different conceptions of culture. I think that in an interesting kind of way, Du Bois was an indisputable radical democrat in his ideology—though I'm not so sure he was an indisputable radical democrat in his temperament, in his personality. I think he was shaped at a time when his temperament and personality were much more rooted in a kind of elitist formation essentially, and yet he never allowed that to impede or obstruct his sensitivities and his inclusivity when it came to the suffering of other people. That is part of his greatness to me, even though I tend to accent a much more radical democratic temperament, personality, and way of being in the world.

CHB: Again, he saw the problem himself. He revised the concept of the Talented Tenth, because he wondered about it. He again admitted that he had been naïve, idealistic, because what he had counted on was character, and he had become aware of the fact that you could not count on that. So when he revised his concept of the Talented Tenth, he was contemplating how to actually realize his concepts and how to solve the problem of organization.[24] And this essay shows to me that there was a certain helplessness on his part, but then, aren't we all at a loss when it comes to organization? It is so difficult a task.

CW: Oh absolutely. Yes, I think it's true. And I do think that at the center of his conception of the Talented Tenth was an ethos of service to the poor, service to those who have been left behind, as it were, or in the religious sense, service to the least of these—echoes of the twenty-fifth chapter of Matthew— and I like that core very much. It's just that early on in 1903, when he put forward that notion, it was deeply bourgeois and elitist. In the 1940s, when he revised it, he had been radical- ized by Marxism; he had been radicalized by the Communist movement. And so he knew that that ethos of service had to be now cast in such a way that the class elitism of 1903 had to be rejected, and also the sexist elitism.

CHB: He was a nineteenth-century person in that regard, but he moved forward.

CW: Yes, he had come a long way from where he was in the early part of the twentieth century. Of course, you are absolutely right, "The Damnation of Women" from *Darkwater* is a good example. I was blessed to take courses with his second wife, Shirley Graham Du Bois. She was an intellectual powerhouse. She was on fire for justice and would not put up with any kind of patriarchal mess from anybody. She taught at Harvard in the early 1970s. She was something, and she had wonderful memories and reminiscences of her husband.[25]

CHB: And Du Bois then writes in *Darkwater* about servants, female servants.

CW: Yes, yes. Absolutely. "The Servant in the House"; that's powerful.

CHB: What I appreciate is his self-reflexivity on his own develop- ment, his self-criticism. It is very honest.

CW: Yes. You wonder, though, whether the major reception of Du Bois's corpus will be providing the launching pad for that American Gibbon I was talking about, i.e., a turning away from Du Bois's challenge and the escalation of the refusal of the de- liberate ignorance, the willful evasion of the realities Du Bois was talking about at the level of empire and white suprem- acy that will constitute the downfall of the American proj- ect. America slowly but surely moves toward a second-world, maybe even a third-world status, with ruins and relics of its great democratic past being completely trampled by the kind of neoliberal obsession with unregulated markets and indifference toward the poor and polarizing politics of scapegoating the most vulnerable. And Du Bois's magisterial corpus sits there and says: "You should have listened. I've spent my whole life trying to get you to listen, to wake up, to heed the challenge that I was talking about because I was concerned both about you but first and foremost about my people that you've been trampling." And there is a very, very good chance that that's where we are headed. The irony would be that the indisputable relevance of Du Bois was not heeded: we didn't listen; we didn't take him seriously. Shame on you, America! Shame on you, the American academy! Shame on you, the American intelligentsia, that your narrow individualism, your truncated rapacious marketeering, your deep dedication to paradigms and frameworks that are too truncated to come to terms with the realities that were undermining your democratic experiment have led to the need for the American Gibbon. That's very much where we are right now.

CHB: Yes, but it is really a question of bringing the more radical Du Bois to the fore. Before I had read more of Du Bois, I used to focus on *The Souls of Black Folk*. That is not to say that this is not a great work, with all the metaphors that have shaped academic discussions such as "the veil" and "double-consciousness." But I am also deeply impressed, in *Dusk of Dawn*, by his metaphor of the cave, which is describing the same caste system[26] but in much more radical terms; or rather, it's darker, more pessimistic, and you hardly ever see it referenced. He plays on Plato's cave, I think.

CW: Absolutely. Straight out of *Republic*. No, it is darker here. It is darker here. He writes:

> No matter how successful the outside advocacy is, it remains impotent and unsuccessful until it actually succeeds in freeing and making articulate the submerged

caste. [. . .] This was the race concept which has dominated my life, and the history of which I have attempted
to make the leading theme of this book.[27]

And yet he is one of those who emerges out of the pro-
vincialism, he shatters the narrowness and becomes the grand
cosmopolitan and internationalist that we know him to be. I
mean, that's one of the reasons why in my own classes I assign
Souls of Black Folk, but I also have students read *Reconstruction*, the 1935 classic, especially the more literary, more metaphoric sections of that text alongside the analytical sections,[28]
because by 1935, he has become someone wrestling with the
legacies of Marx and Freud, wrestling with Lenin's conception of imperialism based on Hobson[29] and others, and that is
a different Du Bois. I mean, there are continuities, but it is a
very different Du Bois.

CHB: When I was thinking about the issues we would be talking
about, I thought your perspective might be that, in the end,
he is just too dark. Where is the hope that you would insist
on? But in contrast, one of your points of criticism in *The Future of the Race* is that you think he partakes in American optimism.[30] So you probably meant a different phase. But what do
you think about Du Bois's optimism or pessimism?

CW: Remember, when he was on the boat and he looks back he
says: "The Negro cannot win in America. I must go international, got to go to Ghana," linked to China, the Soviet
Union, and so forth.[31] I'd have to rethink what I had in mind
when I talked about American optimism. That was certainly
part of his earlier phase. I think the later phase is closer to the
darkness that I was talking about. One of the things that has
always disturbed me about the great Du Bois is that I've never
encountered in his grand works a substantive wrestling with
Chekhov, or I would even say with Russian literary tradition
as a whole: Tolstoy, Gogol, Leskov, Turgenev, Dostoyevsky,
and we could go on and on.[32] And I believe that would have
shattered any cheap optimism or any American optimism that

informs earlier stages of his work. I'm just amazed that there is no wrestling with Kafka; there is no wrestling with even Beckett in the 1950s, from a radical democratic point of view. I want him to hold on to his militancy and radicality in terms of the talk about empire and white supremacy. But I think there is a connection between him running from the blues and him running from Chekhov and running from the Russian literary tradition and running from Kafka and from Beckett. And yet he has his own kind of darkness at which he arrives on his own.

ChB: By way of analysis, on the basis of his sociological training.

CW: Yes, exactly. When he looks at the structural and institutional forces in play vis-à-vis poor and working people, and those Frantz Fanon called "the wretched of the earth,"[33] I think of the Chekhovs and the blues sitting there waiting for him. And yet he arrives on his own, so in that sense I'd have to revise my critique if I was implying that American optimism actually held through all of the phases of his thinking as opposed to just the earlier phases.

ChB: I wonder what he read in terms of literature, since, he quotes in *Souls of Black Folk*—

CW: —A lot of Shakespeare, Balzac.

ChB: Yes. His famous quote: "I sit with Shakespeare and he winces not."[34]

CW: Oh, we know his favorite was Goethe. That's one of the things that I hit him hard on, you see.[35]

ChB: Well, after all, he had spent some time in Germany.[36]

CW: Yes, he was deeply shaped by the German conception of *Bildung*, and at that time—and understandably so—the major stellar figures were Goethe and Schiller, who actually mean much to me, too.

ChB: It's the idea of humanism, I think, that shapes him.

CW: Yes, absolutely. Yet you don't get a serious wrestling with modernist texts at all in his work. There's little Joyce, there's little Proust, there's little Kafka.

CHB: What I wonder is, did he really not read any of them, or did he choose not to comment on them because they were alien to his thinking?

CW: It's a good question. My hunch is that he was certainly aware of them. He was too cosmopolitan and intellectual not to know that Joyce, Eliot, Pound, Proust, Kafka, and Mandelstam and others were around. He may have read Hermann Broch's *The Death of Virgil* [1945] in German, but we have very little evidence for this, and it would be the same in terms of modernist movements and in Afro-American life. What did he think of Charlie Parker? Was he moved by the pianistic genius of Art Tatum? I would like to know.

CHB: And what about Richard Wright and writers of his time?

CW: I think he did read Wright. I recall reading a review of Richard Wright, especially given the Communist overlap, both being members of the Communist culture.[37] Wright was actually a member of the party. Du Bois was not, but they overlapped for a little while before Wright left the party. And what did Du Bois think about Ralph Ellison? I think he did actually write about Ellison, too. So, again, I mean this not so much as a brick thrown at the great Du Bois but as a matter of trying to see what constitutes his edifice and which bricks are missing in the building that he was working on. And I think this again resonates with the concerns about popular culture, the contemporary cultural expressions of his day, and the concern about popular culture as a whole.

CHB: There is a heated debate about religion in Du Bois's work, and most of his biographers think he was an agnostic, if not an atheist, due to his Marxism. There are comments that he makes from which you could conclude that. But then there is an interesting book by Edward Blum, *W. E. B. Du Bois:*

American Prophet, who argues that Du Bois, though certainly not an orthodox Christian, was religious in a way and kept it up.[38] In his view, Du Bois did not just do some window dressing using religious phrases, examples from the Bible, but there was a, let's call it, spirituality that shaped him throughout his life.

CW: I think that Du Bois had a self-styled spirituality that was not wedded to cognitive commitments to God talk. He was very similar to his teacher George Santayana. Santayana used to go to Mass, shed tears weekly as a lapsed Catholic, and would say, "The Mass was too beautiful to be true." So he was moved by the passion and the perceptions and the purpose in the Eucharist but could not make cognitive commitments to any of the claims. Ludwig Wittgenstein was the same way, and I think Du Bois is part of that particular coterie of secular figures who are profoundly religiously musical, to use Max Weber's words; people who resonate deeply with the issues that religious people are wrestling with—what it means to be human, how do you engage in a virtuous life, what kind of character do you cultivate, what kind of sensitivity, what kind of compassion, what conceptions of justice, the centrality of love and empathy—without being religious in terms of belief in God, in the rituals of faith.

And I have a great respect for Du Bois's spirituality, even as a Christian, which makes him in some ways even more of a prophet than most Christians or religious Jews or religious Buddhists and so on, because it means that he was able to sustain himself spiritually without the help of the religious apparatus of tradition. He also didn't fall into the kind of narrow reductionist traps of scientistic, positivistic ties to science, the kind of narrow Darwinism that you get today among the number of the more sophomoric atheists like our dear brothers Christopher Hitchens, Richard Dawkins, and others, who reduce the rich Darwin to narrow scientism. Darwin is the brook of fire through which we all must pass. But you can be religiously sensitive without being religious, and Du Bois certainly was one of the most religiously sensitive of the secular thinkers.

CHB: Du Bois wrote an essay entitled "The Revelation of Saint Orgne"—i.e., Negro—"the Damned," and there is a concept of a new church which, according to Du Bois, should be based on the "word of life from Jeremiah, Shakespeare and Jesus, Buddha and John Brown."[39] And it's a church organized "with a cooperative store in the Sunday-school room; with physician, dentist, nurse, and lawyer to help serve and defend the congregation; with library, nursery school, and a regular succession of paid and trained lecturers and discussion; they had radio and moving pictures"—now: mark that!—"and out beyond the city a farm with house and lake."[40] That's his—Orgne's—concept of a church, and what I think is so interesting about it is what is joined here: not just the secular and Christian traditions but body and soul, mind and body; that is what the church would have to offer to help people come to combine the two, to provide food for body and soul. I have noticed that this concept appears in several of Du Bois's writings, and I'd like to follow up on that because I don't think it has been much commented on, though it seems to be part of his later thinking. At first Du Bois counted on the mind exclusively, and then he changed and said, "No, that's not enough," and although he does not go as far as you wished him to—namely, to take into account the physical expression in dance and music and so on of the African American tradition—as a concept he expresses it in that new church that he thinks is needed to raise people to a higher level.

CW: I think you are right about that. It reminds me of one of my own favorite figures and thinkers, Nikos Kazantzakis, where you have this kind of self-styled spirituality that appropriates Jesus, Buddha, Lenin, Shakespeare. I mean, it's quite a heterogeneous coterie of chaps—not too often women actually—who become part of a kind of ecumenical exemplary group of those who constitute grand examples of high-quality living.

So it's the beauty of life, it's the quality of life, it's the courage, the freedom that these people exemplify.[41] You can go from Socrates to Shakespeare in that regard. And there's something that I've always found fascinating about that, I must say. Again, it has a lot to do with Du Bois's humanism. He is a thorough-going radically democratic humanist drawing on the Renaissance, on the Enlightenment and the Victorian critics. William Morris was probably the most revolutionary of them, but Ruskin played a role, and certain moments in Arnold, certain moments in Carlyle, certain moments in Hazlitt; those are Du Bois's intellectual ancestors. I do think that Du Bois would be again relevant for our day because the religious traditions—be they Christian or Islamic or Judaic—if they are not radically Socratized and humanized, then the fundamentalist wings of all three are going to push us into a living hell, which is to say, radically anti-democratic, radically sexist, racist, xenophobic, capitalist hell. Well, I shouldn't say that radical Islam would be capitalist, though. The fundamental Christians would be capitalist, but not the fundamental Islamic folk; they are just theocratic. Now the fundamentalists in Judaism, that's interesting. They tend to be free-marketeers, too, in general, though there are theocratic manifestations of it, too.

You can just see how badly we need Du Bois today in the midst of our catastrophic circumstances. There is no doubt about it. We need the rigor of his structural and institutional analysis, the religiously musical sensitivity to the things that religion is wrestling with as opposed to simply the truth claims of the God belief or the truth claims of the faith appropriated by religious people, and, probably more than anything else, his acknowledgement of subaltern peoples and voices, and just how crucial those voices are in helping us come to terms with our crisis. There is a sense in which Du Bois's witness is such a thoroughgoing indictment of the transatlantic intelligentsia. It really is. If you were to examine much of the intellectual work of the transatlantic intelligentsia—from Europe

and the US—there is not just a relative silence around Du
Bois's work but a relative silence about the issues and problematic that Du Bois is coming to terms with. It's a very sad
state of affairs when you look at the kind of pre–Du Boisian
condition of much of the transatlantic intelligentsia. And it
says much about how far we have *not* come; how cowardly,
how deferential, how careerist, how narrow so many of our
beloved colleagues in the academy can be.

CHB: Well, you pay for it. And he paid for it.

CW: Absolutely. There is a cost to be paid. But I love Martin Luther
King Jr.'s remarks in his "Honoring Dr. Du Bois" address.[42] I
recall talking with John Hope Franklin before he died about
his decision to attend this event, because when they had the
celebration of Du Bois's birthday at Carnegie Hall, most of
the intelligentsia, including Black intellectuals, would not
come within a mile or two miles of the gathering; they were
just scared. They were afraid; they didn't want to be tainted
with the Communist brush during the anti-Communist hys-
teria and frenzy that was then taking place. But, thank God,
Martin Luther King Jr., along with John Hope Franklin and
a few others, had the courage to attend. This is when brother
Martin laid out his statement:

> We cannot talk of Dr. Du Bois without recognizing that
> he was a radical all of his life. Some people would like
> to ignore the fact that he was a Communist in his later
> years. It is worth noting that Abraham Lincoln warmly
> welcomed the support of Karl Marx during the Civil War
> and corresponded with him freely. In contemporary life,
> the English-speaking world has no difficulty with the fact
> that Sean O'Casey was a literary giant of the twentieth
> century and a Communist or that Pablo Neruda is gen-
> erally considered the greatest living poet though he also
> served in the Chilean Senate as a Communist. It is time
> to cease muting the fact that Dr. Du Bois was a genius
> and chose to be a Communist. Our irrational obsessive

anti-Communism has led us into too many quagmires to be retained as if it were a mode of scientific thinking. [. . .] Dr. Du Bois's greatest virtue was his committed empathy with all the oppressed and his divine dissatisfaction with all forms of injustice.[43]

This is powerful stuff. This is very, very powerful stuff. King is right. Martin King is absolutely right. Good God Almighty.

Martin Luther King Jr., 1964

CHAPTER THREE

Moral Fire

MARTIN LUTHER KING JR.

After having spoken about the two towering male figures of the Black tradition of activists and intellectuals in the nineteenth and first half of the twentieth centuries, Frederick Douglass and W. E. B. Du Bois, we decided to focus next on Martin Luther King Jr. Du Bois died aged ninety-five on August 27, 1963, that is, on the eve of the famous March on Washington for Jobs and Freedom, passing on the baton, as it were, to King, who delivered his celebrated "I Have a Dream" speech before the Lincoln Memorial.

Though our exchange had been motivated by politics from the very beginning, the dramatic political events of 2011—with the anti-government protests in Spain, the Arab Spring, and the emerging Occupy Wall Street movement in the United States—brought an urgency to our transatlantic conversations. We knew that if we wanted to bring the precious Black prophetic voices into the current debates and struggles for freedom, justice, and economic equality, we would have to wrest them from a collective memory that had reduced their radical messages to inoffensive sound bites. The most evident example of a sanitized national icon was Martin Luther King Jr., a fact that strengthened our decision to select him for the subject of our next talk, which took place in August 2011. Our project gained further momentum when the dialogue on King was accepted for publication in the German journal *Amerikastudien/American Studies*.[1] The idea of a book took shape—and we sped up.

CHRISTA BUSCHENDORF: You consider Martin Luther King Jr. the "most significant and successful organic intellectual in American history."[2] Your claim that "never before in our past has a figure outside of elected public office linked the life of the mind to social change with such moral persuasiveness and political effectiveness" seems to be based on the following interconnected assumptions: first, that the vocation of the intellectual is to "let suffering speak, let victims be visible, and let social misery be put on the agenda of those in power,"[3] and, second, that "moral action is based on a broad, robust prophetism that highlights systemic social analysis of the circumstances under which tragic persons struggle."[4]

The following quotation by Martin Luther King Jr. is particularly pertinent in view of the present global crisis of capitalism, which drives more and more people into poverty:

> I choose to identify with the underprivileged, I choose to identify with the poor, I choose to give my life for the hungry, I choose to give my life for those who have been left out of the sunlight of opportunity. [. . .] This is the way I'm going. If it means suffering a little bit, I'm going that way. If it means sacrificing, I'm going that way. If it means dying for them, I'm going that way, because I heard a voice saying, "Do something for others."[5]

"Let us march on poverty," King suggested in 1965.[6] To highlight the increasing plight of the poor in the United States almost half a century later, Tavis Smiley and you recently undertook the "Poverty Tour" through eighteen cities, talking to Americans of all colors who struggle to make ends meet.[7] In his mission statement, Tavis Smiley quotes from King's declaration, thus it seems to be particularly apt to speak about Martin Luther King Jr. at this very moment—his historical significance to America and his relevance in the present.

CORNEL WEST: One of the great prophetic voices of the twentieth century, Rabbi Abraham Joshua Heschel, said that the future of America depends on the American response to the legacy of

Martin Luther King Jr.[8] Martin himself had said that the major issues in the America that he would soon die in—what he called a "sick country"—were militarism, materialism, racism, and poverty. Those four, for him, were going to be the fundamental challenges. And I think he was prophetic in this sense: when we look at the role of the military-industrial complex—the role of the Pentagon, the share of the national budget, the ways in which militarism has been routinized and institutionalized and recently outsourced; then the materialism, which is really very much tied to corporate media in the various ways in which it produces its weapons of mass distraction that try to pacify and to render the citizens sleepwalking by means of stimulation and titillation; then when you look at racisms, beginning with the "new Jim Crow" that Michelle Alexander talks about[9]—with the prison-industrial complex in ways in which legacies of white supremacy are still very much operative, even though in some ways more covert than before; and then the last one—poverty—which is very much tied to the Wall Street oligarchic and plutocratic complex—so, when you think about the military-industrial complex, the corporate-media multiplex, the prison-industrial complex, and the Wall Street oligarchic and plutocratic complex, those four complexes have really squeezed most of the juices or sucked most of the life out of the democratic experiment. And this was what Martin was talking about.

So, I think, in fact, when brother Tavis and I were on that Poverty Tour and said, "Look, we are trying to make the world safe for the legacy of Martin Luther King," that it was really responding to Heschel and saying, "You know, since 1968, what has been the response of the country to Martin on all four issues?" When we look at wealth inequality increasing, hyper-incarceration; when we use brother Loïc Wacquant's language, from his brilliant book *Punishing the Poor*[10]—the kind of emptying of souls given the debased and decayed culture that is produced day-in and day-out by the corporate media, Martin's characterization of America as a sick country really makes more and more sense, and I think more and more people are seeing that. Part of the problem is, I think, the death of Martin in some sense signified that America was in deep need of a revolution. He used the language of revolution, the need of a revolution in priorities, revolution in values, the need for a transfer of power from oligarchs to the people. America was deeply in need of a revolution, but he wondered whether America was only capable of a counter-revolution, and therefore all he could do was just bear witness and be willing to live and die for what he understood at the end of his life as democratic socialism or kind of a radical redistribution of power and wealth, as he put it. He used to say, over and over, every day he would put on his cemetery clothes. That was all he could do. And in some ways I think he was right; you just have to be coffin-ready for this bearing of witness and struggle in the midst of a very sick country run by greedy oligarchs and avaricious plutocrats whose interest is very entrenching, whose power is mighty. It's not almighty. Rebellion could make a difference; civil disobedience could have some impact. But the kind of fundamental rise of a revolutionary social movement is very, very unlikely given the powers that be.

CHB: It was a long process for him, too, to discover what you were just talking about: the power of these forces.

CW: But it's funny, though, because it's two things about Martin people tend to overlook. Coretta Scott King told me one time that when she went out with Martin on their first date, it was the first time in her life she ever met a Socialist, that Martin was already calling himself a Socialist and was part of the intercollegiate Socialist movement.[11] The other interesting thing is that when Martin was called by the Nobel Prize committee and told that he had won, he said that he didn't deserve to win if Norman Thomas had not yet won. Norman Thomas, of course: Princeton undergraduate, Union Theological Seminary grad, left the church, became head of the Socialist Party, ran for president six times—three times against Franklin Roosevelt—and actually was supported by John Dewey.[12] So that even as a very young man, especially under Chivers—there was a professor named Walter Chivers at Morehouse who was a Socialist—[13]

CHB: And sociologist—

CW: And sociologist too, absolutely. So they read a lot of Marx, and Martin was very influenced by this brother. So that in an interesting kind of way—even though a lot of people think that Martin really began as a liberal and was radicalized as a result of the movement and the pressures of Stokely Carmichael and the pressures of those in SNCC[14] and, of course, Stanley Levison, who had been a Communist, and Bayard Rustin, who was a Socialist[15]—in fact, as Coretta has suggested, he actually began early on as a Socialist but knew that he could never use that language in the Jim Crow South or even America. And so it became a matter of a kind of confirmation of what Norman Thomas and others had been talking about in the thirties and forties. Even in the early sixties, Norman Thomas was one of his great heroes. Martin is a very fascinating figure in that regard. He really is.

CHB: But don't you think there was a change in him, after all? At least I think he talks about that himself—that once he went to Chicago and lived there among the poor, that this was yet another dimension to him. Or was it just that when he was confronted with that situation in the ghetto, he thought he had to speak out, that he had to be more explicit, that he had to drop his careful distance in rhetoric to socialist or Marxist phrases in order to get his message across. Or is it both?

CW: I think there were two things going on when he moved to 1550 South Hamlin Avenue in Chicago. I was just there at the apartments with brother Tavis in the very room where he and Coretta lived, and then when we met Bernice and Martin Luther King III and laid the wreath a couple of days later, they talked about living in Chicago—because he brought the kids with him to Chicago—that, on the one hand, Martin had little experience in the North. Boston and Philadelphia had been the only places where he had spent time, and Boston in some ways was an aberration as opposed to Chicago and Detroit, as opposed to even Los Angeles or New York, with high concentration of Black folk, even Washington, DC. To move to Chicago was to recognize that the ways in which Jim Crow Jr. in the North operated, as opposed to Jim Crow Sr. in the South. The dynamics were different. It was more entrenched in the North in terms of getting at some of the economic causes, but it was much more visible in the South, because the apartheid was right in your face, you know, and the violence was right in your face. And so he knew he had to come to terms with class issues in the North in a way that he just didn't in the South. But in addition, I think—and here, of course, it goes beyond Norman Thomas—that when Martin became a critic of American imperialism—because that happened roughly at the same time: he moves to Chicago in '66; he is already being pushed by SNCC to come out against the war; then he reads *Ramparts* magazine and sees the bodies of those precious Vietnamese children, and decides he must speak out: he can't be against violence in Mississippi and not also be against violence in Vietnam—that being forced to come to terms with class in Chicago and forced to come to terms with empire in Vietnam does in fact change him and sharpen his analysis, even given his earlier socialist sensibilities and sentiment. It really does. But it's in the heat of battle, it's in the context of intense struggle that Martin begins to have this clarity, and, ironically, it's the clarity that intensifies his dance with mortality.

ChB: And toward the end it becomes a battle not just against all these forces you mentioned but against his own activist groups, because they become anxious that he is going too far. And he is very isolated.

CW: Absolutely. At the time he is shot dead, 72 percent of Americans disapprove of him and 55 percent of Black Americans disapprove of him.[16] He is isolated. He is alienated. He is down and out. He is wrestling with despair. He is smoking constantly; he is drinking incessantly. He is, in many ways, more and more—not so much distant but having more difficulties with Coretta, who was heroic in her own ways. His relations with the various women and so forth are increasing as a way of what he called dealing with his anxiety, getting relief from the deep anxiety of living under the threat of death and all of the vicious attacks and assaults on his character by Black writers like Carl Rowan[17] and leaders like Roy Wilkins and Whitney Young[18] and within his own organization, the Southern Christian Leadership Conference,[19] people seeing him becoming more radical.[20] And that too is something that's not talked about as much as it should: that Martin King started very much as a patriot, that he was part of that generation of the Black bourgeois formation, where the Declaration of Independence had nearly the same status as the Bible, not as much, but it nearly did.

ChB: The American civil religion.

CW: Exactly. It's just so tied into his own Christianity.

ChB: But the interesting question here is, to me, is it patriotism or is it some kind of universalism? Because what he appeals to when he refers to the Declaration of Independence is the declaration of equality of people. So often in the past, as we have seen in Douglass and Du Bois, there was a conscious reference to those values that, at the same time, are values of the United States of America, and thus there is an interrelation between universalist values and patriotism, because you might be proud of your country if you believe that it represents those values.

CW: That's true. But I think—maybe I could be wrong because I am fundamentally opposed to any version of American exceptionalism—American exceptionalism is not just self-justifying but one of the most self-deceiving concepts in the history of the nation. There is a distinctiveness to the American democratic experiment, but America is in no way a nation as chosen, in no way a nation that God smiles at and winks at and shuns others. I think Martin King, early in his career, did subscribe to a form of American exceptionalism, and in that sense, there still is an interplay between universal values and the fact that America enacts or embodies those values at their best.

But I believe at the end of his life he felt that American exceptionalism was a major impediment for the struggle for justice in America and around the world; he had discovered that it was Gandhi that had influence; he had discovered that South African struggles for democracy were as inspiring as anything Thomas Jefferson had to offer. Maybe it was a matter of growing and maturing and recognizing that internationalism was the only way to go. I recall listening to a sermon of his in '68, '67/'68, where he says that he has to recognize now more than ever that his commitment is fundamentally to a struggle for justice that doesn't just transcend the US context but views the US context alongside of the international context. You see, when he began in '55, '56, '57, that's not his language. Now, you would think as a Christian preacher—which is his fundamental vocation—every flag would be beneath the Cross. And Martin did always believe that the Cross was about unarmed truth and unconditional love. Those are the two pillars that he always talked about: unarmed truth and unconditional love, across the board. And that is an internationalism; every flag is beneath that. But that American exceptionalism, you see, sneaks back in again, and lo and behold, the United States becomes that very special case that embodies it more than anybody else. And the next thing you know—going back to American civil religion—it's providential. And even if America somehow died out, it would undoubtedly bounce back, rooted as it was in that heroic errand into the wilderness—an American jeremiad that our dear brother Sacvan Bercovitch talked about with such an insight.[21] And Martin was a part of that for much of his calling and career. But I think at the end he was beginning to let that go. Malcolm X had already let it go a long time before, though we must not forget Martin reaching out through his personal lawyer Jones[22] to Malcolm, joining him in his efforts to put the United States on trial at the UN for the violation of the human rights of Blacks.

CHB: But it was easier for Malcolm X to see through the deception because of his upbringing that left him no—or hardly any—illusions to begin with, whereas King rose in the academy and had a successful career, and so it's the upbringing that very much shaped him.

CW: That's exactly right. Even in fraternity—Martin King was an Alpha like myself, as were W. E. B. Du Bois and Paul Robeson and Duke Ellington, Jesse Owens, Adam Clayton Powell Jr., Donny Hathaway, John Hope Franklin.[23] All of these were Alphas—and we Alphas do tend to move in patriotic ways. But you look at Du Bois: he swerves from US patriotism; Robeson: swerves; and Martin at the very end: swerves. That's what's fascinating. That's a very difficult thing to do, to break like that. Someone like myself, I had the privilege of building on their breaks, you know, with the Black Panther Party and others. I had already learned lessons as a young lad that America didn't have this special providential role in the history of the world, ordained by God to embody democracy, given its history of what it did to indigenous peoples and crushing the workers, enslaving Black folk, and so on. But there is something about that Black middle-class incorporation and formation in the South as a "PK," as a preacher's kid, that made it much more difficult for Martin to break and made his break more heroic. Very much so. Martin—there simply is no one like him in the history of the American experience because he really is an intellectual, but he never really has a lot of time to meditate and reflect. But he has a deep tie to the life of the mind, and his calling is rooted in his Christian faith, unlike Douglass and unlike Du Bois.

CHB: How did he talk about the possibilities of combining religious faith and socialism? It was not really a problem for him, or was it?

CW: I think that because he was part of the Black prophetic tradition, he always connected religious faith with social change, and socialism just became one particular end and aim of social change that he began to take very seriously. Black prophetic tradition has always rooted spirituality and religiosity with social transformation. And this is where you can show that present-day America is so profoundly decadent, especially in the age of Obama—it is demeaning, devaluing, and marginalizing the Black prophetic tradition, which has been the primary tradition that has contributed to the renewal and regeneration of American democracy.

CHB: Could it be that this moral change is based on a change of social conditions that people are confronted with, so that something like the hope that is embodied in Christian prophetic faith is hard to maintain, hard to sustain, when in your social conditions you see hardly any future for your kids, for yourself?

CW: Yes, but you think through 244 years of slavery, that kind of American terrorizing and traumatizing and stigmatizing of Black folk, and we still kept the Black prophetic tradition alive. You are right. I think the social conditions that you are talking about have as much to do with the changes in the culture, with market forces so fundamentally undermining family and community, with corporate media filling the void with narcissism and materialism and individualism and those distractions. So that during slavery we could keep the Black prophetic tradition alive by lifting our voices—music was fundamental in sustaining Black dignity and sanity—and families still had networks, even given that the slaveholders attempted to destroy the Black family. Whereas in contemporary late-capitalist culture, there is such a distraction from empathy and compassion and community and non-market values as a whole, and you cannot have the Black prophetic tradition without non-market values. I mean, one of the problems since Martin's death is when it comes to leadership. You have either the fear of being killed because the FBI, the CIA, and the repressive apparatus of the nation-state might kill you quickly—as was the case in the 1960s—not just Martin but Fred Hampton, Bobby Hutton,[24] and a lot of others—or the other alternative is just buying people, so that you end up with

Black leaders today, most of whom are just up for sale. All you got to do is just give them a bit of money, give them access to corporate position, give them access to the White House, give them access to whatever status they want and they are paid off. So you either get killed or bought. And Martin, I mean, one of the reasons why he stands out so is that there was no price that he was ever willing to accept to be bought—and in that he was like Malcolm and like Fannie Lou Hamer.[25] He was not up for sale, and that's just so rare. It's almost alien to us, really; it's alien to us that corporate America couldn't buy off everybody. The White House couldn't incorporate him. He supported Lyndon Johnson intensely when LBJ helped to break the back of US apartheid, and then two and a half years later, LBJ was calling him a nigger preacher he wished would go away because of Martin's opposition to the war. And Martin refused to support him in '68, and LBJ decided to withdraw from the race. You see, that's something. Even among the Black intelligentsia, Black leadership, and the Black community as a whole, many were talking about Martin like a dog. Here he is willing to die for folk, and they are still talking about him so bad. He refuses to be bought, you know. He doesn't want to be popular in the community if he can't have integrity. It's a very rare thing.

CHB: And now he is no longer able to defend himself, because in public memory he has not been turned into a radical leader, but as you always say, he has been sanitized, and it's that sanitized King that has survived, and it is the radical King that has disappeared. Or maybe, due to the increasing suffering and the increasing crisis of capitalism, he is being rediscovered. One instance I noticed recently was when Tavis Smiley talked on National Public Radio about King's speech "Beyond Vietnam," which is not very well known.[26] It is interesting to juxtapose the "I Have a Dream" speech with the "Beyond Vietnam" speech, but the latter is the forgotten or repressed Martin. I wonder how you see it, whether the more radical Martin has a chance to be rediscovered now.

CW: The radical Martin is highlighted in what brother Tavis Smi-
      ley has done in the National Public Radio show on the "Be-
      yond Vietnam" speech. And *that* Martin cannot but come
      back. So that the kind of, as you say, sanitized, sterilized Mar-
      tin, the deodorized Martin, the Martin that has been San-
      taclausified,[27] so that the Santa Claus that he now becomes,
      jolly old man with a smile giving out toys to everybody from
      right-wing Republicans to centrists to progressives, is op-
      posed to the version of King who took a stand on the side of a
      class war and of an imperial battle, which is actually closer to
      the truth. He really did take a fundamental stand: "I choose
      to identify with the underprivileged, I choose to identify with
      the poor." That sounds like Eugene Debs; that sounds like
      Jim Larkin of the Dublin working-class 1913 strike; it sounds
      like all of the great freedom fighters of the last hundred and
      fifty years in modern times.[28] Now *that* Martin is so scary; *that*
      Martin requires so much courage; *that* Martin requires all of
      us to pay such a price, that *that* Martin will live and come
      back, precisely how is the open question.
         I have the feeling that *that* Martin, in some ways, is going
      to be much more in the possession of people outside of the
      United States, in Brazil, in Africa, in Asia, than in America,
      since *that* Martin is really a prophetic figure for the world
      more than he is for America. I think he is too much for Amer-
      ica. He is too honest; he is too truthful; he is too loving for a
      culture that is fearful of the truth and is fearful of a genuine
      love especially of poor people. There will be voices in Amer-
      ica that will try to hold on to that later Martin, but I think the
      kind of hysteria—let's use the wonderful word of Tennessee
      Williams—the hysteria of America doesn't allow it to really
      come to terms with the deep truth of its history, and in that
      sense *that* Martin is repressed. That's why all this notion of
      people walking around with the juxtaposition on the same
      shirt—Malcolm, Martin, Obama—is such a joke. And in peo-
      ple's minds, they really think all three are identical, and you
      say, "What? Wait a minute. Do you understand?" I mean, you
      got Obama, who is the friendly face of the American empire,

with drone-dropped bombs killing innocent people, at home crushing the poor with policies that are pro–Wall Street and pro-oligarchy and pro-plutocracy. And you got Martin, who is with the poor folk who Obama is crushing, and Malcolm with the poor folk who Obama is crushing, especially the later Malcolm, who is a revolutionary even more so than Martin in some way. And you see all three of those and you can see the level of confusion and obfuscation that is taking place in America, which reinforces why the counter-revolution of the deeply conservative reactionary forces is triumphing.

CHB: But it's so easy because the media play into it. I read that you thought that the radical King in your own time, early as a young man at Harvard, was not yet the voice you listened to.[29] This would change in the next decade; that's what you said. And I wondered about that: Did it change in the eighties? Did you then read "Beyond Vietnam"? Did it resonate with the Left at that time?

CW: You know, I had already read the radical Martin and had great respect for the radical Martin, and as a Christian I have very deep ideological affinities with him in terms of religious sensibility. But what was lacking in Martin—and I continue to say it is lacking in Martin—was his refusal to identify or immerse himself in youth culture.

See, what Malcolm had was a style that resonated more with young people. Martin's style had difficulties, and even as a young person and as a young Christian, I could identify much more with Malcolm the way I could identify with Huey Newton,[30] Angela Davis,[31] and Stokely Carmichael.[32] It had something to do with church and the church leadership styles that Martin as a preacher tended to. And as a Southern preacher, too, a Black Southern preacher, his style was more distant from northern California rhythm and blues, funk orientation. Now, Malcolm himself was very conservative in some ways, especially as a member of the Nation of Islam, where they don't even have music in their rituals, you see, but you could just tell in his style that he was closer to the styles in youth culture. There was a certain swagger; there was a certain sincerity in keeping it real, which is what the funk is all about. So there were elements of James Brown, George Clinton, Bootsy Collins, Lakeside, Ohio Players. You could feel it in Malcolm, whereas in Martin, you couldn't feel that.

CHB: That's the same with the Du Bois we talked about. And it's again the upbringing. It would have been quite difficult for them to step beyond certain limits that are produced by a bourgeois upbringing and bourgeois values and the emphasis on turning children into "civilized" human beings.

CW: That's true, but part of it is choices. Habitus is fundamental, but there is still choice. You can think of figures who come out of this same context as Du Bois who fundamentally chose to identify with the blues the way Du Bois did not, see what I mean? Duke Ellington, bourgeois to the core, but that Negro genius that he was—you could see him identifying with Biggie and Tupac. He had that kind of capacious personality. Louis Armstrong—Negro genius that he was—of course, from the street, so he is a little different. You could see Louis sit down with Ice Cube and probably kicking and having a good time, you know what I mean, whereas with Du Bois that's not going to take place. You cannot see him sitting down with Billie Holiday; Billie Holiday would scare him to death. And I think that there is a sense in which George Clinton would scare Martin King to death: "George, what is all that hell, man? You know, I love you, but damn man, I don't understand, I don't understand." "Come on Martin, get into the groove!" That's not his style, and that's just something missing in Martin from my own point of view, just in terms of my own orientation. And it's not a major thing, but I do think that the appropriation of Martin by young people is ongoing here and around the world—because I mean youth culture has been Afro-Americanized around the globe now—so there is a sense in which any appropriation of Martin is going to be effected by the Afro-Americanization that is already taking place among young people in Asia, Africa, Europe, Central

America. He comes out of a different habitus that has its own specificity and distinctiveness. There is no doubt about that.

CHB: What about the space, the social space of the church today? You talked about the moral decline, and the church was always the institution that would provide a space for self-assertion, even in those much worse times such as slavery and militant Jim Crow in the South. What about young people and the church today? Is it only for the middle class, something you do on Sunday because it's proper to do? Or is there still real power in the churches?

CW: I was blessed to be at the Progressive Baptist Convention just a few weeks ago, which is the convention that Martin helped found when he was booted out of the National Baptist Convention in 1961, with Gardner Taylor,[33] who was the mentor of Martin King. He is now ninety-five years old. Brother Tavis Smiley and I were blessed to interview Reverend Taylor in front of the Progressive Baptist Convention, and it was something, because you look out, you see only about twenty-five hundred people there. Twenty years ago you would have seen ten thousand. That's the result of the decline of the denominations. So, two basic phenomena are taking place: First, the impact of market culture on the Black church is the decline of denominations, so you get the rise of nondenominational churches, so many of the members of Progressive Baptists joined the nondenominational churches. And the second phenomenon is the Pentacostalization of the nondenominational churches, you see. So that here you get Pentacostals, which is, of course, a denomination founded by Black Baptists, the fastest-growing denomination in the whole world, which places stress on the third person in the Trinity, on the Holy Ghost, the Holy Spirit and highly individualist salvation. Most Pentecostal churches shy away from direct political involvement or action. In addition, you get nondenominational churches growing. You end up with a towering figure like Bishop T. D. Jakes,[34] who is a spiritual genius, a great preacher, but doesn't have a whole lot of political courage. I could go on and on. Another towering figure is Bishop Glen Staples,[35] my dear brother, nondenominational and very much tied to working and poor people and politically active. Pentacostalism is still, in style, too funky for the well-to-do, the Black elites, you see, so that what happens is you get the breakdown of denominations, the Pentacostal styles becoming hegemonic.

But the prophetic element associated with the old denominations, like progressive Baptists, is lost. So that you have some prophetic folk, like Bishop Staples—and there are few like him—but for the most part, it really is a matter of spiritual stimulation and titillation that has market parallels and market stimulation and titillation, and these nondenominational churches really don't have the rich prophetic substance of courage, compassion, sacrifice, and risk. For example, there is the story that Wacquant and others tell about the $300 billion invested in the prison-industrial complex, the Marshall Plan for jails and prisons, so you get these escalating, exponentially increasing numbers of prisons, but most churches don't have prison ministers. So you get a sense how far removed they are from the suffering of the people. Now, the preachers probably have one or two Bentleys, some have Lamborghinis, but they don't have prison ministers, whereas the Progressive Baptist Convention in the 1950s, they are so attuned to the suffering of the people that wherever the people were being dominated, in whatever form they were dominated, they had a ministry that's somehow connected. And so in that sense, the market-driven religiosity of much of the Black church these days is counter to the prophetic sensibility of Martin—what Martin King was all about—and that's one of the major, major things missing in contemporary America. The two outstanding exceptions are my mentor, Reverend Herbert Daughtry, pastor of the House of the Lord Pentecostal Church, in Brooklyn, founder of the National Black United Front, an exemplary Black freedom fighter, and my dear brother Father Michael Pfleger, pastor at historic Saint Sabina, in Chicago, whose prophetic leadership is deeply grounded in King's witness and legacy.[36]

CHB: You associated the liberal Black church with social analysis, with an insight that goes with the preaching of how you can cope with these conditions, but you're saying that this element is basically lost these days?

CW: For the most part. I mean you get a J. Alfred Smith in Oakland, one of the great prophetic figures; Freddy Haynes or Carolyn Knight, major prophetic figures, or Reverend Dr. Bernard Richardson, Reverend Toby Sanders, Dr. Barbara King, or Reverend Dr. M. William Howard Jr., Reverend Dr. William Barber.[37] Of course, the great Vincent Harding—scholar, activist, teacher—is the reigning dean of King-like prophetic witness. So you have some exceptions, but generally speaking it's lost, and it's exacerbated in the age of Obama, because identification with Obama could easily become—in the eyes of Black leaders—an identification with the Black prophetic tradition. So that Obama displaces the Black prophetic tradition; people think they are doing something progressive and prophetic by supporting our Black president given the history of white supremacy in America, counter-hegemonic, countervailing and so forth, you see. And given the trauma of overcoming blatant legalized racism, Obama is counter-hegemonic, but it's overshadowed by his identification with the oligarchs, with his identification with the imperial killing machine and so forth. But that small sliver gives these Black leaders the sense of "I'm very progressive. I'm with the Black president. The right wing hate him, right wing want to kill him, right wing tell lies about him, but we are taking a stand," you see. And so it's very deceiving, very confusing, and very obfuscating in terms of any clear social analysis of the relations of domination and of power in American society.

CHB: So often the argument is "But isn't there progress? Not just that visual, symbolic progress, but the African American middle class is growing, after all, so what are you talking about?"

CW: Yes, it's true. And they could use that argument up until 2008, when the financial catastrophe took place owing to the greed of Wall Street bankers, when Black people lost 53 percent of their wealth.[38] So we are seeing the relative vanishing of the Black middle class, most of whom had wealth in their homes; large numbers lost their homes. The predatory lending that was connected to the market bubble that burst—those bad loans were for the most part given to Black and brown lower-middle-class people. They've lost their homes, and so there is a transformation taking place. For example, even in the churches, they used to preach prosperity gospel, but now with the lack of prosperity, the material basis of their theology is called into question.

CHB: Yes, I think, what you are talking about—the vanishing of the middle class—is a global development. But probably disproportionately so in the African American community, as always.

CW: Absolutely. In America, whites lost 16 percent wealth, while brown people lost 66 percent wealth. It was worse among Latinos than among Blacks, who lost 53 percent. On a global scale, you do have the middle class contracting with oligarchic and plutocratic power expanding. Now, for the seven past months,[39] 75 percent of corporate profits were based on layoffs, so corporations are actually able to make big money by cutting costs, which are primarily labor costs. And then, of course, they are sitting on $2.1 trillion that they are hoarding because they are scared that the next collapse is going to leave them dry. So that what happens is that the Black middle class loses—a Black *lumpenbourgeoisie* under the American bourgeoisie. We never really had a solid Black bourgeoisie, E. Franklin Frazier says in '57,[40] and he is absolutely right. Even given the unprecedented opportunity the last forty years, the Oprah Winfreys, the Michael Jordans, and so on, once you shave off the entertainers who make big money, we are still beneath the American middle class in terms of wealth. And right now the white household in America has twenty times more wealth than the Black: $113,000 for the average white family, Black is $5,000, Hispanic is $6,000.[41] And we are not even talking of the social neglect and economic abandonment of the poor, which is the kind of thing brother Tavis and I were accenting on the Poverty Tour. That has had no visibility since Martin was killed. Marian Wright Edelman has been heroic trying to make it visible, but she has had difficulty making it visible.[42] Part of Tavis's creative genius as a media figure is his ability to gain access to media sites to make things visible, so that even without a social movement you can go on a Poverty Tour and get the whole nation talking about poverty, from *Nightline* to CNN to C-SPAN to the *New York Times*, *Washington Post*. That's unprecedented in so many ways. But in the absence of a social movement, that's one of the best things you can do to try to shape the climate of opinion, try to have some impact on the public discourse in the country.

CHB: And that influence is stronger, more powerful than in King's days.

CW: Yes. That's true. Because King's social movement was an attempt to dramatize issues of injustice, and the Poverty Tour, which is what brother Tavis and I did, really is an attempt to dramatize the issue of poverty without a social movement. Now, I think that the aim of putting a smile on Martin's face in the grave is the highest criterion of a freedom fighter in America. And to put a smile on his face is to be willing to live and die and bear witness on behalf of those who are wrestling with all four of those issues: militarism, materialism, racism, and poverty. Now, I would include patriarchy and sexism—I would include homophobia as well—even though he didn't talk about them, so that when we are talking about racism, we are talking about a species of xenophobia. We could really just say xenophobia as a whole, so it includes anti-Semitism; it includes anti-Arab racism, anti-Muslim sensibility, and so on. But my hunch is that's probably the best we can do.

I think Sheldon Wolin is probably right with his notion of fugitive democracy,[43] where it is a matter of trying to generate and galvanize people to be organized and mobilized to bring power and pressure to bear, but know that the powers that be are going to either kill you, try to absorb you and incorporate you, or lie about you or try to undermine your movement by those weapons of mass distraction that we talked about before. It's very difficult to conceive of how the kind of revolution that Martin really wanted can take place given current arrangements. Now, it could just be a matter of my limited imagination, but the Frankfurt School and Wolin and the others just make more sense to me. And I think that's one reason why you have fewer persons who really want to put a smile on Martin's face, because the possibilities of actualizing what he was calling for tend to be so small, and most people don't want to fight for something that they don't think can be actualized or realized—especially in America—rather quickly.

CHB: It always impresses me that Noam Chomsky, an intellectual I appreciate very much, who is so marginalized—naturally—sharply analyzes the situation and sees the difficulties you were just talking about—of how change could come about—and yet always believes that people can do it. And I wonder how he sustains this belief, which seems to be based on some insight that it is possible.

CW: We just had him at Princeton, and I had a chance to speak to him and introduce him, and brother Noam, deep down he is a Cartesian, he really is. So he believes in not just the power of reason but the power of transparency and the power of clarity as themselves fundamentally just agents of change. Beckett, Chekhov, Schopenhauer, they are not part of his world. I think he has a limited grasp of the role of the nonrational, and so he easily pushes it aside, so he really believes that once people are exposed to the clear analysis that he has, somehow they will catch on.

CHB: That's what Du Bois believed.

CW: For a while, that's right. He really believed that it is ignorance standing in the way.

CHB: I think it's, on the one hand, rationality versus irrationality, but on the other hand, it's also about the interrelation of mind and body, because so much of how we look at the world, our perceptions, our orientations, are deeply ingrained in our bodies, and as embodied dispositions, they are persistent. Thus, according to Pierre Bourdieu, a change of habitus occurs only under certain conditions, mainly in moments of crisis.[44] So that is something that one has to address.

CW: You've got to come to terms with that. What happens is that the Cartesian element has its place because reason does have a role to play, but it can become a fetish; it can become an idol; it can become a form of false religiosity in order to sustain your optimism, and in some ways I think that's true for Noam. You know who I think is a better example is my dear brother Howard Zinn. I just wrote an introduction to his writings on race that was recently published.[45] Because Howard— like Noam—really believed in the power of reason, clarity, transparency, and analysis. But he also had a deep sensitivity to body, to nonrationality—or maybe nonrationality is not a good word—to trans-rationality—what culture is about—and so Howard had such a long view of things. Reminds me a little of Raymond Williams's wonderful book *The Long Revolution*,[46] which needs to be read and reread over and over again. And in that sense he is a little closer to reality in a way, whereas I think people like Wolin, they understand all the things that go into social transformation, and it's always messy, always.

CHB: What about King in that respect? What do you think?

CW: I think King always understood the mess, and I think once he hit those issues of class in Chicago and empire in Vietnam, the mess became more and more Beckett-like, which means all you can do is try to lay bare illuminating analysis and try to live a life committed to justice and love and truth. That's all you could do at that point. It's just a matter of integrity, because what you are up against is such a mess, in a very technical sense—which is a term which Beckett uses,[47] rather than

Being in Heidegger—and King understood that, he really did. And you wonder though—I mean, he died at thirty-nine—if he had lived to be sixty, what would Martin have done? That's still a question. Some say he would have been a professor in Union Theological Seminary. So he would have been an activist but would be teaching as well, because you have to be able to sustain yourself with something; you can't be an intense activist every week of your life the way he had done this from twenty-six to thirty-nine—thirteen years—you just can't do that, you know, especially if you had kids and grandkids and things. But you never know. I know Martin would have been fundamentally in solidarity with the struggles of poor people. I really do. And I think that he would have been a countervailing voice and a countervailing force against the Obama administration, and he would have spoken out very loudly. Now, he spoke out very loudly among Black politicians of his day, when he said that the US Congress was turning "the war on poverty into a war against the poor."[48] And when he supported Carl Stokes as mayor, and Stokes refused to invite Martin on the stage when he won,[49] Martin was very hurt. Martin was too radical. He had come out against Vietnam already. He was very hurt, and he would say over and over again, "These Black politicians kind of sell out just as quickly as any white politician. It's about the people!"

Now you see, Huey Newton and company, they loved that about Martin; even Amiri Baraka,[50] who Martin met before he died. Baraka was just telling me about that wonderful encounter that he and Martin had in '68 in March prior to the death in April, and they loved that about Martin, because they knew that his critique of Black bourgeois politicians was a powerful one. Though he supported these folks, they used him; they used his prowess, his charisma for their campaign, and then they win and they won't touch him with a ten-foot pole. Martin said: "What the hell is going on here?" They know what they do, you know. They know what they do. They got the big business community, the permanent government, to relate to and so forth.

I think if Martin had lived, he would have been critical of the later rule of Mandela as president of South Africa, given his complicity with the business class and given his willingness to in some ways downplay the plight of the poor of South Africa as he moved into the mainstream. You can see the same kind of Santaclausification, the same kind of complicity with the business elites in South Africa, the embrace by Bill Clinton, the embrace by Richard Stengel, the managing editor of *Time* magazine, so that any time now you talk about Mandela, Clinton and Stengel pop up rather than Sisulu and Slovo,[51] who were revolutionary comrades of the revolutionary Mandela, who spent twenty-seven and a half years in prison, you see. Martin would understand the ways that people's names are promoted and sustained by corporate money and elites who protect their names, but he would resist that kind of sanitizing, which is to say he would be critical of the way that he has been sanitized, too. In some ways it's probably an inevitable process, but even given its inevitability, it has to be criticized, because it is a shift away from the truth. And there's a distancing from the truth. He would still have great respect for Mandela, don't get me wrong, but he would be critical of that process. I think Mandela was critical of this process himself. He told me that when we met, when I gave that Mandela lecture and talked about the Santaclausification of Mandela himself in Africa. I think Martin would resonate with that. No doubt. There is no doubt that the great Nelson Mandela was the most courageous of men and most genuine of revolutionaries—yet as president of South Africa he ruled in a neoliberal manner.

Ella Baker, 1964

CHAPTER FOUR

The Heat of Democratic Existentialism

ELLA BAKER

Our project gained momentum, and so did the Occupy movement. The demonstration camp in New York City's Zuccotti Park triggered the vital question of all political movements—and especially grassroots movements—how to organize and mobilize. No figure embodies more convincingly than Ella Baker the genius of grassroots organizing in the civil rights movement. Her deep commitment to democratic decision making turned her into an ideal choice for our next conversation, which took place in summer 2012, when the Occupy movement was at its height. With Ella Baker we opened up the field of the female voices within the Black prophetic tradition. The women, in contrast to their charismatic male companions, had not just been sanitized but, worse, marginalized.

CHRISTA BUSCHENDORF: In our three previous conversations we talked about Frederick Douglass, W. E. B. Du Bois, and Martin Luther King Jr. Even when we consider the tremendously rich tradition of African American intellectuals and activists, these were obvious choices. After all, all three were considered towering figures, if not the most towering intellectuals of their time, by their contemporaries as well as by posterity. To many, our choice to speak about Ella Baker will be much less evident, although she clearly belongs to the exclusive group of

long-distance runners, i.e., freedom fighters who devote their
whole lives to the struggle for freedom and justice. However,
her life's work is more difficult both to access and to assess.
First, as a highly skillful organizer, she often became an indispensible member of the organization for which she chose to
work, but she never stood in the limelight of the movement.
Second, while she held concise theories of social change and
political action, she never put them down in writing. There
is no memoir; there is no collection of essays. There are just
speeches, a few newspaper articles, and interviews, but apart
from that, we rely on biographers who consulted her papers
and spoke to the people who knew her personally. Third, her
very theory of political action is decidedly group-centered in
that she firmly believed in a kind of grassroots organizing that
would allow the poor and oppressed to get actively involved in
the fighting. To Baker, the ideal activist was not the charismatic
figure of the prophet who mobilizes the masses by mesmeriz-
ing speeches but an unassuming person who helps the suppressed to help themselves. As she put it in 1947, "The Negro
must quit looking for a savior, and work to save himself."[1] And
twenty years later, with regard to the Student Nonviolent Coordinating Committee, which she cofounded, she maintained,
"One of the major emphases of SNCC, from the beginning,
was that of working with indigenous people, not working for
them, but trying to develop their capacity for leadership."[2]

If, then, Ella Baker may not be as obvious a choice as
Douglass, Du Bois, and King, she nevertheless is, I think, a
very obvious choice for you. So could you just start by giving
us an assessment of why you cherish her personality and her
work in the civil rights movement?

CORNEL WEST: I think in many ways Ella Baker is the most relevant of our historic figures when it comes to democratic forms
of leadership, when it comes to a deep and abiding love for
not just Black people in the abstract or poor people in the
abstract, but a deep commitment to their capacities and their
abilities to think critically, to organize themselves, and to think

systemically, in terms of opposition to and transformation of a system. When we think of the Occupy movement—we do now live in the age of Occupy in this regard—and Ella Baker's fundamental commitment to what Romand Coles calls "receptivity"—Coles's work also was quite powerful in terms of Ella Baker's legacy[3]—learning to receive from the people, not just guide, not just counsel, not just push the people in a certain direction, but to receive from the people the kinds of insight that the people themselves have created and forged in light of a tradition of ordinary people generating insights and generating various visions. And so it's grassroots in the most fundamental sense of grassroots. And I don't think that even Douglass, in all of his glory, and Du Bois, in all of his intellectual genius, and King, in all of his rhetorical genius, have that kind of commitment to the grassroots, everyday, ordinary people's genius in this sense. And of course, there is a gender question as well: her powerful critique of patriarchal models of leadership, including especially messianic models of leadership, which ought to be a starting point for any serious talk about organizing and mobilizing and social change in the twenty-first century.

In addition, I was just in dialogue with my dear brother Bob Moses.[4] He spent a whole year at Princeton, and his office was right across the hall from mine. Of course, for him, Ella Baker is the grandest figure in radical democratic praxis, and he is very much a disciple of Ella Baker. He is quite explicit about that, very explicit that charismatic leadership, messianic leadership is something that he rejects across the board. But I think what comes through is that Ella Baker has a sensitivity to the existential dimension of organizing and mobilizing, and what I mean by that is that for her political change is not primarily politically motivated. This goes back to her early years in the Black Baptist women's missionary movement. When she talks about humility with the people, not even for the people but with the people, when she talks about service alongside the people, and when she talks about everyday people, everyday people's capacities becoming more and more manifest at the center of the movement, not something that is just used and manipulated by messianic leaders, but at the center of the movement, that's a kind of democratic existentialism of a sort that I see in her work—and I see in Bob Moses's. But you see it in very few people's works.

There are elements of this in some of the anarchists, and that's why I have a tremendous respect for anarchism, because anarchism has this deep suspicion of hierarchy, be it the state in the public sphere, corporations in the private sphere, or cultural institutions in civil society. We know Baker worked with George Schuyler, who called himself an anarchist in the 1930s. He ended up a reactionary right-wing brother, but he earlier called himself an anarchist.[5] We also know Bayard Rustin was an anarchist, called himself an anarchist quite explicitly.[6] We know that Dorothy Day called herself an anarchist, quite explicitly, till the day she died.[7] This is a great tradition I have great respect for, and I see it among my young brothers and sisters of all colors in the Occupy movement, even though I don't consider myself an anarchist. I do see similarities between Ella Baker's position and the council Communist tradition that called for Soviets without Bolsheviks, that called for workers' councils without a revolutionary vanguard party that served as managerial manipulators of the people in the councils, so that the self-organization of working people was the kind of radical organizing among everyday people without any managers, experts, or party members telling them what to do. And there is some overlap between Herman Gorter and Anton Pannekoek and some of the early council Communists that mean much to someone like myself coming out of a deep democratic tradition.[8] And so, ironically, Ella Baker, the very figure who one would think would be marginal vis-à-vis these male-type titans, ends up being the most relevant in light of our present dark times of political breakdown, economic decline, and cultural decay.

CHB: It is so interesting that the Occupy movement is definitely leaderless, tries to be leaderless and group-centered, which has great advantages. For one thing, you can't decapitate a movement easily by just killing one of its charismatic leaders. But more than that, as you just explained, it gives the group much more power, a power that it otherwise delegates to a representative. But even if we say today that this is why Ella Baker is more important, when we think back, what is your stance on the fact that after all we also needed a Martin Luther King Jr.? What, then, is to your mind the relation between those two forces, the charismatic leader-figure and the group-centered work that Ella Baker did?

CW: When Ella Baker says that the movement made Martin, Martin didn't make the movement, she is absolutely right, and so for me the greatness of Martin King has to do with the ways in which he *used* his charisma and *used* his rhetorical genius and *used* his courage and willingness to die alongside everyday people. The critique of Martin would be that the decision-making process in his organization was so top-down and so male-centered and hierarchical that one could have envisioned a larger and even more effective mass movement, especially when it came to issues of class, empire, gender, and sexual orientation. When he hit economic justice for janitors and the poor, and when he hit issues of American imperialism in Vietnam, he would not have been just dangling all by himself if there had been more political education and cultivation among the people in the organization and the community. And Ella Baker—who was shaped by the South, went to Shaw University in North Carolina, and then straight to New York City, where she runs the West Indian newspaper, and she is working with George Schuyler during his anarchist years, interacting with leftists, interacting with various progressives, but always rooted, always grounded—offered a deep democratic alternative to the model of the lone charismatic leader.

One of the things about Ella you might recall is that—and Bob Moses was telling me this, it was so striking—right in the middle of the movement, she pulled out to take care of her niece. And people said, "Wait a minute, this is something that you have been waiting for. This is the moment. The cameras are here." "I got my roots," you see, "my niece needs to be taken care of. She is, after all, by herself." And people would say, "Oh, but that's part of the gender question. She had to think of herself as a carer and nurturer." But, no, no, she puts things in perspective. Her caring for her niece in those years that her niece needed her was part and parcel of her calling as someone who is of service. But for Ella, her calling embraced both service to her family and service to the movement. For her, humility and service flow across the board, and so I think that her critique of the great Martin Luther King Jr. ought to be integral to any discussion about Martin Luther King Jr. She brings to her critique humility, service, and love; her own willingness to sacrifice. She's the kind of unassuming character who doesn't need the limelight at all in order to have a sense of herself. She doesn't need the camera. You know what happens is that these charismatic leaders become ontologically addicted to the camera. And it's a very sad thing to behold. You see it in Jesse Jackson, despite his rhetorical genius and great contributions to our struggles. We see it in Al Sharpton, despite his talent for adaptability and service. You saw it in the later years of Huey Newton, as great as he was in his early years. Angela Davis has resisted it. Bob Moses also resisted it. Stokely Carmichael—even given his greatness, incredible love for the people, and the deep influence of Ella Baker—was still much more tied to the charismatic model.[9] My dear brother the charismatic Reverend Dr. Jeremiah Wright—largely misunderstood and underappreciated—was demonized by the media and will, in the long run, be vindicated. But, like Ella, prophetic giant Dr. James Forbes Jr. defies these seductions.

CHB: One wonders, of course, whether there is not a natural relation between the possibility of becoming such a charismatic leader and a certain degree of narcissism, so it is an even greater accomplishment of those figures who do not develop in terms of egocentricity, and yet are great leaders. Baker often criticized the mostly male cofighters she had to put up with. As she recalled, they took it for granted that when there was a meeting she would take care of the people, so that they would have something to eat and drink, that the coffeemaker was running. Thus, there was always that double concern of hers. For she was not at all a person who was content with those everyday services to the movement; she had great foresight. In fact, this to me is another important feature of hers: the way she understood the whole process, namely, as something that would go on for a long time, because nothing would be accomplished in ten years or twenty years, but that nevertheless you would have to bring all your strength to it, even if you did not see much progress. She was looking ahead and willing even to pass on the baton to the next generation, to the next person who was there to serve, and that is one of her great strengths.

CW: Absolutely. There is a fundamental sense in which the age of Occupy is the age of Ella Baker. Even given the deep contributions of the legacies of Douglass and King—we could add Malcolm; we certainly would add Du Bois as well—for Ella Baker, you know, when you radically call into question the distinction between mental and manual labor, then that frees you up to engage in forms of activities in the movement that allow for a natural flow, from caring for the homeless, cooking food for the elderly, and reading Gramsci on what it means to be an organic intellectual all in the same afternoon, because these are all just functions of a freedom fighter, functions of an organic, catalytic figure, where the intellectual is not somehow either isolated or elevated and therefore distinct from the manual, tactile, touch, hands-on-activity.

You know, when I talked about Ella's democratic existentialism, it is relevant to me in terms of your point on narcissism and charismatic leaders, because anyone who is a long-distance freedom fighter has to have a tremendous sense of self-confidence, and the real challenge is how do you have this tremendous sense of self-confidence when you are being targeted by assassination attempts or threats; when you are rebuked, scorned, lied about, or misunderstood. You need self-confidence in order to keep going in a community and a network, but how do you hold on to self-confidence without sliding into self-indulgence? The only weapon against narcissism is a belief in self and a greater cause than the self that is severed from an obsession with self as some grand messianic gift to the world. And I think you could see elements of this in the other figures that we talked about: Douglass and King and Du Bois had unbelievable self-confidence, and at their best, they are Ella Baker–like; at their worst, they are narcissists. And of course, this is a struggle in the human soul in each and every one of us. But the major weapon against narcissism for me is a kind of spirituality or a spiritual strength that accents, on the one hand, gratitude—what it means to be part of a long tradition that has produced you and allowed you to have the self-confidence—because self-confidence doesn't drop down from the sky; it is cultivated over many, many years owing to earlier people, antecedent figures who had the same kind of self-confidence—so gratitude on the one hand, as a kind of democratic piety in that sense, if piety is understood as the debts you owe to those who came before tied to the tradition and community and legacy of struggle, and on the other hand, there is an indescribable joy in serving others. This joy in serving others is qualitatively different than pleasure in leading others.

CHB: And a third factor in combatting narcissism may be the belief in the cause, or do you take that for granted?

CW: That's true, the depth of your commitment to the cause. And that is, I think, very important, because when you really get at the complicated core or the mediated essence of Ella Baker, it really has so much to do with this kind of democratic gratitude of being in a tradition of struggle, of being an agent of change and transmitter to the younger generation, which allows you to make a Pascalian leap in belief in the capacities of everyday people, because it's a kind of leap of faith that you are having in their capacity to cultivate themselves. You

don't need messianic leadership; you don't need a revolutionary party; you don't need professionals and experts coming in
from the academy and telling you x, y, and z. You are in conversation with them, but they don't need to have an elevated
status. But it's that democratic gratitude on the one hand, and
it is that deep spirituality that actually I think was rooted initially in Baker's early Black Baptist experiences and the model
of her blessed mother, and then the depth of her belief, in the
cause, what she calls the cause of humanity.

CHB: Indeed, it wasn't just a particular cause, as important as the
civil rights movement she had actually worked for was to
her—she was in the NAACP for some twenty years. She said
explicitly that she worked for so many organizations and campaigns, more than thirty, I think, but in truth, she said, she
worked for a movement that is greater than all these particular struggles.[10]

CW: It would be wonderful if one were to meet members of a progressive organization and you asked them who do you work
for and they would say not the organization, whatever it is,
but I'm working for the freedom of human beings around the
world; I'm working for the cause; I'm working for justice, and
this organization is a means toward that end, this organization
is a vehicle or conduit through which my commitment to the
cause for humanity, the cause for social justice, the cause for
human dignity, beginning with poor and working people and
those Frantz Fanon called the wretched of the earth. She always kept that in mind. So even when it comes to the kind of
organizational chauvinism—organizations clash because they
are trying to gain access to a certain kind of turf on a terrain—she would look at that and say, "Oh, you are missing the
point." SCLC people wanted to know how she could make
that move from interim executive director of SCLC—before
Wyatt Tee Walker was to take it over in 1960—how she could
make that move so smoothly from SCLC to SNCC, when
the tension between SCLC and SNCC was so intense. She
is the only one who carries over and becomes a hero for the

young people. She's already an older person; the young people trusted her.

CHB: She never attempted to tell them to do it her way, but she
listened and engaged in what you would call, I assume, a Socratic dialogue.

CW: Oh, absolutely, a Socratic dialogue in the deepest sense. I'll
never forget Bob Moses recalling one of the meetings where it
was clear that SNCC was collapsing. It was right near the end,
very intense conversations, and Ella Baker was sitting there.
You could just see the internal pain, and more and more, the
young people were looking toward her to intervene to save and
rescue the organization. And she just sat there and listened,
and afterward people were saying like, "Damn, if Martin and
the others had been there, they would have come to our rescue. Can't you see this is the only way? We need this almost
Hobbesian sovereign, you know what I mean, to help impose
some order, so we can sustain an organization that we worked
so hard for. We don't understand your silence." And she said,
"It's up to you. It's up to you all. You all got to work it out. I
am just one voice." And of course, someone said, "We want
to hear that one voice!" Sometimes, you know—Bob Moses is
like this, too—sometimes you just wonder whether they could
be too reticent and too reluctant to speak. Their democratic
humility is never false, but their democratic receptivity could
be more balanced with bold democratic voicing.

CHB: She was convinced that if a movement cannot find a way from
within the group to go on, then it is no longer relevant. It
has to be replaced. It might have had its time, done its work.
And when she moved from SCLC to SNCC, it was in part, I
think, because she was frustrated, owing to what you talked
about earlier about hierarchy and the male chauvinism, which,
for example, never allowed her to have this post of executive
director fully. It was always interim. She showed that she could
do it, but she was a woman, so it was not acceptable to the
male-dominated group at that time. So she moved, because

she had more confidence in the radical thinking of the young, and she thought it was needed at that moment. Now, within SNCC, there were different developments, and I think at one point—it may have been earlier in their development than the moment you talked about—two groups within SNCC fought each other, and at that point she tried to reach a compromise with this idea: let's have two strains; let's have two subgroups that follow their agenda, and let's see how far this takes us. And it was accepted at the time, but that was probably already foreshadowing a conflict within the group, and she would have been the last one to fight for something that she thought, "Well, if it can't sustain itself, it is not worth fighting for. It has to be replaced. This is what a revolutionary process is about."

CW: And she understood it so very, very well. Again, that has something to do with the kind of revolutionary patience that she had which I am associating also with this radical democratic receptivity that Romand Coles has talked about with such insight. You know, we do have to pay tribute in so many ways to Joanne Grant and Barbara Ransby and Romand Coles and others who really have not just thought through and theorized but thrown their hearts and minds and souls into the radical democratic praxis of Ella Baker.[11] Because on the one hand, she seemed to be rather reluctant to write a book about what she was doing, or write a memoir about her life, all of those things, in some ways mitigating against her commitment to radical democratic praxis, and yet we know there was always a theoretical dimension to it,[12] because she was just so brilliant; she was so reflective, introspective, and spiritual all at the same time.

CHB: To come back to one of your points as to education and how it might work when you try to educate a group not by preaching, not by lecturing from top to bottom, but by engaging in a dialogue—it takes a long time to begin with.

CW: Absolutely. I think that the major limitation of Ella Baker's global historical work and witness is the tremendous clash

between democratic time and market time. With the commodification of cultures around the world, most of us, if not
all of us, live in market time, even if we are on the margins of
the larger imperial system of our day. And market time is fast;
it's quick; it's push-button; it's 24/7 cycles of media. Whereas
democratic time, which has to do with the kind of organizing
and mobilizing Baker was doing, requires a long revolution,
in the language of the great Raymond Williams.[13] And it's
a long memory, in the language of Mary Frances Berry and
John Blassingame, who wrote that wonderful book together,
Long Memory.[14] So, you get a long revolution, a long memory,
a long struggle within democratic time; in market time: quick,
quick, quick, quick, quick. And the charismatic leadership is
very much tied to market time. It's fast, you see. You want
to get the cameras to see those precious kids get mistreated
in Birmingham, boom, flash. It's all around the world, quick,
quick, quick. Congress has to do something; the president has
responded, telephone calls. And Martin knew that he had to
live in some way between times, right on the thin edge between democratic and market time. But that slow, bottom-up,
democratic organizing that Ella talked about has always been
associated with some of the best social movements.

For example, Saul Alinsky, who in some ways we associate these days with the Industrial Areas Foundation of my
dear brother Ernesto Cortés[15]—they have been at this form
of organizing in democratic time for thirty years, and you end
up with some elected officials and local groups,[16] two elected
city councilmen, and people say, "Damn, a whole generation
and you got a union in place." And of course, they have done
amazing things in terms of raising consciousness, because it's
not just reflected in the electoral process. But from a market
perspective, of course, you might say, "Eh, that's all you come
up with in twenty-five years? When we got all these babies
who die, we got all these struggles going on, and that's the
best we can do?" And I think that's the challenge, maybe limitation is too strong a word, but it's a real challenge for the
genius of Ella Baker.

CHB: And even more so today than in her time, because of the speed.

CW: Yes, hyper-capitalism, absolutely.

CHB: So the question is, how can change be brought about with the powers that be? Should we, like anarchists, work locally and change the system on the level of the local community and go on from there, and change it radically at a particular place and in a particular moment and thus make at least a small difference, rather than battling and struggling in market time and being shot dead or defeated? The question becomes the more urgent when we look at what we are fighting for and against right now and compare it to the past, when Ella Baker—just as you and many others still do in the present—talked about poverty and civil rights.

CW: But I wonder—here my own view becomes more manifest and pressing—when you look at it from the perspective of the powers that be, what do they find most threatening? That's always a measure, you see. And they are threatened by any serious challenge to their oligarchic power, to their profit-driven economic system and their cultural forms of distraction that keep the masses pacified. And I think that in the long run, they are more threatened by Ella Baker's mode of engagement; in the short run, they are more threatened by Martin King's mode of engagement, because for the FBI and the CIA and other repressive apparatuses in the nation-state in which we live, that patience and that receptivity, you can keep track of that more easily, and you can infiltrate it quicker,[17] whereas if the people who don't have revolutionary consciousness but do have a love for one leader, they see that leader shot down and mistreated, they are more likely to rebel. Now, that's not revolutionary action; that's rebellion.[18] And given the constraints of the system, in which electoral politics is so much dominated by big money and so forth, it's the rebellions that have played a fundamental role in getting concessions from the powers that be, more so than the long-term organizing that's quiet on the margins, hardly visible. When you have two hundred cities going up in flames, the powers that be have to concede something. They could go fascist and say, "No concessions at all," or they can be moderate and say, "We have to give a little bit. We have to be open for the expansion of the middle class. We have to bring in a relatively privileged people from the working class: women, Black folk, brown folk, red folk, or whatever." This middle class of color is a *lumpen-bourgeoisie* beneath the wealthier white bourgeoisie.

But I do think that—this is the Chekhov in me, of course[19]—I think that the cycles of domination and the cycles of death and the cycles of dogmatism are so deeply entrenched in human history, that more than likely the best we can do is to break the cycle. And even what we call revolution, when you think you really have broken the cycle in, say, the Soviet Union, Cuba, or what have you, the same cycle comes right back in new clothing. The men are heroic against the white supremacist powers, but look what they're doing to the women, and the straights are heroic, but look what they are doing to the gay brothers and lesbian sisters and bisexuals and transsexuals and so forth. Or the elderly seem to be heroic, but look how they are demeaning the youth—these different kinds of cycles. And, so, I am not suggesting that there are no breakthroughs or progress or betterment or amelioration, but Ella Baker is most relevant because she tells a fundamental truth about the need for democratic organizing. King becomes highly relevant in our time, less relevant than Ella in regard to democratic leadership. Ella Baker and Fannie Lou Hamer stand above Martin Luther King in their democratic existentialism; their democratic leadership and horizontal organization stand above his messianic leadership and hierarchical organization. All three have a love supreme for the people that is so visible, that cannot be denied. King's organizing fits well with market time and his murder generated massive outrage, and you end up with a real rupture in the cycle. It's not a change in the system, but it's a rupture in the cycle, and the powers that be have to make some concessions, you see. But deep democratic revolution requires the democratic existentialism of Ella Baker and Fannie Lou Hamer.

CHB: Back to the kind of organizing Baker practiced. I think one could distinguish even within her work the very patient, slow-pace education of groups and what follows from that and what she herself, I think, saw as the need for a more radical pushing of groups. That's why, to go back to that, she joined the youth and cofounded SNCC, because she hoped that, from that more radical group, less bourgeois, less concerned with respectability, and more radical in a broad sense, that something like a rupture might result, even out of a group. I think that was her hope. So she tries to do both, patient grassroots organizing and speeding up the process through work with radical groups, which I think is particularly difficult. And one would have to ask oneself how far she got, but do you see the possibility of radicalizing groups, too, so that they work like charismatic leaders?

CW: Yes. You see, in my own view, that kind of crucial radicalizing of the group toward a more revolutionary consciousness becomes one of the essential elements in the rebellion. That is to say, when the rupture takes place and the system must just stop and respond rather than just keep going on and trying to deny the suffering of the people who are revolting. Now, whether in the end that generates the kind of system change that she wanted and I want, I don't know. But in my more Chekhovian thinking, I can see not so much a cycle but a spiralling, where these systems of domination and oligarchies reemerge and the hierarchies reemerge, the anti-democratic forms reemerge, and that revolutionary consciousness is this deep democratic consciousness suspicious of those hierarchies, suspicious of those oligarchies, and so on.

Here Clausewitz's philosophy of war[20] plays an important role for me—not in a moral sense but a crass political sense, in terms of just how cruel the struggle for power is and how gangster-like these thugs are who run things at the very, very top, who would kill anybody and do anything to reproduce their power. You see, you look at the number of times Martin went to jail, while Ella hardly ever went to jail—stark contrast! And when you talk about rupture, you're talking about a threefold moment of, first, hitting the streets—and Ella is already in the streets—and, second, being willing to go to jail, and, third, being willing to be killed. If you don't have those three elements, you don't have a movement. That is to say, you have to have people who are willing to take that kind of risk, and you need the blood of those martyrs to help fertilize the movement, which is not to view those martyrs as instruments, because they are still human beings, but that's the historical process. That's how bloody it is. It is just a fact. It can't be denied. When you juxtapose Ella Baker to Martin King, you see, one of the reasons why Martin's death generated the rebellions it did was because all three of those moments were satisfied and in a way in which they were not satisfied for Ella. Now, that's partly again a matter of both gender and theory. She called him the "Great One" and had her powerful critiques, but she never denied his deep love for the people, you see, just like she had that deep love for the people, as everybody who knew her, like Bernice Reagon, one of the great artists of the movement,[21] would say over and over again. But that's an interesting contrast when you think about it.

CHB: But I still wonder about certain aspects of that contrast. Now, Ella Baker could not have been the charismatic leader,[22] so the group did not feel represented by her. No one could have that identifying moment one had with King. So when you say this is threefold—you go to the street, you go to jail, and you get killed—she would not have gotten killed; it was not very likely. But does that really mean that revolt can only happen with the model of the charismatic leader? If we look again at the Occupy movement today, people go to the street; they are willing to go to jail; they are even willing to die. But there is no charismatic figure, and yet you have these three moments, or would you still make a distinction as to their effectiveness?

CW: That's an interesting question. You see, I think that when you satisfy all three of those moments in light of the Ella Baker model, I am not so sure that the death or deaths that take place could have the same galvanizing effect as the death of a highly charismatic, highly visible figure who touched the hearts, minds, and souls of people, you see. And because precious ordinary people are in a condition of catastrophe and wrestling with desperation, for them to break out of a mindset that is deferential to the powers that be, it is only a love that they have for someone they identified with, who was out there speaking on their behalf, that has the power to move them to rebellion.

CHB: It's very interesting, because both models work with the insight that it is not enough to understand a problem and then act politically; you need the emotional involvement. In the first model, we have the love toward a leader that you identify with and who acts for you. Now, Ella Baker would have said, "This is not my model, because it harms the potential activity of the group, of the masses, if they delegate. So I want the other model. What then is my means of arousing emotion? It is personal connections. People have to interconnect." And, again, you can say, and rightly so, it is so slow; it takes time to bring this process to a point that it becomes efficient. But to her it was the emotional binding of people that she would say is needed, but it works differently and, again, slower, not in market time.

CW: Exactly. I think, in the end, we have to say that there should be no discussion of Martin Luther King Jr. without Ella Baker, which is to say they are complementary. These two figures, voices, tendencies in the Black freedom movement, and particularly in the human freedom movement in general, they say something to young people these days in the age of Obama. See, Obama ends up being the worst example of messianic leadership, captured by a vicious system that is oligarchic domestically and imperialistic globally and uses the resonances of this precious freedom struggle as a way of legitimating himself in the eyes of both the Black people and the mainstream Americans, and acting as if as community organizer he has some connection to Ella Baker, which is absurd and ludicrous in light of him running this oligarchic system and being so proud of heading the killing machine of US imperial powers. So that when young people—who now find themselves in an even more desperate situation given the present crisis—think about the legacy of Martin King and the legacy of Ella Baker in the age of Obama, it compounds the misunderstandings and misconstructions, and sabotages the intellectual clarity and political will necessary to create the kind of change we need. To use jazz metaphors, what we need would be the expression and articulation of different tempos and different vibrations and different actions and different witnesses, so it's antiphonal; it's call-and-response, and in the call-and-response, there are Ella Baker–like voices tied to various kinds of deep democratic witnesses that have to do with everyday people organizing themselves. And then you've got the Martin-like voices that are charismatic, which are very much tied to a certain kind of messianic leadership, which must be called into question, which must be democratized, which must be de-patriarchalized. And yet they are part of this jazz combo.[23]

CнB: But it means we need to turn our attention to Ella Baker, because historically she has had—and understandably so, given the strong effect of charismatic leaders—she has had much less attention in the historical reception of the movement.

CW: Yes. Absolutely. And again, one of the ironies—I never met Ella Baker, but I recall taking my class down to the film *Fundi* when I was at Union Theological Seminary thirty years ago.[24] I was overwhelmed by it. Oh I was overwhelmed by it. It hit me so hard, because I just so much resonated with Ella. I could see Curtis Mayfield in her; I could see Bessie Smith in her; I could see the great gospel artist Shirley Caesar in her; I could see Aretha Franklin in her. And nothing moves me more than that level of artistic engagement with suffering and transfiguring it into vision and witness. I said to myself, "Ella Baker is one of the most charismatic figures I've seen on film, and yet she is fighting against charisma"; you know what I mean. So, what happens is, her critique of charisma goes hand in hand with an enactment of a kind of quiet, unassuming charisma, which swept me away.

Now, it could be that I am just tied to charisma in various forms, but I do think that you get ordinary people like Louis Armstrong; this brother is charismatic—and a genius—to the core. Now, with Ella Baker, you see it in the way she interacts. You look in her eyes and you get a sense of how she is reading people when she is silent that has its own kind of charisma, you know. Maybe it's a charisma to be deployed in democratic time in the service of the self-organization of everyday people. Martin's charisma is more usable in a market time, though it is just as genuine as Ella's charisma. I think, in the end, Ella's is probably closer to my own soul, but in terms of how you deal with this vicious system in which we find ourselves, you can see why Martin's love, which is continuous with Ella's love, becomes indispensable, and his death is nothing but an extension of his love. I mean, Martin's death is nothing but the love-ethic at work, just as Ella's long-distance struggles are extensions of a love-ethic at work, and both of them encountered that love-ethic in the Black family, initially in the Black church. And yet both, in the end, were scandalized by the Black church, which is to say they both end up on the margins of it, even as they are products of it. For brother Martin and sister Ella, it is a privilege to live and die for everyday people.

CHB: But for reasons that have nothing to do with their spirituality but rather with their outspoken political opinions in terms of how, for example, they use the word *socialism*.[25]

CW: That's right. Explicitly, publicly.

CHB: Yes, and the demand for the change of the system—they re-
semble each other very much in what they demand, certainly
the later King and, well, maybe even the early Baker,[26] but
certainly the later King.

CW: That's very true. Now, the speech that she gave in defense
of Puerto Rican independence in Madison Square Garden is
something that the film *Fundi* and other scholars have made
much of, and there she engages in explicit talk about colonialism, imperialism, some things that she had always talked about
but that now were more publicly projected. And to be publicly
associated with a Puerto Rican independence movement—of
the great Pedro Albizu Campos and Lolita Lebrón—that was
perceived to be an extension of the kind of terrorist attack on
the US Congress.[27] You know, for anybody, let alone a Black
woman, to be associated with that kind of movement, which
in the eyes of the public was nothing but crude terrorism, required a level of courage, which brings us back to that willingness to take a risk even in her own quiet—and in this case, not
so quiet—way, because she was quite eloquent in her speech
in front of thousands of people in Madison Square Garden.
Absolutely. Absolutely.

Malcolm X, 1964

CHAPTER FIVE

Revolutionary Fire

MALCOLM X

We agreed that a conversation about Malcolm X was a must, although he is undoubtedly the most controversial of the Black prophetic figures. Among too many white Americans he is often seen as a proponent of reversed racism, if not of hatred and violence. But even the Black community has been divided in assessing his status as a political leader. While the working poor respected his eloquence and honesty, and the "old" middle class was horrified, the "new" lower-middle class, especially students, greatly admired his rhetoric and sincerity. In part, the controversy is due to the continuous juxtaposition between Malcolm X and Martin Luther King Jr., a false opposition that is based on one-sided public images and that has led to a sanitized Martin and a demonized Malcolm, a gross mistake that overlooks what they share in common and how much they overlap.

In the fall of 2012, Occupy Wall Street was evicted from public spaces in a concerted action by law enforcement all over the United States, from New York City to Oakland. When we met in January 2013 for our dialogue on Malcolm X, it seemed to be the perfect time to discuss his revolutionary fire and its legacy among the younger generation.

CHRISTA BUSCHENDORF: You have repeatedly written about Malcolm X. In *Prophesy Deliverance!*, for example, you positioned Malcolm X as "the transitional figure who stands between King and the Black Marxists."[1] In your essay "Malcolm X and

Black Rage," you compared him with both his mentor Elijah Muhammad and Martin Luther King Jr., claiming that "Malcolm X articulated black rage in a manner unprecedented in American history. His style of communicating this rage bespoke a boiling urgency and an audacious sincerity." And you went on to state: "His profound commitment to affirm black humanity at any cost and his tremendous courage to accent the hypocrisy of American society made Malcolm X the prophet of black rage—then and now."[2] As to Malcolm X's cultural and political influence on yourself and Black fellow students at Harvard, you stressed in our dialogue on Martin King his attraction in terms of his style, his swagger, in contrast to the much revered, but to the youth less appealing, respectable King. And you pointed out that you would identify with Malcolm X's political vision rather than listening to the voice of the "Great Man who died for us,"[3] a viewpoint, as you add, that was to shift in the next decade. In fact, more recently you seem to have been highlighting the relevance of King. How then would you assess the impact of Malcolm X on African American political struggle and your own fight for justice and freedom today?

CORNEL WEST: Malcolm X is the great figure of revolutionary *parrhesia* in the Black prophetic tradition. The term *parrhesia* goes back to line 24A of Plato's *Apology*, where Socrates says, the cause of my unpopularity was my *parrhesia*, my fearless speech, my frank speech, my plain speech, my unintimidated speech. Malcolm is unique among the figures in the prophetic tradition to the degree to which he was willing to engage in unintimidated speech in public about white supremacy. We have had a number of Black figures who have done that in the Black context, but not in public the way Malcolm did. In that sense, he represents the standard. He reminds me of jazz musicians like Charles Mingus, who are always tied to the underdog, always looking at the world from below, but speaking so clearly.

Now what was he saying? Brother Malcolm begins where Marcus Garvey[4] left off, which is to say he represents a Black Nationalist tradition. But he is a revolutionary within that Black Nationalist tradition. And, like Garvey, he begins with the idea that the world has made being Black a crime—I intend to make it a virtue. White supremacy had told Black people that Black history is a curse, Black hope is a joke, and Black freedom is a pipe-dream, and you are locked in; you are trapped in a white-supremacist maze or labyrinth, and there is no way out. And Marcus Garvey, Elijah Muhammad, and the others came along and said: "The Negro is unafraid." So what Malcolm does is, he begins with this notion of the world making being Black a crime. He responds to this condition of being cursed and trapped by courageously exemplifying what it is and means to say: "I am unafraid. I will speak my mind." He is able to do so because of the love of Elijah Muhammad. Malcolm Little was a gangster, a street-gangster and hustler. And in the cell in Massachusetts,[5] he feels the love of the Honorable Elijah Muhammad—who is, of course, often viewed as a hater because he did believe that white people were devils, and he is wrong about that.[6] But Elijah Muhammad had a deep love of Black people, and he loved Malcolm Little into giving him the self-confidence to become Malcolm X.

Now, back to Garvey. Garvey also said that as long as Black people live in America, most of them will live lives of ruin and disaster, especially the poor and working class. Malcolm took that very seriously. When he looked at Black life in America, he saw wasted potential; he saw unrealized aims; he saw ruin and disaster. He saw forms of self-hatred and self-destruction running amok. So he is building on this Black Nationalist tradition that says, "America you have a weak will to justice when it comes to Black people and poor people. America, we have no disappointment in you because we have no expectations of you. You have no soul, you have no conscience when it comes to the plight of Black people, either enslaved, Jim Crowed, ghettoized, hated, despised, lynched, subjugated, whatever." This Black rage, viewed through the narrow lens of the American mainstream as Black revenge, sits at the center of Malcolm's soul. And there is just no one like him in terms of having the courage to risk life and limb to speak such painful—not just unsettling in the Socratic sense, but painful—truths about America, truths that are so difficult to come to terms with that they seem to be too much for the country. It's unbearable for the country to really look at all the rape, the violation, and the exploitation of Black people over four hundred years. It echoes Patrice Lumumba, when he told the king of the former Belgian Congo: "We shall never forget these scars, no matter how much reconciliation, no matter how much integration even, we shall never forget these scars."[7] That's Malcolm.

It reminds me of Faulkner when he says: "Memory believes before knowing remembers."[8] Memory of scars, memory of lynching, memory of being despised and spit on, rebuked and scorned—it's not a victim's mentality, as my right-wing brothers and sisters would put it, because there is and ought to be Jewish memory of pogroms, Jewish memory of Shoah and Holocaust; there is and ought to be Indigenous peoples' memory of dispossession of land and genocidal attack. It is that fundamental role of memory that Malcolm always invoked.[9] And to think that someone in a brief twelve-and-a-half years of his ministry could have had this kind of impact at the level of psyche and spirit is unique in modern history. Malcolm was a revolutionary prophet in speech and in spirit, and I think we need to hear him now as much as we need to hear Martin and Ella and Du Bois.

CHB: Malcolm X said that "the best thing that a person can be is sincere."[10] I think his sincerity is something that also made him so convincing to Blacks when they listened to him, because it was clear he would not put on a show, he would not engage in any sweet talk, but he would stand for what he presented to them.

CW: That's exactly right. The young hip-hop generation talks about "keeping it real." Malcolm was as real as it gets. James Brown talks about "make it funky." Malcolm would never deodorize his discourse; it was always: "Bring in the funk, bring in the truth, bring in the reality." There is a fundamental sense in which Malcolm specialized in de-niggerizing Negroes. He took the nigger out of them. To niggerize a people is to make them afraid and ashamed and scared and intimidated, so that they are deferential to the powers that be. They scratch when it doesn't itch; they laugh when it ain't funny. They wear the mask, as Paul Laurence Dunbar wrote in his great poem.[11] And Malcolm came along and said, "No. I will take that nigger out of you. I'm gonna take it out of you." There is a wonderful motto on Elijah Muhammad's newspaper, founded by Malcolm X: "Islam dignifies." A niggerized people must be dignified. And if they are dignified in the right way and take that nigger out of themselves, they can stand up like human beings, with a steeliness in their backs and a heartiness in their hearts and a fortitude in their soul that allows them to think for themselves and work for themselves in the name of a self-respect and self-determination that was required if Black freedom was not to be a pipe dream, if Black history was not to be a curse, if Black hope was not to be a joke, and if being Black was not to be a crime.

CHB: It is an interesting strategy, if you think of the relation between the established who define you as an outsider and how difficult it is to get out of the range of the defining power. So what do you do? You reach out to another tradition, in Malcolm X's case, Islam, and that tradition gives you the possibility of a different self-definition in turn. But is there not at the same time a certain problem, if you then operate within a tradition that is not the common one within the Black community?

CW: Absolutely. Because you don't have any roots that resonate deeply in the culture of the people that you are speaking to. Islam did not have any deep roots in the history of Black people the way Christianity did. That's one of the reasons why Marcus Garvey always remained a Christian. His father, Marcus Sr., was very isolated but a great man; he always stood straight in Jamaica. His mother was Methodist. Garvey himself allowed for Muslims, atheists, different kinds of Christians to constitute his movement. But he had that deep Christian sensibility, whereas Malcolm, coming out of Elijah, went radically against the grain. He would identify with Christians like Nat Turner and John Brown and some of the great insurrectionists, or even the Deacons for Defense, who had their guns to defend themselves in North Carolina, with Robert Williams that influenced the Black Panther Party later on.[12] They were Christians coming out of the churches, but Malcolm, Elijah, they were starting something that was new in the States.

CHB: But not central.

CW: That's right. You know I have had wonderful dialogues with my dear brother Minister Louis Farrakhan, and I would push him on the issues of patriarchy and homophobia, anti-Semitism, and he always pushed me in his own powerful way.[13] But I used to tell him that the Nation of Islam could never become a mass movement among Black people because there is no music in their ritual. And music has really been the fundamental means by which Black people have been able to preserve sanity and dignity and, at our best, integrity. And to have no music in your ritual is an over-reaction against what Elijah Muhammad understood to be the naïve emotionalism of many Black churches. We should remember that Elijah Muhammad was Reverend Elijah Poole in the Baptist church before he was a Muslim, so he had his own Black Baptist roots, as it were. But he wanted to look outside to get a different vantage point. Christianity was, in the view of Elijah Muhammad and Malcolm X, a tool of the white man; it was an extension of white supremacy. You had the white Jesus looking like Michelangelo's uncle on the wall, rather than the Palestinian Jew that he was with a swarthy complexion and linked to Northern Africa as well as the Middle East. And they were right about that. Christianity had been whitewashed and Europeanized in a fundamental way, and there was no doubt that the white supremacy in the Christianity that the slaves appropriated was pervasive. Yet the prophetic tradition within the Christian context was able to listen, to resonate with much of what Malcolm X was talking about, even as we remained Christian. The theological genius of James Cone is the best example of the Christian response to Malcolm.[14]

CHB: I think, in terms of tactics, Malcolm X was so clever as to combine Muslim belief and Christian belief, in that in his speeches he would use Christian stories from the Bible, which were more familiar to his audience.

CW: Absolutely. And I think both the Honorable Elijah Muhammad and Malcolm X always looked at the world from below, echoes of the twenty-fifth chapter of Matthew: What you do for the least of these—the prisoner, the poor, the stranger, the widow, the fatherless, the motherless, the weak, the vulnerable—has lasting value. Even as Black Muslims, they could resonate with that theme, so they invoked Hebrew prophets, Isaiah, Amos; they invoked Jesus, emphasizing that sense of coming from below, looking at the world from below. One of my favorite formulations of Malcolm X is the epigraph in my chapter "The Crisis of Black Leadership" in *Race Matters*, where he tells the white mainstream: "You all say you respect me. If you can't respect the brother and sister on the block, the Black brother and sister on the block, then you don't really respect me."[15] And that's missing these days among most Black leaders. They think they are respected in some isolated, individualistic way as a Black person, and yet their second cousin is despised and held in contempt by the same white people or white establishment that respects them. And Malcolm says: "Wait a minute, this is a contradiction. Something wrong is going on here. Of course, we are individuals. We understand that. But the ways in which you separate me from my brother and sister on the block is just a way of viewing me as exceptional, incorporating me and still turning your eye or being indifferent toward my folk, my own family, community, slice of humanity." Malcolm would never, ever sell out to the powers that be. There would never be enough money, position, power, whatever that would allow him to violate his integrity and what I would call his magnanimity. And that's what makes Malcolm stand out these days, because everybody is up for sale, everything is up for sale. And if Malcolm were around and looked and saw all of these folk who have sold out he'd say: "I didn't know there was such a mass movement of house Negroes."

Who would have thought that the expansion of the Black middle class would lead toward a re-niggerization of Black professionals, because that is really what you have. You have Black professionals who have big money, a lot of prosperity, but are still scared, intimidated, have low self-respect, don't take a stand, don't want to tell the truth about the situation, let alone say, "If you don't respect the brother and sister on the block, the ones you send into prison, then you don't respect me." All they want is position, status, and cash. You see, Malcolm is too much of a challenge to them. That's another reason why we need him, because he shakes us, doesn't allow us to sell out in that way.

CHB: I'd like to come back to the point you make as to the importance of music. As far as I know, Malcolm X—at least during the phase when he was a member of the Nation of Islam—would not often refer to music or use musical metaphors, probably owing to the restrictions imposed by the leaders. And yet, one associates him in his appearance, in his rhetoric with music, with the tradition of jazz, especially.

CW: Malcolm was music in motion; he was Black music in motion; he was jazz in motion, and, of course, jazz has improvisation, swing, and the blues, as brother Wynton Marsalis says, those three fundamental elements. Malcolm could be improvisational; he could be so lyrical and so funny all at the same time, and in the next minute shift and be serious and push you against the wall. The way he spoke had a swing to it, had a rhythm to it; it was a call and response with the audience that you get with jazz musicians. And he was the blues. Blues is associated with catastrophe, and Malcolm would say over and over again: "You are not going to get something detached and disinterested from anybody who is sitting on the stove and the stove is burning their behind, no, they're going to holler out, they are going to respond deeply and viscerally."[16] He never forgot the Black folk on the stove. He never forgot the prison system: Black folk on the stove. Massive unemployment: Black folk on the stove. Indecent housing: Black folk on the stove. Inadequate healthcare: Black folk on the stove. And from the very beginning, from slavery to Jim Crow, so that the sense of catastrophe, the sense of emergency, the sense of urgency, the sense of needing to get it out, to cry out, to shout, somehow allowed that fire inside of his bones to be expressed with power and with vision. He never lost that. He never, ever lost that. The great Amiri Baraka has the same fire—literary genius, spiritual warrior, a Black revolutionary who never sold out. And that's so rare these days.

When you think about the legacy of Malcolm, you think, for example, of the great Reverend Walter Newton of Monroe, Louisiana, pastor of Bethel Baptist church.[17] He was full of fire. His son, Huey Newton, was full of fire, too. Yes, Huey was a preacher's kid. Walter was just like Malcolm's father, he was known to be always demonstrating, wouldn't allow his wife to work in the white households, would stand in front of the police telling them the truth. That's what Huey was exposed to when he was young. And Huey understood Malcolm's spirit. And so did the Black Panther Party, Bobby Seale,[18] Ericka Huggins,[19] and so many others. They understood Malcolm's spirit. The same is true of Amiri Baraka. Malcolm changed that brother's life from Le Roi Jones to Amiri Baraka.[20] There was something in Malcolm's sincerity, something in his integrity and his willingness to live and die that hit people so. He hit me hard too. Malcolm means the world to me, because he was someone with a deep love for people, in his case, especially, a love for Black people, and a willingness to speak the truth knowing that he would be crucified, knowing he would be demonized, knowing that he would be misunderstood, misconceived and yet continuing on in the Black context as well as the larger national and international context. And for someone to say I'm gonna bring the US government before the United Nations for the violation of human rights[21]—wow. Lord, Lord, that's my kind of brother!

CHB: I think, in a way, you break his message down to a core that would then also allow you to make the connection with the other figures, whereas in public discourse Malcolm X is usually separated from them owing to his demonization. In fact, the way you talked about why he is so important to you, you might even exchange the name and put in Martin Luther King, and there would be so many resonances, despite the differences with regard to certain issues.

CW: That's true. I think James Cone's great book on Martin and Malcolm is still the best juxtaposition we have.[22] He understands that the two go hand in hand. You can't talk about the one without the other. As for me, Malcolm has a revolutionary fire that Martin didn't have; Martin has a moral fire from the very beginning that Malcolm didn't get until later. Malcolm's love for Black people is so strong and so intense that early on it leads him to call white folk devils and give up on them, and I think he is wrong about that. Martin never did that, but Martin doesn't have the revolutionary fire that Malcolm had until the very end of his life. And by revolutionary fire I mean understanding the system under which we live, the capitalistic system, the imperial tentacles, the American empire, the disregard for life, the willingness to violate law, be it international law or domestic law. Malcolm understood that from very early on, and it hit Martin so hard that he does become a revolutionary in his own moral way later in his short life, whereas Malcolm had the revolutionary fire so early in life. It's just that he had to continually grow into his analysis of the system, when he embraces critiques of imperialism and capitalism, and he just tells the truth: "It looks like vultures to me."[23] He just lays it out.

Now, Malcolm wasn't talking that way in the 1950s, because he hadn't been exposed to it. But he never allows the analysis of the system to override or displace his understanding of the psyches, the souls, and the culture of Black people. You have to hold both at the same time, your analysis of the system—capitalism, imperialism, patriarchy, homophobia, these days, the ecological catastrophe owing to the capitalist domination—but at the same time, the need for an unleashing of the fire of the soul and an acknowledgment of the power of the spirit that fortifies us in order to fight. You can't be a warrior or a soldier without having your spirit intact, without having your sense of self-respect, self-regard, and self-esteem intact, and Malcolm always understood this fundamental truth.

CHB: The fact that he would keep the systemic analysis in the background was in part probably due to the restrictions of the Nation of Islam in terms of political engagement. He was not supposed—

CW: To be too politically involved. I hear what you are saying. The thing is, Elijah Muhammad did give Malcolm more freedom than he gave the other ministers, partly because Malcolm was just so charismatic, attracting so much attention. But at the same time, it's also true that Elijah Muhammad's own programs were not revolutionary programs at all—despite their powerful impact on many Black people, especially young Black men.

CHB: Malcolm stood out in that regard. But he becomes more politicized, consciously speaking about the system, about capitalism, later, after his break with Elijah Muhammad. What is interesting, though, in your talking about Malcolm is that you don't seem to rely on that break in your interpretation. As important as the change in Malcolm is—and I am sure you agree that it is—what you are saying is that there is a continuity that we must not overlook.

CW: I think that Malcolm X's break with Elijah Muhammad and
      the Nation of Islam was primarily driven by his deep love for
      Black people, and he did not see the Nation of Islam speak-
      ing to the suffering of Black people in the way that he would
      have liked. Now, we know there is a personal issue in terms
      of Elijah Muhammad's relations with women and so forth,
      but politically and ideologically, Malcolm was driven into a
      more radical direction because he could not accept some of
      the theology of the Nation of Islam, that part that was still
      waiting for the mother plane to arrive, waiting for the reign
      of the white man to come to an end, which was not princi-
      pally a matter of Black action but still divine action. So that
      even given Elijah Muhammad's critique of Christian pie-in-
      the-sky theology, he still had an otherworldly element in
      his Black Muslim theology. And Malcolm was just more and
      more talking about human action and collective agency and
      organization on the ground.

      I think it's impossible to understand the greatness of a
      Stokely Carmichael without understanding the impact of Mal-
      colm's talk about human agency and collective insurgency,[24]
      without any reference to any kind of otherworldly powers.
      By the time you get to the Black Panther movement, SNCC
      in its last stage, and then the League of Revolutionary Black
      Workers, Ken Cockrel, General Baker, Darryl Mitchell,[25] and
      others, you see Malcolm's legacy. Other legatees of Malcolm
      X today, like Mumia Abu-Jamal[26] and Assata Shakur,[27] grand
      figures that they are—most of them are in jail; they've been
      actually in jail for twenty, thirty years—were real warriors;
      those were the real soldiers, and the counterintelligence pro-
      gram of the FBI knew these were the ones to target.[28] Roger
      Wareham of the December 12 movement[29] went to jail for so
      many years; Elombe Brath, and H. Rap Brown[30]—these are
      the ones we don't really talk about because the system ran
      them down even though they are still holding on. And yet we
      need to take them very seriously.

      There are hundreds of political prisoners right now in
      America's jails who were so taken by Malcolm's spirit that they

became warriors, and the powers that be understood them as
warriors. They knew that a lot of these other middle-class
leaders were not warriors; they were professionals; they were
careerists. But these warriors had callings, and they have paid
an incalculable and immeasurable price in those cells. Many
changed their names; some became Muslims; they had that
same Malcolm X–like spirit. The grand artist and legendary
educator Haki Madhubuti was deeply influenced by Malcolm
X,[31] and Sonia Sanchez[32] and others on the female side. The
great Toni Morrison, she has got a Malcolm X spirit in her
sense of being an intellectual warrior, a kind of literary soldier, as it were, even given all of the white acceptance in the
establishments of our day, and I think Toni Morrison would
be the first to acknowledge the tremendous impact on her of
Malcolm's revolutionary sincerity and his revolutionary love
and his willingness to pay the ultimate price.

CHB: In regard to organization, Malcolm X was really not as important as others we have talked about in terms of organizing, although he did his own organizing once he was independent. He
founded two organizations, the Muslim Mosque Incorporated
and the Organization of Afro-American Unity. We have talked
about these prophetic activists in terms of organic intellectuals,
so in what sense does he fit into that Gramscian model?

CW: I think that Malcolm was indeed an organic intellectual,
which is to say, he was a countervailing force and a counter-
hegemonic voice against the powers that be. And by using all
of the various linguistic tools that touch people's souls and
hearts and minds and body simultaneously, his critiques and
visions connected with the people. During his life his major
weapons were his fierce intellect, undeniable sincerity, and
oral power of presentation. After his death his autobiography
emerges as another kind of intellectual weapon. There is a
sense in which Malcolm actually lives in a very powerful way
among large numbers of people through the autobiography,
even more than for people who saw him speak physically.

CHB: So the organizing itself would not be necessarily part of the organic intellectual?

CW: For Gramsci, the war of position includes raising the consciousness of people and motivating them to fight for justice. Malcolm specializes much more in these activities than in building and sustaining organizational structures.

CHB: Malcolm X once said if you inspire the people, if you bring them to the political sense, you don't have to worry any longer; they become active themselves.[33] So that would explain why he thought he could, through his rhetorical power, lead the path to a revolutionary spirit in the people.

CW: I think that's true. In that sense he sounds like Ella Baker. I think if Malcolm were to choose between a Luxemburgist versus a Leninist conception of organization, where a Luxemburgist would put much more stress on the radical consciousness arising among the people themselves, and the people themselves creating their own organization—the so-called spontaneity thesis, or more spontaneous forms of organization—versus Lenin, where you get professional revolutionaries who then go out and bring the masses inside of a vanguard party, then Malcolm would be highly suspicious of a Leninist orientation. He would be much closer to a Luxemburgist one.

   Just before he was shot, in New York in the Audubon Ballroom, Malcolm had planned on setting up his own mosque. He was a Sunni Muslim leader. When we think what it means to be a revolutionary Muslim in this day and age, when people are looking for ways in which Islam is compatible with democracy, compatible with progressive politics, compatible with revolutionary politics, Malcolm is a looming example of that. But he was going to be a Sunni Muslim clergyman with his own mosque, reaching out with his own organizations and programs for the poor. He would have relations with left wing-organizations, but he would not be a member of left-wing organizations. It's a fascinating development that could have taken place, that could have created a paradigmatic model of what it means to be a revolutionary Muslim in the way in which King at the end of his life becomes a revolutionary Christian, and both perspectives begin more and more to overlap. Their critiques of capitalism and imperialism led the FBI and the CIA to view them and their followers as the most fundamental and formidable threat to the status quo in the history of America. There would have been nothing like it, especially at a moment when so many of the white middle-class youth were responding against the draft, responding against the Vietnam War, upset deeply with Jim Crow in the South—all converging at the same time, Good God Almighty. You have such a fiery situation for social change; there is no doubt about it.

CHB: I think this is especially true for the US, because as we said in one of our other conversations, the Black Power movement had the difficulty of being too secular, not being able to stay in contact with Black masses who did not want to hear too secular a message.

CW: That's exactly right. But it's very interesting in our present moment, where there is a rising atheistic movement in the country. Now nearly 20 percent of Americans call themselves atheists,[34] and there are various atheistic clubs and atheistic groups in the Black community as well. Secularism is becoming more widespread, and it's a fascinating thing to see. Even as a Christian I think that a lot of this atheism is very healthy, because in many ways it is a rejection of the idolatry in the dominant churches; it's a rejection of the gods—small "g"—who are being worshipped in mainstream America and in mainstream Black America, and that kind of atheism is always healthy for prophetic religious people. It's healthy precisely because it allows people to freely think for themselves and engage in wholesale rejection of forms of idolatry, and, you see, the prophetic is predicated on critiques of idolatry. It is true that my atheistic brothers and sisters do not accept conceptions of God linked to love and justice as I do. But the atheistic movement itself can be one of the carriers of the prophetic tradition in its rejections of forms of idolatry that I find very healthy.

And we haven't had enough conversation about this in the country, let alone in Black America. You think of somebody like Bill Maher, my dear brother, who has played such an important role in giving me tremendous exposure around the country and the world in his TV shows, who is a proud atheist, a progressive atheist whose prophetic witness is undeniable. We could give many other examples in terms of popular culture; we have always had a number of prophetic atheists in the academy. If my only options for belief in God were the idols of our market culture, I would be an atheist too. But the Black prophetic tradition that produced me provides rich views of God that yield moral integrity, spiritual fortitude, and political determination.

CHB: I am so surprised that you maintain secularism is on the move, whereas from a European perspective, my hunch would be that religiosity is on the move again, that there has been a major backlash as to the secular force of enlightened humanism in the last ten, twenty years or so.

CW: Things have changed; the numbers are now turning in a very different direction. The new data that just came out in 2012 reported that 18 percent of the country call themselves atheists.[35] It's a major leap; it's the highest in the history of the country. Brother Robert Ingersoll[36] and brother Clarence Darrow,[37] two exemplary atheists back in the 1910s and '20s, are coming back now with tremendous force. I love their prophetic witness.

Much of the force of Malcolm's prophetic witness is his critique of idolatry in America. And again, that coincidence of critiques of idolatry from prophetic secular figures and critiques of idolatry from prophetic revolutionary Islamic figures like Malcolm or prophetic revolutionary Christian figures like the later King is fascinating. Du Bois is secular in so many deep ways, yet as we saw, he has a profound spirituality. Frederick Douglass began as a religious man and seems to have ended up agnostic. Ella came out of the church, but she was agnostic, too, I think.

CHB: Well, I think all these prophetic figures saw what Christianity could do to the suppressed, namely to suppress them even more. It was a tool, as you said before, of white supremacy. So there was always the ambivalence about the dangers of the church as an oppressive institution on the one hand, and on the other hand, the benefits of religion that might carry you on in your struggle.

CW: That's exactly right. And although we are unable to actually do a longer reflection on the great James Baldwin, we should not overlook the sublime fact that he exemplifies the prophetic tradition in a literary form and a political form on a very high level. When he left the church, as he says in order to preach the gospel,[38] he was agnostic from fourteen years old until he died. So he had the church in his heart and in his soul in terms of love, love, love, because he is on the love train; he is a love supreme kind of brother, like the one and only John Coltrane. But Baldwin is secular in terms of any cognitive commitments to God; he is agnostic to the core.

CHB: I'd like to come to another issue that plays such a great role with all the activists, namely their stance vis-à-vis self-defense, the question as to whether to fight with military weapons or not. We have the position of nonviolence of Martin Luther King; we have Ella Baker's pacifism; and we have the notion of self-defense in the case of Malcolm, which has always been exaggerated as militancy. Where do you stand on that?

CW: Martin thought that there was something distinctive about the Negro, that we had certain peculiar spiritual gifts that allow us to withstand suffering and pain and respond by opting for a nonviolent strategy. It's almost a kind of implicit moral superiority that we had accumulated over time that didn't allow us to engage in that kind of gangster-like activity, whereas with Malcolm, you know, Malcolm would say over and over again: "I am the man you think you are. What do

you think you would do after four hundred years of slavery
and Jim Crow and lynching? Do you think you would respond
nonviolently? What is your history like? Let's look at how
you have responded when you are oppressed. George Washington—revolutionary guerrilla fighter!"[39] Malcolm was just
so direct. One could easily imagine his response to Johnny
Carson if he'd been on *The Tonight Show* and had been asked,
"Well, what do you think about the Negro problem? What
does the Negro really want?"—"Well, brother Johnny, what
do *you* really want? Do you want your children to live in a
safe neighborhood, do you want a job with a living wage, do
you want decent health care, do you want respect for yourself
and your community? There is no Negro problem. We want
what you want. We are the people you think you are. If you
are in our situation, what do you think you would want? And
how would you go about getting it?" As has been reported,
Richard Nixon says in his files: "If I was a Black man I would
be head of the Black Panther Party. If I was a Black man I
wouldn't put up with all this violation and exploitation. I'm
Richard Nixon." And all Malcolm would say is: "Listen to
the Man." You see what I mean. There is that line in Du Bois
where he says that if in fact the slave insurrectionists were
whites struggling against Black supremacy, they would be heroes in every corner of the European world.[40] So Malcolm was
saying explicitly: "Be honest, y'all."

So when it comes to self-defense, it's a matter of "by any
means necessary," as he said in the great Oxford Union Debate.[41] "Oh, my God, does that mean you pick up the gun?"
"Do *you* have a history of picking up the gun? Did *you* drop
the bombs on Nagasaki and Hiroshima? Whose history are
we talking about? We are human beings, man. We just like
you in that sense." Now Martin would come back and say,
"Malcolm, you are scaring them, brother. Oh, you got them
so upset. They get so scared; they gonna be harder on us now
than ever." And Malcolm would say: "I'm not talking about
strategy; I'm talking about the truth at this point. But Martin,

we got to be honest, the community you are leading—even given your spiritual and moral ideals and vision—that's how they really think. Most of them are just scared. They are scared to the core, and as long as they stay scared, they don't even follow you in any serious way." So you can imagine the juxtaposition there.

If there was an imaginary meeting between Malcolm and Martin it would go as follows: Malcolm would say: "Brother Martin, Garvey and others have told us that the vast majority, the masses of Black people, will never be treated with dignity. They will always live lives of ruin and disaster tied to the prison system in the hoods and the projects. There might be spaces for the middle classes, but there will never be for the masses." And Martin would say: "No, I can't believe that. I just can't. We've got to redeem the soul of America." Malcolm would say: "There is no soul, Martin." "That can't be true, Malcolm." But then Martin would come back to Malcolm and say: "So what you gonna do after you tell your truths? You gonna follow Elijah and create a Black state in the Southern United States that has the same chance as a snowball in hell?" Malcolm would come back and say: "But the chance of your integration full-scale is a snowball in hell too! It's gonna be a truncated integration. It's gonna be assimilation; it's gonna be the bourgeoisification of Black people. Some may go all the way up to the White House, but even when they get to the White House, they still going to have the crack houses; they still gonna have the prison-industrial complex, and if he doesn't say a mumbling word about the new Jim Crow, that's going to get worse and worse, and unemployment will be getting worse and worse. So even with a Black person in the White House, Garvey is still right." You see.

And then Martin and Malcolm would look at each other with tears flowing down their faces because both of them love Black folk so, and they bend over and say: "Let's sing a song. Let us sing a song." You know what I mean. Maybe a little George Clinton, maybe a little Stevie Wonder. We need some

Aretha Franklin here; we need some Billie Holiday and some Sarah Vaughan and some Curtis Mayfield. "Sing a song, Martin!" And Martin would say: "We gonna go crazy." "No, we just gonna keep on pushin'." Because it ain't a question of what is at the moment credible; it's a matter of what has integrity, of what is true, what is right, and what is worthy of those who struggled and died for us and for the precious children. That's what brings Martin and Malcolm together.

That's what we need so much more now in our situation, because when you actually look at what some of the revolutionary solutions are, they seem to be so far-fetched, and usually when people see that, they say: "Let me go back to my careerism; let me go back to my individualism; let me go back to my hedonism; let me go back to my narcissism." And Martin and Malcolm, with tears flowing as they both, in their sacrificial and magnificently loving ways, say: "No, just because the solutions are far-fetched, it doesn't mean you sell your soul for a mess of pottage. That's not the conclusion. This is not only about being successful. This is fundamentally about being faithful to the freedom struggle that has brought us as far as it has."

CHB: And Ella Baker would be right there and say: "The revolutionary process takes a long, long time, and we have to have the patience to maintain it, to keep it going."

CW: That's exactly right, that revolutionary patience. Eldridge Cleaver wrote a piece years ago in a magazine on revolutionary patience. He was still a revolutionary at that time; he hadn't become a right-wing Republican. But it's a very difficult and very powerful notion of revolutionary patience, of keeping your integrity even when the rest of the world seems to want to sell everything and everybody, or buy everything and everybody.

CHB: And claiming that the problem has gone, after all.

CW: That's the denial that goes hand in hand with the careerism.

CHB: I would like to address the question of nationalism at this point, because you have been such a critic of nationalism. How does that affect your appreciation of Malcolm X?

CW: Because I am such a critic of all forms of nationalism, be they Italian, German, Ethiopian, Japanese, American, or Black nationalism, I appreciate the progressive revolutionary versions of all of those nationalisms.[42] That's why somebody like Walt Whitman still means much to me, although he is very much a nationalist. And Malcolm is a nationalist; he really is a Black Nationalist, though he represents a very revolutionary and progressive wing of it. I think nationalism is the dominant form of idolatry of modernity, and therefore internationalism and universalism for me has to be always at the center of how I think about the world and how I analyze the world. But we do come in specific human bodies, communities, nations; and therefore we do have to talk about gender and color and race, class and nation. Malcolm's internationalism is something that, especially at the end of his life, becomes highly attractive and, in the end, indispensable for any serious talk about social change. The same is true with Martin, especially at the very end. Martin actually shifts from being a US patriot to becoming a serious revolutionary internationalist.

But I have to be honest that Malcolm's revolutionary Black Nationalism is something that cannot be overlooked. Think of Manning Marable's powerful biography[43]—Manning was my very dear brother; I loved him very deeply, respected him dearly—I think that the fervor and the fire of Malcolm's revolutionary Black Nationalism doesn't come fully through in the text. I think that the book Herb Boyd and Amiri Baraka and others published in response to Marable's book is a very important dialogue.[44] They make that point—and they are on to a very important insight there—that you can't view Malcolm through the categories of mainstream leftist analysis. Malcolm as Social Democrat—that does not capture his fervor and his fire. That's why I started this interview with Garvey, because Garvey was not a revolutionary Black Nationalist the way Malcolm was. But there is no Malcolm X without Marcus Garvey. There is no Malcolm X without Elijah Muhammad. It's inconceivable. It's impossible given his own personal pilgrimage, his own individual trajectory into becoming the great prophetic revolutionary figure that he was, and therefore we really have to wrestle with this issue of nationalism. How could it be that this Black Nationalist tradition dishes out such remarkable revolutionary fervor and insight?

CHB: I think this is true of all our prophetic figures: they are more complex than we sometimes can deal with. We have to look at the various aspects, because it's also true that Malcolm X did have notions of socialism, certainly of anti-capitalism. To come back to nationalism, I think what it achieves is it transcends the individualism once you have group thinking, a we-identity, a we-consciousness that makes you stronger. From your point of view, it is unfortunate when this we-identity is a national one, is a patriotic one. But then again, many of these intellectuals start with a patriotic sense of we-identity, which incorporates a civil rights struggle, and then move on to a fight for human rights. And there is a clear pattern of this shift, certainly in Du Bois; in King, too; and especially in Malcolm X. We can't stop at civil rights; we have to move on to human rights, and then the struggle becomes international, and that's another kind of we-identity. It is no longer limiting because it turns into a freedom to unite and identify with ideals that could be shared by all.

CW: Shared by all, the species. And it even—as our animal rights brothers and sisters would say—includes all sentient beings. But because nation-states have been the shells into which most of the democratic possibilities have to filter, you have to deal with nationalisms and nation-states; there is no doubt about that. It's just that you have to be able to have a we-consciousness that transcends nationalisms, and that is why the transnationalism and internationalism of the progressives and revolutionaries is so fundamental. I used to sit at the feet of Harry Haywood, who wrote a great autobiography called

Black Bolshevik.[45] He was probably the most famous Black Communist in the twentieth century. He was the first to put forward the Black-nation thesis in the Soviet Union in the 1920s. And here he was, tied to an internationalist movement, Communist movement, that still was trying to get them to see that Black people constituted a nation that required its own self-determination and its own freedom and liberation. So, somehow, he is wrestling with the we-consciousness of Black people as a Black nation and the we-consciousness of being a Communist, which is the human race as a whole. And Harry Haywood and others who come after, such as the Communist Labor Party, led by Nelson Perry, was very important for the Black-nation thesis in the 1970s, which built on Haywood's early work. We need to go back to some of those discussions given the interdependence and the international struggles today. I used to argue with brother Haywood, and I was very young and he was an old man, but we would go at it. I said that I believed in Black peoplehood, but not Black nationhood; that we were a distinct people who had created ourselves over against the emergence of a US nation-state that didn't want to treat us with dignity and oftentimes didn't want us here other than to exploit our labor. That means we are so tied into the emergence of the US nation-state and we are often tied to the nationalism, tied into the patriotism as well as tied into the chauvinism, because every nationalism that I know has been patriarchal, class-ridden, homophobic, and usually xenophobic, so that you have to be profoundly suspicious of all forms of nationalism. Yet nationalism is the very terrain upon which you must work.

And I think part of the problem of the Black prophetic tradition is that some of us are so eager to become flag-wavers that we don't want to bear the cross of internationalism that highlights the struggles of poor peoples here in our nation and all around the world. And that's a fundamental question: Are you going to be a flag-waver or a cross-bearer? I use the cross here in a metaphoric sense, not just in a Christian sense. Malcolm was a cross-bearer rather than a flag-waver. In our day, the age of Obama, most Black leaders are flag-wavers; they don't want to be cross-bearers at all. That's the last thing they want to be. They want the acceptance of the US nation-state; they want the acceptance of the US mainstream. So they are silent on drones; they are silent on the centrality of the new Jim Crow in terms of Black life; they are silent on the trade union movement being crushed; they are silent on the Wall Street criminality. And this is the challenge of the Black prophetic tradition at its best, with Malcolm the exemplary revolutionary wing. Not every member of the Black prophetic tradition is a revolutionary like Malcolm. He's a very special kind of brother. He really is. There is no Black prophetic tradition without the Malcolms and others, but he is very distinct in this regard. But at the same time, if we don't come to terms with this challenge, then we end up being just these deferential flag-wavers, thinking that somehow we are keeping alive the Black prophetic tradition. This self-deception must be shattered—in each and every generation.

CHB: What do you think about the legacy of Malcolm X? For a long time there was no strong legacy, but it picked up again in the nineties, when, as critics would claim, he entered popular culture. What becomes of him in being appropriated by popular culture? Is it really a genuine Malcolm, in your sense, that is evolving there, or is it just an icon that is about memory, maybe even nostalgia about a dead man, rather than evoking a revolutionary struggle?

CW: On the one hand, the centrality of memory of the revolutionary wing of the Black prophetic tradition—Malcolm is a grand example of that—the memory of him and the others is very important. That's why, in a certain sense, I thank Spike Lee, Denzel Washington, and the others who forced us to talk about Malcolm.[46] Now, in a highly commodified country, Malcolm will become commodified.[47] In a country obsessed with patriotism, they will designate a stamp for him. That's the last thing he wanted. "I want a free people. I don't want a stamp."

CHB: As to the stamp, to me it exemplifies the demonized Malcolm. The photograph chosen is quite unbecoming, showing a strained, almost sinister facial expression that is highlighted by the unnatural twist of his eyes. This image enforces the marginalization from the point of view of the mainstream.

CW: The fact that the establishment authorizes the stamp with that image is part of the paradox; that's part of the contradiction. But to keep alive the memory, even when you have the stereotype, you have the occasion to call it into question and therefore constitute a continuation of the conversation, because to wipe him completely out of memory, that's the sad thing. You go to a group of young people—Let's say I would go to Newark and talk and write on the board "Malcolm X," they would say: "Malcolm the tenth, who was he?" That's to wipe out his memory, you see what I mean. Whereas when you say "Malcolm X," "Yeah, didn't brother Spike make a movie about that Negro"—they wouldn't say "Negro"; they use the n-word— "make a movie about that nigger? Yeah, I don't know too much about him, but Spike was getting it on, Spike was getting it on." At least you have a hook to say, "Well, let's see who Spike was talking about." Now, granted, you get the critiques of Spike's film from brother Amiri Baraka, brother Maulana Karenga, and the others.[48] And that's wonderful, because they are veteran revolutionaries themselves, and they want to preserve the integrity of the memory of Malcolm. And Spike is the younger generation, and Spike is not a revolutionary. He is a courageous and gifted artist and a towering figure in a deeply racist Hollywood trying to make movies about Black people as full-fledged human beings. And he is close to Obama, too. He has his critique of Obama, I think, but he is very close to Obama, raised big money for Obama. But I do thank Spike for having the courage to take Malcolm's greatness on. And no one can do full justice to Malcolm in a film, book, or interview. It's just a fact. Even James Baldwin's script, which, I am sure, was powerful—I never read it—but he couldn't do justice to Malcolm, no way.[49] And even, for example, the New Black

Panthers—and of course, you know Bobby Seale and the others have criticized them and in some ways condemned them: "This is not a continuation of what we were doing; they are too anti-white; they are too xenophobic"—and brother Bobby Seale has got some very good points to make, but I still have a certain love for the New Black Panther Party. They can learn; they can grow; but they have a certain fearlessness like Malcolm. Why? Because they talk about his courage, and you can be courageous and still xenophobic—you need to call it xenophobia—but they are at least willing to stand up and at least keep certain organizations going, and they can mature the way Malcolm himself matured.

In our time, the spirit of Malcolm X is most clearly expressed in the revolutionary politics of *Black Agenda Report*, led by my dear brother Glen Ford and brother Bruce Dixon and sister Nellie Bailey, sister Margaret Kimberley, brother Anthony Monteiro, and sister Leutisha Stills.[50] I also discern his spirit in the courageous work of my dear brother Carl Dix of the Revolutionary Communist Party, led by brother Bob Avakian,[51] as well as the prophetic witness of Chris Hedges, Glenn Greenwald, and Larry Hamm.[52] Needless to say, the lives and work of the great Harry Belafonte and renowned James Cone still speak loudly.[53] The dramatic art of brother Wren Troy Brown's great Ebony Repertory Theatre is a sign of hope, as are the scholarly works of Robin D. G. Kelley, Imani Perry, Katie Geneva Cannon, Emilie Townes, Matthew Briones, Andre Willis, Michael Hanchard, Leonard Harris, Eddie Glaude, Gerald Horne, Farah Jasmine Griffin, Lucius Outlaw, and others. And the musical artistry of Dead Prez, KRS-One, Immortal Technique, Brother Ali, Jasiri X, Javon Jackson, Ravi Coltrane, Rah Digga, Mos Def, E-40, Erykah Badu, Jill Scott, India.Arie, the Last Poets, James Mtume, Lupe Fiasco, and others keep the memory of Malcolm X's legacy alive. But the issue of memory in a commodified society is always difficult; it's very hard, and that's part of our challenge. Malcolm's revolutionary *parrhesia*—that unintimidated, fearless, frank, plain speech and putting your body on the line—is the core of our challenge. This kind of prophetic witness can never fully and thoroughly be crushed. Even when you kill the body, the words still linger in the air, and it touches people. People take it and run and do with it what they will, and that's part of breaking that cycle of hatred and domination that we talked about in relation to Ella Baker. But you and I know it is impossible to even think about the Black prophetic tradition without making Malcolm X a central figure in it, regardless of what the main-stream thought then, thinks now, or will think in the future.

Ida B. Wells, 1893

CHAPTER SIX

Prophetic Fire

IDA B. WELLS

We wanted to end our conversation on a high note full of the prophetic fire we started with. Thus in January 2013, we met on two consecutive days to discuss first Malcolm X and then Ida B. Wells. As far apart as they are in time and as different as they are in social background, they share an uncompromising radical spirit that is expressed in fearless speech. Yet such boldness is the more extraordinary in a woman, let alone a woman in the nineteenth century. As a female voice in the Black prophetic tradition, Wells, like Ella Baker, has often been a victim of public amnesia. We want to honor her outstanding example of prophetic witness by giving her the last word.

CHRISTA BUSCHENDORF: With Ida B. Wells, we go back to the nineteenth century, where we started. Historically speaking, she stands between Frederick Douglass and W. E. B. Du Bois, and she knew both men personally. Wells was the pioneering figure in the anti-lynching campaigns of her day, and the way in which she courageously and undauntedly took up a difficult and dangerous struggle against prejudices about the "beastly nature" of the Black man, certainly renders her a worthy candidate in our series of long-distance freedom fighters in the Black prophetic tradition. Like Du Bois, she was shaped by Victorian America, and her bourgeois background means that evaluating her from today's point of view is difficult. We have to contextualize her, and so we will try to get at her core by doing just that. So could you start by assessing Ida B. Wells's importance in the tradition of the Black struggle for freedom?

CORNEL WEST: Ida B. Wells is not only unique, but she is the exemplary figure full of prophetic fire in the face of American terrorism, which is American Jim Crow and Jane Crow, when lynching occurred every two and a half days for over fifty years in America. And this is very important, because Black people in the New World, in the Diaspora, Brazil, Jamaica, Barbados, were all enslaved, but no group of Black people were Jim Crowed other than US Negroes. And what I mean by Jim Crow is not just terrorized, not just stigmatized, not just traumatized, but, what we talked about before, niggerized. Black people were first reaching citizenship after the most barbaric of all civil wars in modern times—750,000 dead, we are told now.[1] Black people are made slaves, then citizens, then are remade into subjects who are subjected to an American terrorist order—despite Black resistance. They are no longer slaves in the old sense, yet not citizens, but sub-citizens, namely subjects, namely Negroes, namely niggers who are wrestling with this terror.

Why is this important? Because, I would argue, Jim Crow in some ways is as important as slavery in understanding the mentality, understanding the institutions, and understanding the destiny of Black folk. A lot of people want to jump from slavery into the civil rights movement. But, no, right when the American social order was providing opportunities for white immigrants all around the world between 1881— Let's begin with the pogroms that escalate in Russia at the time with the death of the tsar[2] and the waves of white immigrants who come to the United States and who begin to gain access to some of the opportunities afforded here—that is precisely the time in which Jim Crow emerged. It consolidates in the 1890s, along with the American imperial order in the Philippines and Cuba, Guam, and other territories. So you get six million people of color outside the United States, and you get the terrorized, traumatized, stigmatized order, which is a Jim Crow order, in the United States. That's the context for Ida.

Why is she so unique? Well, the textbook version of Black history is the following. You get W. E. B. Du Bois versus Booker T. Washington: The nice little deodorized discourse of Booker T., who is tied to the white elites, who has access to tremendous amounts of money, who has his own political machine, moving in to take over Black newspapers and pulling Black civic organizations under his control while refusing to say a mumbling word publicly about lynching, which was the raw face of American terrorism against Black people. Then you get Du Bois, who did want to talk about civil rights, who did want to talk about political rights, but in no way targeted the lynching face of American terrorism the way Ida B. Wells did. Ida B. Wells, in so many ways, teaches us something that we rarely want to acknowledge: that the Black freedom movement has always been an anti-terrorist movement, that Black people in America had a choice between creating a Black al-Qaeda or a movement like Ida B. Wells's, which was going to call into question the bestiality and barbarity and brutality of Jim Crow and American terrorism and lynching, but would do it in the name of something that provided a higher moral ground and a higher spiritual ground given her Christian faith, not opting for a Black al-Qaeda that says, "You terrorize us; we terrorize you. You kill our children; we kill your children." No, not an eye for an eye, a tooth for a tooth, where we end up both blind and toothless. She said: "We want a higher moral ground, but I'm going to hit this issue head-on."

And that is in so many ways relevant today, because we live in an age in which people are talking about terrorism, about terror, all the time. Here we have much to learn from an Ida B. Wells, who was born a slave, orphaned young—both her parents die of yellow fever in Hollis Springs, Mississippi. She makes her way with two of her sisters to Memphis, is run out of Memphis, even as she begins to emerge as a prophetic voice in *Free Speech and Headlight*, a newspaper that she begins to edit, and then with the lynching of three men in

Memphis, brother Tom and brother Calvin and brother Will, on March 9, 1892,[3] the white elite puts a bounty on her head, because she wants to tell the truth—like Malcolm X, *parrhesia* again, the fearless speech. Thank God for T. Thomas Fortune, who welcomed her to New York and invited her to write for his newspaper, the *New York Age*.[4] And this was where she published the two classics, *Southern Horrors*, in 1892, and *A Red Record*, in 1895.

And it is important to use the language of American terrorism, because we live in an age where, when people think of terrorism, they usually think of a very small group of Islamic brothers and sisters, whereas, of course, terrorism has been integral to the emergence and the sustenance of the American democratic experiment, beginning with indigenous peoples and slavery. But after the Civil War, we get a new form of terrorism—crimes against humanity—that sits at the center of American life, and Ida B. Wells forces us to come to terms with that.

CHB: Maybe we should mention the interim of Reconstruction, because right after the Civil War the situation was improving in terms of political power of Blacks. And what Ida B. Wells reveals then—in contrast to the understanding of most people, including Black people, including Douglass—what she reveals is that it is in reaction to the very success of Black people, their rising on the social ladder, their becoming respectable, learned, and a political power, too, that terrorism sets in. And she saw through the story that was fabricated at the time that this was all about Black men wanting white women; she saw that it was a pretext; that, in fact, what this was all about was a reaction to a change of the hierarchical order, and, of course, especially in the South, where white people did not want Black people to rise. And I think that is the truth she told in all fearlessness, a truth that was very important even for Blacks to understand.[5]

CW: I think that's very true. Actually, I would go to 1876 and 1877 with the so-called Compromise, which is a capitulation that allowed for the withdrawal of the military troops in the South, which would allow for states' rights to become predominant, which would allow for white supremacists powers to take over so that the Ku Klux Klan and the White Citizens' Councils would move into positions of power culturally, economically, and politically, and so Black folk would be subject to that kind of terror. The troop withdrawal allowed for an emerging reconciliation between the former foes, the Confederacy and the Union. Now the South and the North are able to view themselves more and more as a family, and they are unified by the scapegoat, they are unified by these Black folk who are sacrificed with the withdrawal of the troops.

It had much to do, of course, with the fact that other issues were emerging, issues of depression, issues of international relations, and they were just tired of dealing with the so-called race question; they were tired of dealing with the legacy of white supremacy. So that even great figures like William Lloyd Garrison—for whom I have tremendous respect, who gave his time, energy, and life to abolish slavery—do not engage in the kind of follow-through to deal with the vicious legacy of white supremacy after the Civil War. Now that slavery is over, the notion is "Thank God, it's all done; the business is over."

Now, let me tell a story. I was at West Point the other day and was talking to a number of students and professors there. The biggest picture in the library they have at West Point is of Robert E. Lee, who was superintendent of West Point when he was part of the Union army, but was only a colonel in the Union army. He became a general in the Confederate army. And the painting they have of him is in Confederate attire, with a Black slave bowing in the right corner. So Lee is a general in the army of rebels and traitors against West Point. They were telling me that the reconciliation on the military front began when the soldiers from the South joined the soldiers in the North in the Spanish-American War, so that the imperial front becomes a space for them of coming together. Then, by the end of the Spanish-American War, lo and behold, West Point embraces the memory of Robert E. Lee.

Then, in 1971, President Nixon tries to force them to have a monument to Confederate troops and Confederate soldiers. Nixon appoints Alexander Haig to establish the monument. There was Black opposition—they had just admitted Black soldiers to West Point in the sixties—the Black cadets strongly rejected the idea; there was tremendous disarray, and West Point gave up on the idea. So you see, this tribute to the legacy of white supremacy remains integral to West Point, past and present.

So on the imperial front, after Reconstruction, the white Southerners and the white Northerners were able to come together, subordinate the peoples of color in Hawaii, in Guam, in the Philippines, in Puerto Rico, and domestically subordinate the Black folk, so that, lo and behold, the Confederate and the Union view themselves as part of a cantankerous family not really at odds over whether the Union ought to exist or not, but a cantankerous family whose members have more in common than what separates them. And there is a united front against Black folk internally and brown folk externally, and to me this is really important, because Ida B. Wells is willing to speak courageously and sacrificially and candidly about the brutality of American terrorism at home and acknowledge the terrorism abroad.[6]

Unlike Booker T. Washington, Ida B. Wells publicly denounced lynching. Du Bois is not really hit by the issue until he sees the knuckles of lynching victim Sam Hose on display in Atlanta, gives up his detached, disinterested, scientific orientation and becomes a political activist—now this is seven years after Ida B. Wells has a bounty on her head!

CHB: True. But it needed that confrontation, and he reacts to the experience, whereas Ida B. Wells has that experience earlier; she is in the South. And in the Memphis lynching, one of the three victims, Tom Moss, was one of her close friends; she was godmother to his daughter. So I think it is about the immediate confrontation, and when Du Bois is confronted, it changes his life just as much as it changed her life.

CW: That's true. But you know, Du Bois is in Nashville in the
     1880s as a student at Fisk University and then teaches those
     two summers there in a small town in Tennessee, so he must
     have heard about the lynching and the terror.

CHB: In his autobiography he writes about that very different kind
     of— He would not call it terror but a kind of discrimination
     of Blacks in the South that he was not used to. But as far as I
     remember, he does mention lynching, but it is the lynching of
     Sam Hose that, as he puts it, "startled me to my feet."[7]

CW: Exactly. But there is something about—and I love it—sister
     Ida B. Wells's rebellious spirit. As a youth, she had a deep
     suspicion of authority.[8] She reminds me of Malcolm, and
     Malcolm reminds me of her in terms of this willingness to be
     candid and honest about any sources of pain and suffering,
     and you speak to it directly regardless of the price, regardless
     of what burden goes along with it, or whatever cost you have
     to pay.

CHB: The first time she was so courageous was when her parents
     had just died and the community decided to distribute the
     children, her five younger siblings, to be adopted by other
     families, and as a young girl of sixteen, she says: "No. No way.
     You can't do that. Give me a job instead, and I will take care
     of my brothers and sisters." It was unheard of for so young
     a woman to be the independent head of a family, and it was
     highly suspicious, and she got the reaction of the community
     in the form of really vicious slander: when Dr. Gray, a white
     physician, returned the savings her dying father had entrusted
     to him, and when the community noticed the transaction tak-
     ing place in the town square, she is immediately suspected of
     prostituting herself. So we see early in life the bravery of a
     young woman who would take the responsibility for her fam-
     ily, which was something that did not fit into the Victorian
     model of womanhood, and thus people resented it and con-
     sequently suspected her of a transgression of quite a different
     type. That is the first moment when you see her courage.

CW: So true. Then we get her Rosa Parks–like act of protest on the
      railroad train. That's still very early in her life. She refuses to
      give up her seat in the first-class ladies' coach and is removed
      by force. She takes it to the court; she wins; the case goes to
      a higher court; she loses; she must pay fees, but she takes a
      stand. You are so right about this willingness of this young,
      militant, uncompromising, bold, and fearless woman.

ChB: And she sacrifices, because she can't finish school, and when
      later she attends a graduation ceremony at her former school,
      she is in tears because she was not able to graduate. That was
      the price she had to pay. She makes up for it with her own
      tireless efforts to learn and to read, but it is a price she has to
      pay for speaking out and for taking care of her family.[9]

CW: And as a teacher taking care of the family, she discovered
      that she was being paid thirty dollars a month and the white
      teachers are being paid more than twice that much. She could
      already see the deeply racist practices there. And we should
      note, of course, her summers at Fisk University. Like Du
      Bois, she did spend time at Fisk University. But it also shows
      she has a tremendous drive for studying and love of learning,
      not just for knowledge in the abstract but also the very pro-
      cess of coming to know, the very process of being committed
      to exploring, a sense of intellectual adventure, trying to be
      culturally cultivated in a variety of different ways by means of
      voracious reading, conversation, dialogue.

ChB: As a young woman teaching, she reaches out to young men.
      In part, of course, she is looking for a partner; that was natural
      at her age. But sometimes what she wants is a companion to
      talk with and to be inspired by, someone who is an intellec-
      tual, and she loves these discussions but has the problem of
      decorum, because she is admonished that this is not done. You
      need a chaperone, all these rules of etiquette against which
      she often rebels.[10] Another point, though, in terms of learning
      and aspiring to more learning: she is never allowed to teach
      above the fourth grade, and at one point she realizes that this

is unsatisfactory—and here her activist side comes to the fore. She wants to be more influential by becoming a journalist and discovers that this is her true vocation. She writes: "It was through journalism that I found the real me."[11]

CW: You know, Ida B. Wells was the first Black correspondent to a major white newspaper, the *Daily Inter-Ocean* in Chicago, when she was on her tour in Britain, forming the British Anti-Lynching Society—not because Britain had a lynching problem. Britain was deeply racist, but they never had a Jim Crow system. Yet progressive British whites were deeply concerned about the lynching taking place in America. And Ida went there in the 1890s twice and helped form that society and wrote various articles back to that Chicago newspaper. But as a journalist, she had a vocation to tell the truth at an observational level. It reminds me in some ways of the great text of Theodore Weld and Angelina Grimké, *American Slavery As It Is*,[12] which became a best seller in 1839. And it was observational; it was like William Cobbett[13] in England or Harriet Martineau,[14] where you observe and picture for your audience in a dramatic fashion the suffering and the misery of your fellow human beings, in this case of Blacks vis-à-vis a white audience. And what Ida B. Wells does as a journalist is not just report in a regular way, but she presents these dramatic portraits with statistics, with empirical data, but also stories. Ida was saying: "Let me tell you about these seventeen lynchings, where the myth was to protect white womanhood's purity and so forth. No, there was a fear of economic competition. No, there was a sense of arbitrary targeting of these Black men that had nothing to do whatsoever with white sisters." So you are right about the journalistic vocation and the calling. And, my God, journalism is about dead in America today, given that most journalists are extensions of the powers that be, but in those days there was prophetic witness, and Ida B. Wells was one of the great pioneers of this prophetic journalism.

ChB: Yes, she was what today we would call an investigative journalist, because she often travelled to the places where the lynching had happened and she investigated what was going on there. And then she found out what you just said about the pretext of lynching and the truth. But sometimes she was too radical even for her time. In May 1892, in the context of the Memphis lynching, she warned her white male fellow citizens that they should not go too far:

> Eight Negroes lynched since last issue of the *Free Speech*. Three were charged with killing white men and five with raping white women. Nobody in this section believes the old thread-bare lie that Negro men assault white women. If Southern white men are not careful they will over-reach themselves and a conclusion will be reached which will be very damaging to the moral reputation of their women.[15]

But here, as in so many other cases, when she was really radical, she had to cope with the consequences, and the consequences were severe, because, in this case, with her insinuation of consensual relationships between white women and Black men, she had enraged the white elite of Memphis, who in reaction formed a "committee" of leading citizens who completely demolished the printing office of the *Free Speech*.[16] But often she was even too provocative for her journalist colleagues, so even at a time when, as you pointed out, journalism was more substantial, she went over the top sometimes.

CW: Yes, when you think of the history of American journalism, people often evoke Upton Sinclair and even Jack London and other muckrakers who were investigating various forms of social injustice and social misery. But Ida B. Wells was there ten, fifteen years before. *The Jungle* was published by 1906,[17] while Ida B. Wells was already there in 1892. As to her radicality, it shows in her statement about the Winchester rifle: that ought to have a place of honor in every Black household.[18] Now that's going to get our dear sister into a whole lot of trouble. She sounded like Deacons for Defense, Robert Williams down in North Carolina, the Black Panther Party, Huey Newton, which is about self-defense: arm yourself and make sure you police the police, so the police do not kill you.[19]

CHB: And, again, it was the incident of the lynching in Memphis, when she herself bought a revolver and said, "Well, if I'm attacked, I won't die like a dog, but I will see to it that someone else—"

CW: "—Goes before me."[20] Now, you would not hear that out of a Booker T. Washington or W. E. B. Du Bois, maybe a William Monroe Trotter.[21] I could hear William Trotter saying something like that, actually. But when you are so far ahead of your time, full of so much prophetic fire as Ida B. Wells—and then, when she marries Ferdinand Barnett, Ida B. Wells-Barnett— the level of loneliness is intense. You feel all by yourself, isolated, misunderstood, and misperceived. We see this over and over again in our prophetic figures. This is something she probably exemplifies more so than any of the figures that we have examined.

CHB: And in part because she is a woman, and you expect less of that kind of blazing spirit of hers, that militancy, in a woman.[22] As I said before, she did not succumb to the image of the Victorian woman, although she grew out of an education that was very strict, teaching her to adhere to that very model, and you see the impact of that education in her early years,[23] before she renounced that ideal, and said, "To hell with it, I am here to do something for others." For example, when her case against the railroad was overthrown, she said she was very disappointed because with her trial she had wanted to achieve something for her people.[24] The responsibility she feels as an activist is her focus now, and she is less occupied with respectability and proper behavior. At the same time, she always has to defend herself, because she is so often attacked for being a woman who is—

CW: Independent and free-thinking. Now, of course, in that case against the railroad, her lawyer is bought off by the railroad. They pay a bribe to him, and he actually succumbs, you know. This Negro, he is selling his soul, while she is fighting for justice. So she has to get a white lawyer who has more integrity in order to fight her case, and yet at the same time she doesn't give up on the Negro; she just recognizes how cowardly some of these bourgeois Negroes can be. When we think of two classic texts by Evelyn Higginbotham and Kevin Gaines on the politics of respectability and the difficulty of women, especially in a Victorian period in which respectability has such weight and gravity,[25] we see an obsession with gaining access to status and stature, with a sense of decorum and tact. Ida B. Wells is able to show that bourgeois respectability is usually a form not just of moral blindness and political cowardice, but it is also a form of conformity that hides and conceals some of the more vicious realities going on in that day. Picture this: Ida B. Wells is focusing on the barbarity of American terrorism while the mainstream is preoccupied with the politics of respectability. Most female citizens of the time are trying to prove to the male normative gaze that they are worthy of being treated in a certain kind of way. All the burden is on them: "You have to show yourself worthy for us to be accepting of you." And Ida B. Wells shatters that, so that the cost that she has to pay at that time is enormous, and yet she comes back to us as, in some ways, a contemporary, for we take for granted the emptiness of these forms of respectability she attempted to shatter at tremendous personal cost.

CHB: To come back to her loneliness, she was active in so very many organizations, it's incredible, but they were bourgeois organizations, Christian organizations, that is, all middle-class organizations, and working within those groups, her base was the middle class. Especially later on, when she lived in Chicago, she was often lonely because she went too far for the middle-class sensibilities, and the sensibilities of middle-class women in particular, and she was not ready to compromise. In fact, she often scolded herself for her temper and told herself that she would have to be more reticent, and when she failed and refused to compromise, she ended up being marginalized within an organization that in some cases she had founded herself.

CW: Over and over again. I think there was a kind of a myth of Ida B. Wells-Barnett that she was difficult to get along with, when, in fact, she would advocate the truth.[26] You can go right down the row: Her critique of Booker T. Washington about his reticence to say a word about American terrorism,[27] and he comes at her very intensely: "Oh she is ridiculous."[28] Her critique of W. E. B. Du Bois, who did take her name off of the list at the founding of the NAACP, and she comes at him, too. Her mistreatment by Black women in the Black club movement that she had helped initiate; there was an Ida B. Wells Club in Chicago, and she didn't get enough respect from them. Mary Church Terrell[29] and Margaret Washington, the wife of Booker T. Washington, both became presidents in the Black club movement organization that Ida B. Wells-Barnett created, while she herself was never, ever a national president. But also her willingness to take on powerful white sisters, like Mary Ovington in the NAACP. They clashed, and Wells was explicit about her critique of Ovington's paternalism, her racist and sexist arrogance toward her.[30] The same would be true with the famous case of Frances Willard. When Willard is in England, Wells attacks her: "Well, you are talking about woman's rights in America, and you are pushing it here in England, you haven't said a mumbling word about lynching." "Well, maybe I have." "Well, where is it then?" Willard got caught, she was exposed, and Ida was quite explicit about that.[31] But we have that kind of willingness with Wells to tell the truth, Black men, white men, white women, Black women. Other than Ferdinand and the kids and the Sunday school class she so loved and taught for ten years,[32] there is not a whole lot left. Jane Addams[33] was a friend, of course, but Wells had a critique of Jane Addams, too. So you would want to say: "Ida, this is Socratic and prophetic all the way down. How does one cope with this loneliness?" She reminds me of my dear sister, comrade, and coauthor bell hooks[34] for all of her courage, consistency, and compassion.

CHB: And yet Wells is so untiring in her activities. There is always so much she is doing at the same time, so that she is active instead of becoming discouraged or even depressed.

CW: That's a good point: she is forever going at it. Even though, you know, there are moments in *Crusade for Justice*, her great classic autobiography, that bring tears to your eyes, when she feels as if she was often abandoned by her own people[35] and never really appreciated by the movements that she helped initiate and create. She was willing to stand alone—her view was, "I don't mind being the lonely Negro who stands up for truth"—and yet I also get a sense that she did yearn and long for some kind—not just of comradeship but an appreciation of the depth of her sacrifice and the breadth of her contribution to the movement.

CHB: There is something else linked to that, namely, that so many times her emphasis is on the unity of Black people, or rather the lack of it. In her autobiography, she quotes extensively from a provocative address W. T. Stead delivered at Bethel AME Church in Chicago in 1894, in which he exclaimed: "You people have not been lynched enough! You haven't been lynched enough to drive you together! [. . .] Any ten-year-old child knows that a dozen persons fighting as one can make better headway against ten times its number than if each were fighting singlehanded and alone."[36] Wells-Barnett herself makes that point often, and like Stead, gets angry that it seems to be impossible for Blacks to show the cohesion that is needed for effective political fight. Unity, coherence in political struggle was of great importance to her, and she was often disappointed that she couldn't make herself understood to her co-fighters.[37]

CW: I think that one of the loneliest roads to travel is to be a de-niggerized Black person among a niggerized people. She sees the great potential of Black people, but she also sees the fear, the insecurity, the inferiority complexes, the cowardliness, the conformity, the complacency, the apathy, the inertia among the people. I guess she felt what the great Harriet Tubman is known to have felt when she went into the belly of the slavocracy beast so many times: "I rescued many slaves, but I could have saved a thousand more if the slaves knew they were slaves." Mentally, psychically, spiritually, they were still tied to the master, and the decolonizing of the mind, heart, and soul had to go hand-in-hand with an attempt to break from the institution of slavery, and I think this is something Ida B. Wells was wrestling with during the phase of American terrorism and Jim Crow. She was dealing especially with middle-class Negroes, because you are right that so much of her world was still circumscribed by a middle-class world. I think she had a deep love for poor Black people, but she was not a part of the organizations of poor Black people. Now as a Baptist, she was a member of the largest denomination of Black people as a whole, with large numbers of poor Black people. The best friend I have ever had—my dear brother James Melvin Washington—wrote the great book on Black Baptists called *Frustrated Fellowship*.[38] Sister Ida was deeply frustrated with Black Baptists who were often stratified by class in local churches. This class division made it difficult for Ida B. Wells to be able to fully be what she would have liked to be, which was a freedom fighter grounded in the organizations of Black people across the board, poor, working class, rural, urban, whatever.

CHB: But although she was not based in the poor people's organizations or activities, she would always work for them, and she went to their neighborhoods, and then, again, she was disappointed by the ladies in the clubs with whom she wanted to work in those neighborhoods, because they would say: "Oh no, we won't go there."[39] She was ready to do just that and to be on the spot for the poor people to try to improve their situation. But it is really a question whether it was feasible for her as a member of the middle class to do what Ella Baker later did. I wonder was it feasible, historically? It's something that we should not hold against her, because she might have risked losing what she needed to engage in a successful fight, namely being grounded in the middle class on whose support and money she depended.

CW: Scholars like sister Hazel Carby and Angela Davis[40] and others have made the points—and rightfully so—that you already have a focus on the workplace in terms of the kind of violation and rapes of Black women in the white household, given the role of the white men with Black women working as domestic maids. And the women's club movement was focused on the workplace in a way in which Du Bois and Washington were not. In the case of Ida B. Wells, you get the focus on the workplace and the lynching, and then, of course, you also have the focus on prophetic civic institutions that generate a certain kind of prophetic civic consciousness.

CHB: She also emphasizes women's suffrage.

CW: And women's rights, absolutely. But when you think of Black women grounded in and attuned to poor people's struggles, as, for example, in the arts, as the emergence of the great blues singers Ma Rainey and Bessie Smith—and the first wave of the blues singers were primarily women before the men take over—and most of these talented sisters came from poor communities. There is no doubt that Ida B. Wells is one of the great crusaders for justice during the period of American terrorism in its raw form in the face of Black people. One can't think of any greater figure, and yet when it comes to issues of poverty, race, and gender, we think of Fannie Lou Hamer; we think of Ella Baker; we think of Victoria Garvin;[41] we think of subsequent freedom fighters, who hit those issues—legendary Angela Davis, now, Michelle Alexander come to mind. So that it is not in any way to put down the great Ida to acknowledge her middle-class context. But it is about how we appropriate, critically engage a giant like Ida B. Wells so that we can learn, and so that we can build on not just her great example but on her witness that connects us to the example of so many others at the time. But in terms of political affiliation—unlike Du Bois, King, Baker, and Malcolm X—she did not side with socialism, let alone Marxism. Yet throughout her life she stayed committed to the plight of working-class Blacks.[42]

CHB: There is very little about African American culture in her autobiography. It is very focused on the political situation.

CW: And you know that culture plays an important role, because she is in the church every Sunday.

CHB: Right, and that is, of course, an issue. One of the many battles she fights is the integration of the YMCA and YWCA.[43] And she makes a very interesting point, namely—and I admire her sharp, analytical mind—she is discussing the crime rates in Chicago on a panel, and the statistics show crime rates among Black people are high. Now, the usual explanation is essentialism, naturalization, they are what they are. But she contradicts the common rationalization by pointing out that all the organizations of uplift that serve the white population are closed to Blacks:

> The statistics which we have heard here tonight do not mean, as it appears to mean, that the Negro race is the most criminal of the various race groups in Chicago. It does mean that ours is the most neglected group. All other races in the city are welcomed into the settlements, YMCA's, YWCA's, gymnasiums and every other movement for uplift if only their skins are white. [. . .] Only one social center welcomes the Negro, and that is the saloon. Ought we to wonder at the harvest we have heard enumerated tonight?[44]

CW: It's a social-historical explanation.

CHB: Exactly, and that is her strength in terms of her intellect, in terms of the kind of analysis she undertakes, systemic analysis, which was her forte when she revealed what was behind the

lynching, because that's a sociological argument as well. And
she is avant-garde here, too.

CW: It's amazing.

CHB: In *A Red Record*, for example, she explicitly refers to sociology:

> The student of American sociology will find the year
> 1894 marked by a pronounced awakening of the public
> conscience to a system of anarchy and outlawry which
> had grown during a series of ten years to be so common,
> that scenes of unusual brutality failed to have any visible
> effect upon the humane sentiments of the people of our
> land.[45]

So she talks about sociology when this is still a new discipline,
and not only that, but she understands sociological thinking,
and she does so when she talks about lynching and then later
on when she talks about institutions of uplift in the city. She
was ahead of her time.

CW: Way ahead of her time, light-years ahead of her time. That is
so true. Now, when you think, though, the same figure would
work with Frederick Douglass and write with Frederick Douglass in a pamphlet in protest against the World's Fair in Chicago in 1893,[46] but also would work with Du Bois,[47] as well
as with Garvey,[48] it's very interesting, and especially with the
great preacher in Chicago, Reverend Junius Caesar Austin Sr.
He worked with Garvey, with A. Philip Randolph; he was pastor at the Pilgrim Baptist Church; he was called the "Dancing Preacher"—no one like him. He had Mahalia Jackson in
the choir; he had Thomas A. Dorsey, considered the father
of Black gospel music, playing the piano, with the Dancing
Preacher preaching every Sunday in Chicago. Now, that's culture; it's religious culture, but that's culture, and it would be
fascinating to know what Wells actually thought about those
cultural dimensions you were talking about. Now, of course,
Chicago was also the great center for the blues, probably the
greatest center for American blues other than the Mississippi

Delta, for so many Mississippi folk went straight up to Chicago. But she doesn't tell us too much about that more secular form of Black culture,[49] but we know it had tremendous impact on her in a variety of different ways. But what a life, what scope and what depth, bringing together so much of the best of the Black prophetic tradition in terms of being willing to bear witness and lay bare the truth, speak out with courage, keep somehow a love flowing, even given the kinds of betrayals by Black men and white men, and Black women and white women. It is an extraordinary life!

CHB: I would like to raise the question that we addressed with regard to all our figures, namely, how she fits the category of an organic intellectual.

CW: I would argue that Ida B. Wells-Barnett is the most courageous Black organic intellectual in the history of the country, because when you look at what she faces: lynching, American terrorism, especially with vigilante activity of citizens condoned by the nation-state—and when the powers that be are able to use the repressive apparatus of the nation-state to come at you, you have to wait to get to Martin King to get another courageous intellectual like that, or Huey Newton. Imagine the raw power of the American racist imperial state coming down on you in that way—allowing its citizens to kill at whim, blow up homes, and so forth—and she remains as strong as ever, with her Winchester rifle and the Holy Ghost. It's hard to think of a more courageous organic intellectual. Garvey as an organic intellectual and leader—he goes to prison, he is wrongly incarcerated, and so forth, but I don't think he ever has to deal with the raw violence coming at him like Ida. I don't think Malcolm had this raw repressive apparatus of the nation-state coming at him in that way. We know that it was targeting him, but not in that way. It's not until we get to King and Huey Newton that organic intellectuals are targeted by raw state power like that faced by Ida B. Wells-Barnett. And we must keep in mind, she is a Black woman organic intellectual being targeted.

CHB: I mentioned her immensely broad activities in various organizations and the projects she takes care of. For example,
she founds the first Black kindergarten in Chicago, and she
also creates a social center with a reading room. This is in
the Chicago phase, when she is still active in national issues
like the anti-lynching campaign, woman's suffrage, and so on,
but at the same time concentrates very much on local politics
and projects focusing on helping the people in her hometown.
And I am wondering whether you see a parallel to the development of the Occupy movement, which started as a movement in the streets and now has shifted. Occupy still exists,
but it exists in other forms, often local activities, for example,
supporting people to prevent them from being evicted from
their homes, activities like that.

CW: She certainly is so multicontextual in her radical activism.
She is a radical reformist moving from a variety of different
organizations all connected with a commitment to justice,
but it's rare to see someone involved on so many different
terrains and spheres and fronts and still with a family, with
children, with a husband, brother Ferdinand, who is a highly
distinguished citizen and freedom fighter in his own right.
I do think that the Occupy movement could learn from the
kind of decentralization, the kind of differentiated forms of
activism that she engaged in herself while still trying to keep
that prophetic fire burning. I think you are absolutely right
about that. We said that the age of Occupy is the age of Ella
Baker; we could argue that the age of Occupy is Ella Baker in
a deep sense in terms of organizing and Ida B. Wells-Barnett
in terms of the multicontextual. Today, of course, it's ecological, anti-corporate, critiques of globalization, of the oligarchs
and plutocrats who rule around the world, but it's still a general principle of multicontextual activism that we see enacted
in Ida B. Wells-Barnett.

If Ida is to be judged by the great leaders of her time, when
you think of Booker T. Washington and W. E. B. Du Bois,
and T. Thomas Fortune and Mary Church Terrell, and Mary

McLeod Bethune,[50] these are towering figures in their own right, but she would certainly be the most militant, the most outspoken, and, in many ways, the most courageous. Well, we don't want to overlook George Washington Woodbey, the Black Socialist preacher who ran with Eugene Debs in 1908 as vice president.[51] He was militant; he was uncompromising; and he was already connected to critiques of capitalism and imperialism and so forth. He was pastor at San Diego Mt. Zion Baptist Church for decades, a great towering figure who also deserves to be part of this great pantheon. But in the end, I think, we have to come back to sister Ida. We must learn from her in terms of moral integrity, spiritual fortitude, and political determination.

Last Words on the Black Prophetic Tradition in the Age of Obama

The great irony of our time is that in the age of Obama the grand Black prophetic tradition is weak and feeble. Obama's Black face of the American empire has made it more difficult for Black courageous and radical voices to bring critique to bear on the US empire. On the empirical or lived level of Black experience, Black people have suffered more in this age than in the recent past. Empirical indices of infant mortality rates, mass incarceration rates, mass unemployment, and dramatic declines in household wealth reveal this sad reality. How do we account for this irony? It goes far beyond the individual figure of President Obama himself, though he is complicit; he is a symptom, not a primary cause. Although he is a symbol for some of either a postracial condition or incredible Black progress, his presidency conceals the escalating levels of social misery in poor and Black America.

The leading causes of the decline of the Black prophetic tradition are threefold. First, there is the shift of Black leadership from the voices of social movements like those in this book to those of elected officials in the mainstream political system. This shift produces voices that are rarely if ever critical of this system. How could we expect the Black caretakers and gatekeepers of the system to be critical of it? This shift is part of a larger structural transformation in the history of mid-twentieth-century capitalism in which neoliberal elites marginalize social movements and prophetic voices in the name of consolidating a rising oligarchy at the top, leaving a devastated working class in the middle, and desperate poor people whose labor is no longer necessary for the system at the bottom.

Second, this neoliberal shift produces a culture of raw ambition and instant success that is seductive to most potential leaders and intellectuals, thereby incorporating them into the neoliberal regime. This culture of superficial spectacle and hyper-visible celebrities highlights the legitimacy of an unjust system that prides itself on upward mobility of the downtrodden. Yet, the truth is that we live in a country that has the least upward mobility of any other modern nation![1]

Third, the US neoliberal regime contains a vicious repressive apparatus that targets those strong and sacrificial leaders, activists, and prophetic intellectuals who are easily discredited, delegitimated, or even assassinated, including through character assassination. Character assassination becomes systemic and chronic, and it is preferable to literal assassination because dead martyrs tend to command the attention of the sleepwalking masses and thereby elevate the threat to the status quo.

The central role of mass media, especially a corporate media beholden to the US neoliberal regime, is to keep public discourse narrow and deodorized. By "narrow" I mean confining the conversation to conservative Republican and neoliberal Democrats who shut out prophetic voices or radical visions. This fundamental power to define the political terrain and categories attempts to render prophetic voices invisible. The discourse is deodorized because the issues that prophetic voices highlight, such as mass incarceration, wealth inequality, and war crimes such as imperial drones murdering innocent people, are ignored.

The age of Obama was predicated on three pillars: Wall Street crimes in the financial catastrophe of 2008; imperial crimes in the form of the USA PATRIOT Act and National Defense Authorization Act, which give the president sweeping and arbitrary power that resembles a police or neofascist state; and social crimes principally manifest in a criminal justice system that is in itself criminal (where torturers, wire tappers, and Wall Street violators of the law go free yet poor criminals, such as drug offenders, go to prison). This kind of clear and direct language is rare in political discourse precisely because we are accustomed to be so polite in the face of crimes against humanity. The role of the Black prophetic tradition has always been to shatter the narrow and deodorized discourse in the name of the funky humanity and precious individuality of poor people. How rarely this takes place today! The profound failings of President Obama can be seen in his Wall Street government, his indifference to the new Jim Crow (or prison-industrial complex) and his expansion of imperial criminality in terms of the vast increase of the number of drones since the Bush years. In other words, the Obama presidency has been primarily a Wall Street presidency, drone presidency, mass surveillance presidency unwilling to concretely target the new Jim Crow, massive unemployment, and other forms of poor and Black social misery. His major effort to focus on poor Black men was charity and philanthropy—not justice or public policy.

The state of Black America in the age of Obama has been one of desperation, confusion, and capitulation. The desperation is rooted in the escalating suffering on every front. The confusion arises from a conflation of symbol and substance. The capitulation rests on an obsessive need to protect the first Black president against all forms of criticism. Black desperation is part of a broader desperation among poor and working people during the age of Obama. The bailout of Wall Street by the Obama administration, rather than the bailout of homeowners, hurt millions of working people. The refusal of the Obama administration to place a priority on jobs with a living wage reinforced massive unemployment, and the sheer invisibility of poor people's plight in public policy has produced more social despair among weak and vulnerable citizens. The unprecedented historical symbolism of the first Black president has misled many if not most Black people to downplay his substantial neoliberal policies and elevate his (and his family's) brilliant and charismatic presence. Needless to say, the presence of his brilliant and charismatic wife, Michelle—a descendent of enslaved and Jim-Crowed people, unlike himself—even more deeply legitimates his symbolic status, a status that easily substitutes for substantial achievement. The cowardly capitulation of Black leadership to Obama's neoliberal policies in the name of the Black prophetic tradition is pathetic. The role of the NAACP, National Urban League, and Black corporate media pundits, who so quickly became Obama apologists, constitutes a fundamental betrayal of the Black prophetic tradition. The very idea of Black prophetic voices as an extension of a neoliberal and imperial US regime is a violation of what the Black prophetic tradition has been and is. This violation enrages me when I think of the blood, sweat, and tears of the people who created and sustained this precious tradition. The righteous indignation of the Black prophetic tradition targets not only the oppressive system that dominates us but also the fraudulent figures who pose and posture as prophetic ones while the suffering of the people is hidden and concealed. To sell one's soul for a mess of Obama pottage is to trash the priceless Black prophetic tradition. Is it not hypocritical to raise one's voice when the pharaoh is white but have no critical word to say when the pharaoh is Black? If the boot is on our neck, does it make any difference what color the foot is in the boot? Moral integrity, political consistency, and systemic analysis sit at the center of the Black prophetic tradition.

Since the rise of the neoliberal regime, the Black struggle for freedom has been cast or reduced to an interest group, one among other such groups in American politics. Even the motto of the Black Congressional Caucus, the apex of Black elected officials, is "We have no permanent friends or permanent enemies—only permanent interests." How morally empty and ethically deficient this motto is— no reference to moral principles, ethical standards, or grand visions of justice for all; just permanent interests, like the Business Roundtable for Wall Street oligarchs, the American Israel Public Affairs Committee (AIPAC) for the security of Israel, or the National Rifle Association for gun ownership. The Black prophetic tradition indeed includes interests but goes far beyond such narrow calculations and stresses a moral high ground of fairness and justice for all. The Black prophetic tradition surely begins on the chocolate side of town, but like the blues and jazz, it has a universal message for all human beings concerned about justice and freedom.

It is no accident that the "permanent interests" of the Black Congressional Caucus so quickly became Black middle-class interests given the neoliberal regime to which they were accommodating. To be a highly successful Black professional or politician is too often to be well adjusted to injustice and well adapted to indifference toward poor people, including Black poor people. The Black prophetic tradition is fundamentally committed to the priority of poor and working people, thus pitting it against the neoliberal regime, capitalist system, and imperial policies of the US government. The Black prophetic tradition has never been confined to the interests and situations of Black people. It is rooted in principles and visions that embrace these interests and confront the situations, but its message is for the country and world. The Black prophetic tradition has been the leaven in the American democratic loaf. When the Black prophetic tradition is strong, poor and working people of all colors benefit. When the Black prophetic tradition is weak, poor and working class people are overlooked. On the international level, when the Black prophetic tradition is vital and vibrant, anti-imperial critiques are intense, and the plight of the wretched of the earth is elevated. What does it profit a people for a symbolic figure to gain presidential power if we turn our backs from the suffering of poor and working people, and thereby lose our souls? The Black prophetic tradition has tried to redeem the soul of our fragile democratic experiment. Is it redeemable?

—CW

NOTES

Introduction: Why We Need to Talk About Black Prophetic Fire

1. Cornel West, "Pragmatism and the Tragic," in West, *Prophetic Thought in Postmodern Times*, vol. 1, *Beyond Eurocentrism and Multiculturalism* (Monroe, ME: Common Courage Press, 1993), 45; cf. Cornel West, "Pragmatism and the Sense of the Tragic," in West, *Keeping Faith: Philosophy and Race in America* (New York: Routledge, 1993), 114.

2. West, "Pragmatism and the Tragic," 32.

3. Cornel West, *Race Matters* (New York: Vintage, 1994), 147.

4. James Baldwin, "Down at the Cross," in *The Fire Next Time* (New York: Vintage, 1992), 26; cf. Pierre Bourdieu, *Pascalian Meditations* (Stanford, CA: Stanford University Press, 2000), 170.

Chapter One: It's a Beautiful Thing to Be on Fire

1. "The Meaning of July Fourth for the Negro," speech at Rochester, New York, July 5, 1852, in *Frederick Douglass: Selected Speeches and Writings*, ed. Philip S. Foner (Chicago: Lawrence Hill Books, 1999), 188–206 (hereafter cited as *Selected Speeches*). One of Douglass's most powerful orations, it is best known in its abbreviated version published by Douglass himself, with other extracts from his speeches, under the title "What to the Slave Is the Fourth of July?" in an appendix to his autobiography *My Bondage and My Freedom* in Frederick Douglass, *Autobiographies*, ed. Henry Louis Gates Jr. (1855; New York: Library of America, 1994), 431–35.

2. Angela Davis's first lecture as an assistant professor of philosophy at the University of California at Los Angeles was on Frederick Douglass. "Angela said for a people in slavery 'the first condition of freedom is an open act

of resistance—physical resistance, violent resistance.'" Howard Moore Jr., "Angela—Symbol in Resistance," in *If They Come in the Morning: Voices of Resistance*, ed. Angela Y. Davis et al. (New York: Third Press, 1971), 191–92. See also chap. 3, n. 31.

3. Toward the end of his life, Douglass gave two speeches against the "frequent and increasing resort to lynch law in our Southern States." "Lynch Law in the South" was published in the renowned *North American Review* (July 1892); reprinted in *Selected Speeches*, 746. According to the editor, "[A]ll the fire of his early years returned as Douglass struck out hard against the defenders of lynching" (*Selected Speeches*, 746). Provoked by the outcry it caused, Douglass extended his attack in his last major address, "Why Is the Negro Lynched?" published in a pamphlet entitled *The Lesson of the Hour* (1894); reprinted in *Selected Speeches*, 750–76.

4. "Oration in Memory of Abraham Lincoln, delivered at the unveiling of the Freedmen's Monument in Memory of Abraham Lincoln, in Lincoln Park, Washington, D.C., April 14, 1876," in *Selected Speeches*, 616–24. The sculptor Thomas Ball had designed the statue that Douglass criticized later for presenting "the Negro on his knees when a more manly attitude would have been indicative of freedom" (615). Yet Douglass failed to come up to his own standards expressed in his 1852 oration (see above, n. 1), when he had demanded: "We have to do with the past only as we can make it useful to the present and to the future" (193).

5. Owing to a result of a highly contested election, the nineteenth president of the United States, Rutherford B. Hayes, was inaugurated in early March 1877 as a result of the so-called "Compromise of 1877," which allowed the Republicans to claim the presidency in exchange for ending the implementation of Reconstruction in the Southern states. Immediately afterwards, Hayes appointed Douglass United States Marshal of the District of Columbia, and despite substantial opposition, Douglass was confirmed by the Senate on March 17, 1877. According to Douglass, one of the reasons against his appointment was that "a colored man at the *Executive Mansion* in white kid gloves" should perform the ceremony "of introducing the aristocratic citizens of the republic to the President of the United States" (*Life and Times of Frederick Douglass Written By Himself*, in *Autobiographies*, 856). Although Douglass had protested the diminishing Republican commitment to Reconstruction during the election campaign, he was silent when the newly elected president decided to withdraw federal troops from the South.

6. "Yeah, brother, you find me in a crack house before you find me in the White House." Jeff Sharlet, "The Supreme Love and Revolutionary Funk of Dr. Cornel West, Philosopher of the Blues," *Rolling Stone*, May 28, 2009.

7. Michael Lind, *The Next American Nation: The New Nationalism and the Fourth American Revolution* (New York: Free Press, 1995).

8. Herman Melville juxtaposes the illusion of individual autonomy with the reality of social interdependence, when, in chap. 108 of *Moby-Dick*, he has Ahab, the epitome of human hubris, complain about his dependence on the carpenter who is in the process of crafting an artificial leg for him: "Here I am, proud as a Greek god, and yet standing debtor to this blockhead for a bone to stand on! Cursed be that mortal inter-indebtedness which will not do away with ledgers." *Moby-Dick or The Whale* (Evanston: Northwestern University Press/Newberry Library, 1988), 471–72.

9. The two prominent Abolitionists authorize, as it were, Douglass's narrative; see William Lloyd Garrison's preface and a letter by Wendell Phillips to Douglass in *Narrative of the Life of Frederick Douglass, an American Slave. Written by Himself* (1845), in Douglass, *Autobiographies*, 3–10, 11–13.

10. Cornel West with David Ritz, *Brother West: Living and Loving Out Loud* (Carlsbad, CA: Smiley Books, 2009).

11. Douglass, *Narrative*, in *Autobiographies*, 33.

12. Douglass, *My Bondage and My Freedom* (1855), in *Autobiographies*, 169.

13. Douglass, *Life and Times* (1881; rev. 1893), in *Autobiographies*, 492.

14. For an extended argument, see Christa Buschendorf, "'Properly Speaking There Are in the World No Such Men as Self-Made Men': Frederick Douglass's Exceptional Position in the Field of Slavery," in *Intellectual Authority and Literary Culture in the US, 1790–1900*, ed. Günter Leypoldt (Heidelberg: Winter Verlag, 2013), 159–84.

15. Douglass, *Narrative*, in *Autobiographies*, 97.

16. Ludwig Andreas Feuerbach, *The Essence of Christianity* (1841), trans. from the second German edition by Marian Evans (London: Chapman, 1854; New York: Blanchard, 1855). Based on a fundamental critique of Hegelian idealism, Feuerbach interpreted religion anthropologically, claiming that God is a mere projection of human beings that reflects their desire for self-transcendence.

17. In 1860, Douglass read Feuerbach's *Essence of Christianity* with his German friend Ottilie Assing, who seems to have tried to convert Douglass to agnosticism and in a letter to Feuerbach (1871) claimed, "Douglass has become your enthusiastic admirer." See Maria Diedrich, *Love Across the Color Lines: Ottilie Assing and Frederick Douglass* (New York: Hill and Wang, 1999), 227–29. See also the allusion to Feuerbach in a letter by Assing to Douglass (Jan. 6, 1879), in which she encouraged him to write a sequel to his second autobiography that "would furnish an abundance of [. . .] highly interesting material, and of all things your conversion to free thinking, how through your

own courage and strength, with Feuerbach tendering a helping hand to you as it were, you broke the chains of a second bondage." *Radical Passion: Ottilie Assing's Reports from America and Letters to Frederick Douglass*, ed., trans., and introduced by Christoph Lohmann (New York: Peter Lang, 1999), 351. Douglass, however, preferred not to mention Feuerbach in *Life and Times*.

18. In Douglass's 1846 report of his visit to the Scottish town of Ayr, the birthplace of "the brilliant genius," he describes the social position of the poet in terms reminiscent of his own recent experiences: "Burns lived in the midst of a bigoted and besotted clergy—a pious but corrupt generation—a proud, ambitious, and contemptuous aristocracy, who, esteemed a little more than a man, and looked upon the plowman, such as was the noble Burns, as being little better than a brute." Philip S. Foner, *The Life and Writings of Frederick Douglass*, vol. 1., *Early Years, 1817–1849* (New York: International Publishers, 1950), 153. The eighteenth-century poet was a stern critic of false claims of authority, a passionate spokesperson for the working poor, and a resolute defender of the dignity of the common man. Not surprisingly, "Douglass had a special fondness for the highland singer shared by many American Negroes." Arna Bontemps, *Free At Last: The Life of Frederick Douglass* (New York: Dodd, Mead, 1971), 127. Almost fifty years after his tour through Scotland, Douglass connected the suppression of independent thinking in his former life as a slave with Burns's poem "Man Was Made to Mourn": "Obedience was the duty of the slave. I in my innocence once told my old master that I thought a certain way of doing some work I had in hand the best way to do it. He promptly demanded, 'Who gave you a right to think?' I might have answered in the language of Robert Burns, 'Were I designed your lordling's slave, / By Nature's law designed, / Why was an independent thought / E'er placed in my mind?' But I had not then read Robert Burns. Burns had high ideas of the dignity of simple manhood." "The Blessing of Liberty and Education" (1894), in *The Frederick Douglass Papers*, series 1, *Speeches, Debates, and Interviews*, vol. 5, *1881–95*, ed. John W. Blassingame and John R. McKivigan (New Haven, CT: Yale University Press, 1992), 565.

19. "Hereditary bondmen, know ye not / Who would be free, themselves must strike the blow?" Douglass quotes the famous couplet from Lord Byron's *Childe Harold's Pilgrimage*, canto ii, stanza 76, at the end of chap. 17 of *My Bondage and My Freedom*, in which he describes the long victorious battle with the notorious slave breaker Covey, a victory that Douglass considered the turning point in his life as a slave (*Autobiographies*, 287). Douglass's library contained both *The Works of Robert Burns* (1837) and *The Works of Lord Byron* (New York: Blake, 1840). See William L. Petrie and Douglas E. Stover, eds.,

Bibliography of the Frederick Douglass Library at Cedar Hill (Fort Washington, MD: Silesia Companies, 1995).

20. John T. Grayson is still at Mt. Holyoke, where he conducts research on the women in Douglass's life.

21. *Autobiographies*, 431, 432.

22. See Christa Buschendorf, "The Shaping of We-Group Identities in the African American Community," in *The Imaginary and Its Worlds: American Studies after the Transnational Turn*, ed. Laura Bieger et al. (Hanover, NH: Dartmouth College Press/University Press of New England, 2013), 84–106.

23. Here and elsewhere in our dialogue, West refers to the title of what has become the classic of anticolonialism by the trained psychiatrist, Marxian revolutionary humanist, and activist Frantz Fanon: *The Wretched of the Earth* (1961), trans. Constance Farrington, preface by Jean-Paul Sartre (New York: Grove Press, 1963); new edition, trans. Richard Philcox, foreword by Homi K. Bhaba (New York: Grove Press, 2004). For Fanon's influence on the Black Power movement, see David Macey's acclaimed biography, *Frantz Fanon* (2000; London: Verso, 2012), 23.

24. "Inasmuch as ye have done it to the least of these my brethren, ye have done it unto me." Matthew 25: 40.

25. In reflecting upon critiques of optimism, West mentions major French and German eighteenth-century Enlightenment thinkers. Voltaire's most famous work, *Candide, or Optimism* (1759), is a satire on philosophic optimism represented by the protagonist's mentor Pangloss. In *Rameau's Nephew* (written between 1760 and 1774), Denis Diderot criticizes contemporary French society in the form of a highly satirical philosophic dialogue. The major philosopher of German idealism, Immanuel Kant, postulated man's exercise of rationality and self-determination (*What Is Enlightenment?* 1784), but in his philosophy of religion he saw a propensity of human beings toward radical evil (*Religion within the Boundaries of Mere Reason*, 1793). The playwright and critic Gotthold Ephraim Lessing put his ideal of brotherly love and religious tolerance into his drama *Nathan the Wise* (1779); in his various contributions to contemporary theological controversies he was known for his position of critical questioning.

26. John Stauffer, "Frederick Douglass's Self-Fashioning and the Making of a Representative American Man," in *The Cambridge Companion to the African American Slave Narrative*, ed. Audrey Fisch (Cambridge, UK: Cambridge University Press, 2007), 210.

27. "An organic intellectual, in contrast to traditional intellectuals who often remain comfortably nested in the academy, attempts to be entrenched

in and affiliated with organizations, associations, and, possibly, movements of grass-roots folk." Cornel West, *The American Evasion of Philosophy: A Genealogy of Pragmatism* (Madison: University of Wisconsin Press, 1989), 234. The conception of the "organic intellectual" stems from the Italian thinker in the Marxist tradition, Antonio Gramsci, who discusses it in his essay "The Intellectual Selections from the Prison Notebooks." See Gramsci, *Selections from the Prison Notebooks*, trans. and ed. Quintin Hoare and Geoffrey Nowell Smith (New York: International Publishers, 1971), 5–23. West has appropriated Gramsci's core concept of hegemony ("the set of formal ideas and beliefs and informal modes of behavior, habits, manners, sensibilities, and outlooks that support and sanction the existing order") and his view of "organic intellectuals as leaders and thinkers directly tied into a particular cultural group primarily by means of institutional affiliations" to the Black prophetic tradition as early as *Prophesy Deliverance! An Afro-American Revolutionary Christianity* (Philadelphia: Westminster Press, 1982; Louisville, KY: Westminster John Knox Press, 2002; anniversary ed. with a new preface by the author), 119, 121. In his book on American pragmatism, West explains why his own concept of prophetic pragmatism "is inspired by the example of Antonio Gramsci [. . .] the major twentieth-century philosopher of praxis, power, and provocation" whose "work is historically specific, theoretically engaging, and politically activistic in an exemplary manner" (*American Evasion of Philosophy*, 231).

28. The English journalist William Cobbett (1763–1835) investigated the difficult living conditions of the English rural population on the basis of first-hand observations published under the title *Rural Rides* in 1830.

29. There seems to be no evidence that Douglass read the liberal political journalist and literary critic William Hazlitt (1778–1830), who is considered one of the greatest essayists in the English language.

30. Douglass possessed several volumes of the works of John Ruskin, who was not only the major art historian of the Victorian era but also an early critic of modern industrial capitalism whose utopian vision of human society was to inspire many Socialists. It is interesting to note that Douglass owned not only studies in art history, e.g., *Lectures on Architecture*, but also three famous Ruskin lectures, "Work," "War," and "Traffic," collected in *The Crown of Wild Olive* (New York, n.d. [1866]); see *Bibliography of the Douglass Library*, s.v. Ruskin.

31. An avid disciple of Ruskin, the prolific writer of poetry and fiction and staunch Socialist William Morris applied Ruskin's concept of the revival of craftsmanship to the art of textile design and in 1861 founded a decorative arts firm together with the artists Edward Burne-Jones, Dante Gabriel

Rossetti, and others. But as with Hazlitt, there is no evidence of Douglass's reception of Morris.

32. The Scottish philosopher, historian, and essayist Thomas Carlyle published *Sartor Resartus* in 1831, followed by *The French Revolution* (1837) and *On Heroes and Hero Worship and the Heroic in History* (1841). For Carlyle's 1849 "Occasional Discourse on the Nigger Question," see *Collected Works*, vol. 11, *Critical and Miscellaneous Essays: Collected and Republished in Six Volumes*, vol. VI (London: Chapman and Hall, 1870), 169–210.

33. James McCune Smith, "Introduction," in Douglass, *My Bondage*, in *Autobiographies*, 132.

34. On Douglass's reading of Emerson, see Stauffer, "Frederick Douglass's Self-Fashioning," 205. In addition, there are references to Emerson in Douglass's published papers. In his early years in the North he regularly attended popular lectures, and among the lecturers he heard was Emerson; see *Frederick Douglass Papers*, vol. 1: *1841-46*, xxiii; and in a manuscript (ca. 1865), he "discusses Emerson's comments on producers and poets" (*Frederick Douglass Papers*, series 1, vol. 3: *1855-63*, 620).

35. Gay Wilson Allen, *Waldo Emerson: A Biography* (New York: Viking Press, 1981).

36. Lawrence Buell, *Emerson* (Cambridge, MA: Belknap Press of Harvard University Press, 2003). Referring to Emerson's address on British emancipation, Buell states: "Never before had he so firmly associated himself in public with any social reform movement, on the same platform with noted activists like Frederick Douglass" (251). Buell also presents evidence from Emerson's papers that Douglass knew Emerson's *Representative Men*: soon after its publication, on February 5, 1850, Douglass had written Emerson to ask for a copy (368, n. 14).

37. *Frederick Douglass and Herman Melville: Essays in Relation*, ed. Robert S. Levine and Samuel Otter (Chapel Hill: University of North Carolina Press, 2008).

38. See Sterling Stuckey's article "Cheer and Gloom: Douglass and Melville on Slave Dance and Music," in ibid.: "Melville's evocation of the music described by Douglass is so faithful to its tragic joy-sorrow quality that, as we shall see, blues form and feeling shape and suffuse his writing style at critical junctures in the novel" (71).

39. See also William V. Spanos, *The Legacy of Edward W. Said* (Urbana: University of Illinois Press, 2009).

40. William V. Spanos, *Herman Melville and the American Calling: Fiction After Moby-Dick, 1851–1857* (Albany: State University of New York Press,

2008); and William V. Spanos, *The Errant Art of Moby-Dick: The Canon, the Cold War, and the Struggle for American Studies* (Durham, NC: Duke University Press, 1995). Meanwhile Spanos has published the third volume "in a trilogy whose essential aim is to retrieve Herman Melville's subversion of the myth of American exceptionalism": *The Exceptionalist State and the State of Exception: Herman Melville's* Billy Budd, Sailor (Baltimore: Johns Hopkins University Press, 2011), xi.

41. In the last and programmatic chapter of *The American Evasion of Philosophy*, "Prophetic Pragmatism," West explains that he defines his conception of pragmatism as "prophetic" because "it harks back to the Jewish and Christian tradition of prophets who brought urgent and compassionate critique to bear on the evils of their day. The mark of the prophet is to speak the truth in love with courage—come what may" (233).

42. Robert S. Levine, *Dislocating Race and Nation: Episodes in Nineteenth-Century Literary Nationalism* (Chapel Hill: University of North Carolina Press, 2008).

43. Charles Sumner served as US senator from Massachusetts from 1851 to 1874. A staunch and eloquent spokesman for the abolition of slavery and a harsh critic of Lincoln's moderate politics toward "slave power," he remained a strong advocate for civil and voting rights for the freedmen after the Civil War. One of Sumner's colleagues and friends was the German American Carl Schurz, who, as a student, had fought in the German Revolution of 1848, and after his emigration to the United States in 1852 brought his belief in democratic principles to the fight for the emancipation of slaves. Schurz served as a brigadier general in the Union army, held political posts under Presidents Lincoln and Hayes, and became the first German American to be elected to the US Senate (Missouri), in 1869.

44. See Levine, *Dislocating Race and Nation*, 209.

45. For Collins's remark, "Give us the facts, we will take care of the philosophy," see Douglass, *My Bondage*, in *Autobiographies*, 367.

46. See John Stauffer, *Giants: The Parallel Lives of Frederick Douglass and Abraham Lincoln* (New York: Twelve, 2008), 87–88.

47. The novel *The Autobiography of an Ex-Colored Man* was published anonymously in 1912 because Johnson was afraid it might harm his reputation as a diplomat; it appeared under his name in 1927 (by Knopf) with an introduction by Carl Van Vechten. James Weldon Johnson, *Along This Way: The Autobiography of James Weldon Johnson* (New York: Viking Press, 1933).

48. This was prior to Obama's retreat on green issues such as the Keystone Pipeline.

49. Frederick Douglass, "West India Emancipation," speech delivered at Canandaigua, NY, August 3, 1857, in *Selected Speeches*, 367. In this speech Douglass again quotes Byron: "Who would be free, themselves must strike the blow" (366); see also above n. 19.

50. "I had reached the point, at which I was *not afraid to die*." In Douglass, *My Bondage*, in *Autobiographies*, 286. Douglass cites Patrick Henry in connection with his first attempt at escape and points out that "incomparably more sublime" is "the same sentiment, when *practically* asserted by men accustomed to the lash and chain—men whose sensibilities must have become more or less deadened by their bondage" (312).

51. Douglas A. Blackmon, *Slavery by Another Name: The Re-Enslavement of Black Americans from the Civil War to World War II* (New York: Random House, 2008).

52. Leon F. Litwack, *Trouble in Mind: Black Southerners in the Age of Jim Crow* (New York: Knopf, 1998). See also Isabel Wilkerson, *The Warmth of Other Suns: The Epic Story of America's Great Migration* (New York: Random House, 2010).

53. W. E. B. Du Bois, *Dusk of Dawn: An Essay Towards an Autobiography of a Race Concept* (1940), in *The Oxford W. E. B. Du Bois*, ed. Henry Louis Gates Jr. (New York: Oxford University Press, 2007). The nineteen-volume edition of Du Bois's works is dedicated to Cornel West.

54. "The anti-slavery platform had performed its work, and my voice was no longer needed. [. . .] A man in the situation in which I found myself has not only to divest himself of the old, which is never easily done, but to adjust himself to the new, which is still more difficult. [. . .] But what should I do, was the question. I had a few thousand dollars [. . .] saved from the sale of 'My Bondage and My Freedom,' and the proceeds of my lectures at home and abroad, and with this sum I thought [. . .] [to] purchase a little farm and settle myself down to earn an honest living by tilling the soil." Douglass, *My Bondage*, in *Autobiographies*, 811, 812.

Chapter Two: The Black Flame

1. This conversation was recorded in the summer of 2010 and was first published under the title "'A Figure of Our Times': An Interview with Cornel West on W. E. B. Du Bois," in the *Du Bois Review* 10, no. 1 (2013): 261–78.

2. Cornel West, "W. E. B. Du Bois: The Jamesian Organic Intellectual," in West, *American Evasion of Philosophy*, 138–50.

3. Cornel West, "Black Strivings in a Twilight Civilization," in *The Future of the Race*, ed. Henry Louis Gates Jr. and Cornel West (New York: Vintage,

1997), 53–112, 180–96, 55; reprinted in *The Cornel West Reader* (New York: Civitas, 1999), 87–118, 571–79.

4. Ibid., 55.

5. West alludes to the main work of the eminent eighteenth-century British historian Edward Gibbon, *The History of the Decline and Fall of the Roman Empire*, in six volumes (1776–88).

6. In *Dusk of Dawn*, Du Bois carefully registers his intellectual development from both conformity with the Puritan work ethic ("My general attitude toward property and income was that all who were willing to work could easily earn a living; that those who had property had earned it and deserved it and could use it as they wished; that poverty was the shadow of crime and connoted lack of thrift and shiftlessness. These were the current patterns of economic thought of the town of my boyhood" [9]) and consent to the ideology of the "White man's burden" ("French, English and Germans pushed on in Africa, but I did not question the interpretation which pictured this as the advance of civilization and the benevolent tutelage of barbarians" [21]) to insights into the international scope of the problem of labor and property, which he first gained during his studies at the University of Berlin in 1892–1894, when he "began to see the race problem in America, the problem of the peoples of Africa and Asia, and the political development in Europe as one [23]."

7. *The Negro* covers African history and cultures and contains one chapter each on the slave trade and on "The Negro in the United States" (New York: Holt, 1915). Cf. Du Bois on the sequence of his writings on Africa in the foreword to *The World and Africa: An Inquiry into the Part Which Africa Has Played in World History* (1946; Oxford, UK: Oxford University Press, 2007): "Twice before I have essayed to write on the history of Africa: once in 1915 when the editors of the Home University Library asked me to attempt such a work. The result was the little volume called *The Negro*. [. . .] Naturally I wished to enlarge upon this earlier work after World War I and at the beginning of what I thought was a new era. So I wrote *Black Folk: Then and Now* (1939), with some new material and a more logical arrangement. But it happened that I was writing at the end of an age which marked the final catastrophe of the old era of European world dominance. [. . .] I deemed it, therefore, not only fitting but necessary in 1946 to essay again not so much a history of the Negroid peoples as a statement of their integral role in human history from prehistoric to modern times" (xxxi). By 1946, Du Bois views the history of European colonialism from a Marxian perspective: "I have also made bold to repeat the testimony of Karl Marx, whom I regard as the greatest of modern philosophers, and I have not been deterred by the witch-hunting which always follows mention of his name" (xxxii).

8. Studies on Du Bois as "sociological pioneer" have increased considerably in the past decade. On Du Bois's exclusion from the canon of sociology in the past and the increasing recognition of his work in the social sciences, see the introduction to *The Social Theory of W. E. B. Du Bois*, ed. Phil Zuckerman (Thousand Oaks, CA: Sage, 2004). See also Robert A. Wortham's numerous publications on Du Bois's sociology, especially on the sociology of religion: "Du Bois and the Sociology of Religion: Rediscovering a Founding Figure," *Sociological Inquiry* 75, no. 4 (2005): 433–52; "W. E. B. Du Bois, the Black Church, and the Sociological Study of Religion," *Sociological Spectrum* 29:2 (2009), 144–72; "W. E. B. Du Bois and the Scientific Study of Society: 1897–1914," in *W. E. B. Du Bois and the Sociological Imagination: A Reader, 1897–1914*, ed. Robert A. Wortham (Waco, TX: Baylor University Press, 2009), 1–20. For the neglect of Du Bois within the discipline of sociology on the one hand, and his achievements in the fields of urban and rural sociology, the sociology of race, gender, religion, as well as education and crime on the other hand, see *W. E. B. Du Bois*, ed. Reiland Rabaka (Farnham, UK: Ashgate, 2010). Drawing upon Michel Foucault's theories, Rabaka has written extensively on Du Bois; most relevant with regard to Du Bois's innovative transdisciplinary method is his monograph *Against Epistemic Apartheid: W. E. B. Du Bois and the Disciplinary Decadence of Sociology* (Boulder, CO: Lexington Books, 2010). For a broader approach that situates Du Bois and other Black sociologists in the field of US-American sociology, see the seminal study by Pierre Saint-Arnaud, *African American Pioneers of Sociology: A Critical History*, trans. Peter Feldstein (Toronto: University Press, 2009 [French original, 2003]. Saint-Arnaud summarizes Du Bois's significance as follows: "[G]iven the enormous scope of the task Du Bois had assigned himself—that of rehistoricizing the Negro 'problem,' which the Anglo-American paradigm viewed through an ahistorical lens—he had to *invent* sociohistorical analysis as such. He had to revolutionize his field in order to make room for black sociology" (143).

9. To be more precise, no review of *The Philadelphia Negro: A Social Study* (Boston: Ginn & Co., 1899) appeared in the *American Journal of Sociology*, at the time the only American journal in that field; moreover, as Saint-Arnaud puts it, "As for the possibility that Du Bois might actually publish a paper in the *Journal*, it was completely out of the question" (*African American Pioneers*, 155). Cf. Du Bois's comment on the academic neglect of the Atlanta University studies on the social condition of African Americans he and his team of social scientists undertook between 1896 and 1914: "Our reports were widely read and commented upon. On the other hand, so far as the American world of science and letters was concerned, we never 'belonged'; we remained unrecognized in learned societies and academic groups. We rated merely as Negroes studying

Negroes, and after all, what had Negroes to do with America or science?" *Autobiography of W. E. B. Du Bois: A Soliloquy on Viewing My Life from the Last Decade of Its First Century* (New York: International Publishers, 1968), 145.

10. Du Bois, *Dusk of Dawn*, 67.

11. See Du Bois: "Once in a while through all of us there flashes some clairvoyance, some clear idea, of what America really is. We who are dark can see America in a way that white Americans can not." "Criteria of Negro Art," *Crisis* 32 (October 1926): 290.

12. "A Klee painting named 'Angelus Novus' shows an angel looking as though he is about to move away from something he is fixedly contemplating. His eyes are staring, his mouth is open, his wings are spread. This is how one pictures the angel of history. His face is turned towards the past. Where we perceive a chain of events, he sees one single catastrophe which keeps piling wreckage upon wreckage and hurls it in front of his feet. The angel would like to stay, awaken the dead, and make whole what has been smashed. But a storm is blowing from Paradise; it has got caught in his wings with such violence that the angel can no longer close them. This storm irresistibly propels him into the future to which his back is turned, while the pile of debris before him grows skyward. This storm is what we call progress." Walter Benjamin, "Theses on the Philosophy of History" (1940), in *Illuminations*, ed. Hannah Arendt, trans. Harry Zohn (New York: Harcourt, Brace & World, 1968), 257–58.

13. "I did not understand at all, nor had my history courses led me to understand, anything of current European intrigue, of the expansion of European power into Africa, of the Industrial Revolution built on slave trade and now turning into Colonial Imperialism; of the fierce rivalry among white nations for controlling the profits from colonial raw material and labor—of all this I had no clear conception. I was blithely European and imperialist in outlook; democratic as democracy was conceived in America" (Du Bois, *Dusk of Dawn*, 16–17).

14. See Du Bois on his earlier faith in the power of enlightenment: "The Negro Problem was in my mind a matter of systematic investigation and intelligent understanding. The world was thinking wrong about race, because it did not know. The ultimate evil was stupidity. The cure for it was knowledge based on scientific investigation" (*Dusk of Dawn*, 30). By 1940, Du Bois had developed a more differentiated view: "Admitting widespread ignorance concerning the guilt of American whites for the plight of the Negroes; and the undoubted existence of sheer malevolence, the present attitude of the whites is much more the result of inherited customs and of those irrational and partly subconscious actions of men which control so large a proportion of their deeds. Attitudes and habits thus built up cannot be changed by sudden assault"

(ibid., 98). In hindsight, Du Bois himself names the theoretical munitions that allowed him to transform his position: "My long-term remedy was Truth: carefully gathered scientific proof that neither color nor race determined the limits of a man's capacity or desert. I was not at the time [in 1906] sufficiently Freudian to understand how little human action is based on reason; nor did I know Karl Marx well enough to appreciate the economic foundations of human history" (ibid., 145).

15. See Du Bois's concept of "the negro co-operative movement" (*Dusk of Dawn*, 106–9).

16. Loïc Wacquant, *Punishing the Poor: The Neoliberal Government of Social Insecurity* (Durham, NC: Duke University Press, 2009).

17. Du Bois stresses that in the South he "had accepted and embraced eagerly the companionship of those of my own color" (*Dusk of Dawn*, 17). He describes his first encounter with "the frenzy of a Negro revival in the untouched backwoods of the South" in the beginning of chap. X of *The Souls of Black Folk* (1903; New York: Modern Library, 2003), 190–91.

18. See Du Bois's self-characterization in *Dusk of Dawn*: "In general thought and conduct I became quite thoroughly New England. [. . .] I had the social heritage not only of a New England clan but Dutch taciturnity. This was later reinforced and strengthened by inner withdrawals in the face of real and imagined discriminations. [. . .] The Negroes in the South, when I came to know them, could never understand why I did not naturally greet everyone I passed on the street or slap my friends in the back" (9).

19. The book ends with a credo, as it were, a praise of "tragicomic hope" that "is wedded to a long and rich tradition of humanist pursuits of wisdom, justice, and freedom from Amos through Socrates to Ellison. The high-modern moments in this tradition—Shakespeare, Beethoven, Chekhov, Coltrane— enact and embody a creative weaving of the Socratic, prophetic, and tragicomic elements into profound interpretations of what it means to be human. These three elements constitute the most sturdy democratic armor available to us in our fight against corrupt elite power." Cornel West, *Democracy Matters: Winning the Fight Against Imperialism* (New York: Penguin, 2004), 217.

20. The essay referred to is entitled "Of Beauty and Death." It juxtaposes the enjoyment of beauty in nature with the painful experience of social death under Jim Crow in a dialogue with a female friend, "who is pale and positive," and accuses the first-person narrator, a persona of Du Bois, of being "too sensitive." *Darkwater: Voices from Within the Veil* (1920; New York: Washington Square Press, 2004), 171.

21. "The Souls of White Folk." It is interesting to note that in this essay, Du Bois anticipates the negative reaction of white readers to his collection of

essays, fiction, and poetry: "My word is to them mere bitterness and my soul, pessimism" (Du Bois, *Darkwater*, 21). As David Levering Lewis points out in his "Introduction," in "many of the mainstream American newspapers and periodicals the standard reproach was similar: *Darkwater* was tragically infected with its author's bitterness" (xvi).

22. Ibid., 35–36.

23. As Du Bois stated in the manifesto "Krigwa [= Crisis Guild of Writers and Artists] Little Theatre Movement," "a real Negro theatre" should be "About us, By us, For us, and Near us," *Crisis* 32 (July 1926): 135. "I believed that the pageant, with masses of costumed colored folk and a dramatic theme carried out chiefly by movement, dancing and music, could be made effective. [. . .] I wrote and staged an historic pageant of the history of the Negro race, calling it 'The Star of Ethiopia.' Before a total attendance of thirty thousand persons, we played it on the floor of an armory with three hundred fifty actors" (*Dusk of Dawn*, 136). After this first performance in New York in 1913, the pageant was reproduced in Washington in 1915 and in Philadelphia in 1916. It should be pointed out that Du Bois clearly understood that the genre was doomed to fail due to the competition from technically advanced media: "But alas, neither poetry nor pageants pay dividends, and in my case, they scarcely paid expenses. My pageant died with an expiring gasp in Los Angeles in 1925. But it died not solely for lack of support; rather from the tremendous and expanding vogue of the motion picture and the power of the radio and loud speaker. We had no capital to move into this field and indeed in face of monopoly, who has. Yet, my final pageant took place significantly in Hollywood Bowl, and was still a beautiful thing" (137). On the popularity of the pageant in America as a genre of political struggle in general and Du Bois's pageant in particular, see Soyica Diggs Colbert's interpretation of *The Star of Ethiopia* in her informative study *The African American Theatrical Body: Reception, Performance, and the Stage* (New York: Cambridge University Press, 2011), 48–90.

24. See "The Talented Tenth Memorial Address" (delivered at the Nineteenth Grand Boulé Conclave, Sigma Pi Phi, 1948); reprinted in Gates and West, *Future of the Race*, 159–77. In his attempt "to re-examine and restate the thesis of the Talented Tenth" (159), Du Bois concedes that he erroneously "assumed that with knowledge, sacrifice would automatically follow. In my youth and idealism, I did not realize that selfishness is even more natural than sacrifice" (161). Conceptually, the major shift is from individual to "group-leadership," or the "Guiding Hundredth," which then "calls for leadership through special organization" (168, 177).

25. See Shirley Graham Du Bois's portrait of her husband in *His Day Is Marching On: A Memoir of W. E. B. Du Bois* (New York: Lippincott, 1971),

which not only conveys Du Bois's superior intellect, stalwart courage, and prophetic vision but also his sharp wit and (oftentimes mischievous) humor. On her own political activism, which has all too often been neglected, see Gerald Horne and Margaret Stevens, "Shirley Graham Du Bois: Portrait of the Black Woman Artist as a Revolutionary," in *Want to Start a Revolution? Radical Women in the Black Freedom Struggle*, ed. Dayo F. Gore et al. (New York: New York University Press, 2009), 95–114.

26. "It is difficult to let others see the full psychological meaning of caste segregation. It is as though one, looking out from a dark cave in a side of an impending mountain, sees the world passing and speaks to it; speaks courteously and persuasively, showing them how these entombed souls are hindered in their natural movement, expression, and development. [. . .] It gradually penetrates the minds of the prisoners that the people passing do not hear; that some thick sheet of invisible but horribly tangible plate glass is between them and the world. They get excited; they talk louder; they gesticulate. [. . .] They may scream and hurl themselves against the barriers, hardly realizing in their bewilderment that they are screaming in a vacuum unheard and that their antics may actually seem funny to those outside looking in" (Du Bois, *Dusk of Dawn*, 66).

27. Ibid., 67.

28. In *The American Evasion of Philosophy*, West calls *Black Reconstruction* the "most significant product of Du Bois' encounter with Marxist thought" (146) and gives an example of Du Bois's "graphic and hyperbolic language": "America thus stepped forward in the first blossoming of the modern age and added to the Art of Beauty [. . .] and to Freedom of Belief [. . .] a vision of democratic self-government. [. . .] It was the Supreme Adventure, in the last Great Battle of the West, for that human freedom which would release the human spirit from lower lust for mere meat, and set it free to dream and sing. And then some unjust god leaned, laughing, over the ramparts of heaven and dropped a black man in the midst. It transformed the world. It turned democracy back to Roman Imperialism and Fascism; it restored caste and oligarchy; it replaced freedom with slavery and withdrew the name of humanity from the vast majority of human beings." Du Bois, *Black Reconstruction in America: An Essay Toward a History of the Part Which Black Folk Played in the Attempt to Reconstruct Democracy in America, 1860–1880* (New York: Harcourt, Brace, 1935), 29–30; cf. West, *American Evasion of Philosophy*, 147.

29. John A. Hobson (1858–1940) was an English economist and prolific writer best known for his critique of imperialism as a consequence of modern capitalism.

30. See West: "The last pillar of Du Bois's project is his American optimism. Like most intellectuals of the New World, he was preoccupied with

progress. [. . .] Du Bois tended to assume that U.S. expansionism was a sign
of probable American progress. In this sense, in his early and middle years,
he was not only a progressivist but also a kind of American exceptionalist. [. . .]
Du Bois never fully grasped the deeply pessimistic view of American democracy behind the Garvey movement" ("Black Strivings," 71–72). In a footnote
to this passage West highlights the importance of two essays by Du Bois, one
of which he mentions above: "Du Bois confronts this pessimism most strik-
ingly in two of the most insightful and angry essays in his corpus—'The White
World,' in *Dusk of Dawn* (1940), and 'The Souls of White Folk,' in *Darkwater*
(1920)" (West, "Black Strivings," 187n27).

31. "I just cannot take any more of this country's treatment. We leave for
Ghana October 5 and I set no date for return. [. . .] Chin up, and fight on, but
realize that American Negroes can't win." Du Bois quoted in Gerald Horne,
*Black and Red: W. E. B. Du Bois and the Afro-American Response to the Cold War,
1944–1963* (Albany: State University of New York Press, 1986), 345; see also,
West, *American Evasion of Philosophy*, 149.

32. For an extended argument regarding the similarities between "the
Russian sense of the tragic and the Central European Jewish sense of the
absurd and the black intellectual response to the African-American predicament," and Du Bois's neglect of this connection, see West, "Black Strivings,"
76–79, 184n14, 187–90n29.

33. See chap. 1, n. 23.

34. For the passage we refer to, see chap. VI of *The Souls of Black Folk*
entitled "Of the Training of Black Men": "I sit with Shakespeare and he winces
not. Across the color line I move arm in arm with Balzac and Dumas [. . .] I
summon Aristotle and Aurelius and what soul I will, and they come all graciously with no scorn or condescension" (109–10).

35. See West, "Black Strivings," 190–91n30.

36. On the influence of German and European culture and manners in
general on his education, see the chap. "Europe 1892 to 1894" in Du Bois,
Autobiography.

37. Du Bois wrote a very positive review of Wright's 1941 photo-history
12 Million Black Voices: A Folk History of the Negro in the United States (photo
direction Edwin Rosskam); he was more skeptical of Wright's autobiography
Black Boy (1945), which he considered "as a work of art patently and terribly
overdrawn" (see reviews nos. 104 and 115 in *Book Reviews by W. E. B. Du Bois*,
ed. Herbert Aptheker (Millwood, NY: KTO Press, 1977), and he was highly
critical of Wright's book *Black Power: A Record of Reactions in a Land of Pathos*
(New York: Harper, 1954): "Naturally I did not like Richard Wright's book.

Some of his descriptions were splendid but his logic is lousy. He starts out to save Africa from Communism and then makes an attack on British capitalism which is devastating. How he reconciles these two attitudes I cannot see." Letter to George Padmore, December 10, 1954, in *The Correspondence of W. E. B. Du Bois*, vol. III, *Selections, 1944–1963*, ed. Herbert Aptheker (Amherst: University of Massachusetts Press, 1954), 375.

38. Edward J. Blum, *W. E. B. Du Bois: American Prophet* (Philadelphia: University of Philadelphia Press, 2007).

39. "The Revelation of Saint Orgne, the Damned," commencement address, 1938, Fisk University; reprinted in *W. E. B. Du Bois Speaks: Speeches and Addresses, 1920–1963*, ed. Philip S. Foner (New York: Pathfinder, 1970), 111.

40. Ibid.

41. Nikos Kazantzakis (1883–1957) is best known for his novels *Zorba the Greek* (1946; trans. 1952), *The Greek Passion* (1948; trans. 1954), *The Last Temptation of Christ* (1951; trans. 1960), and *Saint Francis* (1954; trans. 1962). He also wrote the play *Buddha* (1941–1943; trans. 1983) and the epic poem *The Odyssee: A Modern Sequel* (1938; trans. 1958). In 1928, while Kazantzakis worked at the first version of the *Buddha*, a verse tragedy he later destroyed, he also developed ideas for a screenplay on Lenin that he hoped to turn into a film; see *The Selected Letters of Nikos Kazantzakis*, ed. Peter Bien (Princeton, NJ: Princeton University Press, 2012). Another link between Du Bois and Kazantzakis is their interest in the Bolshevik Revolution and the Russian experiment in Communism, which led them both to travel to Russia in the 1920s. In 1927, Kazantzakis was a guest of the Soviet government for the celebrations of the tenth anniversary of the revolution, and in his letters from Moscow, he praised "the atmosphere [. . .] filled with spirit, every race has come to worship at the red Bethlehem" (*Selected Letters*, 278). See also his travel book *Russia: A Chronicle of Three Journeys in the Aftermath of the Revolution*, trans. Michael Antonakes and Thanasis Maskaleris (Berkeley, CA: Creative Arts Book, 1989). Cf. Du Bois's summary of his impressions of Russia during his trip in 1928: "Yet, there lay an unforgettable spirit upon the land" (*Dusk of Dawn*, 143); see also chap. IV, "The Soviet Union," *Autobiography*, 16–25.

42. Just forty days before he was assassinated, Martin Luther King Jr. spoke at an event marking the hundredth anniversary of Du Bois's birth, at Carnegie Hall in New York City, "Honoring Dr. Du Bois," in *Black Titan: W. E. B. Du Bois*, ed. John Henrik Clarke et al. (Boston: Beacon Press, 1970), 176–83.

43. Ibid., 181–82, 183.

Chapter Three: Moral Fire

1. The first and slightly different version of this chapter appeared as "We Need Martin More Than Ever" in *Amerikastudien/American Studies* 56, no. 3 (2011): 449–67. A shortened version was published in the German political journal *Die Gazette* (Summer 2013), translated into German by Marlon Lieber.

2. Cornel West, "Prophetic Christian as Organic Intellectual: Martin Luther King, Jr.," in *The Cornel West Reader*, 426; first published in Cornel West, *Prophetic Fragments: Illuminations of the Crisis in American Religion and Culture* (1988; Grand Rapids, MI: Eerdmans Publishing, 1993), 3–12.

3. Quoted in James Cone, "'Let Suffering Speak': The Vocation of a Black Intellectual," in *Cornel West: A Critical Reader*, ed. George Yancy (Malden, MA: Blackwell, 2001), 108.

4. Cornel West, "Introduction: The Crisis in Contemporary American Religion," *Prophetic Fragments*, ix-xi; reprinted in *The Cornel West Reader*, 338.

5. Martin Luther King Jr., "The Good Samaritan," sermon at Ebenezer Baptist Church, Atlanta, August 28, 1966; quoted in David J. Garrow, *Bearing the Cross: Martin Luther King, Jr., and the Southern Christian Leadership Conference* (New York: Vintage, 1988), 524.

6. "Let us march on poverty, until no American parent has to skip a meal so that their children may march on poverty, until no starved man walks the streets of our cities and towns in search of jobs that do not exist." Martin Luther King Jr., "Our God Is Marching On!" speech, Montgomery, AL, March 1965, in *I Have a Dream: Writings and Speeches That Changed the World*, ed. James M. Washington (New York: Harper, 1992), 123.

7. See Tavis Smiley and Cornel West, *The Rich and the Rest of Us: A Poverty Manifesto* (New York: Smiley Books, 2012).

8. Abraham Joshua Heschel, descended from a highly distinguished family of Polish Hasidic rabbis, was able to escape to London shortly before the German invasion of Poland, from where he emigrated to the United States in 1940. One of the leading Jewish theologians of the twentieth century and an advocate of interreligious dialogue, Heschel—on the basis of his study of Hebrew prophets and what in his University of Berlin doctoral dissertation he called "prophetic consciousness" (*Die Prophetie*, 1936)—insisted on combining religious commitment with social activism. He supported the civil rights movement, e.g., by taking part in the Selma-Montgomery march, and he spoke out against the Vietnam War (see, for instance, a publication on behalf of the interfaith group Clergy and Laymen Concerned About Vietnam, Robert McAfee Brown, Abraham J. Heschel, and Michael Novak, *Vietnam: Crisis of Conscience* (New York: Association Press, 1967). Heschel was one of

the speakers at New York's Riverside Church on April 4, 1965, when King gave his controversial speech "Beyond Vietnam," also known as "A Time to Break Silence." As Heschel wrote in 1972: "Would not our prophets be standing with those who protest against the war in Vietnam, the decay of our cities?" See Michael A. Chester, *Divine Pathos and Human Being: The Theology of Abraham Joshua Heschel* (London: Mitchell, 2005), 195.

9. Michelle Alexander, *The New Jim Crow: Mass Incarceration in the Age of Colorblindness*, foreword by Cornel West (New York: New Press, 2010).

10. Loïc Wacquant, *Punishing the Poor: The Neoliberal Government of Social Insecurity* (Durham, NC: Duke University Press, 2009).

11. Though Coretta King chose not to reveal this in her autobiography, she did mention that "Martin had, of course, read Karl Marx, who, he said, had convinced him that neither Marxism nor traditional capitalism held the whole truth, but each a partial truth." Coretta Scott King, *My Life with Martin Luther King, Jr.* (London: Hodder and Stoughton, 1970), 71. Cf. King's statement about their first date: "I never will forget, the first discussion we had was about the question of racial and economic injustice and the question of peace." *The Autobiography of Martin Luther King, Jr.*, ed. Clayborne Carson (New York: Warner, 1998), 35. King's autobiography contains an extended passage on Marxism, in which King criticizes the "materialistic interpretation of history," the "ethical relativism," and the "political totalitarianism" of the "Communist writings" of Marx and Lenin on the one hand, yet acknowledges that Marx had made him "ever more conscious [. . .] about the gulf between superfluous wealth and abject poverty" on the other hand (*Autobiography*, 21). As early as 1952, King, in a letter to his wife, addressed the failure of the capitalist system: "So today capitalism has out-lived its usefulness. It has brought about a system that takes necessities from the masses to give luxuries to the classes" (ibid., 36). By 1967 King did not hesitate to publicly question the capitalist economy, for example, when, in his last Southern Christian Leadership Conference (SCLC) presidential address, he spoke about "restructuring the whole of American society" and declared "that one day we must come to see that an edifice which produces beggars needs restructuring" and that "you begin to ask the question, 'Who owns the oil?'" In summary, he claimed, "When I say question the whole society, it means ultimately coming to see that the problem of racism, the problem of economic exploitation, and the problem of war are all tied together." "Where Do We Go From Here?" in *A Testament of Hope: The Essential Writings and Speeches of Martin Luther King, Jr.*, ed. James M. Melvin Washington (San Francisco: HarperCollins, 1991), 250. For a thorough and differentiated assessment of King's adoption of ideas of Marxism and democratic socialism, see Adam Fairclough, "Was Martin Luther King a

Marxist?," *History Workshop Journal* 15 (Spring 1983): 117–25; reprinted in *Martin Luther King, Jr.: Civil Rights Leader, Theologian, Orator*, vol. 2, ed. David J. Garrow (Brooklyn, NY: Carlson, 1989), 301–9.

12. Like King, Norman Thomas was very much influenced by Walter Rauschenbusch, a leading voice of the Social Gospel movement. And, like King, Thomas believed in nonviolent activism in the tradition of Gandhi and spoke out fervently against US militarism. Apart from Rauschenbusch's Christian concept of socialism, it was the extreme poverty and utter despondency of the working class of all colors, which Thomas witnessed as a social worker in lower Manhattan and later as a pastor of the East Harlem Church and which turned him toward a socialist critique of capitalism. In the chapter "The Negro," in his study *Human Exploitation in the United States* (New York: Frederick A. Stokes, 1934), 258–83, he discusses at length the interrelation between Black economic exploitation in the twentieth century and "the plantation psychology"; in emphasizing in particular the economic and psychological factors of lynching, he draws upon the case studies in Arthur Raper's *The Tragedy of Lynching* (Chapel Hill: University of North Carolina Press, 1933). He supported major civil rights campaigns, and though physical frailty prevented him from joining the Selma marches in 1965, he was one of the speakers at the March on Washington in August 1963. In 1965, King wrote an article about Thomas entitled "The Bravest Man I Ever Met," *Pageant* 20 (June 1965), in which he praised him for his undaunted commitment to the cause of justice and equality. For further details on Thomas's fight for racial justice and his relations with King, see Harry Fleischman, *Norman Thomas: A Biography: 1884–1968*, with a new chapter, "The Final Years" (New York: Norton, 1969), 323–24; and Raymond F. Gregory, *Norman Thomas: The Great Dissenter* (New York: Algora, 2008), 250–51, 271–72. West is an honorary chairman of the Democratic Socialists of America, the institutional heir of Norman Thomas's legacy.

13. Walter R. Chivers taught sociology at Morehouse College from 1925 to 1968. For his impact on other Black sociologists, his devotion to teaching, and his activism based on his early experiences as a social worker, see Charles V. Willie, "Walter R. Chivers—An Advocate of Situation Sociology," *Phylon* 43, no. 3 (1982): 242–48. John H. Stanfield, who considers King "a public sociologist par excellence," puts great emphasis on the Morehouse curriculum, with its stress "on thinking sociologically to promote the public good of racial justice," and maintains that Chivers, "who was the chief black community researcher for Arthur Raper's (1933) *The Tragedy of Lynching*" (see above, n. 12) "had a profound influence on King." Stanfield, s.v. King, *The Blackwell*

Encyclopedia of Sociology, vol. 5, ed. George Ritzer (Oxford, UK: Blackwell, 2007), 2465–67.

14. The Student Nonviolent Coordinating Committee (SNCC), an essential organizational force in the sit-ins, freedom rides, and voter-registration activities, turned more radical in the mid-1960s and under its new chairman, Stokely Carmichael (Kwame Ture), propagated "Black Power." A seminal text that presented "a political framework and ideology" of this revolutionary faction of the movement was *Black Power: The Politics of Liberation in America*, by Stokely Carmichael and Charles V. Hamilton (New York: Random House, 1967), vi; an enlarged edition with a new afterword by both authors critically discussing their concepts appeared in 1992. It clearly stated the necessity for a grassroots model: "The power must be that of a community" (ibid., 46). On SNCC's concept of Black Power, see also Stokely Carmichael, "What We Want," *New York Review of Books*, September 1966; reprinted as "Power and Racism" in *Stokely Speaks: From Black Power to Pan-Africanism* (1971; Chicago: Chicago Review Press, 2007), 17–30. For confrontations between Carmichael and King, see Garrow, *Bearing the Cross*, 481–85; for King's critique of Black Power politics, see the chap. "Black Power" in Martin Luther King Jr., *Where Do We Go from Here: Chaos or Community?* (1967; Boston: Beacon Press, 2010), 23–69.

15. Both Stanley David Levison, a Jewish businessman and member of the Communist Party who had been introduced to King by Bayard Taylor Rustin in the mid-1950s, and Rustin himself were close advisors to King. The FBI's supposition that Levison was a Communist agent prompted the wiretapping of Levison and King, and led Robert Kennedy to exert great pressure on King. See Taylor Branch, *Parting the Waters: America in the King Years, 1954–63* (New York: Simon & Schuster, 1988), 516–18, 835–38. Rustin, a Quaker, champion of nonviolent struggle, and one of the most important organizers of the movement, withdrew from the front line when his homosexual orientation was used to compromise King. Thus, *Brother Outsider* (Nancy Kates and Bennett Singer, dir. [California Newsreel, 2002]) is an appropriate title for a documentary on Rustin's life. For a study that analyzes Rustin's marginal position from the perspective of relational sociology, see Nicole Hirschfelder's PhD dissertation, "Oppression as Process: A Figurational Analysis of the Case of Bayard Rustin," University of Tübingen, 2012.

16. Per a May 22, 1967, Harris poll.

17. Carl T. Rowan was a highly successful and influential journalist in the 1960s. His syndicated columns were published in more than a hundred American and international newspapers, and in addition, he had contracts as a

weekly radio and TV commentator. In 1964 and 1965, he was director of the US Information Agency and, thus, became the first black man to be present in meetings of the National Security Council. In a *Reader's Digest* article published in September 1967, Rowan distanced himself from King, whose civil rights activism he had formerly covered very favorably ("Martin Luther King's Tragic Decision"). It is interesting to note that in a speech given February 14, 1965, Malcolm X, speaking about tokenism, mentioned Rowan: "Tokenism benefits only a few. It never benefits the masses. [. . .] So that the problem for the masses has gone absolutely unsolved. The only ones for whom it has been solved are people like [. . .] Carl Rowan, who was put over the USIA, and is very skillfully trying to make Africans think that the problem of black men in this country is all solved." *Malcolm X Speaks: Selected Speeches and Statements*, ed. George Breitman (New York: Pathfinder, 1990), 174.

18. Roy Wilkins, executive secretary of the National Association for the Advancement of Colored People in the 1960s, was an impassioned spokesman for the civil rights movement, yet a staunch critic of militant voices. His friend Whitney Moore Young Jr., who firmly believed in operating within the system, became famous for his successful work as executive director of the National Urban League.

19. The Southern Christian Leadership Conference (SCLC) was founded in early 1957 as an organization that endorsed forms of nonviolent protest. King became its first president, and Ella Baker was its first and—in the beginning—only staff member.

20. On the fear of these and other prominent African Americans that King's radical criticism of the Vietnam War might harm the civil rights movement, see Henry E. Darby and Margaret N. Rowley, "King on Vietnam and Beyond," *Phylon* 47, no. 1 (1986): 49–50.

21. Sacvan Bercovitch, *The American Jeremiad* (Madison: University of Wisconsin Press, 1978).

22. On Clarence B. Jones and the plan to put the United States on trial at the UN, see also below, chap. 5, n. 21.

23. There has been an increase in the last decade in scholarly attention toward Black Greek-letter organizations. For an account of the origins and legacy of the Alphas, see Stefan Bradley, "The First and Finest: The Founders of Alpha Phi Alpha Fraternity," *Black Greek-Letter Organizations in the Twenty-First Century*, ed. Gregory S. Parks (Lexington: University Press of Kentucky, 2008), 19–39.

24. Fred Hampton, leader of the Chicago chapter of the Black Panther Party, was twenty-one years old when he was assassinated in a Chicago police raid in December 1969; Bobby Hutton, treasurer of the Black Panther Party,

was not yet eighteen when, on April 6, 1968, he was shot dead by Oakland police.

25. Fannie Lou Hamer began her work in the civil rights movement as a voter registration activist, and although she experienced severe physical abuse by law enforcement officers, she refused to be intimidated and remained committed to the struggle for civil rights, e.g., as a candidate of the Mississippi Freedom Democratic Party for Congress in 1965. Like King, she would call America "a sick place," and like Malcolm X, she insisted on fighting not just for civil rights but for human rights; see, for example, her speeches "America Is a Sick Place, and Man Is on the Critical List" (May 27, 1970) and "Nobody's Free Until Everybody's Free" (July 10, 1971), in *The Speeches of Fannie Lou Hamer: To Tell It Like It Is*, ed. Maegan Parker Brooks and Davis W. Houck (Jackson: University Press of Mississippi, 2011).

26. Tavis Smiley's well-known PBS television special called *Beyond Vietnam* is the best treatment of this historic speech. For the speech, see "A Time to Break Silence," in *Testament of Hope*, 231–44.

27. Cf. the seminal volume of essays by Vincent Harding, *Martin Luther King: The Inconvenient Hero* (Maryknoll, NY: Orbis, 2008, rev. ed.), in which he challenges the "amnesia" vis-à-vis the national hero and quotes the poem "Now That He Is Safely Dead," by Carl Wendell Himes Jr., who, as early as 1977, wrote: "Dead men make / such convenient heroes: They / cannot rise / to challenge the images / we would fashion from their lives" (3).

28. "Eugene Debs was one of the greatest trade unionists as well as the leader of the US Socialist Party. His crusade against vast wealth inequality was legendary, yet despite his own antiracist views, he could not convince his organization to integrate with peoples of color" (West, *Democracy Matters*, 53). Like Debs, Jim Larkin was a Socialist and a trade union leader who, during his stay in the United States, became a speaker for the Socialist Party of America and supported Debs's presidential campaign. A famous legend has it that he once "unbuttoned his shirt to reveal a cross, and told his largely atheist [New York] audience: 'There is no antagonism between the Cross and social-ism. [. . .] I stand by the Cross and I stand by Karl Marx.'" See Emmet O'Con-nor, "James Larkin in the United States, 1914–1923," *Journal of Contemporary History* 37, no. 2 (2002): 185.

29. "At that time [in the early seventies], MLK was a grand example of integrity and sacrifice but, in sharp contrast to Malcolm X, not a distinct voice with a credible politics in our Harvard conversations. [. . .] King was for us the Great Man who died for us—but not yet the voice we had to listen to, learn from and build on. This would change in the next decade." Cornel West, "Introduction: The Making of an American Democratic Socialist of African

Descent," in West, *The Ethical Dimensions of Marxist Thought* (New York: Monthly Review, 1991), xv–xxxiv; reprinted in *The Cornel West Reader*, 6–7.

30. In 1966, Huey P. Newton cofounded the Black Panther Party, which he and his combatant Bobby Seale conceptualized under the influence of Malcolm X and on the basis of writings by revolutionaries such as Mao Zedong, Frantz Fanon, and Che Guevara. Though the Black Panthers established armed self-defense patrols that often led to violent confrontations with the police, they also ran social programs, e.g., the children's breakfast program and free clinics.

31. Angela Y. Davis has been a radical activist since her youth, an associate of the Black Panther Party and a member of the Communist Party of the United States. For her early years of activism, her trial and acquittal of the charge of first-degree murder in the early 1970s, which had turned her into an internationally known and supported political prisoner, see Angela Davis, *An Autobiography* (New York: Random House, 1974). In her latest book, *The Meaning of Freedom*, a collection of unpublished speeches, she emphasizes the interconnectedness of the issues of power, race, gender, class, and mass incarceration, arguing for, among other things, the abolition of the prison-industrial complex. *The Meaning of Freedom*, foreword by Robin D. G. Kelley (San Francisco: City Lights Books, 2012). See also above chap. 1, n. 2.

32. For Stokely Carmichael, see above, n. 14.

33. Dr. Gardner C. Taylor, recognized for his elegant rhetorical style, is yet another prominent example of spiritual leadership and social activism.

34. Thomas Dexter Jakes maintains the television ministry of the Dallas-based Potter's House, which he founded in 1996.

35. Glen A. Staples is pastor of the Temple of Praise in Washington, DC.

36. "Under the dynamic leadership of Rev. Herbert Daughtry, the National Black United Front (composed of black Christians, Marxists, nationalists, and left-liberals) has established itself as the leading voice of progressive black America. Far beyond liberalism and indifferent to social democracy, this Christian headed-group is staunchly anti-US imperialist and vaguely pro-Socialist with a black nationalist twist. With the founding of the African Peoples' Christian Organization in March 1983, Rev. Daughtry has extended his vision by supplementing the National Black United Front with an exclusively Christian organization, especially for those prophetic black Christians demoralized and debilitated by the secular ideological battles in NBUF: Rev. Daughtry continues to head both organizations" (West, *Prophetic Fragments*, 71). Daughtry's most well-known book is *No Monopoly on Suffering* (Trenton, NJ: Africa World Press, 1997), with an introduction by Cornel West. The

well-respected Father Pfleger is the John Brown of contemporary America—a white leader profoundly committed to Black freedom. West has preached annually in his church for fifteen years. See Robert McClory, *Radical Disciple: Father Pfleger, St. Sabina Church, and the Fight for Social Justice* (Chicago: Chicago Review Press, 2010).

37. J. Alfred Smith Sr., pastor emeritus of Allen Temple Baptist Church, in Oakland, clearly reveals his commitment to the tradition of prophetic Christianity in the title of his 2004 autobiography: *On the Jericho Road: A Memoir of Racial Justice, Social Action, and Prophetic Ministry*, with Harry Louis Williams II (Downers Grove, IL: InterVarsity Press, 2004). Frederick Douglas Haynes III is senior pastor at Friendship-West Baptist Church, Dallas. Rev. Dr. Carolyn Ann Knight studied under Cornel West at Union Theological Seminary, where she received a master's of divinity and a master's of sacred theology; she earned a doctor of ministry from United Theological Seminary in Dayton, Ohio. She founded "Can Do" Ministries, devoted to the spiritual and intellectual advancement of youth, and she was professor of preaching at Interdenominational Theological Center in Atlanta for many years. She is one of the great preachers of her generation. Rev. Dr. Bernard Richardson is the dean of Howard University's historic Andrew Rankin Memorial Chapel and professor at Howard University's Divinity School. West has preached in this chapel annually for the past twenty years. Rev. Toby Sanders is pastor of the Beloved Community, former president of the Trenton Board of Education, and "dean" of the New Jersey STEP prison/college program (directed by Margaret Atkins), in which West teaches philosophy with 140 brothers/students in Rahway. Rev. Dr. Barbara King is the founder/minister of the Hillside Chapel and Truth Center in Atlanta. Rev. Dr. M. William Howard Jr. is the pastor of Bethany Baptist Church in Newark, New Jersey, and was the first Black president of the National Council of Churches. Rev. Dr. William Barber is one of the grand King-like figures in our time.

38. For statistics on housing and wealth distribution quoted in this passage and the next, see the Pew Research Center analysis based on 2009 government data: Rakesh Kochhar et al., *Twenty to One: Wealth Gaps Rise to Record Highs Between Whites, Blacks, Hispanics* (Washington, DC: Pew Research Social and Demographic Trends, July 26, 2011), http://www.pewsocialtrends.org/2011/07/26/wealth-gaps-rise-to-record-highs-between-whites-blacks-hispanics.

39. West refers to the period between December 2010 and August 2011.

40. E. Franklin Frazier, *Black Bourgeoisie* (Glencoe, IL: Free Press, 1957).

41. Kochhar, *Twenty to One*. For soaring corporate profits based largely on layoffs, see, for example, Floyd Norris, "As Corporate Profits Rise, Workers'

Income Declines," *New York Times*, August 5, 2011. The figure of $2.1 trillion is based on Federal Reserve statistics released in 2011 and discussed widely, e.g., by Jacob Goldstein on National Public Radio, September 20, 2011.

42. Marian Wright Edelman, a civil rights attorney, graduate of Yale University Law School, the first African American woman admitted to the Mississippi Bar, and promoter of the Poor People's Campaign, is best known for her indefatigable work on behalf of poor children, e.g., with the Children's Defense Fund.

43. Wolin defines democracy as a "project concerned with the political potentialities of ordinary citizens, that is, with their possibilities for becoming political beings through the self-discovery of common concerns and of modes of action for realizing them." Consequently, democracy "seems destined to be a moment rather than a form." Sheldon S. Wolin, "Fugitive Democracy," *Constellations* 1, no. 1 (1994): 11, 19.

44. Though Bourdieu argues that "there is an inertia [. . .] of habitus" (*Pascalian Meditations*, 160), he also emphasizes that habitus can be "practically transformed" and even "*controlled* through awakening consciousness and socioanalysis." Pierre Bourdieu, *In Other Words: Essays Towards a Reflexive Sociology*, trans. Matthew Adamson (Cambridge, UK: Polity, 1994), 116.

45. *Howard Zinn on Race*, introduction by Cornel West (New York: Seven Stories Press, 2011).

46. Raymond Williams, *The Long Revolution* (London: Chatto, 1961).

47. This was also a favorite word of Fannie Lou Hamer's, who would say in many of her speeches that to be born Black in America is to be born in a mess.

48. Garrow, *Bearing the Cross*, 562.

49. On King's support for Carl Stokes's 1967 election campaign for mayor of Cleveland, see ibid., 580.

50. For Huey Newton and Amiri Baraka (LeRoi Jones), see also chap. 5. Baraka passed away on January 9, 2014.

51. Both Walter Sisulu, secretary general of the African National Congress (ANC), 1949–54, and Joe (Yossel Mashel) Slovo, a Lithuanian Jew whose family had emigrated to South Africa when he was eight years old, were members of the South African Communist Party and of the Umkhonto we Sizwe, "Spear of the Nation," the armed wing of the ANC, led by Mandela.

Chapter Four: The Heat of Democratic Existentialism

1. See Barbara Ransby, *Ella Baker and the Black Freedom Movement: A Radical Democratic Vision* (Chapel Hill: University of North Carolina Press, 2003), 170.

2. Ibid., 273.

3. "Receptivity" is a core concept of Romand Coles's theory of radical democracy that proposes the practices of listening and one-on-one relations in grassroots organizing. In an essay on both Cornel West and Ella Baker, Coles submits an extraordinarily perceptive reading of West's work, emphasizing the passages that testify to West's listening rather than his voicing, while at the same time offering a candid critique by juxtaposing West's "incredible passion and charisma" to Ella Baker's "democratic receptivity," because Coles "still think[s] that Cornel West has a great deal to learn from Ella Baker and from Bob Moses" and wants to push him beyond certain limits he discerns in his work. Romand Coles, "'To Make This Tradition Articulate': Practiced Receptivity Matters, Or Heading West of West with Cornel West and Ella Baker," in Stanley Hauerwas and Romand Coles, *Christianity, Democracy, and the Radical Ordinary: Conversations Between a Radical Democrat and a Christian* (Cambridge, UK: Lutterworth Press, 2008), 79, 53, 81.

4. Baker took Robert Parris Moses, a "deeply spiritual young man with a sharp intellect and a perceptive ear" (Ransby, *Ella Baker*, 248), under her wing. For an instructive summary of his educational background, his beginnings as an activist in SNCC, and his excellent rapport with Baker, see ibid., 248–52. Ransby highlights their "similar sensibilities": "Both were intellectuals, thoughtful and analytical, yet at the same time practical and personable. Both were deeply attentive to ideology and the ideological implications of certain tactical decisions, but both were equally willing to do the messy, hands-on work necessary to implement those ideas" (ibid., 251).

5. Baker and Schuyler were close friends in the 1930s; she was a founding member of the Young Negroes' Cooperative League (YNCL), launched by Schuyler in 1930, and became its national director. Among the various factions of anarchism, the economic model of the cooperative as a third way between capitalism and state Marxism was the most prominent concept during the Great Depression. As Schuyler wrote in 1930: "Cooperative democracy means a social order, in which the mills, mines, railroads, farms, markets, houses, shops and all the other necessary means of production, distribution and exchange are owned cooperatively by those who produce, operate and use them. Whereas the Socialists hope to usher in such a Utopia society by the ballot and the Communists hope to turn the trick with the bullet the cooperator (who is really an Anarchist since the triumph of his society will do away with the state in its present form—and I am an Anarchist) is slowly and methodologically doing so through legal, intelligent economic cooperation or mutual aid." *Pittsburgh Courier*, November 15, 1930; quoted in Ransby, *Ella Baker*, 87. Baker considered the cooperative movement as a path toward radical social

change, toward "the day," as Baker wrote in 1935, "when the soil and all of its resources will be reclaimed by its rightful owners—the working masses of the world." "Youthful City Workers Turning to Cooperative Farming," *Amsterdam News*, May 11, 1935; quoted in Ransby, *Ella Baker*, 86. For Du Bois's propagation of cooperative economics in the 1930s, see *Dusk of Dawn*.

6. For Bayard Rustin, see chap. 3, n. 15.

7. Best known as the cofounder of the Catholic Worker Movement and writer for the *Catholic Worker*, Dorothy Day, who converted to Catholicism in 1927, combined her anarchist and socialist convictions with a fervent religious belief. See Cornel West, "On the Legacy of Dorothy Day," *Catholic Agitator* 44, no. 1 (February 2014): 1–3, 6; and Cornel West, "Dorothy Day: Exemplar of Truth and Courage," a lecture given at Maryhouse Catholic Worker, New York City, November 8, 2013, the 114th birthday of Dorothy Day (http://www.youtube.com/watch?v=AcMmXSMqJag). For the anarchist thought of Day, Bayard Rustin, and Henry David Thoreau, see Anthony Terrance Wiley's Princeton PhD dissertation (2011), "Angelic Troublemakers: Religion and Anarchism in Henry David Thoreau, Dorothy Day, and Bayard Rustin."

8. Dutch poet and activist Herman Gorter and Dutch astronomer and theorist of council Communism Anton Pannekoek both criticized Lenin and the party dictatorship of the Bolsheviks. See, for example, Gorter's pamphlet *The World Revolution* (1923) and Pannekoek's *Lenin as Philosopher: A Critical Examination of the Philosophical Basis of Leninism* (1948; rev. ed., edited, annotated and with an introduction by Lance Byron Richey (Milwaukee: Marquette University Press, 2003). There is also a recent English translation of Pannekoek's 1946 *De arbeidersraden, Workers' Councils* (Edinburgh: AK, 2003), with an introduction by Noam Chomsky.

9. And yet, Baker's influence on Carmichael is evident in the following remark: "He [the Southern Negro] has been shamed into distrusting his own capacity to grow and lead and articulate. He has been shamed from birth by his skin, his poverty, his ignorance and even his speech. Whom does he see on television? Who gets projected in politics? The Lindsays and the Rockefellers and even the Martin Luther Kings—but not the Fannie Lou Hamers." Stokely Carmichael, "Who Is Qualified?" (1966), in *Stokely Speaks*, 13.

10. Though Baker's focus was the Black freedom struggle, she also dealt with international issues, e.g., the Vietnam War, the Puerto Rican fight for independence, and South African apartheid, as well as national problems of inequity, such as poverty, social injustice, unequal education, and discrimination against women (Ransby, *Ella Baker*, 5).

11. West refers to the following two biographies on Baker: Joanne Grant's *Ella Baker: Freedom Bound* (New York: John Wiley, 1998) and Barbara Ransby's *Ella Baker and the Black Freedom Movement* (cited above, n. 1). For Coles's work, see "'To Make This Tradition Articulate,'" above, n. 3.

12. It would be a mistake to consider Ella Baker as an activist exclusively rooted in practice. In fact, her practice was informed by theoretical reading; for example, according to a friend, "Ella Baker was a student of Marx and we used to debate that often" (Ransby, *Ella Baker*, 68); for further information on Baker's education in Harlem, "a hotbed of radical thinking" (Baker, quoted in ibid., 64), see "Harlem during the 1930s: The Making of a Black Radical Activist and Intellectual" (ibid., 64–104). Ransby summarizes Baker's logic of practice as follows: "Baker's theory of social change and political organizing was inscribed in her practice. Her ideas were written in her work: a coherent body of lived text spanning nearly sixty years" (ibid., 1).

13. Williams, *Long Revolution*.

14. Mary Frances Berry and John Blassingame, *Long Memory: The Black Experience in America* (New York: Oxford University Press, 1982).

15. Saul David Alinsky, a student of sociologist Robert Park at the University of Chicago, was a pioneer of community organizing, and his book *Rules for Radicals: A Pragmatic Primer for Realistic Radicals* (New York: Random House, 1971) has been an influential manual of grassroots organizing. Alinsky established the community organizing network the Industrial Areas Foundation (IAF) in 1940. With his first organizing project, the Back of the Yards Neighborhood Council, located in an industrial area next to the Chicago stockyards, Alinsky joined two basic social forces of the neighborhood: organized religion (the Catholic church) and organized labor. It not only improved the living conditions of the people but also their understanding of the importance of self-organizing: "The organizations and institutions of the people back of the yards feel that the only way that they can get their rights is through a community organization that is built, owned, and operated by themselves rather than by outside interests which in many cases are basically opposed to many of the fundamental objectives which these people want." Alinsky, "Community Organizing and Analysis," *American Journal of Sociology* 46 (May 1941): 807. Ernesto Cortés, trained by the Industrial Areas Foundation in the early 1970s, is now cochair and executive director of the West/Southwest regional network of the IAF.

16. According to West, the best treatment of these issues is Jeffrey Stout's *Blessed Are the Organized: Grassroots Democracy in America* (Princeton, NJ: Princeton University Press, 2010).

17. The FBI considered Baker potentially subversive and observed her for decades, but due to her unconventional behavior and her frequency in changing affiliations with various organizations, the agency, as Ransby puts it, "did not know what to make of this middle-aged hell-raiser who defied categorization" (Ransby, *Ella Baker*, 129).

18. For an extended discussion of the possibilities of Black rebellions and revolutions in the United States, see Harold Cruse's volume of essays *Rebellion or Revolution?* (New York: Morrow, 1968).

19. Among the artists who have inspired West, Chekhov, "the great writer of compassion" ("Chekhov, Coltrane and Democracy," *The Cornel West Reader*, 555), ranks first. In a 1992 interview with the Hungarian philosopher Eva L. Corredor on Georg Lukács's philosophy of history, West accounts for his own "deep Chekhovian strain" by pointing out that though, for Chekhov, love and service are not linked to an optimistic view of life, we are not condemned to cynicism: "What is so great about Chekhov? I think he understood this better than others, that we are able to love, care [*sic*] and serve others—and this is so true of his life and his art—but we are able to do that with there being no deep faith in life or human nature or history or what-have-you. And then it does not mean that we are anti-life, it does not mean that we are cynical toward it, it is simply there" ("The Indispensability Yet Insufficiency of Marxist Theory," *The Cornel West Reader*, 228). See also West's comments on his boundless enthusiasm, especially in the mid-1970s, for Russian literature in general and for his favorite writer, Chekhov, in particular: "Chekhov is the deep blues poet of catastrophe and compassion, whose stories lovingly depict everyday people wrestling with the steady ache of misery and yearning for a better life" (West, *Brother West*, 92–94).

20. In his philosophy of war, Carl von Clausewitz (1780–1831) famously defined war as "an act of violence intended to compel our opponent to fulfil our will." Of the three elements of war that, according to Clausewitz, form "a fascinating trinity" (violence, chance, and reason), West here obviously thinks of the first: "primordial violence, hatred and enmity, which are to be regarded as a blind natural force." Clausewitz, *On War*, ed. Michael Howard and Peter Paret (Princeton, NJ: Princeton University Press, 1984), 89.

21. Singer and songwriter Bernice Johnson Reagon, "one of Ella Baker's political daughters" (Ransby, *Ella Baker*, 12), was active in the civil rights movement, for example, as a member of the Freedom Singers, organized by SNCC. Reagon composed and performed "Ella's Song" for the documentary film *Fundi* (see n. 24 below); reprinted as an epigraph in Grant's biography, *Ella Baker*.

22. This statement should not be misconceived as referring to the individual Ella Baker. In fact, Baker was known for being "a powerful speaker who talked without notes from her heart to the hearts of her audience. Very forceful, with a strong voice that projected even without a microphone. Her speeches [...] were to the point [...] very human and warm." This observation by one of her female coworkers in the NAACP is quoted in Ransby, *Ella Baker*, 131. Notwithstanding her personal rhetorical power and charismatic gifts, as a woman, Baker would not have been considered suited for the male-denoted model of charismatic leadership. On gender divisions in African American leadership, see Erica E. Edwards, *Charisma and the Fictions of Black Leadership* (Minneapolis: University of Minnesota Press, 2012).

23. For today's legacy of Martin Luther King and Ella Baker, see the movements of the Dream Defenders, led by Philip Agnew, and Moral Mondays, led by Rev. Dr. William Barber.

24. The 1981 documentary *Fundi: The Story of Ella Baker* was directed by Joanne Grant, who comments on the film's title as follows: "The designation 'fundi' seemed to characterize her. *Fundi* [...] is a Swahili word which denotes the person in a community who passes on the wisdom of the elders, the crafts, the knowledge. This is not done in an institutional way, a way which Baker would have rejected, but as an oral tradition, handed down from one generation to the next" (Grant, *Ella Baker*, 143).

25. For example, Baker maintained in an interview in 1977: "The only society that can serve the needs of large masses of poor people is a socialist society." Wesley Brown and Aeverna Adams, interview with Ella Baker, New York, 1977; quoted in Grant, *Ella Baker*, 218.

26. The radicalism of Ella Baker's political thinking derives from the systemic critique she advocates: "In order for us as poor and oppressed people to become a part of a society that is meaningful, the system under which we now exist has to be radically changed. This means we are going to have to learn to think in *radical* terms. I use the term radical in its original meaning— getting down to and understanding the root cause. It means facing a system that does not lend itself to your needs and devising means by which you change that system." Ella Baker, "The Black Woman in the Civil Rights Struggle," speech given at the Institute for the Black World, Atlanta, 1969, in the possession of Joanne Grant, in Grant, *Ella Baker*, 227–31; see also, Ransby, *Ella Baker*, 1, 377.

27. At the behest of Pedro Albizu Campos, leading activist and president of the Puerto Rican Nationalist Party, Lolita Lebrón, together with three companions, led an attack on the House of Representatives on March 1, 1954,

demanding a free Puerto Rico. For Ella Baker's involvement with the Puerto Rican Solidarity Organization (PRSO), see Ransby, *Ella Baker*, 354–55. The keynote address Baker gave at a Puerto Rican Independence rally in New York's Madison Square Garden took place in 1978. In 1979, after having served twenty-five years in prison, Lebrón and her companions were pardoned by President Jimmy Carter.

Chapter Five: Revolutionary Fire

1. West, *Prophesy Deliverance!*, 143.
2. West, *Race Matters*, 135–36.
3. *The Cornel West Reader*, 7.
4. The Jamaican activist Marcus Garvey was one of the most important and influential Black leaders of the early twentieth century; he succeeded in mobilizing the Black masses with his commitment to Black Nationalism and Afrocentrism, and with his message of Black self-esteem and independence. Like the later Du Bois, Garvey was convinced that organizing a mass movement called for a "cultural nationalism" that offered resplendent parades and pageants endowed with such paraphernalia as gaudy uniforms, banners, and nationalist anthems. Malcolm X's parents were Garveyites. His father, Earl Little, was active in local branches of Garvey's organization, the Universal Negro Improvement Association, and he would often take his favorite son, Malcolm, to UNIA meetings. "The meetings always closed with my father saying several times and the people chanting after him, 'Up, you mighty race, you can accomplish what you will!'" Manning Marable, *Malcolm X: A Life of Reinvention* (New York: Viking, 2011), 27.
5. In 1946, Malcolm X was sentenced to eight to ten years in prison for burglary, for which he served seven years. In 1948, owing to his sister Ella's indefatigable endeavors, he was transferred to Norfolk Prison Colony in Massachusetts, a particularly progressive institution emphasizing rehabilitation. It was at Norfolk that his siblings introduced him to the Nation of Islam and where he subsequently started a rigorous program of self-education that would turn him, paradoxically, into a free man: "From then until I left that prison, in every free moment I had, if I was not reading in the library, I was reading on my bunk. [. . .] [M]onths passed without my even thinking about being imprisoned. In fact, up to then, I had never been so truly free in my life." *The Autobiography of Malcolm X* (1973), with Alex Haley (New York: Ballantine Books, 1992), 188.
6. Elijah Muhammad (born Elijah Robert Poole) led the Nation of Islam from 1934—the year its founder, Wallace D. Fard, disappeared—until his death in 1975. Fard's and Muhammad's religious teachings were not congruent

with orthodox Islam, as Malcolm X realized during his pilgrimage to Mecca. Like Garvey, Elijah Muhammad propagated Black pride and separatism as the only means to gain independence from white domination. The strict dietetic rules and moral laws aimed at the acquisition of a discipline that was to impede whites' control over Blacks. Malcolm X, who "had believed more in Mr. Muhammad than he believed in himself" (ibid., 335), was profoundly shaken when he found out that the adored leader had not adhered to his own moral principles; see also the chapter "Out" in *Autobiography*.

7. Here, as elsewhere in our dialogue, West indirectly hints at remarks by Malcolm X. At the founding rally of the Organization of Afro-American Unity (OAAU), modeled on the Organization of African Unity, Malcolm X praised Patrice Lumumba as "the greatest man who ever walked the African continent. He didn't fear anybody. He had those people so scared they had to kill him. They couldn't buy him, they couldn't frighten him, they couldn't reach him." In his speech in Harlem's Audubon Ballroom on June 28, 1964, Malcolm X quoted from Lumumba's "greatest speech," addressed to the King of Belgium at the ceremony of the proclamation of the Congo's independence (June 30, 1960), advising his Black audience that they "should take that speech and tack it up over [their] door" because, as Malcolm X suggests, Lumumba's message was just as relevant to African Americans as it was to Africans: "This is what Lumumba said: 'You aren't giving us anything. Why, can you take back these scars that you put on our bodies? Can you give us back the limbs that you cut off while you were here?' No, you should never forget what that man did to you. And you bear the scars of the same kind of colonization and oppression not on your body, but in your brain, in your heart, in your soul, right now." Malcolm X, *By Any Means Necessary: Speeches, Interviews, and a Letter by Malcolm X*, ed. George Breitman (New York: Pathfinder, 1970), 64–65.

8. William Faulkner, *Light in August*, opening of chap. 6 (New York: Modern Library, 1012), 110.

9. One instance in which Malcolm X highlighted the importance of history and memory for a people was, again, the speech at the founding rally of the OAAU. In it, he quotes from and expounds upon the propositions in the "Statement of Basic Aims and Objectives of the Organization of Afro-American Unity," written by a committee. The OAAU demands "a cultural revolution to unbrainwash an entire people": "This cultural revolution will be the journey to our rediscovery of ourselves. History is a people's memory, and without a memory man is demoted to the level of the lower animals." "Armed with the knowledge of our past, we can with confidence charter a course for our future. Culture is an indispensible weapon in the freedom struggle. We must take

hold of it and forge the future with the past." Malcolm X, *By Any Means Necessary*, 54–56.

10. This is Malcolm X's answer to Black reporter Claude Lewis's question about how he wanted to be remembered, in an interview that took place in New York in the last months of his life. Peter Goldman, *The Death and Life of Malcolm X* (1973; Urbana: University of Illinois Press, 2013), 238. See also Malcolm X's statement on March 12, 1964: "I am not educated, nor am I an expert in any particular field—but I am sincere, and my sincerity is my credentials" (*Malcolm X Speaks*, 20).

11. Paul Laurence Dunbar, "We Wear the Mask," in *The Collected Poetry*, ed. Joanne M. Braxton (Charlottesville: University Press of Virginia, 1993), 71.

12. On Robert Williams, see chap. 6, n. 19.

13. None of these debates with the long-time leader of the Nation of Islam exists in print. Though West does not ignore "the disagreeable views of Farrakhan," he insists on the minister's "deep love and service for his people. [. . .] He bravely stood up against white supremacy at a time in our history when to do so required courage and character" (West, *Brother West*, 186). "We agree on highlighting black suffering," West wrote in a statement justifying his participation in Farrakhan's Million Man March in 1995 ("Why I Am Marching in Washington," *Million Man March/Day of Absence: A Commemorative Anthology*, ed. Haki R. Madhubuti and Maulana Karenga (Los Angeles: University of Sankore Press, 1996), 37.

14. In three seminal studies James Hal Cone developed a Black theology of liberation that addressed the questions of what it meant to be a Black Christian during the Black Power movement and what the example of the life of Jesus could contribute to the liberation of oppressed Black people suffering from the legacy of white supremacy: *Black Theology and Black Power* (New York: Harper & Row, 1969; Maryknoll, NY: Orbis Books, 1997), followed by *A Black Theology of Liberation* (Philadelphia: J. B. Lippincott, 1970; Maryknoll, NY: Orbis Books, 1990) and *The Spirituals and the Blues* (1972; Maryknoll, NY: Orbis Books, 1991). See also Cornel West's homage to Cone, "Black Theology and Human Identity," in *Black Faith and Public Talk: Critical Essays on James H. Cone's* Black Theology and Black Power, ed. Dwight N. Hopkins (Maryknoll, NY: Orbis Books, 1999), 11–19.

15. "No matter how much respect, no matter how much recognition, whites show towards me, as far as I'm concerned, as long as it is not shown to every one of our people in this country, it doesn't exist for me" (1964), quoted in West, *Race Matters*, 35.

16. See Goldman, *Death and Life of Malcolm X*, 14.

17. For a vivid portrait of his father, see Huey P. Newton's autobiography *Revolutionary Suicide* (1973), especially chap. 4, "Changing," in which he states, for example: "When I say that my father was unusual, I mean that he had a dignity and pride seldom seen in southern Black men. Although many other Black men in the South had a similar strength, they never let it show around whites. To do so was to take your life in your hands. My father never kept his strength from anybody." Huey P. Newton, with J. Herman Blake, *Revolutionary Suicide* (New York: Penguin, 2009), 29.

18. See also chap. 3, n. 30. On the famous murder trial of Bobby Seale and Ericka Huggins, which ended in acquittal on all charges, see the detailed account by Donald Freed, *Agony in New Haven: The Trial of Bobby Seale and Ericka Huggins and the Black Panther Party* (New York: Simon and Schuster, 1973). See also Seale's presentation of the major years of the party's history, *Seize the Time: The Story of the Black Panther Party and Huey P. Newton* (New York: Random House, 1970), as well as his autobiography, *A Lonely Rage: The Autobiography of Bobby Seale* (New York: Times Books, 1978).

19. It is significant that although Ericka Huggins was a high-ranking Black Panther Party leader, at first in the Los Angeles chapter and then as a founder and leader of the New Haven chapter of the BPP, she and so many other female revolutionary activists are far less known than the party's male leaders, just as the party's multifaceted community services have been downplayed. For a long time, scholarship focused almost exclusively on the militant male image of the party, as it had in part been encouraged by male members themselves and certainly enforced by the media. For a revisionist reading of the BPP history, see Ericka Huggins and Angela D. LeBlanc-Ernest, "Revolutionary Women, Revolutionary Education: The Black Panther Party's Oakland Community School," in *Want to Start a Revolution?*, 161–84, with further references to the neglected women's contributions to the revolutionary work of the BPP. For a highly balanced and differentiated assessment of the crucial role of women in the BPP, and the difficulties both male and female members of the party had with gendered power relations, see "A Woman's Party," in Mumia Abu-Jamal, *We Want Freedom: A Life in the Black Panther Party* (Cambridge, MA: South End Press, 2004), 159–84; on Abu-Jamal, see below, n. 26. Interestingly, Abu-Jamal draws attention to Ella Baker's "collectivist model of leadership": "In essence, Baker was arguing against civil rights organizations mirroring the Black church model—a predominantly female membership with a predominantly male clergy—and for the inclusion of women in the leadership of these organizations. Baker was also questioning the hierarchical nature of these groups'

leadership" (ibid., 159). For an emphasis on BPP community services, see *The Black Panther Party: Service to the People Programs*, ed. David Hilliard (Albuquerque: University of New Mexico Press, 2008). In the foreword, West, who as a student participated in the BPP Free Breakfast for Schoolchildren Program, highlights the avant-garde character of the party's political vision: "The Black Panther Party [. . .] was the highest form of deniggerization in niggerized America. The Black Panther Party was the greatest threat to American apartheid because it was indigenous in composition, interracial in strategies and tactics, and international in vision and analysis. It was indigenous in that it spoke to the needs and hopes of the local community. [. . .] It combined bread-and-butter issues of everyday people with deep democratic empowerment in the face of an oppressive status quo. It was interracial in that it remained open to strategic alliances and tactical coalitions with progressive brown, red, yellow, and white activists. And it was international in that it understood American apartheid in light of anti-imperial struggles around the world" (x).

20. For the great impact Malcolm X had on Amiri Baraka (LeRoi Jones), see, for example, "The Legacy of Malcolm X, and the Coming of the Black Nation," in Baraka's collection of "Social Essays" entitled *Home* (1966; New York: Akashi Classics, 2009), 266–79, as well as the new introduction to the reprint, in which he highlights the significance of Malcolm X for the development that Baraka defines as "the open dialectic of the Afro-American national movement, splitting one into two, because my generation—though clearly we had to love and respect Dr. King—rejected that call ['If any blood be shed, let it be ours!'] with our whole-ass selves. Why? Because Malcolm X had begun to appear, and he said, 'Be peaceful, be courteous, obey the law, respect everyone; but if someone puts his hand on you, send him to the cemetery'" (17).

21. In the last months of his life, Malcolm X frequently talked about the necessity of seeking international alliances and of holding the United States responsible for human rights violations. The most extensive passage can be found in one of his most famous speeches, which he entitled "The Ballot or the Bullet," in which, on April 3, 1964, he told his Black audience: "They keep you wrapped up in civil rights. And you spend so much time barking up the civil-rights tree, you don't even know there's a human-rights tree on the same floor. When you expand the civil-rights struggle to the level of human rights, you can then take the case of the black man in this country before the nations in the UN. You can take it before the General Assembly. You can take Uncle Sam before a world court." *Malcolm X Speaks*, 34–35. According to the FBI files on Martin Luther King Jr., two months after this speech, in June 1964, there was a meeting between Malcolm X and representatives of several civil

rights organizations; among others, King's lawyer, advisor, and friend Clarence Jones attended and was authorized to speak for King (who at the time was in jail). As the FBI report maintains, "Jones said that in 'reflecting on today's conference the most important thing discussed was Malcolm X's idea that we internationalize the question of civil rights and bring it before the United Nations.' [. . .] Jones stated that 'we should present the plight of the Negro to the United Nations General Assembly in September of this year.'" Michael Friedly and David Gallen, *Martin Luther King, Jr.: The FBI File* (New York: Carroll & Graf, 1993), 242.

22. James H. Cone, *Martin & Malcolm & America: A Dream or a Nightmare?* (Maryknoll, NY: Orbis Books, 1991; 20th anniversary ed., 2012). See Cone's recapitulatory statement: "We should never pit them against each other. Anyone, therefore, who claims to be for one and not the other does not understand their significance for the black community, for America, or for the world. We need both of them and we need them *together*. Malcolm keeps Martin from being turned into a harmless American hero. Martin keeps Malcolm from being an ostracized black hero" (ibid., 316).

23. "You can't operate a capitalistic system unless you are vulturistic; you have to have someone else's blood to suck to be a capitalist." Speech at the Audubon Ballroom, December 20, 1964, quoted in *Malcolm X Speaks*, 121. For a more elaborate use of the metaphor of the vulture, see the following statement by Malcolm X: "It is impossible for capitalism to survive, primarily because the system of capitalism needs some blood to suck. Capitalism used to be like an eagle, but now it's more like a vulture. It used to be strong enough to go and suck anybody's blood whether they were strong or not. But now it has become more cowardly, like the vulture, and it can only suck the blood of the helpless. As the nations of the world free themselves, then capitalism has less victims, less to suck, and it becomes weaker and weaker. It's only a matter of time in my opinion before it will collapse completely." "The Young Socialist Interview," January 18, 1965, *By Any Means Necessary*, 165–66.

24. In his speeches, Carmichael would highlight the importance of preserving the spirit of the radical Black tradition: "We must listen to Malcolm very closely, because we have to understand our heroes. We cannot let them be used by other people, we cannot let them be interpreted by other people to say other things. We must know what our heroes were saying to us—*our* heroes, not the heroes of the white left or what have you." *Stokely Speaks*, 178; for references to Douglass, Du Bois, and contemporary activists, see also ibid., 62–63, 74–75.

25. The League of Revolutionary Black Workers (LRBW) was a radical organization formed in the aftermath of the Detroit riots in 1969 by auto

industry workers who were frustrated with inhumane working conditions and dissatisfied with the neglect of Black workers' interests in the United Auto Workers union. Kenneth Cockrel and General Gordon Baker Jr. were members of the LRBW's executive committee, and Darryl Mitchell was one of the founding members. For a detailed history, see James A. Geschwender, *Class, Race, and Worker Insurgency: The League of Revolutionary Black Workers* (New York: Cambridge University Press, 1977); it is interesting to note that the classic *Detroit, I Do Mind Dying: A Study in Urban Revolution*, by Dan Georgakas and Marvin Surkin (New York: St. Martin's Press, 1975) was reissued with a foreword by Manning Marable in 2012 by Haymarket Books.

26. Mumia Abu-Jamal, former member of the Black Panther Party and prolific radio journalist and writer, was sentenced to death for allegedly killing a police officer in 1982; the sentence was commuted to life imprisonment in 2012. For the defense's view of the trial, see Abu-Jamal's attorney Leonard I. Weinglass's "The Trial of Mumia Abu-Jamal," in Abu-Jamal's book of autobiographical reflections, *Live From Death Row*, introduction by John Edgar Wideman (Reading, MA: Addison-Wesley, 1995), 195–215. In that book's "Musings on Malcolm" (133–36), Abu-Jamal affirms the significance of Malcolm X for the Black Panthers and stresses the continuity of Malcolm X's fight against systemic racism: "Malcolm, and the man who returned from Mecca, Hajii Malik Shabazz, both were scourges of American racism. [. . .] He stood for— and died for—*human* rights of self-defense and a people's self-determination, not for 'civil rights,' which, as the Supreme Court has indeed shown, changes from day to day, case to case, administration to administration" (136). See also Mumia Abu-Jamal, *Death Blossoms: Reflections from a Prisoner of Conscience*, foreword by Cornel West (Farmington, PA: Plough Publishing House, 1997). West's foreword ends with the urgent question that has motivated the making of *Black Prophetic Fire*: "Will we ever listen to and learn from our bloodstained prophets?" (xii). The Black prophetic fire of Pam Africa and Ramona Africa of the MOVE organization has helped keep the cause of Mumia Abu-Jamal alive—along with the efforts of many others. In his more recent conversations with Marc Lamont Hill, Abu-Jamal also refers to some other great figures of the Black radical tradition; for example, in an extended exchange on Du Bois, he reveals that "my favorite Du Bois book isn't *The Souls of Black Folk*, it's *Darkwater*, which is far rougher and harder and angrier." Mumia Abu-Jamal and Marc Lamont Hill, *The Classroom and The Cell: Conversations on Black Life in America* (Chicago: Third World Press, 2012), 70. See also the excellent documentary film by Stephen Vittoria, *Long-Distance Revolutionary: A Journey with Mumia Abu-Jamal* (Street Legal Cinema, 2013), which clearly situates Abu-Jamal in the Black prophetic tradition, both by references to predecessors

such as Douglass and Malcolm X and by interviews with current intellectuals and activists such as Angela Davis, Alice Walker, and Cornel West.

27. Assata Shakur has been a radical activist since her student days in the mid-sixties; she was a leading member of the Harlem branch of the Black Panther Party but left the BPP for its members' want of an awareness of the Black historical tradition. As she claims in her autobiography, the "basic problem stemmed from the fact that the BPP had no systematic approach to political education. They were reading the *Red Book* [by Mao Tse Tung] but didn't know who Harriet Tubman, Marcus Garvey, and Nat Turner were." Shakur, *Assata: An Autobiography* (1987; Chicago: Lawrence Hill Books, 1999), 221. As to her own steps in self-education, Shakur emphasizes the importance of learning about "Black resistance": "You couldn't catch me without a book in my hand after that [after "i found out about Nat Turner"]. I read everything from [. . .] Sonia Sanchez to Haki Madhubuti (Don L. Lee). I saw plays by Black playwrights like Amiri Baraka and Ed Bullins. [. . .] A whole new world opened up to me" (175). She joined the more radical BPP split-off, the underground Black Liberation Army (BLA). In the so-called New Jersey Turnpike shootout trial, she was found guilty of the murder of a state trooper; she escaped prison in 1979 and eventually fled to Cuba, where she has been granted political asylum since 1984. Classified as a "domestic terrorist" since 2005, the FBI placed her on the Most Wanted Terrorists list in May 2013.

28. As stated in a letter by J. Edgar Hoover in March 1968, the FBI's Counterintelligence Program (COINTELPRO) defined the following five very distinct long-range goals: to prevent "the *coalition* of militant black nationalist groups," to prevent violence on the part of these groups, to prevent them from gaining respectability, and to prevent their growth. In the context of the Black prophetic tradition, the second of these five goals is particularly interesting: "Prevent the *rise of a 'messiah'* who could unify, and electrify, the militant black nationalist movement. Malcolm X might have been such a 'messiah'; he is the martyr of the movement today. Martin Luther King, Stokely Carmichael, and Elijah Muhammed [*sic*] all aspire to this position. Elijah Muhammed is less of a threat because of his age. King could be a very real contender for this position should he abandon his supposed 'obedience' to 'white, liberal doctrines' (nonviolence) and embrace black nationalism. Carmichael has the necessary charisma to be a real threat in this way." This letter and other excerpts from the FBI's BPP files are reprinted in a booklet that speaks to the problem raised by West: Dhoruba Bin Wahad, Mumia Abu-Jamal, and Assata Shakur, *Still Black, Still Strong: Survivors of the U.S. War Against Black Revolutionaries* (New York: Semiotext/e, 1993), 245.

29. Roger Wareham, human rights attorney and long-time political activist, is a member of the New York–based December 12 movement, a nongovernmental organization committed to Malcolm X's legacy of bringing the United States before a world court for its continued violations of Black peoples' human rights.

30. Elombe Brath, graphic artist and long-time activist in the Pan-African movement, was one of the founders of the African Jazz-Arts Society and Studios (AJASS), a collective of Black artists active in the mid-1950s and considered a forerunner of the famous Black Arts Movement (BAM); it was launched by Amiri Baraka after the assassination of Malcolm X. In 1967, H. Rap Brown followed Stokely Carmichael as SNCC chair. While in Attica Prison (1971–1976), Brown converted to orthodox Islam, changed his name to Jamil Abdullah Al-Amin, and became a devout Imam. After a shooting in 2000, he was convicted of murder and sentenced to life in prison without parole. His memoir about growing up Black in America abounds with psychosociological reflections—reminiscent of Fanon's (see chap. 1, n. 23) analysis of the pathology of oppression—such as the following: "When a race of people is oppressed within a system that fosters the idea of competitive individualism, the political polarization around individual interests prevents group interests." H. Rap Brown, *Die Nigger Die! A Political Autobiography*, foreword by Ekwueme Michael Thelwell (1969; Chicago: Lawrence Hill Books, 2002), 16.

31. In the preface to his collection of poems *Don't Cry, Scream* (1969), Haki R. Madhubuti (Don L. Lee) defined his poetics as follows: "Blackpoetry is like a razor; it's sharp & will cut deep, not out to wound but to kill the inactive blackmind." In *Liberation Narratives: New and Collected Poems 1966–2009* (Chicago: Third World Press, 2009), 61. His poetry bears witness to his deep commitment to the Black prophetic tradition. In the collection *Killing Memory, Seeking Ancestors* (1987), Madhubuti pays homage to Malcolm X by asking: "if you lived among the committed / this day how would you lead us?" And he gives the answer: "it was not that you were pure. / the integrity of your vision and pain, / the quality of your heart and decision / confirmed your caring for local people, and your / refusal to assassinate progressive thought / has carved your imprint on the serious." "Possibilities: Remembering Malcolm X," in *Liberation Narratives*, 278.

32. Sonia Sanchez has repeatedly expressed great admiration for and deep gratitude to Malcolm X, most famously in her poem of mourning "Malcolm," from the collection *Home Coming* (Detroit: Broadside Press, 1969), 15–16, and in her play *Malcolm Man/Don't Live Here No Mo'* (1972). In her prose poem "Homegirls on St. Nicholas," Sanchez vividly describes how her life changed radically when she first heard Malcolm X speak, even so "I didn't

want to hear him. His words made my head hurt. [. . .] Why did he bring his
hand-grenade words into my space?" But when Malcolm X "demanded, 'Do
you know who you are? Who do you really think you are? Have you looked
in a mirror recently brother and sister and seen your Blackness for what it is?'
[. . .] something began to stir inside me. Something that I had misplaced a
long time ago in the classrooms of America. On that cold wet afternoon, I
became warm again." *Wounded in the House of a Friend* (Boston: Beacon Press,
1995), 52–53. See also her remarks on Malcolm X in a collection of interviews,
especially in the conversation with David Reich (1999), where she states that
Malcolm X "became our articulator": "Malcolm articulated all that we
thought. For many of us, Baraka and the rest, he gave us his voice." *Conversations with Sonia Sanchez*, ed. Joyce A. Joyce (Jackson: University Press of
Mississippi, 2007), 90, 89.

33. "I for one believe that if you give people a thorough understanding
of what it is that confronts them and the basic causes that produce it, they'll
create their own program. And when the people create a program, you get
action." Speech at a meeting of the Organization of Afro-American Unity on
the evening of December 20, 1964, *Malcolm X Speaks*, 118–19. As in his famous
"Message to the Grass Roots," delivered in November 1963, Malcolm X sets
off the people against the leaders by emphasizing the latter's propensity to
control rather than ignite the revolutionary fire. Earlier that day, Malcolm X
had appeared with grassroots activist Fannie Lou Hamer at the Williams
Institutional CME Church in Harlem and had invited her to attend the evening meeting at the Audubon Ballroom; see *Malcolm X Speaks*, 114–15.

34. For West's statements on rising secularism here and below, see statistics on religiously unaffiliated Americans released by the Pew Research Religion and Public Life Project, *Nones on the Rise: One in Five Adults Have No
Religious Affiliation* (Washington, DC: Pew Research Center's Forum on Religion & Public Life, October 9, 2012), http://www.pewforum.org/2012/10/09
/nones-on-the-rise-religion/.

35. Ibid.

36. Robert Green Ingersoll was one of the most popular freethinkers of
the late nineteenth century and considered one of the best lecturers, if not the
best orator, of his time. Though he was best known for his controversial talks
on agnosticism (or atheism: in contrast to common understanding, according
to which an agnostic claims not to know whether God exists, as opposed to
an atheist who denies God's existence, Ingersoll did not think it made sense
to distinguish between the two), he delivered speeches on a broad range of
topics, and in the name of humanism advocated racial equality, women's rights,
and civil liberties. In a speech in honor of Walt Whitman, "Liberty in

Literature," given in the presence of the poet (two years before he delivered a much-praised eulogy at Whitman's funeral), Ingersoll, referring to Shelley, Lord Byron, and Robert Burns, praises the prophetic quality of great poets: "The great poets have been on the side of the oppressed—of the downtrodden. They have suffered with the imprisoned and the enslaved. [. . .] The great poets [. . .] have uttered in all ages the human cry. Unbought by gold, unawed by power, they have lifted high the torch that illuminates the world." *Walt Whitman. An Address. Delivered in Philadelphia, Oct 21, 1890* (New York: Truth Seeker Co., 1890). It does not come as a surprise that Frederick Douglass and Ottilie Assing (see chap. 1, n. 17) were on friendly terms with Ingersoll; see Diedrich, *Love Across the Color Lines*, 358. In a meeting in Washington, DC, to protest the 1883 Supreme Court decision that found sections 1 and 2 of the 1875 Civil Rights Act unconstitutional, Ingersoll—introduced by Douglass—condemned the Court's decision and painted its effects in gruesome colors: "The masked wretches who, in the darkness of night, drag the poor negro from his cabin, and lacerate with whip and thong his quivering flesh, will, with bloody hands, applaud the Supreme Court." Ingersoll, "Address on the Civil Rights Act," *The Works of Robert G. Ingersoll*, vol. XI, *Miscellany* (New York: C. P. Farrell, 1900), 2. See also Susan Jacoby's *The Great Agnostic: Robert Ingersoll and American Freethought* (New Haven, CT: Yale University Press, 2013), 111, and in that book, her "Letter to the 'New' Atheists," who, according to Jacoby, have largely ignored Ingersoll (192–202).

37. Clarence Seward Darrow was a renowned lawyer. Among his famous cases was his defense of John T. Scopes, put to trial for teaching evolution in a classroom in Dayton, Tennessee. In his autobiography, Darrow devotes three chapters to this trial, which he had taken on "solely to induce the public to stop, look, and listen, lest our public schools should be imperilled with a fanaticism founded on ignorance." *The Story of My Life*, with a new introduction by Alan M. Dershowitz (1932; New York: Da Capo Press, 1996), 276. See also the chapter "Questions without Answers," in which Darrow discusses the belief in God (385–95). Together with Wallace Rice, Darrow compiled *Infidels and Heretics: An Agnostic's Anthology* (1928; New York: Gordon Press, 1975). The current revival of atheism mentioned by West is reflected, for example, in the following recent publications: *In the Clutches of the Law: Clarence Darrow's Letters*, ed. and with an introduction by Randall Tietjen (Berkeley: University of California Press, 2013), and *Attorney for the Damned: Clarence Darrow in the Courtroom*, ed. and with notes by Arthur Weinberg; foreword by Justice William O. Douglas (1957; Chicago: University of Chicago Press, 2012).

38. See Baldwin's address to the World Council of Churches, July 7, 1968, "White Racism or World Community," in *Collected Essays* (New York: Library

of America, 1998), 749–56. Referring to his credentials as a speaker, Baldwin says: "I never expected to be standing in such a place, because I left the pulpit twenty-seven years ago. [. . .] And I want to make it clear to you that though I may have to say some rather difficult things here this afternoon, I want to make it understood that in the heart of the absolutely necessary accusation there is contained a plea. The plea was articulated by Jesus Christ himself, who said, 'Insofar as you have done it unto the least of these, you have done it unto me'" (749). In his autobiographical essay "Down at the Cross," originally published in the collection *The Fire Next Time* (1963), Baldwin rejects Christianity's claim of the monopoly on morals: "It is not too much to say that whoever wishes to become a truly moral human being [. . .] must first divorce himself from all the prohibitions, crimes, and hypocrisies of the Christian church" (Baldwin, *Collected Essays*, 314). Yet he also admits that the church service held great attractions for him: "The church was very exciting. It took a long time for me to disengage myself from this excitement, and on the blindest, most visceral level, I never really have, and never will. There is no music like this music, no drama like the drama of the saints rejoicing, the sinners moaning, the tambourines racing, and all those voices coming together crying holy unto the Lord" (306). In a 1965 interview, Baldwin explicates, "I'm not a believer in any sense which would make any sense to any church, and any church would obviously throw me out. I believe—what do I believe? [. . .] I believe in love. [. . .] [By love] I don't mean anything passive. I mean something active, something more like a fire, like the wind, something which can change you. I mean energy. I mean a passionate belief, a passionate knowledge of what a human being can do, and become, what a human being can do to change the world in which he finds himself." James Mossman, "Race, Hate, Sex, and Colour: A Conversation with James Baldwin and Colin MacInnes" (1965), in *Conversations with James Baldwin*, ed. Fred L. Standley and Louis H. Pratt (Jackson: University Press of Mississippi, 1989), 48. It is interesting to note that Sonia Sanchez ends her homage to James Baldwin, written on the occasion of his passing away in 1987, by thanking him "for his legacy of fire. A fine rain of words when we had no tongues. He set fire to our eyes. Made a single look, gesture endure. Made a people meaningful and moral. Responsible finally for all our sweet and terrible lives" ("A Remembrance," *Wounded*, 34).

39. See Malcolm X's speech at the Williams Institutional CME Church in Harlem, December 20, 1964: "I'm not for anybody who tells black people to be nonviolent while nobody is telling white people to be nonviolent. [. . .] Now if you are with us, all I say is, make the same kind of contribution with us in our struggle for freedom that all white people have always made when they were struggling for their own freedom. You were struggling for your

freedom in the Revolutionary War. Your own Patrick Henry said 'liberty or death,' and George Washington got the cannons out, and all the rest of them that you taught me to worship as my heroes, they were fighters, they were warriors" (*Malcolm X Speaks*, 112–13).

40. See Du Bois, "The Propaganda of History," in *Black Reconstruction*, 594.

41. Excerpts from Malcolm X's contribution to the Oxford Union Society debate December 3, 1964, are available in *By Any Means Necessary*, 176–77, 182. The question debated was "Extremism in the defense of liberty is no vice, moderation in the pursuit of justice is no virtue." Almost fifty years later, on November 22, 2012, Cornel West took part in the Oxford Union Society debate on this motion: "This House would occupy Wall Street." Both speeches can be accessed on YouTube.

42. For an in-depth exploration of Black Nationalism, see Michael Lerner and Cornel West, *Jews and Blacks: A Dialogue on Race, Religion, and Culture in America* (New York: Penguin, 1996), 91–114; reprinted as "On Black Nationalism," in West, *The Cornel West Reader*, 521–29.

43. Marable, *Malcolm X*. For an account of the immense difficulties Marable faced in collecting factual evidence on Malcolm X, see his article "Rediscovering Malcolm's Life: A Historian's Adventure in Living History," *Souls* 7, no. 1 (2005): 20–35; reprinted in *The Portable Malcolm X Reader*, ed. Manning Marable and Garrett Felber (New York: Penguin, 2013), 573–600.

44. See the first collection of essays published in reaction to Marable's biography, *By Any Means Necessary: Malcolm X: Real, Not Reinvented; Critical Conversations on Manning Marable's Biography of Malcolm X*, ed. Herb Boyd, Ron Daniels, Maulana Karenga, and Haki R. Madhubuti (Chicago: Third World Press, 2012), which offers a wide range of critical opinions. It opens with Sonia Sanchez's poem "Malcolm" (see above, n. 32) and contains essays by Mumia Abu-Jamal, Amiri Baraka, and many others who, above all, seek to affirm the radical Black tradition. See also *A Lie of Reinvention: Correcting Manning Marable's Malcolm X*, ed. Jared A. Ball and Todd Steven Burroughs (Baltimore: Black Classic Press, 2012), which contains contributions by, among others, Mumia Abu-Jamal, Amiri Baraka, and Herb Boyd. Though most statements criticize Marable's extensive use of conjecture in presenting his arguments, the most severe critique, voiced repeatedly against Marable's portrayal, is that the historian deprived Malcolm X of the political radicalism of his message and turned him into a "mainstream-leaning, liberal Democrat" (6).

45. Harry Haywood, *Black Bolshevik: Autobiography of an Afro-American Communist* (Chicago: Liberator Press, 1978). In the context of the Black

prophetic tradition, it is interesting to note that Haywood praises Du Bois as a pioneer of historical revisionism with his *"tour de force, Black Reconstruction,* and the epilogue, 'Propaganda of History,' which contained a bitter indictment of the white historical establishment" (95).

46. West refers to the 1992 Hollywood film *Malcolm X,* directed and cowritten by Spike Lee, with Denzel Washington in the title role. Given the fierce political struggle over Malcolm X's legacy, it is not surprising to learn that, though the screenplay was largely based on *The Autobiography of Malcolm X,* the film was highly controversial, both during the long history of planning and production, and after its release.

47. On the iconization and commodification of Malcolm X, see Angela Davis's "Meditations on the Legacy of Malcolm X," in *Malcolm X in Our Own Image,* ed. Joe Wood (New York: St. Martin's Press, 1992), 40–41.

48. For the criticism by Baraka and others, see, for example, Evelyn Nieves, "Malcolm X: Firestorm Over a Film Script," movie section of the *New York Times,* August 9, 1991. The new book by activist-scholar Maulana Karenga on Malcolm X as a moral philosopher promises to be a major contribution to our understanding of Malcolm. West wrote the introduction to this text.

49. In 1966, Baldwin accepted the offer by Columbia Pictures to write a screenplay based on *The Autobiography of Malcolm X,* although he had "grave doubts and fears about Hollywood. [. . .] The idea of Hollywood doing a truthful job on Malcolm could not but seem preposterous. And yet—I didn't want to spend the rest of my life thinking: *It could have been done if you hadn't been chicken.* I felt that Malcolm would never have forgiven me for that." Baldwin, "To Be Baptized," from the essay collection *No Name in the Street* (New York: Library of America, 1998), 413. In an interview, Baldwin commented on his disagreements with Hollywood as follows: "To put it brutally, if I had agreed with Hollywood, I would have been allowing myself to create an image of Malcolm that would have satisfied them and infuriated you, broken your hearts. At one point I saw a memo that said, among other things, that the author had to avoid giving any political implications to Malcolm's trip to Mecca. Now, how can you write about Malcolm X without writing about his trip to Mecca and its political implications? It was not surprising. They were doing the Che Guevara movie while I was out there. It had nothing to do with Latin America, the United Fruit Company, Che Guevara, Cuba . . . nothing to do with anything. It was hopeless crap. Hollywood's fantasy is designed to prove to you that this poor, doomed nitwit deserves his fate." Interview with Jewell Handy Grasham (1976), in Standley and Pratt, *Conversations with James Baldwin,* 167. See also Baldwin's screenplay *One Day, When I Was Lost: A Scenario,* based on *The Autobiography of Malcolm X.*

50. *The Black Agenda Report: News, Commentary & Analysis from the Black Left* is a radio and TV program launched in 2006 by long-time radio journalist Glen Ford, life-long activist and community organizer Bruce Dixon, and legendary Harlem activist Nellie Bailey, as well as writer and peace activist Margaret Kimberley and political scientist and activist Leutisha Stills.

51. Carl Dix, self-proclaimed "veteran revolutionary fighter from the '60s," is cofounder of the Revolutionary Communist Party, USA (RCP), established in 1975, and has been a committed activist, for example, on behalf of Mumia Abu-Jamal and as a leading voice in the campaign against New York Police Department's "stop and frisk" practice; see his article "Why I Am Getting Arrested Today" (*Huffington Post*, October 21, 2011), in which he explains the rationale behind the act of civil disobedience, during which he was joined by thirty other activists, including Cornel West. Dix and West have conducted several public dialogues entitled "In the Age of Obama: What Future for Our Youth?" as well as a series of "Mass Incarceration Dialogues." Bob Avakian has been RCP chair since its founding; for his unwavering commitment to radical political activism, see *From Ike to Mao and Beyond: My Journey from Mainstream America to Revolutionary Communist; a Memoir* (Chicago: Insight Press, 2005). Avakian wrote his life story on the suggestion of Cornel West; see preface (ix).

52. Chris Hedges, Pulitzer Prize–winning journalist, best-selling author, and activist, was a foreign correspondent for the *New York Times* (1990–2005) and is now a regular columnist for *Truthdig*. In November 2011, Hedges, West, and others held a mock trial of Goldman Sachs in Zuccotti Park, New York. Glenn Greenwald practiced law as a litigation attorney specializing in constitutional law and civil rights before he became an award-winning journalist and best-selling author; he gained worldwide fame in June 2013 due to his involvement in publishing whistleblower Edward Snowden's documents on US surveillance practices in the *Guardian*. (For Margaret Kimberley, see above, n. 50.) Larry Hamm—a distinguished Princeton University graduate—is the legendary founder and leader of the revolutionary People's Organization for Progress.

53. The best anthology on the Black prophetic tradition remains *African American Religious Thought*, edited by Cornel West and Eddie Glaude Jr. (Louisville, KY: Westminster John Knox Press, 2003).

Chapter Six: Prophetic Fire

1. See Guy Gugliotta, "New Estimate Raises Civil War Death Toll," *New York Times*, April 2, 2012. Gugliotta's report is based on a study by J. David Hacker, a demographic historian from Binghamton University in New York whose recalculation increased the death toll by more than 20 percent.

2. The assassination of Tsar Alexander II, in 1881, which, according to contemporary rumors, was committed by Jews, set off a wave of pogroms that lasted until 1884; this in turn led to considerable Jewish emigration to the United States.

3. In her autobiography, Wells claims that the lynching in Memphis "changed the whole course of my life." *Crusade for Justice: The Autobiography of Ida B. Wells*, ed. Alfreda M. Duster (Chicago: University of Chicago Press, 1970), 47 (hereafter cited as *Crusade*). The three men—Thomas Moss, Calvin McDowell, and Will (Henry) Stewart, whom Wells calls both "Henry" and "Lee"; see *Crusade*, 47, 64—co-owned and ran a cooperative grocery store, the People's Grocery, located opposite a white grocery store that had enjoyed a monopoly in the densely populated suburb of Memphis.

4. Like Wells, T. Thomas Fortune was a pioneering journalist and newspaper editor as well as a staunch activist. Fortune founded the Afro-American League in 1890, a more militant precursor of the NAACP, which faltered for lack of funding. For several years, Wells and Fortune supported each other, but their paths diverged in 1898, when Fortune, due to several personal and financial blows, grew more and more desperate and turned to Booker T. Washington for help. Washington then subsidized the *New York Age* and offered assistance; see Paula J. Giddings, *Ida: A Sword Among Lions; Ida B. Wells and the Campaign Against Lynching* (New York: Harper Collins, 2009), 191.

5. It was the Memphis lynching that opened Wells's eyes: "Like many another person who had read of lynching in the South, I had accepted the idea meant to be conveyed—that although lynching was irregular and contrary to law and order, unreasoning anger over the terrible crime of rape led to the lynching; that perhaps the brute deserved death anyhow and the mob was justified in taking his life" (*Crusade*, 64). But the three men "had committed no crime against white women. This was what opened my eyes to what lynching really was. An excuse to get rid of Negroes who were acquiring wealth and property and thus keep the race terrorized and 'keep the nigger down'" (ibid.).

6. But as her biographer, Paula Giddings, points out, even radically minded Blacks like Ida B. Wells-Barnett and her husband, Ferdinand Barnett, who were highly critical of the imperialist politics of the United States, felt obliged to support Black troops: "Even those like Ida and Ferdinand, who loathed the imperialist impulses that the soldiers carried out in the rebellious Philippines and elsewhere, took pride in their tenacity and courage and supported them with fund-raising parties" (Giddings, *Ida*, 467). Yet, "Ida and Ferdinand helped organize a mass meeting at Chicago's Bethel Church to demand freedom for the Cubans and to deplore the killing of the island's Afro-Cuban military hero, Antonio Maceo y Grajales" (378).

7. The passage referred to builds up toward the experience of violence: "My knowledge of the race problem became more definite. I saw discrimination in ways of which I had never dreamed; the separation of passengers on the railways of the South was just beginning; the separation in living quarters throughout the cities and towns was manifest; the public disdain and even insult in race contact on the street continually took my breath; I came in contact for the first time with a sort of violence that I had never realized in New England; I remember going down and looking wide-eyed at the door of a public building, filled with buck-shot, where the editor of the leading paper had been publicly murdered the day before" (Du Bois, *Dusk of Dawn*, 15). And, in fact, Du Bois recalled that "lynching was a continuing and recurrent horror during my college days," but it was, indeed, more than a decade later when, in the late 1890s, while he was working as a social scientist at Atlanta University, that the case of Sam Hose affected him deeply (34). It is interesting to note that Wells-Barnett published a pamphlet on the Hose case: *Lynch Law in Georgia* (1899).

8. As Wells herself puts it in her diary: "I think of my tempestuous, rebellious, hard headed wilfulness, the trouble I gave, the disposition to question his [W. W. Hooper, president of Rust College (formerly Shaw University)] authority." *The Memphis Diary of Ida B. Wells*, ed. Miriam DeCosta-Willis (Boston: Beacon Press, 1995), 78.

9. "As I witnessed the triumph of the graduates and thought of my lost opportunity a great sob arose in my throat and I yearned with unutterable longing for the 'might have been'" (ibid., 78). Wells had been expelled from Rust College for her insubordination, and once she had to earn a living as a teacher, she was not able to continue her formal education.

10. As Patricia A. Schechter puts it in her highly instructive article "'All the Intensity of My Nature': Ida B. Wells, Anger and Politics," *Radical History Review* 70 (1998): 48–77: "Her 'anomalous' craving for social autonomy or platonic male friends suggests the limited range of social identities available to single middle-class black women. One was either a wife, a former wife, or a wife-to-be—all else was strange or irregular" (52–53).

11. Giddings, *Ida*, 69; see also Wells, *Crusade*, 31. As journalist Lucy Wilmot Smith notes, Wells, who "has been called the Princess of the Press [. . .] believes there is no agency so potent as the press in reaching and elevating a people" (quoted in *Crusade*, 33). The praise she received by contemporary journalists highlights the fearlessness of her speech. For example, T. Thomas Fortune writes: "She has plenty of nerve and is as sharp as a steel trap" (ibid.).

12. *American Slavery As It Is: Testimony of a Thousand Witnesses* (New York: American Anti-Slavery Society, 1839) was compiled by Theodore Dwight

Weld, one of the founders of the American Anti-Slavery Society; the sisters Sarah Grimké and Angelina Grimké Weld, staunch Abolitionists and early advocates for women's rights, contributed to the volume by bearing witness to the cruelties of slavery they had experienced at their father's plantation in South Carolina.

13. On William Cobbett, see chap. 1, n. 28.

14. On an extended visit to the United States between 1834 and 1836, Harriet Martineau became engaged in the Abolitionists' fight against slavery, closely observed American society (*Society in America*, 1837), and reflected upon the methods of social investigations (*How to Observe Morals and Manners*, 1838). The two books on America established her as a pioneer in sociology *avant la lettre*.

15. Wells, *Crusade*, 65–66.

16. See Giddings, *Ida*, 214. "They had destroyed my paper, in which every dollar I had in the world was invested. They had made me an exile and threatened my life for hinting at the truth. I felt that I owed it to myself and my race to tell the whole truth" (Wells, *Crusade*, 62–63).

17. The Socialist journalist and novelist Upton Sinclair investigated the working conditions in the Chicago meatpacking industry and published his findings at first as a serialized novel in 1905 in the Socialist paper the *Appeal to Reason*. In a review of the 1906 Doubleday edition, Jack London famously called *The Jungle* "the *Uncle Tom's Cabin* of wage slavery"; repr. in *Jack London: American Rebel; a Collection of His Social Writings Together with an Extensive Study of the Man and His Times*, ed. Philip S. Foner (New York: Citadel, 1947), 524.

18. "The lesson this teaches and which every Afro-American should ponder well, is that a Winchester rifle should have a place of honor in every black home, and it should be used for that protection which the law refuses to give. When the white man who is always the aggressor knows he runs as great a risk of biting the dust every time his Afro-American victim does, he will have greater respect for Afro-American life. The more the Afro-American yields and cringes and begs, the more he has to do so, the more he is insulted, outraged and lynched." Ida B. Wells, *Southern Horrors: Lynch Law in All Its Phases* (New York: New York Age Print, 1892), 70.

19. Robert F. Williams recounts the story of how, in 1957, "a Negro community in the South [in Monroe, North Carolina] took up guns in self-defense against racist violence—and used them" in his book *Negroes With Guns* (New York: Marzani and Munsell, 1962), 39, which he wrote in exile in Cuba, from where he broadcast *Radio Free Dixie*. In the prologue, Williams invokes "an accepted right of Americans, as the history of our Western states prove, that where the law is unable, or unwilling, to enforce order, the citizens

can, and must, act in self-defense against lawless violence," and claims that "this right holds for black Americans as well as whites." His example inspired Huey P. Newton and the Black Panther Party; see Timothy B. Tyson, *Radio Free Dixie: Robert F. Williams and the Roots of Black Power* (Chapel Hill: University of North Carolina Press, 1999).

20. "I had bought a pistol the first thing after Tom Moss was lynched, because I expected some cowardly retaliation from the lynchers. I felt that one had better die fighting against injustice than to die like a dog or a rat in a trap. I had already determined to sell my life as dearly as possible if attacked" (Wells, *Crusade*, 62).

21. Like Wells-Barnett, William Monroe Trotter, newspaper editor of the radical *Boston Guardian*, lifelong activist, and cofounder of the Niagara Movement, was known for his fearlessness and militancy. He and Wells-Barnett were often marginalized by more moderate activists. For example, they belonged to the militant faction of the group that prepared the founding of the NAACP, and Du Bois did not think them fit to appear on the list of the Founding Forty.

22. When, in 1909, Wells-Barnett had successfully fought against the reinstatement of a sheriff who had been involved in a lynching in Cairo, Illinois, the *Springfield Forum* praised her as "a lady in whom we are justly proud" and who "towers high above all of her male contemporaries and has more of the aggressive qualities than the average man" (December 11, 1909, quoted in Giddings, *Ida*, 487). Yet the common reaction to female aggression or anger expressed in public was repression or defamation. See Schechter, "'All the Intensity of My Nature,'" which—based on extensive research—highlights the pressure exerted on (Black) female radical activists like Wells, accomplished by an instrumentalization of etiquette that asked women to suppress feelings of rage.

23. In fact, she even published an essay in 1885 on the ideal of "true womanhood," "Woman's Mission," in the *New York Freeman*, edited by T. Thomas Fortune. As Giddings notes in *Ida*, her "well-received essay had made her an authority on the subject," "the nineteenth-century idea of the ideal woman who possessed the Victorian-era virtues of modesty, piety, purity, submission, and domesticity—virtues denied by the conditions that faced black women during slavery and deemed essential to not only their uplift but that of their families, and the community" (12, 86–87).

24. She writes in her diary: "I felt so disappointed for my people generally. I have firmly believed all along that the law was on our side and would, when we appealed to it, give us justice. I feel shorn of that belief and utterly discouraged, and just now, if it were possible, would gather my race in my arms

and fly away with them. O God, is there no redress, no peace, no justice in this land for us?" Entry for April 11, 1887, in the unpublished diary of Ida B. Wells, quoted by her daughter Alfreda M. Duster in the introduction to *Crusade*, xvii.

25. Evelyn Higginbotham, *Righteous Discontent: The Women's Movement in the Black Baptist Church, 1880–1920* (Cambridge, MA: Harvard University Press, 1993); Kevin Gaines, *Uplifting the Race: Black Leadership, Politics, and Culture During the Twentieth Century* (Charlotte: University of North Carolina Press, 1996).

26. See Trudier Harris in her introduction to Wells-Barnett's *Selected Works*: "While she was certainly celebrated by blacks, some of them nevertheless painted her as egotistical or as a crazy woman, a loner who did not represent the sentiments of the majority of forward thinking black intellectuals." *Selected Works of Ida B. Wells-Barnett*, compiled with an introduction by Trudier Harris (New York: Oxford University Press, 1991), 11.

27. In her autobiography, *Crusade for Justice*, Wells expresses her critique by juxtaposing her own "radical" political goals with Washington's policy, a technique that renders the latter downright absurd: "Our policy was to denounce the wrongs and injustices which were heaped upon our people, and to use whatever influence we had to help right them. Especially strong was our condemnation of lynch law and those who practiced it. Mr. Washington's theory had been that we ought not to spend our time agitating for our rights; that we had better give attention to trying to be first-class people in a jim crow car than insisting that the jim crow car should be abolished; that we should spend more time practicing industrial pursuits and getting education to fit us for this work than in going to college and striving for college education. And of course, fighting for political rights had no place whatsoever in his plans" (265). After the publication of Du Bois's *The Souls of Black Folk*, in 1903, when his critique of Washington was ardently debated among whites and Blacks, the "Barnetts stood almost alone in approving them [Du Bois's views] and proceeded to show why. We saw, as perhaps never before, that Mr. Washington's views on industrial education had become an obsession with the white people of this country. We thought it was up to us to show them the sophistry of the reasoning that any one system of education could fit the needs of an entire race; that to sneer at and discourage higher education would mean to rob the race of leaders which it so badly needed; and that all the industrial education in the world could not take the place of manhood" (281).

28. Not only did Wells-Barnett publicly oppose Washington's lenient attitude toward lynching, but she would also repeatedly criticize him sharply for certain political moves, for example, when in 1900 he launched a new

organization, the National Negro Business League, in order to counterbalance the Afro-American Council and its Anti-Lynching Bureau headed by Wells-Barnett (see Giddings, *Ida*, 423–26). In reaction to Wells-Barnett's attack in an editorial, Washington's mouthpiece, secretary Emmett J. Scott, wrote: "Miss Wells is fast making herself so ridiculous that everybody is getting tired of her" (426).

29. Wells-Barnett's great rival, Mary Church Terrell, a highly educated teacher, journalist, and lifelong activist, also advanced the Black women's club movement. In fact, according to Angela Davis, "Mary Church Terrell was the driving force that molded the Black women's club movement into a powerful political group." Davis, "Black Women and the Club Movement," in Angela Davis, *Women, Race & Class* (New York: Vintage, 1983), 135. Though Davis praises Wells and Terrell as "unquestionably the two outstanding Black women of their era," she also states that regrettably their "personal feud, which spanned several decades, was a tragic thread within the history of the Black women's club movement" (136).

30. Mary White Ovington, born to white progressive Unitarians who were active in the struggle against slavery and for women's rights, was one of the cofounders of the NAACP and served this organization in various functions for thirty-eight years. It was during the founding phase of the NAACP that the two women collided, when Du Bois had taken Wells off the list of the so-called Founding Forty, and Wells felt that Ovington approved of his decision (see Wells, *Crusade*, 325). Wells settled her account with Ovington by making her responsible for the fact that the NAACP "has fallen short of the expectations of its founders," because it "has kept Miss Mary White Ovington as chairman of the executive committee. [. . .] She has basked in the sunlight of the adoration of the few college-bred Negroes who have surrounded her, but has made little effort to know the soul of the black woman; and to that extent she has fallen far short of helping a race which has suffered as no white woman has ever been called upon to suffer or to understand" (327–28).

31. Wells devotes a whole chapter ("Chapter VIII: Miss Willard's Attitude") of *A Red Record: Tabulated Statistics and Alleged Causes of Lynchings in the United States, 1892–1893–1894* (Chicago: privately published, 1895), 138–48, to this battle with the national president of Woman's Christian Temperance Union, Frances E. Willard; see also "A Regrettable Interview," Wells, *Crusade*, 201–12. Willard's voice was a potent one; after all, she headed the era's largest and most powerful organization of white women. The more harmful for the Black community was her claim that Black men were excessively indulging in both alcohol and sex—and here she "quotes" an anonymous voice from the South—and consequently became an omnipresent threat to Southern women:

"The colored race multiplies like the locusts of Egypt. The grog-shop is its center of power. 'The safety of woman, of childhood, of the home is menaced at a thousand localities at this moment, so that the men dare not go beyond the sight of their own roof-tree'" (Wells, *Red Record*, 142).

32. According to Wells-Barnett, teaching Sunday school turned her life in Chicago into "one of the most delightful periods. I had a class of young men ranging from eighteen to thirty years of age. [. . .] Every Sunday we discussed the Bible lessons in a plain common-sense way and tried to make application of their truths to our daily lives. I taught this class for ten years" (*Crusade*, 298–99).

33. Jane Addams's famous Chicago settlement project of Hull House was a great model to Wells-Barnett; in fact, she regarded Addams as "the greatest woman in the United States" (*Crusade*, 259) and must have been proud to be called the "Jane Addams among Negroes" by a Danish visitor to the United States (Giddings, *Ida*, 538). However, Wells-Barnett's admiration for the out-standing social reformer did not prevent her from sharply criticizing Addams for failing to question the common charge of rape in an article that condemned lynching on legal grounds. See Jane Addams, "Respect for Law," *New York Independent*, January 3, 1901, and Wells-Barnett's response, "Lynching and the Excuse for It," *Independent*, May 1901. Both articles are reprinted in Bettina Aptheker's unearthing of this dispute, *Lynching and Rape: An Exchange of View*, by Addams and Wells, occasional papers, no. 25 (New York: American Institute for Marxist Studies, 1977). See also Maurice Hamington, "Public Pragmatism: Jane Addams and Ida B. Wells on Lynching," *Journal of Speculative Philosophy* 19, no. 2 (2005): 167–74, which presents this debate as "a wonderful example of public pragmatist philosophy" between the two activists who, despite Wells's critique, would continue to collaborate "on behalf of civil justice despite their public disagreement" (173).

34. See hooks and West, *Breaking Bread*.

35. An early experience of a lack of support in the Black community was when, in 1889, she wrote an article in the Memphis *Free Speech and Headlight* about the poor conditions in Black schools while she was still working as a teacher. As a result of her criticism, the school board did not reelect her. "I had taken a chance in the interest of the children of our race and had lost out. The worst part of the experience was the lack of appreciation shown by the parents. They simply could not understand why one would risk a good job, even for their children. [. . .] But I thought it was right to strike a blow against a glaring evil and I did not regret it. Up to that time I had felt that any fight made in the interest of the race would have its support. I learned then that I could not count on that" (*Crusade*, 37). Wells's belligerent fight

for justice would isolate her throughout her life. As her youngest daughter, Alfreda, remembered: "I've seen my mother shed tears after she'd come home from some organization where she worked so hard to try to get change . . . and had met with just obstinate antagonism" (Giddings, *Ida*, 623). See also Thomas C. Holt, "The Lonely Warrior: Ida B. Wells-Barnett and the Struggle for Black Leadership," in *Black Leaders of the 20th Century*, ed. John Hope Franklin and August Meier (Urbana: University of Illinois Press, 1982), 39–61, especially 58.

36. *Crusade*, 123. As Wells states, the British journalist and reformer William T. Stead "had come late to visit the World's Fair and remained for three months writing his book *If Christ Came to Chicago* and welding the civic and moral forces of the town into a practical working body" (122–23). Stead's book *If Christ Came to Chicago! A Plea for the Union of All Who Love in the Service of All Who Suffer* (1894) became a best seller. See Joseph O. Baylen, "A Victorian's 'Crusade' in Chicago, 1893–1894," *Journal of American History* 51 (December 1964): 418–34.

37. As early as 1891, Wells was aware of the importance of concrete organizational measures for the purpose of unification. Having attended the second national Afro-American League convention, in Knoxville, Tennessee, she complained that the gathering had not addressed the "gravest questions": "How do we do it? What steps should be taken to unite our people into a real working force—a unit, powerful and complete?" (quoted in Giddings, *Ida*, 170).

38. James Melvin Washington, *Frustrated Fellowship: The Baptist Quest for Social Power* (Macon, GA: Mercer, 1986); paperback edition 2004, with a new preface by Quinton H. Dixie, foreword by Cornel West.

39. In May 1910, owing to Wells-Barnett's initiative, the Negro Fellowship League Reading Room and Social Center opened its doors on State Street amid the saloons and gambling houses of Chicago's Black Belt. While Wells-Barnett "was lifted to the seventh heaven and cheerfully went about the work of helping to select the library," there was "great objection among some of our members to going there. Some of them took the ground that State Street was beneath their consideration" (*Crusade*, 304).

40. West alludes to Hazel Carby, *Reconstructing Black Womanhood* (New York: Oxford University Press, 1987), and Angela Y. Davis, *Women, Race & Class* (New York: Vintage, 1983), especially chap. 5, "The Meaning of Emancipation According to Black Women" (87–98).

41. Like Wells, Victoria (Vicki) Garvin (1915–2007) was a long-distance radical, yet, until recently, her lifelong political activism has been unduly neglected (and for this reason is highlighted in this note). Her work focused

on, but was by no means limited to, the struggle for Black workers' rights. In the 1950s, she served as executive secretary in the New York chapter of the National Negro Labor Council (NNLC) and as vice president of the national NNLC, an organization suspected by other unions to be (and in 1951 by the US attorney general officially declared) a Communist front. Garvin belonged to a network of leftist women who had been radicalized in the 1930s and had held on to their radical convictions even when they came under attack during the McCarthy era; see the seminal study by Dayo F. Gore, *Radicalism at the Crossroads: African American Women Activists in the Cold War* (New York: New York University Press, 2011), which unearths the largely neglected history of Black women radicals of the 1950s. See also Gore's article, "From Communist Politics to Black Power: The Visionary Politics and Transnational Solidarities of Victoria (Vicki) Ama Garvin," in the essay collection *Want to Start a Revolution?*, 71–94. In the late 1950s, Garvin moved to Africa and in 1961 settled in Accra, Ghana, where she was a member of the African American community headed by W. E. B. Du Bois and Shirley Graham Du Bois, and where she also met Malcolm X again, with whom she had collaborated closely in Harlem. Encouraged by Du Bois, Garvin accepted an invitation to go to China, where from 1964 to 1971 she taught English at the Shanghai Foreign Language Institute. See the biographical information in the highly instructive article on Black radical activists, e.g. Robert Williams, Huey Newton, and Amiri Baraka, embracing Mao's cultural revolution, in Robin D. G. Kelley and Betsy Esch, "Black Like Mao: Red China and Black Revolution," *Souls* 1, no. 4 (September 1999): 6–41. Back in the United States in the 1970s, Garvin continued her struggle for social justice by working as a community organizer, joining rallies on behalf of political prisoners such as Mumia Abu-Jamal, and through speaking engagements, for example, in March 1981, when she appeared with Harry Haywood in a presentation attended by Cornel West; see West, *Prophesy Deliverance!*, 176. As Gore aptly puts it in *Radical Crossroads*: "Her distinct political legacy rests not in official titles but in revolutionary experience and solidarity efforts that always combined local organizing with a global vision" (73).

42. As to party politics, the Barnetts remained loyal to the party of Lincoln, but Wells-Barnett actively supported unions, for example, in the mid-1920s, she assisted the young Brotherhood of Sleeping Car Porters and Maids (BSCPM), under its new Socialist leader A. Philip Randolph, in its struggle against strong resistance in Chicago, the seat of the Pullman Company (Giddings, *Ida*, 634–41).

43. *Crusade*, 302. Ironically, due to the initiative of the Jewish philanthropist Julius Rosenwald, a successful campaign led to the erection of a YMCA

for African Americans, in 1913. See Giddings: "In the past there would have been more debate among the Chicago black leadership about the propriety of supporting an all-black institution in lieu of demanding that the white-only Y accept African Americans. But by 1912, need, appreciation of the effort by prominent whites, and a growing sense of, and desire for, the black community's emergence as an entity in and of itself resulted in blacks, with few exceptions, supporting the effort" (*Ida*, 506).

44. *Crusade*, 301–2.

45. Wells, *A Red Record*, 75.

46. Wells gives a lively account on her collaboration with Douglass at the 1893 Chicago World's Fair in her autobiography (*Crusade*, 115–20). According to Wells, the pamphlet was turned into "a creditable little book called *The Reason Why the Colored American Is Not in the World's Columbian Exposition*. It was a clear, plain statement of facts concerning the oppression put upon the colored people in this land of the free and home of the brave. We circulated ten thousand copies of this little book during the remaining three months of the fair" (117).

47. Wells-Barnett's relations with Du Bois were strained after Du Bois took her off the list of the NAACP's Founding Forty (see above, n. 30). As Giddings suggests, Wells-Barnett's "ideology and militant views were something that the civil rights organization could, literally, not afford" (*Ida*, 497).

48. On Wells-Barnett's relations with Garvey, see *Crusade*, 380–82. Garvey applauded her by counting her among the "conscientious workers [. . .] whose fight for the uplift of the race is one of life and death" (Giddings, *Ida*, 585). Garvey invited her several times to address his Universal Negro Improvement Association (UNIA) in the fall of 1918, when Wells-Barnett and other radical activists, e.g., William Trotter and A. Philip Randolph, were elected to represent the UNIA at the Versailles Peace Treaty negotiations (but were denied passports by the government). In 1919, Ferdinand Barnett defended Garvey in a libel case; see Giddings, *Ida*, 619.

49. As an exception to the rule, Wells-Barnett recounts her support of Robert T. Motts, who turned his saloon into the Pekin Theater, with its company of Black actors and an African American orchestra. It is typical of Wells's broad-mindedness that, trying to convince other socially active women to collaborate with Motts, she argues "that now [*sic*] Mr. Motts was engaged in a venture of a constructive nature, I thought it our duty to forget the past and help him, that if he was willing to invest his money in something uplifting for the race we all ought to help" and that, furthermore, she "felt that the race owed Mr. Motts a debt of gratitude for giving us a theater in which we could sit anywhere we chose without restrictions" (*Crusade*, 290). In contrast to her

autobiography, the few entries of her short Chicago diary passed down to us clearly manifest her love of music and her regular attendance at concerts, shows, and movies. See *The 1930 Chicago Diary of Ida B. Wells-Barnett*, included in the *Memphis Diary*.

50. Younger than Wells, Mary Jane McLeod Bethune lived to support the election campaign of Franklin D. Roosevelt in 1932 and became a close friend to First Lady Eleanor Roosevelt. Bethune was both a devoted educator (best known for having founded a school for Black girls in Daytona Beach, Florida, in 1904) and an activist focusing on various Black women's associations (she was president of the Florida chapter of the National Association of Colored Women and in 1935 founded the National Council of Negro Women, which united twenty-eight different organizations).

51. In *Prophesy Deliverance!*, West presents Woodbey as a case of an "alliance of black theology and Marxist thought," who "devoted his life to promoting structural social change and creating a counter-hegemonic culture in liberal capitalist America" (126).

Conclusion: Last Words on the Black Prophetic Tradition in the Age of Obama

1. Jason DeParle: "Harder for Americans to Rise from Lower Rungs," *New York Times*, January 4, 2012.

WORKS CITED

Abu-Jamal, Mumia. *Death Blossoms: Reflections from a Prisoner of Conscience.* Farmington, PA: Plough Publishing House, 1997.

———. *Live From Death Row.* Reading, MA: Addison-Wesley, 1995.

———. *We Want Freedom: A Life in the Black Panther Party.* Cambridge, MA: South End Press, 2004.

Abu-Jamal, Mumia, and Marc Lamont Hill. *The Classroom and the Cell: Conversations on Black Life in America.* Chicago: Third World Press, 2012.

Addams, Jane, and Ida B. Wells. *Lynching and Rape: An Exchange of View.* 1901. Occasional papers, no. 25. Edited by Bettina Aptheker. New York: American Institute for Marxist Studies, 1977.

Alexander, Michelle. *The New Jim Crow: Mass Incarceration in the Age of Colorblindness.* New York: New Press, 2010.

Alinsky, Saul D. "Community Organizing and Analysis." *American Journal of Sociology* 46, no. 6 (May 1941): 797–808.

———. *Rules for Radicals: A Pragmatic Primer for Realistic Radicals.* New York: Random House, 1971.

Allen, Gay Wilson. *Waldo Emerson: A Biography.* New York: Viking Press, 1981.

Aptheker, Herbert, ed. *Book Reviews by W. E. B. Du Bois.* Millwood, NY: KTO Press, 1977.

Avakian, Bob. *From Ike to Mao and Beyond: My Journey from Mainstream America to Revolutionary Communist; a Memoir.* Chicago: Insight Press, 2005.

Baldwin, James. *Collected Essays.* New York: Library of America, 1998.

Ball, Jared A., and Todd Steven Burroughs, ed. *A Lie of Reinvention: Correcting Manning Marable's Malcolm X*. Baltimore: Black Classic Press, 2012.

Baraka, Amiri. *Home: Social Essays*. 1966. New York: Akashi Classics, 2009.

Baylen, Joseph O. "A Victorian's 'Crusade' in Chicago, 1893–1894." *Journal of American History* 51 (December 1964): 418–34.

Benjamin, Walter. "Theses on the Philosophy of History." 1940. In *Illuminations*, edited by Hannah Arendt. Translated by Harry Zohn. New York: Harcourt, Brace & World, 1968.

Bercovitch, Sacvan. *The American Jeremiad*. Madison: University of Wisconsin Press, 1978.

Berry, Mary Frances, and John Blassingame. *Long Memory: The Black Experience in America*. New York: Oxford University Press, 1982.

Bin Wahad, Dhoruba, Mumia Abu-Jamal, and Assata Shakur. *Still Black, Still Strong: Survivors of the War Against Black Revolutionaries*. Edited by Jim Fletcher, Tanaquil Jones, and Sylvère Lotringer. New York: Semiotext/e, 1993.

Blackmon, Douglas A. *Slavery by Another Name: The Re-Enslavement of Black Americans from the Civil War to World War II*. New York: Random House, 2008.

Blum, Edward J. *W. E. B. Du Bois: American Prophet*. Philadelphia: University of Philadelphia Press, 2007.

Bontemps, Arna. *Free At Last: The Life of Frederick Douglass*. New York: Dodd, Mead, 1971.

Bourdieu, Pierre. *In Other Words: Essays Towards a Reflexive Sociology*. Translated by Matthew Adamson. Cambridge, UK: Polity, 1994.

———. *Pascalian Meditations*. Translated by Richard Nice. Stanford, CA: Stanford University Press, 2000.

Boyd, Herb, Ron Daniels, Maulana Karenga, and Haki R. Madhubuti, ed. *By Any Means Necessary: Malcolm X: Real, Not Reinvented; Critical Conversations on Manning Marable's Biography of Malcolm X*. Chicago: Third World Press, 2012.

Bradley, Stefan. "The First and Finest: The Founders of Alpha Phi Alpha Fraternity." In *Black Greek-Letter Organizations in the Twenty-First Century*, edited by Gregory S. Parks, 19–39. Lexington: University Press of Kentucky, 2008.

Branch, Taylor. *Parting the Waters: America in the King Years 1954–63*. New York: Simon & Schuster, 1988.

Brown, H. Rap. *Die Nigger Die! A Political Autobiography*. 1969. Chicago: Lawrence Hill Books, 2002.

Brown, Robert McAfee, Abraham J. Heschel, and Michael Novak. *Vietnam: Crisis of Conscience*. New York: Association Press, 1967.

Buell, Lawrence. *Emerson*. Cambridge, MA: Belknap Press of Harvard University Press, 2003.

Buschendorf, Christa. *"The Highpriest of Pessimism": Zur Rezeption Schopenhauers in den USA*. Heidelberg: Winter Verlag, 2008.

———. "'Properly speaking there are in the world no such men as self-made men': Frederick Douglass's Exceptional Position in the Field of Slavery." In *Intellectual Authority and Literary Culture in the US, 1790–1900*, edited by Günter Leypoldt, 159–84. Heidelberg: Winter Verlag, 2013.

———. "The Shaping of We-Group Identities in the African American Community: A Perspective of Figurational Sociology on the Cultural Imaginary." In *The Imaginary and Its Worlds: American Studies after the Transnational Turn*, edited by Laura Bieger, Ramón Saldívar, and Johannes Voelz, 84–106. Hanover, NH: Dartmouth College Press/University Press of New England, 2013.

Byron, George Gordon. *The Works of Lord Byron*. New York: Blake, 1840.

Carby, Hazel. *Reconstructing Black Womanhood*. New York: Oxford University Press, 1987.

Carlyle, Thomas. "Occasional Discourse on the Nigger Question." 1849. In *Collected Works*. Vol. 11, *Critical and Miscellaneous Essays: Collected and Republished in Six Volumes*, vol. VI. London: Chapman and Hall, 1870.

Carmichael, Stokely. *Stokely Speaks: From Black Power to Pan-Africanism*. 1971. Chicago: Chicago Review Press, 2007.

———. "What We Want." *New York Review of Books*, September 1966.

Carmichael, Stokely, and Charles V. Hamilton. *Black Power: The Politics of Liberation in America*. New York: Random House, 1967.

Chester, Michael A. *Divine Pathos and Human Being: The Theology of Abraham Joshua Heschel*. London: Mitchell, 2005.

Clarke, John Henrik, et al., ed. *Black Titan: W. E. B. Du Bois*. Boston: Beacon Press, 1970.

Clausewitz, Carl von. *On War*. Edited by Michael Howard and Peter Perct. Princeton, NJ: Princeton University Press, 1984.

Colbert, Soyica Diggs. *The African American Theatrical Body: Reception, Performance, and the Stage*. New York: Cambridge University Press, 2011.

Coles, Romand. "'To Make This Tradition Articulate': Practiced Receptivity Matters, Or Heading West of West with Cornel West and Ella Baker." In *Christianity, Democracy, and the Radical Ordinary: Conversations Between a Radical Democrat and a Christian*, edited by Stanley Hauerwas and Romand Coles, 45–86. Cambridge, UK: Lutterworth Press, 2008.

Cone, James H. *Black Theology and Black Power*. 1969. Maryknoll, NY: Orbis Books, 1997.

———. *A Black Theology of Liberation*. 1970. Maryknoll, NY: Orbis Books, 1990.

———. "'Let Suffering Speak': The Vocation of a Black Intellectual." In *Cornel West: A Critical Reader*, edited by George Yancy, 105–14. Malden, MA: Blackwell, 2001.

———. *Martin & Malcolm & America: A Dream or a Nightmare?* Maryknoll, NY: Orbis Books, 1991.

———. *The Spirituals and the Blues*. 1972. Maryknoll, NY: Orbis Books, 1991.

Cruse, Harold. *Rebellion or Revolution?* New York: Morrow, 1968.

Darby, Henry E., and Margaret N. Rowley. "King on Vietnam and Beyond." *Phylon* 47, no. 1 (1986): 43–50.

Darrow, Clarence. *Attorney for the Damned: Clarence Darrow in the Courtroom* (1957). Edited and annotated by Arthur Weinberg. Chicago: University of Chicago Press, 2012.

———. *Infidels and Heretics: An Agnostic's Anthology*. With Wallace Rice. 1928. New York: Gordon Press, 1975.

———. *In the Clutches of the Law: Clarence Darrow's Letters*. Edited by Randall Tietjen. Berkeley: University of California Press, 2013.

———. *The Story of My Life*. 1932. New York: Da Capo Press, 1996.

Daughtry, Herbert. *No Monopoly on Suffering*. Trenton, NJ: Africa World Press, 1997.

Davis, Angela Y. *An Autobiography*. New York: Random House, 1974.

———. "Black Women and the Club Movement." In *Women, Race & Class*. New York: Vintage, 1983.

———. *The Meaning of Freedom*. San Francisco: City Lights Books, 2012.

———. "Meditations on the Legacy of Malcolm X." In *Malcolm X in Our Own Image*, edited by Joe Wood, 36–47. New York: St. Martin's Press, 1992.

Davis, Angela Y., et al., ed. *If They Come in the Morning: Voices of Resistance*. New York: Third Press, 1971.

Diedrich, Maria. *Love Across the Color Lines: Ottilie Assing and Frederick Douglass*. New York: Hill and Wang, 1999.

Douglass, Frederick. *Autobiographies*. Edited by Henry Louis Gates Jr. New York: Library of America, 1994.

———. *Frederick Douglass: Selected Speeches and Writings.* Edited by Philip S. Foner. Chicago: Lawrence Hill Books, 1999.

———. *The Frederick Douglass Papers.* Series 1. Edited by John W. Blassingame and John R. McKivigan. New Haven, CT: Yale University Press, 1992.

———. "Lynch Law in the South." *North American Review* (July 1892): 17–24.

Du Bois, Shirley Graham. *His Day Is Marching On: A Memoir of W. E. B. Du Bois.* New York: Lippincott, 1971.

Du Bois, W. E. B. *Autobiography of W. E. B. Du Bois: A Soliloquy on Viewing My Life from the Last Decade of Its First Century.* New York: International Publishers, 1968.

———. *Black Reconstruction in America: An Essay Toward a History of the Part Which Black Folk Played in the Attempt to Reconstruct Democracy in America, 1860–1880.* New York: Harcourt, Brace, 1935.

———. *The Correspondence of W. E. B. Du Bois.* Edited by Herbert Aptheker. Amherst: University of Massachusetts Press, 1954.

———. "Criteria of Negro Art." *Crisis* 32 (October 1926): 290–97.

———. *Darkwater: Voices from Within the Veil.* 1920. New York: Washington Square Press, 2004.

———. *Dusk of Dawn: An Essay Towards an Autobiography of a Race Concept.* 1940. Oxford, UK: Oxford University Press, 2007.

———. *The Negro.* New York: Holt, 1915.

———. *The Oxford W. E. B. Du Bois.* Edited by Henry Louis Gates Jr. Oxford, UK: Oxford University Press, 2007.

———. *The Philadelphia Negro: A Social Study.* Boston: Ginn, 1899.

———. "The Revelation of Saint Orgne, the Damned." Commencement speech, 1938, Fisk University. Reprinted in *W. E. B. Du Bois Speaks: Speeches and Addresses, 1920-1963,* ed. Philip S. Foner, 100–23. New York: Pathfinder, 1970.

———. *The Souls of Black Folk.* 1903. New York: Modern Library, 2003.

———. *W. E. B. Du Bois Speaks: Speeches and Addresses, 1920–1963.* Edited by Philip S. Foner. New York: Pathfinder, 1970.

———. *The World and Africa: An Inquiry into the Part Which Africa Has Played in World History.* 1946. Oxford, UK: Oxford University Press, 2007.

Dunbar, Paul Laurence. *The Collected Poetry.* Edited by Joanne M. Braxton. Charlottesville: University Press of Virginia, 1993.

Edwards, Erica E. *Charisma and the Fictions of Black Leadership.* Minneapolis: University of Minnesota Press, 2012.

Fairclough, Adam. "Was Martin Luther King a Marxist?" *History Workshop Journal* 15 (Spring 1983): 117–25.

Fanon, Frantz. *The Wretched of the Earth*. French original, 1961. Translated by Constance Farrington. Preface by Jean-Paul Sartre. New York: Grove Press, 1963. Richard Philcox translation, New York: Grove Press, 2004.

Feuerbach, Ludwig Andreas. *The Essence of Christianity*. 1841. Translated from the second German edition by Marian Evans. London: Chapman, 1854; New York: Blanchard, 1855.

Fisch, Audrey, ed. *The Cambridge Companion to the African American Slave Narrative*. Cambridge, UK: Cambridge University Press, 2007.

Fleischman, Harry. *Norman Thomas: A Biography: 1884–1968*. New York: W. W. Norton, 1969.

Foner, Philip S. *The Life and Writings of Frederick Douglass*. Vol. 1, *Early Years, 1817–1849*. New York: International Publishers, 1950.

Foner, Philip S., ed. *Jack London: American Rebel: A Collection of His Social Writings Together with an Extensive Study of the Man and His Times*. New York: Citadel, 1947.

Frazier, E. Franklin. *Black Bourgeoisie*. Glencoe, IL: Free Press, 1957.

Freed, Donald. *Agony in New Haven: The Trial of Bobby Seale and Ericka Huggins and the Black Panther Party*. New York: Simon & Schuster, 1973.

Friedly, Michael, and David Gallen. *Martin Luther King, Jr.: The FBI File*. New York: Carroll & Graf, 1993.

Gaines, Kevin. *Uplifting the Race: Black Leadership, Politics, and Culture During the Twentieth Century*. Charlotte: University of North Carolina Press, 1996.

Garrow, David J. *Bearing the Cross: Martin Luther King, Jr., and the Southern Christian Leadership Conference*. New York: Vintage, 1988.

Gates, Henry Louis, Jr., and Cornel West. *The Future of the Race*. New York: Vintage, 1997.

Georgakas, Dan, and Marvin Surkin. *Detroit, I Do Mind Dying: A Study in Urban Revolution*. New York: St. Martin's Press, 1975.

Geschwender, James A. *Class, Race and Worker Insurgency: The League of Revolutionary Black Workers*. New York: Cambridge University Press, 1977.

Giddings, Paula J. *Ida: A Sword Among Lions; Ida B. Wells and the Campaign Against Lynching*. New York: Harper Collins, 2009.

Goldman, Peter. *The Death and Life of Malcolm X*. 1973. Urbana: University of Illinois Press, 2013.

Gore, Dayo F. "From Communist Politics to Black Power: The Visionary Politics and Transnational Solidarities of Victoria (Vicki) Ama Garvin." In *Want to Start a Revolution?*, edited by Dayo F. Gore et al., 71–94.

———. *Radicalism at the Crossroads: African American Women Activists in the Cold War.* New York: New York University Press, 2011.

Gore, Dayo F., Jeanne Theoharis, and Komozi Woodard, ed. *Want to Start a Revolution? Radical Women in the Black Freedom Struggle.* New York: New York University Press, 2009.

Gramsci, Antonio. *Selections from the Prison Notebooks.* Translated and edited by Quintin Hoare and Geoffrey Nowell Smith. New York: International Publishers, 1971.

Grant, Joanne. *Ella Baker: Freedom Bound.* New York: John Wiley, 1998.

Gregory, Raymond F. *Norman Thomas: The Great Dissenter.* New York: Algora, 2008.

Hamer, Fannie Lou. *The Speeches of Fannie Lou Hamer: To Tell It Like It Is.* Edited by Maegan Parker Brooks and Davis W. Houck. Jackson: University Press of Mississippi, 2011.

Hamington, Maurice. "Public Pragmatism: Jane Addams and Ida B. Wells on Lynching." *Journal of Speculative Philosophy* 19, no. 2 (2005): 167–74.

Harding, Vincent. *Martin Luther King: The Inconvenient Hero.* Maryknoll, NY: Orbis Books, 2008.

Haywood, Harry. *Black Bolshevik: Autobiography of an Afro-American Communist.* Chicago: Liberator Press, 1978.

Higginbotham, Evelyn. *Righteous Discontent: The Women's Movement in the Black Baptist Church, 1880–1920.* Cambridge, MA: Harvard University Press, 1993.

Hilliard, David, ed. *The Black Panther Party: Service to the People Programs.* Albuquerque: University of New Mexico Press, 2008.

Hirschfelder, Nicole. "Oppression as Process: A Figurational Analysis of the Case of Bayard Rustin." PhD dissertation, University of Tübingen, 2012.

Holt, Thomas C. "The Lonely Warrior: Ida B. Wells-Barnett and the Struggle for Black Leadership." In *Black Leaders of the 20th Century*, edited by John Hope Franklin and August Meier. Urbana: University of Illinois Press, 1982.

hooks, bell, and Cornel West. *Breaking Bread: Insurgent Black Intellectual Life.* Boston: South End Press, 1991.

Horne, Gerald. *Black and Red: W. E. B. Du Bois and the Afro-American Response to the Cold War, 1944–1963.* Albany: State University of New York Press, 1986.

Horne, Gerald, and Margaret Stevens. "Shirley Graham Du Bois: Portrait of the Black Woman Artist as a Revolutionary." In *Want to Start a Revolution?*, edited by Dayo F. Gore et al., 95–114.

Howard, Michael, and Peter Paret, ed. *On War.* Princeton, NJ: Princeton University Press, 1984.

Huggins, Ericka, and Angela D. LeBlanc-Ernest. "Revolutionary Women, Revolutionary Education: The Black Panther Party's Oakland Community School." In *Want to Start a Revolution?*, edited by Dayo F. Gore et al., 161–84.

Ingersoll, Robert Green. *Walt Whitman. An Address.* New York: The Truth Seeker, 1890.

———. *The Works of Robert G. Ingersoll.* New York: C. P. Farrell, 1900.

Jacoby, Susan. *The Great Agnostic: Robert Ingersoll and American Freethought.* New Haven, CT: Yale University Press, 2013.

Johnson, James Weldon. *Along This Way: The Autobiography of James Weldon Johnson.* New York: Viking, 1933.

———. *The Autobiography of an Ex-Colored Man.* New York: Alfred A. Knopf, 1927.

Kazantzakis, Nikos. *Russia: A Chronicle of Three Journeys in the Aftermath of the Revolution.* Translated by Michael Antonakes and Thanasis Maskaleris. Berkeley, CA: Creative Arts, 1989.

———. *The Selected Letters of Nikos Kazantzakis.* Edited by Peter Bien. Princeton, NJ: Princeton University Press, 2012.

Kelley, Robin D. G., and Betsy Esch. "Black Like Mao: Red China and Black Revolution." *Souls* 1, no. 4 (September 1999): 6–41.

King, Coretta Scott. *My Life with Martin Luther King, Jr.* London: Hodder and Stoughton, 1970.

King, Martin Luther, Jr. *The Autobiography of Martin Luther King, Jr.* Edited by Clayborne Carson. New York: Warner, 1998.

———. *I Have a Dream: Writings and Speeches that Changed the World.* Edited by James M. Washington. New York: Harper, 1992.

———. *A Testament of Hope: The Essential Writings and Speeches of Martin Luther King, Jr.* Edited by James M. Washington. San Francisco: Harper-Collins, 1991.

———. *Where Do We Go From Here: Chaos or Community?* 1967. Boston: Beacon Press, 2010.

Lerner, Michael, and Cornel West. *Jews and Blacks: A Dialogue on Race, Religion, and Culture in America.* New York: Penguin, 1996.

Levine, Robert S. *Dislocating Race and Nation: Episodes in Nineteenth-Century Literary Nationalism.* Chapel Hill: University of North Carolina Press, 2008.

Levine, Robert S., and Samuel Otter, eds. *Frederick Douglass and Herman Melville: Essays in Relation*. Chapel Hill: University of North Carolina Press, 2008.

Lind, Michael. *The Next American Nation: The New Nationalism and the Fourth American Revolution*. New York: Free Press, 1995.

Litwack, Leon F. *Trouble in Mind: Black Southerners in the Age of Jim Crow*. New York: Knopf, 1998.

Lohmann, Christoph, ed. *Radical Passion: Ottilie Assing's Reports from America and Letters to Frederick Douglass*. Translated by Christoph Lohmann. New York: Peter Lang, 1999.

London, Jack. *Jack London: American Rebel; a Collection of His Social Writings Together with an Extensive Study of the Man and His Times*, 517–24. Edited by Philip S. Foner. New York: Citadel, 1947.

Macey, David. *Frantz Fanon: A Biography* (2000). London: Verso, 2012.

Madhubuti, Haki R. *Liberation Narratives: New and Collected Poems, 1966–2009*. Chicago: Third World Press, 2009.

Marable, Manning. *Malcolm X: A Life of Reinvention*. New York: Viking, 2011.

———. "Rediscovering Malcolm's Life: A Historian's Adventure in Living History," *Souls* 7, no. 1 (2005): 20–35.

Marable, Manning, and Garrett Felber, ed. *The Portable Malcolm X Reader*. New York: Penguin, 2013.

McClory, Robert. *Radical Disciple: Father Pfleger, St. Sabina Church, and the Fight for Social Justice*. Chicago: Chicago Review Press, 2010.

Melville, Herman. *Moby-Dick; or The Whale*. 1851. Evanston: Northwestern University Press/Newberry Library, 1988.

Moore, Howard, Jr. "Angela—Symbol in Resistance." In *If They Come in the Morning: Voices of Resistance*, edited by Angela Davis et al., 191–92.

Mossman, James. "Race, Hate, Sex, and Colour: A Conversation with James Baldwin and Colin MacInnes." 1965. In *Conversations with James Baldwin*, edited by Fred L. Standley and Louis H. Pratt, 46–58. Jackson: University Press of Mississippi, 1989.

Newton, Huey P. *Revolutionary Suicide*. With J. Herman Blake. New York: Penguin, 2009.

O'Connor, Emmet. "James Larkin in the United States, 1914–1923." *Journal of Contemporary History* 37, no. 2 (2002): 183–96.

Pannekoek, Anton. *Workers' Councils*. 1946. Edinburgh: AK, 2003.

Petie, William L., and Douglas E. Stover, ed. *Bibliography of the Frederick Douglass Library at Cedar Hill*. Fort Washington, MD: Silesia, 1995.

Rabaka, Reiland. *Against Epistemic Apartheid: W. E. B. Du Bois and the Disciplinary Decadence of Sociology.* Boulder, CO: Lexington Books, 2010.

Rabaka, Reiland, ed. *W. E. B. Du Bois.* Farnham, UK: Ashgate, 2010.

Ransby, Barbara. *Ella Baker and the Black Freedom Movement: A Radical Democratic Vision.* Chapel Hill: University of North Carolina Press, 2003.

Raper, Arthur. *The Tragedy of Lynching.* Chapel Hill: University of North Carolina Press, 1933.

Rowan, Carl T. "Martin Luther King's Tragic Decision." *Reader's Digest,* September 1967.

Ruskin, John. *The Crown of Wild Olive.* New York, n.d. [1866].

Saint-Arnaud, Pierre. *African American Pioneers of Sociology: A Critical History.* French original, 2003. Translated by Peter Feldstein. Toronto: University of Toronto Press, 2009.

Sanchez, Sonia. *Conversations with Sonia Sanchez.* Edited by Joyce A. Joyce. Jackson: University Press of Mississippi, 2007.

———. *Home Coming.* Detroit: Broadside Press, 1969.

———. *Wounded in the House of a Friend.* Boston: Beacon Press, 1995.

Schechter, Patricia A. "'All the Intensity of My Nature': Ida B. Wells, Anger and Politics." *Radical History Review* 70 (1998): 48–77.

Seale, Bobby. *A Lonely Rage: The Autobiography of Bobby Seale.* New York: Times Books, 1978.

———. *Seize the Time: The Story of the Black Panther Party and Huey P. Newton.* New York: Random House, 1970.

Shakur, Assata. *Assata: An Autobiography.* 1987. Chicago: Lawrence Hill Books, 1999.

Sharlet, Jeff. "The Supreme Love and Revolutionary Funk of Dr. Cornel West, Philosopher of the Blues." *Rolling Stone,* May 28, 2009.

Smiley, Tavis, and Cornel West. *The Rich and the Rest of Us: A Poverty Manifesto.* New York: Smiley Books, 2012.

Smith, J. Alfred, Sr. *On the Jericho Road: A Memoir of Racial Justice, Social Action, and Prophetic Ministry.* With Harry Louis Williams II. Downers Grove, IL: InterVarsity Press, 2004.

Spanos, William V. *The Errant Art of Moby-Dick: The Canon, the Cold War, and the Struggle for American Studies.* Durham, NC: Duke University Press, 1995.

———. *The Exceptionalist State and the State of Exception: Herman Melville's Billy Budd, Sailor.* Baltimore: Johns Hopkins University Press, 2011.

———. *Herman Melville and the American Calling: Fiction After Moby-Dick, 1851–1857.* Albany: State University of New York Press, 2008.

Stanfield, John H. "King, Martin Luther (1929–1968)." In *Blackwell Encyclopedia of Sociology*, edited by George Ritzer. Oxford, UK: Blackwell, 2007.

Stauffer, John. "Frederick Douglass's Self-Fashioning and the Making of a Representative American Man." In *The Cambridge Companion to the African American Slave Narrative*, edited by Audrey A. Fisch, 201–17. Cambridge, UK: Cambridge University Press, 2007.

———. *Giants: The Parallel Lives of Frederick Douglass and Abraham Lincoln*. New York: Twelve, 2008.

Stout, Jeffrey. *Blessed Are the Organized: Grassroots Democracy in America*. Princeton, NJ: Princeton University Press, 2010.

Thomas, Norman. *Human Exploitation in the United States*. New York: Frederick A. Stokes, 1934.

Tyson, Timothy B. *Radio Free Dixie: Robert F. Williams and the Roots of Black Power*. Chapel Hill: University of North Carolina Press, 1999.

Wacquant, Loïc. *Punishing the Poor: The Neoliberal Government of Social Insecurity*. Durham, NC: Duke University Press, 2009.

Washington, James Melvin. *Frustrated Fellowship: The Baptist Quest for Social Power*. Macon, GA: Mercer, 1986.

Weld, Theodore Dwight, ed. *American Slavery As It Is: Testimony of a Thousand Witnesses*. New York: American Anti-Slavery Society, 1839.

Wells-Barnett, Ida B. *Crusade for Justice: The Autobiography of Ida B. Wells*. Edited by Alfreda M. Duster. Chicago: Chicago University Press, 1970.

———. *The Memphis Diary of Ida B. Wells*. Edited by Miriam DeCosta-Willis. Boston: Beacon Press, 1995.

———. *A Red Record: Tabulated Statistics and Alleged Causes of Lynchings in the United States, 1892–1893–1894*. Chicago: Privately published, 1895. Reprinted in *Selected Works of Ida B. Wells-Barnett*, compiled by Trudier Harris, 138–252. New York: Oxford University Press, 1991.

———. *Selected Works of Ida B. Wells-Barnett*. Compiled by Trudier Harris. New York: Oxford University Press, 1991.

———. *Southern Horrors: Lynch Law in All Its Phases*. New York: New York Age Print, 1892. Reprinted in *Selected Works of Ida B. Wells-Barnett*, compiled by Trudier Harris, 14–45. New York: Oxford University Press, 1991.

West, Cornel. *The American Evasion of Philosophy: A Genealogy of Pragmatism*. Madison: University of Wisconsin Press, 1989.

———. "Black Strivings in a Twilight Civilization." In *The Future of the Race*, edited by Henry Louis Gates Jr. and Cornel West, 53–112, 180–96. New York: Vintage, 1997.

———. "Black Theology and Human Identity." In *Black Faith and Public Talk: Critical Essays on James H. Cone's* Black Theology and Black Power, edited by Dwight N. Hopkins, 11–19. Maryknoll, NY: Orbis Books, 1999.

———. *Brother West: Living and Loving Out Loud.* With David Ritz. Carlsbad, CA: Smiley Books, 2009.

———. *The Cornel West Reader.* New York: Civitas, 1999.

———. *Democracy Matters: Winning the Fight Against Imperialism.* New York: Penguin Press, 2004.

———. *The Ethical Dimensions of Marxist Thought.* New York: Monthly Review, 1991.

———. *Keeping Faith: Philosophy and Race in America.* New York: Routledge, 1993.

———. "On the Legacy of Dorothy Day." *Catholic Agitator* 44, no. 1 (February 2014): 1–3, 6.

———. *Prophesy Deliverance! An Afro-American Revolutionary Christianity.* 1982. Anniversary ed. with a new preface by the author. Louisville, KY: Westminster John Knox Press, 2002.

———. *Prophetic Fragments: Illuminations of the Crisis in American Religion and Culture.* 1988. Grand Rapids, MI: Eerdmans Publishing, 1993.

———. *Prophetic Thought in Postmodern Times.* Vol. 1, *Beyond Eurocentrism and Multiculturalism.* Monroe, ME: Common Courage Press, 1993.

———. *Race Matters.* New York: Vintage, 1994.

———. "Why I Am Marching in Washington." In *Million Man March/Day of Absence: A Commemorative Anthology,* edited by Haki R. Madhubuti and Maulana Karenga, 37–38. Chicago: Third World Press, 1996.

West, Cornel, and Eddie Glaude Jr., ed. *African American Religious Thought.* Louisville, KY: Westminster John Knox Press, 2003.

Wiley, Anthony Terrance. "Angelic Troublemakers: Religion and Anarchism in Henry David Thoreau, Dorothy Day, and Bayard Rustin." PhD dissertation, Princeton University, 2011.

Wilkerson, Isabel. *The Warmth of Other Suns: The Epic Story of America's Great Migration.* New York: Random House, 2010.

Williams, Raymond. *The Long Revolution.* London: Chatto, 1961.

Williams, Robert F. *Negroes With Guns.* New York: Marzani and Munsell, 1962.

Willie, Charles V. "Walter R. Chivers—An Advocate of Situation Sociology." *Phylon* 43, no. 3 (1982): 242–48.

Wolin, Sheldon S. "Fugitive Democracy." *Constellations* 1, no. 1 (1994): 11–25.

Wortham, Robert. "Du Bois and the Sociology of Religion: Rediscovering a Founding Figure." *Sociological Inquiry* 75, no. 4 (2005): 433–52.

———. "W. E. B. Du Bois, the Black Church, and the Sociological Study of Religion." *Sociological Spectrum* 29, no. 2 (2009): 144–72.

Wortham, Robert, ed. *W. E. B. Du Bois and the Sociological Imagination: A Reader, 1897–1914.* Waco, TX: Baylor University Press, 2009.

Wright, Richard. *Black Power: A Record of Reactions in a Land of Pathos.* New York: Harper, 1954.

X, Malcolm. *The Autobiography of Malcolm X.* With the assistance of Alex Haley. New York: Ballantine Books, 1992.

———. *By Any Means Necessary: Speeches, Interviews, and a Letter by Malcolm X.* Edited by George Breitman. New York: Pathfinder, 1970.

———. *Malcolm X Speaks: Selected Speeches and Statements.* Edited by George Breitman. New York: Pathfinder, 1990.

Yancy, George, ed. *Cornel West: A Critical Reader.* Malden, MA: Blackwell, 2001.

Zinn, Howard. *Howard Zinn on Race.* New York: Seven Stories Press, 2011.

Zuckerman, Phil, ed. *The Social Theory of W. E. B. Du Bois.* Thousand Oaks, CA: Sage, 2004.